INTERMEDIATE
MICROECONOMICS

INTERMEDIATE
MICROECONOMICS

Robert W. Clower
University of South Carolina

Philip E. Graves
University of Colorado

Robert L. Sexton
Pepperdine University

HARCOURT BRACE JOVANOVICH, PUBLISHERS
and its subsidiary, Academic Press

San Diego New York Chicago Austin Washington, D.C.
London Sydney Tokyo Toronto

ISBN: 0-15-541496-8
Library of Congress Catalog Card Number: 87-81893
Printed in the United States of America

To Our Families

Those who have handled sciences have been either men of experiment or men of dogmas. The men of experiment are like the ant; they only collect and use; the reasoners resemble spiders, who make cobwebs out of their own substance. But the bee takes a middle course; it gathers its material from the flowers of the garden and of the field, but transforms and digests it by a power of its own. . . . Therefore from a closer and purer league between these two faculties, the experimental and the rational (such as has never yet been made), much may be hoped.

Francis Bacon, *Novum Organum*, 1620
(trans. R. Ellis and James Spedding, 1857)

Preface

*R*ecent decades have witnessed profound changes in economic analysis. Years ago the professional journals were as innocent of mathematics as principles texts are today, and most students of intermediate microeconomics would finish the course having learned more about social and economic institutions than about the formulation and analysis of economic models. Today the same students are likely to end the session with partial derivatives glazing their eyeballs and with hardly any notion of the actual working of any economic system, least of all the one they know best. As Martin Shubik has so aptly put it:

> The consumer with his indifference curves confronts the price system which functions smoothly for the individually operated profit-maximizing firm. The owner combines factors by setting marginal everything equal to marginal everything else. Supply and demand curves are obtained and for three quarters of a semester the God-given, institution-free, frictionless markets of upper-class Western, utilitarian man function in neo-Newtonian fashion.*

Not that anyone would wish to return to the Good Old Days; progress *has* blessed us, though the blessings are mixed.

This textbook is not intended to resist the tide of formalism, for that would be misguided as well as quixotic. The purpose of this book is to harness some energy from that tide to support a fresh analysis of individual and market behavior whose institutional structure bears some resemblance to the world in which we live. The book is designed to give the student a feel for economic institutions and a sense of perspective in dealing with unsolved economic problems; it does not attempt to make the student an expert in solving technical exercises to which the answers are already known.

As suggested by its title, the book is for undergraduate courses in which the instructor wishes to provide a more intensive training in microeconomic theory than is

---

*"A Curmudgeon's Guide to Microeconomics," *Journal of Economic Literature*, Vol. 8 (June 1970), p. 406.

customarily attempted in elementary courses. The argument is essentially nonmathematical, but for those who use a more mathematical approach we have included calculus in the footnotes.

To help students get a better feel for economic theory we feature many boxed examples and applications of microeconomics throughout the text. Some of these are intended to reinforce the student's comprehension of the analysis while others are used to demonstrate the usefulness of theory in the real world.

One of the goals of this textbook is to bridge the gap between micro- and macroeconomics. For example, an optional chapter on stock and flow analysis in supply and demand (Chapter 4) is used to assist in understanding durable goods, inventories, and business cycles. Other examples of this "bridge" are the chapter on the theory of interest (Chapter 16) and section 21.9, on money and consumer good inventories, in the chapter on asset management and intertemporal income allocation (Chapter 21). It is our belief that strong microeconomic foundations are of paramount importance in understanding macroeconomics. The text is also particularly strong in its coverage of factor price determination (Chapters 13–18), an area, in our opinion, that is treated too lightly in most microeconomics textbooks.

Organization and Content

An outline of the four parts of *Intermediate Microeconomics* follows.

Part 1, the introduction, is composed of Chapters 1–4 and covers such topics as methodology, goals and decision-making by economic agents in the market system, and supply and demand from both a flow and a stock/flow perspective. Chapter 1, "The Role and Method of Economic Analysis," provides an introduction to the scientific approach. Chapter 2, "The Economic System: Consumers, Producers, and Market Transactions," offers a novel treatment of the nature of economic decision units and the nature of markets. This material naturally precedes the supply and demand analysis that is reviewed in Chapter 3. Chapter 4, "Stocks and Flows in Supply and Demand," serves as an important bridge to macroeconomics. This unique but optional chapter allows the student to understand how microeconomic tools shed light on familiar macroeconomic problems such as the impact of changed stock demands on inventory holdings, hence on production and income.

Part 2, "Price and Output Determination," contains Chapters 5–12, which deal in depth with the optimizing behavior of individuals in their roles as consumers and producers. Chapters 5 and 6 present the standard consumer behavior model and emphasize the pervasive theme of the text—that there are many unsettled issues in economics. Rather than present theory as the dogmatic "absolute truth," out goal is to prepare students to think for themselves about economic matters. After completing consumer theory, we turn in Chapters 7 and 8 to "The Theory of Production" and "The Costs of Production," the output and supply side of final product markets. The last four chapters in this section describe price and output determination in various market situations: "Competitive Price Determination" (Chapter 9), "Monopoly" (Chapter 10), "Monopolistic Competition" (Chapter 11), and "Oligopoly" (Chapter 12).

Turning in **Part 3** to how the output is distributed, the text offers thorough coverage of factor markets. We believe that input or factor markets are as critical as output markets in microeconomics and are typically treated in too cursory a manner. Thus we have provided six chapters that cover the subject fully: "Theory of Factor Pricing" (Chapter 13), "The Pricing of Labor Services" (Chapter 14), "Capital Investment" (Chapter 15), "The Theory of Interest" (Chapter 16), "Rents and Quasi-Rents" (Chapter 17), and "Theory of Profits" (Chapter 18).

Part 4, "Efficiency, Exchange, and Intertemporal Issues," contains four chapters that pursue a diverse range of topics. Chapter 19, "General Equilibrium," has an algebraic as well as a graphical presentation to reinforce the understanding of general equilibrium. This is followed by Chapter 20, "Welfare Economics." Chapter 21, "Asset Management and Intertemporal Choice," is one of the most difficult in the book. However, we believe that it is richer in content than the standard treatment on this subject. Chapter 22, "Market Failures: Public Goods and Externalities," is the final chapter.

Alternative Formats

With such a full menu of topics, there are many ways to use this textbook in a one-quarter, a one-semester, or a longer format. Those on a tight schedule might select only the core chapters (1–3, 5–10, and 13). A class stressing micro-macro interrelations would want to include Chapters 4 (Stocks and Flows"), 16 ("Theory of Interest"), and 21 ("Asset Management and Intertemporal Choice"). Additional readings and lectures on specific microeconomic topics to supplement the text can be added as time permits.

Pedagogical Devices

- **Applications**   Each chapter features numerous solved problems, presented in boxes throughout the text. Some of these are intended to reinforce earlier concepts while others are intended to be thought provoking. Our belief is that problem solving stimulates students, creating active, thoughtful readers. These applications are denoted by boldface page numbers in the index.

- **Graphs**   We have taken care in constructing the graphs, realizing that they are of vital importance in microeconomics texts. Detailed captions accompany each graph; caption topics are denoted by italic page numbers in the index. The use of color, shaded areas, and bold lines all assist in making the graphs appealing and easy to understand.

■ ***End-of-Chapter Aids*** Every chapter ends with a **Summary** listing the important concepts and a list of **Words and Concepts for Review**. The **Review Questions** at the end of the chapters are answered in the Instructor's Manual. A **Supplementary Reading List** has been included for outside assignments and for the curious reader. Several chapters conclude with an appendix containing material related to the chapter but presented separately to provide flexibility. In a class with a serious time constraint, the appendixes can easily be omitted without loss of continuity. Chapter 3, "Supply and Demand," includes an appendix on econometrics as it relates to supply and demand; Chapter 7, "The Theory of Production," has an appendix on linear programming; Chapter 13, "Theory of Factor Pricing," has an appendix that discusses the adding up problem in factor pricing (Euler's Theorem) and the Cobb-Douglas production function; and Chapter 19, "General Equilibrium," has an appendix on input-output analysis.

Supplementary Material

■ ***Study Guide*** Prepared by Carol Tremblay of Kansas State University, the Study Guide contains many useful elements to further the student's understanding of microeconomic theory: an outline of each chapter, a chapter review (summary), exercises (definitions of key concepts, problems, multiple-choice questions) with answers, and a generous number of stimulating quotations throughout.

■ ***Instructor's Manual*** The manual also contains an outline of each chapter, a list of learning objectives, the answers for the end-of-chapter text questions, and a test bank with essay questions, problems, and multiple-choice questions. Answers are given at the back of the manual for the problems and multiple-choice questions in the manual. In addition, the Instructor's Manual contains a **market game** that enables students to participate in mock markets. The game demonstrates how prices are determined in various market structures.

We are thankful to the many people who helped us in the preparation of this book. The economists who reviewed earlier drafts and made numerous helpful suggestions are Jack E. Adams (University of Arkansas at Little Rock), Peter H. Aranson (Emory University), Scott E. Atkinson (University of Georgia), John C. Dutton (North Carolina State University), David Finifter (College of William and Mary), James Hess (North Carolina State University), Albert N. Link (University of North Carolina), and Henry N. McCarl (University of Alabama). In addition, we have benefited from the comments of our colleagues Ron Batchelder (Pepperdine University), Gary Galles (Pepperdine University), Edward Morey (University of Colorado-Boulder), and Don Waldman (University of Colorado-Boulder). Excellent word processing assistance was provided by Sandy Hagmann.

R. W. C., P. E. G., R. L. S.

Contents

PART 1
Introduction / 1

1
The Role and Method of Economic Analysis / 3

4
Stocks and Flows in Supply and Demand / 67

PART 2
Price and Output Determination / 85

5
The Theory of Consumer Behavior and the Determinants of Demand / 86

8
The Costs of Production / 172

9
Competitive Price Determination / 207

10

Monopoly / 244

11

Monopolistic Competition / 276

12
Oligopoly / 291

PART 3
Factor Price Determination / 323

13
Theory of Factor Pricing / 324

14

The Pricing of Labor Services / 348

15

Capital Investment / 377

16
The Theory of Interest / 392

17
Rents and Quasi-Rents / 406

PART 4
Efficiency, Exchange, and Intertemporal Issues / 437

22
Market Failures: Public Goods and Externalities / 496

PART 1

Introduction

1

The Role and Method
of Economic Analysis

1.1 INTRODUCTION

Economic analysis allows decision makers to evaluate the consequences of alternative actions and thus provides a basis on which to make intelligent choices. For business leaders, consumers, workers, union officials, and government policymakers, economic analysis provides a guide to planning. Given the goals of individuals and organizations, economic principles may be used to evaluate various policies in terms of their efficiency (are the benefits greater than the costs?) and equity (are the benefits and costs "fairly" distributed?).

Economic analysis also provides a basis on which we can predict future events. Business firms are always concerned with trends in the prices of the goods they buy and sell. By studying price-determining forces in their industries and using economic principles to analyze their particular situations, businesses can often make very good predictions about future prices. Similarly, households are interested in and affected by movements in the general price level. If, on the basis of economic analysis, we know that a general increase in the demand for goods that is not accompanied by a comparable increase in the supply of goods will lead to price increases, then we can predict that the general price level will rise during periods of war, national emergency, or large increases in the money supply. An imbalance between supply and demand at initial prices is almost inevitable in such situations.

Prediction enables people to avoid undesirable outcomes. The knowledge of economic principles is a particularly important factor in determining what governmental action should be taken to avoid unfavorable developments in the economy. If the general price level rises rapidly following a period of high defense spending (as in wartime), then some knowledge of the causes of the increase is essential if effective control measures are to be introduced. Only through careful economic analysis is it possible to predict the consequences of alternative control policies and to select the

3

policies that are likely to yield the desired results.

Finally, economic analysis provides us with a basis for judging the performance of various segments of the economy and of the economic system as a whole. For example, if maximization of aggregate real income is accepted as a goal of the economic system, then unemployment should not be undesirably large. If at any time many persons are unemployed, a knowledge of the principles that determine employment levels is necessary to decide whether this unemployment is due to an inherent weakness in the structure of the macroeconomy or to particular microeconomic factors (minimum-wage legislation, welfare programs that discourage people from keeping jobs even if they are able to find them, unwise union policies, immobility of workers due to ignorance and lack of resources, and so forth).

Despite the great utility of economic analysis, we must not expect the impossible. The operation of an economic system is much too complex to be characterized by a few simple laws; given the difficulties of developing economic theories that predict observable events with a high degree of accuracy, we cannot expect to forecast and control economic activity with more than moderate success. By and large, therefore, we must treat economic principles as tools of analysis to be applied in particular cases and as aids in selecting data that require further study. As John Maynard Keynes once remarked:

> The object of our analysis is not to provide a machine or method of blind manipulation, which will furnish an infallible answer, but to provide ourselves with an organized and orderly method of thinking out particular problems; and, after we have reached a provisional conclusion by isolating the complicating factors one by one, we then have to go back on ourselves and allow, as well as we can, for the probable interactions of the factors amongst themselves. This is the nature of economic thinking.

Test your skills of analysis by referring to Box 1-1.

1-1   True or False?   There is so much variety in the behavior of different people that economic theory cannot possibly lead us to any meaningful conclusions about human behavior.

False.   Often group behavior is more predictable than individual behavior. When the weather gets colder, more firewood will be sold. Some individuals may not buy firewood, but we can predict with great accuracy that a *group* of individuals will establish a pattern of buying more firewood. The same is true of gasoline in the summertime. After all, if human behavior could not be predicted, then how could insurance companies be profitable? Insurance companies are not concerned with predicting one individual's behavior; they work under the premise that variability in individual behavior is minimized in average or group behavior. Most economic theory similarly focuses on market outcomes that involve large numbers of individuals.

1.2 MAJOR DIVISIONS OF ECONOMIC ANALYSIS

If the world were simple enough or if human ingenuity were great enough, then all areas of scientific knowledge could be brought within the reach of a single unified theory. But that is not the way it is. Empirical science is divided into three main categories—physical, biological, and social—which are further separated into countless specialized fields. The only element of unity in the entire scheme is the acceptance by all scientists of certain broad standards of scholarly conduct in the development, presentation, and evaluation of their work.

Contemporary economics is divided into overlapping segments according to **subject matter** (price theory, econometrics, industrial organization, welfare economics, development, trade, monetary theory, and so on); **theoretical perspective** (micro or macro, partial or general, static or dynamic); **mode of presentation** (literary or mathematical); and **analytical objective** (positive and explanatory or normative and prescriptive). A closer inspection of these segments is necessary to understand how the content of this book relates to the broader field of economics.

1.3 MICROECONOMICS AND MACROECONOMICS

Microeconomic analysis is just what the term suggests—a study of the behavior of individual households and business firms and of individual markets, considered in isolation or in groups, aimed at providing a logically coherent description of the structure and working of a market economy. Microeconomic analysis is the bread-and-butter item on any menu of economic theory. Once you understand microeconomics, you will have acquired a tool that is essential to all economic analysis. The rest of the menu is interesting, some of it is nutritious, and most of it is intellectually palatable; but all of it would amount to very little without microeconomics as its foundation.

Macroeconomics analysis is a legacy of the "Keynesian Revolution" of the late 1930s, which directed the attention of economists away from the analysis of individual decision units and individual markets and encouraged them to look at the overall behavior of the economic system as reflected in a few *aggregative measures* of economic activity, including gross national income and output, employment, investment, consumption, the stock of money, and the general price level. In recent years, some economic theorists have reduced formal macroeconomic analysis to a special type of microeconomic analysis centered around four or five aggregate markets instead of several hundred or several million individual markets.

There is some question whether contemporary statements of macroeconomic theory accurately characterize the aggregative behavior of the economic system. Some economists have gone so far as to suggest that aggregate economic behavior depends on interactions among individual consumers and firms that can be described only by completely reformulating the established theories of individual and market behavior. Perhaps this is an extreme position, but it is a reasonable analogy to treat an economic system involving millions of individuals and goods like a volume of gas with billions of molecules in motion. Even if we could say exactly how each individual behaves in isolation, we could not infer from this how a group of mutually interdependent individuals would act, any more than we could infer how a gas behaves from an analysis of its separate molecules.

Though this book will focus on microeconomics, the topic is in some respects inextricably intertwined with macroeconomics. (See Box 1-2.)

1.4 PARTIAL AND GENERAL EQUILIBRIUM ANALYSIS

General equilibrium analysis is often described as the part of microeconomic analysis which focuses on mutual interrelationships among the prices and outputs of all goods traded in the economic system. **Partial equilibrium analysis** is the special type of general equilibrium analysis which isolates and examines one or more individuals, firms, or markets while assuming that all other factors in the economy remain constant. Partial equilibrium analysis is most clearly reflected in modern textbook accounts of the supply-and-demand determination of the market price in isolated markets. If you were estimating the demand for automobiles, for example, you would incorporate the price of substitutes (such as public transportation), the price of complements (tires, oil, gasoline), and income; but you would generally ignore the price effect of many unrelated goods (pillows, pencils, aspirin). Both general and partial equilibrium analyses are useful; the nature of the problem being considered dictates which type of analysis to use. As is appropriate to its content, this book mainly employs partial equilibrium analysis.

1.5 STATICS AND DYNAMICS

A clear distinction between *statics* and *dynamics* can be made through a mechanical illustration. Imagine a room in which a pendulum (consisting of a "bob" on a string) is suspended from a domed ceiling by a hook. We can ask several kinds of questions about the behavior of the pendulum. First, if the pendulum is suspended at a particular point and left undisturbed, what will be the ultimate position of its bob? Clearly, the bob will lie directly below the hook on which it is hung, at a distance given by the

---

1-2   True or False? *Microeconomics* is relatively insignificant for macroeconomic topics.

False.   Both microeconomics and macroeconomics are primarily concerned with explaining things in the large. *Microeconomics* analyzes things in the small to better understand the large. The study of microeconomics has helped economists increase their understanding about many macro topics, including foreign trade, interest rates, economic growth, and the price level.

length of string that connects it to the hook. In this example of (informal) **static analysis**, our only concern is to describe the **equilibrium state** of a physical system which will be maintained indefinitely in the absence of external "shocks." The familiar textbook discussion of the determination of market equilibrium price in terms of the intersection of demand and supply curves provides an example of static analysis applied to an economic system.

Second, we can ask how the equilibrium position of the bob will be affected if the hook is withdrawn and screwed into another location on the ceiling. Clearly this procedure will be followed by some erratic movements in the bob; but when the pendulum has once again come to rest, the new equilibrium position will differ from the old only by virtue of the change in the hook's location. This illustrates what economists call **comparative statics**, the study of variations in equilibrium positions corresponding to specified changes in underlying data. An economic example is provided by textbook discussions of the effects of changes in demand on the equilibrium price when supply conditions remain unchanged.

Third, we can ask how the pendulum behaves over time, starting from some arbitrary date on which the position of the bob is given. This question is much more complicated than the previous two. To answer it, we must engage in **dynamic analysis**, dealing explicitly with a variable representing "time" in order to characterize the *motion* of variables with equilibrium values. Note that static analysis is a special case of dynamic analysis. In a static analysis, we deal only with equilibrium states; in a dynamic analysis, equilibrium states correspond to a specific choice of "initial conditions." In particular, the states of the system at all dates after some initial point in time coincide exactly with the state of the system at the initial point in time; that is, the "motion" of the system is *stationary* in an equilibrium state.

Serious dynamic analysis requires the use of some fairly complicated mathematical tools and is therefore not a suitable topic for elementary or intermediate microeconomic texts; hence we shall deal in this book primarily with comparative statics. Even in elementary discussions, however, it is desirable to indicate, at least qualitatively, how economic systems are likely to behave out of equilibrium. Without such information, the very notion of equilibrium becomes almost meaningless. Knowing the equilibrium values is much less useful if movement between equilibria essentially takes *forever* than if movement between equilibria is rapid. (Recall that instantaneous adjustment is implicitly assumed in principles accounts of supply and demand.)

1.6 LITERARY AND MATHEMATICAL ANALYSES

The current trend in economic analysis is toward mathematical analysis of theoretical ideas. The virtues of the mathematical approach are evident in long-established and essentially developed sciences such as theoretical mechanics. In unsettled research sciences such as economics and microphysics, however, the use of mathematics is more of a mixed blessing. Although mathematical analysis contributes greatly to clarity and precision of argument, it also encourages users to place more stress on logical form than may be desirable in areas where questions of subject matter and conceptual perspective have yet to be resolved.

Mathematical analysis cannot be carried out effectively without the frequent use of words; on the other hand, literary analysis cannot be carried out efficiently without the occasional use of symbols and graphs and at least the implicit use of mathematical ideas. It has been suggested that literary analysis constitutes a form of "intellectual masochism," that it is simply wrongheaded to insist on splitting fine hairs with a blunt instrument when sharper (mathematical) tools are readily available. A considerably weaker case can be made for the mathematical analysis of economics than can be made for the mathematical analysis of physics. The most active areas of modern physics rely, though, as much on literary as on mathematical modes of analysis.

However, many key concepts in economics can be more easily understood when calculus or even set-theoretic topological methods are employed. Consequently, mathematical footnotes will appear throughout this text to add precision to the discussion. No advanced mathematics beyond the use of graphs appears in the text itself.

1.7 POSITIVE AND NORMATIVE ECONOMICS

It is important in every science to make a conceptual distinction between the analysis of *what is* and the analysis of *what ought to be*—between the description of observed behavior without regard to its moral or social consequences and the evaluation of behavior in terms of desired goals. This distinction is relatively easy to make in the physical sciences: a biochemist who is intellectually fascinated with the study of poisonous gases may pursue research without thinking about the harmful uses of such gases. Such distinctions are more difficult for social scientists: it seems almost immoral for a student of *human* behavior to view the subject matter dispassionately, treating people as if they were viruses or ants while ignoring their present condition (and, even worse, the fate of society). In principle, however, detachment is possible; **positive economics** (the study of "what is") can be separated from **normative economics** (the study of "what ought to be.") In practice, economists are no more likely than atomic physicists to refrain from making judgments about the social implications of their work.

The distinction between positive and normative is rarely absolute. Normative economics can be carried on in a completely "scientific" way by considering the social implications of alternative sets of value judgments without committing to any particular set. Conversely, positive economics must rely on some value judgments (the judgment that the pursuit of positive knowledge is worthwhile, for example, or the judgment that capitalistic forms of economic organization are interesting and not necessarily negative objects of study). Therefore, it is pointless to suggest that economists ought or ought not to pursue their research "objectively." Economists who are deeply concerned about contemporary social problems will naturally direct their efforts toward positive studies in order to facilitate desirable solutions to such problems. Other economists are simply unconcerned about society; they can be as fascinated with economies that are descending a staircase to Hell as with economies that are riding an escalator to Heaven.

A long-debated question now arises: Should economists make policy recommendations? On the one hand, it can be argued that such recommendations are beyond the scope of economics as a scientific study, since they are made in terms of goals (such as the maximum wealth of a nation) whose desirability can only be postulated rather than be determined by objective analysis. On the other hand, it may be argued that economic analysts are in a peculiarly advantageous position to make policy suggestions. We will not attempt to settle this long-debated issue here. We merely observe that the *ethical* content of most policy recommendations is so slight when compared to the *scientific* content—that is, positive analyses of the consequences of alternative policy actions—that the entire "science versus ethics" issue becomes of minor concern. In recent years, most policy debates among economists have focused on how the economic system works, not on social goals. Those who want economists to recommend policy should be wary of accepting their advice; the present state of positive economic knowledge is highly imperfect. (See Boxes 1-3 and 1-4.)

1.8 ECONOMICS AND SCIENCE: FACT OR FICTION?

Contrary to popular opinion, the bulk of all knowledge commonly regarded as scientific is expressed in terms not unlike the stories told by writers of serious fiction—and this resemblance is not accidental. The novelist tries to persuade us that a story could

1-3 True or False?   The following two statements are examples of normative economics: Income is concentrated in the hands of relatively few wealthy individuals. It is only fair that the government step in and make income and wealth more equal.

False.   The first statement is a *positive* statement because it describes what is observed. The second statement is a *normative* statement because it implies that some action *ought* to be taken. One important difference is that most positive statements can be *tested;* normative statements cannot be tested because they are based on value judgments.

1-4 True or False?   Economists, like most social scientists, find little to agree on.

False.   Most economists agree on certain issues: rent control, import tariffs, export restrictions, price controls on natural gas, and many others. Specifically, economists usually argue that market forces should be allowed to work freely and that economic analysis can predict certain phenomena with a high degree of success. For example, if Florida suffers a severe winter and frost ruins the state's orange crop, then the price of oranges will rise (all other things being equal).

almost be true; the scientist tries to persuade us that certain events fall into a meaningful pattern. It may appear that the scientist does not (or is not supposed to) invent the underlying "facts" of the story, whereas the novelist is not so constrained. However, a scientist does select *certain* facts from among many facts that could have been chosen, just as a novelist chooses from an infinite number of possible characters and situations only those certain to make the story most persuasive. In either case, the artist "invents" the story. Therefore we should not be surprised to find *order* in economic or social theory any more than we are surprised to find order in a good novel. Scientists would not bother to write about "life" if they were not convinced that they had stories worth telling.

What makes a story worth telling? When we look for order in nature, we cannot automatically suppose that the "facts" are a sufficient basis for understanding observed events. The basic problem is that the facts of a complex world simply do not organize themselves. Understanding requires that a *conceptual order* be imposed on these facts to counteract the confusion that would otherwise result. For example, objects of different weights falling freely in the air do not travel at *precisely* the same rate (largely because of differing wind resistance). Yet this piece of information is generally much less significant than the fact that falling bodies do travel at *almost* the same rate (which presumably would be identical in a vacuum). By focusing on the most significant fact— the similarity rather than the difference—Galileo was able to impose order on the story of gravity.

When choosing a set of facts to weave into a story (a theory), a scientist views events not as they *actually appear* but as they *would appear* if certain outside complications were ignored. To interpret the impact of rising housing prices on the quantity of housing desired, economists must ignore the impact of increasing wealth, population, and other contributing factors. Failing to do so would obscure the central insight that people tend to buy less housing at higher prices. If Galileo had focused his attention on a falling feather and a falling brick, the persuasive story of how objects *generally* fall might never have been written. In the same way, rising incomes lead to a greater demand for housing and can result in higher housing prices. The casual observer of these "facts" who concludes that people buy *more* (not less) housing at higher prices would be confusing *correlation* with *causation*. That is, higher prices and more housing purchases occur together, but the *causation* is that higher incomes lead to both increased purchases and higher prices, not that higher prices lead to increased purchases. Without a story—a theory of causation—scientists could not sort out and understand the complex reality that surrounds us.

1.9 SCIENTIFIC EXPLANATION

Scientific stories exhibit a cumulative character that is lacking in works of fiction. Stories told by one scientist are seized upon by others, reworked, expanded, and passed on to other scientists with similar interests. During these ongoing efforts to tell a better story, scientists must share certain common ground rules governing the arrangement, analysis, and communication of ideas. Since each science deals with different events and problems, each has certain procedures that are peculiar to it. Thus, the "experimental method" plays a crucial role in biology, physics, and chemistry, where repeatable controlled experiments are possible; this experimental method has a lesser (but growing) role in economics, where individual events ("experiments") are generally neither controlled nor repeatable.[1] Nevertheless, the sciences are more like various breeds of cats or dogs than like entirely different species. Though the different disciplines may vary in details of approach, all conform to a common logical structure and conceptual orientation.

What makes a good scientific story or "theory"? A theory should provide the reader with enough information to figure out what the storyteller is saying—that is, what is supposed to cause what. A theory should also give a sense of the story's importance and of how the story fits in with other stories the reader already knows. A good scientific story will also be so phrased as to force us to ask "if/then" questions. For example, *if* the price of good X increases, *then* the quantity demanded of good X will fall.

1.10 WHY ECONOMISTS DIFFER

While professional economists differ frequently on economic policy questions, there is probably less disagreement than the media would have people believe. Disagreement is common in most disciplines: seismologists predict earthquakes at different times; historians argue over the authenticity of manuscripts; psychologists differ on proper ways to raise children; nutritionists debate the merits of large doses of vitamin C.

As indicated earlier, some of the differences which divide economists are based on normative social goals and noneconomic consequences of economic policies. For instance, economists who are philosophically opposed to any encroachment on individual decision making will be skeptical of governmental involvement in the economy unless overwhelming objective evidence shows that the intervention will have profound positive economic consequences. Other economists, more concerned with what they consider an unfair or unfortunate distribution of income, wealth, and power, may view governmental intervention as a desirable method of righting injustices that exist within the economy.

Philosophical differences aside, economists may differ on the applicability of a given economic theory to the policy in question. Suppose two economists have identical philosophical views which lead them to the identical conclusion that unemployment should be reduced to end injustice and hardship. The first economist believes that the government should lower taxes and increase spending to reach the objective, while the second believes that the government should increase the amount of money in public hands through a variety of banking policies. The two economists differ partly

---

[1]For an example of experimental economics, see Don L. Coursey and Vernon L. Smith, "Price Controls in a Posted Offer Market," *American Economic Review*, vol. 73, no. 1 (March 1983), 218–21.

1-5   Will what is a good theory for an individual always be a good theory in the aggregate?

No.   What is true for an individual may not be true for everyone, and it's not just because of taste differences. Suppose it is a beautiful fall afternoon, and you are one of 100,000 spectators in a football stadium. It would, you suspect, be a lot easier for you to get out of the parking lot if you were to leave early in the fourth quarter rather than at the end of the game. However, if one of the teams opened up the game to go ahead by 40 points and everyone decided to leave at once, then it would be a different story. Thus, what is true for the part is not always true for the whole. Other examples are standing up at a rock concert to get a better view or studying harder to get an "A" (in a course graded on a curve). These examples highlight the problem of aggregation, whether it be in microeconomics or macroeconomics.

because the empirical evidence regarding the cause of unemployment appears to support either theory. Some data suggest government taxation and spending policies are effective; other evidence supports the view that the prime cause of the unemployment lies with faulty monetary policy. (Still other evidence suggests that over long periods neither approach is of much value in reducing unemployment, which may be part of our existence no matter what macroeconomic policies we follow.) Note that these disagreements are of a type that, like earthquake prediction, are likely to become less important over time as our science advances and new evidence and understanding will tend to make one economic story become more convincing than the other possible stories. (See Box 1-5.)

What makes one story come to be accepted over others? Some economic storytellers do a recognizably better job of holding constant other variables, as is appropriate. Also, information tends to become better over time—either because we have longer time periods to analyze or because data can be assembled to answer a specific question. Moreover, as statistical techniques for analyzing the available data improve, some of these techniques are becoming more accepted than others. Finally, human behavior may actually change over time, so a theory that explained behavior fairly well in the past is replaced by another theory that is more relevant to current behavior.

1.11 A FINAL COMMENT

We have taken what will seem to some a rather odd methodological stance. The "modern" view is that one should, as a scientist, select that one theory among all the competing theories which *predicts* the best. We submit that very little in the way of scientific progress is actually made this way. Sometimes different theories can each best explain different aspects of the same thing (as with the wave and particle theories of light in physics). Questions of realism of assumptions also cannot be decided defin-

1-6   True or False?   A good theory always predicts well.

False.   Some theories predict and explain; others just explain. Theories that both predict and explain make very convincing stories, but some stories, such as Darwin's theory of evolution, have done quite well without giving "the reader" much foresight. After all, the theory of evolution doesn't tell us when or whether we will lose our "baby toes" or gain additional fingers. Nevertheless, many scientists are convinced that this theory is rich in explanatory power.

itively. Theoretical models should be tested by any means possible, whether by direct tests of assumptions or indirect comparisons between observable behavior and the hypotheses flowing from various theories. Hidden assumptions are a major source of the mistrust and contempt that so many people feel for economics and economists. As Nobel laureate Sir John Hicks once observed: "Pure economics has a remarkable way of producing rabbits out of a hat—apparently *a priori* propositions which apparently refer to reality. It is fascinating to try to discover how the rabbits got in; for those of us who do not believe in magic must be convinced that they got in somehow." The trouble is that economists too often fail to communicate to others their own knowledge about "how the rabbits got in." We do not propose to make that mistake, at least consciously, in this book.

Scientific advance stems, as Amelie Rorty notes, from "our ability to engage in continuous conversation (rhetoric) testing one another, discovering our hidden presuppositions, changing our minds because we have listened to the voices of our fellows. Lunatics also change their minds, but their minds change with the tides of the moon and not because they have listened, really listened, to their friends' questions and objections."[2] (See Box 1-6.)

SUMMARY

1. Economic analysis provides a basis for evaluating the consequences of alternative actions, judging the performance of the economy, predicting future events, and planning.

2. Microeconomics and macroeconomics are both usually interested in explaining things in the large. Microeconomics analyzes things in the small to better understand the large.

3. General equilibrium emphasizes mutual interdependence and gives us insight into the overall performance of the economy. Partial equilibrium analyzes part of the system (one or more individuals, firms, or markets) in isolation, holding other things constant.

---

[2]Amelie Rorty, "Experiments in Philosophic Genre: Descartes' Meditations," *Critical Inquiry* (March 1983), p. 562.

4. Static analysis refers to a state which will be maintained indefinitely if not disturbed by some external shock. The position that is maintained is called the equilibrium state.

5. Comparative statics is the comparison of equilibrium states after an external shock. Dynamic analysis observes the *motion* of variables once an equilibrium state has been altered.

6. Positive economics covers analysis dealing with hypotheses that are generally testable by reference to facts; normative economics is not "testable" in the same way since it relies on value judgments.

7. Like other scientists, economists are involved in storytelling. Economists try to persuade their readers, select their facts, and "invent" their stories. That is, economists are looking for a theory of causation (a story).

8. Stories are often seized upon by others, then reworked, expanded, and passed on again. Thus there must be consistent ground rules. All scientific disciplines conform to a common pattern in logic and concept.

9. Economists disagree on normative issues or on the validity of a particular economic theory (story). However, on many issues in economics there is much common ground.

WORDS AND CONCEPTS FOR REVIEW

theoretical perspectives
mode of presentation
analytical objective
microeconomic analysis
macroeconomic analysis
general equilibrium analysis
partial equilibrium analysis

static analysis
equilibrium state
comparative statics
dynamic analysis
positive economics
normative economics

REVIEW QUESTIONS

1. What is the purpose of economic theory?

2. What are economic principles? What is an economic model?

3. If the results anticipated from the use of an economic principle in a particular case do not occur, what are likely to be the sources of the difficulty?

4. Discuss the statement: "Economic theory does not provide the answers to a particular question but rather serves as a guide to the facts necessary to obtain an answer."

5. In what sense can empirical studies show that a principle is not applicable in a particular case, yet never prove that a principle is applicable?

6. Why is empirical work completely futile without some analytical framework?

7. It has been suggested that the only difference between macro- and microeconomics is that the former deals with larger numbers. Does this seem to you a suitable basis for the distinction? Discuss.

8. "The generality of a theoretical model cannot be determined except in relation to another theoretical model that is similar in structure, or in relation to a particular set of phenomena that the model purports to describe." Give some examples to illustrate this proposition.

9. Classical hydrodynamics deals with the properties of "ideal fluids" that are entirely lacking such properties as viscosity and friction. No such fluid exists in practice; even air is highly "imperfect," as the possibility of heavier-than-air flight indicates. Evidently classical hydrodynamics is highly unrealistic; do you suppose that it is also useless? Discuss.

10. In economic analysis, an equilibrium position is often described as an "optimum." Do you see any danger in this association of ideas? Discuss.

11. Should economists make policy recommendations? What if two economists offer different recommendations? How does one decide which economist, if either, should be trusted?

12. Distinguish between partial and general equilibrium theory.

13. What aspects of the behavior of the pendulum of a grandfather clock would you mention if you were analyzing its static properties; that is, how would you describe the equilibrium position of the pendulum? Would a dynamic analysis of the behavior of the pendulum involve anything more in the way of general principles? Discuss.

14. Can a definition be "right" or "wrong"? Explain.

SUGGESTED READINGS

Blaug, Mark. *The Methodology of Economics: Or How Economists Explain.* Cambridge, England: Cambridge University Press, 1980.

Friedman, Milton. "The Methodology of Positive Economics." In Milton Friedman (ed.). *Essays in Positive Economics.* Chicago: University of Chicago Press, 1953, pp. 3–43.

Knight, Frank. *The Economic Organization.* New York: Harper and Row, 1965.

Koopmans, Tjalling. *Three Essays on the State of Economic Science.* New York: McGraw-Hill, 1957.

McCloskey, Donald. "The Rhetoric of Economics." *Journal of Economic Literature* (June 1983), pp. 481-517.

Nagel, Ernest. "Assumptions in Economic Theory." *American Economic Review* (May 1963), pp. 211-19.

Pirsig, Robert. *Zen and the Art of Motorcycle Maintenance.* New York: Bantam Books, 1974.

Stigler, George. *The Theory of Price,* 4th ed. New York: Macmillan, 1987, Chapter 1.

2

The Economic System: Consumers, Producers, and Market Transactions

2.1 INTRODUCTION

The first step in any theoretical analysis is posing a problem and deciding provisionally which phenomena require investigation in order to solve the problem. If our problem is describing the workings of a market economy, we must start with a reasonably definite conception of the nature of such an economy—its human and material components, its institutional setting, and its characteristic modes of operation.

2.2 BASIC DECISION UNITS

In keeping with a division that occurs in every actual economy, we begin by distinguishing two primary types of decision-making units: *households* and *business firms*.

Households consist of persons (most commonly, families) who utilize funds from current or past income either to acquire goods and services for the satisfaction of personal wants or to purchase assets to add to previously accumulated savings. Each household ordinarily contains at least one factor owner whose provision of input (or **factor**) units to business firms—labor, land, money capital, entrepreneurial services—yields income in the form of wages, rent, interest, or profit.

Firms consist of persons who undertake and carry on production activities. A firm may be a single individual (say, a dentist) or an extensive organization with the legal status of a corporation. In theoretical work, we generally do not distinguish one kind of firm from the other, since the technical operations of the two may be similar. We *do* distinguish a firm, which is a decision unit, from a plant or enterprise, which is a technical production unit. In general, a firm may own and operate any number of distinct plants or enterprises.

For some purposes, it is useful to group firms into **industries**—groups of firms producing goods that are technically similar or close substitutes for one another. Thus the retail grocery industry consists of firms operating retail grocery stores, the steel industry consists of steel-manufacturing enterprises, and so forth. In the real world, of course, industries do not have sharp boundaries. The products of one group of firms shade off gradually into those of another, and brands at opposite ends of the quality scale may be poorer substitutes for one another than each is for some entirely different good. Sellers of low-priced cars may compete more directly with bus companies, for example, than with sellers of the most expensive cars. As a rule, however, the definition of an industry is relatively clear in practice. For example, various brands of washing machines are substitutes for one another much more than they are substitutes for television sets.

In the real world, households are not always easy to distinguish from firms. Indeed, much of existing economic theory—strictly speaking, all of it—could be stated in such a way as to eliminate separate mention of households and firms. Firms are, at heart, merely collections of households—"intermediaries" between household production and household consumption. The only reason these collections are formed is because costs of production are lower than if all goods were produced within the household.

The distinction is convenient for purposes of exposition, however, for it permits us to discuss separately decisions that are made primarily to satisfy immediate human desires. For similar reasons, it might be desirable explicitly to recognize types of transactors other than households and business firms: cooperatives, labor unions, charitable organizations, government agencies, and the like. Transactors of these kinds play distinctive and important roles in actual economic life, but they do not fit easily into existing theoretical frameworks. Except in occasional asides, we shall ignore the existence of such transactors in the remainder of this book.

2.3 THE FUNCTIONS OF DECISION UNITS

Since everyone is familiar with households, their functions require little comment. It should be emphasized, however, that a major activity of some households is the management of an **asset portfolio**—various forms of accumulated wealth such as cars, stocks, real estate, and money. In this respect certain households are more like banks or insurance companies than run-of-the-mill consumers, who are essentially concerned with earning and spending wage income. Note also that since households typically consist of several people, some of their decisions are bound to represent compromise solutions to "conflict of interest" problems like those arising in large business firms.

The business firm, considered as an entity distinct from the individuals who own and manage it, performs several functions. First, it acquires ownership or rental of productive factors (such as raw materials, buildings, and labor) and retains title to products produced by those inputs until they are disposed of in the market. In order to acquire factor services prior to the sale of products, the firm must possess money capital, which the owners may obtain from their own funds, from previously accumulated profits, or from outside borrowing. Second, the firm coordinates production activities. In a market economy, firms must make decisions about types and quantities of goods to be produced and offered for sale, about methods of production (and thus types and quantities of factors to be used), and frequently about prices. Third, the firm must predict future market conditions and make present decisions in the light of these projections.

In a static society, the firm's management functions would involve only routine decisions once a satisfactory program of products, factor combinations, outputs, and prices had been attained. But in a changing and growing world, the firm's owners must constantly revise their estimates of future prospects and adjust their policies gradually in the light of realized results. Decisions may stem from informed judgments about the future, but those in charge can never be certain about the correctness of their forecasts. If forecasts are accurate, or if the firm is lucky, it may earn excellent profits and growth; this good fortune need not be shared with factor suppliers, at least in the short run. But if forecasts are inaccurate, or if the firm is unlucky, then the shoe is on the other foot—for the firm contracts in advance for most factor services and makes most payments prior to the sale of products; moreover, lenders of money capital have a prior claim on any positive earnings that the firm's owners may enjoy. To be sure, factor suppliers run some chance of loss: workers might not get their full pay, and investors might not receive favorable returns on their investments. But the greatest loss, like the greatest gain, falls to the firm's owners, the coordinating agents who direct its development. (See Box 2-1.)

2.4 THE PERFORMANCE OF FUNCTIONS WITHIN THE FIRM

Decisions obviously must be made by human beings. Which persons or groups of persons within the firm actually perform its various functions? To answer this question, we must classify business firms into two groups: those in which the owners and managers are the same persons and those in which the two groups are largely separate.

In the first case, regardless of the legal form of organization, the persons who own the enterprise constitute the entrepreneurial group making the policy decisions, so they must perform the management functions. Since, as owners, the entrepreneurial

---

2-1   True or False?   For a firm to be profitable, it must be large.

False.   Many smaller firms have witnessed phenomenal profits and growth rates, especially in the computer industries. Small firms are just as likely to show a profit as large firms. Adapting well to *change* is what is critical; large firms may be no better able to anticipate, observe, and react to change than are small firms.

group directly controls the disposition of earnings, it obtains the profits in the event of success and bears the greatest loss in the event of failure. Under proprietorship and partnership forms of business organization, even the owners' personal property may be taken to satisfy the firm's debts.

Matters are more complicated in the second case. The typical corporation is owned by large numbers of relatively small stockholders who are not in a position to influence the management of the enterprise and are not interested in doing so. Even the holders of relatively large blocks of stock are rarely interested in management policies, concerning themselves only with dividend payments and increases in the market value of their holdings. The typical part-owner of a large corporation performs no entrepreneurial functions beyond the purely nominal one of ownership, plus the provision of money capital. Thus, the part-owner's position differs very little from that of a bondholder, except that there is a somewhat greater risk of loss. The stockholder does receive a share of the earnings, of course, provided that the persons controlling the enterprise decide to make dividend payments; however, profits earned by the enterprise do not necessarily accrue directly to the stockholders. Most large corporations are avid savers on their own account, thereby raising the value of the firm (hence stock prices).

The primary functions of large corporations are performed by the executive group—top management officials or business leaders of the enterprise. These persons typically own only a small percentage of the corporation's total stock, though these holdings may constitute a major part of individual managers' personal wealth and income. In some cases, the stock holdings of the management group will be too small to give them a direct financial stake in the firm's operations, except as these operations affect their salaries and bonuses. Technically, the executives are always responsible to the stockholders; but the influence exercised by the latter is, in practice, often very limited. (See Box 2-2.)

2.5 GOALS OF DECISION UNITS

It is conceivable that atoms of hydrogen and oxygen suffer traumatic shocks when chemistry students force them to fuse into water molecules; but even if physical objects had feelings, these would be ignored by physical scientists, who have devised models for analyzing physical behavior that are valid regardless of such considerations. Social scientists might follow the same procedure; after all, human beings are just material objects from one point of view. In practice, however, it has not seemed sensible to formulate theories about human behavior without taking explicit account of **purposeful action**. That is, human beings might not follow mechanical patterns of behavior, but they do respond in certain characteristic ways to opportunities that offer them chances to increase their material welfare or social prestige. In dealing with economic phenomena, economists generally have found it convenient to proceed partly on the basis of mechanical descriptions of observable regularities in behavior (as in the physical sciences) and partly on the basis of maximization assumptions that impute goal-seeking behavior to individuals.

2-2 Do business firms have a social responsibility?

It is observed that some companies carry on educational enrichment programs for communities, take on projects in lower-income areas (like improving inner city school systems or assisting in urban housing projects), subsidize public television, or become involved in cleaning up the environment. Are such actions appropriate activities of the firm?

The opponents of firms engaging in projects indicating social responsibility believe that executives are responsible for making as large a profit as possible without violating laws or ethics. Indeed, making high profits (or at least seeking them) can be argued to be *itself* an act of social responsibility: as a society we want to convert *low* value goods into *high* value goods

through production—and profit-seekers attempt this. Moreover, it is claimed that executives have no right to spend the firm's money on social programs. Let individual firm owners— stockholders or proprietors—spend as they wish on social concerns.

On the other hand, some social problems (such as pollution) may be caused by the firm. The firm might feel obliged to take care of the costs they have imposed on the community. Furthermore, many social programs might be considered long-run profit maximization. Such programs often create customer loyalty and respect which bring in greater profits in the long run.

The assumption that individuals act purposefully does not, in itself, say anything about behavior; it merely implies that whatever individuals do is done with a purpose! To get any mileage out of the assumption, we must specify not only what is to be maximized but also what are the alternative choices facing the individual.

It must be recognized from the outset that no assumption of a single goal pursued by every type of economic unit can be entirely satisfactory; if our assumption is very general it will yield no useful implications, and if it is very specific it will apply only to a limited number of cases. The best procedure to follow, therefore, is to start with a very general assumption that is open to a variety of different interpretations and later introduce additional specializing assumptions as required to deal with particular cases. The assumption traditionally adopted in economic analysis is that each decision unit seeks to maximize its own economic well-being, where "economic well-being" is assumed to be some function of the quantities of goods produced, consumed, and traded by the unit. The application of this assumption to household consumers encounters relatively few difficulties. Its application to business firms poses certain problems, however, especially in cases where ownership and management are separated.

2.6 MAXIMIZATION OF HOUSEHOLD SATISFACTION

With regard to households, the maximization assumption is formulated to relate quantities of various goods to an imaginary magnitude of satisfaction called **utility**. Utility is assumed to increase with an increase in the quantity of any good consumed by the household and to decrease with an increase in the quantity of any factor service that the household makes available to firms or other households. In choosing among alternatives that involve the purchase and sale of goods, the household is constrained, of course, by the requirement that the value of its purchases at any time cannot be greater than the value of whatever money or goods or services it supplies to finance them; market exchange is a peculiar kind of two-way street in which traffic (demands for goods) is permitted to move in one direction only when a volume of traffic (supplies of goods) of equal money value simultaneously moves in the opposite direction.

The nature and implications of the maximization assumption will be developed later. Here we merely observe that it implies, among other things, that households will seek to purchase units of any given good from the cheapest available source of supply and to sell units of any factor (such as their labor) to the highest bidder, with allowances made for differences in quality in the first instance and for differences in working conditions in the second.

2.7 MAXIMIZATION OF BUSINESS PROFITS

Business firms operate much like households in some respects, supplying their workers as well as their managers and owners with services that yield direct satisfaction. For the most part, however, business firms function as technical intermediaries; that is, they carry out production activities not for their own sake but to provide income to the households of their owners. Hence the appropriate way to formulate the maximization assumption in this case is to relate quantities of goods used as factor inputs and quantities produced as final outputs to a magnitude called **profit**. Like households, firms are limited in their choices of market activities by the requirement that the value of goods purchased at any point in time cannot exceed the value of resources available for financing them; moreover, offers to sell goods imply a demand for money or other goods of equal value in exchange. Firms are also constrained by technological conditions: outputs cannot be produced in unlimited quantities from given quantities of inputs. These specifications will be elaborated later. Already, it should be clear that the assumption of **profit maximization** entails much more than a mere greedy pursuit of financial gain; the behavior of firms depends not only on external market circumstances but also on existing social legislation, the personal attitudes of business managers towards their work force, and numerous other elements that effectively determine "technological conditions."

2.8 PROFIT MAXIMIZATION: SOME QUALIFICATIONS

By and large, businesses operate under conditions of considerable ignorance and uncertainty about prices, prospective sales, costs, and so forth. This being so, there is no objective way to determine whether a firm "really" seeks to maximize profit, because various firms (and various managers of the same firm) may have very different ideas about future circumstances and may therefore operate on very different assumptions about the relation between present inputs and outputs and expected profitability. One choice of inputs and outputs may promise high gains with great uncertainty, while another may promise moderate gains with little risk. Some kind of subjective weighing of risk factors will enter into the definition of profit in these circumstances. Similarly, one strategy of pricing may offer short-run gains at the expense of long-run losses (customer "ill will") while another offers moderate returns over a long period of time. Such return streams over time must be *discounted* to the present, and different decision makers have different discount rates. Opinions may differ among firms and their managers about the relative "profitability" of one strategy as compared with another.

Another qualification of profit maximization results from the separation of ownership and management in large corporations. The typical owner—the stockholder—has little voice in the making of decisions. The typical executive may have interests that diverge more or less from those of the owners; he or she may strive for power and prestige within the business community in ways that either do not affect profits or affect them adversely. Executives can always rationalize actions taken in pursuit of personal rather than corporate goals on the ground that they are "in the long-run interest of the corporation," appearances to the contrary notwithstanding. One should not make too much of this, for there is a tendency among corporate officials to regard their corporation as a separate entity, distinct from the stockholders who own it, and to identify their own welfare with that of the corporation even though they may not themselves receive any portion of its net profits. Almost all executives regard their firm's profits as the best measure of their own professional success. If executives fail to earn as high a rate of return as informed stockholders believe possible, the stockholders may revolt and seek a new set of executives. Failure to earn a normal rate of return can also endanger the continued existence of a firm, for if it continues for long enough, a firm will be forced into bankruptcy and reorganization. Finally, a satisfactory rate of profit is essential for continued expansion of the firm. Profits directly provide funds for expansion and facilitate acquisition of additional capital. Growth of the enterprise not only increases executives' income but also enhances their prestige and power.

When there are true conflicts of interest between owners and managers, the managers' interests often prevail. Executives might, for example, oppose a projected expansion (or a "takeover" by others of their firm) that would be profitable to the firm over a period of time but involved bringing in new stockholders who might gain control of the firm and eliminate the present management. In other instances, executives might dispose of current assets at a heavy loss in order to obtain funds to meet pressing obligations which, if ignored, would lead to immediate reorganization. Most drastically, management is likely to delay complete liquidation of an unprofitable business beyond the point at which it should be undertaken in the stockholders' interests. The managers not only dislike seeing the firm to which they have long been attached disappear but also seek to avoid loss of their positions. Through undermaintenance of plant and equipment, depletion of inventories, failure to cover depreciation charges, and sale of assets, the firm may continue to operate until the owners' equity is completely dissipated, whereas earlier liquidation might preserve a substantial portion of the stockholders' money capital.

Many apparent qualifications to the profit-maximization assumption have to do not with the goal itself but with the vigor displayed in pursuing it. Particularly at junior levels, managers in large-scale businesses may be less energetic than those in individual enterprises. Management of a large business can easily become overcautious. The desire to maintain the status quo—to protect the positions of present executives—may encourage managers to avoid changes that appear profitable for fear that expected gains will not materialize. Since profits seldom accrue directly to executives, the dynamic qualities of management characteristic of smaller enterprises may be overwhelmed by fear of "rocking the boat." The large corporation's complex structure may itself discourage change. The goals of top, middle, and lower management often diverge; and top management may have difficulty in getting enough information from lower echelons to ensure that its policies are carried out. (See Box 2-3.)

2.9 ALTERNATIVES TO PROFIT MAXIMIZATION

If profit maximization is not to be regarded as the primary goal of business firms, what alternatives might seem reasonable? Several have been proposed.

1. **Satisfactory Profits.** Business firms may aim at a "satisfactory" rate of profit rather than a maximum figure. Top management may be more concerned with a steady growth in earnings than with higher but fluctuating earnings.

    Short-run acceptance of a goal of "satisfactory" profits does not necessarily involve failure to seek maximum returns over the long run. Management may, for example, believe that long-run profits will be greater if the firm avoids full exploitation of all temporary situations, which might allow high profits for a time but encourage the development of new firms. However, emphasis upon "satisfactory" profits does affect the firm's reactions in the short run. If a firm is attempting to maximize short-run profits, an increase in demand will almost of necessity lead to a price increase; but if it is seeking only "satisfactory" profits, prices may be left unchanged.

2-3   Define economic profits. Can a firm maximize these profits? If so, is it best to maximize profits precisely?

Economic profits are defined as revenue minus costs, where costs are the opportunity cost of using the productive resources. Whether firms can or want to maximize economic profits depends, of course, on how we define the term "maximizing economic profits." One could argue that with incomplete information firms do not know their demand and cost curves and hence cannot determine how either total revenue or total cost will vary as their behavior changes. If long-run profit maximization is the goal, then perhaps only the "fittest" firms will survive, although "fitness" is difficult to determine at any point in time.

Profit-maximizing firms will, however, gradually accumulate financial assets, and non-profit-maximizing firms will be eventually eliminated. Also, to maximize profits precisely may have costs greater than benefits: information (like all economic goods) is costly to acquire, so firms might try to do as well as they can subject to the constraints of information and uncertainty.

2. Sales Maximization. William Baumol has argued that maximization of *sales,* rather than of profits, is the primary goal of the management of larger businesses, given a satisfactory rate of profit. Sales are a more readily observable measure of management success than profits, particularly in light of most firms' conviction that their share of total industry sales is of primary importance for long-term success. Baumol also suggests that there is a closer correlation between the salaries of executives and the gross sales of their businesses than between salaries and net profits; thus executives are more concerned about the former than the latter.

3. Nonpecuniary Goals. In both small, owner-managed enterprises and large corporations, the persons making decisions are often influenced by nonpecuniary motives, which may take precedence over profit maximization. If prestige is very important to the executives, they may undertake policies that enhance their standing in the community or in the industry but do not contribute to profit maximization. Moreover, most business leaders seek power over as large a "business empire" as possible. While in many cases profit maximization is the best path to expansion, in other cases it may not be. History offers many examples of business firms that undertook unprofitable expansions merely because the executives wished to exercise authority over more extensive empires. Such policies are more likely to be followed in large corporations, in which executives do not directly benefit from profits, than in small enterprises; but they are not absent even in the latter.

Large firms sometimes follow policies that they regard as best serving the interests of the community or nation as a whole, even though not directly advantageous for profit maximization. Such firms may be reluctant to cut wages or lay off workers in a depression, in the (possibly correct) belief that such action will aggravate the decline in economic activity. Or, for apparently humanitarian reasons, they might not fire nonproductive employees, for example those impaired by health or age-related difficulties.[1]

Businesses operate within a complicated and restrictive framework of legal and social institutions. They rarely seek to maximize profits by taking illegal action, though criminal behavior is certainly not unknown. Furthermore, they are likely to avoid certain practices which, although legal, are contrary to accepted standards of business practice. Thus, they may avoid price cutting if such practices are generally frowned upon by other firms.

4. Preference Maximization. The preceding remarks suggest that for a more satisfactory analysis, the profit-maximization assumption should be replaced by a more general assumption of "utility maximization" which includes various goals besides profit maximization. Such an assumption would seem particularly desirable in situations of ignorance and uncertainty; in such cases the profit-maximization rule is inadequate because executives are confronted by a

---

[1]However, if such policies are known in advance, employees may be willing to work for less; this "employer-insurance" represents an *implicit* contract which may well be consistent with profit maximization (note, for example, the Japanese practice of providing a lifetime job).

group of possible outcomes with different degrees of probability, rather than a single profit potential. Further progress in certain areas of economic analysis may require such an assumption. But the complexity of the overall analysis would be tremendously increased if profit maximization were replaced by a broader goal such as utility maximization.

2.10 THE NATURE AND GOALS OF DECISION UNITS: THEORY AND PRACTICE

It should be clear on the basis of the preceding discussion that the "households" and "firms" of theoretical analysis, although modeled after flesh-and-blood consumers and hard-driving business executives, cannot be more than pale and imperfect reflections of real people. To avoid confusion about these matters, it may be helpful to think of theoretical households as typical consumers rather than specific individuals. In effect, the theory deals with statistical stereotypes, decision-making units that conform to the behavior of an "average" household. The models will conform much less well to the behavior of any specific household—professional households, households with three children, "hard-hat" households, black households, and so on. Thus it is not a criticism of a theory of household behavior to say that its implications are contradicted by the behavior of any particular individual; the issue is seldom whether the theory applies to particular people but rather whether it provides a reasonably accurate description of average behavior.

A similar set of observations applies to the concept of a "firm." No actual business firm could possibly be as simple as the firms considered in theory. Whereas we generally deal in theory with single-product firms, actual firms typically produce many different outputs. Actual businesses use inputs at earlier dates to produce at later (sometimes much later) dates, meanwhile holding large stocks of raw materials and goods in process; firms considered in theory are usually regarded as instantaneous converters of raw materials into finished outputs. Actual firms stumble and fumble about rather than adjusting their operations decisively to changing conditions; theoretical firms are treated as if they not only knew exactly what they should do at any point in time but also were sometimes able to jump immediately from one situation to another without any time delay and without any cost.

As with households, therefore, so with firms it is essential to view decision units as "average" or typical representations. It may happen that simplifications introduced into theoretical work ignore features of the real world that are crucial in describing actual behavior, in which case the theoretical analysis may be worthless. But these simplifications can also be benign—they may facilitate analysis and permit us to derive useful conclusions that might have been obscured by a more complex theory. It is no use doing theoretical work in an empirical science with one's head in the clouds; potential flaws in basic assumptions should be borne in mind at every stage. But neither is it sensible to scorn a theory for lack of realism before its implications for observed behavior have even been revealed.

As in bridge or physics or drama, so too in economics: one learns best by doing. We have said enough about economic theory and the economic system to set the stage for interested learners; it only remains to raise the curtain for the play to begin.

SUMMARY

1. A household is a group of one or a few people who provide business firms with labor, land, money capital, or entrepreneurship (in various combinations) in exchange for wages, rent, interest or profit.

2. A firm is a group of people who undertake and carry on production activities. It may consist of one person or thousands (including stockholders, managers, and employees). A firm is a decision unit, while a plant is a technical production unit.

3. Markets do not have sharp boundaries.

4. The firm must acquire ownership of production factors or their services, coordinate production activities, and make decisions in an environment of incomplete information and uncertainty.

5. Business firms can be usefully classified into two groups: those in which owners and managers are separate and those in which they are the same.

6. Individuals act purposefully—that is, people do things with a purpose.

7. Households seek to maximize utility (satisfaction).

8. Businesses seek to maximize profits subject to the constraints of technology.

9. The goal of profit maximization is the topic of some debate among economists: Instead of aiming for maximum profits, top management may choose to accept satisfactory levels of profit with stable growth rates, may seek to maximize sales as an alternative to profits, or may focus on prestige and other so-called nonpecuniary goals.

10. When studying the behavior of households and firms, it is best to think in terms of average or typical representations.

WORDS AND CONCEPTS FOR REVIEW

households
firms
industries
asset portfolio
factors
purposeful action
utility

profit
profit maximization
satisfactory profits
sales maximization
nonpecuniary goals
preference maximization

REVIEW QUESTIONS

1. Imagine three people stranded on an island. One of them claims all rights to the only source of water (a small spring), another claims possession of the only indigenous source of food (a grove of coconut trees), while the third takes possession of a canoe and becomes the sole source of protein (fish). Theorize about trading possibilities in this situation: Will trade take place? If so, will it occur randomly, or will definite trading posts be established? What factors will govern rates of exchange among the goods traded? How will rates of exchange be expressed: in terms of one good, in terms of an arbitrary unit of account such as dollars, or what? How often will individuals trade; specifically, will they have any reason to trade in large lots rather than small?

Under what conditions will production specialization lead to greater total output? (These are not simple questions. Some possible answers are suggested in later chapters, but you should try to work some of them out at this stage.)

2. What is the difference between a firm and an industry? Between a firm and a plant?

3. As the term *industry* is usually used, does potato farming constitute an industry? Law practice? University teaching?

4. Would you regard firms producing toasters, refrigerators, and air conditioners as constituting separate industries, or is each an element of the electrical appliance industry? Discuss.

5. What are some examples of firms operating in more than one industry?

6. Business firms perform what major functions?

7. What are the principal characteristics of the two major types of business firms?

8. What is meant by maximizing?

9. If you operated a small restaurant, what factors might serve as constraints on profit maximization?

10. What is the significance of uncertainty for the goal of profit maximization?

11. In a large-scale firm, is it more realistic to assume that top management is seeking to maximize profits for the firm or personal income for management personnel? How might these two goals not be conflicting? In what types of situations may they conflict?

12. Are large firms or small firms more likely to be influenced by nonpecuniary goals? Explain.

SUGGESTED READINGS

Baumol, William. *Economic Theory and Operations Analysis,* 4th ed. Englewood Cliffs, NJ: Prentice-Hall, 1977, Chapter 15.

Cyert, Richard M. and March, James G. *A Behavioral Theory of the Firm.* Englewood Cliffs, NJ: Prentice-Hall, 1965, Chapter 7.

Machlup, Fritz. "Theories of the Firm: Marginalists, Behavioral, Managerial." *American Economic Review* (March 1967), pp. 1–33.

Scherer, Frederick M. *Industrial Market Structure and Economic Performance.* Chicago: Rand McNally, 1980, pp. 29–41.

Williamson, Oliver E. "The Modern Corporation: Origins, Evolution, Attributes." *Journal of Economic Literature* (December 1981), 1537–68.

3

Supply and Demand

3.1 INTRODUCTION

Like scissors, which function by the interaction of two distinct blades, so do supply and demand interact to determine value (price) and quantities exchanged. But supply and demand do not operate in a void. Prices and quantities exchanged of various outputs and inputs (such as land, labor, and capital) are also affected by the structure of markets—that is, the prevailing relationships among potential buyers and sellers. The price and the output of a good is normally different, for example, if the entire supply is controlled by one firm than if it is provided by a large number of independent sellers. The number of buyers and the relationships prevailing among them likewise affects price and output, although independent competitive behavior is more pervasive on the demand side. The nature of markets for factor units affects the prices paid for them, and thus the costs of producing the products made with them and the distribution of income among factor owners.

3.2 THE CONCEPT OF A MARKET

A **market** consists of a group of buyers, sellers, and middlepersons in sufficiently close contact with one another to carry on exchange under stipulated rules or customs. For some goods, such as gravel, markets are numerous and more or less isolated. Since transportation costs are so high relative to selling prices that the good will not be shipped any substantial distance, buyers are in contact only with local producers. Price and output are thus determined in a number of small markets, and total production of gravel is the sum of the amounts of output determined separately in each of the markets. In other industries, markets are nationwide. Automobile manufacturers, for example, sell to dealers throughout the country and determine (wholesale) price and output on the basis of considerations relating to the entire economy.

Perfection in Market Conditions

Price and output are determined not only by market relationships prevailing among buyers and sellers but also by the absence or presence of other institutional factors that affect the behavior of both the buyer and the seller. The two major considerations of this type are the extent of knowledge about market conditions and the mobility of factors such as labor and capital. Deviations from perfect knowledge or perfect mobility of factors are known as **imperfections**.

A market characterized by complete absence of imperfections, as well as by purely competitive market conditions (many buyers and sellers of a homogenous product), is described as **perfectly competitive**. In this type of market, all sellers and buyers have complete knowledge of market conditions, and frictions restraining the immediate adjustment of price and output are absent. Because producing units have complete knowledge of costs and market conditions, they are able to maximize profits at all times. Because factor units are freely mobile, they will always move quickly to the most attractive employments.

The concept of perfection in markets may be applied to nonpurely-competitive markets as well. In monopolistic competition, for example, perfection requires perfect factor mobility and complete knowledge on the part of sellers about cost and demand conditions. In oligopoly, perfection requires that firms know the reactions of their competitors to their own policies, along with other data pertinent to profit maximization.

The assumption of perfection is frequently useful as a first approximation in the development of an analysis, in order to make it manageable. Actually, all markets are characterized by substantial imperfections. There are two major types: imperfect knowledge and imperfect mobility.

Imperfect Knowledge

Factor owners and business firms rarely, if ever, possess all the information they need to attain maximization goals. Workers may be unaware of employment alternatives. Persons about to establish new business enterprises have only limited knowledge of profit possibilities. Despite improved techniques, sellers have inadequate knowledge of potential sales at various price levels and imprecise knowledge of how actual costs will vary with production levels. Information about income possibilities, sales, and costs depends upon the institutions and technology of the period—the state of education, the state of market research and cost analysis techniques, the activity of government agencies in preparing and distributing information about job and profit possibilities, trends in national income, and so on. Because of imperfect knowledge, outputs of various goods differ from what they would otherwise be, and both resource allocation and income distribution are affected. Too many producers enter some lines of production, while others make unwarranted plant expansions or fail to make other changes which would be profitable. Prices may be set at levels that do not maximize profits, and production may exceed or fall short of the quantities that can be sold at profitable prices.

Mobility of Factor Units

There are numerous restrictions, in practice, on the **mobility of factors**—that is, the movement of factors of production from one use to another. Many specialized factors are not easily adaptable to changing conditions. Machinery constructed for one purpose is often completely unsuited for any other use. A railroad grade, including expensive bridges and tunnels, is ordinarily useless for any purpose except railroad operation. Apple trees cannot produce anything but apples.

In some instances the transfer of resources, although possible, is not feasible because of costs of transference; streetcar rails on abandoned lines are often left in the pavement because costs of removal are prohibitive. As a result of nonadaptability, resources will be continued in a particular use long after they have ceased to yield the return which was necessary to bring them into the field.

Labor likewise is not entirely adaptable. Persons trained in certain lines of work cannot easily shift to employment requiring different skills. For example, "human capital" embedded in economics professors may be ill suited to producing television sets or football games. Geographical mobility of labor is seriously restricted by costs of moving, by family ties, and by preferences for living in certain areas. Workers are typically reluctant to shift away from present employers and occupations to move to other areas.

Markets and Pricing: a Caveat

In every advanced economy, a large portion of productive resources is devoted to market activities. What comes to mind? Wholesaling, retailing, advertising, banking, and transport, to name just a few. Most of us spend substantial amounts of our scarce labor resources traveling to work, banks, and stores. One must be either very young or very dead to be ignorant of the general nature of markets and trade. Nevertheless, it is hard to *define* a market. How do we throw together all the different markets such as supermarkets, department stores, drug stores, and restaurants? After all, an incredible variety of exchange arrangements exists in the real world—organized securities markets, wholesale auction markets, foreign exchange markets, real estate markets, labor markets, and so forth. The problem of defining a market is further aggravated by goods being priced and traded in various ways at various locations by various kinds of buyers and sellers. In short, narrow definitions tend to be too specific while broad definitions tend to be too vague.

In the past, economists have dealt with this problem by ignoring it, either leaving the reader to decide what a market is or defining "a market" in such a broad fashion to make the concept of little value—as "an area where supply and demand interact to determine price." Although such definitions are relatively harmless, they are also uninformative. In fact, one comes away from most theoretical models with such a vague idea of markets that one might almost suppose prices and quantities to be determined by "ghostly forces" (supply and demand) rather than by people.

The reason why it is so difficult to define a market is that there is no such "animal" as *a* market. The closest we can get to defining a market is as "an organized set of institutional arrangements (a set of rules or customs) for the negotiation of exchange between buyers and sellers." This excludes elementary barter (where there is nothing "organized" about trading arrangements) and includes highly organized markets with no particular physical location (such as markets for foreign exchange). At the heart of this definition is the presumption of an exact set of institutional arrangements governing trading.

3.3 ABSOLUTE AND RELATIVE PRICES

In the past fifty years, very few goods have fallen in **absolute price**—that is, the price one pays in dollars and cents. There have been a few well-known examples of falling absolute prices—the personal handheld calculator, the video recorder, the home computer, and so on—but the evidence suggests that *most* prices have risen in money terms. The value of a dollar in terms of goods has fallen. (See Box 3-1.)

Absolute price increases are not important at all because money wages are also rising. Reiterating, it is the price of one good relative to another—the **relative price**—that is crucial. If the price of movies rises relative to all other goods, we could predict that less people would go to the movies. They would look for substitutes like bowling or watching television, or they would just go to the movies less frequently. (See Box 3-2.)

3-1   True or False?   During the period 1960 to 1973, the price of gasoline at the pump rose markedly, but the quantities demanded of gasoline did not fall. This phenomenon reveals a flaw in the so-called law of demand.

False.   While it is true that gasoline prices rose significantly, so did just about everything else— including wages. As it turns out, the *relative* price of gasoline did not change much during this period; and thus we would not expect a fall in the quantity demanded (holding other things, especially income, constant).

3-2   True or False?   All other things being equal, when compared with a childless couple, a couple with young children is more likely to dine out at an expensive restaurant than at an inexpensive restaurant.

True.   The key to this question is relative prices. Add a $10 babysitting charge to the cost of an inexpensive meal and to an expensive meal:

inexpensive		expensive	
babysitting	$10	babysitting	$10
meal for two	$10	meal for two	$40
	$20		$50

The babysitter cost raises the total price of the inexpensive meal by 100% and the total price of the expensive meal by only 25%. Thus the price of an expensive meal (relative to an inexpensive meal) for couples with children is lower. So for those with small children we would predict a greater *proportion* of dinners out to be at expensive restaurants. Note, however, that those with young children are also expected to go out less often (going out to either type of restaurant is *relatively* more expensive than staying home for them).

3.4 THE CONCEPT OF DEMAND

In a market economy, characterized by freedom of choice, consumer demand plays a major role in determining product prices and resource allocation. Firms will produce only those goods for which demand is adequate to support prices at levels that cover production costs, and the quantities produced will in turn influence the employment and earnings of factor units. To clarify these concepts and relationships, we begin our discussion of consumer demand with an account of the nature and determinants of demand.

The demand of an individual buyer for a product, known as *individual demand,* is a schedule of the amounts of the product which the person would buy at various possible prices in a particular time interval. A shopper enters a store to buy oranges for use during the coming week. Finding the price to be 60 cents a pound, she buys four pounds. Had the price been 70 cents for oranges of the same grade, she might have bought three pounds; had it been 80 cents, she might have bought none at all; at 50 cents, she might have bought five pounds. Her demand for oranges at the particular time is the schedule of the various amounts that she would purchase at the various possible prices. (Such a schedule is illustrated in Table 3-1.) The fact that the shopper might not be consciously aware of the amount that she would purchase at prices other than the prevailing one does not alter the fact that she has a schedule, in the sense that she would have bought various other amounts had other prices prevailed. It must be emphasized that the schedule is a list of alternative possibilities; at any one time, only one of the prices will prevail, and thus a certain determinate quantity will be purchased.

The data in Table 3-1 can be plotted graphically, as shown in Figure 3-1. The data as given provide a series of points which, when connected by a continuous curve, constitute the demand curve. This procedure provides by interpolation estimates of quantities demanded at prices between those for which information is given. In graphs employed for price and output analysis, price is always plotted on the vertical axis and quantity on the horizontal axis.

In the typical market, there are numerous buyers, each with his own individual demand schedule. The horizontal sum of these schedules, known as *market demand*—or more commonly, **demand**—is thus a schedule of total amounts that

TABLE 3-1

Individual Demand Schedule of a Consumer for Oranges, Week of December 10–16

Price (cents)	Quantity Demanded (pounds)
80	0
70	3
60	4
50	5
40	7

FIGURE 3-1

Individual Demand Curve of a Customer for Oranges of a Certain Grade, Week of December 10–16

The demand curve records the pounds of oranges a consumer desires at various prices in a given week holding all other factors fixed. Since the individual desires more oranges at lower prices, the demand curve slopes downward.

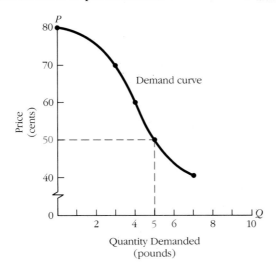

would be purchased in a given time interval by all buyers in a particular market at various possible prices. The demand for oranges in a particular market for a certain week might appear as shown in Table 3-2 and illustrated graphically in Figure 3-2. Although the actual quantities that would be purchased at prices other than the prevailing one may not be known, the schedule is nevertheless determinate in that total purchases would shift to various other definite amounts if the price were to change.

When a good is homogeneous, in the sense that buyers have no preferences for particular brands of the good and thus no preference for the product of any particular

TABLE 3-2

Market Demand Schedule for Oranges in a Particular Market, Week of December 10–16

Price (cents)	Quantity Demanded (pounds)
80	40,000
70	60,000
60	75,000
50	90,000
40	120,000

██████████
FIGURE 3-2

Market Demand Curve for Oranges of a Certain Grade in a Particular Market, Week of December 10–16
The horizontal sum of the individual demand curves defines the market demand curve, the schedule of quantities of oranges desired by all consumers in the market at alternate prices, *ceteris paribus.*

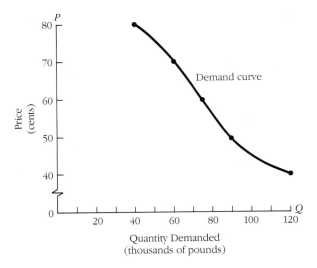

Quantity Demanded
(thousands of pounds)

seller, the concept of market demand is precise; the various individual demand schedules can be added without conceptual difficulty. But when the product is differentiated, the concept of market demand, although still useful, becomes less precise. With differentiation, individual buyers have preferences for brands of particular producers; a buyer's schedule is not, for example, for "cola" but for a particular brand of cola. The amount that he is willing to buy depends upon the brands available, and he may demand less of the good if his favorite variety cannot be obtained. Likewise, with differentiation, the selling prices of firms may not be identical; in one situation some brands may sell for $3.00, some for $4.00, and others for $2.00; in another situation (perhaps of lessened demand or increased supply) they may sell for $1.80, $2.30, and $1.30 respectively. Thus there is no clear-cut market demand schedule of certain amounts being purchased at particular prices. Instead, the schedule must be regarded as showing the total amounts of particular brands that would be purchased at various possible levels of a pattern of prices, with the fact recognized that the amounts which individuals will buy are different for the various brands. Even with these qualifications, the concept of "market demand" has significance. It is useful to be able to speak of "an increase in the demand for automobiles," for example, even though what is meant by demand is a set of closely related demands for particular kinds of cars rather than the demand for a single homogeneous good.

The Demand Function

The concept of demand, as defined in the previous section, describes a functional relationship between two variables: the price of a product and the quantity of the product demanded. As a general rule, however, the demand for any given product depends on a host of other considerations besides price. Strictly speaking, therefore, other influences should be taken into account explicitly by introducing additional independent variables into the demand function. These other variables would represent such things as prices of other goods, income, number of buyers (consumer population), tastes, and expected future prices.[1] Depending on the problem we wished to consider, then, we might treat demand not as a function of price alone (all other variables fixed in value) but alternatively as a function of income alone (prices and so on constant) or as a function of other prices alone, and so forth.

Note, however, that when we speak of demand or the demand function without further qualification, we mean by this the special and simple form of the demand function in which price is the only explicit independent variable and all other influences are implicit "shift" parameters (that is, variables which, if their values are altered, produce a shift on the graph of the demand function relating quantity to price).

Changes in Demand

Since *demand* is defined as a schedule of amounts which would be purchased at various alternative prices, a change in demand occurs only if persons will buy larger or smaller quantities at particular prices as a result of a change in one or more of the "shift" parameters noted in the preceding section. A **change in demand** may affect the entire schedule or only portions of it. An increase in demand is shown in Table 3-3 and is illustrated graphically in Figure 3-3. The change in demand is reflected in an entirely new demand curve (D_1 in Figure 3-3).

A change in demand must be distinguished clearly from a **change in quantity demanded** resulting from a price change. The latter is illustrated by a movement along an existing curve from one point to another. A change in the price of a good is

---

[1] A memory device to help you remember the **demand shifters** is the Old English word PYNTE. Each letter represents an important demand parameter:

P—the *price* of related goods; the prices of substitutes (such as butter and margarine) and complements (such as hamburgers and french fries), which vary with individual preferences, will affect demand.

Y—is the symbol economists often use to denote *income,* which usually increases, but can decrease, demand.

N—*number* of people, which increases demand.

T—*tastes;* these changes affect demand but are not easily charted.

E—*expected* future prices (expecting prices to fall in the future lowers current demand).
Any and all of the preceding will shift the demand curve.

TABLE 3-3

Increase in Demand

Price (cents)	Quantity Demanded (pounds)	Quantity Demanded after Change (pounds)
80	40,000	55,000
70	60,000	78,000
60	75,000	93,000
50	90,000	105,000
40	120,000	132,000

FIGURE 3-3

Illustration of an Increase in Demand
When the price of a related good, income, the number of consumers, tastes, or expected future prices change, the demand curve shifts. An increase in demand is illustrated by a rightward shift in the demand curve. The quantity demanded increases for every price.

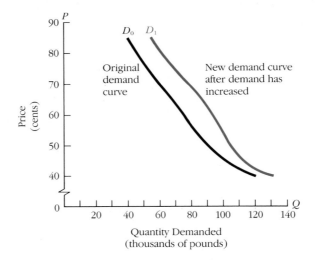

not said to cause a change in the demand for the good, since demand is defined as the entire schedule of the quantities which would be purchased *at various possible prices.*

3.5 SUPPLY

As with demand, economists consider several factors to be important in determining supplier willingness to provide goods and services. One factor, again, is the price of the good. While behavior will vary among individual suppliers, it is hypothesized as the **Law of Supply** that other things equal, *the quantity supplied will vary directly with price.* The higher the price of the good, the greater the quantity supplied; the lower the price of the good, the smaller the quantity supplied.

Why do suppliers behave in this fashion? While a detailed, rigorous answer will absorb much of our attention later in this book, a brief response is that firms supplying goods and services have incremental (or marginal) costs which increase as output increases, at least in the short run; hence higher prices are necessary to coax additional output from profit-maximizing firms (recall the principles discussion of setting $P = MC$ for the competitive firm).

The law of (short-run) supply expressed above is illustrated in Table 3-4 and Figure 3-4. Again oranges are the product, but now we are considering the amount of oranges that farmers, operating through grocer middlepersons, are willing to provide to consumers during the weekly time period. Note that the *supply curve* is upward sloping as you move from left to right; movements along this curve are called **changes in the quantity supplied.**

Changes in "supply" shift the entire curve. An increase in supply shifts the curve to right; a decrease shifts it to the left. Shifts in the supply curve may occur for reasons unrelated to the price of the good, including the price of other goods, expectations of future prices, factor prices, technology, tampering, or taxes.[2] If production costs rise, say because of a wage increase, then other things constant we would expect a decrease in supply; when this happens, the whole curve shifts to the left.

The market supply curve for a product represents the horizontal summation of the supply curves of individual suppliers, much the same as the market demand curve summarizes the demand responses of many consumers.[3] In the case of supply, an

---

[2]Just as we had a memory device for demand shifters, we also have one for **supply shifters.** It's called PEST. The letters represent:

P—the price of related goods

E—expected future price.

S—suppliers input price (for example, steel or labor in automobile production).

T—technology, tampering, or taxes.

[3]There are, however, complications, to which we shall return later.

TABLE 3-4

Market Supply Curve for Oranges in a Particular Market Week of December 10–16

Price (cents)	Quantity Supplied (pounds)
80	110,000
70	90,000
60	75,000
50	50,000
40	30,000

FIGURE 3-4

Hypothetical Supply Curve, Oranges
The market supply curve for oranges depicts the relationship between price and the quantity of oranges offered for sale by all suppliers, *ceteris paribus*. The supply curve is positively sloped because grocers are willing to sell more oranges at higher prices. The dots indicate quantities of oranges that suppliers (grocers, acting as middlepersons) will provide at various prices; the line connecting the dots is a supply curve.

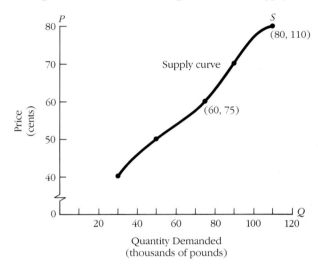

increase in the number of suppliers leads to an increase in supply, denoted by a rightward shift in the supply curve; while an exodus of suppliers leads to a decrease in supply, denoted by a leftward shift in the supply curve.

3.6 EQUILIBRIUM PRICE AND QUANTITY

Enough has been said for now about demand and supply separately. How do they operate together to answer the first fundamental question of economics—namely, what do we produce and in what quantities?

The market solution to this basic question is classic in its simplicity: *Output will tend to be at that price where the quantity demanded equals the quantity supplied.* This level of output is called an **equilibrium quantity** and the price associated with it is called an **equilibrium price** because they are a quantity and a price that tend not to change until something else—the price of related goods, income, expectations of future relative prices, tastes, or technology,—changes and leads to a new equilibrium. As long as these other factors remain unchanged, however, price and quantity will tend to remain at their original equilibrium levels. (For a more precise understanding of equilibrium conditions, see the stock/flow approach discussed in Chapter 4.)

The equilibrium market solution is easily depicted. Consider again the orange example. Figure 3-5 and Table 3-5 combine the demand curve for oranges (Figure 3-2) with the supply curve (Figure 3-4). At a price of 60 cents per pound, the community is

FIGURE 3-5

Market Demand and Supply Schedules for Oranges in a Particular Market (December 10–16)

Market equilibrium requires that quantity demanded equal quantity supplied. This occurs at the intersection of the demand and supply curves. In this example, equilibrium price is 60 cents and equilibrium quantity is 75,000 pounds. A price higher than 60 cents creates a surplus, and price will be driven down to reduce the excess supply. Similarly, a price less than 60 cents will result in a shortage, and buyers will offer higher prices to eliminate the excess demand.

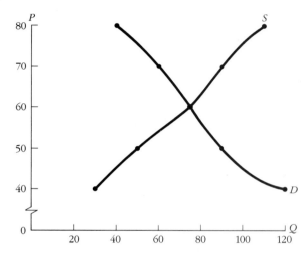

TABLE 3-5

Market Demand and Supply Schedule for Oranges in a Particular Market (December 10–16)

Price (cents)	Quantity Demanded	Quantity Supplied
80	40,000	110,000
70	60,000	90,000
60	75,000	75,000
50	90,000	50,000
40	120,000	30,000

willing to buy 75,000 pounds of oranges per week; local grocers also are willing to supply 75,000 pounds at this price. Both the demanders and the suppliers are "satisfied" (in the sense that they can do what they want at that price—neither may be "happy" about the price!). At any other price this is not the case. At 70 cents a pound, the quantity demanded is 60,000 but the quantity supplied is 90,000. At that price a *surplus* exists—grocers are supplying more than they can sell and are earning no revenue on the unsold oranges. To ease the predicament, grocers will cut their price to get rid of the unsold surplus (or if the oranges rot, the next batch will be priced lower and less will be ordered). What if the grocers cut back the price to 50 cents a pound? Not only will they get rid of any previously accumulated surplus, but they will find the weekly quantity demanded (90,000 pounds) greater than the 50,000 pounds that they are willing to supply at this low price. So at 50 cents a pound a *shortage* exists. Only at 60 cents a pound does neither a shortage nor a surplus exist. Thus this is the equilibrium price, one that will remain until the demand or supply curves are moved by some consideration other than the price of oranges.

3.7 CHANGES IN EQUILIBRIUM PRICE AND QUANTITY

In reality, of course, prices and quantities do change fairly frequently. Why? Because *factors other than the price of the good itself are altered,* leading to a change in demand (shift in the demand curve) and/or a change in supply (shift in the supply curve).

Suppose incomes rise and people, now more affluent, increase their demand for oranges. That means that the demand for oranges at any given price will be greater than before. Thus the demand curve shifts to the right (see Figure 3-6). What is the impact on equilibrium price and quantity? As indicated in the figure, both price and quantity will increase. Let D_0 represent the original demand curve and D_1 the demand curve prevailing after the increase in income. The supply curve remains unchanged, as a rise in general income levels does not directly influence the grocer's ability or desire to supply more oranges. The new equilibrium price and quantity are higher; people are buying more oranges and paying more for them because of the increase in demand. We can say that there has been "an increase in quantity supplied," as there has

FIGURE 3-6

An Increase in Demand for Oranges
At any given price, the amount of oranges that consumers want to purchase is greater than before; therefore, a change in a nonprice factor (for example, income or number of consumers) has increased consumer demand. The demand curve shifts to the right (from D_0 to D_1) and increases the equilibrium price and quantity.

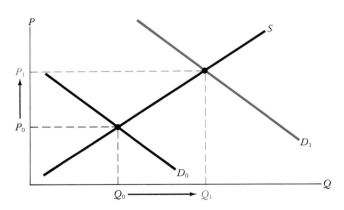

been a movement along a supply curve (as opposed to a shift in the curve) because of the shift in demand. We should *not* say that there has been an "increase in supply," since we reserve that expression for *shifts* in the supply curve.

In general, equilibrium quantities increase over time (except for inferior goods), while equilibrium *real* prices may be rising or falling. It is in fact a common occurrence for both equilibrium price and equilibrium quantity to increase over time. This is not a refutation of the Law of Demand (which says that when prices rise, quantity demanded falls) since nonprice factors will have worked to increase both supply and demand above earlier levels. In short, many factors have worked to shift both the demand curve and the supply curve to the right over time. (See Box 3-3.)

Similarly, shifts in supply curves reflecting changes in supply will influence both price and quantity even if consumers have not changed in their basic willingness to buy the product at any given price. Take the calculator example. The sharp decrease in equilibrium price and large increase in equilibrium quantity during the late 1970s reflected primarily an increase in supply, as illustrated in Figure 3-7. If supply were to decrease, perhaps because of an expensive labor settlement, the reverse would hold. Equilibrium price would increase, but equilibrium quantity would fall. Again, we can say "quantity demanded has increased" and "supply has increased" in the case of Figure 3-7; but we *cannot* say "demand has increased" because that expression is reserved for shifts in the demand curve reflecting changes in demand factors unrelated to the price of the good. (See Boxes 3-4 and 3-5.)

3.8 ELASTICITY OF DEMAND

The concept of elasticity relates to the *relative* responsiveness of a given variable to changes in the values of another variable to which it is functionally related. By using

3-3   In ski resorts like Sun Valley and Aspen, hotel prices are higher in March than in June. Why is this the case? If the June hotel prices existed in March, what problem would arise?

In the (likely) event that supply is not altered significantly, demand is chiefly responsible for the higher prices in the prime skiing months. If prices were maintained at the off-season rates all year long, excess demand would exist. And it is this excess demand at the off-peak prices that causes prime-season rates to be higher.

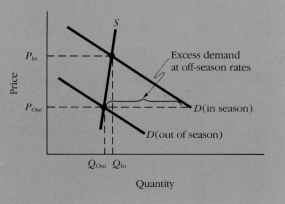

FIGURE 3-7

Impact of Increased Supply

When the quantity supplied increases for every possible price, supply has increased due to a change in a supply curve shifter such as technology or falling input prices. The rightward shift in supply reduces the equilibrium price but raises equilibrium quantity.

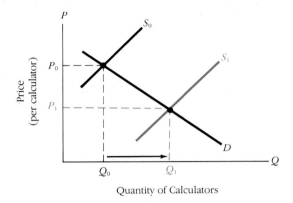

Quantity of Calculators

percentages, the units of measurement (say, ounces versus pounds or quarts versus gallons) do not affect the outcome, reducing one possible source of confusion. With the demand function relating quantity demanded to price, for example, elasticity refers to the relative percentage response of quantity demanded to a percentage change in price. If one is relating demand to income, price being treated as a given parameter, elasticity refers to the relative percentage response of demand to a percentage change in income. With a function relating the demand for one good to the price of another good, elasticity refers to the relative percentage effect of a percentage change in the price of one good on the demand for the other. The terms price elasticity (or, more commonly, elasticity), income elasticity, and cross-price elasticity are given to these three concepts. Each will be considered in turn.

3-4 Why are strawberries more expensive in winter than in summer?

Assuming that consumers tastes and income are fairly constant throughout the year, the answer lies on the supply side of the market. The supply of strawberries is lower when strawberries are out of season and more abundant when in season.

Again we see that if prices do not adjust we will be out of equilibrium. In this case there will be excess supply if prices are not lowered when strawberries come into season. And it is this excess supply that drives the price down.

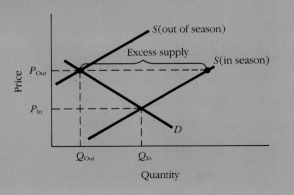

3-5 With improvements in telecommunication technology, we can anticipate lower costs of production and lower prices for phone calls in the future. Graph this phenomenon. What happens to the equilibrium price and quantity? What happens if there is a simultaneous increase in demand due to a rise in income?

With an increase in supply, the price of phone calls will fall and the quantity demanded (and exchanged, in equilibrium) will rise. If there is a simultaneous increase in demand, equilibrium quantity rises but the impact on equilibrium price now becomes indeterminate—that is, we need to know the magnitude of the increase in demand in order to determine whether the price will rise or fall.

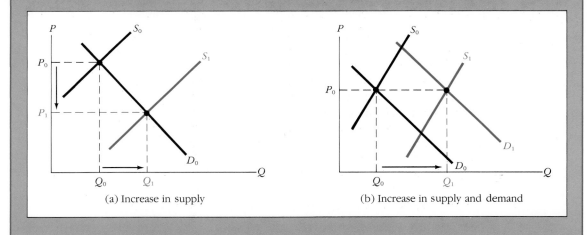

(a) Increase in supply   (b) Increase in supply and demand

Price Elasticity

A reduction in price (ceteris paribus) will result in an increase in the quantity demanded. **Price elasticity** measures the proportional magnitude that quantity demanded increases as price falls. More specifically, price elasticity may be defined as the relationship between a given percentage change in price and the consequent percentage change in quantity demanded; thus the numerical coefficient of elasticity is obtained by dividing the percentage change in quantity demanded by the percentage change in price:[4]

$$e_p = \frac{Q_0 - Q_1}{Q_0} \div \frac{P_0 - P_1}{P_0} \quad \text{or} \quad \frac{\Delta Q}{Q} \div \frac{\Delta P}{P}$$

[4]Note that this can be rewritten $(\Delta Q/\Delta P) \cdot (P/Q)$ which for small changes is the derivative, $(dQ)/(dp)$, of the demand function multiplied by the inverse of the average quantity per unit of price, Q/P. Hence the elasticity of any function is the slope function divided by the average function.

where Q_0 and P_0 represent the initial quantity and price, and Q_1 and P_1 represent values of the same variables after the change. The negative sign, indicating the inverse relationship between price and quantity demanded, is in practice often omitted.

When the changes in price and quantity are of significant magnitude, the exact meaning of the term "percentage change" requires clarification, and the terms *price* and *quantity* must be defined more precisely. The issue is this: Should the percentage change be figured on the basis of price and quantity before or after the change has occurred? For example, a price rise from $10.00 to $15.00 constitutes a 50-percent change if the original price ($10.00) is used in figuring the percentage, or a 33⅓-percent change if the price after the change ($15.00) is used. For *small* changes this distinction is of little consequence, but for large changes it is significant. The most common approach is the use of the midpoints between the old and new figures for both price and quantity demanded. In the formula the sums of the prices (here $10.00 plus $15.00) and of the quantities before and after the change, respectively, may be used instead of the averages of these, since the result will be exactly the same. (A fraction is not altered by dividing both its numerator and denominator by 2.) The formula thus becomes:

$$e_p = \frac{Q_0 - Q_1}{Q_0 + Q_1} \div \frac{P_0 - P_1}{P_0 + P_1}$$

The elasticity of demand for a good also has implications for the behavior of the total outlay or expenditure on the good (price times quantity purchased) as the price changes. When the elasticity exceeds one (numerically), total outlay will rise as the price declines, since the quantity demanded increases at a relatively greater rate than that at which the price falls. If a price is cut in half and the quantity demanded more than doubles, obviously more money is being spent on the good than before. If elasticity is less than one, the total outlay will be less at low prices than at high, since a given price reduction will be accompanied by a proportionately smaller increase in quantity demanded. If the elasticity is one, the relative changes in price and quantity are the same, and total outlay will be the same regardless of the price.

On the basis of elasticity, particular segments of demand schedules[5] can be grouped into three major classes:

1. *Elastic demand segments*—those with elasticity numerically greater than one $(e > 1)$. In this case the price change is accompanied by a more-than-proportionate change in quantity demanded; total outlay is greater at lower prices than at higher ones. In the limiting case of perfect elasticity, an increase in price causes the quantity demanded to fall to zero; at a certain price and at any lower figure the quantity demanded is infinite.[6] In Table 3-6, a typical elastic demand is illustrated along with a perfectly elastic schedule.

---

[5]An entire demand schedule would rarely have the same elasticity throughout (a rectangular hyberbola, for example, would have an elasticity of 1 throughout the range of the curve).

TABLE 3-6
Elastic Demand

Price (cents)	Typical Elastic Demand		Perfectly Elastic Demand	
	Quantity Demanded	Total Outlay	Quantity Demanded	Total Outlay
50	8	$4.00	0	0
40	12	4.80	0	0
30	20	6.00	0	0
20	35	7.00	Infinite	Infinite
10	80	8.00	Infinite	Infinite

TABLE 3-7
Inelastic Demand

Price (cents)	Typical Inelastic Demand		Perfectly Inelastic Demand	
	Quantity Demanded	Total Outlay	Quantity Demanded	Total Outlay
50	8	$4.00	8	$4.00
40	9	3.60	8	3.20
30	11	3.30	8	2.40
20	14	2.80	8	1.60
10	19	1.90	8	0.80

2. *Inelastic demand segments*—those with elasticity less than one ($e < 1$). In this case the price change is accompanied by a less-than-proportionate change in quantity demanded; total outlay is greater at higher prices. The limiting case is a perfectly inelastic demand; here the quantity demanded is the same, regardless of the price. A typical inelastic schedule and one of perfect inelasticity are illustrated in Table 3-7.

3. *Demand segments of unitary elasticity*—those with elasticity of one ($e = 1$). In this case, lying between the previous two, the percentage change in quantity demanded is the same as the percentage change in price. If price is cut in half, the quantity

---

[6]Strictly speaking, the quantity demanded is not defined but is said to be infinite. Individual and total demand schedules cannot be perfectly elastic; the fact that incomes are limited prevents persons from buying infinite amounts of any positively priced good. However, the market demand schedules confronting individual sellers may appear to be approximately perfectly elastic from the standpoint of the sellers themselves.

demanded doubles; total outlay is the same regardless of the price. The demand curve is a rectangular hyperbola in this case (graph the data in Table 3-8 to see what such a demand curve looks like). It is unlikely that any demand schedule would possess exactly unitary elasticity over a substantial range; the case merely constitutes the dividing line between elastic and inelastic segments. Table 3-8 shows a demand of unitary elasticity.

At any given price/quantity point on a graph of a demand curve, an inelastic demand will appear as a steeper curve than an elastic demand. A perfectly inelastic demand will appear as a vertical line, a perfectly elastic demand as a horizontal line. A demand of unitary elasticity appears as a rectangular hyperbola. These are illustrated in Figure 3-8. Great care, however, must be taken in estimating elasticity from the slope of the curve, beyond the extreme limiting cases; when segments of curves appear on different portions of the graph, the relative slope tells little about elasticity. A straight-line demand curve with a constant slope will change elasticity continuously along its course, since the denominators of the fractions in the formula are continuously changing while the numerators remain unchanged. The top half of a linear demand schedule is elastic. The midpoint is unitary elastic and the bottom half is inelastic regardless of slope (use the definition of elasticity to convince yourself of this). For example, in Figure 3-8(d), if you complete the demand curve where it intersects the price axis, it becomes clear that this graph represents the lower portion of the demand curve—the inelastic region. (See Box 3-6.)

TABLE 3-8
Demand of Unitary Elasticity

Price (cents)	Quantity Demanded	Total Outlay
50	8	$4.00
40	10	4.00
30	13⅓	4.00
20	20	4.00
10	40	4.00

3-6   True or False?   A poor harvest is always bad for farmers.

False.   Without a simultaneous reduction in demand, a reduction in supply due to weather will mean higher prices. If demand for the product is inelastic over the pertinent portion of the demand curve, the farmers' total revenue will rise. Clearly, if some farmers lose their entire crop, they are worse off; but *collectively* farmers can profit from events that reduce crop size—and usually do, since most agricultural demands are inelastic. (Note: what is total revenue for producers is total outlay for consumers.)

FIGURE 3-8

Various Demand Elasticities
The price elasticity of demand measures the responsiveness of quantity demanded to a change in price. Part (a) shows that a minute change in price evokes an infinite response in quantity demanded; hence, demand is perfectly elastic. A fair response to price changes is exhibited by the relatively elastic demand curve in part (b), whereas rigid responses are captured by the relatively inelastic demand curve in part (d) and the perfectly inelastic demand curve in part (e). The case of constant, unitary elasticity is reflected in the demand curve in part (c).

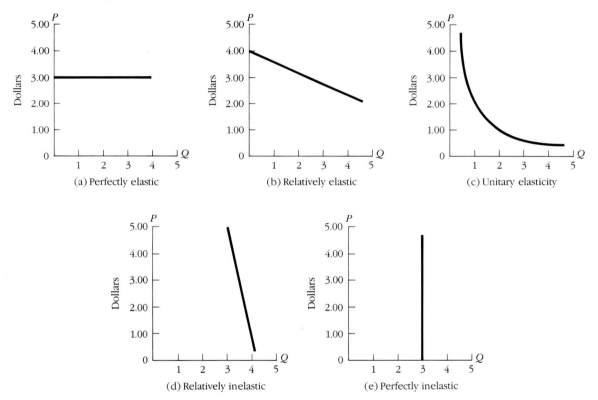

Because of shifts in supply and demand curves, researchers have a difficult task when trying to establish price elasticity of demand. Despite this difficulty, Table 3-9 has been constructed with estimates of price elasticity of demand for certain goods. As you would expect, certain low-priced goods like salt, matches, and toothpicks are very inelastic. This is because these items form an insignificant part of most people's total budget; hence the quantity demanded is relatively insensitive to price in the relevant region. On the other hand, foreign air travel is much more sensitive to price (elastic) since available substitutes are much more plentiful. In Table 3-9, we see that the price elasticity of demand for foreign air travel is roughly 2; that is, a 1-percent increase in price will lead to a slightly less than 2-percent reduction in quantity demanded.

TABLE 3-9
Price Elasticities of Demand for Selected Goods

Good	Short-Run	Long-Run
Movies	.9	3.7
Air Travel (foreign)	.1	1.8
Jewelry and watches	.4	.7
Theatre and opera	.2	.3
Gasoline	.2	.5
Medical insurance	.3	.9
Physician services	.6	—
China and glassware	1.5	2.6
Radio and TV Repairs	.5	3.9

Source: H. S. Houthakker and Lester D. Taylor, *Consumer Demand in the United States: Analysis and Projections,* 2nd ed. (Cambridge, MA: Harvard University Press, 1970).

It should be noted that while many of these elasticities appear low, the elasticity of demand for a specific item (such as a brand of gas or type of watch) will be much larger than the more general category.

Income Elasticity

While the most widely employed demand relationship is that relating price and quantity demanded, use is also made of the function which relates demand to income (the so-called "Engel curve"). Specifically, this is a measure of the relationship between a relative change in income and the consequent relative change in demand, ceteris paribus. Expressed symbolically, the **income elasticity of demand** is given by the formula:[7]

$$e_y = \frac{\dfrac{Q_0 - Q_1}{Q_0 + Q_1}}{\dfrac{Y_0 - Y_1}{Y_0 + Y_1}} = \frac{\dfrac{\Delta Q}{\overline{Q}}}{\dfrac{\Delta Y}{\overline{Y}}} = \frac{\Delta Q}{\Delta Y} \cdot \frac{\overline{Y}}{\overline{Q}}$$

Here the percentage change in purchases (demand) is divided by the percentage change in income. The response may be positive or negative. For most goods, an

---

[7]Again, for small changes, this becomes

$$\frac{dQ/dY}{Q/Y}$$

or the marginal function divided by the average function.

increase in income should result in an increase in purchases, but the degree of elasticity may vary substantially. For example, if income were to rise by 10 percent and a consumer increased her purchases of X by 15 percent, then the income elasticity, 15%/10%, would be positive 1.5. As distinguished from "normal" goods, the relationship for "inferior" goods is negative; as incomes rise, people tend to buy fewer units of these goods. A good such as hamburger may, of course, be normal over some range (switching from beans to hamburger as income rises) but inferior over some other range (switching from hamburger to steak at still higher incomes).

Cross-Elasticity of Demand

Another useful demand measure relates the price of one good to the demand for another; the concept of cross-elasticity describes the behavior of this functional relationship. As coffee prices rise, to what extent does the demand for tea rise? Say the price of coffee (X_1) rises by 10 percent, and as a consequence the quantity of tea (Q_2) purchased rises 20 percent. If this were the case, then we would know that coffee and tea are substitutes since $e_p(X_1, X_2)$ is positive, or more precisely, 20%/10% = +2. As long as the sign on the cross-price elasticity coefficient is positive, the goods are substitutes. If the coefficient was negative, the two goods would be complements (like hot dogs and hot dog buns).

As before, **cross-elasticity of demand** may be defined as the relationship between a certain percentage change in the price of one good (here P_{x_1}) and the consequent percentage change in the demand for another good (Q_{x_2}):[8]

$$e_{p(x_1, x_2)} = \frac{Q_{x_2}^0 - Q_{x_2}^1}{Q_{x_2}^0 + Q_{x_2}^1} \div \frac{P_{x_1}^0 - P_{x_1}^1}{P_{x_1}^0 + P_{x_1}^1} = \frac{\Delta Q_{x_2}/\overline{Q}_{x_2}}{\Delta P_{x_1}/\overline{P}_{x_1}} = \frac{\Delta Q_{x_2}}{\Delta P_{x_1}} \cdot \frac{\overline{P}_{x_1}}{\overline{Q}_{x_2}}$$

Consumer Surplus

Whenever prices and/or quantities change there is a change in consumer welfare or utility. Economists have developed a concept called **consumer surplus** to measure these changes. Consumer surplus is useful in benefit/cost studies or in measuring welfare losses due to monopoly or other market imperfections.

The height of the demand curve at any quantity level shows the consumer's marginal willingness to pay for an increment in quantity. The greater the height of any particular demand curve, the greater the consumer's marginal willingness-to-pay for that good. It follows that the area under the demand curve up to some quantity level is total willingness-to-pay for all units up to that level, as seen in Figure 3-9.

However, what a consumer is required to pay for a good is usually less than what the consumer is willing to pay. For example, say the price of contact lenses is $100. If

---

[8]As with earlier footnotes, the first term in the final expression (for small changes) is the derivative of the demand relationship, dQ_{x_2}/dP_{x_1}, while $\overline{P}_{x_1}/\overline{Q}_{x_2}$ is the inverse of the average relationship.

FIGURE 3-9

Demand and Total Willingness to Pay
An individual's demand curve shows the maximum amount the consumer is willing to pay for each unit of a commodity. The area under the demand curve represents the total willingness to pay for all units of the good and measures the dollar value of the benefits received by the consumer from the good.

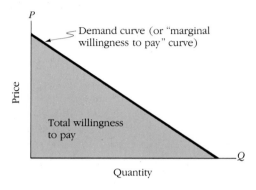

FIGURE 3-10

Consumer Surplus
A buyer receives consumer surplus when consumption benefits exceed expenditures on a commodity. The buyer is willing to spend the amount represented by the area A plus B for Q_0 units of the product. At the price P_0, however, the buyer pays only B amount and earns a consumer surplus equivalent to area A.

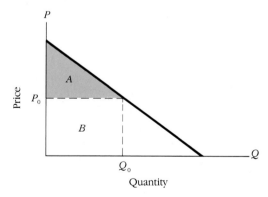

the consumer did not place a value of at least $100 on those lenses, the contacts would not be purchased. On the other hand, if someone was willing to pay $200 for the contacts but was only required to pay the market price of $100, then he would receive a surplus of $100. This monetary difference between what the consumer is willing to pay and what he is required to pay is called consumer surplus. This is depicted graphically in Figure 3-10 as the area under the demand curve and above the market price

━━━━━━━━

FIGURE 3-11

A Consumer Surplus Calculation
The dollar value of the consumer surplus (the shaded area) can be calculated by using the
formula for the area of a right triangle, (base × height)/2. In this example, the base is 10
units, the height is $20, and therefore, the consumer surplus equals $100.

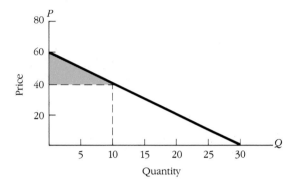

(area A). Area A and B represent total willingness-to-pay for quantity Q_0, while area B is
the amount the consumer is required to pay for quantity Q_0 rather than go without.
The difference is the consumer surplus area A. For example, suppose that the price of
good X is $10, but the consumer is willing to pay $15 for the first unit, $12 for the
second unit, and $9 for the third unit. How much consumer surplus will this individual
receive? First it is important to note the generality of the fact that if the consumer is a
buyer of several units of a good, the earlier units will have greater consumer surplus
because marginal willingness-to-pay falls as greater quantities are consumed in any
period. This is demonstrated by the consumer's willingness-to-pay $15 and $12 successively for the first two units. Thus the consumer will receive $5 of consumer surplus
for the first unit and two dollars of consumer surplus for the second unit. The third
unit would not be purchased, since the required price is greater than the consumer's
willingness-to-pay.

To measure consumer surplus geometrically (in the simple case of linear
demand[9]), we just need to figure out the area of a triangle (base × height/2). In Figure
3-11 we find that this is simply 10($60 − $40)/2 = $100 of consumer surplus, for a
situation in which 10 units of some good are purchased at a price of $40 with the given
demand relation.

────────────────

[9]More generally, one would integrate the demand curve (if this is possible!) from zero to
the final unit purchased and from the resulting area subtract the (rectangular) price times
quantity area to arrive at (net) consumer surplus. In more advanced treatments, the notion
of consumer surplus is given a more precise definition. Fortunately, in many cases, the
practical difference between consumer surplus as discussed here and more sophisticated
constructs is small.

SUMMARY

1. Prices and outputs are affected by the structure of markets.

2. Market behavior depends on information available on market conditions.

3. Markets are comprised of buyers, sellers, and middlepersons operating in close contact under a set of rules or customs.

4. Lack of knowledge and immobility of factors lead to imperfections in the perfectly competitive model.

5. The important price to consider in microeconomics is the relative price—the price of one good relative to another.

6. The law of demand states that there is an inverse or negative relationship between price and quantity demanded.

7. The law of supply states that there is a positive or direct relationship between price and quantity supplied.

8. Equilibrium price and quantity occur where quantity demanded is equal to quantity supplied.

9. Shifts in the demand and supply curves are caused by changes in something other than own-price.

10. Price elasticity measures the relative magnitude that quantity demanded changes as price changes; it is *independent* of the units chosen to measure either quantities or prices.

11. There are three major segments on a straight-line demand curve: elastic ($e > 1$) in the top half, unit elastic ($e = 1$) at the midpoint, and inelastic ($e < 1$) in the bottom half.

12. Income elasticities proportionately relate demand to income; cross-price elasticities show the percentage change in the demand for one good resulting from a given percentage change in the price of another.

WORDS AND CONCEPTS FOR REVIEW

market
imperfections
perfectly competitive
mobility of factors
absolute price
relative price
demand
change in quantity demanded
law of supply
changes in quantity supplied

equilibrium quantity
equilibrium price
surplus
shortage
demand shifters
supply shifters
price elasticity
income elasticity of demand
cross-elasticity of demand
consumer surplus

REVIEW QUESTIONS

1. What is a "market"?

2. What imperfections may occur in market conditions?

3. What is the difference between an increase in demand and an increase in quantity demanded? Show each graphically.

4. What are several possible causes of a decrease in demand?

5. Why does the supply curve have a positive slope?

6. Which variables cause the supply curve to shift?

7. What is the general meaning of the concept of elasticity as relating to demand schedules?

8. How are price elasticity, income elasticity, and cross-price elasticity of demand different?

9. What is the formula used to obtain a numerical coefficient of the price elasticity of demand?

10. Suppose that when a firm reduces price, its total revenue from the sale of the product increases. Will the coefficient of demand elasticity over this range be positive or negative? Will it exceed or be less than one? Why?

11. Landing in a strange country, you are told that a beer costs 1,000 gubbles (the *gubble* being the local currency). Is this a "high" price? How could you find out if it *was* a high price? What does this say about the truth of our assertion that only *relative* prices matter in microeconomics?

12. A bakery finds that if it raises the price of bread from the present price of 75 cents a loaf to 85 cents, it sells none at all. What is the nature of the elasticity of demand for bread from this firm?

13. With an elastic demand, will total revenue (price times quantity) be greater at low prices or at high prices? Why?

14. With a demand of unitary elasticity, what happens to total revenue as price changes? Why?

15. What is the formula for income elasticity of demand? Is the relationship negative or positive? Explain.

16. What is the formula for cross-elasticity of demand? Give several examples of complements and substitutes, noting the sign of cross-elasticity of demand in each case.

SUGGESTED READINGS

Alchian, A. and Allen, W. *Exchange and Production: Competition Coordination and Control,* 3rd ed. Belmont, CA: Wadsworth, 1983. Chapters 2, 3, 4.

Hayek, F. A. Von. "The Use of Knowledge in Society," *American Economic Review,* 35 (September 1945) pp. 519–30.

Marshall, A. *Principles of Economics,* 8th ed. London: Macmillan, 1920, Book III: Chapters 1, 2, 3.

APPENDIX   ECONOMETRICS AND SUPPLY AND DEMAND

Econometrics is the branch of economics which employs economic theory and statistical methods "as analytical foundation stones and economic data as the information base."[10] The word

---

[10]George Judge et al., *The Theory and Practice of Econometrics* (New York: Wiley, 1985), p. 1.

Econometrics literally means "economic measurement," which is of course the main task of all empirical research in economics. As a matter of practice, however, the word *econometrics* ordinarily refers only to empirical research that measures economic relationships in explicitly mathematical terms. From this point of view, econometrics is best regarded as an applied branch of mathematical economics. Any economic relationship that can be expressed as a mathematical equation may thus be considered a potential object of econometric study. Such relations include supply and demand functions, production functions, cost functions, equations and inequalities used in linear programming problems, and so forth. To state the matter another way, we may say that econometrics is concerned with the empirical measurement of economic relations that are sufficiently simple to be expressible in mathematical form. The potential scope of econometrics, thus conceived, is relatively broad. At the present time, it obviously cannot provide answers to all economic questions, or even to most of them. However, econometrics is a potentially promising approach to the study of economic phenomena. This appendix explains the nature of the econometric approach, some of its basic concepts and methods, and its merits and weaknesses.

The Nature of Econometrics

A hypothetical example will help clarify the basic features and objectives of econometric study. Suppose that the government planned to initiate a crop-restriction program in order to raise farm prices and increase farm incomes. Historical data on average farm production and average market prices indicate that a particular volume of production sometimes sells at one price level and sometimes at another. This knowledge, by itself, gives no indication of the extent to which changes in farm production result in changes in price. For the crop-restriction program to be successful, however, government econometricians must estimate approximately a year in advance the probable level of prices that will be associated with any given level of production. To do this, they will need accurate quantitative estimates of the demand and supply functions of various agricultural goods.

For example, if they know the exact nature of the demand curve for wheat, econometricians can predict the equilibrium price of wheat with a given level of production—that is, the price that will clear the market. If they can estimate the size of the wheat crop in the coming year based on information from previous years about rainfall, prices, acreage planted, and similar factors, they can then predict the approximate price of wheat for that particular year. The only way to discover the actual demand curve for wheat is to study data from past years on wheat consumption, wheat prices, and similar magnitudes. Economic theory suggests that the demand curve is downward sloping, but it does not provide precise information about the shape of the demand curve or the factors that control its position. In other words, economic theory provides qualitative but not quantitative information about the demand curve. It is the task of econometrics to develop this quantitative information.

To obtain some idea of the quantitative properties of the demand curve, one must initially assume that the quantity of wheat demanded depends on certain measurable data such as the price of corn, the price of beans, national income, and population, as well as the price of wheat. Historical measures of these data may then be used to arrive at a provisional estimate of the extent to which each of the factors influences the demand for wheat. If some of the factors appear not to influence demand at all, they may be eliminated from the relations originally suggested by economic theory. If all of the factors studied do not suffice to provide a satisfactory explanation of observed variations in quantity demanded, certain additional data may have to be introduced into the relation suggested by economic theory in order to arrive at a satisfactory quantitative description of the demand curve for wheat.

Econometrics can seldom provide precise knowledge of economic relations by this procedure. Though the results are only approximate at best, they may provide sufficiently accurate quantitative content to the purely qualitative relationships of economic theory to permit quantitative rather than qualitative predictions. For example, while on the basis of economic theory alone, it is possible only to say that a 10-percent increase in wheat production will lead to a *lower* price of wheat, econometric analysis may make it possible to say that a 10-percent increase in wheat production will lead to a *decline of approximately 20 percent in the price of wheat*. From a practical point of view, there is a vast difference between the two statements.

Thus the first major task of econometrics is to provide quantitative supplemental information to the purely qualitative statements suggested by economic theory and by everyday experience. To the extent they are accurate, these quantitative relationships facilitate specific quantitative predictions of future events—the second major task of econometrics. The use of quantitative relationships to make predictions provides the crucial test of the accuracy of these relationships; to the extent that predictions are inaccurate, the quantitative measurement of economic relationships has not been entirely satisfactory.

The Scope of Econometrics

Econometrics potentially includes within its scope all work in economics that is concerned with empirical data—that is, with the explanation of observed phenomena. As a practical matter, however, econometric work is largely confined to certain problems of the type included in partial equilibrium theory and in income and employment theory. The first category includes estimating supply and demand functions (emphasized in this chapter), forecasting price in a single market, and estimating cost curves and production functions. In the income theory field, attention has been given to forecasts of consumer demand at various levels of income and to estimates of the demand for money. Several large-scale econometric studies (such as the DRI, Wharton, and Chase Econometrics models) have dealt with the overall behavior of the United States economy; similar attempts have been made to describe many other economic systems. The projects have not been entirely successful from a predictive point of view, but they have yielded much valuable factual knowledge. Perhaps more importantly, at this stage in the development of econometrics, they have indicated areas in which further theoretical and empirical research will be needed if future projects are to be more fruitful.

Concepts and General Approach of Econometrics

Since econometrics seeks to add quantitative content to relationships of economic analysis, it must concern itself not only with data collection and statements of theoretical analysis but also with interrelationships between them. Specifically, it must select data in terms of relations suggested by economic analysis and at the same time adapt these relations in such a fashion as to permit quantification of them with available data and techniques. These concerns must be considered in greater detail.

Preliminary Research and Data Collection   Starting from a given collection of facts about a particular situation, the econometrician's first task is to decide what portion of the information already available is relevant to the task at hand and what further information is required. Neither task is simple.

Suppose that an econometrician is seeking to estimate the demand for a single commodity—corn. For this purpose, she will gather as much information as possible about past production, consumption, and price; but no collection of statistics on corn alone will allow her to estimate the demand for corn unless by remote chance the demand for corn is independent of all other aspects of economic activity. The problem may be clarified by an illustration, as shown in Figure 3-12. With quantities of corn consumed measured on the horizontal axis and prices of corn on the vertical axis, a collection of historical quantity/price data may be represented by a *scatter diagram* in which each point corresponds to a single historical observation. If the scatter diagram is of the nature indicated in Figure 3-12(a), curve D might be regarded as a reasonable estimate of the demand curve for corn. If the scatter diagram is as represented by Figure 3-12(b) or Figure 3-12(c), on the other hand, no single estimate of the demand curve would seem more logical than another; on the contrary, some factor other than price obviously is influencing the consumption of corn, and further information must be sought.

Actually, the evidence provided by the scatter diagram of Figure 3-12(a) is just as ambiguous as that in the other two cases. Although the scatter of points appears to show an obvious demand curve, it could represent a *collection* of demand curves, each point being on a different curve, as illustrated in Figure 3-13. Indeed, if it were known that hog production had been increasing steadily for a number of years, the second interpretation of the scatter in Figure 3-12(a) might seem more plausible than the first; one would not expect the position of the demand curve to be unchanged, year after year, if the number of hogs was increasing. Moreover, we have been implicitly assuming that the observed scatter diagram represents observations on price and quantity demanded, when in fact those observations are market observations on price and the *intersection* of demand and supply. The supply curve *and* the demand curve both move over time, and they become quite difficult to "identify" as separate curves.

The implication is that facts alone never speak for themselves, and no interpretation of factual data can ever be regarded as final unless one knows the precise nature of the process by which the data are generated. In the case of economics, the nature of the data-generation process is seldom known with any precision.

FIGURE 3-12

Scatter Diagrams
Identification of the demand curve requires more information than just past observations on price and quantity. Each observation is an equilibrium point and represents the intersection of the demand and supply curves. Since demand and supply shift over time due to changes in the shift parameters, the price-quantity data points do not map out the demand curve.

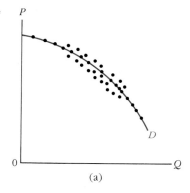
(a)

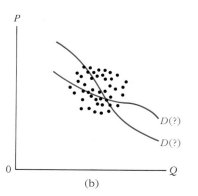
(b)

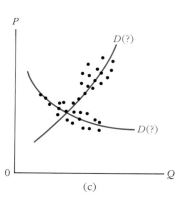
(c)

FIGURE 3-13

Demand Curve Ambiguity

Each observation plotted in Figure 3-12(a) may represent a point on a different demand curve.

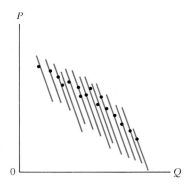

To deal with problems like this, econometricians are forced to undertake "fishing expeditions." Starting with certain basic facts, they cast a net as widely as possible to discover other facts that might have a bearing on the interpretation of the original collection of data. In the given case, researchers must obtain information about factors other than price—such as prices in other markets, production and consumption of related commodities, consumer income, government purchasing programs—which may influence the consumption of corn. They must also investigate the process by which the price of corn is determined, acquiring information about the production and marketing of corn. It may happen, for example, that the amount of corn supplied to the market comes partly from current production and partly from existing stocks. In this case the behavior of the market will depend partly on changes in stocks, making the data required to describe variations in price and consumption more difficult to obtain and more complicated to analyze.

To add to the complications already mentioned, the consumption, production, and price reactions observed during one period may be the result of previous events. To take this possibility into account, it may be necessary to attach some references to factual data—that is, to work with scatter diagrams in which the various points are dated. This will almost inevitably increase the range of admissible interpretations of the data and so increase the difficulty of arriving at definite conclusions about the nature of the process by which the data are generated.

Theoretical Considerations   The role of economic theory in econometrics is to provide a set of "hooks" upon which facts of particular kinds may be hung. In effect, the econometrician starts with a vast collection of hooks, most of them unencumbered by facts; he then proceeds from one hook to another, asking in each case whether the kinds of facts a particular hook is designed to hold are relevant to the problem at hand. If the hooks are few in number or difficult to discern (that is, if the theory is narrow in scope or ambiguous in meaning), the econometrician may easily overlook relevant facts and arrive at a poor solution to his problem. Alternatively, he may recognize the inadequacy of the theory and be forced to devote as much attention to searching for additional hooks as looking for facts. The ideal situation is one in which the basic theory is relatively comprehensive and reasonably precise, but this is not always the case in practice.

Necessary Modifications in the Theoretical Analysis   Even if existing theory is adequate, the data actually available to the econometrician are not likely to conform exactly to specifications suggested by theory. Where theory required daily or weekly data on prices and quantities, for example, the econometrician may have to settle for quarterly or annual figures. Similarly, where theory refers to data involving quantities with adjustments to equilibrium completed, the econometrician is forced to work with actual quantities, which are not likely to reflect complete attainment of equilibrium. Difficulties of this kind cannot be overcome by ignoring them; the basic theory must be modified so that it can be used to interpret actual data.

Likewise, in the course of an econometric study, certain calculations often cannot be performed unless relations suggested by existing theory are first simplified. For example, as a practical matter, econometric work is often confined to *linear relations* (represented geometrically by straight lines) rather than *nonlinear relations* (represented geometrically by curves other than straight lines). The precise form of a linear relation is determined simply by its *slope* relative to the axes on which the variables included in the relations are measured. The form of many nonlinear relations, on the other hand, can be specified only if much additional information is provided.

The importance of this difference can be illustrated by examining the usual two-dimensional curve. If the "curve" in question is a straight line, then one number (representing the slope of the curve relative to the X axis) suffices to determine the *form* of the relation, and another number (representing, for example, the point at which the line crosses the X axis) suffices to fix the *position* of the line. If the curve contains bends or kinks, however, as it would if it were part of a circle, knowledge about the slope and position of one section of the curve would not indicate the nature of the curve in other sections. The use of such nonlinear relations in econometrics is becoming increasingly common. There is, however, no need to use more complicated relations without first attempting to get along without them, and most curves can be approximated fairly well, within a limited range, by straight lines.

Other kinds of simplifications are also used in econometric work, as will be indicated in more detail below. Though these simplifications are useful in avoiding various practical difficulties, their use involves the introduction of new and essentially untested hypotheses about the form of relations suggested by economic theory. An important task of econometric research, therefore, is to select simplifications that permit practical work but do not materially alter the character of the original theoretical model.

The Formulation of Econometric Models

In current practice, most econometric analyses follow a standard pattern. The data relevant to a given problem are first divided into two classes: data to be interpreted by the theory and data to be taken as given. The variables of the theory are then divided into two corresponding categories, *endogenous* and *exogenous,* according to the same principle; and a series of theoretical *structural relations* or *structural equations* is established relating the endogenous variables to one another and to the exogenous variables. The purpose of this procedure is to arrive at a system of relations (simultaneous equations) which can be used to determine the "unknown" values of the endogenous variables in terms of the "given" values of the exogenous variables.

A Typical Model   A theory intended to describe price determination in a single market—say, the market for corn—could be represented by a system of three linear *structural equations:*

$$d_c = a_1 p_c + B_1 h \quad \text{(demand)}$$
$$(1) \qquad s_c = a_2 p_c + B_2 r \quad \text{(supply)}$$
$$d_c = s_c \qquad\qquad \text{(market clearance)}$$

In this system, $d_c, s_c,$ and p_c are *endogenous variables* representing the current demand, supply, and price of corn. The symbols h and r represent *exogenous variables* and describe the current stock of hogs and annual rainfall. The symbols $a_1, a_2, B_1,$ and B_2 represent given constants called *structural parameters.* The particular values assigned to these structural parameters determine the precise form of the structural relations of the system and so determine indirectly the equilibrium values of the endogenous $d_c, s_c,$ and p_c corresponding to given values of the exogenous variables h and r.

A geometric interpretation of system (1) is presented in Figure 3-14. The lines $d_c{}^1, d_c{}^2,$ and $d_c{}^3$ represent three out of an indefinitely large number of possible positions of the demand "curve" corresponding to a *given value* of the structural parameter a_1 (which fixes the slope of each of the demand lines) and *three different values* $h_1, h_2,$ and h_3 of the exogenous variable h (stock of hogs). The extent to which changes in the value of h alters the position of the demand relation depends on the magnitude of the structural parameter, B_1; for example, if B_1 were twice as great, the demand lines illustrated in the figure would be more widely spaced. Similarly, lines $s_c{}^1, s_c{}^2,$ and $s_c{}^3$ represent three possible positions of the supply "curve" corresponding to a given value of the structural parameter a_2 (which fixes the slope of each supply relation) and three different values $r_1, r_2,$ and r_3 of the exogenous variable r (rain). The "shift effect" of changes in the variable r will depend on the magnitude of the structural parameter B_2. The line corresponding to the equation $d_c = s_c$ cannot be drawn explicitly in this graph because the variables

FIGURE 3-14

The Market for Corn
This geometric representation of the system of linear structural equations highlights the three endogenous variables, quantity demanded, quantity supplied, and price, and the two exogenous variables (or shifters) stock of hogs and rainfall. Each demand curve corresponds to a different quantity of hogs, and has a slope equal to the structural parameter a_1. The slope of the supply curve is a_2, and different levels of rainfall produce different supply curves.

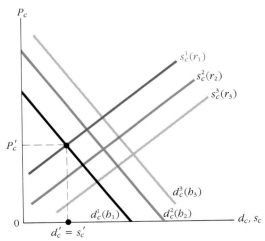

d_c and s_c are not measured on separate axes. However, this market clearance condition will be satisfied at the intersection of the supply line and a demand line for given h and r.

Suppose, for example, that h has the particular value h_1 while r has the particular value r_1, and that h_1 and r_1 represent particular numbers such as 3 million hogs and 40 inches of rain. The corresponding demand and supply relations are represented by d_c^1 and s_c^1, and the equilibrium price is given by p_c^1 (a particular number determined by the market clearance equation $d_c^1 = d_s^1$). Different values of the exogenous variables r and h would determine different demand and supply lines, and so a different equilibrium price. Moreover, different values of the structural parameters a_1 and a_2 would result in demand and supply lines with different *slopes,* and thus a different equilibrium price. Finally, different values of the structural parameters B_1 and B_2 would determine different *positions* of the demand and supply lines, and so, once more, different equilibrium prices.

Thus we see that the implications for price and quantity determination of the system of equations (1) differ depending on the particular values assigned to the exogenous variables h and r and the structural parameters a_1, a_2, B_1, B_2. That is to say, the particular equilibrium values of the endogenous variables d_c, s_c, and p_c that satisfy the three equations in system (1) vary according to the internal structure of the system as determined by the particular values of the structural parameters a_1, a_2, B_1, B_2 and the external factors affecting the system as determined by the particular values of the exogenous variables h and r.

Models and Structures   A general system of equations such as (1), with the values of the structural parameters not specified exactly, is called a *model.* If *specific* values are assigned to the parameters of the system, the system is known as a *structure* rather than a model. In other words, every model is an infinite class of different possible structures. The model is essentially *qualitative* in character; each structure represents a particular *quantitative* form of the model.

In these terms, the purpose of econometric study may be restated as follows: First, the study seeks to establish, with the aid of economic theory, a tentatively acceptable model, which is in purely qualitative terms. Next, on the basis of empirical data about past values of the endogenous and exogenous variables, it seeks to determine the particular quantitative structure contained within the model—that is, a set of values of the structural parameters of the model, which produces a set of values of the endogenous variables in accord with actual data of past experience. This structure can then be used to predict the magnitudes of endogenous variables in future periods, on the assumption that the parameters and exogenous variables for these future periods will be the same as in the past or will change in some specified way.

Models with Error Terms   An obvious difficulty with this procedure is that no structure contained in a linear model (or for that matter, in any theoretical model) is likely to yield predictions that are completely accurate. Even with the most careful work and the most ingenious theories, errors are bound to occur because of imperfections in data, omission of relevant exogenous variables, unanticipated nonlinearities, and unforeseen changes in the behavioral and institutional character of the situation being studied.

To take some of these difficulties into account, and also to avoid working with models that are known in advance to provide a false picture of reality, it is standard econometric practice to introduce certain latent (unobservable) *error terms* into every econometric model. The model described by the system of relations (1), for example, would normally be written in the form

$$(2) \qquad \begin{aligned} d_c &= a_1 p_c + B_1 h + u_1 \\ s_c &= a_2 p_c + B_2 r + u_2 \\ d_c &= s_c + u_3 \end{aligned}$$

with the additional error variables $u_1, u_2,$ and u_3 in each relation representing various unknown factors not otherwise taken into account in the model.

With a model of this kind, together with certain assumptions about the nature of the error variables, $u_i,$ the purpose of econometric study may be modified as that of determining the structure contained in the model which is *most nearly* in accord with known facts—that is, determining values of the structural parameters which lead to predicted values of the endogenous variables $d_c, s_c,$ and $p_c,$ that differ as little as possible from their observed values.

The Complexity of the Models   The preceeding discussion gives only a hint of the possible complexity and generality of econometric models. Systems may involve 150 or more equations, consider not only current but also past (lagged) values of both endogenous and exogenous variables, and work with nonlinear as well as with linear relations.

Problems of Estimation

While the collection of data and construction of provisional theoretical models constitute more than half the battle in most econometric studies, the remaining task is not merely a matter of routine computation. This would very nearly be the case if models which provided perfectly accurate simulation of observed economic phenomena were feasible, for straightforward calculations would suffice to indicate whether a model did or did not provide a precise description of available empirical data.

In actual practice, however, there are major complications. First, available empirical data do not always provide enough information to permit the econometrician to say whether a chosen model is satisfactory; in order to carry out an analysis, it may be necessary to reformulate the model or to search out additional data. Second, even if available data appear to provide some information about the adequacy of a given theoretical model, this information may not be sufficiently detailed or exact to permit the econometrician to choose a single "best" structure from the set of structures contained within a given model. Third, there are various alternative methods of calculating numerical estimates of the structural parameters in any given model, and different methods do not always lead to the same results. The advantages and disadvantages of different methods of calculation are difficult to determine on logical grounds. Each of these problems merits brief discussion.

The Identification Problem   A simplified example will illustrate the first problem of estimation mentioned above: situations in which available empirical data do not permit the econometrician to decide whether a chosen model is or is not worthwhile. Suppose that price in a given market is known to be determined by current supply and demand forces, in the sense that the market price always adjusts immediately to the level required to make quantity supplied equal to quantity demanded. But with available data on prices and quantities exchanged, it may not be possible to distinguish between supply and demand relations because the data on quantity exchanged represent both quantity supplied and quantity demanded at the equilibrium. This problem is called the *identification problem* because of the impossibility in such cases of separating the data for the various structural relations in the theoretical models—that is, of identifying the data for a particular relationship.

The difficulty is most easily appreciated by considering the price/quantity data that relate to various demand and supply curves. If, for example, a shifting demand curve is combined with a fixed supply curve (as in Figure 3-15), this will yield a series of "observable" equilibrium points on the supply curve. But the *same* series of "observable" points could just as well have been generated by a shifting demand curve combined with a *shifting* supply curve, as illustrated in Figure 3-16.

FIGURE 3-15

Increasing Demand with a Fixed Supply
The price-quantity observations may be the equilibrium points of a stable supply curve
with shifting demand curves over time.

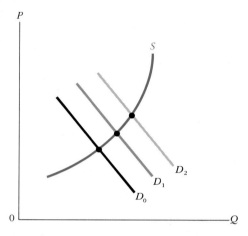

FIGURE 3-16

Increasing Demand with a Decrease in Supply
The price-quantity observations in Figure 3-15 may be equilibrium points of shifting
supply and demand curves over time. Connecting the three equilibrium points might give
a misleading impression of supply.

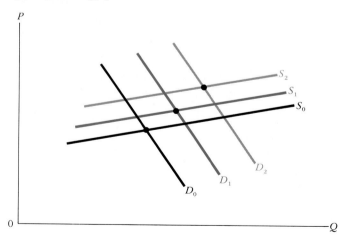

From a given set of structural relations and given information about shifts in these relations, it
is possible to obtain precisely one set of "observable" points; but the *reverse* operation, that of
obtaining a given set of structural relations and shifts from a given set of "observable" points,
cannot be carried out in the absence of additional information. If it is known, for example, that

the supply curve shifts from year to year according to the amount of rainfall, whereas the demand curve does not shift at all, it may be possible to *identify* the demand curve from observable price/quantity data. Similarly, if the demand curve shifts only in response to changes in income and the supply curve shifts, as before, only in response to changes in rainfall, then both the supply and the demand curves may be empirically identifiable.

There are various ways of adding extra information to a theoretical model in order to lessen identification problems. Some structural parameters may be assumed to have positive signs and others to have negative signs. Still other parameters may be assumed to have the value zero; that is, they may be assumed to be absent from some equations. Assumptions can also be made about the values of the error terms in various structural equations. For example, it may be assumed that the average value of the error is zero, implying that "errors" in one direction are offset by "errors" in the opposite direction, at least in any long series of observations.

Whatever procedure is followed in order to achieve theoretical identifiability of the structural relations of an econometric model, the relations of the model still might not be identifiable in practice. This will happen, for example, if the factors that *might* lead to shifts in structural relations *in fact* do not happen to vary significantly during the period for which empirical data are available. As an illustration, let us consider an attempt to analyze the effect of income changes on demand. Even if the supply curve is absolutely fixed, empirical data on price, quantity exchanged, and income will not provide an indication of the nature of the supply curve if, during the period of observation, income does not vary. All observable price/quantity points will be the same, and will simply indicate the intersection of the given demand and supply curves.

The Problem of "Goodness of Fit"   The second type of problem described earlier—namely, one arising because empirical data are not sufficiently exact or detailed to indicate whether a particular theoretical model provides a good explanation of observed events—may be described as the problem of "goodness of fit."

This class of problem may be illustrated with a supply/demand model in which the demand equation is identifiable. With a scatter diagram of the sort illustrated in Figure 3-17, one would

FIGURE 3-17

Goodness of Fit
The estimated demand curve fits the data well and generates confidence in the model estimates. Actual observations are close to the estimated model.

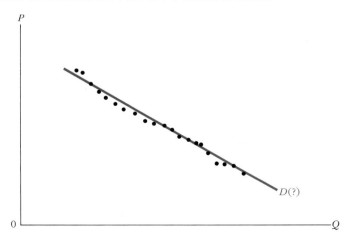

have no difficulty estimating the form of the demand relation. The data would indicate very clearly that a straight-line estimate of the demand curve is entirely appropriate. Matters would be very different, however, if on the same assumptions the scatter diagram was of the type shown in Figure 3-18. An embarrassingly large number of different demand relations would all seem to fit these data about equally well.

Unfortunately for econometrics, situations of the latter kind are common. The typical econometric model is too complicated, and the data available for estimating the relations of the model are too varied, to permit the investigator to discover by simple inspection whether a provisionally satisfactory model is likely to provide a "good" or a "bad" fit to the data. If one could say, on the basis of casual inspection of empirical data, that a given structure did or did not provide a reasonable explanation of the data, one could use such knowledge to check the efficiency and validity of various techniques for calculating numerical estimates of structural parameters. But the contrary situation is more common in practice: No clear indication of the empirical validity of a theoretical model can be obtained until after the structural parameters in the model have been estimated; and even then there may be considerable room for doubt unless the particular estimation technique (that is, the particular method for calculating numerical estimates of the structural parameters) is somehow known in advance to yield reliable results. In any event, the net result is a great increase in the amount of work required compared to what would be necessary if the usefulness of the model could be ascertained by simple inspections at an early stage in the process.

Choice of Estimation Techniques   In many situations, the econometrician faces a serious dilemma. Simple inspection of empirical data will not indicate whether a given model can be used to provide a satisfactory explanation of the data. To make any progress at all, the data must be processed by one of several possible methods so as to yield numerical estimates of the structural parameters in the given model. The values of the endogenous variables, calculated on

FIGURE 3-18
A Poor Fit
The data do not fit any of the potential demand curves well. Confidence in the estimated model is limited in this case.

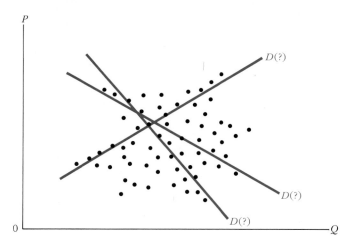

the assumption that the structural parameters of the model are as estimated, may then be compared with observed values of the same variables to determine whether the model's theoretical predictions are satisfactory.

If the results of this comparison are unsatisfactory, however, the econometrician may have difficulty deciding which factors are responsible for the failure. Are the data inaccurate? Is the model unsatisfactory? Or is the technique used to calculate estimates of the structural parameters in the model a poor one? The complexity of economic phenomena is such that reliable techniques of estimation are essential if econometric studies are to be fruitful; but reliable techniques of estimation are extremely difficult to establish because of the complexity of the models needed to describe economic phenomena.

Much of the difficulty springs from the fact that all of the estimation techniques currently used in econometrics are basically designed to apply to experimental data of the kind studied in physics, chemistry, and the biological sciences, where it is possible to maintain some degree of control over sources of error in the construction of models and the measurement of phenomena. Most of the data of economics, however, are nonexperimental in character. Economists have to take whatever factual information is provided by the everyday working of the economic system; they cannot ordinarily arrange experiments in which individuals, communities, or countries are subjected to controlled changes in external conditions and studied like bugs in a laboratory.

The problem would not be serious if different techniques of estimating structural parameters applied to the given data always yielded similar answers; but this is not the case. Neither would it be a serious problem if the theoretical models used in econometrics were known to be capable of simulating observed phenomena with a high degree of accuracy; but this is not true, either. As matters stand, the derivation of empirically significant estimates of structural parameters remains a major unsettled problem of contemporary econometrics. Future progress will depend as much upon the solution of this issue as upon the collection of better data and the construction of improved theoretical models.

Conclusion

Several important limitations of contemporary econometric research have been indicated in the preceding discussion. Some of these limitations will become relatively more important over time, while others will become less important.[11]

On the other hand, it is essential to recognize that econometric research is a unified activity in the sense that every aspect of such research has a direct bearing on every other aspect. Thus, improved data may lead to improvement in estimation techniques, which in turn may lead to the construction of theoretical models that can be used satisfactorily to describe nonexperimental data. While econometric research faces many serious and unsettled problems, it is important to note that the *problems of econometric research are essentially the same as the problems of empirical economic research in general.* Every science has problems of this kind, many of them far from completely resolved. In this regard, there is no reason to suppose that the problems of economics are any more serious than the problems of, say, nuclear physics or psychology or political science.

---

[11]For an engaging, accessible discussion of econometric difficulties, see E. Leamer, "Let's Take the Con Out of Econometrics," *American Economic Review,* Vol. 73 (March 1983) pp. 31–43.

Scientific progress is a gradual phenomenon, even in the best of circumstances. Economics in general, and econometrics in particular, have not displayed especially rapid rates of progress in the past; but neither has progress been slow. The fact that more and more professional economists are becoming interested in econometrics research indicates that they do not consider the present limitations of econometric work to be permanent. The same fact gives us reason to hope that the results of future econometric research will greatly expand our knowledge about quantitative characteristics of the economic system. Perfectly accurate measurement of econometric relations is an impossibility in any case; but even approximate measurement is better than no measurement at all.

4

Stocks and Flows in Supply and Demand*

4.1 INTRODUCTION

Our discussion thus far has dealt with **flow variables**—variables that have a time dimension, such as the quantity of wine purchased in Los Angeles in 1987. Here we must know not only *how much* wine was purchased, but also *over what duration:* days, months, or years. (After all, 40,000 cases a day is clearly more than 40,000 cases a year.) The other kind of variable we must distinguish is a **stock variable**. A stock variable (inventories being of interest here) has *no* time dimension, an example being an inventory level of 1,000 cases of wine in a store. It should be remarked that many goods are a mix of both stock and flows. Automobiles and household appliances are in the form of stocks on hand, yet they provide a service flow over many periods. In a pure stock economy, assets can be exchanged only for other assets; in a pure flow economy, income (the flow return to the owner of a factor input) can only be consumed.

To ignore the distinction between stocks and flows would considerably hinder our understanding of business cycles. Explicit analysis of savings, investments, and growth processes is conceptually possible only in the context of a stock/flow model. The terms supply and demand, unless properly addressed to include stock and flow analysis, may conceal as much as they reveal about the *forces* governing market behavior.

The term *supply* of a good can refer either to the quantity of the good in existence at any particular moment (stock) or to the rate or flow at which it is currently being produced (quantity per day, per month, per year). Similarly, the term *demand* for a

---

*This chapter presents material that is a bit more difficult than that of earlier chapters. Teachers without particular interest in macroeconomic issues or durable goods may wish to omit this material.

good refers either to the quantity of the good that individuals possess at a particular moment (stock) or to the rate at which it is currently being consumed (flow).

In everyday discussion, one can usually infer from the context whether a speaker refers to stock or flow aspects of any activity. If a strike is in progress in the automobile industry and car production is currently at a standstill, the term *supply* will normally refer to stocks already in the hands of dealers. Alternatively, if the industry is operating normally, stocks in existence at any moment are typically small relative to yearly output; in this case, the term *supply* almost always refers to the annual rate of production. In economic analysis, however, there is no contextual basis for distinguishing between the two interpretations; we must either make the distinction explicit or risk serious confusion and misunderstanding (See Box 4-1.)

4.2 STOCKS, FLOWS, AND EXCHANGE

If the activity of exchange involved nothing more than a matching of what is produced with what is consumed, then the distinction between stocks and flows wouldn't matter much. In fact, stocks could be ignored altogether on the grounds that they would have little impact on the ultimate equilibrium of supply and demand. However, the real world is not so simple. Often contracts are written that obligate one party to deliver goods to another party in exchange for money. In most cases, goods promised for delivery are already held as inventories; production flows do not move directly from business firms to consumers, but instead pass through an intermediate stage in which they are temporarily held as **inventories** (a stock). Also, goods delivered to consumers seldom flow directly into consumption; on the contrary, they normally are used to replenish household inventories (stocks) and aren't consumed physically for days or even months after they are purchased. For example, wine producers keep large stocks of wine on hand, while wine consumers often have inventories ranging from a few bottles to cellars containing hundreds or thousands of bottles.

It may appear that we are making a great fuss about a minor matter. Surely it cannot matter all that much if we ignore household and business inventories and suppose that trade proceeds as if such inventories did not exist. But if we wish to provide a discussion of short-run *disequilibrium* situations, then it is unwise to ignore from the

---

4-1   True or False?   The salary that one makes is a stock variable.

False.   A salary, whether it be paid by the hour, the month, or the year, is a *flow* of money income. All your assets considered at *one moment* would be a stock variable. Other stock variables might be the value of your car or house, the value of a company's inventories or assets, and so on.

outset an aspect of the real world—inventory depletion or build-up—that is known to be an important source of economic variability. To appreciate just what is involved, one need only consider the number of automobiles, new and used, that are held by American households and firms—or indeed the quantity of money held. While some kinds of inventories truly are minor and can be safely ignored, no serious analysis of market behavior can proceed on the assumption that all inventories fall into this category. In the discussion that follows, therefore, we shall treat the case in which inventories are important as the rule rather than the exception.

4.3 STOCK DEMAND AND SUPPLY

If an individual offers to *sell* units of a given good, this indicates a willingness to deplete current inventory holdings. The person is said to have **stock excess supply**—that is, excess stock of this good. Similarly, if an individual offers to *buy* units of a given good, this implies a willingness to add to present inventory holdings. The person who wants to "stock up" is said to have **stock excess demand**. (See Box 4-2.)

Individuals may wish to hold inventories for various reasons: to provide a reserve against future predicaments, to serve as a hedge against inflation, or to avoid the high cost of frequent small-lot exchange transactions. In normal circumstances, only the last of these motives is important. Why the last one? Because it costs nearly as much in terms of time and effort to buy or sell a small quantity as a large quantity; so if an individual trades always in small lots, the total cost of trading a given quantity of goods during a given period of time will be vastly greater than if she trades infrequently in relatively large lots. To appreciate the importance of this consideration, one needs only to reflect on observed behavior. Do you buy gum by the stick or by the pack? Do you cash small checks every day or larger ones every week? Do you purchase gasoline by the gallon or by the tank? Needless to say, business firms are much more conscious than households of the costs that can be avoided by holding relatively large average inventories and buying and selling in relatively large lots. But the factors governing holdings of trade inventories are essentially the same for both households and business firms. (See Box 4-3.)

4-2 True or False?   Producers hold inventories of goods all the time; however, this is not the case with consumers.

False.   Of course consumers hold inventories. Why have a refrigerator if you don't store food? Virtually all durable goods (which typically yield consumer service flows) are held as inventories. Our clothes, TVs, and automobiles are all inventories.

4-3   How does consumption affect the stock of a good—say, ice cream in your freezer?

If you continue to eat ice cream regularly without replenishing your inventories, the stock will fall. The only way to add to the stock is to put more ice cream into the freezer (increase market purchases) than you take out (presumably to consume).

Individual holdings of inventories depend on many factors—political, institutional, and technological—that lie outside the immediate scope of economic analysis. It can be shown, however, that an individual's willingness to hold stocks of any particular good will vary inversely with the good's market value, ceteris paribus. The higher the price of a good, the greater the amount of wealth it represents. Any time wealth is used to replenish inventories, the opportunity to earn interest on that wealth or to consume other goods is forgone. The cost is relatively greater for high-priced goods than for low-priced goods.

We assume, then, that the **stock demand** for any given commodity is a decreasing function of its market price, as illustrated by the stock demand curve D in Figure 4-1. This curve is drawn on the assumption that the values of all variables relevant to stock demand other than market price are fixed. If any of these values should change, the position of the stock demand curve would shift.

FIGURE 4-1

Stock Demand and Supply

The stock demand curve represents the quantity of a particular commodity that transactors are willing to hold as inventories at various prices, *ceteris paribus.* People want fewer holdings, the greater the price. Thus, the stock demand curve slopes downward. The stock supply curve depicts the amount of the commodity available at a point in time. Stock supply cannot respond to price changes.

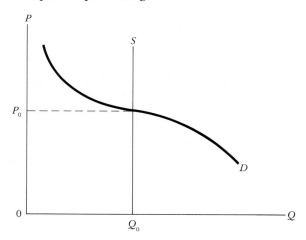

Unless all goods purchased are instantaneously consumed (as, perhaps, with a restaurant meal), when any individual offers to buy units of a given good, this implies a willingness to add to present inventory holdings. The desire to add to inventories under current market conditions we shall call "stock excess demand." (See Box 4-4.)

The quantity of any good actually held by individuals at any given moment is a legacy from the past, as is the aggregate stock of the good available to the economy as a whole. Thus, at any moment, the aggregate stock is "frozen" and cannot be changed. Of course an individual can increase his stock of a good right now (by acquiring more of it in exchange from somebody else), but the economy-wide (aggregate) stock of that good is not affected. While the future magnitude of a stock supply of a good can be altered by human action, its *current* level is simply a fact. This is illustrated in Figure 4-1 by drawing the stock supply curve, S, as a vertical line to indicate that the quantity of existing stocks is independent of current market price.

Evidently, the quantity of a good demanded to hold at any moment will be equal to the quantity actually in existence only at one particular level of market price—namely, that level at which the stock demand curve intersects the stock supply curve (P_0 in Figure 4-1). At any other price, either stock demand will exceed stock supply (stock excess demand will be positive), or stock supply will exceed stock demand (stock excess supply will be positive). This difference between stock demand and supply implies a desire on the part of some individuals to alter their existing holdings. Consumers or firms may each have *either* stock excess demands or stock excess supplies, depending on whether they wish to build up or deplete their inventories at the current market price. Normally, for example, an increase in stock demand (stock excess demand at current prices) from consumers will lead to depleted firm inventories, transferring the stock excess demand to firms; the firms are then likely to increase production, a flow, to eliminate their stock excess demands.

4.4 FLOW DEMAND AND SUPPLY

Individual holders of a good who wish to alter current stocks may do so by changing their present rate of consumption (or production) or by changing current market purchases (or sales). The stock of any good held by individuals in the aggregate will

---

4-4 Name some occurrences that would cause the stock demand curve to shift to the left.

- A new shopping center opens that is closer to your home.
- A more fuel-efficient automobile lowers your transportation costs.
- You become a vegetarian, and we are considering your stock demand curve for meat.

- Your stockbroker forecasts a major decline in "stock" prices. Your stock demand for stocks might fall *now:* you may sell now in anticipation of replenishing stocks at lower prices later.

vary over time only if aggregate production of the good currently differs from aggregate consumption; otherwise, trades among individuals involve nothing more than a redistribution of existing stocks. Current levels of aggregate production and consumption thus play a crucial role in determining the rate of change of stock supplies of various commodities—which in turn directly influences prevailing levels of stock excess demand. In order to complete the groundwork for demand and supply analysis of market behavior, we must deal with the determinants of aggregate production and consumption. There is, to be sure, some consideration to timing and lags given in traditional accounts of supply and demand—but that consideration comes mainly in the distinction between the "market," "short-run," and "long-run" periods. *Within* each of those periods, the impact of time is ignored by implicitly or explicitly assuming instantaneous equilibration. As students perceive the power of the "period simplifications" for certain problems (partial equilibrium problems), they forget that these simplifications are abstractions from the impact of time in the real world. Unfortunately, for *other* problems, these simplifications hinder an understanding of supply and demand in the real world.

We begin by noting that the quantity (flow) of any given good that individuals in the aggregate are willing to produce at any given moment is an increasing function of its current market price: the higher the price, the greater the quantity supplied. Similarly, we suppose that the quantity (flow) of any given good that individuals in the aggregate are willing to consume at any given moment is a decreasing function of its current market price. These assumptions are illustrated in Figure 4-2, where the flow demand

FIGURE 4-2

Consumption Flow Demand and Production Flow Supply
The flow demand curve shows the quantity demanded for consumption of a particular product at alternate prices over a specified period of time—a day, a week, a year. The quantity supplied at various prices over a given period, the production flow supply curve, slopes upward because producers will want to produce greater amounts of a commodity in response to higher prices.

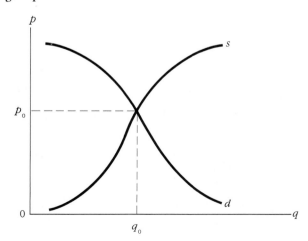

curve d represents the relation between market price and desired consumption, and the flow supply curve s represents the relation between market price and desired production. In general, the position and form of the flow demand and supply curves depend upon many factors in addition to current market price, including population, income, suppliers input prices, technology, and other factors that are usually considered in supply and demand analysis. The desired rate of consumption evidently will be equal to the desired rate of production only at one particular value of market price (p_0 in Figure 4-2). At any other price, flow excess demand or flow excess supply will occur.

We now must consider flow demand and supply together with stock demand and supply to understand what occurs when exchanges take place in actual markets. Increases in *market* demand may stem from desires either to consume more or to add to stocks. There is no obvious way to know which motive is at work. Similarly, increased supplies to the market may come from either increased production or attempts to reduce stocks on hand. (See Box 4-5.)

4.5 MARKET DEMAND AND SUPPLY

Throughout the preceding discussion, we have been careful to emphasize that decisions about rates of production and consumption and desired holdings of inventories are separate and distinct from decisions about quantities demanded for purchase or offered for sale; *the laws of market exchange are related to, but not derivable from, the laws of production and consumption.* That is, supply is more than merely the horizontal summation of marginal cost of production schedules; demand is more than merely the horizontal summation of individual consumption demands. To understand these distinctions, we must establish the relation between stock demands and supplies, flow demands and supplies, and market offers to buy and sell.

It is customary to define market demand as a relation that indicates, for each possible level of market price, the quantity of a good that individuals in the aggregate are willing to purchase per unit of time. Similarly, it is customary to define market supply as a function that indicates for each possible level of market price the quantity of a

---

4-5 Can *actual* stocks be different from *desired* stock?

Yes, for a *particular* price. However, price will tend to move in the market if desired stock holdings differ from actual stock holdings. If, for example, people collectively (buyers and sellers) have more than they want of a good, efforts to get rid of the excess stocks will lower price. At this lower price, production will be lower and consumption will be higher. Hence *flow* behavior is affected by excess stock demands or supplies: this stock/flow interaction is critical to macroeconomic activity where, for example, the circular flow of income will be affected by the demand for stocks of money.

good that individuals in the aggregate are willing to sell. An initial difficulty with these concepts is that they do not permit us to distinguish between *purchases for use* (flow) and *purchases to hold* (stock), or between *production for sale* (flow) and *production for stockpiling* (stock). To state the same difficulty in another way, we can hardly suppose that the quantity of a good that individuals are willing to purchase depends only on market price; it must also depend on current stocks held. Similarly, we can hardly suppose that quantity offered for sale depends only on market price; it must also depend on current stocks held. The conventional definitions of market demand and supply are flawed by their failure to explicitly recognize these facts—the emphasis in traditional texts is always on the rather special case where stock excess demands are zero for all transactors.

We may remedy this difficulty most conveniently by supposing that market demand, measured as a flow, is an increasing function of stock excess demand of all households and firms whose desired stocks currently exceed actual holdings. That is, if consumers want to increase their stocks (if they have stock excess demands), then they must increase the inflow by purchasing in the market more than they want for personal consumption. This implies that the **market demand** for any good is a function of its current market price and of stocks currently held by prospective purchasers of the good. Similarly, we suppose that market supply, measured as a flow, is an increasing function of stock excess supply of all transactors whose actual stocks currently exceed desired holdings. That is, if businesses have too much stock in inventories (stock excess supply), they will offer more for sale to increase their market outflow. This implies that the **market supply** of any good is a function of its current market price and of stocks currently held by prospective sellers of the good.

These relations are illustrated in Figure 4-3 by the market supply and demand curves $s(S_{firm})$ and $d(S_{consumer})$. In general, the position of the curves will depend on the distribution as well as the total quantity of stocks, $S_{consumer}$ and S_{firm}, that are held by buyers and sellers. (See Box 4-6.)

4-6   Imagine you owned a redwood hot tub. In terms of stocks and flows, what would you call the water already in the hot tub? How about the water that entered into the hot tub through the garden hose? Or the water that drained out through a leak in the bottom of your hot tub? Finally, how would you change the stock of water in the hot tub?

The water already in the hot tub is a stock, while the water flowing in (garden hose) and flowing out (leak) are both flow variables. If the leak were to become smaller and there was more water entering into the hot tub via the garden hose than leaving through the leak, the stock of water in the hot tub would increase. Remember this little formula:

Stocks will ↑ if inflows > outflows
Stocks will ↓ if inflows < outflows

FIGURE 4-3

Market Demand and Supply
The market demand curve measured as a flow depends upon current stocks held.
Deviations of desired stocks from actual stocks will shift the market flow demand curve.
Stock holdings of a commodity are also a market supply curve shifter. At price p_1, quantity
supplied exceeds quantity demanded creating excess flow supply. Excess flow demand
exists at p_2. Buyers will offer higher prices until the price reaches p_0.

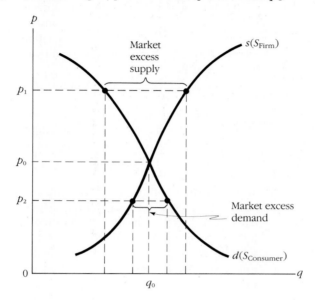

4.6 MARKET EQUILIBRIUM

Taking the word *equilibrium* in its usual sense to mean an "absence of motion," we
shall say that a market is in equilibrium if, and only if, market price and quantity traded
do not change over time. This definition merely permits us to recognize an equilibrium situation when we see one; it does not allow us to say what conditions must be
met if market price and quantity are to be stationary over time, much less to describe
how such an equilibrium might be attained. To say anything about these matters, we
must introduce explicit assumptions about the forces governing market price and
quantity at each moment.

In describing the behavior of market price, we assume (following Chapter 3) that
market price tends to rise whenever market demand exceeds market supply and to fall
whenever market supply exceeds market demand. More precisely, we assume that the
rate of change of price at any time is an increasing function of market excess demand at
the same moment. The usual rationale for this assumption runs something like the
following:

Suppose that the market demand and supply curves for a particular good as of a certain date $t = 0$ are represented by the curves $d(S_{consumer})$ and $s(S_{firm})$ in Figure 4-3. Suppose, further, that the market price at time $t = 0$ is at p_1, so that market supply currently exceeds market demand. In these circumstances, some sellers may fail to sell anything at all, and many sellers will sell less than they would like to at the prevailing market price. Accordingly, some sellers will attempt to improve their position (partly at the expense of other sellers) by asking less than the prevailing market price. The result will be a tendency for market price to decline over time. Alternatively, suppose that market price at time $t = 0$ is at p_2, so that market demand currently exceeds market supply. In this case, some buyers may be unable to purchase anything at all, and many will be unable to buy all they want. Accordingly, some buyers will offer better terms in an attempt to move to the head of the buying queue. The result will be a tendency for market price to rise over time. (See Box 4-7.)

Therefore, in order for market equilibrium to occur at any given time:

1. stock excess demand and stock excess supply must equal zero; and
2. market (flow) excess demand and market (flow) excess supply must equal zero. (If the first condition holds, another way to express the second condition is: actual production flows must equal actual consumption flows.)

Note that market equilibrium does *not* imply an absence of "motion" or "change." *Individual* holdings of stocks will vary more or less continuously over time. For example, a typical household may replenish its inventories of consumer goods at the end of each week and then run down its holdings during the course of the week to meet daily requirements. Business holdings of inventories will constantly fluctuate in much the same manner and for similar reasons. However, in the midst of all these changes, *average* holdings of inventories and *average* levels of production, consumption, and trade will be constant from period to period so long as equilibrium prevails.

4-7   True or False?   Since market price tends to rise when a good is in excess demand and to decline when it is in excess supply, it is only natural to suppose that market price will be stationary over time if market demand is equal to market supply.

False.   This may be seen most easily by supposing that price at time $t = 0$ is at p_0 in Figure 4-3—that is, at the level where the market demand and supply curves intersect. At the initial instant, no force will be acting to drive market price either up or down. However, if current production at price p_0 exceeds current consumption at the same price (and there is no reason why this should not be so), aggregate stocks will be increasing, which means that the market demand and supply curves (whose positions depend on $S_{consumer}$ and S_{firm}) will be shifting over time. Indeed, only if both producers and consumers are each holding exactly their respective desired stocks of inventories will production and consumption coincide with no stock changes. Thus the "equilibrium" defined by the intersection of the market demand and supply curves at time $t = 0$ will be strictly transitory in this case, for market demand will shortly cease to be equal to market supply.

4.7 MARKET DISEQUILIBRIUM

The statement of conditions for market equilibrium does little to advance our understanding of market behavior and, in particular, of the impact of market behavior on business cycles. To gain additional insight into this problem, we must deal directly with disequilibrium states and attempt to describe the adjustment process through which the market ultimately approaches a state of equilibrium. For this purpose, we shall work directly with the stock and flow demand and supply curves shown in Figure 4-4.

Suppose that market price and existing stocks are initially at levels P_0 and S_0, which are consistent with market equilibrium when stock demand is represented by the curve D_0 and flow demand and supply are represented by the curves d_0 and s_0. Also suppose that actual levels of production and consumption always adjust quickly to desired levels as indicated by prevailing market (flow) demand and supply conditions. (In other words, leave aside the time it takes for consumers to increase consumption of a good whose price falls or for firms to increase production of a good whose price rises.) What will happen to market price and to quantities produced, consumed, and held if at some *instant* of time $t = 0$ the stock demand curve shifts to the left in Figure

Adjustment to Change in Stock Demand
Stock demand declines from D_0 to D_1 in part (a) due to lower transportation costs. Households delay their next shopping trip and the flow demand curve falls from d_0 to d_1 and sales decline from q_0 to q_1 in part (b). Inventory costs for businesses rise and firms are willing to supply more at each possible price to work off excess inventories; s_0 shifts right to s_1 in part (b). At the original price, P_0, there is excess flow supply and price will fall. Stocks of inventories eventually fall from S_0 to S_1 as consumption rises and production declines due to lower prices. Flow demand and supply return to original levels but stock supply remains at S_1.

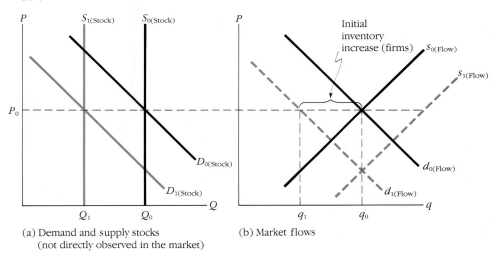

(a) Demand and supply stocks (not directly observed in the market)

(b) Market flows

4-4(a), say from D_0 to D_1 (perhaps in response to an improvement in transportation facilities that encourages households to shop more frequently and hold smaller average inventories)?

The shift in stock demand will produce an almost immediate increase in inventories held by business firms; households will work off their excess stocks $(Q_0 - Q_1)$ by delaying their next shopping trip until their initial inventories have been reduced to conform with their revised shopping schedules (d_0 falls in the market to d_1); hence there will be a temporary dip in business sales and a consequent accumulation of undesired inventories in the hands of retailers (seen in Figure 4-4(b) as the excess supply at P_0 with the initial supply curve and the new demand curve). The increase in business inventories will increase business costs, for business firms will now have to pay out more in interest charges, and perhaps crowding will become a problem with enlarged holdings of inventories. The effect of this increase in costs will be to shift the market (flow) supply curve to the right, say from s_0 to s_1, indicating that at each possible level of market price, producers will wish to supply somewhat larger quantities per unit of time to rid themselves of excess inventories.[1]

Since market demand has decreased due to consumer stock excess supply, and since market supply has increased due to firm stock excess supply, market price will fall. Although production will fall at this lower price, the costs of changing production plans will make many firms reluctant to alter their normal production operations to meet what appears to them (correctly) as a temporary drop in sales. Thus the response of the market to the initial decline in stock demand will consist partly of a reduction in price (tending to reduce existing stocks through increased consumption) and partly of a reduction in quantity produced (reducing existing stocks even more quickly). As soon as surplus inventories are eliminated, production, consumption, and market price will tend to return to their initial equilibrium levels. That is, d_1 will return to d_0 as purchases in the market again correspond to flow demands for consumption (rather than to changes in desired stock holdings); similarly, s_1 will return to s_0 as offers to sell in the market again correspond to flow production supplies (rather than to changes in desired stock holdings). The only permanent effect of the original decline in stock demand will be a reduction in aggregate inventories (from S_0 to S_1 in Figure 4-4(a)), unless this reduction permanently alters the positions of the flow demand and supply

---

[1]We are abstracting from another response that the firm might make, in combination with the response of increasing the supply to the market. The firms may also reduce *production* flows at the original price P_0. Such a response may seem inconsistent with profit maximization since the marginal cost curve has not shifted and, recalling economic principles, $p = mc$ is the condition for profit maximization. But that profit maximization condition presumes that production and sales are equivalent, which is not the case here as firms are unable to sell current production. The response of adjusting production *before* market prices adjust may be of particular importance in the macroeconomics setting. However, we shall ignore changes in production flows as an *initial* response to inventory build-up; we shall soon see that production flows will fall, in any event, as market price begins its (rapid) fall.

curves (which is not likely, for reasons which will become clear in later chapters).[2] (See Box 4-8.)

Disequilibrium adjustment processes associated with shifts in stock demand are relatively straightforward to analyze. Matters become more difficult if we consider adjustments initiated by shifts in flow supply (resulting from, say, technological progress) or in flow demand (resulting from, say, changes in household dietary habits). The initial effect of such changes clearly will be to produce steady accumulation or decumulation in existing commodity stocks. Stock demand will shortly come to differ from stock supply, and market price and quantities produced and consumed will proceed to change thereafter in much the same fashion as indicated in the preceding example. The market ultimately should settle down to a new equilibrium—at a permanently lower level of market price if the adjustment process was initiated by a rightward shift in flow supply, at a higher level of market price if the process was initiated by a rightward shift in flow demand. To describe the actual adjustment process in any detail, however, is beyond the scope of this text. Reduced to fundamentals,

---

[2]The reader may find it instructive to calculate the effects of a once-over increase in stock excess demand for a good. Evidently the only permanent consequence of such a change will be an increase in the equilibrium level of aggregate inventories—but the adjustment process leading to this result is worth examining for its own sake.

4-8 Summary of a fall in stock demand (resulting from, say, lower transportation costs).

1. Households will shop more frequently and hold smaller average inventories in the future, that is, stock demand curve shifts left from D_0 to D_1 in Figure 4-4(a).
2. Households will immediately start to work off their excess supply of stock (delay their next shopping trip). This will shift the *market* flow demand curve to the left from d_0 to d_1 in Figure 4-4(b).
3. Business sales fall while families are depleting their inventories in this manner—sales decline from q_0 to q_1 in Figure 4-4(b).
4. Business costs rise because of inventory costs; hence firms will be willing to supply more at each possible market price to rid themselves of excess inventories—s_0 shifts rightward to s_1 in Figure 4-4(b).
5. As a consequence of the preceding shifts, at P_0 there will be substantial excess flow supply that will lead to a temporary fall in price and the amount that is optimally produced (recall $p = mc$ at a profit maximum). Price may not actually fall all the way to the intersection of s_1 and d_1, but it will be moving in that direction.
6. Stocks of inventories fall from S_0 to S_1 as consumption (which is higher at lower prices) and production (which is lower at lower prices) combine to work off the initial excess of inventories.

the problem is to describe the behavior over time of four mutually interdependent magnitudes: market price, commodity stocks, production, and consumption[3]

4.8 STOCKS, FLOWS, AND THE BUSINESS CYCLE

Consider now the impact of disequilibrium on the business cycle. Suppose consumers wished (perhaps because of increased uncertainty about the future) to increase their stock holdings of money. To do this, they must either attempt to sell stocks of other goods or assets (stock excess supply) or reduce their flow consumption of other goods leading to a flow excess supply. But to whom can they sell their stock? In the aggregate, they cannot eliminate the excess stock supply at the going price. The market price could, of course, fall until the existing stock was voluntarily held. In the case of goods, this would involve consumers' adding their sales to the flow supply (production) of firms, a rather odd occurrence given our exchange institutions. Attempts to rid themselves of bonds would result in lower bond prices, hence higher interest rates leading to lower investment demand. Alternatively, and perhaps more plausibly, consumers may reduce their flow demands for goods until their stocks of these goods (in terms of money) have fallen by as much as they had wished to increase their stocks of money. Depending on the size of the increase in the stock demand for money, a considerable period of reduced flow purchases may ensue.

In either case, firms will see, at original market flow supply (and production) levels, steadily increasing inventory levels of either producer goods or consumer goods. These unintended inventory buildups lead to excess stock supplies. Firms must then engage in some combination of cutting prices or cutting production to reduce inventories. Since they are unaware that consumers are still consuming at the same rate (but predominantly out of their stock, not from flow purchases), they may suspect that demand is now lower for their product. They could reduce production (perhaps through temporary layoffs) and work off excess inventories while they wait to see what happens to demand. In this way they will not lose money on goods already in inventories, they will not have to incur any expenses associated with lowering prices, and they will be prepared to increase production should demand pick up again. Unfortunately, the layoffs (and reduced raw material orders) lead to the usual demand-diminishing feedbacks in the aggregate economy. Thus stock and flow interactions importantly affect macroeconomic conditions, and the latter cannot be well understood without reference to the former.

---

[3]The problem would be easy if we could infer the ultimate outcome of any adjustment process by direct inspection of underlying behavior relations—that is, stock and flow demand and supply functions. But such inferences generally are not possible, because we can seldom ascertain from underlying behavior relations anything more than the existence and defining characteristics of equilibrium states. Whether any given equilibrium state will ever be attained—and if so, when and by what route—is an issue that can be resolved only by using highly sophisticated techniques of analysis.

Economics, as taught today, presents the perceptive student with a schizophrenic view of the economic system. In the microeconomic portions of principles courses and in intermediate microeconomics, supply and demand analysis is presented as "the truth," with the usual treatment implicitly converting all demands to flows (as, for example, for the services of an automobile of given quality—this is needed to be able to relate the demand for cars to the demand for lettuce in a time period relevant to some budget constraint).

If however, supply and demand in fact "works," the bright student must surely wonder why half of principles books are devoted to a "nonproblem"—macroeconomics. That is, if inputs and output prices move freely and instantaneously to make market supply equal to market demand, then there are never gluts on output markets or involuntary unemployment in input markets. Hence, neither macroeconomics nor microeconomics, as usually taught, "work." The simple Keynesian macroeconomic model virtually ignores market-clearing entirely, while the standard microeconomic supply and demand model (see Chapter 3) assumes perfect market-clearing. The approach to supply and demand analysis presented here provides a bridge between microeconomics and macroeconomics, and should make both models seem more relevant.

4.9 PARTIAL EQUILIBRIUM ANALYSIS

Even when combined with the preceding discussion, Chapter 3 does little more than scratch the surface of demand and supply analysis; already it is clear that the reach of our questions exceeds the grasp of our analytical apparatus. Two alternatives are open to us: either we must provide additional apparatus, or we must ask less ambitious questions. The first alternative is preferable in principle, but to move in that direction would not be consistent with the objectives of this book. To answer even the simplest questions about dynamic adjustment processes, we should have to present a formidable array of purely mathematical ideas and thereby overlook a wide range of topics of greater economic interest.

Granted that the scope of our questions must be restricted, what direction should we take in the chapters that follow? Numerous routes are possible, ranging from the formal (but elementary) analysis of imaginary economic systems involving just two transactors and two goods to the elaborate description of a wide range of actual markets. We shall follow a middle course that is simultaneously hallowed by tradition, consistent with the essentially practical objectives of this book, and directly related to the conception of demand and supply analysis outlined in this chapter. Specifically, we shall direct our attention to problems that are amenable to solutions within the framework of what is usually referred to as partial equilibrium analysis (see Chapter 1).

In partial equilibrium analysis, we focus attention on one market at a time and deal with adjustments within a single market as if they occurred in *stages* rather than as continuous processes. The neglect of direct interactions among markets may be objectionable in principle, but it is often inconsequential in practice. Even in advanced treatments of microeconomic theory, discussions of multiple-market economic systems seldom get beyond conclusions to the effect that "everything depends on every-thing else." Partial equilibrium analysis does not deny the existence of market inter-actions; it merely leaves the explicit analysis of such interactions to later discussion.

The neglect of direct interactions among variables that are involved in adjustment processes within a single market is more serious. As indicated earlier, the behavior of market price and quantities produced and consumed in situations of market disequi-librium depends in a very complicated way on the precise values assumed by different variables at each moment. In partial equilibrium analysis of such processes, compli-cations of this kind are reduced to a minimum by assuming that the adjustment pro-ceeds in stages (market period, short-run period, and long-run period), in each of which some variables are permitted to vary while others are assumed to be fixed in value. We shall follow this approach in the chapters to come.

SUMMARY

1. A flow variable has a time dimension such as a day or a year; a stock variable refers to a quantity at a given moment and hence has no time dimension.

2. Businesses and households both hold stocks of goods called inventories. Households have purchases for use (flow) and purchases to hold (stock). Businesses have production for sale (flows) and production for stockpiling (stocks).

3. Individuals hold stocks of inventories for various reasons: as a reserve against future pre-dicaments, as a hedge against inflation, and especially as a means of avoiding frequent small-lot exchanges, usually purchases.

4. Stock demand of any good varies inversely with the good's market value. That is, holding high-priced goods in inventories costs more than holding the same quantity of low-priced commodities.

5. Stock supply cannot change at any moment—it is a mere "snapshot" of what's on hand.

6. Excess stock demand and excess stock supply will be zero at only one price. At any other price, individuals will want to alter their existing holdings.

7. Actual stocks may be different from desired stocks; this can be altered by changing the flow.

8. Stocks will always increase if inflows are greater than outflows, and stocks will always decrease if inflows are less than outflows. But for the market *as a whole,* stocks can only decrease if consumption exceeds production, and can only increase if production exceeds consumption.

9. The market supply (or demand) of any good is a function of its current market price and of stocks currently held by prospective sellers (or buyers).

10. In order for market equilibrium to occur at one particular moment, the following condi-tions must be met: stock excess demand and stock excess supply must be zero, flow excess demand and flow excess supply must be zero, and actual production must be equal to actual consumption (the last condition being guaranteed if the first two hold).

WORDS AND CONCEPTS FOR REVIEW

flow variables
stock variable
inventories
stock excess supply
stock excess demand
stock demand

excess flow demand or supply
desired stock
actual stock
market demand
market supply
transactors
undesired inventories

REVIEW QUESTIONS

1. Which of the following represents a stock? A flow?
   (a) Speed of a car
   (b) Distance traveled on a trip
   (c) The water draining from a sink
   (d) Water standing in a bathtub
   (e) Electricity consumption in June
   (f) A skyscraper
   (g) The mass of the moon
   (h) Temperature
   (i) Wind velocity

2. Is national income, measured as an annual flow, likely to be the same on July 1 of a given year as it was on June 1? Explain.

3. What is meant by the term "stock supply"? "Stock demand"? What are the determinants of each?

4. What would be meant by the phrase "stock demand for money"? What could one infer about a person's excess stock demand for money at the instant when he purchases a carton of cigarettes? Discuss.

5. Describe what is meant by the terms "flow supply" (market and production) and "flow demand" (market and consumption)? What factors would be most important in determining the magnitude of each quantity?

6. If flow demand is equal to flow supply, what does this imply about the behavior of stock supply? What if flow supply exceeds flow demand? Explain carefully.

7. Can a market be in equilibrium when flow demand differs from flow supply? When stock demand differs from stock supply? Discuss.

8. Can a market be out of equilibrium when both flow excess demand and stock excess demand are zero? Explain carefully.

SUGGESTED READINGS

Ackley, G. "Commodities and Capital: Prices and Quantities." *American Economic Review* (March 1983) pp. 1–16.

Clower, R. W. "An Investigation into the Dynamics of Investment." *American Economic Review* (March 1954), pp. 64-81.

———. "Stock-Flow Analysis." *International Encyclopedia of the Social Sciences* (1968), pp. 273–77.

PART 2

Price
and Output
Determination

5

The Theory of Consumer Behavior and the Determinants of Demand

5.1 INTRODUCTION

Keeping in mind the major concepts relating to demand and supply schedules, we now address the underlying determinants of demand and demand elasticity (supply will be considered in later chapters). Explaining demand requires an analysis of consumer behavior—that is, decision making by the household. The analysis is based on the assumption that consumers act rationally, seeking to maximize satisfaction gained from given incomes.

According to the Law of Demand, the quantity demanded increases as the price declines; thus, demand curves slope downward from left to right. This relationship is supported by extensive empirical evidence; it can also "usually" be expected from the assumptions that (1) consumers seek to maximize satisfaction; (2) incomes are limited; and (3) the marginal utility—the addition to satisfaction from acquiring an additional unit of a good—falls as additional units of a good are acquired. The Law of Demand can be explained in rather simple terms on the basis of the Law of Diminishing Marginal Utility, or in slightly more general terms by using indifference curves and the Law of Diminishing Marginal Rate of Substitution.

5.2 THE LAW OF DIMINISHING MARGINAL UTILITY

Marginal utility is defined as the addition to total utility or satisfaction that results from the acquisition of an additional unit of a good in a given period of time. While utility is not directly measurable in any usual sense, the concept has meaning in that various goods can be compared and ranked. (In other words, it is an *ordinal* rather than a *cardinal* measure.) Thus a person can compare the satisfaction gained from another car with that obtained from the first car purchased, and the gain from the car with the satisfaction from a trip to Europe; ordering these preferences does not depend on *how much* one good is preferred to another, but merely on the fact that one is preferred to the other.

The Law of Diminishing Marginal Utility describes the behavior of marginal utility as the quantity of a good possessed by an individual varies during a particular time period. According to this "law," as a person obtains additional units of any good, the marginal utility declines; that is, each successive unit adds less to the person's satisfaction than did the previous unit. The first automobile a consumer acquires may yield a great deal of satisfaction by providing a form of transportation more suitable for many purposes than alternative forms. If the person acquires a second car within the given period of time, his satisfaction will increase to a certain extent because, for example, two family members can now use cars at the same time. But the marginal utility—the increase in satisfaction resulting from the acquisition of the second car—is likely to be far less than that resulting from the purchase of the first car. Note that the important thing is the fact that marginal utility decreases, not what *value* that marginal utility takes on; thus, in Figure 5-1, either MU curve could give rise to the same observed behavior).[1]

The Law of Diminishing Marginal Utility involves the mutual interaction of two ideas, individual wants for particular goods are satiable, and different goods are not perfect substitutes for one another in the satisfaction of particular wants. As a person uses more and more units of a good to satisfy a given kind of want, the intensity of the

---

[1]For those familiar with elementary differential calculus, the text discussion to this point may be summarized as follows:

(1) Assume the household decision maker can *rank* any two bundles of goods A and B. In this ranking either A is preferred to B, B is preferred to A, or A and B are indifferent.

(2) Now let a function be defined over quantities of goods in all bundles such that preferences are preserved. That is, if A is preferred to B, the function evaluated at A, $U(A)$, takes on a higher value than when evaluated at B. If A and B are indifferent, $U(A) = U(B)$.

(3) Recognizing that any bundle of goods (such as a shopping-cart full of supermarket items) can be broken into a vector of constituent items, any bundle can be represented as a vector, $(X_1, X_2, X_3, \cdots, X_n)$, where of course many of the X_i will be zero for any particular bundle.

(4) The Law of Diminishing Marginal Utility merely says that while the partial derivatives of

$$U(X_1, X_2, X_3, \cdots, X_n)$$

are all positive, they decline as x_i increases. That is, $\frac{\partial U}{\partial X_i} > 0$ and $\frac{\partial^2 U}{\partial X_i^2} < 0$. Holding constant other goods, additional amounts of a given good make you better off, but at a decreasing rate. Any transformation of the utility function that preserves the rankings among bundles will work equally well in describing preferences.

FIGURE 5-1

Marginal Utility Curves Showing Diminishing Marginal Utility
A marginal utility curve shows the amount of satisfaction for each additional unit of a good. Marginal utility diminishes as a consumer becomes satiated by the good, hence the negative slope. MU_1 represents higher levels of marginal utility than MU_0.

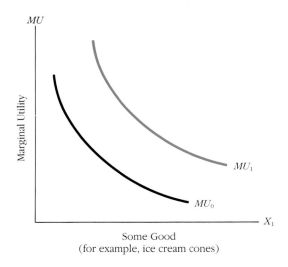

Some Good
(for example, ice cream cones)

want diminishes. Units of the good cannot be transferred to the satisfaction of other wants to produce as much satisfaction as they yielded initially in the satisfaction of the first want because the good is not a perfect substitute for goods best designed to satisfy the second want.[2] For example, as a person consumes more and more salt in various time periods, the desire for it in her food is eventually satisfied within any of those periods. Additional units can be used for other purposes, such as removing ice from sidewalks, but these will add less satisfaction than the initial units used for food. (See Box 5-1.)

The Allocation of Consumer Income

Because marginal utility diminishes as additional units of a good are acquired, a person maximizing satisfaction from limited income must avoid extending purchases of any one good beyond the point at which other goods will yield greater satisfaction for the amount spent. Hence, care must be exercised in the allocation of income among

---

[2]This transfer *could* occur if two goods were perfect substitutes for one another and thus, in an economic sense, essentially the same good.

5-1   Describe the Law of Diminishing Marginal Utility on all-you-can-eat nights at your favorite pizza spot.

A group of your friends and you go to all-you-can-eat pepperoni pizza night once a week. The all-you-can-eat special is available only from 8 P.M. to 10 P.M. Imagine what would happen to the marginal utility of any of the slices of pizza in a night where you consumed eight slices versus another night when you ate only two slices, *ceteris paribus*. Since you are consuming pizza at a higher rate in the former case, the marginal utility of pizza is lower.

various goods. For **maximization of satisfaction**, income should be allocated in such a way that the marginal utility of a unit-of-money's worth (for example, one dollar's worth) of any good is the same for every good. When this situation is realized, one dollar's worth of gasoline will yield the same increment to satisfaction—the same marginal utility—as one dollar's worth of additional bread or apples or theater tickets or soap. If this situation has not been attained, the person can increase total satisfaction by buying more of some goods and less of others. If, for example, the marginal utility of one dollar's worth of apples measures 4 and that of one dollar's worth of bread measures 8, total satisfaction can be increased by buying more bread and fewer apples. The equilibrium is shown by the equation:

$$\frac{MU_1}{P_1} = \frac{MU_2}{P_2} = \frac{MU_3}{P_3} \cdots = \frac{MU_n}{P_n}$$

Alternatively, maximum satisfaction requires allocation of income in such a way that the ratios of marginal utilities of the various goods purchased are equal to the price ratios of the goods. That is, if potatoes cost twice as much per pound as spinach,

5-2   True or False?   Because many goods are not available in small inexpensive units, perfect adjustment of marginal utilities is impossible.

True.   Large consumer goods and almost all durable goods (automobiles, refrigerators) are indivisible and that complicates the process of equating marginal utilities. Here, however, we are concerned with *flow* demands, which are much more divisible than stocks. That is, the *service* flow from an automobile is what gives utility in a certain period, and that service flow can be varied smoothly by getting a slightly better or worse automobile. Indeed, throughout this chapter, think of all goods as being flows entirely consumed within the period, unless otherwise advised.

consumers will adjust their purchases of the two commodities until the marginal utility of a pound of potatoes is twice as great as the marginal utility of a pound of spinach. The equilibrium viewed this way can be shown by a modified version of the previous equation:[3]

$$\frac{MU_i}{MU_j} = \frac{P_i}{P_j} \quad (i, j = 1 \ldots n)$$

(See Box 5-2.)

---

[3]Both of the text equations emerge easily from an income-constrained maximization problem which for simplicity considers maximizing utility by choosing various quantities of only three goods:

$$\text{Maximize:}_{X_1, X_2, X_3} \quad U = U(X_1, X_2, X_3)$$

$$\text{s.t.} \quad I = P_1X_1 + P_2X_2 + P_3X_3$$

Lagrange provides a clever way to incorporate the income constraint into what then becomes a free optimization problem. Rewrite the problem as:

$$\text{Maximize:}_{X_1, X_2, X_3, \lambda} \quad \mathcal{L} = U(X_1, X_2, X_3) + \lambda \, (I - P_1X_1 - P_2X_2 - P_3X_3)$$

The first-order conditions for a maximum (or minimum for that matter, although we shall not be unduly concerned about such possibilities) are that the partial derivatives of $\mathcal{L}$ with respect to the choice variables be zero. That is, at the *top* of the constrained utility "hill," the slope is zero in every direction:

$$\frac{\partial \mathcal{L}}{\partial X_1} = \frac{\partial U}{\partial X_1} - \lambda P_1 = 0$$

$$\frac{\partial \mathcal{L}}{\partial X_2} = \frac{\partial U}{\partial X_2} - \lambda P_2 = 0$$

$$\frac{\partial \mathcal{L}}{\partial X_3} = \frac{\partial U}{\partial X_3} - \lambda P_3 = 0$$

$$\frac{\partial \mathcal{L}}{\partial \lambda} = I - P_1X_1 - P_2X_2 - P_3X_3 = 0$$

Forming the ratio of any two of the first three equations, say the first two, gives the text result:

$$\frac{MU_1}{MU_2} = \frac{P_1}{P_2}$$

Note that the fourth equation, the "trick" of the Lagrangean method, guarantees that the income constraint is satisfied in the neighborhood of the optimum.

In the text graphs, it will be apparent that the tangency of the indifference curve with the budget constraint determines the quantities of the goods purchased when utility is maximized. If a specific function is chosen to represent preferences, the optimal quantities can be derived formally from the simultaneous solution of the first-order conditions above.

The Relationship between Price and Quantity Demanded

It follows as a matter of logic from the Law of Diminishing Marginal Utility and the principle of income allocation that a price reduction of a normal good (and most inferior goods) will lead to an increase in the quantity of that good demanded. The price reduction will lead to reallocation of income, since the old optimum will no longer be optimal.

If the price of coffee declines from three to two dollars a pound, one dollar's worth of coffee is now half a pound instead of a third of a pound; this amount may exceed the marginal utilities of one dollar's worth of substitute goods whose prices remain unchanged. Accordingly, a readjustment in the relative purchases of coffee and other goods is necessary to restore the equality of the marginal utilities of one dollar's worth of all goods purchased. The readjustment will generally involve purchasing more coffee, lowering its marginal utility and raising the marginal utility of the goods substituted away from. In addition to this **substitution effect**, since coffee is cheaper than before, the buyer can buy more of various goods with a given income and some of the income freed may be spent on coffee. That is, with constant nominal income a price decrease leads to a real income increase called the **income effect** of the price change. This income effect will cause more of all goods, including coffee if it is normal, to be bought.

5.3 THE INDIFFERENCE CURVE TECHNIQUE

A more sophisticated approach to the allocation of consumer income and the nature of the demand schedule utilizes indifference schedules and curves to illustrate consumer behavior. The use of indifference curves facilitates explanation of various demand and consumer behavior relationships, avoids the implication of the marginal utility approach that utility can be measured cardinally, and stresses the interrelationships among the demands for goods.

The Indifference Schedule

An indifference schedule indicates various combinations of two goods which will yield a consumer the same total satisfaction. For example, a consumer (or household) may obtain the same satisfaction from the use of three loaves of bread plus four pounds of steak a week as from one loaf of bread and five pounds of steak or ten loaves of bread and two pounds of steak. The consumer's indifference schedule for these two goods, shown in Table 5-1, contains various possible combinations of the two goods which will yield the same satisfaction. (For another level of satisfaction, there would be another pattern of combinations.)

This schedule can be plotted on a graph, with one good being plotted on the vertical axis and the other on the horizontal. The curve connecting the various equally satisfying bundles of X_1 and X_2 is known as an **indifference curve** The curve in

TABLE 5-1

**Various Combinations of Bread and Steak
Yielding a Given Level of Satisfaction to a Consumer**

Steak (pounds)		Bread (loaves)
6	plus	0
5	plus	1
4	plus	3
3	plus	6
2	plus	10
1	plus	15
0	plus	25

Figure 5-2 includes points representing the various combinations contained in Table 5-1. *The curve shows nothing about the absolute amounts of satisfaction obtained but merely indicates the various combinations which will yield equal satisfaction.*

Indifference curves slope downward from left to right under the assumption that, in order to maintain the same level of satisfaction, as more units of one good are added, less units of the other will be required. This merely says that the quantities on the X_1

FIGURE 5-2

An Indifference Curve of a Consumer for Bread and Steak
The combinations of loaves of bread and pounds of steak that give a consumer the same amount of satisfaction are depicted by the indifference curve. The consumer is indifferent among all bundles of bread and steak along this curve.

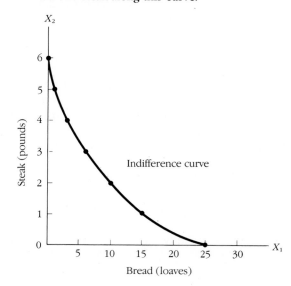

and X_2 axes are "goods" rather than a "good" and a "bad". The slope of an indifference curve measures the **marginal rate of substitution** (MRS) between the two goods—the number of units of one of the goods necessary to replace one unit of the other good in order to maintain the same total satisfaction.[4] For example, the marginal rate of substitution of steak for bread is the number of units of bread which must be added to replace a unit of steak and maintain the same level of satisfaction. Thus, in Table 5-2, with four pounds of steak, three loaves of bread must be added when one pound of steak is eliminated if the same amount of satisfaction is to be obtained. With one pound of steak, ten loaves of bread must be added, if the one pound of steak is eliminated, to

---

[4]Letting $U = U(X_1, X_2)$ and totally differentiating

$$dU = \frac{\partial U}{\partial X_1}\, dX_1 + \frac{\partial U}{\partial X_2}\, dX_2$$

we see how total utility changes as X_1 and X_2 change. Holding utility constant at some level of indifference involves setting $dU = 0$:

$$0 = \frac{\partial U}{\partial X_1}\, dX_1 + \frac{\partial U}{\partial X_2}\, dX_2$$

Since $\frac{\partial U}{\partial X_i} > 0$, if either $dX_1 > 0$ or $dX_2 > 0$ the other *must* be less than zero—otherwise utility would increase. This proves that indifference curves *between goods* must be downward sloping.

TABLE 5-2

The Marginal Rate of Substitution between Bread and Steak for a Particular Consumer

Steak	Bread	Marginal Rate of Substitution of Steak for Bread*
0	25	
		10
1	15	
		5
2	10	
		4
3	6	
		3
4	3	
		2
5	1	
		1
6	0	

*The number of units of bread necessary to replace a unit of steak and maintain a given level of satisfaction.

maintain satisfaction. When a large number of units of bread are necessary to replace a unit of steak, the indifference curve is nearly horizontal; if the number of units of bread required to replace a unit of steak is relatively small, the curve will be nearly vertical.

The Convexity of Indifference Curves and the Principle of Diminishing Marginal Rate of Substitution

A second characteristic of indifference curves, besides their downward slope, is their convexity to the point of origin; that is, the left-hand portion is relatively steep while the right-hand portion is relatively horizontal. In other words, the more units of bread acquired, the fewer units of steak necessary to replace a unit of bread in order to maintain the same total satisfaction. Likewise, the more units of steak, the fewer units of bread necessary to replace a unit of steak. This rule is known as the *Principle of Diminishing Marginal Rate of Substitution*. Reiterating, as additional units of one good are added, the marginal rate of substitution of this good for the other falls; that is, progressively less of the other good will be needed to replace units of the first in order to maintain the same satisfaction.[5]

One way to understand the diminishing marginal rate of substitution is to think in terms of diminishing marginal utility. If you have a relatively large amount of steak (as on the upper left portion of the indifference curve in Figure 5-2), steak will have a low marginal utility: to get additional bread (which has higher marginal utility at low quantities), much steak would be given up. If, however, a point of less steak and more bread were considered (perhaps the middle portion of the indifference curve in Figure 5-2), the marginal utility of steak will be higher (since there is less) and the marginal utility of bread will be lower (since there is more). As a consequence, the amount of steak you would give up for still more bread is smaller (is "diminished"). Considering points at the lower right on the indifference curve in Figure 5-2, you would be very reluctant to give up much of the small amount of steak (which has high marginal utility) for even large quantities of low-marginal-utility bread.[6]

---

[5]Note that the Principle of Diminishing Marginal Rate of Substitution, unlike the downward slope of an indifference curve, cannot be "proven." Rather, it is an empirical regularity which we shall assume; this assumption is, however, quite plausible.

[6]Recall the derivative of footnote 4:

$$0 = dU = \frac{\partial U}{\partial X_1} dX_1 + \frac{\partial U}{\partial X_2} dX_2$$

This can be rearranged, solving for the slope of the indifference curve:

$$\frac{dX_2}{dX_1} = -\frac{\partial U/\partial X_1}{\partial U/\partial X_2} = -\left(\frac{MU_{X_1}}{MU_{X_2}}\right)$$

If one has large amounts of X_2, the ratio on the right is large since MU_{X_2} is small—you would give up a great deal of X_2 to get additional X_1, holding satisfaction constant along an indifference curve. Conversely, if one has relatively small amounts of X_2.

Note, however, that while this discussion of diminishing marginal rate of substitution in terms of diminishing marginal utilities is appealing, it is not at all necessary. One need not assume diminishing marginal utility to yield diminishing marginal rate of substitution (MRS). Indeed, marginal utility of goods could be *increasing,* yet one could still have diminishing marginal rates of substitution. The key is that your willingness to substitute one good for another depends on *relative* quantities consumed—if you have lots of something you will give up more of it (regardless of marginal utility) to get something else than you would if you only had a little. Since diminishing MRS is less restrictive than diminishing marginal utility, we shall adopt this assumption in what follows.

5-3 If indifference curves are in fact convex to the origin, how can one tell whether either or both of the goods are actually "bads"?

Consider the odd-looking circular indifference curves I_0, I_1, and I_2.

These preferences look typical in Region I (the lower left) in that the usual downward-sloping, diminishing marginal rate of substitution behavior is depicted. The other regions have unusual directions of increasing utility, as indicated by the arrows pointing in the direction of increasingly preferred bundles.

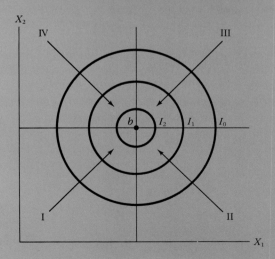

Point b is commonly referred to as the "bliss point"—the point of maximum satisfaction in terms of goods consumption (a person may or may not be "happy" at this point, but it will be preferred to all others). Another way to put it, drawing on the analogy of topographical maps, in which altitude is depicted by "isoclines" like our indifference curves, is that point b represents the top of the "hill of happiness."

Given diminishing marginal rate of substitution, we can now see that Region II represents a case where X_1 is the bad (say, pollution), while X_2 is the good (say, coal production). When the curve bends the other way, as in Region IV, X_2 would be the bad and X_1 the good. The intuition in these cases, and in that of Region III where both goods are bads (say living, without free disposal, in a small condo with $X_1 = 500$ watermelons and $X_2 = 200$ chairs), is not as immediately obvious as in the Region I case. Consider Region II: at the left boundary, X_1 is just becoming a bad and very little of the good would be needed to compensate. But as we get more and more of the bad, it requires larger and larger quantities of the good to compensate for additional amounts of the bad.

■■■■■■■■
FIGURE 5-3

An Indifference Curve of Perfect Substitutes
When two goods are perfect substitutes, the indifference curve is linear. In this example, the consumer is equally satisfied by 6 units of X_1 and 1 unit of X_2, and 6 units of X_2 and 1 unit of X_1. The consumer will always trade 1 unit of X_1 for 1 unit of X_2, so the marginal rate of substitution in this case is constant at -1. Although the MRS is always constant for perfect substitutes, it is not necessarily -1.

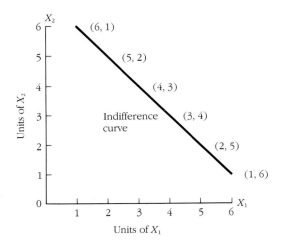

The diminishing MRS principle follows as a matter of logical necessity from the assumptions that particular wants are satiable, that various goods are not perfect substitutes for one another, and that increased quantities of one good do not increase the want-satisfying power of the other. As more units of one good are added, the ability of additional units of this good to satisfy wants falls because the want for which the good is best suited becomes more completely satisfied. Thus a relatively small quantity of the other good (the desire for which is relatively intense, per unit, with a few units being acquired) is needed to replace a unit of the first good and maintain satisfaction. As indicated by the steak/bread example, when the consumer has relatively little of the first good and large quantities of the second, a large additional amount of the second is needed to replace a unit of the first in order to maintain the same level of satisfaction. (See Box 5-3.)

Complements and Substitutes

The ability of one good to satisfy a want depends as a rule upon the quantity of other goods. Many goods are **complements** for each other; that is, the use of more units of

TABLE 5-3
Indifference Scheduling of Two Goods
That Are Perfect Substitutes for One Another

X_1	X_2	MRS
1	6	
		1
2	5	
		1
3	4	
		1
4	3	
		1
5	2	
		1
6	1	

one encourages the acquisition of additional units of the other. Under such circumstances, units of one good cannot be acquired without affecting the want-satisfying power of other goods. Gasoline and automobiles, bread and butter, and coffee and cream are examples of complementary goods. Some other goods are **substitutes** for one another; that is, the more you have of one, the less is your desire for the other. (The relationship between substitutes is thus the opposite of the relation between complements.) Examples of substitutes include coffee and tea, sweaters and jackets, and home-cooked and restaurant meals.

The degree of convexity of an indifference curve—that is, the extent to which the curve deviates from a straight line—depends upon the ease of substitution of the two goods for one another. If two goods are perfect substitutes (such as "left" and "right" socks of the same size, quality, and color), the indifference curve is a straight line (in this case of slope −1). This is depicted in Figure 5-3 based on the data in Table 5-3, since the marginal rate of substitution is the same, regardless of the extent to which one good is replaced by the other.

At the other extreme are two goods among many which are perfect complements, as are (for many persons) coffee and cream. These goods are, for some people, never used separately but are consumed only together. Since it is impossible to replace units of one with units of the other and maintain satisfaction, the marginal rate of substitution is undefined; thus the indifference curve contains a right angle convex to the point of origin, as shown in Figure 5-4 and in the boxed example. The left portion is vertical,

FIGURE 5-4

An Indifference Curve of Goods That Are Not Substitutable

Two goods are perfect complements when they are always used together, such as right gloves and left gloves. A consumer is indifferent between 1 right glove and 1 left glove, and 1 right glove and 5 left gloves, as nothing is gained from the additional 4 left gloves. Similarly, the consumer is indifferent between 1 right glove and 1 left glove, and 5 right gloves and 1 left glove. Hence, perfect complements are represented by L-shaped or right-angle indifference curves. The right angle could, of course, occur at any relative amount. For example, 3 units of X_1 may go with 1 unit of X_2.

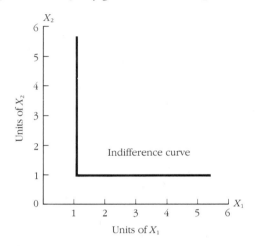

5-4   Draw the indifference curves for a left and right glove.

Because left and right gloves are usually perfect complements, the indifference curve would be L-shaped. For example, point A (2 left gloves and 2 right gloves) and point B (4 left gloves and 2 right gloves) would be equally satisfying. The reason is that the 2 left gloves without mates would be worthless to most individuals. Point C (3 left and 3 right gloves), on the other hand, is on a higher (or further northeast) indifference curve and would be preferred to both point A and B.

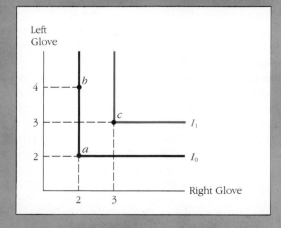

in that an infinite amount of X_2 is necessary to replace one unit of X_1; the right portion is horizontal, since an infinite amount of X_1 is necessary to replace a unit of X_2. In more typical cases, in which the two goods can be substituted for one another but are not perfect substitutes, the indifference curve will be curved as depicted at the outset. The more easily the two goods can be substituted for one another, the nearer the curve will approach a straight line; in other words, it will maintain more closely the same slope throughout. (See Box 5-4.)

Indifference Curves with More Than Two Goods

The typical indifference curve shows the relationship between two goods only, because of the graphical ease of depicting the two-dimensional surface. But the relationships portrayed for two goods are similar to relationships among all of the various goods which a person is interested in acquiring (subject to the fact that for more than two goods *complements* may exist, while if there are only two goods they must be substitutes).[7] This rule can be illustrated by following the procedure of showing one good on the horizontal axis and all other goods (represented by dollars of expenditure on all other goods) on the vertical axis. Prices of all other goods are assumed to be given and unchanged during the analysis. The indifference curve then shows various combinations of purchases of the good under consideration and total expenditures on all other goods (the "composite" good) which will yield the same satisfaction; the curve's slope shows the person's marginal rate of substitution between this good and expenditure on all other goods—in other words, the person's marginal valuation of the good relative to the total amount available for spending and saving. "All other goods" here essentially represents income (if the good under consideration is a small portion of the total budget) and is sometimes referred to as "Marshallian money" (after Alfred Marshall, a pioneer in partial equilibrium analysis).

The Family of Indifference Curves

The discussion up to this point has largely been in terms of a single indifference curve, representing a particular level of satisfaction. But for each consumer and for each pair of goods, there is actually a whole family of indifference curves, each indicating different levels of satisfaction. Four such schedules are presented in Table 5-4 and are illustrated graphically in Figure 5-5.

What are the *properties* of indifference curves such as those depicted in Figure 5-5? The successive **indifference curves never intersect**, since each portrays various combinations which yield a particular degree of satisfaction. If they did intersect, then

---

[7]To see that goods are only substitutes in a two-good world, refer back to footnote 4. To see that complements may exist in a three-good (or more) world, generalize footnote 4 to a three-good world like that formalized in footnote 3. In this manner, it may be seen that depicting perfect complements as an **L**-shaped indifference curve in a two-good world is technically inaccurate. The **L** shape, in fact, depicts zero elasticity of substitution—not perfect complementarity.

TABLE 5-4

**A Pattern of Indifference Curves of a Consumer
for Steak and Bread (pounds and loaves, respectively)**

Schedule I_0		Schedule I_1		Schedule I_2		Schedule I_3	
Steak	Bread	Steak	Bread	Steak	Bread	Steak	Bread
6	0	6	3	6	6	6	10
5	1	5	4.5	5	8.5	5	12
4	3	4	7	4	11.5	4	15.5
3	6	3	10.5	3	16	3	20.5
2	10	2	15.5	2	22	2	28
1	15	1	23	1	31	1	42.5

FIGURE 5-5

A Family of Indifference Curves of a Consumer for Steak and Bread
This indifference map shows a series of indifference curves, each representing a different
level of utility. The most northeasterly indifference curve, I_3, designates the highest level
of utility, and indifference curve I_0 designates the lowest level, because some bundles on
I_3 contain more bread and steak than some bundles on I_0. Note that the consumer need
only be able to rank the bundles ordinally; assigning a numerical (cardinal) value to the
level of satisfaction associated with each indifference curve is not necessary.

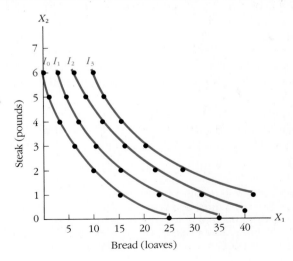

there would be points on either side of the intersection such that a point on the higher curve had more of *both* goods than a point on the lower curve. This point would thus be *preferred.* But this would be in contradiction with the existence of the intersection point, which by definition expresses the fact that the same level of satisfaction must be achieved on both curves since all points on the intersecting curves are indifferent to the intersection point.

Transitivity of preferences is also assumed to characterize indifference curves; that is, the consumer is assumed to choose "consistently." If the consumer is indifferent between one apple and two oranges and between two oranges and one grapefruit, the person should also be indifferent between one apple and one grapefruit. There is no way of knowing—and no need to know—the quantitative differences in satisfaction yielded by combinations that lie on separate indifference curves. The schedules merely show that combinations on one curve yield *more* or *less* satisfaction than combinations on another. If a given combination on one curve contains more of both goods than some combination on another curve, then the curve containing the first combination is said to be preferred to the second; it therefore will lie on a higher indifference curve. Moreover, since more goods will always be preferred to less (as long as they remain goods), *all* combinations on the higher indifference curve will be preferred to *any* combination on lower curves. Geometrically, this means that any combination that lies to the "northeast" (or "north" or "east") of another combination will represent a greater quantity of satisfaction and therefore will lie on a higher indifference curve. (See Box 5-5.)

5-5   Draw indifference curves for all other goods (AOG) and pizza when pizza has to be eaten on the spot.

In area *A*, both AOG and pizza are goods. In order to have another piece of pizza, one would be willing to give up some AOG. In shaded area *B*, this is not the case; the individual "had his fill" of pizza and now would have to be paid to eat any more. Hence it is possible that some goods may become bads after a certain quantity has been consumed.

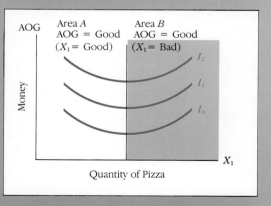

The Budget Constraint Line or Consumption Possibilities Line

A person's schedule of preferences, or family of indifference curves for various goods, is assumed to be independent of the opportunities he or she has for expressing those preferences. But actual purchases depend upon the level of income and on relative prices, with the prices affecting the manner in which one allocates the income among different goods. Possible patterns of expenditures of a given sum of money on two goods may be illustrated on an indifference graph by using a **budget constraint line** or **consumption possibilities line**. Such a line shows the various combinations of the two goods which can be purchased with a certain expenditure, given the prices of the two goods. For example, say that $20.00 is to be spent on bread and steak, and bread costs 80 cents a loaf and steak $4.00 a pound. The consumer can purchase 25 loaves of bread and no steak, five pounds of steak and no bread, or various combinations of the two, such as three pounds of steak and ten loaves of bread or one pound of steak and twenty loaves of bread. The various combinations are shown in Table 5-5 and illustrated in Figure 5-6. Under the assumption that the prices of the goods are independent of the quantities purchased, the budget constraint will necessarily be a straight line.[8] The slope of the line depends upon the ratios of the prices of the two goods. The same principle applies to the expenditure of a person's entire income on the full range of available goods. (See Box 5-6.)

---

[8]If they are not, because of quantity discounts, or because additional purchases drive up prices, the budget line will be a curved line.

5-6   Draw the budget constraint for a situation in which consumers' incomes rise between 1988 and 1989 while the relative price of videocassette recorders fall.

Remember that the slope of the budget constraint denotes relative prices or opportunity costs, since moving along the budget line measures the cost of one item in terms of the other. On the other hand, the position of the budget constraint measures the income of the consumer. In the graph you can see that the consumer can buy more of both goods in 1989 than he or she could buy in 1988. This must mean that income has risen.

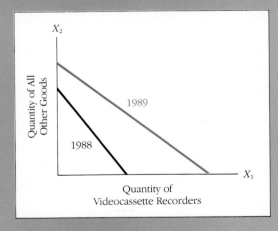

TABLE 5-5

Expenditure Schedule on Bread and Steak, Total Expenditure of $20.00

Bread: price 80 cents (loaves)	Steak: price $4.00 (pounds)
0	5
2.5	4.5
5	4
7.5	3.5
10	3
12.5	2.5
15	2
17.5	1.5
20	1
22.5	0.5
25	0

FIGURE 5-6

Budget Line, Showing Various Combinations of Bread and Steak Which Can Be Purchased with a Total Expenditure of $20.00 (Bread: 80 cents per loaf; Steak: $4.00 per pound)

The budget line shows all combinations of bread and steak that can be purchased with $20.00 when the price of bread is 80 cents per loaf and the price of steak is $4.00 per pound. If the consumer spends all of the $20.00 on bread, 25 loaves of bread may be purchased. If all expenditures are for steak, 5 pounds may be purchased. The slope of the budget line in absolute value is the price of bread divided by the price of steak or .2 (that is, to get another loaf of bread, one must give up one-fifth of a pound of steak).

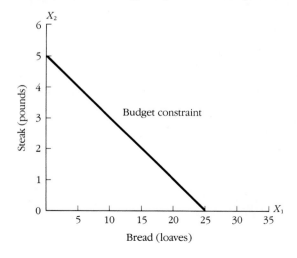

The Quantities Purchased

Given the pattern of indifference curves for two goods, together with the budget constraint line showing the various quantities of the two that can be purchased with the allocated expenditure, the optimum quantities of each good to be purchased can be determined. The point of tangency between the budget constraint line and an indifference curve indicates the quantities of each good which will be purchased in order to maximize total satisfaction. In Figure 5-7, the budget constraint line is tangent to indifference curve I_1 at point *a*: the person will acquire 2½ pounds of steak and 12½ loaves of bread. In order to maximize satisfaction, the consumer must acquire the *most preferred* attainable bundle—that is, reach the highest indifference curve that can be reached with a given expenditure of money. The highest attainable curve is the one to which the budget line is tangent. Any other possible combination of the two goods either would be on a lower indifference curve and thus yield less satisfaction, or would be unobtainable with the given expenditure. The same principle applies to all goods, provided that the Principle of Diminishing Marginal Rate of Substitution is valid. (See Box 5-7.)

In cases where the principle is not valid, and thus indifference curves are not convex to the point of origin, there may be no single optimum combination of goods corresponding to a particular set of prices and level of expenditures. For example, consider the unlikely possibility that an indifference curve is of the character of I_0 in Figure 5-8(a), being convex in part, concave in part. With budget line L_0, there are

5-7   Graph a set of indifference curves for someone who has no preferences for steak (derives no positive or negative utility from steak). In which direction will the consumer's preferences lie? Where will the point of consumer optimum occur? Would the optimum point change if there were a decrease in the price of steak?

The consumer will only be better off moving eastward, as designated by the arrows. Steaks are useless, providing the consumer neither utility or disutility. The consumer will not trade any amount of bread for any amount of steak— this is the case of infinite $\text{MRS}_{(X_1, X_2)}$. In this situation, the consumer's optimum will always be a corner solution on the bread axis (such as point *a* in the graph, where no steaks will be consumed). Notice that even when the relative price of steak falls (dotted line shifts up on steak axis), the consumer's optimum remains unchanged.

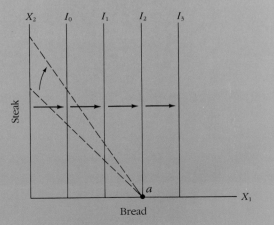

FIGURE 5-7

The Optimum Combination of Purchases of Two Goods

The consumer's most satisfactory, affordable bundle, *n,* occurs where the indifference curve is tangent to the budget line. Bundles on I_3 and I_4 are more appealing to the consumer but are not affordable. The consumer can purchase bundles on I_0, but these provide less satisfaction than *a.*

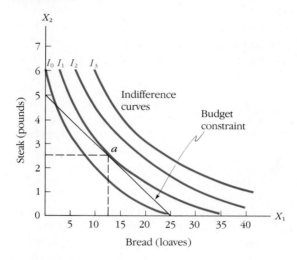

FIGURE 5-8

Oddly Shaped Indifference Curve

Non-convex indifference curves yield unusual utility-maximizing solutions for the consumer. Multiple optima, points *a, b,* and *c,* occur in part (a). Part (b) shows a corner solution, an optimum bundle containing all of one commodity and none of the other commodity.

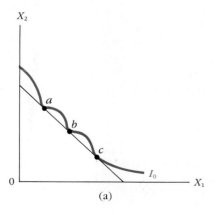

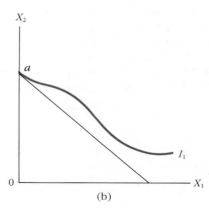

three distinct points of tangency, *a, b,* and *c,* and thus three optimum points, all yielding the same level of satisfaction; but the analysis does not indicate which of these the consumer will select. Or suppose, perhaps more realistically, that the indifference curve and budget constraint line appear as in Figure 5-8(b). Here there is one optimum point, *a,* but this is not a point of tangency. Under such circumstances as these (so-called "corner solutions"), the optimum of the consumer cannot be described in terms of the preceding analysis, and additional assumptions are required.[9]

In typical cases, however, the optimum combination is defined by a point of tangency between the budget line and an indifference curve, where the marginal rate of substitution between the two commodities is equal to the ratios of their prices. As shown in Figure 5-7 at point *a,* the marginal rate of substitution between bread and steak is 5 to 1—that is, five loaves of bread must be added if one pound of steak is eliminated; this is equal to the price ratio 100/20 or 5/1. This relationship follows from the fact that since the curves are tangent at this point, they have the same slope. If this relationship did not hold, the consumer could gain satisfaction by purchasing more of one of the goods and less of the other. If, for example, the consumer were buying such quantities of steak and bread that the marginal rate of substitution was 12 to 1, while the price ratio was 5 to 1, then the addition of one pound of steak would necessitate the loss of only five loaves of bread, whereas the person would be *willing* to sacrifice twelve loaves in order to gain the pound of steak. Substitution would obviously be desirable, and would continue to be so until equality of the two ratios had been obtained. The rule of equality between marginal rates of substitution and price ratios applies to each pair of goods purchased, and thus to all goods. (See Boxes 5-8 and 5-9.)

Preferences in the Immediate Neighborhood

It seems fanciful to suppose that any household goes through a process of choice such as that indicated above. A truer picture of actual budgeting processes might be provided by supposing that the household chooses among alternative feasible budgets in a somewhat haphazard fashion, paying particular attention to budgets that lie in the neighborhood of purchased combinations with which the household is already familiar. The household's situation at the moment of decision thus might be represented by a point *near* some new budget line L_0 (such as point *a* in Figure 5-9) representing the household's actual purchases during the preceding week, and a set of indifference curves that rank alternative budgets in the neighborhood of the point *a.* With this kind of background, the household might select a budget during the current week that lies on the line L_0 and above and to the right of the budget defined by point *a* (for example, point *b* in Figure 5-9); but we could not argue that the household would choose any

---

[9]Mathematically, the "corner solution" corresponds to a situation in which the ordinary constrained optimization technique (The Lagrangean analysis discussed in footnote 3) will not "work." The reason is that a tangency involving positive quantities of both goods does not occur—the highest indifference curve is reached when one of the goods is not consumed. Such cases can be handled formally by Kuhn-Tucker analysis; students well versed in mathematics are encouraged to pursue this technique in more advanced texts.

5-8 True or False? The slope of budget constraint line shows the size of the budget while the position shows us the relative prices (or price ratios).

False. The position of the budget constraint line indicates how much of both goods one can obtain. The further from the origin, the better

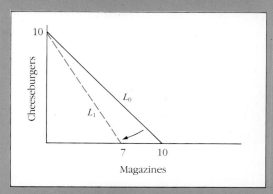

for the consumer—since this implies the capacity to buy more of both goods. A changing slope refers to a change in the relative price between the two goods. If magazines and cheeseburgers are the goods on the graph, which relative price has risen when the budget line shifts from L_0 to L_1? The relative price of magazines has risen. Put simply, if you could have had (with the same money) either *ten* magazines or *ten* cheeseburgers before but now can have either *seven* magazines or *ten* cheeseburgers, magazines must have increased in price relative to cheeseburgers. Moreover, unless you consumed zero magazines before the price rise, you are worse off (lower utility) after the price rise because your new budget constraint encloses a smaller *feasible* set of bundles from which to choose.

5-9 Using indifference curves, show the impact of emission controls on automobiles. Is this a desirable policy to enact?

The imposition of emission controls on automobiles increases the relative price of automobiles. Hence we would expect fewer automobiles to be consumed. The second question is a "trick" question in one important respect: economists can *never* determine from their analysis whether a policy is "desirable" or not. They can, however, determine the relationship between benefits (improved health, visibility) and costs (higher priced cars, more expensive operating costs) and also indicate how these benefits and costs are distributed among individuals.

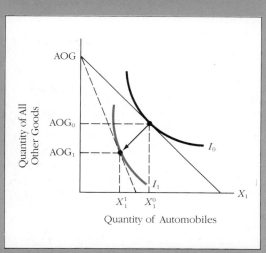

FIGURE 5-9

Neighborhood Preference Map

Households generally choose commodity bundles similar to familiar purchases. The "neighborhood" of bundle *a* includes the commodity bundles in the shaded area.

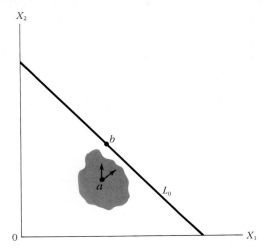

specific budget on the Line L_0, for our present assumptions do not require that preferences be well defined anywhere except in the *immediate* neighborhood of the point *a*. Thus any point on L_0 *might* be chosen.

What would be gained by adopting this outwardly more realistic approach to the problem of household budget selection? Apparently, the only significant improvement would be the explicit recognition that the household might not jump directly from one utility-maximizing budget to another in response to changes in data which alter the position of the budget constraint line. But this improvement could be achieved simply by refusing to suppose that adjustments occur instantaneously. There is no need to throw away the assumption that preferences are everywhere well defined—and if we did throw away this assumption, we would be faced with serious problems trying to describe just how the household reacts to changes in data, for we would have no basis for saying much of anything.

When all is said and done, our interest in the details of consumer choice is limited to showing that a single utility-maximizing bundle is defined under specified (and ideal) conditions, not that such a budget is defined for all conceivable sets of circumstances. The implications of the ideal case are sufficiently complicated in their own right to choke off any interest that we might otherwise have in exploring more realistic possibilities at this point. If realism is to be injected into the discussion, the appropriate place to inject it is at another level of analysis, where empirical evidence can be drawn upon to suggest which of an endless list of possible complications might be worth bothering about in practice. (See Box 5-10.)

5-10　Fertility rates in developing countries are higher in rural areas than urban areas. Using indifference curves, explain why you think this might be so assuming that families are indifferent between rural and urban areas.

The relative price of children is higher in urban areas than rural areas for at least two reasons. First, food and housing are generally more expensive in cities. Second, children have fewer opportunities to be productive in an urban setting. Rural children are quite productive at an early age, doing chores such as planting, weeding, gathering, and fence building. This is not the case in urban areas, where a child's marginal product is close to zero.

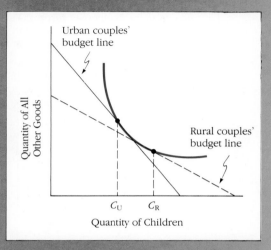

Subsidies and Indifference Curves

The indifference curve is a convenient tool to aid in our understanding of subsidies. In this final section, we will consider two examples demonstrating the effects of subsidies in income as compared to subsidies in price. The first question is whether the poor would be better off with cash or food stamps. The second example has to do with the more general question of subsidizing the price of a good like buses or trains.

Using the indifference curve approach, we can show that the poor would be at least equally as well off receiving cash rather than a subsidy like food stamps.

In Figure 5-10, if the individual's initial position is at a (consuming F_0 amount of food, an amount deemed insufficient by society), the introduction of a food stamp program that allowed the recipient to spend an additional $100 per month exclusively on food would make the consumer better off (bundles on indifference curve I_1 are preferred to those on I_0). However, for the same expense, this individual might be made even better off by receiving $100 in cash. The reason is that the shaded triangle is unobtainable to the recipient of food stamps but not to those receiving a cash payment. Unless the individual intended to spend *all* of the next $100 of additional income on food, he or she would be better off with a choice.

Similarly, subsidizing the price of a good (like education, postal services, mass transportation, or medical services) is usually *not* the best method to assure that society's scarce resources are properly allocated. If the price of a good is subsidized, it

FIGURE 5-10

Cash Grants versus Food Stamp Income Subsidy

With no government assistance, the consumer chooses bundle *a.* The availability of food stamps increases the budget and allows the buyer to purchase bundle *b,* consuming more food and more other goods and attaining a higher level of utility. A cash grant, however, expands the budget set further. The recipient would purchase bundle *c* which contains more nonfood items and less food than bundle *b.* The consumer reaches a higher level of utility with a cash grant than with food stamps.

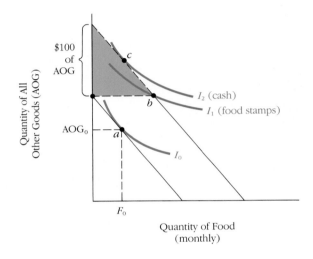

distorts market signals and results in output levels of the subsidized good that are inefficiently large. In other words, the opportunity cost of forgone other goods that could have been produced with those resources is greater than the (marginal) value of the subsidized good. (Recall the ordinary supply and demand diagram for a subsidy from your elementary economics course.) Figure 5-11 shows that if the whole budget constraint is shifted parallel by an amount equivalent to the price subsidy, *ab* (*ab = cd*), then a higher indifference curve can be reached. Since reaching the highest indifference curve subject to the budget constraint maximizes consumer satisfaction, this simple diagram shows that it is better to subsidize income (parallel shift) than to subsidize price (altering the slope), if one is interested in making some group better off.[10] Of course, if you want certain groups (say, the poor) to consume more of *particular* goods (housing or food), rather than just raising their utility you may not wish to give unconstrained income subsidies. Recall that economists can never, in their role as economists, recommend one approach over the other but they can point out the implications of alternative choices.

---

[10]*Note also:* For even this analysis to be correct, the group being subsidized must be small—if the graph referred to society *as a whole* (subsidizing everyone's food or transportation), the budget constraint (really, production possibilities curve in this case) will *not shift at all.* There are no free lunches.

FIGURE 5-11

Cash Grants versus Price Subsidies
A subsidy lowers the price paid for the good, pivoting the budget line to the right, whereas a cash grant causes a parallel shift of the budget line to the right. The consumer chooses bundle A with the subsidy but attains more satisfaction under a cash grant program. More units of the subsidized good and fewer units of other goods are consumed with a subsidy than with a cash grant of equivalent value.

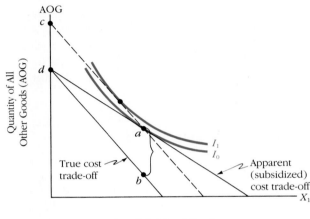

Subsidized Good
(buses, postal services, Amtrak)

SUMMARY

1. Underlying the foundations of the Law of Demand are the assumptions that consumers seek to maximize satisfaction, incomes are limited, and marginal utility falls or that the law of diminishing marginal rate of substitution holds as additional units of a good are acquired.

2. The Law of Diminishing Marginal Utility states that marginal utility declines as successive units of a good are acquired. Utility (marginal and total) is an ordinal measure. That is, goods can be ranked in order of preference, but the utility numbers attached to the ranked bundles do not matter.

3. Transitivity of choices is also assumed to characterize preferences. That is, if bundle I_0 is preferred to bundle I_1 and bundle I_1 is preferred to bundle I_2, then bundle I_0 is preferred to bundle I_2.

4. The interaction of two factors is important in the explanation of diminishing marginal utility: individual wants for any particular good are satiable, and different goods are not perfect substitutes in satisfying particular wants.

5. Maximization of satisfaction requires that income must be allocated in such a way that the marginal utility per dollar of any good is the same for every good. Alternatively, maximization requires the ratios of marginal utilities of the various goods purchased to equal the price ratios of the goods.

6. An indifference schedule (and curve) indicates the various combinations of two goods which will yield a consumer the same total satisfaction. The indifference curve shows us nothing about the absolute amounts of satisfaction obtained; it merely indicates the various combinations which will yield equal satisfaction.

7. The slope of the indifference curve measures the marginal rate of substitution. The marginal rate of substitution is the number of units of one of the goods necessary to replace one unit of the other good in order to maintain the same total satisfaction.

8. Indifference curves for two goods (as opposed to a bad and a good) are convex to the point of origin. The shape of the indifference curves arises from the principle of diminishing marginal rate of substitution.

9. Indifference curves cannot intersect. This would yield the inconsistent result of points having more of all goods being equally satisfying to points having less of all goods.

10. The budget constraint line shows the various combinations of two goods which can be purchased with a certain expenditure.

11. To attain the highest level of satisfaction, one must reach the highest indifference curve obtainable with a given expenditure of money.

WORDS AND CONCEPTS FOR REVIEW

marginal utility
substitution effect
income effect
maximization of satisfaction
indifference curve
marginal rate of substitution
complements
substitutes

indifference curves never intersect
transitivity
budget constraint line (consumption
    possibility line)
preferences in the immediate
    neighborhood

REVIEW QUESTIONS

1. Explain the concept of marginal utility. What is meant by the statement that it is an ordinal rather than a cardinal measure?

2. What is the Law of Diminishing Marginal Utility? Explain its underlying rationale.

3. Explain, in terms of marginal utility, the pattern of allocation of consumer income that is necessary to allow maximization of satisfaction.

4. Why does optimum allocation require that the marginal utilities of the various goods purchased be proportional to their prices?

5. Explain the law of demand in terms of the marginal utility approach.

6. What is an indifference schedule?

7. Why do indifference curves slope downward from left to right? Why do they not intersect?

8. What is meant by the term "marginal rate of substitution"? What is its relation to the slope of an indifference curve?

9. Why are indifference curves convex to the point of origin? What principle is involved in such convexity?

10. What determines the degree of convexity of an indifference curve?

11. What is meant by "transitivity of preferences"?

12. Explain the "budget constraint" line. Upon what assumption is it typically drawn as a straight line?

13. Why is the point of tangency of the budget constraint line and an indifference curve the point of optimum satisfaction?

14. What is the relationship between the ratio of the prices of two articles and the marginal rate of substitution between them at the point of optimum satisfaction?

15. Which of the following statements is best, and why?
(a) "Bundle A is most preferred because it gives highest utility."
(b) "Bundle A gives highest utility because it is most preferred."

SUGGESTED READINGS

Baumol, W. *Economic Theory and Operations Analysis,* 4th ed. Englewood Cliffs, N.J.: Prentice-Hall, 1977, Chapter 9.

Cooter, R. and Rappoport, P. "Were the Ordinalist Wrong About Welfare Economics." *Journal of Economic Literature* (June 1984), pp. 507–30.

Friedman, M. *Price Theory.* Chicago: Aldine Publishing Company, 1976, Chapter 2.

Henderson, J.M. and Quandt, R.E. *Microeconomic Theory,* 3rd ed. New York: McGraw-Hill, 1980, Chapter 2.

Hicks, J.R. *Value and Capital,* 2nd ed. Oxford: The Clarendon Press, 1946, Chapters 1 and 2.

Stigler, G. *The Theory of Price,* 4th ed. New York: Macmillan, 1987, Chapter 4.

6

Indifference Curves
and the
Demand Schedule

6.1 INTRODUCTION

With an understanding of how individuals make decisions founded on their preferences (represented by indifference curves) and on scarcity (reflected in the budget line), consumer theory can now be expanded to examine consumer behavior when prices and income are made variable. Indeed, this analysis lies at the heart of any effort to understand *changes* in consumer behavior.[1]

6.2 THE PRICE CONSUMPTION CURVE

The tangency relationship between the budget line and the pattern of indifference curves indicates the optimum amounts of each of the two goods which will be purchased, given the prices of the two goods and the consumer's total available expenditure. For different possible prices for one of the goods, given the price of the other and given total expenditures, different quantities of the two will be purchased. A change in the price of one of the goods will alter the slope of the budget line since a different amount of the good can be purchased with a given level of expenditure. If, for example, the price of X_1 falls, the budget line will become flatter, since more units of X_1 can be purchased than previously with a given expenditure. Likewise, at all points except that at which no units of X_1 are purchased, the line will be to the right of the old

---

[1]With stable preferences (an unchanging utility function), it is *only* changes in prices or income that can lead to changed behavior. This is the economists' somewhat restrictive approach; yet without good predictive theories of how tastes *change* (from perhaps sociology or psychology), the economists' approach is the only one available to those interested in prediction.

114

one: it rotates outward as a result of the price reduction. Thus the new point of tangency with an indifference curve will be on a higher indifference curve. In Figure 6-1, the point of tangency moves from a to b as a result of the decline in price of X_1 from $20.00 to $10.00; the equilibrium quantity of X_1 purchased increases from two to five units.

Figure 6-2(a) shows a series of points of tangency of the budget line with indifference curves, under the assumption of various possible prices for X_1 ($50.00, $20.00, $13.30 and $10.00), the price of X_2 remaining unchanged at $10.00. A relation known as the **price-consumption curve** (PCC) may be drawn through these points of tangency, indicating the optimum quantities of X_1 (and X_2) at various possible prices of X_1 (given the price of X_2). From this price-consumption curve can be derived the usual demand curve for the good. Thus, from Figure 6-2(a), it can be ascertained that if the price of X_1 is $10.00, five units will be purchased; if the price is $13.30, three and one-half units will be purchased; if the price is $20.00, two units will be purchased; if the price is $50.00, one-half unit will be purchased. These data may be plotted, as in Figure 6-2(b), to derive a demand curve of the usual form. Note that in Figure 6-2(b) the price of X_1 is measured on the vertical axis, and the quantity purchased on the horizontal axis, whereas the axes of Figure 6-2(a) refer to quantities of the two goods. Note also that the quantities demanded, as shown in Figure 6-2(b), are those with the

---

FIGURE 6-1

The Effect of a Decline in the Price of X_1 on the Quantities of X_1 and X_2 Purchased

When the price of X_1 falls from $20 to $10, the budget line rotates outward from vs to vt. With $100 of income, the consumer can now afford to buy 10 units of X_1 if all income is spent on X_1. The optimum bundle of X_1 and X_2 changes from a to b and the consumer increases consumption of X_1 from 2 to 5 units.

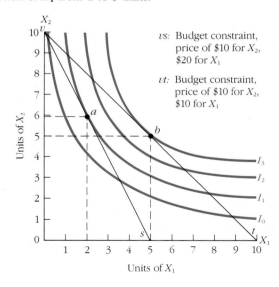

FIGURE 6-2

The Various Combinations of Goods X_1 and X_2 That Will Be Purchased at Various Prices of X_1 and the Demand Schedule for Good X_1

In part (a), the price-consumption curve, PCC, charts the equilibrium combinations of X_1 and X_2 at different price levels for X_1. In other words, the PCC connects the points of tangency between succeeding budget lines and indifference curves. The desired quantity of X_1 for a given price can be read directly from the price-consumption curve diagram. For example, point n indicates that the consumer will buy ½ of a unit of X_1 when the price of X_1 is $50.00 (along budget line vn). Since the demand curve shows the quantity demanded at various prices, $X_1 = ½$ at price of $X_1 = $50.00 is one point on the demand curve in part (b). Similarly, the other points on the demand curve can be plotted.

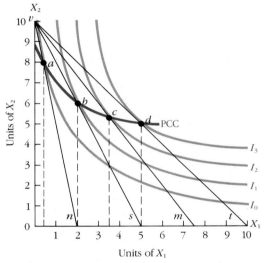

(a) The various combinations of goods X_1 and X_2 which will be purchased at various prices of X_1

(b) The demand schedule for good X_1 derived from the price-consumption curve in graph (a)

consumer's expenditures in equilibrium (at his or her optimum) at the various prices.[2] Essentially, the demand curve is made up of various price and quantity optimum points, in the sense that it indicates the quantities which the consumer will buy at various prices when he or she has attained optimum adjustment of expenditures among the various goods. However, it should be pointed out that one difficulty in constructing demand curves by observing actual consumer behavior is that observation alone will not indicate whether the consumer is at an optimum, and thus whether

---

[2]We prefer to use "optimum" when describing the best choice of the consumer, given prices and income. In a sense, this is also an "equilibrium" in that, unless prices or income change "with stable preferences," the choice will *not* change. We prefer to reserve the term "equilibrium" for the balancing of market forces—supply and demand—that coordinate the optimizing actions of individuals. However, either usage is acceptable, as long as the context is clear.

the observed price-quantity point lies on or off the demand curve. Rather, it is assumed that individuals attempt to maximize satisfaction or utility; hence observed purchases are assumed to occur where (unobserved) indifference curves are tangent to the (observed) budget line. (See Box 6-1.)

The demand curve in Figure 6-2 is of limited significance since it is based upon an analysis of the expenditure adjustments between the good in question and one other, rather than on all goods purchased. However, if the X_2 axis in Figure 6-2 is interpreted to represent expenditures on all other goods (AOG) rather than on one, and the budget line is assumed to represent total expenditures rather than those on two goods

---

6-1   How can one derive a demand curve for record albums from the price consumption curve (PCC)? Assume that the budget constraint is $20 and the price of good X_2 is $1.

Starting off with budget line L_0, we know that we have $20. If we spend it all on record albums and none of it on good X_2, we can buy two albums; this implies that the price of albums is $10 apiece. When the budget line moves to L_1, the price of records falls to $5 apiece (since $20 would, if spent entirely on albums, buy four). At L_2, records are $2 an album. According to the indifference curves in part (a), the consumer will buy one album at $10 (point a), two albums when the price falls to $5 (point b), and five albums when the price

is $2 (point c). In part (b) we convert the consumer's equilibrium points into a demand curve, with a', b', and c' representing the price and quantity demanded points for prices of $10, $5, and $2 respectively. In part (a), the price consumption curve is perfectly horizontal, indicating that the demand curve is unitary elastic. Later in this chapter, we will discuss further the implications of different slopes of the price consumption curve for the elasticity of demand.

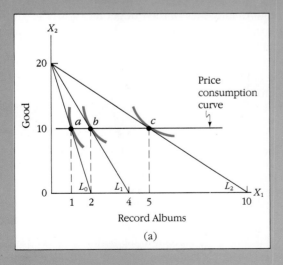

(a)

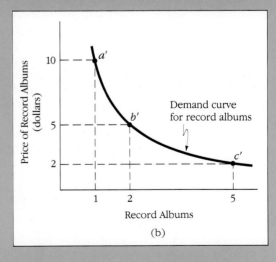

(b)

only, then the demand curve derived from the price-consumption curve reflects the reactions of the quantities of the good purchased in response to changes in the price of the good, with adjustments made between purchases of this good and all others, given a level of total expenditures. The demand curve so derived is called the **uncompensated demand curve**—uncompensated because *real* income is affected by any price change. By contrast, the so-called **compensated demand curve** holds the consumer's utility level constant before and after the price change. (See Box 6-2.)

6.3 THE INCOME EFFECT AND THE SUBSTITUTION EFFECT

With indifference curves, the two distinct types of effects through which a price reduction influences the quantity demanded can easily be seen. When the price of a good declines, the **income effect** enables the person to buy more of this good (or other goods) with a given income; the price reduction has the same effect as an increase in money income. This is reflected by the movement onto a higher indifference curve. For example, in Figure 6-2, if price falls from $20 to $13.30, the consumer can move from indifference curve I_1 to curve I_2, and thus to a higher level of satisfaction. Of course, the entire amount of purchasing power freed might be used to purchase other goods. In some cases the purchasing power freed might be used to buy better quality substitutes for the good whose price changes, and thus the quantity of the good purchased would fall. The more typical effect will be to increase the consumption of good X_1 as a result of the income effect, since income increases will lead to greater demand for normal goods.[3]

The second influence of a price decline upon the quantity demanded is the **substitution effect**. The lower price encourages the consumer to buy larger quantities of this good to replace units of other goods. To the extent that this reaction is significant in a particular case, the point of tangency of the budget line with the indifference curve is moved farther to the right. Thus, in Figure 6-2, the budget line that is parallel to the line vt would be tangent to indifference curve I_2 farther to the right than the point at which vm was tangent. Thus a decline in the price of X_1 would lead to an increase in the quantity purchased even if none of the income freed by the lower price were spent on the good. Hence the substitution effect is always negative (opposite the change in price); lower prices mean higher purchased quantities and vice versa. The

---

[3]The possibility that a price reduction could lead to a quantity reduction, and conversely (upward-sloping demand curves), is however of only theoretical interest; there has never been a properly conducted empirical analysis in real market settings recording such a good referred to as a "Giffen good." However, it is possible that a Giffen good might be observable in experimental settings. The normal downward-sloping demand curve stems from the fact that a price change for most goods will generate a relatively small income effect, since most goods are a small share of the budget. To get the paradoxical upward-sloping demand, the good must be both strongly inferior and important in the budget to offset the substitution effect, which *always* leads to downward-sloping demand. [All compensated demand curves are downward-sloping.]

6-2   Now, show the income and substitution effects for an *increase* in the price of good X_1.

The first thing to show in graph (a) is the relative price of X_1 rising, which means that the budget line rotates inward from L_0 to L_1. (*Note:* The X_2 intercept is *not* changed since neither income nor the price of X_2 has changed. Hence, if all income is spent on X_2 before and after the price increase of X_1, the same amount of X_2 can be purchased.) Where the new indifference curve lies tangent to the new budget line (at point c) is the total effect of the increase in the price of X_1—that is, a reduction of good X_1 from X_1^0 to X_1^1. But within the total effect is the substitution effect and the income effect. First consider how much of the total effect is substituting away from the now-higher-priced good X_1. This can easily be done by taking the new budget line L_1 and drawing a new budget line, L^*, parallel to L_1 but tangent to the old indifference curve I_0. Why? This shows the effect of the new relative price on the old indifference curve—in effect, the consumer is compensated for the loss of welfare associated with the price rise by enough income to return to the original indifference curve, I_0. Remember that as long as L_1 and L^* are parallel, the relative prices are the same; the only difference is the level of income. Thus, we are able to isolate the one effect—the amount of substitution that would prevail without the real income effect—which is the movement from a to b. The movement from b to c is a change in real

income when the relative prices are constant since this move requires a parallel shift in the budget line. Thus the movement from b to c results from the decrease in real income due to the higher price of good X_1 while all other prices have remained constant.

Note that graph (b) looks somewhat different from graph (a). In the present example, the substitution effect (the movement from a to b) is the movement along the original indifference curve occurring due to the higher relative price of X_1. Note, however, that it would take a bit more income, at the new relative prices, to continue to be able to buy the old bundle a (represented by the dashed budget line in graph (b)). In comparing b with b', it is clear that for small price changes they will be virtually indistinguishable. It is the case, however, that b is what one normally would wish to know and b' is a readily observable approximation that doesn't quite hold real utility constant. Remember that the slope of the budget line indicates relative prices; thus by shifting the new budget line next to the old indifference curve, we can see the change that took place holding real income (measured by utility) constant. Then when we make the parallel shift, we see the change in income since the size of the parallel shift just measures the amount of real income change, with relative prices remaining constant.

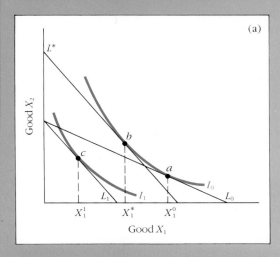

(a)

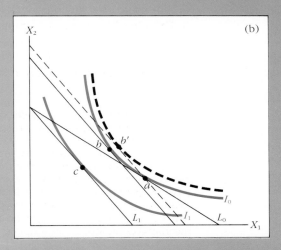

(b)

greater the substitutability of other goods for X_1, the less the curvature in the indifference curve, and thus the greater the extent to which the point of tangency shifts to the right (that is, in the direction of a greater quantity of X_1 purchased) as the price of X_1 falls.

Two cases which show negative income effects are considered in Figures 6-3(a) and (b). In Figure 6-3(a), we see that an increase in income (prices constant) would lead to a decrease in the optimal quantity of X_1 demanded for purchase (going from a to b). If the price of X_1 were decreased, and the resulting increase in real income were offset by a simultaneous reduction in the consumer's money income so that the budget line following this "compensated" change in price were represented by the line L^* in Figure 6-3(a) rather than the line L_1 (the latter corresponding to the situation before money income is reduced), then the consumer would apparently wish to increase purchases of X_1 by moving to the budget a^* from a. That is to say, if we somehow offset the real income effect of the reduction in price, the consumer would increase rather than decrease planned purchases of X_1, substituting the now cheaper good X_1 for the relatively more expensive good X_2 as required by common-sense accounts of the Law of Demand.[4]

The overall effect of the reduction in the price of X_1 can be regarded as the sum of two separate effects: the (negative) substitution effect of the price change (represented in Figure 6-3(a) by the (unobserved) change in purchases of X_1 from X_1^0 to X_1^*, as defined by the "compensated" budget line L^*), and the (negative) income effect of the price change (represented in Figure 6-3(a) by the change in purchases of X_1 from X_1^* to X_1^1, as defined by the "uncompensated" budget line L_1). Clearly, even if the income effect of a price reduction is negative, as in Figure 6-3(a), the total effect still will be to increase quantity demanded if the negative substitution effect is sufficiently large. Indeed, if the quantity purchased is rather small, then the real income change associated with a price reduction will be small and the substitution effect of the price reduction will dominate the income effect. We do not expect to turn up cases in practice in which the overall effect of a reduction in price is to decrease the quantity demanded of the good whose price has declined.

The usual case for inferior goods would be more like that represented in Figure 6-3(b). Here the lines and points are labeled precisely as in Figure 6-3(a), but the

---

[4]Note that there are two types of compensation one could consider. We could, as in the text and in Figure 6-3(a), keep real income the same by allowing the old optimal bundle, a, to be purchased at the new relative price. In fact, this form of compensation will leave the household a bit better off because they will be able to purchase a *more* preferred bundle, a^*. The disadvantage of this approach (the so-called Slutsky decomposition of the income and substitution effects of a price change) is that real income is not *exactly* held constant: a higher indifference curve is reached at the lower price of X_1. However, we could take away a further amount of income to return the consumer to the original level of satisfaction (at which point the new a^* would be indifferent to the original a). This approach, while theoretically preferred, is difficult to implement in practice, since the indifference curves are not observable directly (Figure 6-4 depicts this case). However, it should be noted that for sufficiently small price changes the two concepts become identical. We shall, in the text, take both approaches.

FIGURE 6-3

Total Effect of a Price Reduction for Inferior Goods

As shown in part (a), a reduction in the price of X_1 can decrease the quantity desired of X_1 only if X_1 is an inferior good and the income effect (a^* to b) dominates the substitution effect (a to a^*). In part (b), X_1 is also an inferior good because the additional purchasing power resulting from the price decline (L^* to L_1) reduces the quantity of X_1 desired (a^* to b). The net effect of the decreased price, however, is to increase purchases of X_1 because the negative substitution effect exceeds the negative income effect, as will virtually always be the case even for inferior goods.

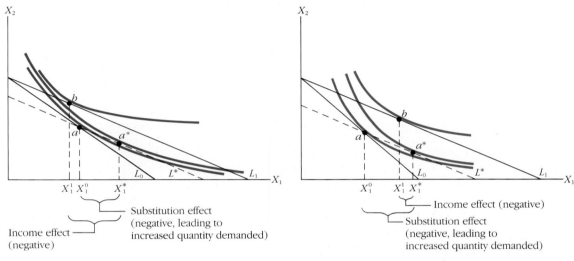

(a) Negative: Price reduction implies a reduction in quantity demanded

(b) Positive: Price reduction implies an increase in quantity demanded

consumer's preferences are different. Again good X_1 is inferior with respect to changes in income, but only to a limited degree. The substitution effect of the price change thus dominates the income effect, and the overall result of a price reduction is to increase the quantity of X_1 demanded for purchase. It is thus clear that the Law of Demand applies in all cases where (1) the good whose price declines is a normal good, or (2) the total expenditure on the good whose price declines is small in relation to total expenditure on all goods—that is, the good is only weakly inferior with respect to changes in income.

Since the terms *small* and *weakly* are ambiguous, we cannot regard the second of the above conditions as saying anything precise. Strictly speaking, the Law of Demand always holds in our theory of consumer behavior only if all goods are normal with respect to changes in income. On any other assumption, the Law of Demand can in principle break down. We thus arrive at a curious situation in which the only general theorem we can state is that a reduction in the price of a good will lead to an increase in quantity purchased if it does not lead to a decrease! We shall adopt the procedure of supposing that all goods are normal (or, at worst, weakly inferior), thus ruling out all cases in which the Law of Demand fails to hold. Our reason for this, as indicated earlier, is analytical convenience. One gets out of a theory just what one puts into it by way of restrictive assumptions. We are, however, as convinced of the practical validity of the Law of Demand as most physicists are convinced of the practical validity of the Second Law of Thermodynamics. Since our theory strictly entails the Law of Demand only on the assumption that all goods are normal or weakly inferior, we impose this restriction on our theory in order to bring it into line with our intuitive (and empirical) beliefs. In doing this, we run the small risk that our theory will at some time be contradicted by factual evidence; but that risk is preferable to the uncertainty of working with a theory that has ambiguous empirical implications. (See Box 6-3.)

Determinants of Elasticity of Demand—Substitutability

The elasticity of demand for a good depends primarily upon the ease of its substitution for other goods in the satisfaction of wants. When several goods are regarded by

6-3   Cigarette and alcohol taxes are imposed to discourage consumption of so-called "undesirable goods." Using indifference curves, show the effect of an increase in taxes on alcoholic beverages. What is the total effect? How much of the change is due to the income effect? How much is due to the substitution effect?

The desired effect is to reduce consumption of alcohol by increasing its relative price. The total effect of the reduction in output is $X_1^0 - X_1^1$. The distance between X_1^0 and X_1^* represents the reduction due to the substitution effect. That is, substitution occurs which favors other goods relative to the now more expensive alcohol or cigarettes. The other component of the total effect is the income effect. The income effect shows the loss in real income due to the price increase. When the price of all other goods and income remain fixed, the consumer *loses* real purchasing power; the feasible area of choice has a triangular portion no longer available to the consumer.

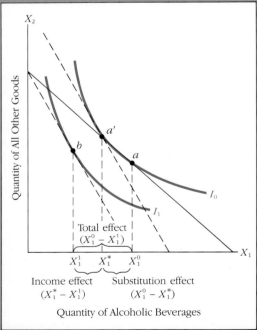

consumers as more or less equally desirable for the satisfaction of particular wants, the demand schedules for each tend to be elastic, since changes in their relative prices cause substantial shifting of relative purchases. Thus an increase in the price of oranges will cause many consumers to purchase more apples, grapefruit, or bananas and fewer oranges. When no satisfactory substitutes are available, price changes will have less effect upon the quantity demanded.

The effects of **substitutability** upon the elasticity of demand may be illustrated by the indifference curve. The greater the ease with which the good in question can be substituted for others (and other goods may be substituted for it), the less the curvature of the indifference curve; that is, the curve will more closely approach a straight line. The smaller the curvature, the greater the extent to which the point of tangency of the budget line with an indifference curve will shift to the right when the price of the good falls; and thus the more the purchases of the good will increase in response to the price reduction.

The significance of the curvature is illustrated in Figure 6-4(a) and (b). In order to show exactly the significance of substitutability, it is necessary to eliminate the income effect on utility by drawing a budget line (L^*) parallel to the new budget line (L_1) after the price change, at a location such that the former is tangent to the old indifference curve (I_0). In Figure 6-4(a), where the curvature of the indifference curve is slight, the tangency of L^* with I_0 (where X_1^1 is purchased) is much farther to the right of the original tangency of L_0 with I_0 (where X_1^0 is purchased) than it is in Figure 6-4(b), where the curvature is greater because the goods are poor substitutes.

FIGURE 6-4

The Significance of Substitutability for the Response of the Quantity of Good X_1 Purchased to Changes in the Price of X_1

When X_1 and X_2 are close substitutes, indifference curves are nearly linear. A decline in the price of X_1 induces a large increase in the purchases of X_1 as the consumer substitutes X_1 for X_2. Corresponding demand curves tend to be elastic. When X_1 and X_2 are not readily substitutable, indifference curves approach the L-shape, and a change in the price of X_1 evokes little change in the quantity of X_1 desired. In this case, demand curves are relatively inelastic.

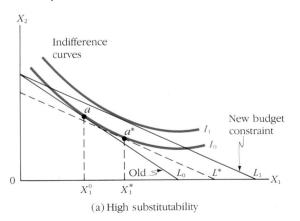

(a) High substitutability

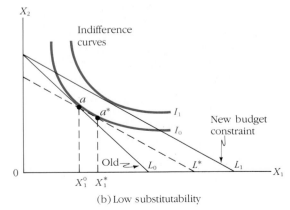

(b) Low substitutability

The same relationships may be expressed in terms of marginal rates of substitution. If the rate falls rapidly, as it will if the goods are poor substitutes, a decline in the price of one good will result in only a relatively slight readjustment in quantities of the two goods purchased to restore equality of the price ratios and the marginal rate of substitution. If the marginal rate of substitution falls slowly, a much greater readjustment in relative purchases will be optimal.

Other Influences on Elasticity

Elasticity is likewise affected by the nature of the want for which the good is being acquired or, in terms of utility, the rate of decline in marginal utility as additional units of the good are acquired. The more quickly the want is satiated, and thus the more rapidly the marginal utility (or the marginal rate of substitution) falls, the less elastic will be the demand. The marginal utility of bread, for example, generally falls more quickly than the marginal utilities of various forms of recreation. The possibility of alternate uses—that is, the ability to use the good to satisfy other wants as well as the original one—lessens the rate of decline in marginal utility.

Elasticity is affected by the closely related considerations of product durability and the time interval for which the schedule is relevant. When goods can be used for a number of years, individual consumers are not in the market for additional units for a considerable period of time after they have made a purchase. But if the goods are not durable, consumers can adjust their rates of purchase at any time and thus are more immediately sensitive to price changes. As a consequence, demand schedules for durable goods are more elastic the longer the period of time over which demand is defined (that is, demand would be more elastic for a price change lasting a year than for a month). The demand for nondurable goods used in conjunction with durable equipment is affected in a similar manner. If someone has installed an oil-burning furnace, she cannot shift from oil to natural gas without substantial additional expense. Thus changes in relative prices of oil and natural gas will not cause an immediate switch from one fuel to the other. But when the furnace is replaced, substitution of the cheaper fuel for the more expensive one may occur.

Apart from considerations of durability, the importance of habit in consumer purchasing causes the demands for many goods, durable or not, to become more elastic over a period of time than they are in a shorter period. People become accustomed to buying certain articles and do not frequently reconsider the desirability of adjusting their purchases. Thus price changes may bring little immediate response. But over a longer period, there is greater likelihood (indeed *requirement,* if prices are higher or income is lower) of reconsidering the desirability of purchases and of seeking substitutes, and the effects of changes in relative prices will be greater. Thus if chicken falls greatly in price, most consumers at first may not consider replacing beef or pork with chicken. But if the price remains at a low level over a period of time, more and more people may revise their purchase patterns to take advantage of the low price of chicken (perhaps through new recipes such as chicken burritos instead of beef burritos). Furthermore, over a longer period, consumers are more likely to become better informed about the existence of lower prices.

The elasticity of the total demand schedule for a good is determined by the elasticities of the individual schedules which underlie it. As the price of a good falls, much of the increase in quantity demanded may come from new purchasers—persons not buying the good at all at higher prices. These may be people with relatively low incomes or those whose desires for the good are relatively weak. For some products, the demand schedules of individual buyers are extremely inelastic, yet the total demand is elastic, since many additional buyers will enter the market at lower prices. Thus the demand for compact disc players may be relatively elastic, even though few individuals buy more than one regardless of the price.

6.4 THE LEVEL OF THE DEMAND SCHEDULE

As noted in Chapter 3, a given *market* demand schedule relating price and quantity demanded is valid only when values of the prices of other goods are given and a host of other "shift" parameters (income, population, tastes, and so on) are held constant. It is useful to consider the relationships between changes in those "givens" which result in shifts in the position and form of the individual demand schedule. The problem may be approached by considering the functional relationship between each of these variables and the quantity demanded, price now being regarded as given instead of variable.

Prices of Other Goods

The first major determinant of the height of a particular demand schedule is the price level of other goods. The influence of the prices of other goods is in part dependent on the good whose price changes. Price changes of close substitutes are far more significant than are those of goods not closely related to the good in question. The demand for oranges is affected much more by the prevailing price of apples than by that of theatre tickets.

The nature of the cross-elasticity of demand between two goods depends upon the relative influences of the income and substitution effects. You may recall from Chapter 3 that the cross-price elasticity formula is as follows:[5]

$$E_{X_2 P_{X_1}} = \frac{5\% \Delta Q_{X_2}}{\% \Delta P_{X_1}} = \frac{\dfrac{\Delta X_2}{X_2}}{\dfrac{\Delta P_{X_1}}{P_{X_1}}} = \frac{\Delta X_2}{\Delta P_{X_1}} \frac{P_{X_1}}{X_2}$$

---

[5]In terms of derivatives, $E_{X_2 P_{X_1}} = \dfrac{dX_2}{dP_{X_1}} \dfrac{P_{X_1}}{X_2}$

As with ordinary price elasticities, one must be careful to consider whether real income is being held constant or not. When the price of one good falls, the income effect (representing the freeing of purchasing power by the price reduction) encourages the purchase of more units of both goods. But the fact that the price of the first good has fallen relative to the price of the second encourages people to substitute the first for the second, and thus to buy less of the second. If the substitution effect outweighs the income effect, the cross-elasticity is positive, and the two goods are regarded as gross substitutes for one another. This situation is illustrated in Figure 6-5. The price of good X_1, fell, causing consumers to substitute away from good X_2 as they buy more X_1. The higher the cross-elasticity, the greater is the ease of substitution. If the articles are perfect substitutes (and thus essentially the same good, from the standpoint of the users), the cross-elasticity is infinite.

There are two types of situations in which cross-elasticity will be negative, in the sense that a decline in the price of one good will lead to an increase in the quantity of the other good purchased. In the first case (shown in Figure 6-6), the income effect of the price change may outweigh the substitution effect. As the price of X_1 falls, if little substitution occurs and the demand for X_1 is inelastic, less of total purchasing power will be spent on X_1 than before, and the amount of X_2 purchased may increase.

The other case of negative cross-elasticity is that of *complementary* goods like bread and butter, where increased use of one gives rise to increased use of the other. A decline in the price of bread stimulates increased use of bread, thus raising the marginal utility of butter and increasing the quantity of butter purchased. If total expenditure on the two items rises, of course, then purchases of other goods must decline to free the necessary purchasing power.

The preceding discussion of own-price and cross-price elasticities can be further clarified with reference to the **price consumption curve** (PCC). Consider Figure

---

FIGURE 6-5

Positive Cross-Elasticity

A decrease in the price of X_1 reduces the amount of X_2 desired from *a* to *b*. The cross-elasticity, the percentage change in purchases of X_2 divided by the percentage change in the price of X_1, is positive and the two goods are substitutes.

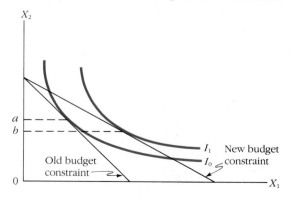

FIGURE 6-6

Negative Cross-Elasticity

Purchases of X_2 increase in response to a decrease in the price of X_1 when the two goods are gross complements.

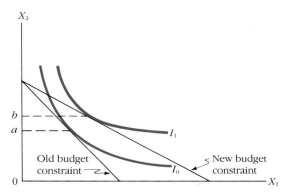

6-7. With fixed money income I, we vary the price of X_1, first from P_1^0 to P_1^1 and then to P_1^2. We know that the price of X_1 is falling during this sequence of price changes since more X_1 can be purchased if all of income is spent on X_1 at P_1^2 than at P_1^1 or P_1^0. Associated with each price will be an optimum combination of X_1 and X_2 which maximizes consumer satisfaction, with points *a, b,* and *c* corresponding to the consumer's best consumption bundles in Figure 6-7. Notice that this price consumption curve first falls, then reaches a minimum, then rises. (The situation where the PCC is at a minimum—locally "flat"—was discussed in earlier boxed material.) For small changes in price about P_1^1, there is *no change* in expenditure on X_2 (the same amount is bought and the price of X_2 is unchanged), hence there is *no change* in expenditure on X_1. That is, when the PCC is flat, own-price changes lead to proportional changes in consumption of the good whose price changes; own-price elasticity is 1. But what about the cross-price elasticity when the PCC is flat? It must be zero! Since there is no change in X_2 consumed when the price of X_1 changes and the PCC is flat, there is said to be an "independence of wants" between the goods. They are neither substitutes nor complements.

What about the upward- or downward-sloping portions of the price-consumption curve?

If the PCC is downward sloping, as at *a* in Figure 6-7, the lowering of the price of X_1 results in less of X_2 being bought. Since the price of X_2 hasn't changed, less is spent on X_2, hence with money income fixed *more* is spent on X_1. It must be the case, then, that the proportional increase in X_1 consumption at lower prices more than offsets the price reduction. That is, the percentage increase in quantity is larger than the percentage price reduction, which means the demand for X_1 is *price elastic* over this range. Hence when the PCC curve is falling the own-price elasticity must be greater than 1. What about the cross-price elasticity? Since lowering the price of X_1 decreases the quantity of X_2 demanded, X_1 and X_2 are **gross substitutes**

FIGURE 6-7

Own-Price and Cross-Price Elasticities and the Price-Consumption Curve
The negatively sloped portion of the PCC indicates that own-elasticity exceeds 1 and that cross-elasticity exceeds zero. At point *b* the PCC is flat, own-elasticity equals 1, and cross-elasticity equals 0. The rising portion of the PCC corresponds to an inelastic portion of the demand curve for X_1 and a negative cross-elasticity.

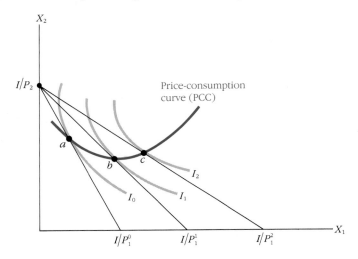

If the PCC is upward sloping, the argument reverses: Since more X_2 is bought when the price of X_1 falls, less is being spent on X_1. Hence the proportional price reduction is larger than the proportional increase in demand at lower prices. Thus, the demand for X_1 is *price inelastic* if the PCC slopes upward. As for the cross-price effect, the price reduction of X_1 causes more X_2 to be purchased, hence X_1 and X_2 are **gross complements** in this case.[6]

Income

A second major determinant of consumption demand is household income. The functional relationship between quantity demanded and income *(ceteris paribus),* and thus the income elasticity of demand, varies greatly among different goods in terms of the nature of consumer preferences and the behavior of marginal utility (or marginal rate

---

[6]The term *gross* here refers to gross of income effects; since the price of X_1 is falling with unchanged X_2 price and unchanged money income, real utility (or real income) is rising. More can be purchased of *both* goods unless no X_1 was bought prior to the price reduction. Note that this is not quite the concept of substitutability or complementarity that one might desire, since the income effect will *tend* to make goods appear complementary (except for inferior goods). Hence, if we only had two goods, they would *have* to be substitutes, holding *utility constant* (indifference curves are downward sloping between goods).

of substitution) as additional units are acquired. The more rapid the rate of decline in marginal utility (or the marginal rate of substitution) as income rises, the lower the income elasticity. High positive income elasticity is characteristic of many so-called luxuries, items not imperative for a minimum living standard but highly desired once incomes reach a certain level. Low income elasticity is characteristic of goods the desire for which is quickly satisfied.

The response of demand to income changes can be illustrated with the use of indifference curves by showing progressively higher budget lines (drawn *parallel* to indicate unchanged relative prices). Larger amounts available for spending, with a given pattern of indifference curves, will result in an **income-consumption curve** (ICC) connecting the best consumption points (tangencies) at each income level. Figures 6-8(a,b,c) show, respectively, goods of high positive, low positive, and negative income elasticity.

As noted in Chapter 3, income elasticity is negative for inferior goods; the quantities purchased will fall as income rises. These are goods like cheap cuts of meat or second-hand clothing, which consumers generally buy only because they cannot yet afford more expensive substitutes. As incomes rise, persons will shift to preferred substitutes and decrease their demand for the inferior goods. Such a case is shown in Figure 6-8(c), where good X_1 is inferior.

Studies of income elasticity of demand for various goods were among the first

---

FIGURE 6-8

Income Elasticity

An increase in income, shifting the budget line to the right and parallel to the original budget line, increases the amount of X_1 desired from a to b in part (a). The income-consumption curve, ICC, shows the optimum combinations of X_1 and X_2 as income changes. The relatively flat slope of the ICC signifies a large response in the demand for X_1 as income changes and a high income elasticity. In part (b), the rise in income induces a smaller increase in the demand for X_1 (a to b). The ICC is steeper, and the income elasticity is lower. The downward-sloping ICC in part (c) indicates that an income boost reduces the demand for X_1 from a to b. Thus, in part (c), X_1 is an inferior good and the income elasticity is negative.

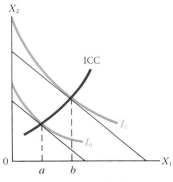

(a) High positive income elasticity

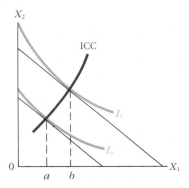

(b) Low positive income elasticity

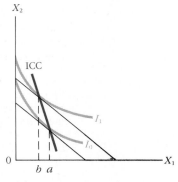

(c) Negative income elasticity

empirical studies in economics. The pioneer work was that of Engel, who discovered the relationships now known as Engel's laws (or, graphically, as Engel curves). Greater availability of data has allowed much more exhaustive research on the question in recent years. One of Engel's laws, that food consumption rises less rapidly than income, has been confirmed many times. Most studies have found elasticities approaching unity for clothing and education, and high elasticities for recreation, personal care, home operation, and other services. There are, of course, significant variations based on family characteristics and preferences. (See Box 6-4.)

The derivation of an Engel curve is straightforward, as shown in Figure 6-9(a) and (b). At the initial money income level M_1, X_1^0 units of X_1 were consumed, as seen in Figure 6-9(a). This point is plotted as point a on the Engel curve for good X_1 in Figure 6-9(b). Doubling income from M_1 to M_2, leads to a somewhat less than doubled X_1 demand, and this combination of income and X_1 demand (M_2, X_2) is plotted as point b in Figure 6-9(b). An equivalent further increase in money income (note that this is now a 50-percent increase) leads to further increases in X_1 demand, as drawn in Figure 6-9(a); this increase is proportionately smaller than the increase in money income. This is plotted as point c' in Figure 6-9(b); connecting all such points yields the Engel curve.

Consumer Preferences—Tastes

The quantities of various goods purchased depend upon the intensity of consumers' preference for the goods, which in turn depends upon a wide variety of social, cli-

---

6-4   Can an income-consumption curve be constructed for a good that is first normal but becomes inferior at higher levels?

Yes. As the budget line moves out from L_0 to L_1 and our new consumer optima point b, this consumer increases consumption of good X_1 and of good X_2. However, when income rises to the level reflected by budget line L_2 and consumer optima point c, the consumer reduces consumption of good X_1 and increases consumption of good X_2. Thus, as income increases, this consumer reduced consumption of good X_1. For example, if income increases slightly, one might consume more hamburger; if income increases still more, one might switch to steak.

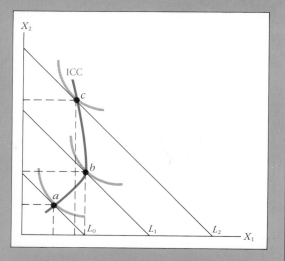

FIGURE 6-9

The Engel Curve: Readily Derivable from the Income-Consumption Curve

The relationship between money income and demand for a commodity is depicted by the Engel curve. Each budget line in part (a) corresponds to a different income level, and each tangent point on the ICC shows the optimum amount of goods X_1 and X_2 for a consumer. The combinations of good X_1 and income along the Engel curve in part (b) can be read directly from the ICC diagram.

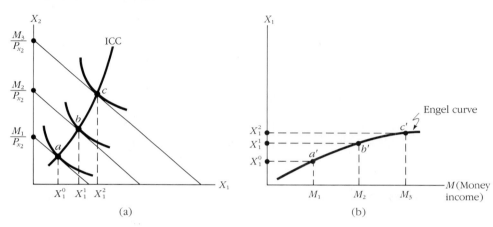

(a)   (b)

matic, demographic and economic factors about which we have little knowledge. In the actual process of decision making, moreover, habit plays an extremely important role, in part because habit buying saves time for the customer. Numerous studies have shown a wide variation in the care exercised in consumer decisions, particularly on consumer durables. Such decisions are also subject to outside deliberate influence in the form of advertising.

Changes in preferences naturally lead to shifts in demand schedules. The power of economic theory, however, stems from the assumption (usually implicit) that tastes are stable, at least over substantial periods of time. *If* tastes are in fact stable, then only changing opportunities (relative prices and income) will alter an individual's behavior. And we are generally much more interested in *changes* in behavior than we are in *levels* of behavior.

Tastes *do* change, though. A person may well grow tired of one type of recreation or mayonnaise or heating fuel and try another type. Changes in occupation, number of dependents, state of health, and age tend to alter preferences. The birth of a baby may cause a family to spend less on recreation and more on food. Illness increases the demand for medicine and lessens purchases of other goods. A cold winter increases the demand for fuel. Changes in customs and traditions also affect preferences; changing styles in clothing, for example, produce significant modifications in demand. In addition, successful advertising campaigns divert purchases from some products to others. Development of new products draws consumer preference away from other goods: digital audio products (for example, compact discs) have replaced analog equipment (for example, record albums), just as the jet very quickly eliminated consumers' preferences for "prop planes."

Expectations about Future Prices

The height of a demand schedule this period, for individuals as well as the market, is affected by expectations about prices in future periods. This influence is in a sense transitory, since consumers will not continue indefinitely to buy in anticipation of future higher prices, nor will they continue to postpone purchases of desired goods if expected price decreases fail to materialize. At any given time, though, expectations may be of substantial importance, and changes in them may produce major shifts in demand schedules. If consumers expect price increases, they may buy large quantities in anticipation of the increases and thus cause substantial increases in demand. If decreases come to be expected, buyers may reduce current purchases drastically. The impact on current demand will, for durable goods, alter current stock holdings which will in turn affect future market demand. That is, expectations leading to greater demand now will lead to less demand in the future for durable goods. (See Chapter 4 on stocks and flows.)

6.5 THE COLLECTION OF DEMAND SCHEDULE DATA

At any time a certain demand schedule exists for each good, in the sense that if definite prices prevail, consumers will wish to purchase certain definite quantities. It is difficult, however, to determine this schedule with any degree of accuracy. For most goods, total sales in particular markets with existing prices can be ascertained; many data are collected by various private and government agencies at the present time. But the figures may not represent optimum quantities, in that consumers may not have completed adjustments to the governing circumstances. Moreover, quantities that would be demanded at other prices can only be estimated with the aid of statistics of sales at various prices in the past. The greatest care must be used in interpreting these statistics, since the changes in sales from one period to another are due not only to price changes but also to changes in other determinants of demand. Incomes, preferences, prices of other goods, and expectations are constantly changing. It is possible to isolate the effects of these other changes by various statistical techniques, but such techniques are by no means entirely accurate or reliable. It is particularly difficult to determine the effects on sales of changes in tastes that may occur during a period for which data are available. Thus, statistical estimates of demand schedules necessarily involve a substantial margin of error. Such work is nevertheless of great value in providing additional information about demand behavior.

SUMMARY

1. The price consumption curve for good X_1 is derived by connecting the tangency points of the indifference curves and budget lines as the price of X_1 changes (holding money income, tastes, and other prices constant).

2. When the price of a good falls (rises), the consumer will be able to buy more (less) of this good or other goods. Thus the price reduction (increase) leads to an increase (decrease) in real income. This income effect of the price decrease is positive for normal goods.

3. The substitution effect of a price change results in a consumer substituting a good which has become relatively less expensive for a good which has become relatively more expensive.

4. Elasticity of demand is influenced by substitutability, the satiability of wants, durability of the product, time intervals, and other factors. The elasticity of the total demand schedule is determined by the individual demand schedules that underlie it.

5. The level of the demand schedule is determined by the price of substitutes and complements, income, consumer preferences (tastes), and expectations about future prices.

6. The nature of the cross-elasticity of demand between two goods depends upon the relative influences of the income and substitution effects. The higher the positive cross-elasticity, the greater the ease of substitution. A negative cross-elasticity means that either the goods are complements or the income effect of a price change outweighs the substitution effect.

7. The income-consumption curves connect the best consumption points (tangencies) at each income level. Goods that are inferior have an income elasticity that is negative. Low-income-elasticity goods are those for which the desire is quickly satisfied as incomes rise. High positive income elasticities usually denote so-called luxury goods.

WORDS AND CONCEPTS FOR REVIEW

price-consumption curve
uncompensated demand curve
compensated demand curve
income effect
substitution effect

substitutability
price consumption curves
gross substitutes
gross complements
income-consumption curve

REVIEW QUESTIONS

1. Distinguish between the price-consumption curve and the demand curve.

2. Explain how the demand schedule can be derived from schedules of indifference curves and budget lines.

3. Distinguish between the income and substitution effect of a change in the price of one good. Illustrate your answer graphically.

4. On the basis of common sense, would you expect purchases of the following goods to be highly responsive or relatively unresponsive to changes in their price? Why?
a) cigarettes   d) theater tickets
b) fur coats   e) insulin
c) appendectomies   f) table grapes

5. It has been said that the utility-maximizing approach to the theory of consumer demand merely tells us that the household acts as it wishes to act—which is not a theory at all. Do you agree or disagree? Explain.

6. List some of the determinants of the elasticity of demand.

7. What determinants establish the height of the demand schedule?

SUGGESTED READINGS

Friedman, M. *Price Theory.* Chicago: Aldine Publishing Company, 1976, Chapter 2.

Henderson, J. M. and Quandt, R. E. *Microeconomic Theory,* 3rd ed. New York: McGraw-Hill, 1980, Chapter 2.

Hicks, J. R. *Value and Capital,* 2nd ed. Oxford: The Clarendon Press, 1946, Chapters 1 and 2.

Stigler, G. *The Theory of Price,* 4th ed. New York: Macmillan, 1987, Chapter 4.

7

The Theory of
Production

7.1 INTRODUCTION

Having completed our discussion of consumer demand, we turn now to the output and supply side of final product markets—the theory of production and cost. Our point of departure is the principle of profit maximization, the assumption that the object of the business firm is to maximize the difference between total revenue and total cost. This requires, among other conditions, that the firm purchase and combine factor inputs in such a way that the total cost of producing any particular level of output is the lowest possible figure, given existing technological and institutional conditions. This chapter is concerned with the reactions of output to changes in inputs of various factors.[1]

The typical business firm manages a substantial portfolio of financial and physical goods, equipment, machinery, land, and buildings. The financial-management side of a firm's activities is not rigidly linked with its production activities. A firm that requires additional space need not purchase a building outright, for it may buy a plant from another business firm or lease space from one of its divisions to provide space for another. Similarly, in deciding how to divide earnings between payments to owners and savings on its own account, a business firm's actions seldom impinge directly on current production decisions. An efficient management will attempt to conduct its production, marketing, and financial management activities so that joint returns are optimized. We first examine the theory of production as an essentially separate branch of the general theory of business behavior.

---

[1]The behavior of cost in response to changes in output will be discussed in Chapter 8. The determination of market prices through the mutual interplay of demand and output-supply considerations will be examined in Chapters 9–12.

7.2 THE PRODUCTION FUNCTION

We begin by supposing that the maximum amount of any product that a firm can produce with any given collection of factor inputs is determined by prevailing institutional circumstances and by the existing state of technical knowledge. The relationship between the inputs and the outputs is expressed symbolically by a **production function** of the general form

$$q = f(V_1, V_2, \ldots, V_n)$$

where the variables $V_1, V_2, \ldots, V_n$ represent quantities of various factor inputs, and the variable q represents the maximum output that the firm can produce with a given set of the input variables. We may assume that the effect of an increase in any of the input variables is, at least up to some limit, to increase output. We may also assume that the proportions in which various factor inputs can be combined to produce a given quantity of output are normally variable. Cases of fixed proportions (at least among ingredients) are found in certain chemical processes; but otherwise, experience indicates that input proportions can be varied significantly with output at a constant level. Thus one type of material can be substituted for another in the production of houses or automobiles; capital equipment may be substituted for labor in the production of long-distance phone calls or secretarial services, and so on.

7.3 TYPICAL OUTPUT BEHAVIOR: ONE VARIABLE INPUT

Suppose that the input of just one factor is varied, while all other inputs are held constant. What will be the behavior of total output in these circumstances? Common sense suggests that output will start at a low (possibly zero) level and increase—perhaps rapidly at first, then more slowly—as the amount of the variable input increases, until the quantity of the variable input becomes so large in relation to the quantity of other inputs that further increases in output become more and more difficult or even impossible. Beyond this point, additional units of the variable input may even result in a decline in total output. The implied pattern of output behavior is illustrated in Figure 7-1 by the curve $q = f(V)$. The intuitive plausibility of this pattern may be strengthened by considering alternative interpretations of the variables V and q.

Suppose that q represents the output (in horsepower) of an electric motor and V represents the input of electric energy (in watts). At zero input, the motor does not turn; as energy input rises, the motor turns with increasing speed and delivers ever-greater amounts of mechanical power until the capacity of the motor (fixed factor) is reached, after which power output does not increase and may even decrease (through overheating of bearings or actual breakdown).

Alternatively, suppose that q represents your cumulative grade point average, while V represents your average weekly input of study hours. Depending on your intelligence, the quality of your personal and college libraries, the competence of your teachers, the personality of your roommate, and other factors, the curve relating your input to your output may be relatively steep or relatively flat, but its general shape will surely be as illustrated in Figure 7-1.

FIGURE 7-1

Total Product Curve: One Variable Input with Fixed Input(s)
The graphical representation of the production function when one input varies and all others are fixed is the total product curve. It shows the potential output produced by various quantities of the variable input V and the fixed inputs.

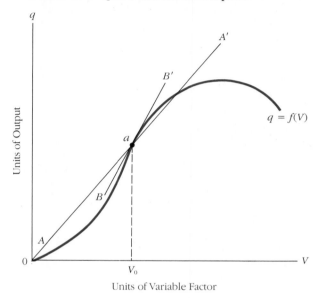

7.4 AVERAGE AND MARGINAL PRODUCTS

To facilitate subsequent analysis, it is convenient to introduce two new concepts at this point: *average product* (AP) and *marginal product* (MP). The **average product** of an input is defined as the ratio of total output to the quantity of the input used; in symbols:

$$AP = \frac{q}{V} = \frac{f(V)}{V}$$

(Strictly speaking, this formula refers to the average product of one input, other inputs being given; in general, therefore, we have one such formula for each distinct input.) The magnitude of this ratio corresponding to any given value of V (say, V_0) is represented in Figure 7-1 by the slope of a straight line (V_{0_a}) connecting the origin with the point on the total product curve that lies directly above V_0 (point a in Figure 7-1). The slope of such a line obviously will vary continuously with variations in V. This is illustrated in Figure 7-2, which depicts in a single chart the total product curve from Figure 7-1 (shown as TP) and the average product curve (AP) that corresponds to it.

FIGURE 7-2

Product Behavior as One Variable Factor Input Is Increased, with Other Factors Fixed

The MP, or slope of the TP curve, reaches a maximum when the TP curve is steepest at its inflection point. MP equals zero when the TP curve is flat at its maximum. The AP, or slope of a ray to the TP curve, is maximum at the steepest ray which is tangent to the TP curve. Thus, AP = MP when AP is maximum. A rising AP curve characterizes stage one, whereas positive but declining productivity designates stage two. Stage three exhibits a negative MP.

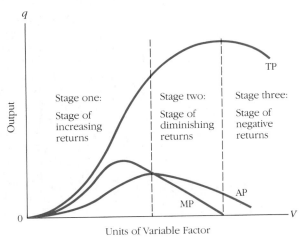

The **marginal product** of any single input is defined as the change in total output resulting from a small change in the input.[2]

$$MP = \frac{\Delta q}{\Delta V}$$

The marginal product of an input can be described as the ratio of a *small change* in output (usually denoted by Δq) to a *small change* in input (denoted by ΔV). For the total curve at the point a, one need only draw the tangent to the curve at that point, where the slope of the tangent is the marginal product. (This slope is approximated by the slope of any line that passes through a and another point on $f(V)$ that lies "close" to the point a.) The slope of the tangent to the total product curve obviously varies continuously with variations in V, and this slope shows the rate at which output increases for small changes in V at various levels of V. This is illustrated by the marginal product curve, MP, as shown in Figure 7-2.

The relation between the AP, MP, and TP curves in Figure 7-2 and Table 7-1 merits close examination. Where the MP curve lies *above* the AP curve, the AP curve rises from

---

[2]The marginal product, then, is the partial derivative of the production function with respect to one input, the values of all other inputs being held constant. If $q = f(V)$, the marginal product is $\frac{\partial q}{\partial V} = f'(V)$.

left to right. This corresponds to the familiar fact that adding a number to a sequence of numbers whose previous average value is less than the number added increases the average value of the sequence. For a similar reason, whenever the MP curve lies *below* the AP curve, the AP curve declines from left to right. Hence, the MP curve intersects the AP curve at the highest point of the latter; where the MP curve lies neither above nor below the AP curve, the AP curve can be neither rising nor falling. Note also that where the TP curve reaches its peak, the MP curve intersects the horizontal axis (the slope of TP is zero); that is, further increases in the input cause total product to decline.

The intersection of the MP curve, first with the peak of the AP curve and then with the horizontal axis, serves to demarcate three stages that are typical of most production processes: an initial stage of *increasing average returns* (where MP exceeds AP); an intermediate stage of *diminishing average returns* (where MP is less than AP but MP is positive); a terminal stage of *negative marginal returns* (where total product declines). The three stages are indicated in Figure 7-2 by the broken lines, one passing through the highest point of the AP curve and the other passing through the highest point of the TP curve. (See Box 7-1.)

TABLE 7-1

Typical Output Behavior with One Variable Factor

Units of Variable Factor V	Total Output q	Average Physical Product q/V	Marginal Physical Product $\Delta q/\Delta V$
1	12	12.00	12
2	28	14.00	16
3	52	17.33	24
4	74	18.50	22
5	91	18.20	17
6	104	17.33	13
7	114	16.29	10
8	120	15.00	6
9	121	13.44	1
10	115	11.50	−6

7-1   If output is 70 units a day with nine workers employed, and would be 73 units if ten workers were employed, what is the marginal product of the tenth worker?

Three units. More precisely, the marginal product of three units is a result of the *change* in workers from nine to ten. It doesn't matter who was first or last, if labor is "homogeneous," but customarily we speak of marginal product in relation to the additional factor unit added (the tenth worker in this example).

7.5 THE BEHAVIOR OF OUTPUT WITH VARYING PROPORTIONS: THE LAW OF DIMINISHING RETURNS

What forces are responsible for the changing rate of output as proportions of the factors are varied? There are two primary considerations:

1. The utilization of certain factor units cannot be effective without a certain minimum number of units of other factors (indivisibilities).
2. The operation of the Law of Diminishing Returns.

The first consideration is obvious; the second requires examination.

The **Law of Diminishing Returns** is one of the oldest and most widely accepted laws in economic analysis. According to this law, if the quantities of certain factors are increased while the quantities of other factors are held constant, beyond a certain point the rate of increase in output, and thus the marginal product of the variable factors, will decline. Since the decline in the rate of increase in output will continue from its onset, eventually the rate of increase in output will drop below the rate of increase in the inputs of the variable factors, and average physical product will also fall. (Were this not the case, the entire world's supply of wheat could be grown in a single flower pot.)

The law is strictly relevant only to those situations in which factor proportions are varied—that is, where some factors are increased in quantity relative to the quantities of others. It is not applicable if all factors are varied in the same proportion, as when the quantities of all factors employed are doubled (perhaps replicating a firm).

The Law of Diminishing Returns is based upon two premises. First, given technology is assumed: the law is relevant to the behavior of output when factor inputs are varied within the framework of available methods and techniques. For clarity of analysis, it is necessary to distinguish clearly between the effects of changes in factor proportions, as such, and the effects of improved technological methods—even though both types of changes may occur at the same time. Second, it is assumed that units of the various factors employed are homogeneous, any unit being of equal efficiency and thus interchangeable with any other unit. The effects of using factor units of varying efficiency, while perhaps important, are distinct from those of varying factor combinations, which underlie the Law of Diminishing Returns. (See Box 7-2.)

7-2 What is responsible for the operation of the Law of Diminishing Returns?

Essentially, marginal physical product decreases because each successive unit of the variable factor has a smaller quantity of fixed factor units with which to work. Once the point is reached at which the number of variable units is adequate to utilize the available fixed factor units efficiently, further increases in the variable factor will add progressively less to total product.

With this preliminary survey of the Law of Diminishing Returns completed, it is now possible to analyze the behavior of average and marginal product in the successive stages of increasing, diminishing, and negative returns.

The Stage of Increasing Returns

The initial rise in marginal and average product is due to the more effective use of fixed factor units (and possibly other variable factor units) as the number of units of the variable factor under consideration is increased. A conveyor belt is of little value with a single worker; as additional workers are added to the assembly line, marginal and average product initially rise.

When the number of variable factors is extremely small, the Law of Diminishing Returns operates negatively relative to the variable factors or, in other words, in a positive way relative to the fixed factor. That is, the quantity of the fixed factor is so great that efficiency of operation is interfered with, and production would actually be greater if some of the fixed factor units were disposed of. There are so many units of fixed factors that in effect they get in the way of other factors.[3] If one man tried to operate a large department store alone—doing work of all types necessary in the store—his energies would be spread so thinly in so many directions that total output (sales) might be less than if he were operating a smaller store (that is, working with less capital). As successive workers were added, up to a certain number, each worker would add more to total product than the previous one.

More significantly, the stage of increasing returns can be attributed to the greater efficiency in the use of certain fixed and variable factor units as they are combined with large quantities of other factors. For example, certain types of capital equipment may require a minimum number of workers for efficient operation, or perhaps any operation at all. With a small number of variable factors, some machines cannot operate at

---

[3]For a broad class of (linearly homogenous) production functions considered later, it is the case that the interpretation of Figure 7-2 is fully symmetric. Just as the marginal product of the variable input being negative in Stage Three means there is too much of that input relative to the fixed input, similarly, in Stage One, there is so much of the *fixed* input that it (unobserved in Figure 7-2) has a negative marginal product when employed with so little of the variable input. Illustrating with the so-called Cobb-Douglas production function:

$$q = V_1^\alpha V_2^{1-\alpha}$$

where V_1 = labor and V_2 = capital.

In Stage One, marginal product is greater than average product, or

$$\frac{\partial q}{\partial V_1} = \alpha V_1^{\alpha-1} V_2^{1-\alpha} > \frac{q}{V_1} = V_1^{\alpha-1} V_2^{1-\alpha}$$

But, for this inequality to hold, α must be greater than 1. Look now at the marginal product of capital:

$$\frac{\partial q}{\partial V_2} = (1-\alpha) V_1^\alpha V_2^{-\alpha} = (1-\alpha) \left(\frac{V_1}{V_2}\right)^\alpha$$

Since $\alpha > 1$, $\partial q/\partial V_2$ is < 0; that is, negative marginal product of the *other* factor.

all, or only at a very low level of efficiency. As additional variable factor units are added, machines are brought into efficient operation, and thus marginal product of the variable factors rises sharply.

Similarly, additional units of the variable factors may permit more effective utilization of their services.[4] Some tasks are inherently difficult for one person alone to perform; adding a second person may far more than double output. This is true, for example, of laying brick on the wall of a house: without a helper, the bricklayer will waste a great deal of time and energy climbing up and down with bricks. Similarly, two persons can get the hay crop into a barn in much less than half the time required for one person, with given equipment and techniques. (See Box 7-3.)

The Stage of Diminishing Returns

The second stage, that of output increasing at a decreasing rate, results from the operation of the Law of Diminishing Returns, once the point is reached at which the number of variable factor units is sufficient to allow efficient utilization of the fixed factors. Further increase in the number of variable factor units results in a decline in marginal product (and eventually average product), because the number of fixed factor units has become smaller compared to the number of variable units.

The exact behavior of total product (and thus marginal and average product) and

---

[4]In a sense, this is an aspect of specialization. Since the primary advantages of specialization are obtained only when all factors can be adjusted, the principal discussion of this question is postponed until Section 7.7.

7-3   True or False?   In some lines of production the stage of increasing returns may never manifest itself at all.

True. If the variable factor units cannot be obtained in small units (for example, if workers cannot be hired for periods shorter than a day or a week), the first unit of the variable factor may carry production out of the increasing returns stage; thus the firm would never be aware that such a stage existed. Only if the variable factor could be added in much smaller units would the stage be noticeable. Thus, in a small store, the adding of one worker may carry operations into the decreasing returns stage: the marginal product of a second worker will be less than that of the first. Likewise, if the fixed factor units are divisible into very small units, increasing returns may never be encountered, since it may be possible to set aside a portion of them and concentrate the work of variable units on only a small portion of fixed factors. More importantly (as will be clarified later), though the first stage *may* exist, we would never expect to observe a firm operating in that range, as more profit can be earned by hiring more of the variable factor.

the actual output figures at which marginal and average product begin to diminish depend upon the nature of the production process and the character of the fixed and variable factor units involved. If the fixed factors consist of a large number of machines that can be operated with small amounts of variable factors (materials and labor primarily), then marginal product is likely to be more or less constant over a substantial range as variable factors are increased, since additional units will be used to operate previously idle machines. Similarly, in a store with given physical plant, portions of the store might simply be closed off when the number of workers is small; as more workers are hired, additional portions of the store would be utilized. Thus, for a substantial range, each successive worker might make possible the same increase in sales volume.

On the other hand, if the fixed factors consist of a large, indivisible, and unadaptable unit—that is, if the group of fixed factors requires certain amounts of variable factors in order to be used at all—then marginal product, after initially rising rapidly, will fall very sharply once the necessary number of variable units has been obtained. For example, if a transit company is to operate one bus run a day between two points, one driver and a certain amount of gasoline are necessary; but the marginal productivity of a second employee on the bus or of additional gasoline is virtually zero. (See Box 7-4.)

The Stage of Negative Returns

The third stage, one which a firm *never* knowingly allows itself to reach, is that in which the use of additional variable factor units actually reduces total output, and marginal product is therefore negative.[5] In such a situation, there are so many units of the variable factor that efficient use of the fixed factor units is impaired. Too many workers in a store make it difficult for customers to shop; too many workers in a factory get in one another's way; too many cooks spoil the soup. In such situations, a reduction in the number of variable units will actually *increase* total output.

---

[5]Only in the bizarre case of a negative factor price—paying the firm to employ people, for example—would a firm knowingly hire inputs with negative marginal product.

7-4   Can you think of a restaurant situation in which fixed factors have a negative marginal product?

When the volume of business is light and only a few waitresses are needed, portions of the dining rooms will be closed off, so that the waitresses will not have to cover unnecessarily large areas. Thus the marginal product of employing the additional land and capital is negative.

7.6 OPTIMUM FACTOR COMBINATIONS: TWO VARIABLE INPUTS

Because marginal product and average product change as factor proportions are varied, and because each factor has a different cost, some factor combinations are more economical than others for the production of a given level of output. A major task of the business firm is the selection of the factor combination which is the optimum, in the sense of allowing lowest cost of producing any given level of output. The optimum factor combination cannot be determined solely on the basis of the production function—that is, on the basis of technological conditions and the behavior of physical output—since the relative economic efficiency of different combinations is dependent upon the prices which must be paid for various factor units. Indeed, even if every country possessed the same technical expertise, basic goods such as food and clothing would still be produced very differently in countries with abundant labor and scarce capital than in countries oppositely endowed.

The Marginal Rate of Technical Substitution

Explanation of the optimum factor combination can be facilitated by the concept of the marginal rate of substitution (usually called **marginal rate of technical substitution**, MRTS, to distinguish it from substitution in consumption along an indifference curve). As applied to factors, the MRTS is the number of units of one factor necessary to replace a unit of another factor and maintain the same level of output.

Suppose, for example, that steel and aluminum are substitutes in the manufacture of washing machines. For the production of a given number of washers, various possible combinations of the two metals (together with given quantities of other factors) may be used, as illustrated in Table 7-2. At one extreme, if only steel were used, ten tons

TABLE 7-2

**Various Combinations of Aluminum and Steel
Which Will Permit an Output of 200 Washing Machines per Day**

Aluminum (tons)	Steel (tons)	Marginal Rate of Technical Substitution of Aluminum for Steel
0	10	
		4
1	6	
		3
2	3	
		2
3	1	
		3/4
4	1/4	
		1/4
5	0	

would be required. At the other extreme, if only aluminum were used, five tons would be required. There are various intermediate combinations; for example if two tons of aluminum are used, three tons of steel will also be needed. Note that the various combinations are alternative possibilities for the production of a given quantity of the product, 200 washers in the example.

For each quantity of aluminum used, there is a marginal rate of substitution of aluminum for steel—that is, a quantity of steel which must be added to allow replacement of a ton of aluminum with steel while producing the same level of output. For example, if five units of aluminum (and no steel) are now being used, only one quarter of a ton of steel must be added to allow the elimination of one ton of aluminum. On the other hand, if two tons of aluminum (and three tons of steel) are now being used, three additional tons of steel must be added to allow reduction of aluminum input to one ton.

The Principle of Diminishing Marginal Rate of Technical Substitution

As illustrated by the data in Table 7-2, the greater the quantity of aluminum used, the smaller the quantity of steel which must be added to allow the elimination of one ton of aluminum. In other words, the greater the extent to which steel is replaced by aluminum, the lower will be the marginal rate of technical substitution—the quantity of steel necessary to replace a unit of aluminum and maintain output. This relationship is known as the **Law of Diminishing Marginal Rate of Technical Substitution**. It is essentially an extension of the Law of Diminishing Returns to the relationship between two factors. The law may be stated more precisely in this manner: As the quantity of any one factor is increased relative to the quantity of the other, output being constant, the number of units of the second which can be replaced by one unit of the first falls, because the marginal product of the first factor falls relative to that of the second.

For purposes of simplicity, Table 7-2 is set up with a diminishing marginal rate of technical substitution of aluminum for steel over the entire range of the table. Actually, if in a particular case there is a stage of increasing marginal returns for the variable factor, the marginal rate of technical substitution will rise initially, since the replacement of aluminum (of which there is too much) by steel (of which there is too little) will facilitate efficiency in production. As soon as the stage of diminishing returns for the factor being increased is encountered, however, the marginal rate of technical substitution will fall.

The rate at which the marginal rate of technical substitution falls is a measure of the extent to which the two factors are substitutes for each other. If they are perfect substitutes—that is, if either factor can be used equally well to produce the product—the marginal rate of technical substitution will not fall. If steel and aluminum can be used equally well to produce all of the metal parts of a washer, the marginal rate of technical substitution will remain unchanged—regardless of the extent to which substitution is carried in either direction.

At the other extreme, two factors may not be substitutes at all for a particular purpose (perhaps in the production of a chemical compound requiring a fixed recipe); here the marginal rate of technical substitution is undefinable, since output cannot be maintained if one factor is replaced by the other. If this relationship exists among all factors used by the firm, the factor combination employed is dictated entirely by technological conditions, and no substitution is possible.[6] (See Box 7-5.)

For purposes of simplification, the marginal rate of technical substitution and its behavior has been explained in terms of two factors. When a firm is using a large number of factors, there are separate marginal rates of technical substitution between each pair of factors employed, and the principles outlined above apply to any two factors, and thus to all of them (as was the case with consumer substitution).

The Isoquant Graph

The various combinations of two factors which will allow the production of a given quantity of output can be illustrated graphically, with the quantity of one factor measured on the vertical axis and the quantity of the other on the horizontal axis. The curve showing the various factor combinations which will produce a given output is known as an **isoquant**. In Figure 7-3, tons of aluminum are measured on the vertical axis, tons of steel on the horizontal axis; isoquant q shows the various combinations of the two factors which will allow the production of 200 washers per day (with given quantities of other factors), based upon the data in Table 7-2.

The slope of the isoquant at any particular point shows the marginal rate of technical substitution between the two factors at that point. Under ordinary circumstances, the isoquant will be convex to the point of origin, because of the Law of Diminishing Marginal Rate of Technical Substitution. The greater the quantity of one factor used, the smaller is the quantity of the other factor needed to replace a unit of the first factor and maintain output. Thus the right-hand portion of the isoquant is almost parallel to the horizontal axis, while the left-hand portion is almost parallel to the vertical axis.

---

[6]These types of production relationships are called "fixed coefficient," or linear technologies.

7-5   True or False?   If two factors are partial substitutes for one another, the marginal rate of technical substitution will vary as factor proportions are altered, ranging in some cases from infinity to values near or equal to zero.

True. Suppose that in the production of washers, either steel or aluminum can be used for most purposes, but steel is essential for some purposes because aluminum lacks sufficient strength for performing the task. In this case, once the quantity of steel has been reduced to the minimum amount required, the marginal rate of technical substitution will become infinite, since output cannot be maintained if substitution is carried further.

FIGURE 7-3

Isoquant Showing Various Combinations of Aluminum and Steel Which Can Be Used to Produce 200 Washing Machines

The isoquant q indicates that 200 washing machines can be produced with 5 tons of aluminum, 10 tons of steel, or 1 ton of aluminum together with 6 tons of steel. All other combinations of aluminum and steel capable of manufacturing 200 washing machines are also charted along isoquant q.

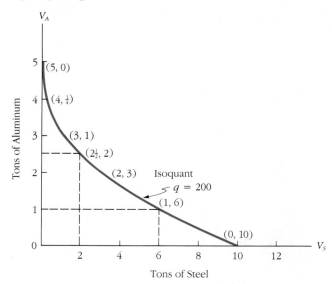

The Isoquant Graph: Increasing and Diminishing Returns

The isoquants in Figure 7-4 indicate alternative combinations of factors V_1 and V_2 that can be used to produce various integral amounts $1, 2, 3, 4, \ldots,$ of an output q (you may think of the integers as representing thousands or millions). Starting at point R in the short run in which the quantity of factor V_1 is held constant at two units, one unit of factor V_2 is needed to increase output from 2 to 3 units moving along RS. To *increase* output by an additional unit (from 3 to 4) then requires *less* than an additional unit of factor V_2—indicating increasing returns. To increase output by yet another unit (from 4 to 5), however, requires *more* than a one-unit increase in factor V_2, and similarly thereafter—indicating that diminishing returns set in after output exceeds 4 units. These relationships are indicated in Figure 7-4 by that fact that the distance between successive isoquants first decreases and then increases as we move along RS.

The Optimum Factor Combination

Knowledge of the marginal rates of technical substitution between two goods does not in itself indicate the optimum quantities of each to use, in the sense of revealing that

▄▄▄▄▄▄▄▄

FIGURE 7-4

Increasing and Diminishing Returns as Shown by the Isoquant Technique
Marginal returns, the additional output obtained when one more unit of the variable input
is hired while other inputs remain fixed, can be observed by fixing input V_1 at 2 units and
examining distances between isoquants. Starting with 0 units of input V_2 and adding one
unit yields 1 more unit of q. To produce another unit of q (from $q = 3$ to $q = 4$) requires
less than 1 more unit of V_2; thus, narrower isoquants imply increasing marginal returns.
Producing the fifth unit of output, however, requires more additional units of input V_2
than were necessary for the fourth unit. Increasing distances between isoquants along a
vertical expansion path indicate a region of diminishing marginal returns.

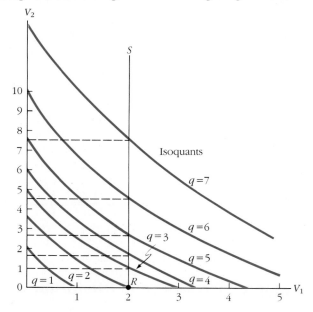

combination which will allow the firm to produce a given level of output at lowest cost.[7]
This combination can be defined only if the costs of the various factors are known as
well as the marginal rates of substitution among them. In the automatic washer example presented in Table 7-2, let us assume that aluminum costs $60 a ton, and steel costs
$30 a ton. Table 7-3 shows the total costs of producing the given number of washers
with various combinations of steel and aluminum, with the assumption that other costs
are constant regardless of the combination of metals employed.

With these data, the least-cost point—and thus the optimum factor combination—is
attained when two tons of aluminum and three tons of steel, are used or when three
tons of aluminum and one ton of steel are used. If the data were broken down in this

---

[7]This is analogous to the theory of consumption—merely knowing preferences does not indicate where on an indifference curve people will consume. How people will actually behave depends on preferences and relative prices at a given level of utility.

TABLE 7-3

**Relative Costs of Producing 200 Washing Machines
with Various Combinations of Steel and Aluminum**

Aluminum (tons)	Steel (tons)	Cost of Aluminum* (dollars)	Cost of Steel** (dollars)	Other Costs (dollars)	Total Cost (dollars)
0	10	0	300	9,000	9,300
1	6	60	180	9,000	9,240
2	3	120	90	9,000	9,210
3	1	180	30	9,000	9,210
4	¼	240	7½	9,000	9,247½
5	0	300	0	9,000	9,300

*Assuming a price of $60 a ton.
**Assuming a price of $30 a ton.

bracket to fractions of a ton, a single combination could be discovered which would allow absolute minimum cost.

The data in Tables 7-2 and 7-3 show that the range of combinations allowing lowest cost is that in which the marginal rate of substitution is 2 to 1, and is thus equal to the ratio of the prices of the two factors (60 to 30). This relationship between the factor-price ratio and the marginal rate of substitution is essential for attainment of the least cost combination.[8] Any deviation from this point will result in an increase in the cost of the added factor of greater magnitude than the reduction in the cost of the replaced factor, and thus in an increase in total cost. For example, on the basis of the data in Table 7-3, if the quantity of aluminum were cut back from two tons to one, the saving in aluminum costs would be $60, whereas the cost of additional steel required to allow production of the same output would be $90 (three tons at $30 per ton). An increase in the quantity of aluminum from three tons to four would add $60 to the cost of the aluminum but would reduce steel costs by only $22.50.

Tangency of the Isoquant with an Isocost Line

The optimum factor combination can be shown graphically by adding to the isoquant graph various **isocost** (equal cost) lines each of which shows the various possible quantities of the two factors which can be purchased with a given outlay of money. The

---

[8]This result should hardly seem surprising in light of consumer utility maximization presented earlier. Maximizing utility, at say, U^*, subject to an expenditure constraint, $\bar{I}$, is formally "dual" to minimizing expenditure (at $\bar{I}$) subject to a utility constraint, U^*. In the present context, minimizing the cost, at say C_0, of producing a given Q_0 will involve the *same* factor quantities demanded as would be the case if one were to maximize quantity producible, at say Q_0, with a cost given to be C_0. This should become quite clear by examining the text graphs.

isoquant shown in Figure 7-3 is reproduced in Figure 7-5 with isocost lines added, showing the various quantities of steel and aluminum which can be purchased with a given outlay of money on the assumption that the prices of aluminum and steel per ton are $60 and $30, respectively. If the given outlay is $210, for example, the isocost line is represented in Figure 7-5 by line A, which indicates that 3½ tons of aluminum can be purchased if only aluminum is purchased, 7 tons of steel if only steel is purchased, and 2 tons of aluminum if 3 tons of steel are used. The isocost relation is a straight line as a matter of mathematical necessity so long as prices paid for factor units are the same regardless of the quantities purchased. There are various possible isocost lines, one for each potential level of outlay on factors, the successive lines being parallel to each other (see lines A, B, and C in Figure 7-5). The farther to the right a line is located, the higher is the level of outlay which it represents.

　　Minimum cost is achieved by choosing the least expensive combination of factor inputs for a given level of output. This combination is represented graphically by the lowest isocost line (the farthest one to the left) which touches the isoquant representing the quantity to be produced. Thus the **optimum factor combination** will be represented by a point of tangency between the given isoquant and the lowest possible isocost line (provided that the isoquant is a smooth curve with diminishing MRTS; if it

---

FIGURE 7-5

**The Optimum Combination of Aluminum and Steel
to Produce 200 Washers per Day**
The isocost lines contain factor combinations that can be hired at the same expense. Minimizing the cost of producing 200 washing machines involves choosing a factor combination on the lowest isocost line that coincides with the 200-unit isoquant. The optimum input combination occurs along the segment between 2 and 3 tons of aluminum.

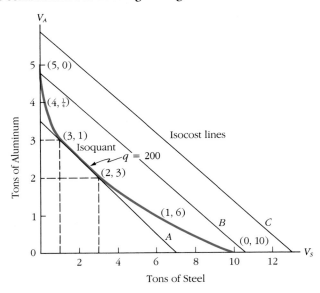

is not, there may be more than one point of tangency and thus more than one "optimum" combination of factors). In Figure 7-5, the tangency condition does not define a single point, but rather a range of points between three tons of steel and two of aluminum, and one ton of steel and three of aluminum. As shown in Table 7-3, it is within this range that the optimum factor combination must lie. If figures for intervals within this range were available, the tangency would appear at a single point, as illustrated in Figure 7-6.

The isocost line which is just tangent to the isoquant allows the acquisition of the necessary factor units with the lowest possible outlay.[9] Any lower line would not allow the purchase of sufficient factors to produce the desired output, while any higher isocost line would entail unnecessarily high factor costs. At any point on the isoquant other than the point of tangency, the outlay on the factors to produce the given output would be higher than that at the tangency point. At the tangency, the slope of the isoquant (which represents the marginal rate of technical substitution between the two factors) is equal to the slope of the isocost line (which represents the ratio of the prices

---

[9]Remember that the isoquant shows the various quantities of the two factors necessary to produce a given output, while each isocost line shows the various quantities of two factors which can be acquired with the expenditure of a given sum of money.

FIGURE 7-6

The Optimum Factor Combination, with Single-Point Tangency
When the isoquant is convex with no flat segments, a single optimum combination can be identified where the isoquant and isocost are tangent. Factor combinations to the northeast of the optimum are more costly, and combinations to the southwest cannot produce the indicated quantity.

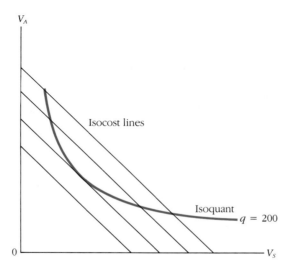

of the two factors), and thus the marginal rate of technical substitution is equal to the ratio of the factor prices.[10]

Factor Price Changes and Factor Substitution

The explanation of the optimum factor combination in the preceding section has, of necessity, been based upon the assumption of given factor prices. It is important, however, to extend the analysis to consider changes in the relative prices of the two factors and consequent changes in quantities of the two factors acquired. The discussion is, as may be suspected, very similar to that of the consumer decision to buy more or less at changed relative prices.

A change in the price of any factor, total output and the prices of the other factors remaining unchanged, will lead to readjustment in factor proportions, since the price change destroys the equality of the price ratio and the marginal rate of technical substitution.[11] The readjustment will continue until this equality is restored. The slower the rate of decline in the marginal rate of technical substitution between two factors, the relatively greater will be the extent of substitution of one factor for another as their relative prices change.

In graphical terms, a change in the price of one factor changes the point of tangency between the isoquant and the isocost line and thus results in a new optimum combination. If the factors are good substitutes, and thus the isoquant has little curvature, the shift of the point of tangency will be substantial (from 0_a to 0_b in Figure 7-7) and the increase in the quantity utilized of the factor which has become cheaper will be relatively great. If the two factors are poor substitutes, the curvature will be sharp and the

---

[10]Formally, to minimize costs, subject to the constraint of producing a fixed quantity

$$\text{Minimize}_{L,K} \quad wL + rK$$
$$\text{s.t.} \quad f(L,K) = \bar{q}$$

where L and K are labor and capital and w and r are wages and rental cost of capital for the same period.

Forming the Lagrangean ($\mathcal{L}$):

$$\text{Minimize}_{L,K,\lambda} = wL + rK + \lambda(\bar{q} - f(L,K))$$

At the optimum least-cost point—the "bottom" of the "valley of costs," we know that small changes in L or K will have a negligible impact on costs or

$$\frac{\partial \mathcal{L}}{\partial L} = w - \lambda f_L(L,K) = 0$$
$$\frac{\partial \mathcal{L}}{\partial K} = f - \lambda f_K(L,K) = 0$$
$$\frac{\partial \mathcal{L}}{\partial \lambda} = \bar{q} - f(L,K) = 0$$

Forming the ratio of the first two equations gives the text result that MRTS = ratio of input prices at the cost minimization. It should be noted that λ is equal to the marginal cost of an added unit of output.

[11]In general, desired total output will be affected by the factor price change. The parallel between the consumer and the firm break down a bit here in that the firm, unlike the consumer, does not maximize output (the analog of utility). Rather, it maximizes profit.

FIGURE 7-7

Readjustment of the Optimum Factor Combination in Response to a Change in the Price of One Factor: High Substitutability

The isoquant for two readily substitutable inputs is nearly linear. An increase in the relative price of input V_2 decreases the slope of the isocost line. The firm will increase its usage of input V_1 substantially from *a* to *b* while continuing to produce the same level of output.

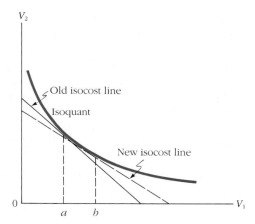

shift in the quantity of the factor acquired will be relatively slight (from 0_a to 0_b in Figure 7-8). (Again, this is but terminologically different from consumer substitution, with the "income effect" being replaced, as we shall see, by both an output effect and a profit-maximizing effect.)

The Scope of Applicability of the Law of Diminishing Returns

The Law of Diminishing Returns is relevant to the behavior of output only when factor proportions are varied. It is most easy to think of this as a situation in which one factor or several factors are increased (or reduced) in quantity while the inputs of the others remain the same. The law is therefore significant under all circumstances (except those of fixed coefficients of production) when a change in relative prices occurs, leading to adjustments of inputs of various factors needed to obtain the optimum factor combination.

The law is also relevant, moreover, for the behavior of total output in any situation in which a firm cannot increase all factors of production in the same proportion. Over a relatively short period of time, some factors of production, particularly capital equipment, cannot be adjusted. Accordingly, as a firm increases output by adding additional inputs of those factors which *can* be adjusted, the Law of Diminishing Returns is encountered in the behavior of product outputs relative to inputs of the variable factors.

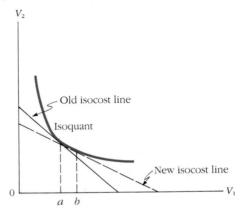

FIGURE 7-8

Readjustment of the Optimum Factor Combination in Response to a Change in the Price of One Factor: Poor Substitutability

The curvature of the isoquant is more pronounced when the two inputs are not easily substituted for one another in production. When the relative price of input V_2 rises, the firm's additional employment of V_1 from a to b is not as great as in Figure 7-7.

7.7 ADJUSTMENTS IN ALL FACTORS: THE PRINCIPLE OF RETURNS TO SCALE

Having considered various situations in which factor proportions have been changed, we turn to the other major segment of the theory of production, which analyzes the behavior of output when *all* factors are varied. For example, if all factors are doubled, will output double or will the new output be more or less than twice as great? The **Principle of Returns to Scale** covers the three possible relationships between an increase in inputs and a consequent increase in outputs when all factors are increased.

1. *Constant returns to scale:* a proportionate change in all inputs produces a proportionate change in output—that is, doubling all inputs results in a doubling of outputs. In other words, as the overall scale of operations is increased, the returns—the marginal product and average product of each factor—are constant.
2. *Increasing returns to scale:* an increase in inputs of all factors results in a more-than-proportionate increase in output. Average total factor product will increase.
3. *Decreasing returns to scale:* an increase in inputs of all factors results in a less-than-proportionate increase in output. Average total factor product will decrease.

It is widely believed that in a typical production activity, when the scale of operations is first increased, increasing returns to scale are encountered; then, with the exhaustion of all economies, returns to scale are constant; ultimately, if expansion is carried far enough, returns to scale decrease.

If one were to think of a two-input production function,

$$q = f(V_1, V_2)$$

the degree of scale economies can be seen by proportionally changing inputs by some amount λ and seeing whether the resulting output is increased by more, the same, or less than λ. This will depend on the magnitude of α in the following expression

$$\lambda^\alpha q = f(\lambda V_1, \lambda V_2)$$

$\alpha = 1 \rightarrow$ constant returns to scale ("linearly homogeneous," "homogeneous of degree 1")

$\alpha > 1 \rightarrow$ increasing returns to scale

$\alpha < 1 \rightarrow$ decreasing returns to scale

Note that, as with the three stages of production, not all of these cases are equally likely to be observed in real-world firm behavior. Production functions are often assumed to be linearly homogeneous in competitive market conditions. If α were greater than 1, average total factor product (output per unit of input) would *rise,* which means that average cost, (input per unit of output) would *fall*—hence, at any given price, firms will wish to produce more, since doing so will raise profit by increasing the spread between price (average revenue) and average cost. Therefore competitive firms will increase production until they are no longer in the range where $\alpha > 1$. Similarly, if α were less than one, average cost would rise; under competitive conditions firms in this region would be undersold (at long-run equilibrium) by firms not operating in this region. (These ideas will become clearer in Chapter 8, which deals more explicitly with the relationship between production functions and cost functions.)

An Isoquant Representation of Returns to Scale

With constant returns to scale, the isoquants representing successive unit increases in output (with adjustments of all factors) will be equidistant on any line extended from the point of origin. Thus in Figure 7-9, segments 0r, rs, st, and so on are of equal lengths; doubling the inputs results in a doubling of outputs. As shown in the lower output range of Figure 7-10, with increasing returns to scale the segments between isoquants (each successive isoquant representing the same increase in output) decrease in length. With decreasing returns the segments increase in length, as also shown in Figure 7-10 for the larger output levels.

Representing constant, increasing, and decreasing returns to scale on a graph does not, however, shed much light on when one would be expected to observe each case. What causes increasing returns to scale?

FIGURE 7-9

Constant Returns to Scale
The expansion path diagrams the optimum factor combinations for different levels of output. The slope of the expansion path is the input ratio. A linear expansion path implies a constant input ratio, and successive points along the expansion path represent proportionate increases in both factors. Equidistant isoquants along a linear expansion path indicate that proportionate increases in inputs—for example, from r to s—boost output by the same proportion.

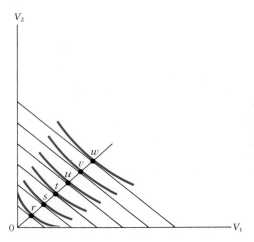

FIGURE 7-10

First Increasing Returns to Scale, then Decreasing Returns to Scale
Doubling the amount of the factors from p to r raises output from 20 to 60, implying increasing returns to scale. At point s, however, doubling inputs to point u increases output from 80 to 120, indicating decreasing returns to scale.

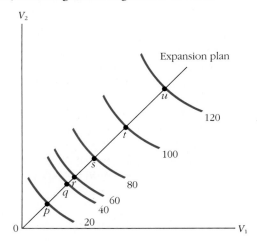

Increasing Returns to Scale

A situation of increasing returns to scale is based, most importantly, on indivisibilities of some factors and on advantages of specialization.

Indivisibilities.   The inability to divide certain factor units into smaller units without either complete loss of usefulness in production or partial loss in efficiency results in a relatively low output per unit of input when operations are conducted on a very small scale. In some instances it is not possible to adjust all factors in the same proportion upward or downward. Certain types of capital goods (for example, presses and road construction equipment) will not perform their function if they are built on too small a scale, since weight is important in their operation. Regardless of how light the traffic on a railroad line, for example, the rails must weigh at least 45 pounds per yard if standard equipment is to be operated; yet rails on the most-travelled lines may not exceed 135 pounds in weight. The traffic density on a heavily used line might be 2,000,000 ton-miles per mile of track annually; on a light-density line the traffic might not exceed 20,000 ton-miles. The latter is only 1 percent of the former, yet the rail required is 33 percent as large. A rail only 1 percent of the weight of the 135-pound rail would not stand the weight of a handcar.

With other capital equipment, small units can be made, but the output per unit of factors used to make and operate them is low. A 5-H.P. engine cannot be built for 1 percent of the cost of a 500-H.P. engine. For physical reasons, larger machines require less material per unit of output for their construction than smaller machines; they likewise require less labor for their construction per unit of product, since it takes little or no more time to assemble a machine designed to produce 100 units a day than to assemble a similar machine designed to produce 50 units. If the machine is very small, more time may actually be required because of the difficulty of working with small parts and obtaining the necessary precision in measurements. In warehouse construction, doubling the building material will more than double the amount of usable space. With a rectangular building, costs of walls need increase only 50 percent for the capacity of the area to double. (See Box 7-6.)

Indivisibilities are also encountered in advertising, research work, and financing. They are likewise encountered in the financing of a business. The cost of floating a bond issue, for example, is to a large extent independent of the size of the issue. Thus, this method of financing—the cheapest method when large amounts of capital are to be obtained—is expensive to a firm until it has expanded beyond a certain size. The refusal of many investors to consider the bonds of any except well-known companies further increases the difficulty of bond financing by small businesses.

Specialization.   The other, closely related cause of increasing returns to scale is the advantage offered by **specialization**. In a very small business, employees must perform a wide variety of tasks. As the size of the enterprise increases, each employee can be used in a relatively specialized job, with a consequent increase in output per worker. The advantages of labor specialization have been recognized at least since Adam Smith analyzed the manufacture of pins, over two hundred years ago.[11] The

---

[11]See his *Wealth of Nations*, Modern Library ed. (New York: Random House, 1937), pp. 7–8.

7-6   Are indivisibilities confined to capital goods?

No. Labor units are not completely divisible either. One operator may be required for each machine, regardless of its size. A freight train requires one engineer, regardless of the tonnage of the train; it is not possible to use a fraction of an engineer on a train of light tonnage. Within limits, in small enterprises, employees may be used to perform several different tasks. But as a practical matter, there are severe limitations to such possibilities. A switchboard operator may serve as receptionist and do word processing too, but this person can scarcely be used at the same time as an elevator operator and window cleaner. A sales clerk in a store may be busy only one third of the time, yet the clerk must be paid for the entire day. In any type of business, it is difficult to utilize each worker to maximum productivity at all times. As an establishment grows, the percentage of labor time not utilized should fall, if management policies are effective.*

---

*Union rules sometimes increase indivisibilities of labor and lessen effective utilization of labor time. Thus a freight train must have a crew of a stated size, though less workers may be needed in certain circumstances.

primary advantages include the greater skill acquired with specialization, the avoidance of wasted time in shifting from one task to another, and the employment of persons best suited to particular types of work.

In managerial activity as well as in other phases of work, advantages of specialization are encountered. As a firm grows in size, personnel relations will be conducted by a specialist; traffic management will be in the hands of a full-time traffic expert instead of someone with half a dozen other tasks. The owner of a small retail store selects the location for the store primarily through guesswork, placing it where sales volume should be high or where there is an available empty low-rent building. In contrast, larger chains have store sites selected by experts with experience in analyzing the relative desirability of different locations.

Specialization is also possible with capital equipment. As a firm increases its scale of operations, it can replace nonspecialized equipment capable of performing a number of tasks with specialized equipment designed for various specific operations, with a consequent increase in output per unit of input.

The importance of the phase of increasing returns depends in large measure upon the type of production process involved. In almost any type, increasing returns are likely when a business expands from a very small initial size because of indivisibilities of labor. If, however, a business utilizes relatively little capital equipment, and if few advantages of labor specialization are obtainable, then increasing returns may very quickly come to an end. On the other hand, if a firm uses extensive amounts of capital goods of types which cannot be used efficiently on a small scale, very substantial increasing returns extending over a great range of output may be encountered. Thus, increasing returns are very important in steel, cement, and automobile production but less important in agriculture and retailing.

Constant Returns to Scale

As a business continues to expand its scale of operations, it gradually exhausts the economies responsible for increasing returns. A firm will eventually grow to the point at which it is using the best type of capital equipment available and is gaining full advantages of labor specialization. Beyond this point, further increases in the scale of operations are likely to produce approximately constant returns for a substantial range of output, the production function being linearly homogeneous. If the entire scale of operations is likely to produce more or less constant returns for a substantial range of output, the production function is linearly homogeneous throughout. If the entire scale of operations is doubled, output will approximately double also.[12] It must be reemphasized that constant returns to scale are relevant only for time periods in which adjustment of all factors is possible. If a firm doubles output in a short period with a fixed physical plant which was previously utilized to normal optimum capacity, returns per unit of the variable factors will decline because of the operation of the Law of Diminishing Returns. But if all factors are varied, as may be possible over a long-run period, the Law of Diminishing Returns is not relevant.

Decreasing Returns to Scale

As a firm continues to expand its scale of operations beyond a certain point, there is apparently a tendency for returns to scale to decrease; thus a given percentage increase in the quantities of all factors will bring about a less-than-proportional increase in output. In some types of production, decreasing returns may follow directly after the increasing returns phase, with no significant intervening period of constant returns. However, on the basis of limited evidence, it appears that a long phase of constant returns is typical.

Decreasing returns to scale for a particular plant must be distinguished from such returns for an entire firm. The former are attributable almost entirely to physical relationships. As the area over which production operations must be coordinated and the territory from which labor supplies must be drawn are increased, this will ultimately result in lower product per unit of input in a given plant. A classic historical example of failure to consider decreasing returns to scale of plant was provided by the Portuguese vessels in the East Indian trade in the sixteenth and seventeenth centuries. As trade flourished, the Portuguese continued to increase the size of their ships in order to provide greater cargo space. But strength and maneuverability could not be maintained as the vessels became larger, and the ships became increasingly vulnerable to storms and attractive to pirates. As a consequence, losses of vessels increased disastrously; and the Dutch, with smaller, faster ships, proceeded to capture the trade.[13]

---

[12]Even in the phase of constant returns, small increases in scale may produce decreasing returns or increasing returns because of indivisibilities. A railroad cannot build half of a new track between two points; if two tracks are inadequate, it may build a third track, which initially will not be used to capacity.

[13]See Ralph Davis, *The Rise of the Atlantic Economies* (New York: Cornell University Press, 1973).

Decreasing returns to scale for the firm itself are usually attributed to increased problems and complexities of large-scale management. Beyond a certain point, continued increases in entrepreneurial labor activity encounter more and more serious difficulties. An increasing percentage of the total labor force is required in administrative work in order to provide coordination of the firm's activities and necessary control over the large numbers of employees. As the firm reaches substantial size, final authority for basic policy must remain in the hands of a group that controls the operation of the business, yet is far removed from the actual level of operations. Managers are forced to make decisions on the basis of second-hand information, on subjects with which they have no direct contact. Furthermore, substantial delay can occur in decision making, since the request for a decision, plus necessary information, must pass up through the chain of command to the entrepreneurial group, whose decision must then pass down to the operating unit.

In order to reduce to a minimum the amount of red tape and delay in making decisions by those out of contact with the situation, responsibility for many decisions must be delegated to subordinate officials. To the extent that such a policy is followed, decisions will be made by persons who lack the knowledge of general business policy, the experience, or the incentive which those at the top level of management possess. As a result, there arises a lack of coordination and unity of policy among various parts of the enterprise. Modern business management attempts to delegate decisions while maintaining a reasonable unity of policy, but the problem can never be eliminated. Scientific management principles merely lessen its seriousness.

The growth of a business likewise increases the amount of division of responsibility and serves to lessen initiative, especially on the part of persons in lower-level jobs who are in a position to note desirable changes. With increased size comes a loss of personal contact between management and workers, with a consequent loss of morale and an increase in labor strife.

The Validity of the Principle of Returns to Scale

The Principle of Returns to Scale has not enjoyed the general acceptance afforded the Law of Diminishing Returns. The initial increase in output per unit of factor which occurs as a firm first increases its scale of operations appears to be confirmed both by commonsense observation and by empirical studies. The ultimate exhaustion of economies of scale likewise seems inevitable. But it is still an open question whether an ultimate decline in output per unit of input is inevitable or is confined to those fields (such as certain types of agriculture) in which management problems are particularly serious because of space considerations.

SUMMARY

1. The relationship between inputs and outputs is called the production function.

2. When the input of just one factor is varied (other inputs held constant), output will start at a low level and gradually increase as the amount of the variable input increases. At some point, as more inputs are added, it becomes increasingly difficult to increase output, and a decline in output may ultimately result.

3. Average product is total product divided by the quantity of the input used. Marginal product is the change in total output resulting from a small change in the amount of the input.

4. The behavior of output as a variable factor is increased relative to some fixed factor can be separated into three stages. In the first stage (increasing returns), average product increases, with marginal product being greater than average product. In the second stage (diminishing returns), marginal product declines and eventually reaches zero while average product declines throughout. In the third stage (negative returns), total product diminishes; hence marginal product is negative while average product continues to decline.

5. As the amount of a variable is increased, the amount of other inputs being held constant, a point ultimately is reached beyond which marginal product will decline. This is the Law of Diminishing Returns.

6. An isoquant shows the various factor combinations which will produce a given output.

7. The marginal rate of technical substitution is the number of units of one factor necessary to replace a unit of another factor and maintain the same level of output. The slope of the isoquant at any one point indicates the marginal rate of technical substitution between the two factors.

8. The Law of Diminishing Marginal Rate of Technical Substitution states that as the quantity of any one factor is increased relative to the quantity of the others, output being constant, the number of the units of the second which can be replaced by one unit of the first falls.

9. The optimum factor combination occurs at the tangency of the isoquant with the isocost line. The isocost lines show the various possible quantities of the two factors which can be purchased with a given outlay of money.

10. A change in the price of any one factor, holding output and other factor prices constant, will require a readjustment in factor proportions until the equality of price ratio and marginal rate of technical substitution is again met. A fall in the price of any factor will lead to increased use of it, and conversely (factor demand curves are downward sloping).

11. There are three possible outcomes with regard to the relationship between the increase in inputs and the consequent increase in outputs when all factors are increased in proportion: *constant returns to scale*—doubling of inputs results in doubling of outputs; *increasing returns to scale*—an increase in inputs of all factors results in a more-than-proportionate increase in output; and *decreasing return to scale*—an increase in inputs of all factors results in a less-than-proportionate increase in output.

WORDS AND CONCEPTS FOR REVIEW

production function
average product
marginal product
Law of Diminishing Returns
marginal rate of technical substitution
Law of Diminishing Marginal Rate of
    Technical Substitution

isoquant
isocost
optimum factor combination
Principle of Returns to Scale: increasing,
    constant, and decreasing
indivisibilities
specialization

REVIEW QUESTIONS

1. Why do firms engage in production?

2. What is a production function?

3. What is the difference between production functions with fixed coefficients and those with variable coefficients? Give an example of the former.

4. How do average physical product and marginal physical product differ?

5. How would you graph the typical behavior of total product as the input of one factor is increased (with given quantities of the other factors)?

6. Why is marginal product equal to average product at the highest level of average product?

7. Why does marginal product fall if the rate of increase in total product falls?

8. Can average product be rising while marginal product is falling? Explain.

9. Upon what premises is the Law of Diminishing Returns based?

10. What is the stage of increasing returns and increasing returns to scale? Indicate the causes of each.

11. a. Contrast the causes of the stage of diminishing returns and those of decreasing returns to scale.

   b. Distinguish between decreasing returns to scale for the plant and for the firm. Why is the latter the more significant of the two?

12. What is meant by the stage of "negative returns"? What can be responsible for negative returns if a firm expands far enough?

13. What is meant by the term "optimum factor combination"?

14. How does one explain the meaning of the term "marginal rate of technical substitution" with respect to factors?

15. Why may the marginal rate of technical substitution of x_2 for x_1 fall as the quantity of x_2 is increased? Why may it rise initially?

16. What is the relationship between the rate of decline in the marginal rate of technical substitution and the degree of substitutability of the two factors for each other?

SUGGESTED READINGS

Baumol, W. J. *Economic Theory and Operations Analysis*, 4th ed. Englewood Cliffs, N. J.: Prentice-Hall, 1977, Chapter 11.

Cassels, J. M. "On the Law of Variable Proportions." In W. Fellner and B. F. Haley, eds. *Readings in the Theory of Income Distribution*. Philadelphia: Blakiston, 1946, pp. 103–18.

Ferguson, C. *The Neoclassical Theory of Production and Distribution*. London: Cambridge University Press, 1969.

Henderson, J. M. and Quandt R. F. *Microeconomic Theory*, 3rd ed. New York: McGraw Hill Company, 1980, Chapter 3.

APPENDIX   LINEAR PROGRAMMING

Few economic problems have simple or precise solutions. In the first place, economic phenomena are inherently complicated, partly because of the great variety of goods and services in a modern economy and the difficulty of describing the processes by which they are produced and distributed. That these processes are largely social rather than physical in nature makes an already arduous task even harder. To make matters worse, the technical and institutional framework of economic activity is subject to constant change. In these circumstances, it is not always possible to formulate economic problems in a clear and meaningful way, and it is hardly surprising that specific solutions can seldom be provided for those problems that can be so formulated. In the second place, much research effort in economics has traditionally been devoted not to describing the world as it is but rather to prescribing how the world ought to be.

   It is an open question whether economic problems will always be this difficult to manage. In recent years, economists have become increasingly aware of the inadequacy of their discipline and have spent considerable effort devising ways and means to diminish the gap between "theory" and "practice."[14] This has included the development, largely since 1930, of *econometrics,* a new branch of economics that is concerned with the empirical measurement of relations described in general economic theory (see Appendix to Chapter 3). Even more recently, the formulation of certain simplified techniques of analysis, commonly referred to as *linear programming,* have made possible the specific numerical solution of problems that have previously been solvable only in vague qualitative terms. Both of these developments have enabled economists to use complex computers in their research and so to solve problems that not long ago would have been unmanageable from a computational point of view.

Linear Programming and Economic Analysis

To appreciate the relation between linear programming and economic analysis, it is helpful to think of the term *programming* as being roughly synonymous with the term *planning.* Almost the whole of microeconomic price theory is concerned with programming in this sense—that is, with the planning behavior of individual consumers and business firms. Typical examples include the consumer's choosing among alternative combinations of goods so as to maximize total satisfaction, the firm's choosing among alternative combinations of factor inputs in order to minimize the total cost of any given level of total output, and the firm's choosing among alternative levels of output in an attempt to maximize total profit.

   In each of these cases, note that nothing is said about the execution of plans. As a general rule, it is simply assumed that an optimal plan (that is, a plan that maximizes satisfaction, minimizes cost, maximizes profit, and so on), once decided upon, can be and is carried into effect. Note also that the relations in terms of which optimal plans are defined are normally represented geometrically by curves (indifference curves, isoquants, total profit curves, and so on), many of which are not straight lines—that is, by *relations that are nonlinear.* Therefore the planning aspects of microeconomic theory consist primarily of techniques that may be called *nonlinear programming.* The only formal difference between this kind of programming and

---

[14]See R. Kuttner, "The Poverty of Economics", *The Atlantic Monthly* (February 1985), pp. 74–84.

what is now called linear programming is that in the latter discipline, various kinds of linear relations are substituted for the usually nonlinear relations of traditional theory. By this procedure it becomes easier to develop quantitative solutions to various problems.

Establishment of Linear Relations

The way in which linear relations are established varies from case to case and is therefore difficult to describe in general terms. The basic idea is simple, however, and is illustrated in Figure 7-11. If we start with a curve (say, an isoquant) such as QQ', we may regard the straight line LL' as a rough approximation to QQ'. A better approximation is provided by the broken line MM', and an even better approximation by the dotted line NN'. Indeed, if with an unlimited number of line segments, the original isoquant QQ' might be approximated to any desired degree of accuracy by means of a "line" with an appropriately large number of "breaks." Or, to use a more technical expression, the isoquant might be approximated by a *piecewise linear relation*. Thus we might say that the difference between traditional programming problems and

FIGURE 7-11

Approximation of Curve by Piecewise Linear Relations
The curve QQ' can be approximated by the straight line LL', but is better approximated by two line segments such as MM', and still better by three line segments such as NN'. The greater the number of line segments, the more accurately the piecewise relations estimate the curve.

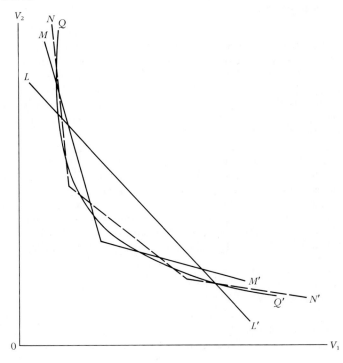

those considered in the modern linear programming literature is a result of the substitution of piecewise linear relations for the nonlinear relations of traditional theory. This is not the whole story, but it does explain a significant part of the outward differences between linear programming and programming of the kind described in traditional price theory.

Scope of Linear Programming

Broadly speaking, linear programming is concerned with the solution of practical and theoretical problems in which some quantity (such as profit, income, the value of national product, aggregate transportation cost, or travel time) is to be maximized or minimized subject to the condition that various technical, institutional, and financial restraints also be satisfied. The subject thus includes the types of problems that in traditional theory involve rational choice among a set of alternative possible plans. But linear programming includes much more than this; many problems that at first do not look like planning problems at all can be treated *as if* they were planning problems and thus be formulated and solved with the same kinds of techniques used to solve the planning problems of individual households or firms. For example, linear programming has been applied with considerable success to broad questions of economic development, interregional trade, general equilibrium analysis, and welfare economics.

Linear Programming: Some Examples

Some specific examples of linear programming problems will help clarify the nature of the methods that it uses and their relations to the methods of general economic analysis. For the sake of simplicity, the examples presented below are drawn mainly from the realm of business practice, but it should be emphasized that the range of problems that can be handled with these and closely related techniques is much wider than these examples might suggest.

The Selection of an Optimal Diet.   A cattle producer seeks to fatten steers for market in the most economical way while meeting various nutritional requirements to ensure high quality of the final product. The rancher has a choice among various mixtures of two foods, hay and cottonseed cake. Both contain a certain quantity of one or more of four nutrients (protein, minerals, vitamins, and calories), so the use of a sufficient quantity of one or both foods will guarantee the satisfaction of any given set of nutritional requirements. Confronted with fixed prices for each of the two foods, the rancher's problem is to choose a diet (that satisfies certain minimal nutrition requirements while minimizing the total cost of feeding a steer.

The essentials of the problem are illustrated in Figure 7-12. Any combination of hay and cottonseed cake represented by a point on or to the right of line P is assumed to satisfy the *minimum* protein requirement (the slope of the line reflects the relative proportions of protein in the two foods); all other points represent food combinations that fail to satisfy this requirement. Similarly, the minimum mineral requirement is satisfied by diets corresponding to points on or to the right of line M, the minimum vitamin requirement is satisfied by points on or to the right of the line V, and the minimum calorie requirement is satisfied by points on or to the right of the line C. These requirements are not satisfied by points that lie to the left of lines M, V, and C. All points on or to the right of the heavy line *abcde* thus represent combinations of cottonseed cake and hay that satisfy all four of the minimum nutrition requirements simultaneously. Any point to the left of the heavy line represents a combination of foods that fails to satisfy one or more of these same minimum requirements. The heavy line thus represents what might be called the lower boundary of *feasible diets*. This boundary is, indeed, a piecewise linear relation of the sort described earlier; it represents a kind of production isoquant in which "nutrition" is

FIGURE 7-12

The Optimal Diet Problem

The cattle producer, wanting to minimize the cost of providing a sufficiently nutritious diet for steers, faces the prices of hay and cottonseed cake reflected in the dotted isocost lines. The combinations of the two foods meeting the minimum daily requirements of protein are charted along *PP*, of vitamins along *VV*, of minerals along *MM*, and of calories along *CC*. Minimum quantities of all four nutrients are contained in the food combinations along *abcde*, the boundary of feasible diets. The optimal diet is *d*, the cheapest diet that provides the necessary nutrition.

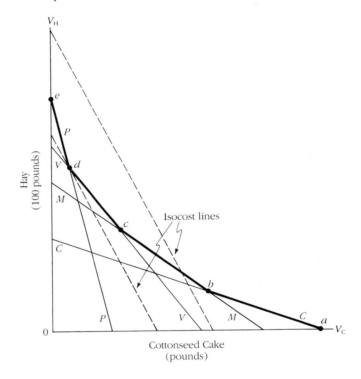

the "output" produced. Diets represented by points to the right of this boundary are, in a sense, wasteful of nutrients; more food is contained in such diets than is strictly necessary for fattening purposes. Diets represented by points on the boundary are just enough, in the nutrient-producing sense, to ensure that cattle are fattened in an appropriate way.

Now, suppose that the unit cost of cottonseed cake and the unit cost of hay are known and constant, regardless of quantity purchased. The various diets that can be purchased for any given level of total cost can be presented graphically by points on an isocost line of the kind shown in Figure 7-12. The cattle producer's problem is to choose a combination of foods on the boundary of feasible diet combinations, line *abcde*, for which total cost is as small as possible. In the present example, such a combination is represented by point *d* in Figure 7-12, since any other point on the boundary *abcde* will lie on a higher isocost line.

There is a clear analogy between this problem and that of a firm choosing a combination of factor inputs so as to minimize total cost for a given level of output; indeed, the main difference is that the present boundary of feasible diets is kinked, whereas the boundary of feasible input combinations in ordinary theory is represented by a smooth isoquant. But there is a considerable gap between principle and practice in the two problems. Whereas existing computational techniques can be used to obtain an explicit numerical answer to the linear programming problem even in cases involving hundreds of foods and nutrients, the analogous problem as posed in ordinary economic theory is ordinarily solvable only in principle. The difference between the two cases lies in the more specialized character of the assumptions underlying the linear programming problem. This would be of no practical advantage if the special assumptions were flatly inconsistent with practical experience, but the truth is that these restrictions are in fair accord with factual knowledge in a surprising number of instances.

Choosing an Efficient Production Process.   The manager of a grain warehouse must arrange for the loading and unloading of a certain number of boxcars each month. Two technically efficient processes are available for this purpose—one involving the use of a motor-driven conveyer belt, the other involving the use of motor-driven grain shovels. The major expenses associated with both processes are fuel and labor costs, but 50 tons of grain per hour can be loaded or unloaded by the conveyer process using three gallons of fuel and one man-hour of labor, whereas two man-hours of labor and one gallon of fuel are required to perform the same task with the shovel process.

The essential characteristics of the two processes are illustrated in Figure 7-13 by the lines $0C$ and $0S$ and the related production isoquants, showing, for each process taken separately, the

---

FIGURE 7-13

The Optimal Production Process
With two available grain-loading processes, the manager can choose only the conveyor process along the expansion path $0C$, only the shovel process along $0S$, or some combination of the two. If the desired output level is 50, the appropriate isoquant is *eabcd.*

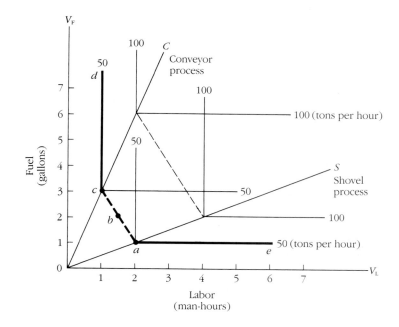

various combinations of fuel and labor required to move either 50 or 100 tons of wheat per hour. If both processes can be used simultaneously, however, certain fuel/labor combinations other than those illustrated can be used to move a given amount of grain. If the conveyer process is used to move 25 out of a required 50 tons an hour, for example, the remaining 25 tons must be moved by the shovel process. The total fuel requirement would then be two gallons (1½ gallons for the conveyor process and ½ gallon for the shovel process), and the total labor requirement would be 1½ man-hours (½ man-hour for the conveyer process and 1 man-hour for the shovel process). This combination is represented in Figure 7-13 by the point *b* on the dotted line joining points *a* and *c*. All mixtures of the two processes that would result in the moving of 50 tons of grain per hour are represented by points on this dotted line. Where a mixture of processes is possible, therefore, the production "isoquant" for grain movements of 50 tons per hour is represented by the broken line *eabcd;* fuel/labor combinations that will permit loading of other quantities of grain can of course be represented by isoquants of the same form. The curve for 100 tons per hour is illustrated on the same figure.

If the warehouse manager is interested in minimizing the total cost of any required grain-moving operation, it is clear that the choice between the two processes (or a combination of the two) will depend on the relative costs of fuel and labor. The present problem is precisely the same as that of the cost-minimizing firm, except that the number of available "processes" is limited to two (or, as at *b,* linear combinations of two). The production isoquants of the warehouse problem would have three "kinks" rather than two if three different processes were available, ten "kinks" if ten processes were available, and so forth. The merit of the linear programming statement of the problem is that it permits extremely complicated practical problems to be formulated and solved in situations where the more general approach of traditional economic theory could not provide specific answers.

The Technique of Linear Programming

The general principles of linear programming are best described by restating one of the preceding examples in mathematical form.

The diet problem is particularly appropriate for this purpose. We may begin by representing quantities of cottonseed cake and hay, respectively, by the symbols x_1 and x_2, and the corresponding dollar prices of these goods by p_1 and p_2. The total dollar cost of any given combination of the goods is then given by the expression

(1)
$$C = p_1 x_1 + p_2 x_2$$

where C represents the number of dollars spent. This is called a *linear equation* in the variables x_1 and x_2 because, for any constant value of the variable C, the expression $C = p_1 x_1 + p_2 x_2$ is represented geometrically by a straight line, as illustrated by the isocost lines in Figure 7-12.

The cattle producer's problem is not simply to choose values of x_1 and x_2 (that is, quantities of cottonseed cake and hay) that make C as small as possible. In the first place, the rancher's range of choice is limited by the requirement that purchases of cottonseed cake and hay be nonnegative, since negative purchases are impossible. This condition is expressed mathematically by writing the expressions

(2)
$$x_1 \geq 0, x_2 \geq 0$$

That is, x_1 and x_2 must be equal to or in excess of zero. Geometrically, these conditions require that points representing feasible diets lie to the right of the "hay axis" and above the "cottonseed cake axis" in Figure 7-12. The conditions are called *inequalities* (in this case, "linear inequalities") because they require that certain numbers (namely, x_1 and x_2) be *different from or equal* to a certain given constant (namely, zero).

In the second place, the producer's range of choice is limited by certain nutritional require-ments as well as by the requirement that total cost be minimized. Specifically, we may suppose that the minimum quantity of protein required is represented by a number b_1, the minimum quantity of minerals by a number b_2, the minimum quantity of vitamins by b_3, and the minimum quantity of calories by b_4. Similarly, we may suppose that the quantity of protein contained in a unit quantity of cottonseed cake is represented by a given number a_{11}, the quantity of protein contained in a unit quantity of hay by a number a_{12}, the quantity of minerals contained in a unit of cottonseed cake by a number a_{21}, and so on (there are eight of these numbers in total, since each of the two foods contains some quantity, perhaps zero, of each of the four nutrients). The various nutrition requirements may then be expressed mathematically by writing the four linear inequalities:

(3)
$$a_{11}x_1 + a_{12}x_2 \geq b_1 \quad \text{(protein requirement)}$$
$$a_{21}x_1 + a_{22}x_2 \geq b_2 \quad \text{(mineral requirement)}$$
$$a_{31}x_1 + a_{32}x_2 \geq b_3 \quad \text{(vitamin requirement)}$$
$$a_{41}x_1 + a_{42}x_2 \geq b_4 \quad \text{(calorie requirement)}$$

Taken in combination, the inequalities (3) define the lower boundary of feasible diets described by the heavy line *abcde* in Figure 7-12 (relevant portions of this figure are reproduced below as Figure 7-14). More specifically, each separate inequality in (3) *directly* represents an *area* on or to the right of one of the dashed lines in Figure 7-14. Taken as a group, therefore, the four inequalities in (3) *indirectly* describe an area of Figure 7-14 within which points repre-senting feasible diets *do not lie:* the area to the *left* of the heavy line *abcde* in Figure 7-14. The upper boundary of this area of nonfeasible diets—that is, the line *abcde* itself—is therefore the *lower* boundary of *feasible* diets.

The term *linear inequality* is used to describe each of the relations in (3) because in the special case in which x_1 and x_2 have values for which the requirements are barely satisfied—that is, values such that the four equations

$$a_{i1}x_1 + a_{i2}x_2 = b_i \quad (i = 1, 2, 3, 4)$$

are satisfied—the equations describing this situation are presented geometrically by straight lines. Each of the inequalities in (3) describes an area in Figure 7-14 that lies on or to the right of one of the dashed lines; the inequalities are referred to as linear inequalities because the area described by any single inequality is bounded on the left by a straight line.

The diet problem may now be stated as that of choosing a pair of numbers (x_1, x_2) that minimizes that value of the linear equation

$$C = p_1x_1 + p_2x_2$$

subject to the condition that the same numbers (x_1, x_2) also satisfy the set of six linear inequal-ities (2) and (3).

The solution of the problem (already presented graphically in Figure 7-12) will clearly depend on the values of the constants that appear in the statement of the problem—that is, on the values of the numbers $a_{11}, a_{12}, \ldots, a_{41}, a_{42}, b_1, b_2, b_3, b_4, p_1,$ and p_2. Thus the numbers $\bar{x}_1, \bar{x}_2$, representing an *optimal diet,* will depend on the form and position of the boundary of feasible diets and on the slope of the isocost line, which is to say that $\bar{x}_1$ and $\bar{x}_2$ will depend on the nutritional content of the two foods, minimal nutrition requirements, and the money prices of the foods purchased. As a general rule, an unlimited number of possible pairs of positive numbers x_1 and x_2 will satisfy the nutrition requirements (the linear inequalities [3]), but only one such pair will also satisfy the requirement that total cost be minimized. It is this *particular* pair of numbers that is denoted by $\bar{x}_1, \bar{x}_2$ and referred to as an *optimal diet.* Other diets that satisfy (2) and (3) are also *feasible* (nonfeasible diets are excluded from consideration by the

■■■■■■

FIGURE 7-14

Areas of Feasible and Nonfeasible Diets Defined by Linear Inequalities

The system of inequalities (3) describes the combinations of the two foods that provide sufficient nutrition. For example, the protein requirement inequality corresponds to the area on or to the right of line e and defines the diets that contain the minimum amounts of protein necessary. All four inequalities, and thus all four nutrient requirements, are met by the diets on or to the right of *abcde*. Diets inside the boundary do not provide sufficient nutrition.

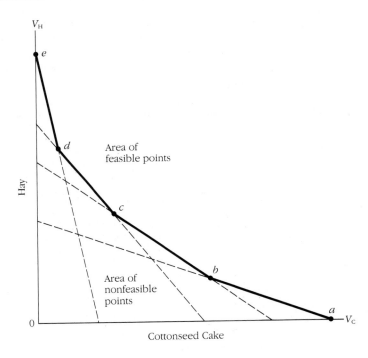

inequality constraints); but the *optimal diet* is the one particular feasible diet which makes the value of C in an equation (1) as small or smaller than any alternative feasible diet.[15]

More Complex Problems

The simple diet problem is probably easier to solve graphically than by using computer techniques. But suppose that we wished to consider a similar problem involving, say, 10 foods and 15 nutritional elements; that is, suppose that the problem required choosing positive or zero

---

[15]If the slope of the isocost line is the same as the slope of one of the lines in terms of which boundary of feasible diets is defined, an infinite number of different diets will minimize total cost. But this is a special case, which would not be frequently encountered in practice.

values of the 10 variables $x_1, x_2, \ldots, x_{10}$ so as to minimize the value of a linear equation

$$C = p_1x_1 + p_2x_2 + \ldots + p_{10}x_{10}$$

subject to 15 linear inequalities of the same form as those given in (3) above. All of the examples given previously—and, indeed, all other linear programming problems—can be expressed in essentially this way. An electronic computer would have no more difficulty with this problem than with one involving only two variables and three inequalities; but no such statement could be applied to a human being armed with pencil and paper! We cannot even visualize geometrically a problem that involves more than three basic variables.

The technique of linear programming involves much more, of course, than the mere feeding of information into hungry computers. The most interesting and important problems of linear programming are not mathematical or computational in character but are concerned instead with the task of interpreting concrete situations in such a way as to make them amenable to linear programming analysis. As a general rule, problems of planning that arise in actual practice do not lend themselves directly to treatment by linear programming techniques. First, it is seldom an easy matter to define a specific objective. A business firm, for example, may wish to maximize its long-run profit and at the same time maximize short-run payments to stockholders, but these two goals may not be consistent with one another. Similarly, a state government wishing to maximize the welfare of its citizens must choose among a wide array of alternative indicators of "welfare" (such as aggregate income, per capita income, leisure, property values). Second, even if a specific objective is defined, it may be difficult to discover the restraints which are operative in a particular situation—that is, which legal, social, financial, and other conditions should be taken into account in pursuing the given objective. Third, even if a specific objective is defined and a given set of restraints is known to apply, the restraints may not be directly expressible as linear inequalities. In actual practice, *precise* linearity of relevant restraints is more likely to be the exception than the rule. Finally, if linearity assumptions appear reasonable, it is always a major task to estimate relevant values of the various constant coefficients that enter into a linear programming problem (prices, nutrition requirements, capacity limitations, final demands, and so on). Once a problem is formulated, the task of finding an answer, or discovering whether an answer is possible, is largely a matter of routine computation which may be done with any one of several standard techniques (the so-called *simplex method* is perhaps the one most frequently used at the present time). But the task of formulations is another matter altogether. Vast ingenuity and intellectual audacity are prime characteristics of the successful linear programming expert.

8

The Costs of Production

8.1 INTRODUCTION

To obtain factor inputs for use in production, a firm must compensate factor owners. These compensations constitute *incomes* to the factor owners and *costs* to the firm. The quantity of output that a firm decides to produce and offer for sale depends upon the relationship between prices and costs. Costs, in turn, depend on the quantities of various factors needed to produce the given output and on the prices paid for factor units. The behavior of cost per unit of output as the firm varies output is determined by the extent of required changes in inputs as output changes. The relationship between price and cost not only governs the firm's output but also influences its decisions on undertaking new business enterprises and liquidating old ones. Thus a discussion of the determinants of output and supply must begin by introducing relevant concepts of cost and describing how various types of costs vary with changes in output.

8.2 THE NATURE OF COST

The term *cost* has a wide variety of meanings. In business, items considered as costs for the purpose of some decisions are very different from those considered for other purposes. For the determination of profit, cost includes only the usual business expenses (including depreciation, interest, rent, and taxes).[1] However, when a firm is calculating the profitability of undertaking a particular expansion or buying new

---

[1] In determining net income in the calculation of income tax liability, the amount of the income tax itself cannot, of course, be treated as a cost.

equipment, it includes in addition to other cost elements an item of return on the money capital used for the investment, even though the money is supplied by the firm itself. The same procedure is followed in pricing various products.[2] For some purposes, though, cost includes far less than it does for profit calculations. If a firm with an idle plant considers whether or not to accept additional orders which can be sold only at a very low price, it might consider only the direct, out-of-pocket costs associated with the additional output. When a railroad decides whether to continue operating a particular passenger train, it considers only the cost resulting directly from operation of that train and not the train's "share" of track maintenance, administrative expenses, or interest on investment.

For purposes of economic analysis, the most satisfactory definition of cost is broader than the concept used in financial accounting but similar to the concept used by business firms for general purposes. Specifically, the term **cost** refers to *the compensations which must be received by the owners of money capital and the units of the factors of production used by a firm if these owners are to continue to supply money capital and factor units to the firm.*

Two elements in this definition require emphasis. The phrase "compensations which must be received by the owners" is used rather than "payments which must be made to the factor owners" because in some instances no formal payment occurs. A person operating a business does not usually "pay" himself interest on funds which he invests in his own business. Yet if he does not receive a return on such funds equivalent to the amount he could get by lending them to others, he will probably end up liquidating the business. Likewise, the phrase "continue to supply the factor units" is used in the definition rather than "supply the factor units" because factor owners may supply factor inputs for a period of time to a firm even though they are getting little or no compensation. The firm will not be able to obtain factor inputs indefinitely, however, if it cannot offer a return comparable to that available in other industries. The owners of a business not yielding a normal return may continue to operate it for some time because they cannot quickly withdraw money capital invested in specialized capital goods. Once the capital goods are worn out, however, the money capital will not be reinvested. (See Box 8-1.)

8.3 EXPLICIT AND IMPLICIT

There are two types of elements in total cost: (1) **explicit costs**, such as wages or rents, which take the form of contractual payments by the business firm to factor owners; and (2) **implicit costs**, which, when covered, accrue directly to the firm or its owners, with no contractual obligations for payment.

---

[2]This is not meant to imply that firms can set their prices on a basis of cost considerations alone. But cost is an element considered; and for this purpose, cost usually includes a "profit" on the firm's own capital.

8-1   True or False?   From the standpoint of a particular business firm, the amount of compensation which owners of factor services must receive is determined by other opportunities which they have.

True. The opportunity is measured by the amounts they could obtain supplying factor inputs to other business firms. Thus if the market price for bar copper is a dollar a pound, a manufacturer who wishes to use bar copper must pay this price, since sellers of the input will not supply it to her for less when they can get a dollar from other buyers. If the current wage rate for laying brick is $80 a day, a contractor must pay $80 a day in order to obtain bricklayers. The same principle applies to factor inputs owned by the firm itself or supplied to it by the owners of the firm. A businessperson who invests $50,000 in his own business could have bought stock—perhaps in General Motors—and for this sum received $2,000 a year in dividends and a (risky) chance of additional capital gains. This sum constitutes a cost for which the business is responsible.

Explicit Costs

The first group consists of the items (other than depreciation charges) that are usually treated as costs in financial accounting: wages and salaries paid; payments for raw materials, fuel, and goods purchased for resale; payments for transportation, utilities, advertising, and similar services; interest on borrowed capital; rent on land and capital equipment leased; taxes. However, not all payments made by business firms are costs. Those made for the purchase of capital equipment involve merely a change in the form of the firm's assets and hence are not costs of producing the output of the particular period in which the assets are purchased. They are charged to capital account, and a depreciation charge—an implicit cost—is set up to recover the amount paid over the period of years during which the equipment will be used. Payments of dividends to stockholders are not explicit costs, but merely withdrawals of profits from the firm by stockholder-owners. Taxes are not true social costs of production, since they do not represent compensation to an input with alternative uses (like labor, capital and other inputs). However, taxes are costs from the perspective of the firm.

Implicit Costs

Costs take the implicit form when factor units and money capital are owned by the firm or its owners. Although the firm is not obligated to make a contractual payment for these factor units, the units represent opportunity costs, since they could be supplied to other producers if they were not used in the business.

In the typical large-scale enterprise operated under the corporate form of organization, the two major implicit costs are depreciation and an average return on money capital supplied by the stockholders. **Depreciation** charges are sums which must be recovered over the life of a capital good to maintain intact the capital sum invested in the item. The sums involved, if actually earned, may be used by the firm for any purpose. But the charges constitute costs and must be earned if the firm is to continue to operate indefinitely.

Likewise, the firm's owners must earn an adequate rate of return on their invested money capital—that is, a rate equal to the figure obtainable from other investments of comparable risk. If the owners have invested $50,000 in the business, they are forgoing a return on this money which they could otherwise have made by lending the money (directly or through bond purchases), by purchasing stock in other corporations, by buying land or buildings, and so on. (See Box 8-2.)

When a firm is earning an amount in excess of all costs, including those of an implicit nature, the additional amount constitutes "excess profit" or "economic profit" and is not in any sense a cost, since the business will be operated on a permanent basis whether or not any such excess sum is earned.

8.4 THE ADJUSTABILITY OF COSTS IN RESPONSE TO CHANGES IN OUTPUT

Of fundamental importance for cost behavior is the extent to which a firm is able to adjust the inputs of various factors, and thus the total magnitudes of the various cost elements, as it varies output. This in turn is affected by the length of time involved. Over a period of time long enough to allow adjustment in all factors, called a **long-run period**, all costs are *variable*—that is, they will change as output changes. The time necessary for adjustments in all factors will vary according to the lifespan of the capital equipment, the ability to obtain additional skilled workers and managerial personnel, and the extent to which capital goods are specialized (usable only for particular purposes). In general, the type of factor requiring the longest adjustment period is the specialized and relatively indivisible form of capital equipment—blast furnaces, dies used in the making of automobile parts, railroad tracks, hydroelectric plants, steamships, grain elevators, and so on. Note that firms never actually operate *in* the long run where everything is variable. At any point in time, inputs are fixed—at zero or some positive amount. Thus the long run is always a *planning horizon* of a length sufficient to vary all inputs.

8-2   True or False?   In smaller businesses, especially those organized as partnerships or individual proprietorships, an implicit cost like the wage which the owner of the firm could make by hiring himself out to another business is less important.

False. A grocer must be able to earn as much from his own store as he could by working for a supermarket chain—or, more exactly, the wage he could get less the value he attaches to the privilege of working for himself. A person may be satisfied with a somewhat smaller return from his own business because he prefers to be his own boss, but this preference has a definite value: If the differential between the store's earnings and the available wage exceeds a certain figure, the alternative of taking a job will become preferable.

Definitionally, in the **short-run period**, some factor units are not adjustable in amount. New capital equipment cannot be obtained or built overnight. Additional skilled labor and management personnel often can be secured only by training new workers. Likewise, with a downward adjustment, specialized capital equipment rarely can be sold for the amount of money invested in it; the firm has the alternative of suffering a heavy loss of invested funds or using the equipment over a long period at a low return. The latter alternative is often preferable.

Fixed factors—those not readily adjustable—consist primarily of capital equipment and top management personnel and are thus often designated by the term **plant**

Fixed Costs

The costs for which fixed factor units are responsible are known as **fixed costs**, while those arising from the use of the variable factors are known as **variable costs**. More precisely, fixed costs may be defined as those which are the same in total amount regardless of the volume of output, even if nothing is produced. The various cost items which are usually fixed in a short-run period may be classified into two major groups: those of a *recurrent* nature, involving actual outlay of money during the period; and those which are *allocable* to the period, the total outlay having been incurred at one time for the benefit of production during several time periods.

Recurrent fixed costs include interest on money borrowed; taxes that are independent of output, such as capital stock taxes and, (to a large extent) the general property tax; the portions of heat, utility, and insurance costs which are independent of output; most rent; and the portions of labor cost (generally salaried managers, as opposed to production workers) not affected by output changes. Even if a plant produces nothing at all, some labor will be needed: night patrol, maintenance employees, clerical and accounting personnel, portions of the administrative staff. These recurrent fixed costs give rise to cash outlays; the firm must obtain the funds from some source—current revenue, accumulated cash surplus, disposition of noncash assets, or borrowing—if it is to continue to operate.

In contrast, allocable fixed costs do not usually necessitate cash outlays during the period, and the firm can continue to operate for a time even if they are not covered. Nevertheless, these items constitute costs in the sense that they must be covered ultimately if the firm is to continue operations. One major example is the portion of depreciation which is a function of the passage of time rather than of usage. The economic life of capital equipment is in part independent of usage, being controlled by the rate of development of new techniques that render old equipment obsolete. The portion of depreciation which is dependent upon usage is a variable cost, but many firms make no effort to separate the time and usage element in total depreciation and assign the entire amount on the basis of time alone, thus in effect treating depreciation entirely as a fixed cost.

The other major allocable fixed cost element is the necessary return on capital supplied by owners. This sum does not have to be earned or paid out in any particular period, but it must be earned over a period of time if the firm is to continue operation. Given the average rate of return and the quantity of money capital invested by the owners, the necessary profit is the same for each year, regardless of the volume of output. The actual profit earned may fluctuate widely, but the necessary return is essentially a fixed cost.

Variable Costs

Variable costs are dependent upon the volume of output and are eliminated if production is not carried on. The major short-run variable costs are those for materials, fuel, electric power, and transportation; most wages, especially for work in direct physical production; and taxes that vary with output, such as those levied upon sales and gross receipts. In addition, other cost items that are primarily fixed costs may be partly variable. Depreciation, as noted above, is a short-run variable cost to the extent that the actual rate of depreciation is affected by usage.

A distinction is sometimes made between **fully variable costs**, which vary more or less in proportion to output, and **semivariable costs**, which change relatively little as output changes. The latter resemble fixed costs but are distinguishable by the fact that they can be eliminated if production is temporarily suspended, whereas fixed costs continue unchanged even if nothing is produced.[3] Semivariable costs reflect indivisibilities of variable factor units: once an indivisible variable factor unit is acquired, it is not fully utilized until output reaches a certain level, and thus the variable cost item for which it is responsible does not vary with small changes in output. For example, if a railroad is to operate freight service at all on a line, a certain train crew—perhaps four workers—will be required. As volume of traffic on the line increases over a very substantial range, the same crew will be sufficient and wages will remain approximately the same. With a small volume of traffic the potential services of the crew are not utilized fully; hence, as output increases, the costs of the crew do not increase significantly. Nevertheless the crew's wages are variable costs rather than fixed costs, since they are not paid if the train does not operate.

As indicated earlier, the distinction between fixed and variable costs is significant only in a short-run period, since over the longer period all factors—and all costs—are variable. The firm can, in the long run, either get completely out of business or expand all inputs as desired if more is to be produced. As already emphasized, firms are *always* in some particular short run (they have some existing fixed plant); the long run is always a planning horizon.

8.5 COST SCHEDULES

A **cost schedule** indicates the total cost of producing various volumes of output; it thus shows the response of cost to changes in output. A long-run schedule shows the costs of producing various amounts of output over a period that is long enough to

---

[3]Under a broader definition, the concept of fixed costs might include some items treated here as semivariable costs.

allow adjustments in all factors in order to obtain the optimum factor combination for each output level.

The costs of producing various amounts of output depend primarily upon three considerations: *the technique of production, the efficiency of the factor units employed,* and *the prices paid for factor units* (including the necessary compensation for factor units owned by the firm).

Profit maximization requires the use of the particular technique of production which will allow the optimum combination of factors (see Chapter 7). In a short-run period, the optimum combination for any given level of output is the least-cost combination possible with the fixed factor units which the firm has on hand. Over a longer period, all factors can be varied, so the firm is free to select the particular short-run combination which is the absolute optimum.

Cost levels are affected not only by available methods of production but also by the efficiency of factor units—the quality of natural resources employed, the types of capital goods available, and the skill of all types of labor including managerial personnel. The better the quality of the resources, for example, the greater the output obtained from a given quantity of resources at the optimum factor combination, and the lower the cost of production (assuming that more efficient inputs are not paid enough more to exactly offset their efficiency—a strong assumption in competitive markets).

Finally, the prices paid for factor units influence cost in monetary terms. The cost of factor units to any one producer is the price which the owner of the unit could obtain from making it available in the next-best use—the opportunity cost. (See Box 8-3.)

8.6 SHORT-RUN COST SCHEDULES

As illustrated in Table 8-1, a **short-run cost schedule** for an individual firm shows the behavior of cost when output is varied with a given plant and fixed factor prices. For most purposes, unit (or average) cost data are more convenient to use than total

8-3   What causes a shift in the cost curve? How about a movement along a cost curve?

Any particular cost schedule is based upon the assumption that factor prices and production technology (represented in the production functions of Chapter 7) are given. When a change in these underlying determinants occurs, the costs of the firm will be *shifted.* An increase in factor prices, for example, will raise cost schedules; the development of new methods of production, the discovery of better quality resources, or improved training of workers will lower cost schedules. It is essential to distinguish clearly between a shift in a cost schedule caused by a change in factor prices or technology and a change in costs resulting from a change in output by the firm. The former is represented graphically by a shifting of a cost curve, the latter merely by a movement along a given cost curve.

TABLE 8-1
Daily Cost Schedule of a Producer

Units of Output	Total Fixed Cost	Total Variable Cost	Total Cost	Average Fixed Cost	Average Variable Cost	Average Cost	Marginal Cost
0*	$20	$ 0	$ 20	—	—	—	—
1	20	30	50	$20.00	$ 30	$ 50.00	$ 30
2	20	56	76	10.00	28	38.00	26
3	20	75	95	6.67	25	31.67	19
4	20	80	100	5.00	20	25.00	5
5	20	105	125	4.00	21	25.00	25
6	20	132	152	3.33	22	25.33	27
7	20	182	202	2.86	26	28.86	50
8	20	320	340	2.50	40	42.50	138
9	20	720	740	2.22	80	82.22	400
10	20	3,000	3,020	2.00	300	302.00	2,280

*If no units are produced, total fixed cost is the same as it would be if production were carried on. No variable costs are incurred. The unit cost columns are blank for zero units because the concept of cost per unit has no meaning if no units are produced.

cost data. **Average cost**[4] is equal to total cost divided by the number of units of output; it consists of two elements—**average fixed cost** (total fixed cost divided by the number of units of output) and **average variable cost** (total variable cost divided by the number of units of output).

The last column in Table 8-1 shows data on **marginal cost**—the increase in total cost which results from the production of an additional unit of output. For example, with five units of output, total cost is $125; with six units, it is $152. Thus the marginal cost of the sixth unit—the amount which the production of the sixth unit adds to total cost—is $27 ($152−$125). Marginal cost depends solely on changes in total variable cost, since total fixed cost is by definition the same for every level of output. A typical pattern of cost curves for a firm is shown in Figure 8-1.

The analysis of short-run cost behavior is based upon the following assumptions:

1. The firm has only a fixed quantity of certain factors, and therefore certain cost items are fixed in total.
2. The fixed factor units require a certain minimum quantity of variable factor units for efficient operation but have at least some degree of adaptability for utilization with varying quantities of other factors.
3. Some types of variable factors cannot be acquired in infinitesimally small units. For example, workers often cannot be hired for periods of less than one day.

---

[4]For simplicity, the term average cost is used rather than average total cost.

FIGURE 8-1

Short-Run Cost Curves of a Firm
SRAC, composed of AVC and AFC, decreases initially because of specialization and
indivisibilities of inputs at low levels of output and then rises because of diminishing
returns at higher levels of output. AFC declines throughout as fixed expenses are spread
over more units of output. The SRMC curve eventually rises due to diminishing returns,
and intersects the SRAC and AVC curves at their minimum points.

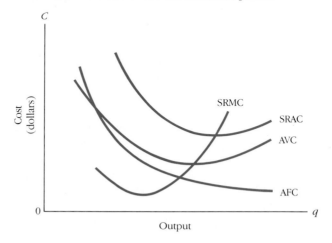

Under these assumptions, as output is increased, average cost will first decline and
then increase, the overall curve being U-shaped. The reasons for this behavior can best
be explained in terms of the reactions to changes in output of the component parts of
average cost: average fixed cost (AFC) and average variable cost (AVC).

Average Fixed Cost

As output increases, AFC declines continuously, since a given sum of total fixed cost is
being spread over successively larger volumes of output. The curve is a rectangular
hyperbola.

Average Variable Cost

Under the assumptions made, AVC will decline initially but ultimately increase. Its
precise behavior is dependent upon the behavior of average physical product (APP) of
the variable factors, under the assumption of given prices for the factor units. If APP
increases as more units of the variable factors are added, then AVC will fall: as each
additional unit of output is produced, the quantity of variable factors required per unit
of output falls. On the other hand, if APP falls, AVC must rise. If APP is constant, AVC will

be unaffected by output changes. These relationships are illustrated in Table 8-2.[5] Each unit of the variable factors (consisting, perhaps, of one worker plus a certain quantity of materials and electric power) is assumed to cost $20. Since APP of the variable factor rises when the number of factor units is increased from one to three, total variable cost rises at a slower rate than output, and thus AVC falls. In the range from three to five units of the variable factor, APP remains constant; total variable cost and total product rise at the same rate, and thus AVC remains constant. With six or more units of the variable factor, diminishing average returns are encountered, APP falls, and AVC rises. We now consider these phases in more detail:

1. The Phase of Declining Average Variable Cost. Under the assumption that the fixed factor units cannot be used effectively without a certain minimum quantity of variable factor units, APP will rise as additional variable units are added, since more effective use is made of fixed factor units. Thus AVC will fall, since the rate of increase in output exceeds the rate of increase in variable factor units. For example, a plant may have a certain set of machines which require five workers for efficient operation. With

---

[5]Since $\text{AVC} = \dfrac{\text{TVC}}{q}$, where q is the output of the firm, then letting (for simplicity) labor (L) be the only variable input (paid a wage, W) we have:

$$\text{AVC} = \frac{\text{TVC}}{q} = \frac{W \cdot L}{q} = \frac{W}{q/L} = \frac{W}{\text{APP}_L}$$

Hence, when APP of the variable factor is rising, AVC must be falling, and vice versa. Costs are, then, inevitably intertwined with the production function relationships discussed in detail in Chapter 7.

TABLE 8-2

Relationship of the Behavior of Average Product of the Variable Factors and Average Variable Cost

Productivity Schedule			Schedule of Variable Costs		
Units of Variable Factor	*Output*	*Average Product per Unit of Variable Factor*	*Output*	*Total Variable Cost*	*Average Variable Cost*
1	5	5.00	5	$ 20	$4.00
2	15	7.50	15	40	2.67
3	30	10.00	30	60	2.00
4	40	10.00	40	80	2.00
5	50	10.00	50	100	2.00
6	54	9.00	54	120	2.22
7	56	8.00	56	140	2.50
8	57	7.125	57	160	2.81

only two or three workers hired, the machines can be used only very ineffectively, and the output per worker will be relatively small. But as the fourth and fifth worker are hired, operation of the machinery reaches a high level of efficiency, so that output per worker is higher and variable cost per unit of product is lower.

The tendency for AVC to fall will be strengthened if the variable factors must be acquired in relatively large indivisible units. It is difficult, for example, to hire workers for only a few hours or to use particular workers on a large number of different tasks. Accordingly, when output is low, a portion of the workforce is not fully utilized; thereafter, a particular percentage increase in output will not require an equivalent percentage increase in labor employed. Thus output per worker will rise, and AVC will fall. The more divisible the units of both fixed and variable factors, the less significant will be the stage of declining AVC. (See Box 8-4.)

2. The Phase of Constant Average Variable Cost.
When the inputs of variable factors have reached such levels that the fixed factors can be employed effectively, and when each variable factor unit is likewise fully utilized, further increases in output over a considerable range may be associated with a more or less constant level of AVC. Through this range of output, a doubling of the variable factors will approximately double the output, and thus the APP and AVC will be roughly constant. This stage will be encountered at relatively low levels of output if fixed factor units are divided into small units because only a small number of variable units are required to operate each fixed unit. If a plant consists of a large number of small identical machines (such as those used in some lines of textile production), efficient operation with a small volume of output can be obtained with only a small labor force. As output is increased, more workers are added and more machines are brought into use; variable cost will be more or less constant per unit of output.

If the nature of a production process is such that operations can be carried on in three shifts of eight hours each, output can be tripled (more or less) from the quantity at which the plant was fully utilized on an eight-hour basis without any significant change in AVC. The ability to vary the speed at which production is carried on likewise increases the range of roughly constant AVC.

Recent empirical studies of cost functions have confirmed the importance of the phase of constant AVC. The phase is not always encountered, however. If the fixed capital requires a certain number of variable units for efficient operation, yet further increases in the number of variable factor units will increase output very little, then the

---

8-4   Can you think of a real-life example of declining average variable costs coupled with greater output per worker?

Extreme examples are found in certain service industries. One bus driver is required whether one passenger or fifty are carried in a bus; as the load increases, the cost per passenger falls.

A movie theatre must have at least one cashier and projectionist on duty while the theatre is open, regardless of the number of customers.

initial phase of decreasing AVC will be followed directly by the phase of increasing AVC.[6]

3. _The Phase of Increasing Average Variable Cost._   Eventually, in any type of business, as output is increased with a fixed plant, AVC will begin to rise because of the decline in APP of the variable factors resulting from the Law of Diminishing Returns. The plant is designed for a certain volume of production; when output is carried beyond this level, the increase in the variable factors necessary to produce the additional output will be relatively greater than the output increase, and AVC will rise. In some production processes the increase will be gradual, as equipment is used longer hours than intended, machinery is operated at a faster rate, and obsolete equipment is placed in use. These adjustments involve some increase in AVC, since maintenance costs rise more than proportionately when machinery is run at a higher rate and older equipment is used. Nevertheless, such adjustments make possible further increases in output without large changes in cost. In some lines of production, however, it may be almost impossible to produce more than the quantity for which the plant was designed; AVC will rise rapidly because a substantial increase in the quantities of the variable factors is required to produce a few more units of output. Once absolute capacity[7] is reached, there are no meaningful AVC figures for larger volumes of output, since such quantities of output cannot be produced. (In such cases, AVC is said to be infinite.)

The Behavior of Average Cost

Since average cost (AC) is the sum of AVC and AFC, its behavior reflects the combined influence of changes in its two constituent elements. As a firm first increases output, AFC must necessarily fall; under the assumptions indicated above, AVC will also fall. As a consequence, AC must fall as well, as illustrated in Table 8-1 and Figure 8-1. The rate of decline will depend upon the relative importance of fixed and variable cost elements, the extent to which fixed factor units consist of large unadaptable units requiring several units of variable factor for efficient operation, and the extent to which the variable factors can be obtained in small units. The rate of decline in AC will be particularly great in large manufacturing establishments with heavy fixed costs and equipment of such nature that effective operation requires a relatively large labor force.

If AVC does not decline initially, or becomes relatively constant once output has

---

[6]If we were to abandon the assumptions that fixed factors require a certain minimum quantity of variable factors for efficient operation and that variable factors cannot be obtained in very small units, then the phase of constant AVC could be encountered initially. It is widely believed, however, that these assumptions are realistic ones, though their significance varies widely in different lines of production.

[7]The term _capacity_ refers in some cases to the "optimum" or "low-cost" level of operation (the minimum of the AC curve), in other cases to the absolute maximum output level possible with the plant. The appropriate meaning should be clear from the context.

reached a certain level, AC will still decline because of the fall in AFC, but the rate of decline will be very low once output has expanded to the point at which fixed costs are a minor element in total cost.

If production is carried far enough, AC must eventually rise. Once the minimum of the AVC curve is reached, AVC will increase and eventually offset the continuing decline in AFC. The speed at which AVC and AC rise will depend primarily upon the nature of the production process, particularly upon the flexibility of the fixed plant—the ability to expand production without a substantial increase in variable factors.

In summary, the **short-run average cost** (SRAC) curve is U-shaped, or ⌣-shaped when AVC is more or less constant over a substantial range of output. Figure 8-2 illustrates the second case. Figure 8-3 illustrates the first case, in which AC falls and rises sharply because the capital equipment is of such nature that a substantial number of workers are required for efficient operation; once the equipment is brought into effective operation, additional output cannot be obtained except by using substantially greater quantities of the variable factor.

The Behavior of Marginal Cost

Since the behavior of marginal cost (MC) depends upon that of total cost, its determinants are the same as those of AC. Certain relationships between MC and AC should be noted, however. When AVC is falling, MC must be less than AVC (but not necessarily falling); likewise, when AC is falling, MC must be less than AC. On the other hand,

FIGURE 8-2

Short-Run Average Cost Curve, with Flexible Plant
When plant size is fixed, but "flexible," the SRAC curve is relatively flat with a large horizontal segment arising from constant returns to scale.

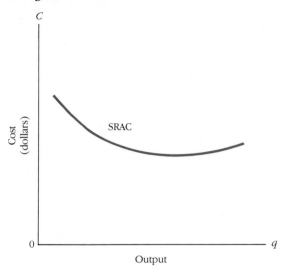

FIGURE 8-3

Short-Run Average Cost Curve, with Inflexible Plant
Inflexible fixed factors become very efficient when variable factors are initially utilized, but once a sufficiently large level of output is reached, large numbers of the variable factors must be added to raise output. The SRAC curve declines sharply and then rises sharply as output increases.

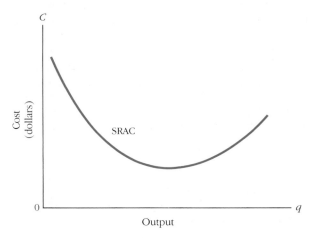

when AVC is rising, MC will be greater than AVC (but not necessarily rising), and when AC is rising, MC must of course exceed AC. Marginal cost is equal to AVC at the lowest point of AVC and is equal to AC at the point of lowest AC. Thus the MC curve intersects both the AVC curve and the AC curve at their respective low points. This relationship is simply a matter of arithmetic: when a number (the marginal cost) being added into a series is smaller than the previous average of the series, the new average will be lower than the previous one; when the number added is larger than the average, the average will rise. (See Box 8-5.)

If AVC is constant, MC and AVC will have the same value, since the production of an additional unit will add to total cost the same amount as the previous average of the

---

8-5   True or False?   If the marginal amount rises, the average will rise.

This is true only if the marginal amount is greater than the average. For example, if you have taken two intermediate microeconomic exams and received a 90% on your first exam and 80% on your second exam, you have an 85% average. If, after some serious "booking," you get a 100% on the third exam (the marginal exam), your average rises to 90%. However, it is possible that the marginal amount could fall and the average still rise. What if your fourth exam was a 94%? Here the *marginal* amount has fallen (you had a 100% on your third test), but the *average* has risen from 90% to 91%.

variable cost. Clearly, adding an amount equal to the previous average will not alter the average.

On the assumption of constant factor prices, the behavior of MC bears a definite relationship to the behavior of the marginal physical product of the variable factors (MPP). When MPP is rising, MC is falling, because each successive unit of the variable factors adds more to total product than did the previous unit, and thus the increase in total cost due to the production of another unit of output will be less than the increase resulting from the production of the previous unit. If the addition of a sixth worker raises output by 45 units a day and the addition of a seventh worker raises output by 65 units, the marginal cost of each of the 65 units is less than that of each of the 45. When MPP is constant, MC will be constant; when MPP is declining, MC will be rising because successive factor units will add progressively less to total output.[8]

The Applicability of the Assumptions

The usefulness of short-run cost analysis depends upon the applicability to actual situations of the assumptions made earlier. The first assumption—that certain factor units are fixed in quantity—follows from the definition of a short-run period and describes the situation which confronts a going concern in relatively short time intervals.

The second and third assumptions relate to the nature of fixed and variable factor units. It was assumed that a certain minimum quantity of variable units is required to utilize the fixed factor units effectively and that at least some of the variable factor units (especially workers) cannot be obtained in very small units. The assumption about fixed factors is relevant to many types of capital equipment in manufacturing; an automobile assembly line, for example, cannot be utilized at all without a certain minimum number of workers. In other lines of production, however, this consideration is much less important. In retailing there is typically no equipment that requires a substantial number of workers to operate. In this type of industry, therefore, there is less likelihood of an increase in APP, and thus an initial decline in AVC from this cause. AFC will of course fall as output increases.

The assumption that variable factor units cannot always be obtained in very small units is more likely to be realized. It is usually difficult to hire a worker for less than a day and it is of course impossible to hire "half a worker." Accordingly, the time of the first workers added will not be fully utilized initially; as output is increased, proportionate increases in inputs of variable factors will not be required, and AVC will fall.

The treatment of technological conditions, factor unit efficiency, and factor prices as

---

[8]Using differentials, and again simplifying as in footnote 5, to the case of labor as the only variable cost component:

$$MC = \frac{d\,TC}{dq} = \frac{d\,TVC}{dq} = \frac{W \cdot dL}{dq} = \frac{W}{dq/dL} = \frac{W}{MP_L}$$

This establishes the text result.

given data is necessary to distinguish the functional relationship of output and unit cost from cost changes due to variations in technology, factor prices, and efficiency. In some instances, however, the price paid for various factor units will change *as a result* of changes in output by the firm; hence the changes are relevant for the nature of a particular cost schedule. When materials are purchased in larger quantities, lower prices are often obtainable. Rate schedules for electric power often provide lower rates per unit for larger quantities than for smaller amounts; shipping in carload or truckload quantities reduces freight costs per unit. When quantity discounts are available, the net cost per unit of the variable factors falls as more units are acquired, and the decline in AVC due to the initial rise in APP per unit of the variable factors is reinforced. In retailing and some other lines of business, the quantity discount feature is of particular importance and is likely to be of greater significance in bringing about an initial decline in AVC than the behavior of APP because of the relative unimportance of capital equipment in these lines of business.

As a firm continues to expand, however, eventually all available quantity discounts will be obtained, and further increases in factor purchases may drive factor prices upward. For example, if a large firm is the principal employer of skilled labor in a certain area, it may eventually exhaust the local supply of this type of labor; further increases in output will necessitate the payment of higher wages to draw workers from other plants or from more distant areas. To the extent that factor prices are increased as output increases, AVC will tend to shift upward. This effect will reinforce the increase produced by the decline in APP. (See Box 8-6.)

Empirical Studies of Short-Run Cost Behavior

The determination of the data in an actual cost schedule of a particular firm is a difficult task, far more so than it might appear at first glance. A firm usually has a reasonably accurate knowledge of average cost at existing output levels but nothing more than a rough estimate of costs at other output levels. Serious attempts to ascertain these data are rare, and the difficulties involved in doing so prevent the results from being entirely accurate. The firm must, however, base its policy upon *some* estimate of cost

---

8-6 True or False? While factor prices may rise as a firm increases output, the additional factor units may be less efficient.

True. The assumption of homogeneous factor units is by no means necessarily realized in practice. Presumably a firm will hire the most efficient workers first. As additional workers are hired, successive workers are likely to be less skilled and less capable, at least in the production of the good in question. Thus the decline in APP and the rise in AVC will be greater than would result from the Law of Diminishing Returns alone, unless the prices paid for less efficient factor units are proportionately lower than those paid for better units. But often they are not.

behavior. Various studies of business policy suggest that firms rarely attempt to ascertain marginal cost as such, seeking instead to determine optimum price and output levels with the use of total and average cost and revenue data. On the whole, however, firms probably have better knowledge of their cost schedules than of their demand schedules, since the latter are dependent upon often unpredictable reactions of customers and competitors.

A number of studies have been made of cost schedules in particular industries, primarily to determine whether the pattern of cost behavior developed by economic analysis accords with actual behavior. Such studies have encountered very serious problems. A major one arises from changes in the underlying determinants of cost schedules—factor prices, techniques of production, and so on—during the period under study. Statistical techniques to isolate cost changes due to output changes from those due to shifts in these other factors are not entirely satisfactory. Also, in any particular period, costs may be affected by the *rate* at which output changes; a sudden increase may cause temporary additions to cost which can be avoided once production is adjusted to the higher volume. Another problem involves the time periods in which costs are recorded. Raw materials might be purchased in large quantities and charged as expenses in a period when output is low (but is expected to increase), then used in a later period when few materials are purchased. The measurement of units of output likewise is a source of difficulty. Most firms produce several types of products, the relative importance of which is likely to change. Finally, the range of output may be relatively narrow, such that only a small segment of the schedule can be computed; the data obtained cannot safely be projected into ranges of output for which no data are available.

A most important discovery is the importance of the phase of constant AVC. Within the ranges of output for some industries for which data were available, AVC and thus MC were found to be relatively constant—like those in Figures 8-4 and 8-5. Therefore, the typical AVC curve would appear to contain an extensive horizontal section rather than being sharply U- or V-shaped.

8.7 COST SCHEDULES WITH LONG-RUN ADJUSTMENTS COMPLETED

The long-run period has been defined as a period sufficiently long for a firm to make desired adjustments in all factors of production employed. The long run, as emphasized earlier, is always a *planning* period, since at any moment firms are inevitably in some short-run situation. In the long run, however, a firm can choose any short-run plant configuration. The actual time interval depends upon the nature of the productive processes and particularly upon the extent to which specialized types of capital equipment requiring a substantial period to construct and having a certain lifespan are utilized. The time needed to allow adjustment of all factors is much greater for a steel mill or railroad than for a service station or grocery store. Over a long-run period, since all factors are adjustable, all costs are variable.

FIGURE 8-4

A Typical Short-Run Average Cost Curve
Empirical studies generally find that the SRAC curve is constant for some output levels.

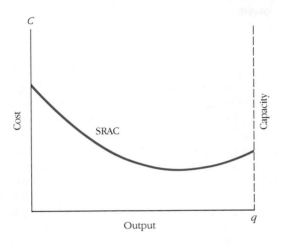

The Nature of the Long-Run Cost Schedule

For each level of output, the long-run cost schedule shows the *lowest possible cost* of production, given a significant time interval for all factors to be adjusted and the absolute optimum factor combination to be attained. In Table 8-1, the total cost of producing ten units is $3,020 with the particular plant. But this plant was designed for

FIGURE 8-5

Another Pattern of Short-Run Average Cost
In this example, the SRAC curve is constant over an even greater range of output.

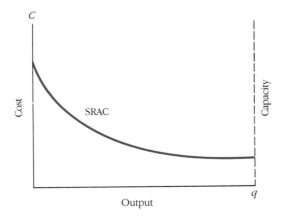

four units per day, a much smaller volume of output. With the plant best suited for ten units, one considerably larger, the total cost of producing ten units per day might be $190. This figure, since it is the lowest possible cost of producing ten units, is the appropriate cost figure for this level of output in the long-run cost schedule. Similarly, for other levels of output, there are certain figures of lowest possible total cost, each with a plant size—a combination of all factors—best suited to the particular output levels.

A typical long-run cost schedule for a firm is illustrated in Table 8-3. The data are obtained from a number of short-run cost schedules, one for each possible size of plant. The data taken for the long-run schedule from each of the short-run schedules are the cost figures for those levels of output for which the particular plant allows the most satisfactory factor combination and lowest cost. From the short-run schedule shown in Table 8-1, the cost data for four, five, and six units of output might go into the long-run schedule, since the plant allows a lower cost for this output range than any other. But for a daily output of seven or eight units, a somewhat larger plant would be more suitable; and the long-run cost figures, taken from the short-run cost data for the larger plant, would be lower than the figures for producing these amounts of output with the smaller plant. For output of three units or less a day, a plant smaller than that for which the data are given in Table 8-1 would allow still lower cost.

By employing isoquant analysis (see Chapter 7), one can easily see why short-run costs are generally higher than long-run costs. Consider Figure 8-6, which depicts at (K_0, L_0) the optimal long-run (and short-run) input bundle to employ if q_0 is the desired output. Any other way of producing q_0 will involve greater cost as long as relative input prices are constant. Suppose that the firm in question has been producing q_0 in this manner and now wishes to produce q_1, a larger output. This would happen, for example, if the price of the good being produced were to rise.

Clearly, the least-cost way to produce q_1, if all inputs were adjustable as in the long

TABLE 8-3

Typical Long-Run Average Cost Schedule of a Firm

Units of Output	Total Cost	Average Cost	Marginal Cost
5	$125	$25.00	—
10	190	19.00	$13.00*
15	263	17.35	14.60
20	340	17.00	15.40
25	418	16.72	15.60
30	498	16.60	16.00
35	579	16.54	16.20
40	664	16.60	17.00
45	751	16.69	17.40
50	845	16.90	18.80

*The increase in total cost of $65 resulting when five additional units are produced, divided by five.

FIGURE 8-6

FIGURE 8-6

A Graphic Illustration of Why Short-Run Costs Are Generally Greater Than Long-Run Costs

In the short run, capital is fixed at K_0. To produce q_1, the firm will hire L_{SR} labor. The short-run cost, represented by the dashed isocost line, exceeds the long-run cost, represented by the isocost line passing through K_{LR}, L_{LR}.

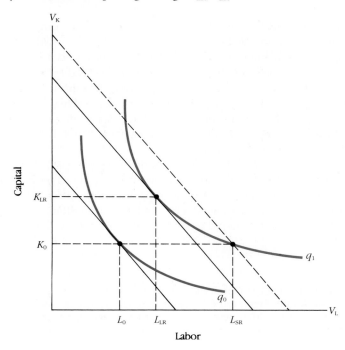

run, would be by employing (K_{LR}, L_{LR}) as shown by the tangency of the isocost line. But, by definition, the short-run period is too short to vary all inputs. Suppose that the stock of capital (plant and equipment) is fixed in the short run at K_0. In this case, the least-cost way to produce q_1 is by employing (K_0, L_{SR}).[9]

Long-Run Average Cost (LRAC) for any output level is determined by dividing the long-run *total cost* for this output by the number of units of output. Long-run average cost may be defined as the lowest possible average cost of producing a particular amount of output with the optimum plant size, and thus factor combination, for that particular amount of output.

---

[9]However, as indicated by the dashed isocost line, the firm could lower the cost of producing q_1 if it could substitute capital for labor until the tangency is reached. An important exercise for the reader would be to depict the situation of Figure 8-6 using long-run and short-run total cost curves and average cost curves. This exercise clarifies greatly how all of the cost and production analysis interrelates.

Each firm has many alternative scales of operation, or plant sizes, which it may build or operate; for each of these there is an appropriate SRAC schedule and curve. The pattern of these curves, for various scales of operation, may be drawn on a single graph, as illustrated in Figure 8-7. For simplification, cost curves of only three possible scales are shown, under the assumption (not unrealistic for many industries) that indivisibilities of some factor units prevent the use of intermediate scales of operation.

Certain relationships among the successive curves should be emphasized. For very small output levels, costs are lowest with plant size $SRAC_1$. Costs with plant size $SRAC_1$ (and larger) are relatively high for these low levels of output because the plants fixed costs are far too high for low levels of output. But beyond the lowest of output, costs with plant size $SRAC_2$ are lower than those with $SRAC_1$. If output levels in this range were produced with plant $SRAC_1$, the plant would be operated beyond designed capacity, and AVC would be high. In contrast, plant $SRAC_2$, designed for a larger volume of output, would be operating close to optimum capacity. For still higher volumes of output, cost is lower with plant $SRAC_3$.

For each level of output, LRAC is represented by the appropriate point on that SRAC curve which reaches the lowest level for the particular output. If a perpendicular line is extended upward from the output axis on a graph containing the various SRAC curves for different-sized plants, the point at which it first strikes an SRAC curve indicates the relevant value of LRAC for that output level. Thus in Figure 8-7, at low levels of output

FIGURE 8-7

Short-Run Average Total Cost Curves and the Long-Run Average Cost Curve
The LRAC curve shows the minimum cost per unit of each level of output. The firm chooses the plant scale coinciding with the lowest SRAC curve for each output level. The LRAC curve, therefore, is the envelope or lower boundary of the feasible SRAC curves.

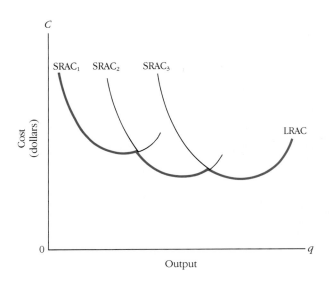

the lowest average cost point is on curve $SRAC_1$; at high levels, it is on $SRAC_3$. The LRAC curve is identical with $SRAC_0$ up to a certain level of output (the intersection of $SRAC_1$ and $SRAC_2$), and so on. The entire long-run average cost curve LRAC (for the output range covered) is indicated in Figure 8-7 by the heavily shaded line. If the LRAC curve is plotted directly from an LRAC schedule such as that presented in Table 8-3, the only portions of the short-run curves which will appear are those which comprise portions of the long-run curve itself. It is important to note that the long-run schedule contains no data which are not to be found in the firm's various short-run schedules.[10]

When all factors are divisible into small units, the successive scales of operation will be close to one another, as in Figure 8-8; and the LRAC curve will be smooth, as shown in Figure 8-9.When indivisibilities prevent small adjustments in plant scale, the short-run curves will be farther apart; and the long-run curves will be irregular, as in Figure 8-7. (The LRMC curve included in Figure 8-9 will be discussed below.)

Reiterating, LRAC curve is often called a *planning curve* since it represents the cost data relevant to the firm when it is planning policy relating to scale of operations, output, and price over a substantial period of time. At any particular time, a firm

---

[10]In mathematical language, the long-run curve is the lower *envelope* of the short-run curves.

FIGURE 8-8

Pattern of Short-Run Average Cost Curves, When All Factors Are Divisible
When fixed factors are divisible, SRAC curves are close together. Each SRAC curve contributes one point to the LRAC curve. Divisibility implies an infinite number of plant scales and a smooth LRAC curve.

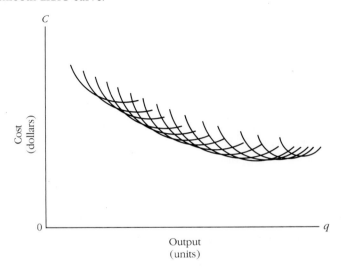

FIGURE 8-9

Long-Run Average Cost Curve Derived from Short-Run Cost Curves in Figure 8-8
The LRAC or envelope curve is smooth when numerous feasible plant scales are available.
Long-run marginal costs are derived from the short-run marginal cost associated with the
least-cost way of producing any quantity (see Figure 8-10).

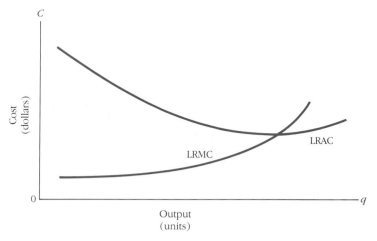

already in operation has a certain plant and must base its current price and output
decisions upon the cost schedule with the existing plant. But when the firm
considers the possibility of adjustment in scale of operations, long-run cost estimates
are necessary.

Note that the LRAC schedule does *not* contain historical data showing what cost has
been in the past with various-sized plants; it shows alternative possibilities at the
present time—what cost would be for various levels of output if various-sized plants
were built.

The Behavior of Long-Run Average Cost

The behavior of LRAC in response to changes in output is controlled by considerations
substantially different from those affecting cost behavior with a particular plant. Short-
run cost behavior is conditioned very largely by the presence of constant quantities of
some factors, which are responsible not only for certain costs being fixed but also for
the nature of the reactions of variable costs to output changes. In a period of time
sufficiently long for the scale of operations to be adjusted, all factors are adjustable, and
the consideration of fixed factors is no longer relevant for cost behavior.

The analysis of long-run cost behavior is based upon the following assumptions:

1. All factors are variable in quantity.
2. Certain factors may be indivisible, in the sense that they cannot be obtained in
   infinitesimally small units, or are relatively inefficient if reduced in size below a
   certain figure.

3. An increase in the quantities of all factors allows greater specialization in the utilization of particular factor units.

4. The managerial factor cannot be multiplied in the same manner as other factors because of the need for maintaining unified control over the entire enterprise.

The major "givens" are the same as those of the short-run schedules: factor prices, technological conditions, and equal efficiency of successive factor units (homogenous inputs).

With these assumptions, the primary determinant of the behavior of LRAC is the manner in which the Principle of Returns to Scale operates in the particular production activity, and thus the behavior of changes in output as the inputs of all factor units are changed. As indicated in Chapter 7, a firm typically experiences increasing returns to scale as it expands its operations initially—in part because of indivisibilities of some factors, especially capital equipment, which make operation on a small-scale basis inefficient and costly, and in part because of advantages of specialization of labor. As a consequence, since output rises at a faster rate than the rate of increase in factor units, total cost rises at a slower rate than output, and average cost falls. Typically, as a firm expands, the low-cost points for the cost curves for successively larger plants will be progressively lower. This is illustrated in Figure 8-7: here the low segment of SRAC$_2$— the segment which constitutes a portion of the LRAC curve— is lower than the low segment of SRAC$_1$, and that of SRAC$_3$ is lower than that of SRAC$_2$. Hence the LRAC curve slopes downward from left to right in the initial stage.

Eventually, however, the economies of large-scale production will be exhausted; otherwise there would just be *one* firm in every industry (whichever got biggest first). The best available types of capital equipment will be employed and utilized to capacity, and full advantage will be gained from specialization. Once a point is reached at which all workers are performing tasks sufficiently limited in scope, further increases in output merely require additional workers doing the same tasks. When output reaches the level at which the stage of increasing returns to scale is succeeded by that of constant returns, total cost and output will increase at the same rate, and average cost will be constant. Especially in industries where little capital equipment is used and thus few economies of large-scale production are available, the stage of constant average cost may begin at relatively low levels of output and extend over a very substantial range. By contrast, wherever there are important indivisibilities and gains from labor specialization, constant average cost will be encountered only after a long phase of decreasing cost.

Eventually, if expansion is carried far enough, decreasing returns to scale (caused, as explained in Chapter 7, by the complexities of large-scale management) will make LRAC progressively greater for successively larger output levels. This rise is likely to be very gradual, however, and is not at all comparable with the rapid rise in average cost in the short run, when expansion of output beyond the designed capacity causes a sharp increase in variable cost and therefore in average cost. (See Box 8-7.)

Under these assumptions, the LRAC curve is ⌣-shaped, the rate of decrease on the left-hand portion being much greater in some industries than in others, the rate of increase in the right-hand portion being very gradual. The exact shape of the curve in any particular case depends upon the manner in which the Principle of Returns to

8-7   True or False?   If forced to sell larger outputs in more distant markets, a firm's average cost may rise as output expands.

True. As a firm increases its output, it often must sell to buyers at greater distances from the plant. Increased transportation costs raise the average cost of production and (joint) distribution. The firm may seek to avoid this by building additional plants in other areas; but if the original location was the one most suited to the particular type of production, costs will be higher in the new plants. A good example of this geographical property is provided by electric power generating plants; despite substantial scale economies of *production*, costs rise when distribution costs are, as appropriate, considered.

Scale operated—that is, the extent to which economies of large-scale production are available, the level to which output must be expanded before economies are completely exhausted, and the extent to which complexities of large-scale management are encountered. Thus, industries in which the lowest possible cost can be obtained with a small volume of output are characterized by a large number of small firms. In other industries, where low cost is obtained only when output reaches a substantial figure, firms tend to grow large in size, and small firms have difficulty competing.

Long-Run Marginal Cost

The concept of **long-run marginal cost** (LRMC) refers to the increase in total cost which occurs when a shift is made to a one-unit-higher scale of production, with optimum factor combinations both before and after the change (see the two representative tangencies in Figure 8-6). Since changes in scale ordinarily cannot be made economically in small increments, LRMC may be regarded more realistically as the increase in total cost which occurs when a transition is made from one scale of output to the next highest scale, divided by the number of units of increase in output which results. That is, if with a scale of plant designed for 20 units per day, total cost is $340, and with the next-largest feasible scale, one designed for 25 units, total cost is $418, then LRMC is $15.60 a unit ($78 increase in total cost divided by five units increase in output).

Long-run marginal cost bears the same relation to LRAC as short-run marginal cost (SRMC) does to short-run average cost (SRAC). Generalization about the relationship of LRMC to SRMC schedules for the various possible plants is more difficult. For any given plant, SRMC will be lower than LRMC for ranges of output up to a certain level, since SRMC is affected only by cost elements which are variable in the short run whereas all cost elements enter into LRMC. Beyond a certain point, however, LRMC will be less than SRMC, since the latter is affected by the effort to get more and more output from a given plant capacity and thus is subject to the Law of Diminishing Returns.

The subtle relationship between LRMC and SRMC requires further explanation. First, in terms of formal derivation, see Figure 8-10. The LRMC curve is derived, at each

FIGURE 8-10

Deriving the LRMC Curve from the SRMC Curves
The SRMC corresponding to the optimum SRAC for each output level equals the LRMC. For example, $SRMC_0$ coincides with the minimum cost plant given by $SRAC_0$ for q_0. Thus, the short-run marginal cost along $SRMC_0$ at q_0 is the long-run marginal cost of producing q_0.

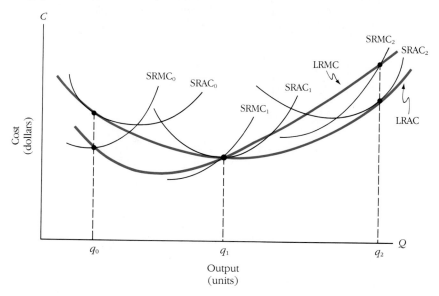

output level, from the short-run marginal cost of production at that output level *if* the least average cost plant is being used to produce that output. Hence, at output level q_0, the short-run marginal cost of production provides one point on the long-run marginal cost curve. Similarly, other points on the SRMC curves corresponding to the least cost of producing q_1 and q_2 (and all other output levels) are used to flesh out the full LRMC curve (see the LRMC curve in Figure 8-10).

A puzzle emerges from examination of points like q_0, q_1, or q_2: unlike with the average cost curves, the LRMC is *not* an envelope of the corresponding SRMCs. Looking at output levels to the left of each of the output levels depicted in Figure 8-10, we see that the short-run marginal cost is *less* than the long-run marginal cost. How can this be?

The answer to the puzzle is most readily seen by returning to an isoquant diagram corresponding to, say, q_0 in Figure 8-10. This is shown as Figure 8-11. Isoquant q' represents the combination of L and K which can produce a smaller amount of output than q_0 of Figures 8-10 and 8-11. In the *short run*, however, capital is fixed at K_0. To produce q' (with the plant designed to produce q_0), a large amount of the variable input, labor, can be released—because the labor remaining, L_{SR}, having a large amount of capital to work with, is very productive. Hence, for outputs smaller than those for which a plant is the least-cost producer, the short-run marginal cost is *less*

■■■■■■■■
FIGURE 8-11

**A Demonstration That the Long-Run Marginal Cost
Can Be *Greater* Than the Short-Run Marginal Cost**
The additional cost of increasing output from q' in the short run is illustrated by the
increase in cost from the isocost containing L_{SR} to the isocost containing L_0. In the long
run, a greater increase in cost occurs from the isocost that goes through L_{LR} to the L_0
isocost. Thus, LRMC > SRMC for output levels *below* the designed plant capacity, while
LRMC < SRMC for output levels *above* the designed plant capacity.

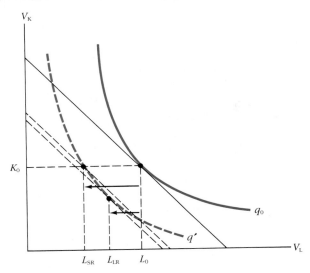

than the long-run marginal cost: *more* of the costly variable inputs are released in the
short run than are released in the long run as output is reduced. The situation is
reversed for outputs exceeding those for which a particular plant is least cost.

The Significance of the Assumptions

The significance of this analysis depends upon the applicability in particular situations
of the assumptions upon which it is based. Each of the assumptions will be examined
briefly.

1. Variability of Factors.   The assumption that all factors can be varied in the
long-run period is valid except in rare cases of unique, specialized resources.

2. Factor Indivisibility.   The assumption that small units of certain factors cannot
be obtained, or are relatively inefficient, appears to be applicable in many lines of
production. It is not possible, for example, to build all types of capital equipment on a
small-scale basis; and some, while they can be built this way, provide relatively low
output per unit of input. Labor often cannot be obtained in very small units, such as
hiring workers by the minute or hour. While these considerations are more important
in some lines of production than in others, both casual observation and careful empir-

ical studies suggest that some indivisibilities are encountered in virtually all lines of production.

3. *Gains from Specialization of Factor Units.* Economies appear typically to be obtainable by utilization of labor and other factor units in more specialized fashion at larger output levels.

Despite the obviously extensive validity of assumptions 2 and 3, it must be recognized that if, in a particular instance, neither assumption is valid, LRAC cannot be expected to decline initially.

4. *Adjustment of the Managerial Factor.* The assumption that the managerial factor cannot be adjusted in the same manner as other factors, with consequent increasing complexities and cost of management as an enterprise grows, is subject to greater question. The problems of large-scale management are, of course, very real. But as business firms grow in size, attention is given to the development and application of the principles of management in an effort to overcome these problems. By this means, firms may succeed in preventing an increase in average cost for a very substantial range of output. Whether this increase can be prevented indefinitely as output is extended is dubious, but a rise in average cost is by no means inevitable over substantial output ranges.

Empirical Studies of Long-Run Cost Schedules

Few producers have precise data about long-run cost behavior, but they are concerned with only a small segment of the cost schedule at any time. They know that costs with a very small plant would be prohibitively high, for example, but they do not care exactly how high these might be. A firm in imperfectly competitive markets does not consider the costs with a plant ten times the present size because it could not possibly sell the increased output at a profitable price. Its attention centers on a much narrower range of plant sizes. If a producer suspects that a change might be desirable, the firm will attempt to figure the cost with various scales of operation, aided by engineering estimates and by data on costs of other firms with larger or smaller scales of operation than its own. Once a plant adjustment is made, the decision is irrevocable for a period of time, even if the cost estimate upon which it is based proves to be erroneous, since additional time is required for further changes.

Empirical studies have been made of long-run cost behavior, but the results have not been at all conclusive. The problems encountered are even more serious than those arising in short-run cost studies. Any attempt to determine the actual long-run cost functions of a single firm from observations of cost with different scales of operation over a period of time is almost entirely futile. Because of the length of the time period necessary to get any substantial number of observations, other determinants of cost—particularly methods of production—change so much that statistical adjustment for them is extremely difficult. As a consequence, most actual studies have taken cost data for several firms of different sizes at a particular time in order to build up a cost schedule typical of firms in the industry. This approach also encounters serious problems, though. Some firms may operate closer to capacity than others, and thus the cost differences will reflect variations in the degree of plant utilization as well as those due to differences in plant size. Differences in age of equipment, quality of product, management efficiency, cost accounting methods, and prices paid for factors prevent exact attainment of the desired results, since the effects of these differences cannot be adequately eliminated.

It is likely that LRAC declines as the scale of operation is increased from a very small size. However, there is much less evidence that increased complexities of management and decreasing returns to scale must eventually cause LRAC to rise as the scale of operation is expanded. There is some evidence that LRAC does *eventually* rise in some industries as operation is expanded, but primarily as a result of the tendency of prices paid for factors and of distribution costs to rise.

8.8 COST CONDITIONS OF THE INDUSTRY

The preceding sections have considered the behavior of cost of the individual firm as it varies with output, on the assumptions that prices paid for factor units are given, except insofar as they may be influenced by changes in the output of the firm itself, and that the efficiency of factor units is given. There is much greater likelihood of changes occurring in factor prices and in factor efficiency when the output of an entire industry changes. The expression "cost conditions of the industry" is given to the relationship between changes in output of an industry and consequent changes in the height of the cost schedules of the individual firms.

There are three possible industry cost conditions: increasing, decreasing, and constant.

Increasing-Cost Industries

In an **increasing-cost industry**, the cost schedules of the individual firms rise as the total output of the industry increases.

Increasing-cost conditions result from **external diseconomies** of large-scale production, primarily increases in factor prices which occur as larger quantities of factors are employed in the industry. When an industry utilizes a large and increasing portion of a factor whose total supply is not perfectly elastic, factor prices will rise. Increasing-cost conditions are typical of "extractive" industries such as agriculture, fishing, mining, and lumbering, which utilize large portions of the total supply of specialized natural resources such as land or mineral deposits. As the output of such an industry expands, increased demand for the resources raises the prices that must be paid for their use. Since additional resources of given quality cannot be produced, greater supplies can be obtained (if at all) only by taking them away from other industries or by using lower-quality (and thus higher-cost) resources. Wheat production is a typical example of an increasing-cost industry. As the output of wheat increases, the demand for land suitable for wheat production rises, and thus the price paid for the use or purchase of the land increases. Farmers owning their own land prior to the output increase do not experience an increase in their expenditure costs, but their total costs increase just as do those of tenant farmers: the opportunity cost of using the land in their own production instead of renting it to others is now greater than before. (See Box 8-8.)

Decreasing-Cost Industries

In a **decreasing-cost industry**, as total output of the industry increases, the firms' cost schedules fall because of external economies of large-scale production—economies, in the sense of cost reductions, which no one firm can gain by its own expansion, but which occur as the industry's total output increases. Consider a new mining region, developed in an area remote from railroad facilities in the days before the motor vehicle. So long as the total output of the mines was small, the ore was hauled by wagon, an extremely expensive form of transport. But when the number of mines increased, and the total output of the region rose substantially, it became feasible to construct a railroad to serve the area. The railroad lowered transportation costs and reduced the cost schedules of all the firms.

Some industries may operate under decreasing-cost conditions in short intervals of output expansion, when continued growth makes possible the supplying of materials or services at reduced cost. As a practical matter, however, external economies are rarely encountered.

It should be noted that when *one firm* produces the entire output of a product in a particular market, the firm may find it profitable to operate at a volume of output less than that of lowest average cost. As a consequence, if the firm increases its sales, its average cost will fall. The term decreasing-cost industry is sometimes defined to include this case, as well as that described in the previous paragraphs. Thus the electric power industry is frequently called a decreasing-cost industry. It should be recognized, however, that in this case the decline in average cost which occurs as output increases involves a movement within a particular cost schedule of an individual firm (and thus along a particular cost curve), whereas the case of decreasing cost due to external economies involves a shifting of the entire cost schedule as more firms enter and existing firms expand.

8-8   True or False?   Increasing-cost conditions may also arise from a reduction in efficiency of production as total output of the industry increases.

True.   In an agricultural area irrigated from wells, for example, increased production—and pumping of water—will lower the water table and increase pumping costs for all farmers in the area. Similar problems arise in oil production: an increase in the number of wells in a field will lessen the pressure and increase the difficulty and cost of getting the oil to the surface. As more and more planes use the New York area airports, the delay in landing increases both costs and accident hazards.

The concept of a decreasing-cost industry cannot usefully be applied to situations in which individual firms in nonmonopoly situations are operating on the decreasing-cost portions of their LRAC curves, as may be typical in many imperfectly competitive fields. Likewise, the concept of a decreasing-cost industry is not used in reference to situations in which average cost declines over a certain period because of the development of new methods of production. This is merely an historical cost change resulting from a shift in one of the determinants of cost, not a cost change due to industry expansion.

Constant-Cost Industries

Constant-cost conditions, where the firms' cost schedules are not affected by changes in the output of the entire industry, occur when an industry does not use factors in sufficient quantities for their prices or efficiency to be affected by changes in the output of the industry. One may think of this case as representing the ability to exactly replicate existing firms as output expands, with no input cost changes. Hence, if industry output doubles, there are just twice as many firms as before, each having unchanged costs. Diagrammatic presentation of the various cost conditions is feasible only for perfectly competitive industries and will be deferred to Chapter 9.

8.9 FURTHER COMPLEXITIES OF COST

The preceding cost analysis has been based upon two simplifying assumptions; effects of changes in certain cost elements upon demand schedules for the product have been ignored, as has the fact that firms frequently produce more than one product. The cost elements for activities which affect sales are known as **selling costs** (in contrast to *production* costs arising from the actual manufacture of the goods). Selling costs are incurred for the purpose of influencing the buyer's choice for the product or service. Their existence creates an interrelationship between cost schedules and demand schedules, which will be considered in Chapter 12.

The production of more than one product by a firm—a practice that is almost universal—gives rise to **common costs**, those which are incurred for the production of two or more products, no one of which is responsible for any particular part of the cost. Thus the cost of maintaining a railroad line is a common cost for freight and passenger traffic. The concept of average cost for each product is no longer precise when common costs are allocated among the various products produced.

8.10 THE PROBLEM OF DISEQUILIBRIUM

Throughout the last two chapters we have tacitly assumed that the cost and revenue estimates of business firms are unaffected by realized results. More specifically, we have ignored possible inconsistencies between the input and output plans of business firms and the factor supply and consumption plans of households. In effect, therefore, we have developed the entire theory of business behavior on the presupposition that no individual firm ever confronts a situation of market disequilibrium.

If we proceeded on the basis of the contrary supposition—that is, assuming that the normal state of a market economy is one of disequilibrium—the first victim would have been our assumption that revenue and cost conditions as seen by business firms are stable functions of time. Without this assumption, we could not have derived even the simplest cost and revenue curves nor stated any simple rules for profit-maximizing behavior. This would have been merely the beginning of a long list of consequences, the total impact of which would have been analytically disastrous.

In defense of this procedure, we might say, first, that it is traditional; second, that the situation described is conceivable if not likely; third, that a theory of equilibrium is a necessary and natural point of departure in the development of theories of disequilibrium. Though the first two points are not without force, the last is the most compelling. Concern with short-run problems of economic adjustment is a relatively recent phenomenon, and the development of theoretical models to deal with such problems is still in its infancy. The theory we have is certainly not complete; but provided we recognize its limitations, it represents our best hope for something better.

SUMMARY

1. Economists broadly define *costs* as the necessary compensations received by the owners of the money capital and factor units used by a firm. Costs, then, are the *opportunity* costs of inputs in their best alternative pursuit. Some private costs, however, are *not* social costs in this sense, notably taxes.

2. There are two types of total costs: explicit and implicit. Explicit costs involve a firm's direct costs such as wages, fuel, and raw materials. Implicit costs refer to the opportunity costs of employing resources elsewhere, in spite of the fact that there is no explicit charge.

3. In the long-run period, all costs are variable. In the short run, however, some costs are fixed such as capital equipment, taxes, and insurance. These fixed costs are independent of output.

4. The cost of producing various amounts of output depends primarily upon three considerations: the technique of production, the efficiency of the factor units employed, and the prices paid for factor units.

5. Short-run cost schedules for a firm show the behavior of cost when output is varied with a given plant when factor prices are fixed.

6. Short-run average cost is equal to total costs divided by the number of units of output. Average total cost is equal to average fixed cost (total fixed costs divided by the number of units of output) *plus* average variable cost (total variable cost divided by the number of units of output).

7. Short-run average variable cost passes through three successive phases as output is increased: the phase of declining average variable cost, the phase of constant average variable cost, and the phase of increasing average variable cost.

8. The long run is a planning period, since at any point firms are always in some short-run situation. The long-run cost schedule shows, for each level of output, the lowest possible cost of producing the particular amount of output given a sufficient time interval. The long-run average cost curve shows alternative possibilities at the *present* time, although production with the best-size plant cannot necessarily begin at the present time.

9. The primary determinant of long-run costs is the manner in which the Principle of Returns to Scale (increasing, constant or decreasing returns to scale) operates in the particular production activity and thus the behavior of changes in output as the inputs of all factor units are changed.

10. Long-run marginal cost is the increase in total costs that occurs when a transition is made from optimal production of one scale of output to the next highest scale, divided by the number of units of increase in output which results.

11. The term "industry cost conditions" describes the relationship between an industry's changes in output and consequent changes in the height of an individual firm's cost schedule. There are three possible industry cost conditions: increasing-cost industries, decreasing-cost industries, and constant-cost industries.

WORDS AND CONCEPTS FOR REVIEW

cost   average cost
explicit costs   average fixed cost
implicit costs   average variable cost
depreciation   marginal cost
long-run period   long-run average cost
short-run period   long-run marginal cost
plant   external diseconomies
fixed costs   increasing-cost industry
variable costs   decreasing-cost industry
fully variable costs   constant-cost industry
semivariable costs   selling costs
short-run cost schedules   common costs

REVIEW QUESTIONS

1. What is the meaning of the concept of cost, as used in economic analysis?

2. What is the difference between expenditure and nonexpenditure costs? Give examples of each.

3. What payments made by business firms are not regarded as costs, at least during the period in which they were made?

4. Which implicit cost is treated as a business expense under usual accounting principles?

5. What is the difference between the concepts of short-run and long-run periods?

6. How are fixed costs and variable costs different? The latter are variable with respect to what?

7. What are the major fixed and variable cost items?

8. Why are all costs variable in a long-run period?

9. What is the difference between fully variable and semivariable costs and between semivariable costs and fixed costs?

10. Is depreciation a cost? Explain.

11. What is your opportunity cost of attending college? Of taking a vacation this summer instead of working?

12. Would you expect each of the following to be (in typical cases in the short run) fixed or variable costs?

    a. sales taxes
    b. property taxes
    c. rent on a factory building
    d. interest on money borrowed to buy additional materials
    e. fire insurance
    f. cost of goods sold
    g. the salary of the president of the company

13. List the major assumptions in short-run cost analysis. Are these assumptions realistic? Compare these with the assumptions used in the analysis of long-run cost behavior.

14. A firm, with a particular plant, has daily fixed costs of $400. Total variable costs for successive quantities of output, per day, are as follows:

Output	Total Variable Cost	Output	Total Variable Cost
1	$200	6	$ 400
2	250	7	450
3	275	8	550
4	300	9	750
5	350	10	1,500

Determine short-run average fixed cost, average variable cost, average cost, and marginal cost.

15. Why does marginal cost reflect solely variable cost?

16. Why does the SRMC curve intersect both the SRAC and the SRAVC curve at their lowest points?

17. If in the short run AVC is falling, must MC be falling? Must MC be less than AVC under these conditions? Explain.

18. Why does AFC decline continuously as a firm increases output?

19. Under what circumstances will AVC decline initially as a firm increases output?

20. Why will AVC eventually rise as a firm continues to increase output?

21. Why is the SRAC curve generally believed to be U-shaped?

22. What significance does the Law of Diminishing Returns have for the behavior of SRAC?

23. Why does the AVC fall if APP of the variable factor is rising?

24. Adding units of variable factors, costing $50 per unit, firm output increases as follows:

Units of Factor	Total Output
1	8
2	20
3	45
4	54
5	60
6	63
7	64

Determine AVC for the range of output for which information is available.

25. Under what circumstances is a firm likely to experience a long range of constant AVC?

26. In what respect does the ability to operate an enterprise on more than one shift affect the behavior of SRAC?

27. Define carefully the term long-run average cost.

28. How is the long-run cost schedule built up from the short-run cost schedules?

29. Why may the LRAC curve be irregularly shaped?

30. Under what conditions will LRAC decline as a firm first expands its scale of operations? Compare the causes of this decline with the causes of decline in SRAC as a firm expands output with a given plant.

31. What may cause an eventual increase in LRAC if a firm continues to expand?

32. Define the concept of cost conditions of the industry.

33. Under what circumstances will an industry be one of increasing cost? Of decreasing cost?

34. Distinguish between external economies and internal economies.

35. What are common costs?

36. Under what cost conditions is it likely that the following industries operate?
   a. lumber production
   b. silver mining
   c. rubber-band production
   d. fishing
   e. corn

SUGGESTED READINGS

Baumol, W. *Economic Theory and Operations Analysis*, 4th ed. Englewood Cliffs, NJ: Prentice-Hall Publishers, 1977, Chapter 11.

Clark, J. M. *Studies in the Economics of Overhead Costs*. Chicago: University of Chicago Press, 1923.

Ferguson, C. E. *The Neoclassical Theory of Production and Distribution*. Cambridge, England: Cambridge University Press, 1969, Chapter 6.

Viner, J. "Cost Curves and Supply Curves." In G.J. Stigler and K.E. Boulding (eds.). *Readings in Price Theory*. Homewood, IL: Irwin, 1952.

9

Competitive Price Determination

9.1 INTRODUCTION

Having completed our analysis of demand and cost, we proceed to describe price and output determination in various market situations: perfect competition, monopoly, monopolistic competition, and oligopoly. Chapter 9 deals with **perfect competition** —a situation in which market prices are treated as known and given to all buyers and sellers, who are assumed to be perfectly informed about the tastes and technology that underlie all prices. Moreover, perfect mobility is assumed to assure that buyers and sellers act on their information when it is in their interests to do so.

In actual practice, perfect competition is likely to be approximated most nearly in markets for standardized goods that are traded by large numbers of buyers and sellers. The essential condition of perfect competition is that buyers and sellers regard the market prices as being beyond their control; that is, they make decisions based on the assumption that they cannot influence the price by their own actions.

9.2 GENERAL CONSIDERATIONS

A perfectly competitive market is likely to be approximated most closely in practice in highly organized markets for securities and agricultural commodities of the kind provided by the New York Stock Exchange or the Chicago Board of Trade. Of the conditions mentioned in the introduction, the most crucial is the requirement that transactors (buyers and sellers) regard prices as something over which they have no direct control. Transactors are most likely to believe that they cannot influence prices when they really cannot do so. However, they may also act upon the assumption that they cannot influence prices even when, in fact, they might be able to do so. For this reason, the theory of perfectly competitive markets can be applicable to a variety of situations that do not satisfy all of the requirements stated above. Even if a market is one in which an imperfectly standardized product is produced by a few sellers whose sale prices are not known to one another—clearly a case in which the usual conditions for perfect competition are not satisfied—the qualitative behavior of prices and quantities nevertheless may approximate that observed in a competitive market if sellers act on the assumption that they cannot influence market price. Nevertheless, the present discussion will focus on situations where all of the usual conditions for perfect competition are satisfied.

Competitive price determination falls into three stages: the market period, the short-run period, and the long-run period. The **market period** is so short that *total stocks* of the good available for sale are *fixed.* The length of the market period depends on the kind of good traded and on conditions affecting its production and consumption. For some goods (Christmas trees on Christmas Eve), the market period may be less than 24 hours; for others the market period may be anything from a few days to a month or longer. In general, one may think of the market period as being so short that *no* inputs can be varied, hence output must remain fixed.

In the next stage, the short run, the period is long enough to vary *some* inputs, but not all; hence output can vary to some extent. This means that existing stocks can be altered by production and consumption flows; that is, existing inventories can be altered. Certain production and consumption features (plant size of firms, for example, or housing or net worth position of households) are prohibitively expensive to vary quickly and are simply treated as fixed.

In the final stage, the long run, there is enough time for buyers and sellers to fully adjust their asset levels and composition as desired, taking into consideration items such as taste and technology. The long-run period might be a year or a decade. Technically speaking, it is a period where all inputs are variable and adjustments are made to bring the economy towards stationary equilibrium.

Of course, any theory or procedure that separates economic decision processes into overlapping time periods and simultaneously treats decisions associated with longer periods as if they were independent of decisions associated with shorter periods must appear artificial. That the artificiality is not only apparent but real must be acknowledged. What must also be acknowledged, however, is the possibility that conclusions born of artificial assumptions may yield significant practical fruit. (See Box 9-1.)

9.3 MARKET PRICE DETERMINATION

We will consider first the determination of the market price—the actual price prevailing at any particular time.

The Average Revenue Curve of an Individual Seller

In a perfectly competitive market, the average revenue function of the individual seller (the relation that indicates for each possible level of output the maximum price per

---

9-1 Why are stock and securities markets a good example of the perfectly competitive model?

One, there are a large number of investors (buyers and sellers) trading with relatively low information costs. Information about stock prices and companies' profit/loss statements are readily available. It is difficult for any individual to make exorbitant profits when information about products and prices flows so freely. This new information is quickly understood by buyers and sellers and incorporated into the price of the stock. Old information (often only as old as a few minutes) is rendered useless and will not make you rich. For example, if a news story breaks on an infestation of the cotton crop, the price of cotton futures will rise immediately and only those that speculated prior to the news or had inside information will make profits. Prices move rapidly in response to news; hence systematic "get rich" schemes are highly unlikely to occur. Even the best analysts on Wall Street have only a *slightly* better than average record over the "long haul."

---

unit for which the seller believes the entire output can be sold) is such that changes in output do not alter the expected price. The seller believes he can sell as much as he wishes to place on the market at the prevailing price. Or, in other words, the demand as seen by the seller is perfectly elastic. A wheat farmer, for example, will act on the assumption that he can dispose of his entire crop at the current market price, for he knows that any change he makes in the quantity offered for sale will have no appreciable effect upon market price. Likewise, he knows that he cannot dispose of his wheat at any figure higher than the current market price; if he attempted to charge a higher price, prospective buyers would simply purchase their supplies from other sources. Thus, if the prevailing market price of the product were $6.00, the farmer's average revenue function would be represented geometrically by a horizontal line, as shown in Figure 9-1. (See Box 9-2.)

To say that producers under perfect competition regard price as a given parameter is not to say that price is constant. The *position* of the average revenue (price) function, as distinguished from its elasticity, will of course vary with every change in the current market price. In effect, sellers are provided with current information about market demand and supply conditions through the medium of price changes; and it is an essential aspect of the perfectly competitive model that sellers respond to the signals provided by such price movements. That is to say, sellers alter their behavior over time in the light of actual experience, revising their decisions in conformity with changes in market price. In this respect, the perfectly competitive model is curiously realistic, for almost alone among models of market price determination it does not assume any knowledge on the part of individual buyers and sellers about total market demand and supply functions. The force of this remark will become clear when we deal in later chapters with price formation under conditions of monopoly, monopolistic competition, and oligopoly.

The concept of **marginal revenue** must also be introduced since it is vital to

FIGURE 9-1

Average Revenue Curve of a Seller of Wheat
Revenue per unit of output equals price in perfect competition and is constant since individual sellers have no power over price. Firm demand, average revenue, price, and marginal revenue, are equivalent in perfect competition and are represented by the horizontal line.

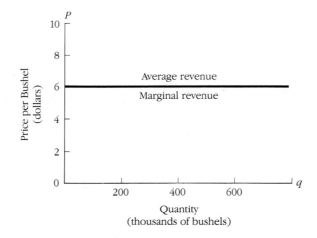

decision-making on the part of all firms. This term refers to the addition to total revenue resulting from the sale of an additional unit of output.[1] In a perfectly competitive market, since additional units of output can be sold without reducing the price of the product, marginal revenue is in each instance identical with average revenue, and the AR curve in Figure 9-1 may also be labeled the MR curve. As will be explained in succeeding chapters, in *imperfectly* competitive markets (monopoly, monopolistic

---

[1]Formally, marginal revenue is the derivative of the total revenue function. Total revenue, TR, is defined simply as the quantity sold times the price at which it is sold:

$$\text{TR} = P \cdot q$$

If price is given (constant with respect to output changes at the firm level) to the firm:

$$\text{MR} = \frac{d\text{TR}}{dq} = P$$

Note that average revenue, AR, which is defined as total revenue per unit, is

$$\text{AR} = \frac{\text{TR}}{q} = \frac{P \cdot q}{q} = P$$

Hence, in perfect competition, AR = MR.

9-2   How is it possible for the average revenue curve of an individual seller to be horizontal, when the market demand curve for the product is not? Why will a wheat farmer act on the basis of a belief that he can sell as much wheat as he pleases without affecting the market price if the total quantity of wheat demanded at each price is a finite amount, and larger quantities can be sold only at lower prices?

This is possible because of the very large number of sellers, all selling identical products. Each producer is providing such a small fraction of the total supply that a change in his own offerings does not have any noticeable effect on market price, and hence the producer does not realize that his sales have any effect at all. In other words, the effect is imperceptible to him. Thus, his average revenue function appears to be horizontal over the entire range of output that he could possibly produce.

competition, and oligopoly), marginal revenue and average revenue are not identical.[2]

For present purposes, then, we need not examine in detail the determinants of *individual* demands in the market period. The individual market period demands will in fact be more closely related to desired stock holdings than to consumption flow

---

[2]For other market structures, price depends on quantity sold (recall the downward-sloping demand curves of earlier chapters):

$$P = f(q) \quad \text{where } \frac{df(q)}{dq} < 0$$

Hence, $TR = P \cdot q = f(q) \cdot q$, and marginal revenue approaches (using the product rule for derivatives):

$$MR = \frac{d\,TR}{dq} = f(q) + f'(q)q$$

$$= P + \frac{dP}{dq}\,q$$

This can be rewritten as

$$MR = P\left(1 + \frac{dP}{dq}\frac{q}{P}\right)$$

$$= P\left(1 + \frac{1}{\frac{dq}{dP}\frac{P}{q}}\right)$$

$$= P\left(1 + \frac{1}{n}\right) \quad \text{where } n \text{ is the price elasticity of demand (negative)}$$

Note that as the price elasticity approaches infinity, MR becomes P; otherwise it is less than P when demand is downward-sloping.

demands, hence may be more volatile than demand over a longer period. But this is not critical for the present: the aggregate effect of these demands, when they interact with aggregate supply, will be to generate a market price to which individual firms react. We turn now to the supply response of firms.

The Concept of Supply

Under the assumption that the average revenue function (price in the competitive case) of a seller is given, the seller has only to decide the amount to place on the market. At any moment, with a given quantity already purchased or produced and on hand, this decision is based upon relative *expected* gains from holding or selling various quantities of the product. Over a longer period of time, the decision involves the determination of the amount to produce, and thus is influenced by the costs of producing at various alternative levels of output. Thus, given the relative expected gains from holding or selling, and the firm's estimates of the costs of producing various amounts of output, the quantity which the firm will offer for sale will depend solely upon the market price. Thus we define supply—the **competitive supply function**—as the relation showing for various possible values of market price the quantities which the seller will offer for sale at that price. The *market* or *total* supply function, in turn, may be defined as the relation showing for various possible values of market price the sum of the quantities which sellers in the aggregate will offer for sale. The **market supply function** is simply the sum of the individual supply functions of all firms selling in a particular market.

So much for definitions and other generalities affecting supply. To say anything specific about the form of competitive supply functions, we must consider the influences that affect profit calculations in market, short-run, and long-run planning periods.

Supply Schedules in the Market Period

We define a market period to be a time interval that is too short to allow production changes, so that sales can be made only from a fixed stock. In industries where production is a continuous process, additional output may be quickly adjusted, and the market period will be very short. Market price will therefore adjust rapidly to the short-run equilibrium level, and the dichotomy between market price and the short-run equilibrium price will be insignificant. In most agricultural industries, however, including many of those for which the perfectly competitive analysis has the greatest applicability, crops are harvested during a short period of the year, and no additional output is possible for another year. In such industries, the period in which only a fixed stock is available and additional output is impossible is relatively long.

With a given stock of goods on hand, a seller has only two alternatives: sell the commodity or hold it for possible future sale. A typical supply schedule of an individual firm in a time interval relevant for market price determination is shown in Table 9-1. The schedule is illustrated graphically in Figure 9-2.

TABLE 9-1

Supply Schedule of an Individual Seller, Fixed Stock of Goods on Hand

Price (dollars)	Quantity Supplied
2.25	0
2.50	800
2.75	1,200
3.00	1,600
3.25	2,000
3.50	2,200
3.75	2,200

FIGURE 9-2

Market Period Supply of an Individual Seller
The market period supply curve is the schedule of prices and quantities a seller is willing to offer for sale in a period too short to vary output. Market period supply depends on the stock on hand, the perishability of the product, expectations regarding future prices, cash needs, and storage costs. At higher prices, the seller will hold less stock for future sale and quantity supplied rises.

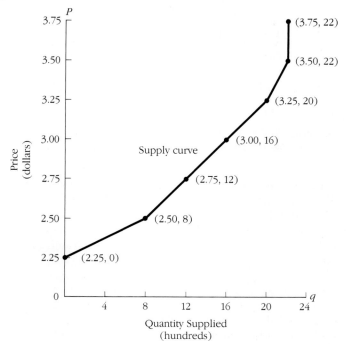

Determinants of Supply. The actual quantities that a particular seller will place on the market at various possible prices will depend upon the stock on hand (under the assumption of a time interval insufficient to allow the production of more units) and **reservation prices**—the prices below which the person will hold, rather than sell, particular parts of the stock of goods. A seller obviously cannot sell more than he or she has at a particular time. A wheat farmer, on a day in October, cannot sell more wheat for delivery now than he has on hand from this year's harvest. But he will not necessarily sell all that he has available. Whether he does or does not depends upon the relationship between the market price and his reservation price, which is determined primarily by his estimate of future prices. If he believes that prices are going down, his reservation price will be low, since he will wish to dispose of his crop while prices are relatively high. On the other hand, if he expects prices to rise, his reservation price will be high, for selling his stock now would involve sacrificing a prospective gain. Expectations about future prices are affected by many considerations including past experience, current reports on price and business trends, views of other persons, and pure guesswork. When sellers become accustomed to receiving prices within a certain range over a period of years, they are likely to regard any price below this figure as unreasonably low and will expect a price rise. Unusually high prices are also frequently regarded as being only temporary.

Reservation prices are also influenced by costs of storage—including rent, interest, and depreciation of goods. The higher these costs, the lower will be the reservation price. For highly perishable goods like lettuce or fresh fish, costs of storage will be prohibitive, and the reservation price will be extremely low. The seller will prefer to realize something from the good rather than have it spoil. The seller's need for cash is also significant. If the seller desires money immediately, then the reservation price will be relatively low, regardless of other considerations. Sellers who do not feel pressed for cash are much more likely to take a chance that prices will rise.

Thus the determinants of market period supply include:

1. stock the seller has on hand;
2. costs of storage;
3. perishability of the product;
4. cash requirements of the seller;
5. expectations of future prices.

Nature of the Supply Schedule of the Individual Seller. The higher the price, the greater the expectation that it will fall and the less the likelihood that it will go still higher (see Table 9-1). Accordingly, at successively higher prices, sellers will be willing to part with successively larger portions of their stocks, since they are less certain that the price will go still higher and are more afraid that a decline will occur. Furthermore, the higher the price, the greater the likelihood that it will exceed the figure to which the seller is accustomed. Finally, at relatively high prices, sellers can obtain cash to meet expenses through the sale of only a portion of their stock.

Total Supply Schedules. The sum of the individual supply schedules in the market constitutes the total or market supply schedule. The nature of the total schedule is the same as that of the individual schedules. At successively higher prices, additional amounts will be placed on the market by those who would make some sales at lower prices, and additional sellers whose reservation prices are so high that they would sell nothing at lower prices will offer units for sale. There are likely to be substantial differences among the schedules of individual sellers, due to differences in stocks of goods on hand, storage facilities, need for cash, and expectations about future trends in prices. It is impossible to generalize about the elasticity of the typical market supply schedule, beyond noting that perishability is significant. When a good cannot be stored at all, the entire stock will be offered for sale regardless of price (vertical supply, in contrast to Figure 9-2), and higher prices will bring forth no larger quantities in the time period under consideration.

Market Price Determination

The market price tends to a level at which the quantity supplied and the quantity demanded are equal. In a perfectly competitive market, with complete knowledge by buyers and sellers about market conditions, the market price would adjust almost instantaneously to a change in either demand or supply. Where imperfections exist, delay is inevitable. Thus, the actual selling price may deviate temporarily from the equilibrium market price. Securities markets and central wholesale markets for goods are relatively well organized, with imperfections at a minimum. In such markets, adjustments occur very rapidly, so current transactions prices may be considered closely to approximate market period equilibrium prices. However, imperfections are widespread and important in the great majority of actual markets, so observed prices may generally be presumed to deviate to some degree from current equilibrium levels. Mathematically, the problem that the "market" solves is that of finding a particular value P_0 of the price variable P which satisfies the demand/supply equality

$$D(P) - S(P) = 0$$

The precise way in which the market solves this problem varies from one market to another, but the general principle is the same regardless of the mechanics of the process. Specifically, if the actual price is for any reason temporarily at a level above the equilibrium value P_0, some sellers will discover that they cannot find buyers at the higher price, because total quantity demanded will be less than the total quantity offered for sale. Consequently, some sellers will offer to sell for slightly less in order to avoid storage, interest, and other costs, and the market price will fall until buyers are willing to purchase the same number of units that sellers wish to sell at the new price. If the price were lower than that at which quantity demanded and quantity supplied were equal, buyers would want to buy more units of the good than sellers would be willing to sell. Accordingly some buyers would offer to pay more in order to get the desired number of units, and the market price would rise until equality of quantity supplied and demanded was attained.

The supply schedule in the market period, and to some extent the demand schedule, are greatly influenced by expectations of future prices. Therefore, market price is typically subject to frequent change as expectations shift.

Cost in the usual sense has little direct influence in the market period. Once a good is produced, there is no way of obtaining money from it except by selling it. A seller may not wish to sell below cost, but this is preferable to allowing the product to spoil or become obsolete. The level of price in the market period is likely to be very sensitive, however, to fears of a possible decline in price. This is a highly significant factor in markets for financial assets as well as for certain agricultural goods.

The determination of the market period equilibrium price is illustrated graphically in Figure 9-3. The curve DD represents the demand function $D = D(P)$, and the curve SS represents the supply function $S = S(P)$. Price will tend to adjust to P_0, the level at which the quantities demanded and supplied are equal; and the quantity exchanged will adjust to the equilibrium level Q_0.[3] (See Box 9-3.)

---

[3]Note that most presentations (recall those from microeconomic principles) depict a *vertical* supply curve for the market period rather than an upward-sloping curve as discussed here. This would be satisfactory if one wished to add the suppliers' demand for their own products (to sell or store) to the ordinary demands of consumers in order to arrive at full market demand. In this case, the demand curve would be flatter by an amount exactly offsetting the difference between our supply curve and one drawn vertically. Market equilibrium price and quantity are unaffected, in any event, and we prefer to isolate seller behavior from buyer behavior.

FIGURE 9-3

Market Price Equilibrium
The intersection of the total market supply and demand curves establishes the market equilibrium price and quantity. Above the equilibrium price, quantity supplied exceeds quantity demanded, and sellers must lower their asking price to avoid storage costs and product spoilage. If price falls short of the equilibrium price, a shortage will induce some buyers to offer higher prices to obtain units of the product. Equilibrium occurs when quantity demanded equals quantity supplied.

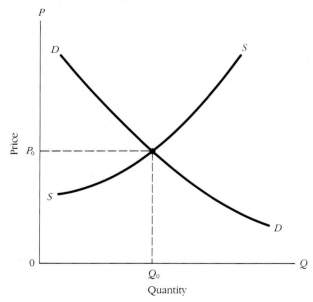

9-3 Suppose you were working at a flower stand and you knew that your flowers would not be fresh tomorrow. How would this affect your pricing behavior throughout the day?

Your reservation price would steadily fall and would depend on how flow demands throughout the day compared to usual. You would like to be able to satisfy all your customers but have few flowers left at the end of the day. It is unlikely that your reservation price would fall to zero, however, as you would presumably take flowers home for your own enjoyment before giving them away. This example would generally apply to all perishable goods, not just flowers.

9.4 OUTPUT AND PRICE IN A SHORT-RUN PERIOD

Over a period of time, firms can adjust output; thus the supply function is dependent upon the rate of output rather than merely upon a firm's willingness to sell from a given stock of goods. In all situations in which output is adjustable—short run or long run—attainment of maximum expected profit requires the adjustment of output to the point at which any additional increase in output, however small, is expected to increase total revenue more than it increases total cost, and any reduction in output is expected to reduce total revenue less than it reduces total cost. Thus marginal profit—the additional profit resulting from the sales of an additional unit of output—will be zero at the **profit maximizing level of output** and negative for changes in output in either direction from this point. Thus the supply function is dependent upon those items influencing marginal cost of production at various levels of output.

The short-run period is defined as an interval long enough to allow adjustment in some inputs, hence in output, but not in all inputs (particularly plant size). During this period, market price will tend toward the short-run supply equilibrium price level, the level determined by the relationship between marginal revenue and the short-run supply function. Firms will adjust output in terms of the relationship between price and short-run marginal cost, and changes in market supply resulting from these output adjustments will bring the market price toward the short-run equilibrium figure.

Short-Run Supply

The short-run supply function is defined as the relationship between various prices and the quantities that will be offered for sale at these prices during a time interval long enough to allow the existing firms to adjust output with given plant capacity. As noted above, because the firms can adjust output, a new determinant of supply becomes significant—namely, cost of production.

The firm will not produce at all unless the price obtainable at least covers *average variable cost* (AVC). These costs would cease if production were suspended; thus operation at a price which does not cover them will worsen the firm's financial position.[4] If a firm cannot obtain enough revenue from the sale of the product to cover the direct wage, raw material, and power costs necessary to produce it, then each additional unit produced will reduce the firm's wealth or increase its debt. Even if the owners of a business desire to continue operation under such circumstances, they cannot do so for very long. Firms will continue to operate when price is below AVC only if the owners believe that prices will rise in the near future and wish to avoid costs associated with closing and reopening the plant and losing experienced personnel.

At price levels equal to or in excess of AVC, a firm will produce in the short-run period even if average total cost is not completely covered. Since fixed costs continue whether the firm produces or not, it is preferable to earn enough to cover a portion of these costs rather than earn nothing at all. Immediate liquidation of a business is not economically feasible, which is the property that defines the short-run period. Money capital invested in specialized capital equipment cannot be withdrawn quickly except at great loss because used capital goods, as a rule, have little resale value.

In the range of prices at which production will be carried on (those which are equal to or above AVC at some level of output), the firm will adjust its output to a level at which *marginal cost* (MC) with the existing plant is equal to *marginal revenue* (MR)—which, in perfect competition, is equal to average revenue (AR) or market price. Until this volume of output is reached, each additional unit produced results in a greater *addition* to the total revenue of the firm (marginal revenue) than to its total cost (marginal cost) and hence is profitable to produce, provided that price covers AVC. If output is carried beyond the level at which MR = MC, additional units will add more to total cost than to total revenue and will thereby either reduce profits or increase losses.

The level of operation of a firm in perfect competition in the short run is illustrated in Figure 9-4. The short-run cost schedule, comparable to those discussed in Chapter 8, is plotted on the same chart with the revenue schedule. The AR curve is a horizontal line at the level of the current market price P_0. This line also indicates marginal revenue, which is identical with average revenue in perfect competition. Since, in this illustration, price is in excess of AVC for some levels of output, the firm will operate; it will produce such a number of units, namely q_0, that MR = MC = P_0, as indicated on the graph by the intersection of the MC and MR curves. Price in this particular instance is also in excess of AC. Figure 9-5 illustrates a case in which price is less than AVC at all ranges of output; hence the firm will not produce ($q_2 = 0$). Figure 9-6 shows a situation in which price is less than AC but in excess of AVC ($q_1 > 0$). In this case, the firm will produce, but at a loss, in the short run. To shut down would make this firm worse off, since it can cover at least *some* of its fixed costs with the excess of revenue over variable cost.

---

[4]Proof: When $\pi(0) > \pi(q^*)$, the firm will shut down. This is equivalent to: $-TFC > Pq^* - TC(q^*)$ or $-TFC > Pq^* - TFC - TVC(q^*)$ or $0 > Pq^* - TVC(q^*)$ or dividing by q^* and rearranging: $AVC > P$. Hence profit at zero output is greater than profit at the optimal positive quantity of output if price does not cover average variable cost.

FIGURE 9-4

Equilibrium Output of the Firm in the Short Run

When marginal cost equals marginal revenue, the corresponding output level maximizes firm profits (or minimizes losses) as long as price is at least as great as average variable cost. Because price exceeds average cost for the firm in this example, the firm reaps positive economic profits in the short run.

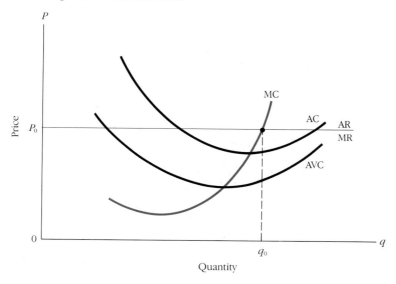

FIGURE 9-5

Revenue and Cost Curves of a Firm in a Short-Run Period, Price Less Than Lowest AVC

The firm ceases to produce in the short run when average variable cost exceeds price. In the long run, this firm would leave the industry. Not even variable inputs can be paid out of revenues, and the firm cuts losses by discontinuing production.

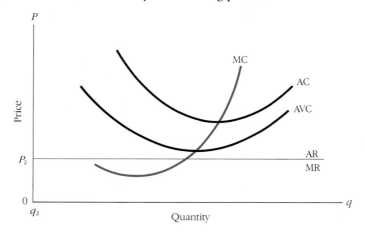

FIGURE 9-6

Revenue and Cost Curves of a Firm in a Short-Run Period, with Price above AVC but below AC

In this case, the firm operates in the short run but incurs a loss because average cost exceeds price. Nevertheless, price is greater than average variable cost, and revenues cover variable costs and partially defray fixed costs. This firm would still leave the industry in the long run unless price rose through exit of other firms.

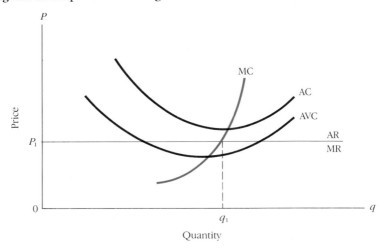

The Short-Run Supply Schedule

At each possible price above the level of lowest AVC, the firm will place on the market that number of units that equates MC to price. Thus the firm's supply schedule can be derived directly from its MC schedule, as illustrated in Table 9-2. The right-hand portion of the table indicates the firm's supply schedule, based on the cost data presented on the left-hand side. At any price below 20 dollars, nothing would be produced, since AVC would not be covered. A price of 20 dollars would cover AVC, and therefore the firm would operate in the short run; four units would be produced, since, with a price of 20 dollars, MC = MR at an output of four units. At 25 dollars, with an output of five units, the firm just covers average total costs, and would be willing to continue producing in the long run. If the price were 27 dollars, six units would be supplied; if it were 50 dollars, seven units; and so on. For output levels six and seven, profits are being earned by the firm; this will, as we shall see, tempt others into this industry.

In graphical terms, the short-period supply curve of an individual competitive seller is identical with that portion of the MC curve which lies on or above and to the right of the point at which the MC curve intersects the AVC curve. As a cost relation, this curve shows the marginal cost of producing any *given output*; as a supply curve, it shows the *optimum output* that the firm will supply at various prices. Thus, as shown in Figure 9-7, the portion of MC above its intersection with AVC is the supply curve. The declin-

TABLE 9-2

Short-Run Cost Schedule and Short-Run Supply Schedule of a Firm Selling in a Perfectly Competitive Market

	Daily Cost Schedule			Daily Supply Schedule	
Units of Output	Average Variable Cost (dollars)	Average Cost (dollars)	Marginal Cost (dollars)	Price (dollars)	Quantity Supplied
1	30	50.00	30	8	0
2	24	34.00	18	12	0
3	20	26.67	12	15	0
4	20	25.00	20	20	4
5	21	25.00	25	25	5
6	22	25.53	27	27	6
7	26	28.86	50	50	7
8	40	42.50	138	138	8

FIGURE 9-7

Short-Run Cost Curve and Supply Curve of a Firm
The quantity supplied by the firm for a given price is the quantity which maximizes profits. Profit-maximization requires that MR = MC, and since P = MR in perfect competition, P will equal MC at the optimum quantity. The $P \geq$ AVC condition ensures that the firm will operate in the short run. Thus, the MC curve on or above the AVC curve is the short-run supply curve for the firm.

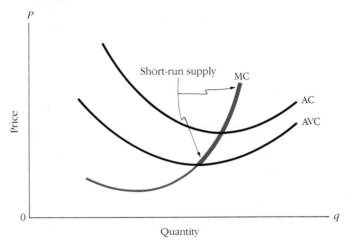

ing portion of the MC curve has no significance for supply, because greater profit can be made by extending production to the quantities for the respective prices on the rising portion of the curve.[5] All units of output in the intervening range will add more to total revenue than to total cost.

Since, beyond the point of lowest AVC, the marginal costs of successively larger amounts of output are progressively greater, larger and larger amounts will be supplied only at higher levels of price. The absolute maximum that the firm can supply, regardless of price, is the maximum quantity that can be produced with the existing plant.

The total short-run supply schedule is very closely related to, and sometimes is equivalent to, the sum of the schedules of the individual firms in the industry. By definition, the short run is too brief for new firms to begin production, and hence the total schedule is the summation of the individual schedules of existing firms. One modification to the summation rule arises from the effect that higher levels of output in an industry may have in raising factor prices for inputs used by existing firms. If this occurs, the quantities supplied at higher prices will be somewhat less than they would appear to be on the basis of a summation of existing individual schedules.

In summary, the **determinants of short-run supply** include:

1. the number of firms;
2. the short-run cost functions of firms (cost being viewed as a function of quantity produced only); and
3. factor prices.

---

[5]Indeed, setting price equal to marginal cost when the latter is downward-sloping corresponds to a profit *minimum* (given positive production) rather than the profit maximum. At a maximum, the rate of increase of marginal profit is *negative* (marginal profit is declining as one moves through the point at which $P = $ MC). Hence, the *second* derivative of the profit function must be negative:

$$\pi = TR(q) - TC(q)$$

Marginal profit $\quad \dfrac{d\pi}{dq} = MR(q) - MC(q)$

$$= P - MC(q) \quad \text{in competition}$$

$$= 0 \qquad \text{at the "top (or bottom) of the profit hill."}$$
$$\text{(that is, } P = MC(q) \text{ at the optimum)}$$

and $\qquad \dfrac{d^2\pi}{dq^2} = \dfrac{-dMC(q)}{dq} < 0 \quad$ if at the top, *rather* than the bottom, of the profit hill.

If marginal costs are increasing as output increases ($dMC(q)/dq > 0$), this condition is met, in light of the minus sign. Hence marginal cost must be increasing in the neighborhood of the optimum.

The Short-Run Equilibrium

The short-run equilibrium price level is the price at which the demand for the product and the short-run supply of the product are equal. At this level, the total amount that sellers will produce and place on the market in each time interval with a given plant is equal to the amount that buyers will purchase in the same time interval at that price. Once sufficient time has passed for firms to complete output adjustments with given plant capacities, the market price will tend to reach the short-run level (apart from possible effects of market imperfections noted in subsequent sections). If market price is temporarily above this level, quantity supplied will increase over time and quantity demanded will decline; thus market price will tend to fall back toward the short-run equilibrium level. Similarly, if for any reason market price is below the equilibrium level, quantity supplied will decline to a figure less than the (larger) quantity demanded at that price, and market price will tend to rise. Accordingly, only at the short-run equilibrium level will the volume of output coming on the market (with given plant capacities) equal quantity demanded. This equilibrium position, one from which there is no tendency for market price to depart, is illustrated in Figure 9-8 (P_0). Once short-run adjustments have been completed, the market supply curve will be at the level SS and will intersect the demand curve (DD) at the same point as that at which the latter is intersected by the short-period supply curve (SRS). Figure 9-9 illustrates a case in which market price (P_0) initially exceeds the short-run equilibrium level. Because market supply (S_0) is relatively low, the quantity actually offered for sale will be only Q_0. With a price of P_0, however, firms will quickly adjust output towards the corresponding short-run equilibrium level Q_2, since at an output Q_0 marginal cost (C) is less than price. As market supply increases, the market supply curve moves to the right until it reaches the level S_1. With this market supply curve, the market price will be P_1, and the quantity produced and sold will be Q_1.

The Relations between Price and Cost in the Short-Run Period

As a consequence of the adjustment of output by firms in the short-run period, certain relationships must exist between equilibrium price and costs, once adjustments are complete. Specifically:

1. $P = MC$ for each firm, as required for short-run profit maximization;
2. $P \geq AVC$, since firms will not operate unless AVC is covered at the short-run equilibrium output.

At the short-run equilibrium output, market price may be either above or below AC, for there is no necessity that fixed costs be covered except in the long run. The actual relation between short-run equilibrium price and AC in particular cases will depend upon the relationship between demand and short-run supply, as indicated above. If demand is sufficiently great, price will be above AC; if demand is relatively low, price will be in the range between AC and AVC.

FIGURE 9-8

**Equilibrium Market Price and Short-Run Equilibrium Price
in a Perfectly Competitive Industry**
The industry short-run supply curve is the horizontal sum of the firm short-run supply
curves assuming that output adjustments do not alter variable input prices. When firms
complete all variable input adjustments, the market supply, short-run supply, and demand
curves intersect at the equilibrium price and quantity.

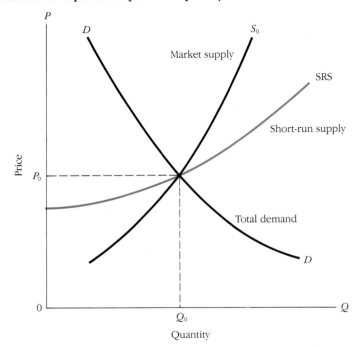

9.5 OUTPUT AND PRICE IN THE LONG-RUN PERIOD

The long-run equilibrium price level is the figure toward which market price and the
short-run equilibrium price tend in a period of time long enough to allow (1) the
completion by firms of desired adjustments in all factor units, and (2) the entry of new
firms, or the departure of old ones. At any one time, adjustments in output with
existing plant are tending to bring the market price to the short-run equilibrium
figure, as described in the previous section. But over a longer period—one that will
allow all firms to make all desired adjustments in plant, new firms to be established,
and unprofitable ones to be discontinued—the various adjustments will bring market
price and the short-run equilibrium figure to the long-run equilibrium level. If all
long-run adjustments are completed, the short-run and long-run equilibrium levels
will be the same, and the market price will be equal to them.

The long-run equilibrium price is determined by the relationship between demand
and long-run supply—the schedule of total amounts that would be forthcoming onto
the market at various price levels in each time interval, over a period sufficiently long

FIGURE 9-9

Adjustment of Market Price to the Short-Run Equilibrium Level

If the market equilibrium price, P_0, exceeds the short-run equilibrium price, P_1, then price (marginal revenue) exceeds marginal cost and firms will supply more to gain profits. Market supply shifts to the right to S_1, reducing price and raising quantity to short-run equilibrium levels.

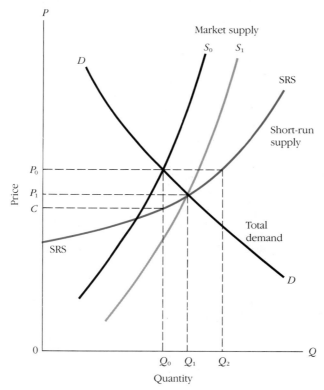

to allow adjustments in the quantities of all factors used. Demand requires little further consideration. Since demand schedules will be more elastic over a longer period than they are at a given time, buyers will make greater readjustments to price changes in a longer time interval than they will immediately after the change has occurred. Long-run supply, however, requires more detailed analysis, since its determinants are not identical with those of supply in the short period.

Long-Run Supply Schedules

In a long-run period, output adjustments of existing firms will differ from those made in the short run because firms are able to adjust the quantities of all factors employed and thereby alter costs that affect short-run equilibrium levels of output. In addition, changes may occur in the number of firms in the industry, which will alter total quantities supplied at various prices and which may also alter the cost curves of existing firms (recall the industry cost conditions of Chapter 8—increasing, constant, or decreasing).

Long-Run Adjustments by Existing Firms.   Whereas price in the short run must only cover average variable cost to ensure that firms continue production, over a long-run period price must cover *all costs*—and thus be at least equal to average total cost—or the owners will liquidate the enterprise and reinvest in other fields. At price levels equal to or greater than the minimum value of average total cost (AC), a firm will adjust plant capacity until long-run marginal cost (LRMC) and short-run marginal cost (SRMC) both equal marginal revenue (MR) and thus price. The plant will be adjusted to a size that allows equality of LRMC and MR and thus permits the most profitable and lowest-cost factor combination for any given volume of output. The firm will produce at the point at which SRMC with this plant is equal to price. The **long-run output equilibrium** position of an existing firm is illustrated in Figure 9-10. At the price P_0, the firm adjusts all factors until the plant with the curve SRAC is attained and q_0 units of output are produced. At this level of output, both SRMC and LRMC will be equal to MR at the prevailing level of market price, P_0.[6]

---

[6]There is one sense in which this reasoning is faulty: If firms really know everything required of them by assumption in perfect competition, they will know that the positive profits depicted in Figure 9-10 cannot last due to entry of new firms. Hence they may build the long-run least-cost plant associated with long-run equilibrium *after* entry of new firms.

FIGURE 9-10

Long-Run Output Equilibrium of Individual Firm
In the long run, the firm chooses the plant scale and output level for which LRMC = MR.
If price covers average cost, the firm will stay in business. P_0 is not the long-run
equilibrium price since the firm is making excess profit.

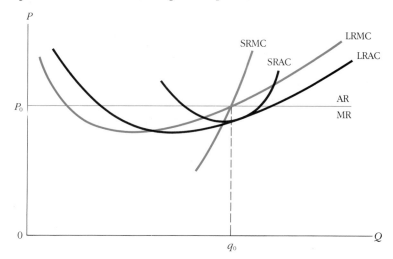

Adjustment in the Number of Firms. The position of long-run output equilibrium illustrated in Figure 9-10 is one in which the prevailing price more than covers the firm's long-run average costs. In these circumstances, the prevailing price cannot represent a long-run equilibrium price because it permits the individual firm to earn excess profits. The existence of excess profits—more precisely, the existence of a situation in which price is above the minimum point on the LRAC curve of any existing or potential producer—will attract new entrants into the industry (or new resources from existing firms). The additional output offered for sale by newcomers will depress price in the market and short-run period, and so force adjustments in long-run output upon existing firms. The number of firms in the industry will become stationary only when price attains a level at which no firm is able to earn excess profits. This is illustrated in Figure 9-11. When long-run adjustments in the number of firms have been completed, price will be at a level P_1 where the AR (which is equal to MR in perfect competition) curve is tangent to the LRAC curve at its lowest point. At this point, the equilibrium level of output, q_1, will be such that price is equal to LRAC, to SRAC with the optimum-size plant, and to both SRMC and LRMC. Tangency of the AR and AC curves is essential for equilibrium in the number of firms in the industry, because if the curves do not touch, AC is not covered; while if they intersect, excess profits will be earned. In the first case, existing firms will leave the industry; and in the second case, new firms will enter.

The reasoning of the preceding paragraphs applies to all firms in the industry. The number of firms in the industry will tend to change over time so long as price differs from the minimum level of LRAC for any firm. Since there is a single market price for

FIGURE 9-11

Long-Run Output Equilibrium of Firm after Elimination of Excess Profit
Positive economic profit attracts new firms into the industry. Short-run industry supply increases, and equilibrium price declines. Entry continues until economic profits are zero—that is, until price equals the minimum long-run average cost for each firm.

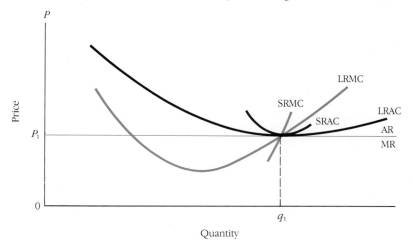

the good, LRAC must be equal to this price for all firms. Therefore only those firms can survive that are capable of producing at a level of LRAC which is no greater than that of any firm. Contradiction between this conclusion and common knowledge about differences in the costs of various firms can be explained. In any given period in which long-run adjustments have not been completed, the statement is not applicable. Many apparent cost differences are short-run phenomena that would disappear over a longer period, since firms having high costs because of obsolete techniques or poor management must either lower their costs (by paying lower salaries to the poor managers, for example) or go out of business. Those firms that appear to have lower costs because of superior resources or management ability do not actually have lower cost schedules if all implicit cost elements are taken into consideration. The owners of superior factor units can command a higher price for them than is paid for standard-quality units. The price differential will, in general, reflect the difference in productivity. (See Box 9-4.)

Long-Run Industry Supply Functions

The nature of long-run industry supply depends on the cost conditions in which the industry operates.

Constant-Cost Industries.   As explained in the preceding section, once long-run adjustments are complete, each firm will of necessity operate at the point of lowest LRAC. Therefore, each firm will supply to the market the quantity of output that it can produce at the lowest possible LRAC. At a price equal to lowest LRAC, the potential *total* supply—taking into consideration changes in the number of firms in the industry—appears to be infinite, if the industry is one of constant cost. In such conditions, total output will increase in the long run to equal demand. Should output be less than this amount temporarily, price will exceed AC and new firms will enter the industry. As a result, market supply will increase (shift rightward) and drive the market price back down to the common AC level. Hence the long-run supply curve for the entire industry—the curve showing the total potential amounts that will be supplied by all firms at

9-4   True or False?   The costs to the firm (either implicit or explicit) using superior factor units are higher than those of firms using standard units; and average cost, including all explicit and implicit elements, is not lower for firms using superior units.

True. For example, a farmer whose land is particularly fertile will have lower labor and capital costs per unit of output than other farmers, but she could rent the land to others at a figure based upon its yield at a price considerably in excess of the rent that could be obtained by the owners of poor land. The rent element in total cost will be greater by the amount of the reduction in her other costs resulting from the use of the good land, and her average cost will be the same as that of neighbors using poorer land.

various prices—may be represented by a horizontal line, as shown in Figure 9-12. At lower prices, nothing will be supplied in the long run, since firms cannot cover AC. Higher prices are of no significance, since prices in the long-run period cannot remain above AC because of entry. The industry long-run supply curve is identical with the long-run cost curve for the industry—the curve showing the locations of the lowest points of the LRAC curves for the firms in the industry with various amounts of total output of the industry. The actual quantity that will be forthcoming on the market (as distinguished from the potential quantity) in each time interval after long-run adjustments have been completed is indicated by the point of intersection of the industry demand curve with the industry supply curve (Q_0 in Figure 9-13).

Increasing-Cost Industries. In an industry of increasing cost conditions, the entry of new firms into the industry will raise the cost schedules of all firms by increasing the prices paid for certain factor units or giving rise to certain diseconomies. Accordingly, the height of the lowest cost figure for the firms depends upon the total number of firms in the industry and will shift as the total output changes.

FIGURE 9-12

Long-Run Equilibrium, Constant-Cost Industry
When industry expansion has no impact on input prices, the industry is one of constant costs. The long-run industry supply curve is the quantity supplied by the industry at alternate prices in the long run. Because long-run average costs are not affected by output, the supply curve is horizontal. Long-run equilibrium price and quantity are determined at the intersection of the total demand curve and the industry long-run supply curve.

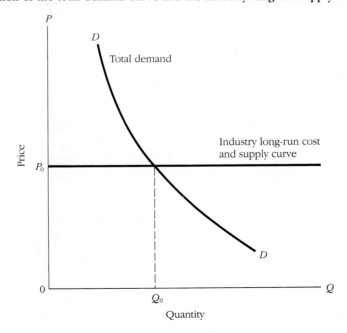

FIGURE 9-13

Industry Cost and Supply Curve, Increasing-Cost Industry
Increases in the number of firms raises the demand for inputs. In increasing-cost industries, the impact on input demand is great enough to raise input prices. Minimum LRAC to each firm rises as industry output increases with the number of firms, and the long-run industry supply curve is positively sloped.

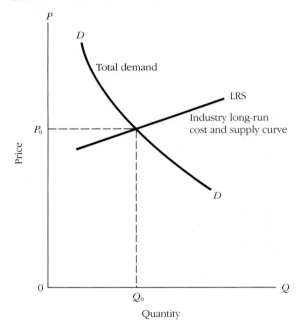

At price levels lower than LRAC at the minimum output of the industry, nothing at all would be produced, and thus the long-run supply would be zero. At a price level equal to minimum LRAC and at each price higher than this, the total quantity supplied would be the amount that would allow AC to equal price. If total output were less, AC would be less than price, so new firms would enter the industry and increase total output. If total output were greater, AC would exceed price, some firms would leave the industry, and the decline in total output would reduce AC and raise price until they became equal.

The long-run supply curve of an increasing-cost industry is illustrated in Figure 9-13. The supply curve slopes upward from left to right, since the level of AC is higher for successively larger volumes of total output. As in constant cost conditions, the industry cost and supply curves are identical since at each price level total industry supply will adjust to the level at which AC = LRMC = P.

The third possible case, illustrated in Figure 9-14, is a decreasing-cost industry, one in which the cost schedules of the firms fall as the total output of the industry increases. From all indications, however, this case is unlikely and therefore of little practical importance.

FIGURE 9-14

Industry Cost and Supply Curve, Decreasing-Cost Industry
Input prices decline with industry expansion in decreasing-cost industries. The minimum points of the LRAC curves fall as the number of firms increases, giving rise to a downward-sloping long-run industry supply curve.

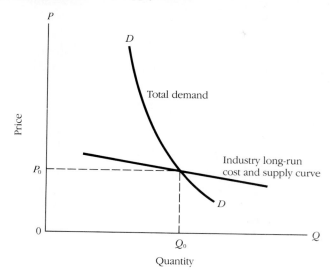

The Long-Run Equilibrium Price

The **long-run equilibrium price** is the figure at which the quantity demanded is equal to the long-period supply, the quantity that will be supplied continuously in a given time interval after long-run adjustments are complete. At higher prices, total output would exceed the quantity demanded; at lower prices, an insufficient amount would be produced to meet the quantity that persons wished to buy. In Figures 9-13 and 9-14, the long-run equilibrium price level is P_0, defined by the intersection of the demand curve with the long-period supply curve—which is, of course, identical with the industry cost curve, the curve that shows the location of the lowest LRAC figures of the firms with various levels of output for the industry. Figure 9-13 depicts an increasing-cost industry, Figure 9-14 a decreasing-cost industry.

In terms of the cost schedules of individual firms, the long-run equilibrium price level is the figure of lowest possible LRAC, which will correspond to a particular short-run plant size. In a constant-cost industry, lowest LRAC and the long-run equilibrium price (which is equal to lowest LRAC) are the same regardless of the demand for the product and the output of the industry. In an increasing-cost industry, the greater the demand for the product (and thus the long-run equilibrium output of the industry), the higher will be the firms' cost schedules, the figure of lowest LRAC, and the long-run equilibrium price. The equilibrium price is, of course, also equal to the firms' LRMC and to SRMC with plants of optimum (lowest-cost) size. (See Box 9-5.)

9-5   Are sexual and racial discrimination more likely in a competitive or noncompetitive environment?

The more competitive the market, the less discrimination (ceteris paribus). In the long run, the perfectly competitive firm receives zero economic profits. Hence any firm discriminating against qualified workers in favor of less-qualified workers would be put at a disadvantage. That is, those firms that hire the less-qualified workers will have higher costs and will eventually be forced out of business.

9.6   THE ADJUSTMENT OF MARKET PRICE TO THE LONG-RUN EQUILIBRIUM LEVEL

At any particular time, market price tends toward the short-run equilibrium level as a result of output adjustments with existing plants. But even if price is at the short-run equilibrium level, changes in plant capacities of existing firms and in the number of firms in the industry will lead to more or less continuous price and output adjustments until market price reaches the long-run equilibrium level. The adjustment toward equilibrium may be illustrated by considering the effects of a change in long-run flow demand and a change in long-run costs.

Readjustments to Change in Demand

The explanation of readjustments in response to a change in flow demand is facilitated if it is assumed that long-run equilibrium has been attained prior to the demand change. This is illustrated in Figure 9-15: the long-run equilibrium price is initially at the level P_{LR}, where the initial demand, D_0, intersects the long-run supply, LRS, as well as the short-run supply, SRS_0. The adjustment can be broken down into three stages:

1. *Rise in market price.* When flow demand increases from D_0 to D_1, quantity purchased for consumption will exceed quantity currently produced and market period stocks will start to decline. The result will be a rapid rise in market price at the initial level of output, leading to a state of market period equilibrium at the price P_M.[7] At this price, desired consumption (indicated along D_1) will equal actual production, but actual production will be increasing because desired production (as indicated by the short-run supply curve SRS_0) will exceed current output. Note that the market period outcome may be very unpopular politically—the higher prices merely transfer wealth to producers from consumers.

---

[7]Note that this assumes complete product perishability, hence no inventories. If inventories are held, as is typical, there would be some market period quantity response as price began to exceed reservation prices of suppliers with a correspondingly lower price at the new demand level.

FIGURE 9-15

Adjustment of Price and Output in Response to Increase in Flow Demand, Constant-Cost Industry

A demand increase to D_1 raises market price to P_M. Market quantity supplied expands, and short-run equilibrium price is established at P_{SR}. Positive profits induce entry and expansion of existing firms, boosting short-run supply to SRS_1. When profits disappear, long-run equilibrium occurs at the original price but at a greater output level.

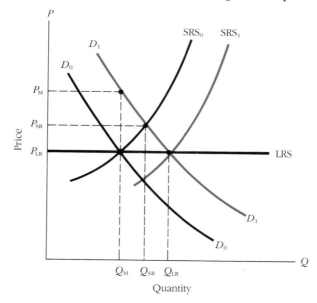

2. *Increase in output and decline in market price to short-run equilibrium level.* At the price P_M, short-run supply (along SRS_0) will exceed flow demand after all market period output adjustments are completed; hence market price, having risen initially to ration the higher demand, will now start to decline. After all short-run adjustments in output and price are made, the market price will be at the level P_{SR} and quantity will have increased to Q_{SR}. Because of the upward slope of the short-run supply curve, which in turn is due to the higher marginal cost of additional output produced with existing plants, the new short-run equilibrium price will still be higher than P_{LR}, hence profits continue to exist.

3. *Increase in plant size and number of firms, and decline in market price to long-run equilibrium level.* At the level of price corresponding to short-run equilibrium, firms already in the industry will find themselves able to increase long-run profit by adjusting fixed capital inputs, and new firms may also appear on the scene. As additions to plant are brought into use (whether by old or new firms), the industry's short-run flow supply curve will shift to the right and this process will continue until all long-run adjustments are completed and short-run supply is represented by SRS_1. In the process, market period changes

in stocks and short-period changes in output will produce a gradual decline in market price until a final position of long-run equilibrium is reestablished in which flow demand is equal to short-run flow supply at a market price that is, in turn, equal to the minimum value of LRAC for every producer.

If the industry is one of *constant cost,* the long-run equilibrium price will be at the same level as prevailed before demand increased; so the only long-run effect of the increase in flow demand will be an increase in industry output, as indicated in Figure 9-15.

If the industry is one of *increasing cost,* as illustrated in Figure 9-16, then an increase in industry output will be associated with higher minimum values of LRAC for individual firms; accordingly, an increase in flow demand will lead, in the long run, to increases in price (from P_0 to P_1) and in industry output (from Q_0 to Q_1).

If flow demand for a good falls, the adjustment to long-run equilibrium is just as indicated above, but in the opposite direction. Market price falls, and firms suffer losses in the market period and reduce their short-run output. Market supply and

FIGURE 9-16

Adjustment of Price and Output in Response to a Demand Increase,
Increasing-Cost Industry

When a demand increase raises price and encourages market period and short-run increases in quantity supplied, then output expansion through the entry of new firms raises production costs in an increasing-cost industry. Firm cost curves shift up and profits are eliminated at a higher price. Long-run equilibrium price and quantity tend to rise in response to a demand increase in an increasing-cost industry.

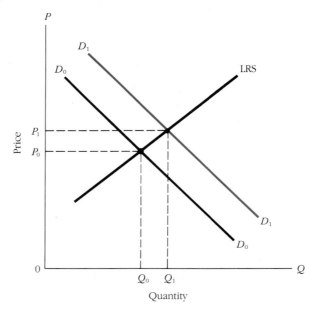

short-run flow-supply curves shift to the left in the long run as existing firms reduce investment in fixed plant and as some existing firms leave the industry. When a new position of long-run equilibrium is finally established, price will be lower than in the initial situation if the industry is one of increasing cost, the same as in the initial situation if constant cost conditions prevail, or higher in the more unusual case of a decreasing-cost industry.

The adjustments outlined above are, of course, oversimplified. The basic determinants of cost—factor prices, methods of production, and so forth—are themselves subject to change over time. Hence the long-run equilibrium is itself constantly changing. The analysis is meaningful, nevertheless, because the direction of movement in market price in any period is controlled by the relationship between the prevailing market price and the short-run and long-run equilibrium price levels. (See Box 9-6.)

Adjustments to Cost Changes

When an increase in cost occurs, there is no immediate effect on market price unless the reservation prices of sellers or demand prices of buyers are affected by the expectation that the cost increase will lead eventually to an increase in price. However, the cost increase will affect both short-run and long-run equilibrium levels and so will lead ultimately to increases in price, once adjustments have occurred in output and in the number of firms. In the short-run period, firms will contract output, since the cost increase will generally raise MC above price. Thus the short-run equilibrium price level will be higher, but by an amount less than the cost increase per unit of product, since reductions in output reduce MC along the new MC curve. Once short-run adjustments are complete, market price will have risen by a sum less than the amount of the cost increase per unit of product. But AC is not yet covered; so the number of firms will

---

9-6   What are the implications, in terms of efficiency (benefits and costs) and equity (the distribution of those benefits and costs) of rent controls? *Hint*: Think about such controls in the context of the market period, the short run, and the long run as discussed above.

Rent controls are politically appealing and have had a long history. Their appeal stems from the pronounced difference between the short-run equity effects (which are viewed as positive by political entrepreneurs) and the long-run efficiency effects (which, while clearly undesirable, occur in a future period of little relevance to the next election). The lower, controlled rent price has only a modest impact on the market period supply, hence, transfers wealth from owners (few in number) to renters (many in number). Since housing is viewed as an important good, and since it represents a major share of the budget, voting support for rent controls is often substantial. In the long run, of course, there will be less housing and the quality of the housing stock at any point in time will deteriorate steadily, if slowly.

decline over time, and market price will rise until it again equals AC. In a constant-cost industry (as illustrated in Figure 9-17), AC will ultimately rise by the amount of the cost increase (per unit of output). In an increasing-cost industry (Figure 9-18), the AC schedules of the firms will fall as the output of the industry declines. The ultimate price increase will be somewhat less than the amount of the cost increase. In a decreasing-cost industry the rise will be greater than the amount of the cost increase. In all cases, output will be less than it was prior to the cost increase. The relative output reduction will be greatest in a decreasing-cost industry and least in one of increasing cost conditions.

9.7 IMPERFECTIONS IN ADJUSTMENTS IN PERFECTLY COMPETITIVE INDUSTRIES

Our analysis of price and output determination in perfect competition has been based on the assumption of an absence of **imperfections** that interfere with adjustments.

FIGURE 9-17

Constant-Cost Industry Long-Run Adjustment of Price to Cost Increase
If costs increase for reasons other than industry expansion, short-run average cost curves shift up. Some firms will cut back on production and others will cease to produce if price falls short of the new AVC. In the long run, some firms will choose a smaller plant and others will go out of business. Short-run industry supply declines and price rises until losses are eliminated. The long-run industry supply curve permanently shifts up since minimum LRAC is now higher for every output level. Equilibrium price rises by the amount of the increase in average cost, and equilibrium output contracts.

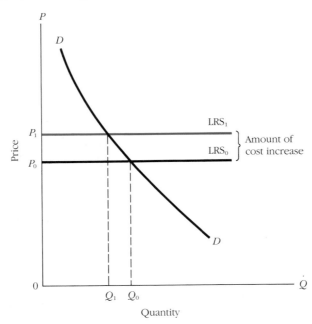

FIGURE 9-18

Increasing-Cost Industry Long-Run Adjustment of Price to Cost Increase
The positively sloped long-run supply curve shifts up by the amount of the increase in minimum average cost for every output level. Price rises by less than the average cost increase, and equilibrium industry output falls.

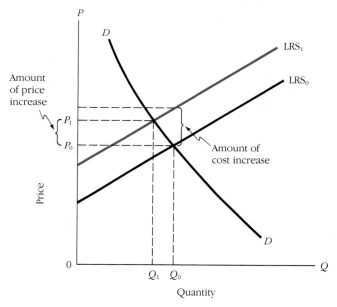

Since imperfections are likely to be of considerable significance in some instances, reference to some leading examples is in order.

Knowledge of Future Prices and Time Lags in Supply Adjustments

In an industry with large numbers of small producers, lack of knowledge of market conditions—coupled with the substantial time lag that often occurs between change in inputs and actual change in output reaching the market—may interfere seriously with market adjustments. Farmers, for example, must base output plans on prices prevailing at the time crops are planted. But they are unaware of the output decisions of other firms; thus the total increase or decrease in output may prove to be too large or too small, relative to demand, when crops actually reach the market. (See Box 9-7.)

Cobweb Models

A similar reaction, but one of a recurrent nature, occurs frequently with crops that require only one season to reach maturity. If price exceeds average cost at harvest time

9-7   An extreme example of time lags in the production process occurs in the growing of certain types of fruit. Apple and walnut trees, for example, do not reach full bearing until 10 to 20 years after planting. In an industry of this type, when the market price exceeds the long-run equilibrium figure, is there a tendency for too many trees to be planted?

When the crops of all new producers reach the market, the supply will be so great that market price will fall below average cost. As a result, some of the firms will be forced to retire from business. A good example of this reaction is provided by the apple industry in the Pacific Northwest during the 1920s and 1930s. During the early 1920s, apple prices exceeded average cost and many new orchards were developed. By the end of the 1920s, the increased supply from the new orchards began to reach the market and prices fell below average cost. The problem was greatly aggravated by the general business depression, which reduced demand at the same time that the increased supply reached the market.

in any year, the next year's crop may be so large that when it comes to market the price falls below average cost. In the following year, production may be reduced so much that price will rise above average cost—and so on. This type of behavior is described by a so-called **cobweb model**

The name originates from the appearance of the graphical presentation of price/quantity behavior in a situation of this sort. Figure 9-19(a) illustrates a case in which the amplitude of the excessive production in alternate years is declining. The D curve is the usual demand curve; it shows the quantities that will be produced at various prices in a particular year—that is, the prices at which various quantities placed on the market can be sold. Curve ss shows the quantities that will be produced and placed on the market in any given year, on the basis of various prices prevailing during the preceding year; it is a "lagged" supply curve. If, in the first year, the actual market price (determined by that year's current supply-demand relationships) is P_1, the quantity that will be supplied the next year is Q_1, as indicated by the curve ss. In that year, because of the increased supply, the price will fall to P_2. Supply the following year will then be Q_2, and price will rise to P_3, only to fall to P_4 the next year, and so on. Eventually, final equilibrium will tend to be reached at price P_0 and quantity Q_0, since each year the amplitude of the fluctuations grows less. Figure 9-19(b) illustrates a case in which the demand and "lagged" supply curves have the same slopes (but of opposite sign). In this case, the fluctuations continue indefinitely at the same amplitude. Figure 9-19(c) shows a case in which the fluctuations grow in amplitude, since the slope of the demand curve is greater in absolute value than that of the lagged supply curve. There is no evidence that this case is found in practice.

For purposes of illustration of the cobweb model, suppose that during the current year potato prices exceed average cost. As a result, next year many farmers will shift acreage from other crops to potatoes. When next year's crop is harvested, market supply will be considerably greater than it is this year. The increase may be so great

■■■■■■■
FIGURE 9-19

Cobweb Models

Part (a) exhibits a lagged supply function S and a demand function D. At price P_1, quantity supplied in the next period expands to Q_1. Consumers, however, are only willing to pay P_2 for Q_1. Producers reduce quantity supplied in the next period, only to find that buyers will pay P_3 for Q_2. This process eventually equilibrates at P_0 and Q_0. In part (b), demand and supply have the same slope, and oscillations continue indefinitely. The amplitude of the fluctuations grows when demand is steeper than supply in part (c).

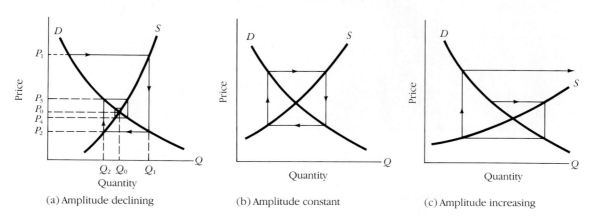

(a) Amplitude declining   (b) Amplitude constant   (c) Amplitude increasing

that market price will fall below average cost. As a result, potato acreage will be reduced substantially the following year, as farmers shift back to other crops. The reduction may be so great that prices will again rise above average cost and lead to another excessive increase in supply. (See Box 9-8.)

Other Imperfections

Knowledge of Cost.   Another source of imperfection is lack of knowledge by sellers of their costs. The typical production unit in perfect competition is small; the average farmer, for example, has very incomplete records and inadequate knowledge of costs. As a result, output is frequently not adjusted to the level that will maximize profit, and short-run supply is different from what it would be if producers calculated marginal cost carefully.

Immobility of Producers.   Another source of imperfection is the unwillingness of small producers, particularly farmers, to abandon their jobs and turn to other types of activity when they are unable to cover costs. They frequently are not skilled in other lines of work; job opportunities may not be plentiful; personal attachment to their jobs may prevent them from leaving even though prices are far below average cost. Farmers and other producers may typically shift quickly from one crop or product to another in response to relative price and profit situations, but they are very slow to leave farming or other production entirely. As a consequence, when prices of large numbers of farm

9-8 Why are there no good examples of cobwebs in which fluctuations *grow* in amplitude?

There are several reasons. First, farmers would be expected to learn from past experience—the basic assumption of a supply curve based strictly on last year's price is at odds with profit-maximization in a world in which farmers possess "rational expectations." Some "crafty" farmers would perceive the price pattern and would plant *more* in years following *low* prices, in anticipation that most farmers would plant less. This behavior, to be expected in the real world, would greatly smooth price fluctuations.

Also, for many crops (such as apples and potatoes) there are multiple uses of varying "durability." Apples can be dried, canned, or frozen when fresh apple prices are low and placed on the market when fresh apple prices are high, effectively eliminating a large portion of the demand for fresh apples. Frozen french fries and powdered mashed potatoes perform a similar price-smoothing function in the fresh potato market.

Such effects, taken together, greatly reduce the price fluctuations one would otherwise expect to observe in the real world.

or other products fall below average cost, readjustment to long-run equilibrium may be very slow.

Governmental Interference. Federal agricultural support programs have introduced another type of imperfection. The federal government has sought to prevent prices of various farm products from falling below certain levels by purchasing the commodities and by other programs designed to reduce supply.[8] Other examples of government interference include guaranteed loans, preferential treatment to small businesses, and general regulatory activity.

Lack of Complete Control over Output. Finally, the influence of climatic conditions upon crop yield, and the consequent inability of farmers to control exactly the volume of output by varying factor inputs, interfere with the attainment of equilibrium prices and cause substantial price fluctuations unrelated to adjustments toward equilibrium levels. Similar imprecision in the input/output relationship affects other production, though to a much lesser degree.

---

[8]Recall that supply reductions will raise revenue in cases such as farming, where demand is inelastic. The combination of higher revenues and lower costs clearly makes farmers *as a group* better off if supply is restricted. Any individual farmer, however, will still wish to supply where marginal cost equals the (higher) price. Such programs obviously interfere with supply adjustments and serve to raise consumer food costs, while actually not greatly helping poor farmers who sell less of their output in the market. Such policies also perpetuate maladjustments in allocation of farmland to various crops. When production becomes excessive in certain lines, consequent price declines should bring about a reduction in production. But if the government artificially holds prices up, the supply adjustment fails to occur.

SUMMARY

1. Perfect competition is a market structure with the following conditions: there are numerous buyers and sellers of a homogenous product; buyers and sellers have perfect mobility and information; and individual buyers and sellers believe that they *cannot* influence price by varying their purchases or sales.

2. There are three stages in the competitive price determination model: the market period, the short-run period and the long-run period. The market period is so short that total stocks of the commodity available for sale are fixed. The short-run period is long enough for existing stocks to be altered but short enough that some production and consumption features are prohibitively expensive to vary and are thus treated as fixed.

3. In the market period, the quantity that a particular seller will place on the market at various prices depends on the amount on hand and reservation prices. Prices below the reservation price mean that the seller will hold rather than sell the current stock.

4. The determinants of market period supply are *stock* on hand, *perishability* of the product, *expectations* of future prices, *cash* "needs," and *storage* costs.

5. The sum of individual supply schedules is equal to the total of market supply schedules. At higher relative prices additional amounts will be placed on the market.

6. The firm will not produce at all unless the price obtainable at least covers average variable cost (AVC).

7. At price levels equal to or in excess of average variable costs, a firm will produce in the short-run period even if total average costs are not completely covered.

8. The firm will adjust its output to a level where marginal cost with the existing plant is equal to marginal revenue.

9. Marginal revenue and average revenue are identical in perfect competition and both are equal to price.

10. The short-run supply curve is the upward sloping portion of the marginal cost curve on or above the intersection of the average variable and marginal cost curves.

11. The determinants of the total short-run supply schedule are the cost functions of existing firms, the number of firms presently in existence, and the size of the industry relative to the size of markets in which factor inputs are purchased.

12. Over the long-run period, price must cover all costs and therefore must be at least equal to average total cost. The plant will be adjusted to a size that allows equality of LRMC and price, and the firm will produce at the point at which SRMC with this plant is equal to price.

13. Since there is a single market price for the good, LRAC must be equal to this price for all firms.

14. The nature of the long-run industry supply depends on the cost conditions in which the industry operates; these conditions are constant cost, decreasing cost, or increasing cost.

15. Market price tends toward the short-run equilibrium level as a result of output adjustments with existing plants. However, changes in plant capacities of existing firms and in the number of firms in the industry will lead to continuous price and output adjustments until market price reaches the long-run equilibrium level.

WORDS AND CONCEPTS FOR REVIEW

perfect competition

market period

short-run period

long-run period

marginal revenue

competitive supply function

market supply function

reservation prices

market price determination

profit maximizing level of output

determinants of short-run supply

long-run output equilibrium

long-run equilibrium price

imperfections

cobweb model

REVIEW QUESTIONS

1. What is meant by the term "perfect competition"? Is it possible for a situation that does not conform to the assumptions of perfect competition to still be described by the perfectly competitive price theory? Discuss.

2. Does the analysis of pricing in perfectly competitive markets assume that sellers have perfect knowledge of total demand and supply conditions? Explain.

3. Explain the concept of a "market period." For what types of products is the concept of the market period, as distinguished from the short-run period, significant?

4. What are the determinants of market period demand and supply?

5. Why will agricultural producers tend to hold their crops off the market if the current price is relatively low? Under what conditions is this behavior unlikely?

6. What is the significance of cost of production for market period excess demand?

7. If the current market price is temporarily above the market period equilibrium level, how will it be brought down?

8. What is meant by short-run supply?

9. (a) Why must price cover AVC if firms are to continue to operate?
   (b) If firms are covering AVC but not all of their fixed costs, will they continue to operate in the short-run period? Why or why not?
   (c) Why is it possible for price to remain above average cost in the short-run period?
   (d) Why would one expect price to equal marginal cost in the short-run period?

10. What is the relationship between marginal cost and the short-run supply function?

11. If market price is above the short-run equilibrium level, by what process will it be brought to the latter? What determines the length of time that this adjustment will take?

12. On the basis of the data given below, can you determine the supply schedule of the firm in the short-run period? If not, why not?

Output	Total Variable Cost	Output	Total Variable Cost
1	$22	6	$ 85
2	32	7	115
3	40	8	155
4	50	9	205
5	65	10	310

13. Why does the short-run supply curve slope upward from left to right?

14. If long-run adjustments are complete, why will firms in perfectly competitive markets of necessity operate at the point of lowest average cost?

15. Why, in an increasing-cost industry, is the long-run industry supply curve identical to the long-run industry cost curve?

16. Draw the long-run supply curve for the industry on the basis of the cost data given below:

Total Output of Industry	Lowest Average Cost Figure for Each Firm
500,000	$47
1,000,000	52
1,500,000	55
2,000,000	59
2,500,000	63
3,000,000	66

17. What determines actual long-run output in a constant-cost industry as distinguished from potential output?

18. Under what circumstances in perfect competition is long-run price dependent upon demand considerations alone? Upon cost considerations alone? Illustrate graphically. Which case is most generally relevant?

19. Explain the cobweb model. If you were a farmer producing a product whose price is subject to these fluctuations, what could you do to increase your profits from a long-run standpoint, provided other farmers do not do the same thing?

20. Why do many farm product prices fluctuate greatly from year to year?

SUGGESTED READINGS

Friedman, Milton. *Price Theory*. Chicago: Aldine, 1976.

Marshall, Alfred. *Principles of Economics*, Book V, 8th ed. London: MacMillan, 1927.

Scherer, F. M. *Industrial Market Structure and Economic Performance*, 2nd ed. Chicago: Rand McNally, 1980.

Stigler, George. "Perfect Competition, Historically Contemplated." In Edwin Mansfield (ed.). *Microeconomics: Selected Readings*, 3rd ed. New York: Norton, 1979.

10

Monopoly

10.1 INTRODUCTION

Imperfectly competitive models of price and output determination are designed to deal with the broad spectrum of market situations that lie outside the realm of perfectly competitive models. Because the empirical significance of perfectly competitive models is commonly believed to be slight, the range of application of imperfectly competitive models is potentially extremely wide. As the situation now stands, though, the imperfectly competitive models—monopoly, monopolistic competition, and oligopoly—are by no means entirely adequate for analysis of particular industries and for recommendations regarding public policy. Nevertheless, they can make significant contributions to an understanding of imperfectly competitive industries.

10.2 IMPERFECTLY COMPETITIVE MODELS: GENERAL CONSIDERATIONS

As noted in Chapter 9, the essential condition for perfect competition is that sellers believe that prices are determined by forces outside their control. Conversely, the distinctive characteristic of imperfectly competitive markets is that individual sellers consider themselves able by one means or another to exert a noticeable influence on market price—by varying quantity offered for sale, by engaging in advertising or other sales promotion activities, by lobbying for favorable legislation, by buying out or otherwise eliminating competing sellers, and so on. The average revenue functions of perfectly competitive sellers consist of the market prices they face; their only decision is how much to produce. The average revenue functions of imperfectly competitive sellers, however, involve both price and sales as variables and are influenced by a number of considerations. Accordingly, a central problem in the general theory of imperfect competition is to explain the **average revenue functions** of individual sellers—that is, the relationships, as seen by the sellers, between the amounts placed on the market and the prices at which these amounts can be sold.

The definition of empirically relevant and theoretically consistent average revenue functions is a particularly difficult problem in oligopolistic markets, where sellers are so few that each seller's revenue prospects necessarily depend directly on the actions, whether anticipated or not, of all other sellers. Such mutual interdependence cannot be entirely ignored even in situations of monopoly and monopolistic competition, but the phenomenon is not of sufficient importance in those situations to require explicit theoretical attention. For this as well as other reasons, therefore, it is convenient to deal separately with different types of imperfectly competitive markets. The present chapter analyzes monopolies—markets where buyers are numerous but where total output of the good offered for sale is controlled by a single firm. The cases of monopolistic competition and oligopoly will be discussed in succeeding chapters.

Average Revenue, Marginal Revenue, and Total Revenue under Monopoly Conditions

The average revenue function of a firm may be regarded as the demand function for the firm's product. The average revenue function indicates the revenue per unit which can be obtained if various amounts of product are placed on the market; the demand function indicates the quantities which the firm can sell at various possible prices; and hence the two must be equal ($TR/Q = P \cdot Q/Q = P$). As noted in Chapter 9, the concept of marginal revenue is defined as the addition to total revenue resulting from the sale of additional units of output. Table 10-1 shows a hypothetical demand schedule for a firm's product and the related revenue schedule, including marginal revenue.

TABLE 10-1

Demand and Revenue Schedules for a Monopolist

Demand Schedule for the Firm's Product		Revenue Schedule from Sale of the Firm's Product			
Price (dollars)	*Number of Units Purchased by Customers*	*Number of Units Sold by Firm*	*Total Revenue (dollars)*	*Average Revenue (dollars)*	*Marginal Revenue (dollars)*
16	1	1	16	16	16
15	2	2	30	15	14
14	3	3	42	14	12
13	4	4	52	13	10
12	5	5	60	12	8
11	6	6	66	11	6
10	7	7	70	10	4
9	8	8	72	9	2
8	9	9	72	8	0
7	10	10	70	7	−2
6	11	11	66	6	−4

The data in Table 10-1 are illustrated graphically in Figure 10-1. The demand curve for the firm's product and the AR curve are identical in form, since the two schedules contain the same data, viewed in two different ways.

With the schedule shown in Table 10-1, average revenue declines as additional units are placed on the market; hence marginal revenue is less than average revenue for all units except the first. Therefore, in the related graph (Figure 10-1), the MR curve lies below the AR curve and declines at a more rapid rate. Each additional unit sold adds less to total revenue than the price (average revenue) received for it, since the price on all units must be lowered to allow additional units to be sold. In the example, in order to sell eight units instead of seven, the firm must lower the price from $10 to $9; thus while the eighth unit sells for $9, it adds only $2 (the difference between $70 and $72) to the firm's total revenue, since seven units could have been sold for $10 apiece instead of $9. Thus marginal revenue is below price. And this is true for any negatively sloped demand curve—for the average revenue (price) to decline, marginal revenue must be below average revenue.[1]

When the demand schedule for a firm's product is elastic (elasticity greater than one), marginal revenue will be positive, because total revenue is greater at lower prices (and larger sales volumes) than at higher prices (and smaller volumes). However, when a demand schedule is inelastic, marginal revenue will be negative because the price reduction necessary to sell an additional unit is relatively greater than the quantity increase, hence total revenue falls (see in Table 10-1 where ten or eleven units are sold). The total price reduction on units which could have been sold at a higher price exceeds the price received from the sale of an additional unit. If the demand schedule is of unitary elasticity, marginal revenue is zero (as in going from a quantity sold of eight to nine in Table 10-1.) The relationship between the elasticity of the demand schedule and marginal revenue is shown in Figure 10-2.

As seen in Figure 10-2, elasticity varies along a linear demand curve. Above the midpoint the curve is elastic ($e > 1$); below the midpoint it is inelastic ($e < 1$); and at the midpoint of the curve it is unit elastic ($e = 1$). How does this relate to total revenue? In the elastic portion of the curve, when the price falls, total revenue rises (mar-

---

[1]For linear demand curves, it is easy to establish that marginal revenue falls at exactly *twice* the rate at which average revenue falls, both beginning at the same point. Let $P = a - bQ$ represent the average revenue or demand relation. Then TR $= P \cdot Q$ or $(a - bQ)Q = aQ - bQ^2$. But the marginal revenue, MR, is just the derivative of total revenue with respect to quantity:

$$MR = \frac{d\,TR}{dQ} = a - 2bQ$$

Hence, both starting at a, the marginal revenue curve has twice the slope of the AR curve. This is, of course, consistent with other related characteristics of linear demand functions. For example, the midpoint is the point of unitary price elasticity; that is, for small changes in price, $P \cdot Q$ (or TR) does not change. But that means that TR is either maximized or minimized at that point—and, indeed, MR $= 0$ at the midpoint of the demand curve. Since MR > 0 for quantities smaller than this and MR < 0 for larger quantities, TR is *maximized* at the midpoint.

FIGURE 10-1

Demand and Revenue Schedules for a Monopolist

The industry demand curve shows the price, or average revenue, of each unit of output. Price exceeds marginal revenue since selling additional units of output requires lowering the price on preceding units.

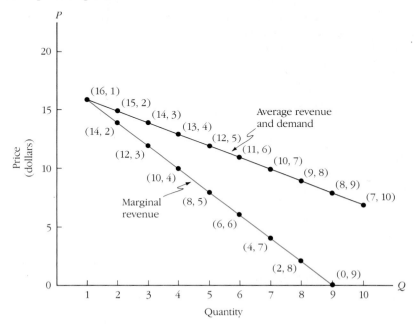

ginal revenue is greater than zero). In the inelastic region of the demand curve, when the price falls total revenue falls (marginal revenue is less than zero). Thus at the midpoint of the linear demand curve, where MR = 0 the total revenue function reaches its highest point.

10.3 PRICE AND OUTPUT DETERMINATION: UNREGULATED MONOPOLY

Monopoly is defined for purposes of economic analysis as a situation in which a single firm supplies the entire quantity of a good offered to buyers in a particular market. Monopolies are virtually nonexistent in basic manufacturing industries at this time, though they did exist around the turn of the century in steel, tobacco, aluminum, and other areas. They occur most commonly now in regulated public utilities and in particular geographic areas where transport costs or similar factors allow a local seller (say a lumber supply firm, a lawyer, or a fabric store) to act as a monopolist within a certain range of prices. (See Box 10-1.)

FIGURE 10-2

**The Relationship between the Elasticity of Average Revenue
and Total and Marginal Revenue**

Along a linear average revenue function, the elastic segment lies above the midpoint, the inelastic segment lies below the midpoint, and the point of unitary elasticity is the midpoint. A high price elasticity of demand indicates that small price reductions will increase quantity considerably. Total revenue rises, and marginal revenue is positive. At unit elasticity, total revenue is maximum. Price and quantity change by the same percentages so total revenue does not change with output and marginal revenue is constant. A modest output response to a price decrease occurs when demand is inelastic. Total revenue declines, and marginal revenue is negative.

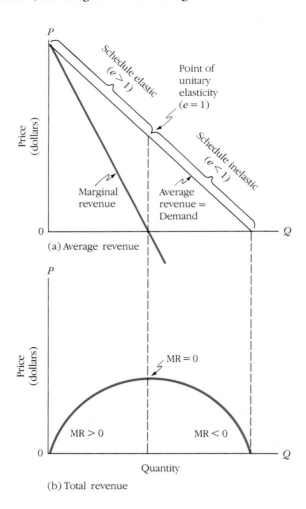

(a) Average revenue

(b) Total revenue

10-1   True or False?   Since every good has a number of more or less close substitutes, monopoly implies complete absence of competition from other commodities.

False. Monopoly does imply an absence of competing sellers in the particular market, and a relatively *low cross-elasticity of demand* between the product and other products. The lack of seller competition leads us to emphasize aspects of market behavior different from those emphasized in our analysis of perfect competition (and monopolistic competition, considered later) and also to extend our argument to include certain kinds of activities (such as advertising and price discrimination) that are entirely absent in perfectly competitive markets. Our treatment of monopoly is nevertheless similar in broad outline to that of perfect competition. Analogies and major differences between the two kinds of market situations will be emphasized.

Monopoly Price Determination in the Market Period

The concept of a market period is defined for monopoly, just as for perfect competition, as an interval of time so short that adjustments in output are impractical. Here we assume a given output rate, not a given stock of goods on hand as in the market period of the perfectly competitive model. If, as is usually assumed, the monopolist deals directly with its customers and so sets its own "asking" price, the price that it sets will be the market price, and demand conditions will be important only insofar as they affect the monopolist's view of future revenue prospects. (See Box 10-2.)

10-2   True or False?   If quantity demanded at the current price is greater than the firm's current output, the monopolist may either meet demand by selling from previously accumulated stock or choke off excess demand by increasing the asking (and the market) price.

True. Which alternative the monopolist adopts will depend on its estimate of the relative advantages of each policy. If the monopolist believes that demand is currently running at an abnormally high level, for example, it may maintain the prevailing price in order to retain customer goodwill and avoid possible expenditures associated with revisions in price. If the current level of demand is considered to be permanent, however, the monopolist will probably raise the asking price—the exact amount depending on its estimate of demand elasticity, the danger of attracting attention from antitrust authorities, the possibility that high prices may encourage buyers to gravitate towards substitute goods offered for sale in other markets, and so on.

Similar considerations apply in situations where quantity demanded at the prevailing market price falls short of current output. The monopolist may either hold price at its current level and watch inventories mount, or cut price in an attempt to reduce storage and other current costs.

Short-Run Pricing—the Average Revenue Function of a Monopolist

The monopolist's problem in a short-run period (a period sufficiently long to permit output to be adjusted with existing plant) is to choose a profit-maximizing level of output such that MR = MC.[2] Thus the monopolist's formal decision problem is the same as that of a competitive seller. There is a practical difference, however: whereas for a competitive seller, knowing the current market price is equivalent to knowing marginal revenue (since MR = P) corresponding to any level of sales, a monopoly seller may find accurate estimation of marginal revenue difficult.

The only objective basis on which a monopolist can arrive at an estimate of its revenue prospects is by referring to past information about actual sales at various prices. If demand conditions are completely stable over time, a little experimentation with different asking prices will provide an accurate impression of the position of the market demand curve and its elasticity in the neighborhood of previously observed price/sales points. If demand conditions fluctuate constantly (for example, because of changes in other prices or preferences), the monopolist can form only a rough statistical estimate of the probable position and form of the short-period demand function; hence the average revenue function on which its marginal revenue calculations are based must be to some degree conjectural.

Then how do we determine the short-run optimum output and price? With the assumption that the monopolist arrives at an estimate of the relevant short-run average revenue function, we may describe the determination of the optimum level of output and price in terms of the relations shown diagramatically in Figure 10-3. The average revenue function of the monopolist is represented by the line AR; the marginal revenue function corresponding to the given average revenue function is therefore defined by the line MR. The factors governing short-run costs of production are assumed to be similar to those of an individual seller operating under conditions of

---

[2]The proof that setting marginal cost equal to marginal revenue maximizes profit is straightforward. By definition, profit equals total revenue minus total cost:

$$\pi(Q) = TR(Q) - TC(Q)$$

At a maximum (or minimum), $d\pi(Q)/dQ = 0$ or

$$0 = \frac{d\,TR(Q)}{dQ} - \frac{d\,TC(Q)}{dQ}$$

But this is exactly the assertion to be proved, that $MR(Q^*) = MC(Q^*)$ at a maximum (or minimum). To guarantee that a maximum, rather than a minimum, is found, the second derivative of $\pi(Q)$ must be *negative* at Q^*, (that is, profits must be falling for output levels a bit above or below Q^*). Imposing this condition yields

$$\frac{d^2TR(Q)}{dQ^2} - \frac{d^2TC(Q)}{dQ^2} < 0$$

This, however, merely says that for a maximum, the slope of marginal revenue is less than the slope of marginal cost. Since the slope of marginal revenue is normally negative (or zero in perfect competition), being on the upward-sloping portion of the marginal cost curve is sufficient.

FIGURE 10-3

Short-Run Adjustment of Price and Output by a Monopolist
Like the perfectly competitive firm, the monopolist's output level coincides with the equality of marginal revenue and marginal cost, providing that the price at which that quantity can be sold is at least as great as average variable cost. The optimum price charged the consumers is P_0. Since price is greater than average cost, this monopolist receives positive profits.

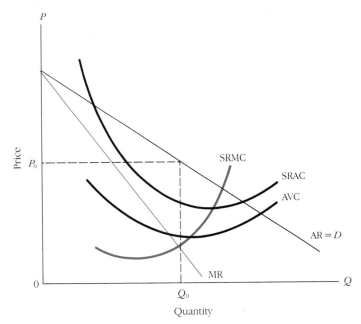

perfect competition; thus we may regard the short-run variable cost function as given, and from it derive the average variable cost curve AVC and the corresponding short-run marginal cost curve SRMC. Finally, we obtain short-run average cost curve SRAC by adding average fixed cost to average variable cost at each possible level of output.

Given the relations shown in Figure 10-3, the firm's short-run optimum level of output, Q_0, is defined by the intersection of the MR curve with the MC curve—that is, by the requirement that output be such that MR = MC, provided AVC is covered by the resulting price. The short-run equilibrium price is given by the AR curve as that value of price P_0 at which buyers will be willing to purchase the quantity of output Q_0—that is, the price at which short-run output will be just equal to short-run quantity demanded.

Another approach to find the optimum monopoly output uses the short-run total cost and total revenue curves, as depicted in Figure 10-4. The output level Q_0 is identical to the output level determined using the marginal approach in Figure 10-3. However, using the total approach, maximum profit is determined by the greatest vertical distance between the SRTC and the TR curve which is at Q_0. At this level of output the

FIGURE 10-4

The Monopolist's Total Revenue and Total Costs: The Short Run
Total revenue less total costs (implicit and explicit) equals profit. Geometrically, the
vertical distance between the total revenue and short-run total cost curves designates
profit. Notice that profit is maximized when the slopes of the two curves—that is, the
marginal revenue and the short-run marginal cost—are equal.

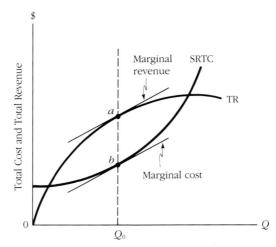

slope of the total cost curve (marginal cost) is equal to the slope of the total revenue
curve (marginal revenue).

Differences and similarities with the perfectly competitive model should be noted.
In monopoly as in competition, the equilibrium value of output is defined by the
requirement that MR = MC. Since the AR curve of the monopolist is downward sloping
rather than horizontal, marginal revenue is less than average revenue at the equilibrium level, whereas marginal revenue is equal to average revenue (and to market
price) in perfect competition.

One difference between perfect competition and monopoly is that the short-run
equilibrium output of a monopolist, unlike the short-run equilibrium output of a
competitive seller, is a determinant rather than a function of market price. Thus our
theory of monopoly output determination does not lead directly to a definition of the
short-run supply function, as does the theory of competitive output determination.[3]

---

[3]On closer inspection, however, it is clear that this supposed difference between perfect
competition and monopoly is more apparent than real. *Under perfect competition, there is
just one equilibrium value of output corresponding to any given average revenue function;
the same is true in the theory of monopoly.* The supply curve of a competitive seller is generated by *varying* the position of the average revenue function; it indicates, for each set of
values of the parameters defining the average revenue function of an individual seller, the
corresponding equilibrium level of output. A similar relation could be established between
the equilibrium output of a monopolist and various levels of the parameters that define the
monopolist's average revenue function. But such a function is not particularly useful for
purposes of analysis (since supply will depend on both cost *and* demand parameters) and
thus is not typically established.

A final point of difference between monopoly and perfect competition concerns the welfare implications of the fact that price exceeds marginal cost under monopoly conditions. Provided that the average revenue function of the monopolist accurately reflects actual market demand conditions, the failure to equate marginal cost with price implies a restriction of equilibrium output and an elevation of price as compared with the results that would occur if the market were perfectly competitive.

Long-Run Adjustments

So long as the situation remains one of complete monopoly, long-run price and output adjustments involve nothing more than readjustments by the firm to bring about equality of LRMC and MR—that is, adjustments in plant to a level such that MR = LRMC = SRMC at the long-run equilibrium level of output.

Clarifying further, maximum profits at a given time require operation at the level at which MC with the existing plant is equal to MR. Over a longer period of time, however, it may be possible to increase profits by adjusting plant size. When this adjustment is complete, MR will be equal both to LRMC and SRMC. Failure to attain equality of MR and LRMC would indicate failure to complete all profitable plant adjustments. Failure to attain equality of SRMC and MR would indicate failure to operate at the most profitable output level with the plant constructed. Figure 10-5 indicates the long-run

FIGURE 10-5

Long-Run Adjustment of a Monopolist
The monopolist chooses the scale of the plant for which MR = LRMC, the scale represented by $SRAC_1$ in this example. In the long run, the monopolist produces Q_L and sell this quantity at price P_L.

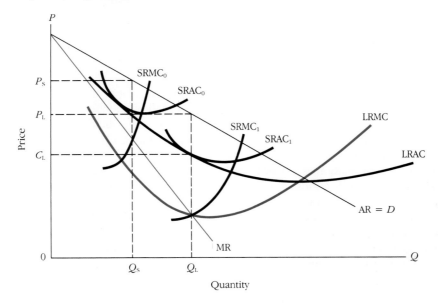

adjustment. Initially, with plant size $SRAC_0$, the firm produces Q_S units (for equality of MR and $SRMC_0$ with plant $SRAC_0$) and sets a price of P_S. But MR does not equal LRMC at the point of most profitable operation, because the plant is too small relative to the demand for the product. Accordingly, the firm increases its plant size to that associated with $SRAC_1$. With this plant, $MR = SRMC_1 = LRMC$ at the point of most profitable operation, Q_L, with corresponding price, P_L.

Under the assumptions of monopoly, no new firms can enter the industry, and thus no other long-run adjustments will take place. In Figure 10-5, the monopolist earns excess profits per unit of output equal to the difference between P_L and C_L. However, a monopolist may or may not have sufficient sales potential to earn more than a normal return on invested capital. Should a monopolist have such a limited sales volume that the firm does not earn even a normal return, then the owners will eventually liquidate the business. A monopoly position in itself is no guarantee of excess profits. If demand is inadequate, lack of competitors is of little benefit to a seller!

10.4 PRICE DISCRIMINATION

The preceding discussion is based on the assumption that the firm sells a given product to all buyers at the same price. Under monopoly conditions, however, such a policy is not always necessary, and is usually not optimal. Some purchasers will buy at higher prices than others, and most individual purchasers will buy more at lower prices than at higher prices. Thus a monopolist will find it profitable to discriminate (where possible) among various buyers, charging higher prices to those willing to pay more and charging individual buyers on a sliding scale for units purchased. This policy is known as **price discrimination**, defined more precisely as the practice of charging different prices to various customers not in accord with differences in costs of producing and handling goods sold to the various customers. Thus discrimination also includes the practice of charging identical prices to various customers when costs differ.

The Conditions Necessary for Discrimination

First, discrimination is possible only with monopoly, or where members of a small group of firms (oligopolists, to be considered later) follow identical pricing policies. Wherever a number of competing firms follow independent policies, discrimination is impossible because competitors will undercut prices charged by others in the high-price markets.

Second, discrimination is possible only if resale from one market to another is impractical; otherwise, goods will flow from the low-price market to the high-price market. Transportation costs may prevent resale. For example, a monopoly producer located at A between two markets, B and C, may charge a differentially higher price in market B than in market C, up to the amount of the B-C freight rate, if demand conditions make such a policy desirable. Also, tariff barriers may prevent the return of goods sold cheaply in a foreign market. The nature of the product may prevent resale;

medical service, for example, is not transferable. Finally, resale may be prevented by contractual agreements forced upon the low-price buyer.

Finally, price discrimination can only occur if the demand curves in various markets are in fact different. If they are not, then $MR_i = MR_j = MC$ at the *same* price—that is, a profit maximizing monopolist would charge the same price in both markets. (See Box 10-3.)

Discrimination will be complete, or "perfect," if it yields the maximum sum buyers will pay on each individual unit sold. That is, the consumer will be stripped of all consumer surplus. Or it may be partial, the buyers being grouped into major classes and the prices varied according to the class.

Perfect Price Discrimination: An Extreme but Informative Case

Perfect price discrimination (sometimes called "first-degree" price discrimination) requires that each buyer be induced to pay the maximum possible sum he is willing to pay for any given quantity rather than forgo use of the good entirely.

Suppose, for example, that a person will buy each week one quart of orange juice if the price is $1.00 a quart, five quarts at a price of 50 cents, and ten quarts at 25 cents. The objective of perfect discrimination is to make the buyer pay $1.00 for one quart, 50 cents for the next four quarts and 25 cents for the last five, and thus make her pay $4.25 instead of $2.50, the price if she could obtain all ten quarts at a 25-cent figure. In this manner the buyer's individual demand schedule effectively becomes the seller's schedule of marginal revenue from the particular buyer, since prices need not be lowered on earlier units if more are produced and sold. The optimum amount to be sold to each buyer is that at which marginal cost is equal to marginal revenue (the AR if the firm could not perfectly discriminate) from the sale to the particular buyer, determined as indicated above.

The charge for the entire group of units sold the customer is the sum of the buyer demand prices for each successive unit ($4.25 in the example above); the buyer is

---

10-3 True or False? **Discrimination is advantageous because some buyers are willing to pay more for a good than others, and because some buyers are willing to pay more for initial units than for subsequent units.**

True. One person may be willing to pay $8,000 for a used car, while another buyer will take the same car only at $6,000; and the first buyer may be induced to acquire an equivalent second used car only if he can get it for $4,000. If a single, uniform price is charged, some buyers will be pushed out of the market completely, others will buy fewer units than they would at a lower figure, and many of those buying the product at the prevailing price would be willing to pay more for some of the units which they are currently buying. Discrimination is designed to gain additional revenue by charging "almost" as much as individuals would be willing to pay for each unit.

required to pay this sum and take the entire amount, under an all-or-nothing bargain. She has only the choice of paying $4.25 for the ten units or not buying the good at all, since the seller will not sell her a smaller number of units. Or, in terms of the usual marginal revenue/marginal cost diagram, the monopolist extends production and sales up to the point at which the MC curve intersects the AR (demand) curve, since the monopolist can sell additional units at successively lower prices without lowering the price on all units sold. Thus the price charged all but marginal buyers will be greater than that indicated by the point on the AR curve at which MC = AR (equals MR, in the perfect price discrimination case).

Market conditions obviously do not permit perfect discrimination to be carried out to any significant extent. One example on a partial scale is to be found in the practice of doctors who vary charges to their customers according to income status. A breeder of fine horses, dealing individually with relatively uninformed buyers in different parts of the country, may be able to carry on perfect discrimination. But apart from such isolated cases, the analysis of perfect discrimination is useful merely to illustrate a type of price-setting procedure that would be advantageous to the firm if it could be employed.

Multipart Price Discrimination

Multipart price discrimination (sometimes known as "second-degree" price discrimination) is much more common than perfect discrimination. This method of discrimination, where discounts are given to those buyers that purchase larger quantities, is often used by public utilities and wholesale traders.

Specifically this form of discrimination allows the monopolist to sell blocks of its output at different prices, charging the greatest amount for the first block and less for successive blocks. In Figure 10-6, the monopolist might sell the first block of output from 0 to Q_1 at price P_1 and then sell the second block Q_1 to Q_2 at the lower price of P_2. Ultimately the monopolist would allow the customer to buy Q_3 at the lowest price it offered (P_3 in Figure 10-6).

The reasoning for multipart pricing is quite simple. Imagine that the monopolist's single-price maximization point (MR = MC) would result in price P_3. If the monopolist charged this price for all the output, total revenue would be the rectangle $0P_3aQ_3$. In contrast, the multipart discriminating monopolist would be able to transfer the cross-hatched areas of consumer surplus to total revenue. Thus, the consumer's loss is the monopolist's gain.

Segmented-Market Price Discrimination

While a firm can seldom exploit fully its profit possibilities in dealings with each buyer, it may be able to segment its total market into several parts on the basis of demand prices and elasticities and charge different prices to different groups of buyers. As seen in Figure 10-7, relatively high prices will be charged in segments where demand is inelastic (Market A) and relatively low prices in segments where demand is elastic (Market B). Accordingly, the firm can advantageously sell a larger quantity than

FIGURE 10-6

Multipart Price Discrimination
The monopolist charges P_1 for units of output up to Q_1, P_2 for units from Q_1 to Q_2, and P_3 for any additional units. In the absence of multipart price discrimination, P_3 would be charged for all Q_3 units of output. Thus, this type of discrimination transfers the portion of consumer surplus in the shaded area to the monopolist.

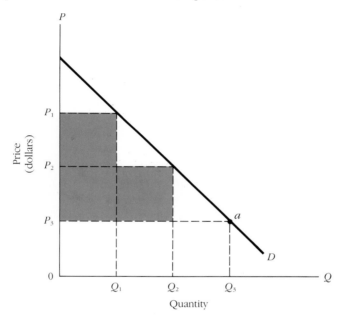

Quantity

under a uniform-price policy. Such a policy is known as **segmented-market price discrimination** (sometimes called "third-degree" price discrimination); here the optimum price is obtained from groups of buyers rather than from each individual buyer.

When segmented-market price discrimination is possible, profits will be maximized by adjusting total output to the level at which the marginal cost of the entire output equals the horizontal sum of the marginal revenues in the various markets. The marginal revenue in each market segment is then set equal to the marginal cost of the last unit produced. Figure 10-7 illustrates the case for two segmented markets. In market A the AR curve is AR-A and the MR curve is MR-A; in market B the two curves are AR-B and MR-B, respectively. Curves AR-T and MR-T show the horizontal sums of the AR and MR schedules in the two markets. Total output will be Q_T, if profits are to be maximized, as determined by the intersection of the MC curve (MC) and MR-T, the curve showing the sum of the marginal revenues in the two markets. The amount sold in each market (Q_A and Q_B, respectively) is the quantity at which marginal revenue in the market is equal to MC at the output level at which MC and the sum of the marginal revenues are equal. This figure is indicated by the point of intersection of the market's MR curve with a line

FIGURE 10-7

Segmented-Market Price Discrimination

Total output for a segmented-market price-discriminating monopolist is that which corresponds to the equality of MC and the total MR curve, the horizontal sum of the MR curves for the two markets. The output is allocated between markets by setting MC on the last unit produced for the entire firm equal to MR in each market.

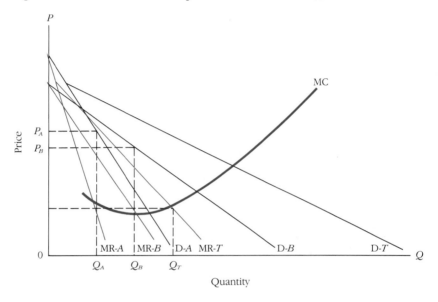

drawn horizontally through the intersection of MC and MR-T.[4] The price charged in each market (P_A in A, P_B in B) is indicated by the point on the market's AR curve directly above this intersection. It is, of course, the price at which the output which yields maximum profit in the market can be sold. The greater the difference in the elasticities of the demand curves in the various markets, the greater will be the optimal price differences, and the larger the increase in profit resulting from discrimination. If demand elasticities are the same in all market segments, there can be no gain from discrimination, as indicated earlier.

The basis upon which markets are segregated depends primarily upon the nature of market conditions and the seller's ability to prevent resale between market segments. The seller seeks to segregate customers in such a way as to produce the maximum difference in elasticity between the various markets. In some instances the basis for segregation is use. Railroad freight rates, for example, vary among goods shipped, largely on the basis of demand conditions.

---

[4]The output sold in each market is not that at which marginal revenue in that market is equal to the marginal cost of producing the particular amount of output sold in that market; the significant marginal cost figure is that of the entire output sold in the two markets.

Markets are frequently segregated on a geographical basis. Products may be sold in a more distant area at a price lower (or higher) than that charged near the site of production because more (or fewer) substitutes are available in distant areas or demand is more (or less) elastic due to competition.

A third basis for segmentation is the direct attempt to group customers on the basis of buying preferences and incomes by providing several brands of a product (sometimes physically identical), each intended for a certain buying group, with prices adjusted to reflect differences in the elasticity of demand. Price differentials may bear little relationship to cost differences. For example, seats in various portions of a theatre are priced in a manner designed to attract different income groups. If a uniform price were charged, lower income groups would not come at all, and those in higher income groups would pay considerably less than they were willing to pay. While it is true that the various seats are not the same "good," the differences in price are often larger than differences in seat "quality."

A fourth basis is the size of the order. Often sellers find it advantageous to make substantial price concessions to large buyers in order to obtain their business—concessions which are not necessary to sell to customers buying smaller amounts. While some such behavior is cost-based (for example, it may cost about as much for a bank to make a very large loan as to make a small loan), much of it is not. (See Box 10-4.)

10.5 ADJUSTMENT OF PRODUCT AND SELLING ACTIVITIES

The discussion up to this point has largely assumed that the product is a standard item, not subject to variation, and that the firm does not engage in activities designed to affect the demand for the product. Actually, however, both elements are subject to variation by the action of the firm, and the point of absolute maximum profit cannot be attained without optimum adjustment in both product and selling activities.

10-4   When airlines offer discounts on their transcontinental flights it is often mandatory to purchase tickets at least a month in advance. Why is this an effective pricing strategy?

This allows the airlines to discriminate against business travelers who often need a flight on the spur of the moment. Thus, the business traveler has a more inelastic demand curve (fewer substitutes). And if the airlines cut prices for these clients their revenues will fall. However, the planned traveler, (perhaps a vacationer) is operating on a much more elastic demand curve. For these travelers there are many substitutes such as other modes of transportation, different destinations, different times, etc. Therefore, the airlines charge lower prices to this group of travelers contingent upon their making earlier reservations. Thus, the airlines can make more money by segmenting the market according to each group's elasticity of demand rather than charging all users the same price.

Adjustment of the Physical Product

Once the firm has selected the product or products it will produce, it must select the exact variety or quality of the product which allows maximum profit. For each potential form of the product, there is a certain cost schedule and a certain demand schedule, and thus a certain possible profit at the level of output for the product where marginal revenue is equal to marginal cost. In general, the higher the quality of the product, the greater the potential sales at various prices; but the cost per unit for producing various quantities will also be higher. Several forms of the product, with optimum price and output levels for each form, will usually allow the greatest profit.

Unfortunately, it is very difficult for the firm to estimate sales corresponding to various forms of the product, because of the difficulty of predicting consumer reaction. Experimentation is sometimes possible ("test-marketing" in target populations), but usually the firm is forced to select the particular forms which, on the basis of rough estimates, appear to yield the greatest net return.

A firm seldom limits itself to one particular quality, finding it advantageous to carry several different brands of the same product, with differences in quality and price. The provision of several different qualities enables the firm to utilize its plant more effectively and to gain greater advantages of large-scale production. The importance of having a "full line" so that shoppers can satisfy their wishes for various types of items (colors and varieties of paints, for example) also may encourage the firm to carry a wider variety of qualities.

Selling Activities

Profit maximization also requires optimum adjustment of selling activities designed to influence the schedule of demand. Costs incurred to carry on these activities are known as **selling costs**, as distinguished from production costs. In practice, a precise line cannot be drawn between the two classes of cost; expenses of packaging, for example, and the salaries of sales personnel, fall partly into each category. But the classification is useful for purposes of analysis.

Selling activity, in turn, may be grouped into two major classes, quality-service competition and direct sales promotion. The former involves improving the quality of the product (or giving the impression of improving it), without altering its basic nature, or adding to the service rendered in conjunction with the sale of the product. A major aspect of quality-service competition is the emphasis placed upon style and deliberate changes in styles to make existing models prematurely obsolete. Whenever style can be emphasized, as with women's clothes and automobiles, firms will deliberately change styles from year to year.

No sharp line can be drawn between the process of selecting the optimum physical product, as outlined above, and that of adjusting quality and service as methods of increasing sales. Both actions affect sales and cost schedules and, if successful, increase the demand for the product. The distinction is essentially one of degree.

Almost universally in monopoly (as in all imperfectly competitive markets, even those with relatively standardized products), firms find it advantageous to increase their sales by using sales representatives, advertising, and other selling activities. Sales promotion, if successful, can raise the demand schedule for the firm's product. Consequently, a greater volume can be sold at the existing price with lower production costs per unit due to scale economies, or price can be raised and thus profit per unit increased. If the addition to total cost resulting from selling activities is less than the increase in receipts (net of any change in production cost), the profits of the firm will increase. (See Box 10-5.)

The Level of Selling Activities. The adjustment of the level of selling activities is influenced by the manner in which sales react as expenditures on selling activities are increased—the "promotional elasticity" of advertising. Apparently, as a firm first increases sales effort, "returns" typically increase in the sense that additional dollars spent on advertising produce successively greater increases in sales. There are two reasons for this phenomenon. First, successful advertising requires repetition, in the sense that repeated suggestions are frequently necessary to influence the actions of the buyers. Thus, if total expenditures on advertising are small, they may have hardly any effect upon sales; thereafter, a relatively limited increase may produce a sharp increase in sales because of the repetition effect. Second, as selling expenditures are increased, more effective means can be used. Division of labor produces advantages in selling as well as in other forms of business activity. Advertising experts can be hired, and nationwide media coverage can be employed.

Eventually, however, increasing returns inevitably give way to decreasing returns, with additional dollars spent on sales promotion producing progressively smaller increases in sales. The economies will eventually be exhausted, along with the exploitation of the best portions of the potential market. Additional sales can be made only to persons who are less interested in the product than those who bought it initially, and greater effort will be required to induce them to buy. Frequently, the additional customers will be more expensive to contact. The old customers can buy additional units only by sacrificing other purchases which offer greater utility than those forgone in

10-5 Why is sales promotion effective?

Sales promotion is effective primarily because consumers have very limited knowledge of the quality of the goods which they are contemplating buying, and their desires are subject to influence. They are not familiar with many goods and frequently have no satisfactory way of even judging the relative desirability of products with which they are familiar. Furthermore, consumer wants may themselves be subject to modification. Persons have certain basic desires for food, clothing, shelter, and so on. But the exact nature of the wants—whether they wish to eat meat or fruit, for example—is subject to change. Many persons have incomes well in excess of the amounts necessary to satisfy the basic "needs" of life. Great opportunity exists for producers to influence these persons to use a portion of their income to make "luxury" purchases.

order to buy initial units of the good. To buy one automobile, a person may need to sacrifice only a portion of the year's savings and a trip to Hawaii. But to buy a second car, he may have to forgo some of the food and clothing to which he has become accustomed.

Attainment of profit maximization requires the selection of the optimum-profit level of selling activities, as well as the most advantageous types. This level, however, cannot be determined independently of decisions on product, output, and price, since the level of selling activities which will maximize profit is not the same at alternative quality, quantity, or price levels. Likewise, product, output, and price cannot be determined independently of the volume of selling activities, since the latter affects both cost and revenue schedules.

At each output level, successively larger selling expenditures will allow higher prices to be obtained but will also increase average cost. For each output level, there will be some level of selling activities at which the relationship between price and average cost allows maximum profit. If the various possible output levels are considered, there will be one level at which, with optimum selling expenditures for that level, profits are maximized. The price set will be that obtainable with the prevailing level of sales expenditure. At this point, full marginal production and selling cost will equal marginal revenue, the demand curve being the one appropriate to that level of selling activities.

In Table 10-2, the profit (or loss) figure is shown for several levels of output, with various levels of selling expenditures. Thus, for example, with one unit of output and selling expenditures of $100, total loss will be $10. Examination of Table 10-2 shows that profits are maximized with four units of output and selling expenses of $400. The price charged (not shown in the table) is that at which the four units can be sold with $400 of selling expenditures.[5]

---

[5]The tabular presentation is adapted from the method used by G. J. Stigler, *The Theory of Price* (New York: Macmillan, 1946), p. 261.

TABLE 10-2

Profits with Various Combinations of Output Levels and Selling Expenditures

Selling Expenditures	Units of Output					
	1	*2*	*3*	*4*	*5*	*6*
	Profits					
$100	−$10	−$ 6	−$ 2	−$ 6	−$20	−$60
200	− 5	− 1	6	12	8	− 4
300	8	18	20	40	20	− 2
400	15	17	60	80	60	10
500	12	15	50	60	30	− 5

The choice of product must also be brought into the picture. For each possible form of product, there will be an optimum price and selling cost combination. For maximum profit, the firm must select that form of product which, with optimum price and selling expenditures, allows the highest profit figure.

Imperfections in the Determination of Selling Activities. Any firm is likely to have extreme difficulty creating a situation in which price, selling activities, and product are all adjusted to levels which allow maximum profits. It is especially hard for a firm to ascertain optimum selling expenditures. The results of sales efforts cannot be predicted in advance; even after sales expenditures have been made, the firm cannot be sure of their exact effect upon its demand schedule. Thus, as a practical matter, the firm's estimate of the optimum sales effort is largely guesswork, more so than decisions in virtually any other phase of business policy. Many firms spend more or less constant amounts annually for sales promotion; others adjust sales expenditures to a certain percentage of expected gross sales; and still others are influenced by current net profit figures. In recent years the so-called "objective and task" method has become widely used, wherein the firm selects certain sales objectives and attempts to estimate the amount of advertising expenditure necessary to obtain them. None of these methods is likely to yield the exact optimum amount, but they are employed because of the lack of more precise techniques for accomplishing the desired goal.

10.6 OBJECTIONS TO MONOPOLY AND WELFARE COST OF MONOPOLY

Monopoly is often considered "bad." What is the basis in economic theory for concerns about the establishment of monopoly power? To begin with, observe in Figure 10-8 that the equilibrium output is achieved where the average total cost of producing the good is not minimized. Per-unit costs of production are at their lowest point where the MC curve crosses the ATC curve, at output 0G. The profit maximizing monopolist, however, will produce a smaller output 0A, an output that requires more resources per unit of output than is possible at higher outputs. Under perfect competition, in the long run, firms produce at the minimum point on their average total cost curves. Monopoly, then, sometimes can be said to promote inefficiency by using more resources per unit of output than are used in perfect competition and by failing to produce units of output having marginal benefits greater than marginal costs. Hence the major objection to monopoly is that, under certain assumptions that are very often realistic, *monopoly leads to a lower output and to higher prices than would exist under perfect competition.* To see why this is so, look at Figure 10-8. In monopoly, the firm produces output 0A and charges a price of 0D. Suppose, however, that we had perfect competition, and that the industry was characterized by constant returns to scale, meaning many small firms could produce output with the same efficiency (at the same cost) as one large firm. Then the marginal cost curve is the sum of the firms' individual marginal cost curves, and the upper portion of that curve might be considered the industry supply curve.

FIGURE 10-8

Profits Derived by a Monopolist

In a perfectly competitive constant-cost industry, price and output would be $0J$ and $0F$. The monopolist, however, sets a higher price, $0D$, and restricts output to $0A$. Per-unit profits equal AR minus ATC (C–B) and total profits equal the area $BCDE$. Since firms are not free to enter, excess profits will not be eliminated in the long run.

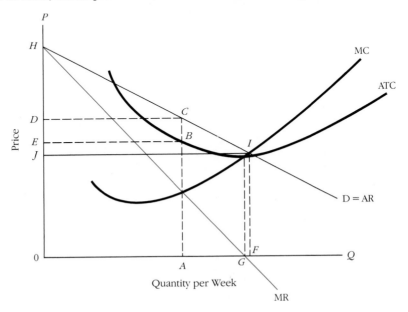

Equilibrium price and quantity would be determined where the MC or supply curve intersects with the demand curve, at output $0F$ and price $0J$. Thus the competitive equilibrium solution provides for more output (AF more) and lower prices (DJ lower) than the solution prevailing in monopoly. This is "unfair" in that consumers are burdened more than under the alternative competitive institutional arrangement and inefficient in that goods producible at costs less than consumer benefits are not produced. In monopoly, the consumer's surplus (the worth to consumers from getting the good for less than they would be willing to pay for all units except the last) is area DCH, while in perfect competition it is the much larger area JIH.

There are secondary objections to monopoly that are sometimes raised. Monopoly involves a concentration of economic power. The monopolist controls significant quantities of inputs and output. Some think that bigness itself is bad in a democratic society for reasons related to justice and equality.

Also, it is argued that a lack of competition tends to retard technological advance. The monopolist becomes comfortable, reaping monopolistic profits, so it does not work hard at product improvement, technical advances designed to promote efficiency, and so forth. Sometimes the example of the American railroads is cited in this regard. Early in this century, railroads had a strong amount of monopoly power, yet they did not spend much on research or development. They did not aggressively try to improve rail transport. As a consequence, technical advances in other transport modes (such as trucks and airplanes) led to a loss of monopoly power. A more contemporary example sometimes cited is the postal service. The United States Postal Service is a government monopoly. Mail is delivered in much the same way today as it was 75 years ago, and no more rapidly. Only very recently have efforts been made to use electronic and computer advances to speed transmission of written messages, and these efforts have largely been stimulated by competing private firms. (It is debatable, in this case, whether the lack of research and development reflects the complacency of a monopolist or instead the absence of the profit motive due to government ownership.)

The notion that monopoly retards innovation can be disputed. Many near-monopolists are in fact important innovators. Companies like International Business Machines (IBM), Polaroid, and Xerox—all with very strong market positions in some instances approaching monopoly secured by patent protection—are important innovators. Indeed, innovation helps firms obtain a degree of monopoly status, as patents give them a monopoly on cost-saving technology. Even the monopolist wants more profits, and any innovation that lowers costs or expands revenues creates profits. Therefore, the incentive to innovate exists in monopolistic as well as competitive market structures. (See Box 10-6.)

10.7 RESTRAINTS ON MONOPOLY PRICE

Even in fields where the monopolist is not subject to regulation, various considerations may deter it from seeking maximum profits and induce it to set a price lower than the one allowing absolute maximum gains. First, barriers against entry are never absolute. If a monopolist sees any chance of new firms developing, it may deliberately hold price below the profit-maximization figure in order to make entry by new firms less attractive and more difficult. Thus the monopolist sacrifices temporary gains in hopes of greater long-term gains.

Second, the firm may be deterred by fear of government regulation. Especially in the United States and Canada, where there are long-standing policies of maintaining competition and public attitudes to monopoly are basically hostile, a firm may be extremely careful to avoid exploiting its monopoly position, thereby warding off antitrust prosecution.

Third, pressures toward the goal of profit maximization are less severe on a monopolist. With competition, a firm is compelled to undertake measures to maximize profit, since failure to do so will likely lead to losses and possible bankruptcy. But a monopolist earning a good rate of profit has much less need to exploit every opportunity to increase profit, especially if the enterprise is a large, widely held corporation. Quite apart from fear of regulation, the monopolist may wish to appear "respectable"—to avoid behavior which seems to the customers to constitute ruthless monopolistic exploitation. A century ago, or even fifty years ago, this attitude was much less prevalent, as indicated by the last-ditch exploitation of shippers by the railroads at that time.

10-6   The output level set by the monopolist is inefficient, but the profits are not. Why?

The net loss due to the failure to produce output having benefits greater than costs is what economists call the **welfare cost of monopoly**. However, society as a whole does not lose additional amounts due to the monopoly profits. Why? Because the profits are *transferred* from consumers to producers, with the monopolists (stockholders and workers) gaining at the expense of consumers who pay a higher price for a monopolist's product than they would if the product were producd by a perfectly competitive firm. This is depicted in the figure below:

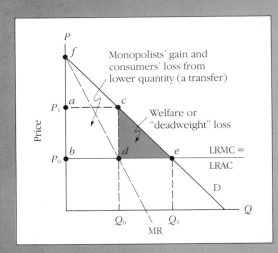

The welfare loss is graphically represented by the area *cde*, for the case of linear demand and constant returns to scale. It is, in this case, the difference between how much the consumers value quantity $Q_1 - Q_0$, which is $Q_0 ceQ_1$, and how much they would have to give up for it, $Q_0 deQ_1$. Under perfectly competitive conditions, the area *fbe* would be the consumers' surplus. However, with the higher monopoly price area *abdc* is transferred from the consumer, becoming part of the monopolist's profits. In sum, the loss to society from monopoly is the area *cde*; the area *abdc* is merely a transfer of consumer surplus to monopoly profits.

The actual amount of the welfare loss from various monopolies throughout the economy is of considerable debate among economists. Estimates vary between one tenth of one percent to six percent of national income. The variation depends on the researcher's estimates of elasticity of demand, on whether firm or industry data are used, on whether adjustments to profits were made (for the inclusion of royalties and intangibles), and on whether the researcher included some proxy for scarce resources used in attempting to create a monopoly. If "creating monopolies" is itself a competitive business, real resources used in creating monopolies will tend to equal the present value of the benefits of having the monopoly in the first place! If this extreme view has merit, there may be no gain to breaking up monopolies.

But today the desire to be regarded as "fair" in exploiting monopoly or semimonopoly positions, like the desire to avoid being regarded as a price chiseler, seems to play some part in molding business behavior and in modifying the profit-maximization goal.

10.8   REGULATED MONOPOLIES

In the public utilities field, a single firm is ordinarily allowed a monopoly in its market area, since operation of more than one firm would prevent the attainment of full economies of large-scale production and interfere with complete utilization of capacity (which often must be extended in advance of needs). However, these monopolies are subject to regulation by governmental agencies, to ensure that they provide adequate service and earn only a "normal" or necessary return on capital.

Regulatory agencies seek to set general rate levels such that the rate (the price) is equal to average cost—which includes a "fair" or average rate of return on investment—and to guarantee that all customers can buy all they wish at this price. Thus, in Figure 10-9, the rate (assuming no discrimination) would be set at P_1, as indicated by the intersection of the AR curve with the AC curve. Because of the difficulty of estimating the elasticity of the demand schedule and of defining a necessary return, the actual rate level would only approximate this figure.

Some critics feel that the establishment of the rate at the level of average cost would be contrary to the principles of economic welfare (as outlined in Chapter 21) unless the utility were operating at the point of lowest average cost and marginal cost happened to equal average cost. It is argued that optimum utilization of resources requires extension of the output of each good to the point at which $MC = P$ (Q_2 in Figure 10-9). If, at the point at which $AC = P$, marginal cost is below price, as it would be if the utility were operating on the downward portion of its AC curve, then additional units of output would add less in cost to the economy (in the sense of resource utilization) than the price charged for them. Thus, optimum utilization of resources requires production of these additional units, moving from Q_1 to Q_2.

FIGURE 10-9

Rate Adjustments of a Regulated Monopoly
Pricing difficulties arise in regulated monopolies because of declining average costs. If regulators choose P_1, economic profits are zero but social welfare is not maximized because the marginal benefits exceed the marginal costs of producing additional units of output. Although optimum social welfare is achieved at P_2, the firm incurs losses and must be subsidized by taxpayers. Two-tiered pricing recovers the losses by charging a fixed fee to users.

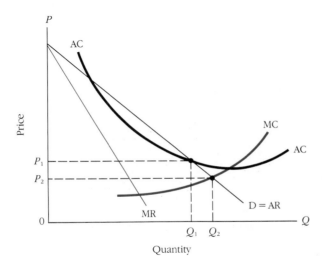

Quantity

In practice, however, output is more likely to be set at the point Q_1 where AC = P rather than at Q_2, with MC = P. For if price is set at the level of marginal cost, the utility will not be able to earn a normal return on its investments or perhaps even cover all of its explicit costs. Hence a subsidy would be required to keep the enterprise in operation. The granting of government subsidies to private enterprise gives rise to a host of difficulties, and the taxes needed to pay the subsidies might themselves interfere with resource allocation. So long as the production of utility service remains in private hands, the use of an average cost basis for regulation of price and output is likely to continue. An alternative approach in such cases is to levy a *fixed* charge for use of the good (say, any use of electricity or any trips on a bus), but then only charge marginal cost prices for any particular use. The charge could be, for example, an annual charge to electricity users or an annual fee for a photo-I.D. for the bus users. With this type of "two-tiered pricing," the fixed fee can cover the losses associated with marginal-cost pricing. (See Box 10-7.)

Discrimination

The possibility of rate discrimination greatly complicates the task of controlling utility rates. From the standpoint of the average cost of providing utility services and the optimum use of resources, discrimination may have merit, since it allows the utility to gain business which it would not otherwise get, lowers the cost per unit for all of the output (assuming operation under decreasing-cost conditions), and encourages operation nearer the point at which marginal cost equals price. In some instances, especially with the railroads, firms would probably be unable to cover costs if discrimination were not practiced. If a single uniform rate were charged on all freight, shipments able to bear only a low rate could not move, and shipments able to bear high rate would be subject to a lower rate than the shippers would be willing to pay, with consequent overall reduction in volume of business and railway revenue. But rate discrimination raises significant questions of equity and economic effects upon customers, to which answers are not easily supplied by the theory of economic welfare. Especially in the transportation field, some of the most difficult problems of rate regulation center around questions of discrimination among shippers of different goods, shipments between different points, and shipments of different individuals.

10.9 MONOPOLY CONTROL: TAXATION

One way to regulate any inequities associated with the profits of monopoly is through taxation. The three methods of taxation used most often are per-unit tax, lump-sum tax, and profit tax.

Per-Unit Tax

If a **per-unit tax** (a tax on each unit sold) is levied on a monopolist, how will this affect price and output? This method of regulating monopolies has an important drawback.

10-7   The actual implementation of a rate (price) that permits a "fair and reasonable" return is more difficult than the analysis suggests. Why do you think this is so?

The calculation of capital costs and values is very difficult, particularly in periods of inflation. In permitting a normal rate of return to the utility's capital, do the regulators value it at its original cost, minus depreciation, or do they value it at replacement cost, specifically the cost today of replacing the capital? In other words, do the rate setters account for the impact of inflation and changing real relative scarcity? This is but one problem that the regulators must face.

Also, in the real world, consumer groups are constantly battling for lower rates while the utilities themselves are lobbying for higher rates so they obtain monopoly profits. Decisions are not always made in a calm, objective, dispassionate atmosphere free of outside involvement. It is precisely the political economy of rate setting that disturbs some critics of this approach to dealing with the monopoly problem. Radical critics who favor nationalization would argue that in the long run the utility companies end up controlling the regulators. The companies have much at stake. Rate-making commissioners become friendly to the companies, perhaps believing that they can obtain a nice utility job after their tenure as a regulator is over. The temptation is great for the commissioners to be generous to the utilities. On the other hand, more conservative observers

usually express concern over the more recent tendency of regulators to bow to pressure from consumer groups. A politician who wants to win votes might succeed by attacking utility rates and promising lower rates. If zealous rate regulators listen too closely to the consumer groups and push rates down to levels below average cost, the industry will be unable to attract capital for expansion. There was considerable concern on that point in past years as utilities faced huge capital requirements in meeting expanding demand, though in recent years demand has expanded far less than anticipated earlier.

While the public regulation of private monopolies has its difficulties, the relevant question is whether any other option is better. Breaking up utility monopolies and permitting multiple firms to operate seems undesirable, given the declining-cost nature of many such industries. It makes little sense to have five companies running electric transmission lines from power plants to every area of a city. Nationalization often leads to politicization of business enterprises and inefficiency of its own. For that reason, most Americans probably accept public regulation of private utilities as being the best, or perhaps the "least bad," of the various alternatives.

The before and after effects of a per-unit tax are seen in Figure 10-10. The before-tax profit-maximizing position of the monopoly firm is denoted by quantity Q_B and P_B. The key to understanding this tax is that it appears to the firm as a variable cost increase because it is attached to each additional unit of output. As you recall from Chapter 8, an increase in variable cost will effect both the long-run average cost and the marginal cost of the firm, vertically shifting both the curves upward to $LRAC_A$ and MC_A. The new price and output will be P_A and Q_A, respectively. A quick glance at Figure 10-10 shows the profit before tax (difference between P_B and C_B times Q_B) to be higher than the profits after tax (difference between P_A and C_A times Q_A).

FIGURE 10-10

Per-Unit Tax

A per-unit tax raises the average and marginal cost of producing each unit of output. LRAC and MC curves shift up, output declines to Q_A, and price rises to P_A. The monopolist and the consumers share the burden of the tax.

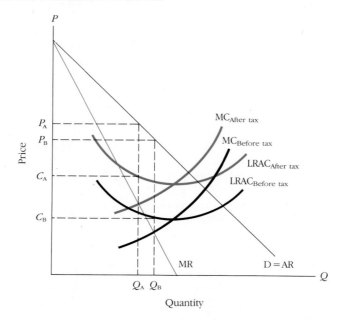

Quantity

Who pays this tax? The producer pays part in the form of reduced profits, and the consumer pays part in the form of higher prices for lower output. The proportion of tax on each depends on the elasticity of the demand and marginal cost curve. However, the tax will cause the monopolist to further reduce output (compared to the competitive case), leading to worsening resource allocation. This approach to controlling monopoly is inefficient (still more goods having benefits greater than cost go unproduced), though administratively straightforward.

Lump-Sum Tax

From the firm's perspective a **lump-sum tax** resembles a fixed cost, in that it is levied on the firm's total output whether it be large or small. The firm must pay this lump-sum tax if it wishes to stay in business. In Figure 10-11, this shifts the LRAC$_{Before}$ up to LRAC$_{After}$. However, the marginal cost curve is unaffected since the tax is the same whether the firm produces one unit a year or 10,000 units a day; that is, marginal costs do not rise with this type of tax. Since the demand and marginal revenue curves are also unaltered, profit maximizing price and output do *not* change (as seen in Figure 10-11). Therefore, a lump-sum tax does not reduce allocative efficiency though it does reduce the monopolist's profits.

FIGURE 10-11

Lump-Sum Tax

As the lump-sum tax is fixed regardless of the level of output, it increases average costs but not marginal costs. Equilibrium price and quantity are unaffected, but profits are reduced.

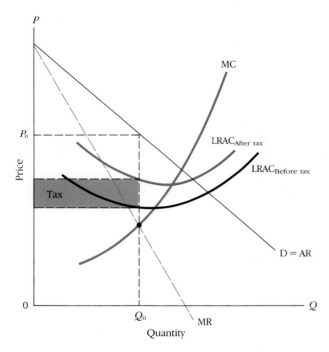

Profits Tax

A **profits tax** will not affect either marginal cost or marginal revenue curves if the profit base is properly calculated (that is, on *economic* profits, not accounting profits). Although it does *not* affect the optimum price and quantity (Q_0 is the profit-maximizing output before and after the tax), it does affect profits, lowering them in proportion to the size of the tax at each output level (see Figure 10-12, where a tax of about 50 percent is depicted).

10.10 THE CASE FOR MONOPOLY

The analysis presented above clearly suggests that monopolies are economically inefficient; noneconomic considerations such as the concentration of power also contribute to opposition to the existence of monopoly. Remember, however, that the notion that monopoly will lead to higher prices and reduced output hinges on the assumption that the monopolist has no inherent efficiencies related to size. However, consider Figure 10-13, where there are economies of scale such that very large firms are more

FIGURE 10-12

Profits Tax

A percentage tax on profits does not affect price or quantity but simply transfers part of the profit to the government.

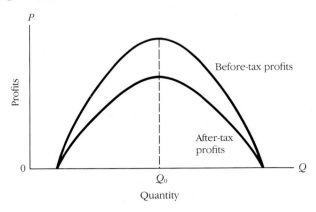

FIGURE 10-13

Appropriateness of Monopoly

In Figure 10-13, economies of scale exist and small firms are inherently inefficient. A good case for monopoly exists, although society may be still better served by effective regulation in such cases.

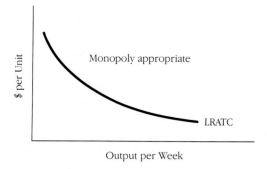

efficient than smaller ones. It is likely that, given demand conditions, the market will accommodate only one large, low-cost firm. In this case, prohibiting monopoly would not lead to higher output and lower prices. The marginal costs of many small producers at any given output would be higher than the marginal cost of the monopolist, so that the supply (MC) and demand curves could intersect at higher prices and lower output in competition than in monopoly.

The decreasing-cost industry depicted in Figure 10-13 is a situation conducive to the formation of a natural monopoly such as an electric power company. In some cases, the average total cost curve may decline over a wide range but then begin to increase again at an output level which would permit two or three firms to operate efficiently, suggesting a "natural oligopoly"; this may be the situation that existed, for example, for many years in the American automobile industry. The growth of world demand and international trade has resulted more recently in a more competitive structure for this industry (the lesson, of course, is that free international trade, in addition to comparative advantage arguments favoring it, also reduces monopoly inefficiency worldwide).

SUMMARY

1. Imperfectly competitive firms can influence market price by such actions as advertising, lobbying for legislation, and varying quantities available for sale.

2. A monopoly is a market where buyers are numerous but the total output of a good with no close substitutes offered for sale is controlled by a single firm.

3. The average revenue curve (demand) for a monopolist's good is downward sloping, meaning that the monopolist must lower its price to sell a larger output.

4. Marginal revenue for a monopolist's good is less than average revenue (demand) for all units except the first.

5. The monopolist attempts to equate MR and MC in the short run. However, the monopolist may find it more difficult to estimate marginal revenue than the perfectly competitive firm.

6. A monopolist's price is higher and its output is lower than a perfectly competitive firm, if cost conditions are similar.

7. The long-run equilibrium level of output for the monopolist requires adjustments to the plant size at which MR = LRMC = SRMC.

8. Possessing a monopoly is no guarantee of excess profits. If demand is inadequate, lack of competitors is of little benefit to a seller.

9. Price discrimination occurs when a monopolist charges different prices to various customers, not justified by differences in cost.

10. Perfect price discrimination requires that each buyer pay the maximum possible sum which he or she is willing to pay—that is, the reservation price for each quantity unit.

11. Multipart price discrimination allows the monopolist to sell part of its output at different prices, charging more for the first block than for successive blocks.

12. Segmented market price discrimination allows the monopolist to segment its total market into several parts on the basis of demand prices and elasticities. The firm will then charge different prices to different groups of buyers.

13. Firms must select the exact variety or quality of the product which allows maximum profit. That is, with each form of the product the demand schedules and cost schedules will differ.

14. The firm must optimally adjust selling activities in order to maximize profits, setting as usual marginal benefits equal to marginal costs.

15. Popular methods of regulating monopolies include taxation (per-unit tax, lump-sum tax and profit tax) and price controls. The profits tax and the lump-sum tax are preferred to the per-unit tax because they do not reduce output and raise the price paid by consumers, ceteris paribus.

16. The smaller output produced in a monopoly market represents a misallocation of resources and hence a welfare cost to society. Goods having benefit greater than (opportunity) cost of production are not being produced; in addition to this inefficiency, most people view monopolies as being inequitable.

WORDS AND CONCEPTS FOR REVIEW

imperfectly competitive models
average revenue functions
monopoly
price discrimination
perfect price discrimination
multipart price discrimination

segmented-market price discrimination
selling costs
welfare cost of monopoly
per-unit tax
lump-sum tax
profits tax

REVIEW QUESTIONS

1. Suppose that a firm is the sole supplier of a particular product, but the cross-elasticity of demand between this product and other products is very high. Is the monopoly analysis useful in explaining behavior in this industry? Explain.

2. Suppose that in a market period, a monopolist finds that the demand for its products at the price set exceeds the market-period current output rate. What will it do? Explain.

3. How does a monopolist estimate the average revenue function?

4. Why is the optimum output level where marginal cost equals marginal revenue?

5. In both monopoly and perfect competition, the optimum output is at the level at which MR = MC, but only in the latter is the optimum level such that P = MC. Why?

6. What is the difference between short-run and long-run adjustments of a monopolist?

7. Can a monopolist always set a price which will cover average cost? Explain.

8. What is meant by "price discrimination"? What conditions are necessary for price discrimination to occur?

9. Why can price discrimination not occur in competitive markets?

10. Suppose that all buyers have precisely the same demand schedules for a good. Is price discrimination profitable? Explain.

11. What is the difference between perfect price discrimination and other forms of price discrimination?

12. In segmented market price discrimination, why are the optimum output levels in each market *not* the levels at which marginal revenue in that market equals marginal cost of the product sold in that market?

13. Determine whether or not price discrimination occurs in each of the following situations; if it does, indicate the reasons why discrimination is advantageous and how customers are segregated:

  a. family fares on airlines and railroads;
  b. lower theater admissions for children or senior citizens than adults;

c. lower fares for regular commuters on railroads and bus lines;

d. higher prices for American subscribers of foreign periodicals than those charged residents of the countries (the differences exceeding differences in postal charges).

SUGGESTED READINGS

Dewey, Donald. *Monopoly in Economics and Law*. Chicago: Rand McNally, 1959.

Harberger, Arnold. "Monopoly and Resource Allocation." *American Economic Review*, 44 (May 1954).

Mansfield, Edwin. *Monopoly Power and Economic Performance*, 4th ed. New York: Norton, 1978.

Posner, Richard A. "The Social Cost of Monopoly and Regulation." *Journal of Political Economy* (August 1975).

Scherer, F. M. *Industrial Market Structure and Economic Performance*, 2nd ed. Chicago: Rand McNally, 1980.

11

Monopolistic Competition

11.1 INTRODUCTION

The monopoly and perfectly competitive models outlined in the two preceding chapters are directly applicable to the analysis of rather limited sectors of the contemporary economy—the former to regulated industries and a few isolated markets, the latter to markets for basic agricultural products and securities. With some modifications, the models are applicable over a much wider range of markets in which conditions approach but do not agree entirely with the assumptions upon which the models were built. Two major types of models involve elements of both competitive and monopoly, in varying proportions. These are monopolistic competition and oligopoly. The former is discussed in this chapter, the latter in Chapter 12.

11.2 GENERAL CHARACTERISTICS OF MONOPOLISTIC COMPETITION

The theory of **monopolistic competition** is based on three primary assumptions: (1) products of various sellers are differentiated; (2) the number of sellers is sufficiently large for each to act independently of the others; and (3) entry of new firms is relatively easy. Thus, unlike perfect competition, monopolistic competition allows individual sellers to influence market price over some range. The various firms recognize the existence of competitors as a group. This limits the prices they can charge and expect to sell a particular level of output; yet they do not consider competitors as individual rivals whose policies will be influenced by their own action. Because of the relatively free entry of new firms, long-run price and output behavior is similar to that of perfect competition; because the firm produces a product that is different than others, there is some degree of monopoly power. In a sense, each seller in a market of monopolistic competition may be regarded as a "monopolist" of its own particular brand of the good—but unlike the firm of the monopoly model, there is competition by firms producing similar brands. (See Box 11-1.)

One required characteristic of monopolistic competition is **product differentiation**—preferences among buyers to deal with particular sellers or to purchase the products of particular sellers. The significant feature of differentiation is the buyers' belief that the various sellers' products are not the same, whether the products are actually different physically or not. An example of a product of which the various brands are identical but buyers believe them to be different is aspirin.

There are various sources of differentiation, depending on the product. Actual physical differences, of course, constitute one source: brands of apparently similar ice cream, beer, or wine differ significantly in taste to many buyers. There are physical differences among various makes of cars which lead some buyers to prefer one make, some another. Prestige considerations can be significant: many persons prefer to be seen using the currently popular make, while others prefer the "off brand." Prestige considerations are particularly important with gifts. Location is a major factor in retailing: people are not willing to travel long distances to shop for items that are minor in their overall expenditure pattern; hence the growth in convenience stores like 7-11 and ARCO minimarts. Service considerations are likewise significant with speedy service being very important to some people, less so to others or at other times. Reliability or "no-hassle" return policies lead many persons to buy at department stores instead of at discount houses, even though the latter may be cheaper. Personal attitudes of storekeepers and clerks is an important influence: the attitude of waiters, for example, may significantly affect choice of restaurants. Since most buyers realize that there is no significant difference among brands of gasoline, their choice might be influenced by credit terms or the location of the service station.

Despite differentiation, many buyers simply select sellers who offer the lowest prices. Accordingly, sellers in a monopolistically competitive market may be expected to discover from experience (if not common sense) that relatively small changes in prices produce relatively large changes in sales. Hence each seller may be presumed to regard the demand for its product as relatively elastic. By the same token, an individual seller who fails to follow price trends initiated by competitors, or fails to respond to the entry or exit of other sellers into its industry, will experience substan-

---

11-1 True or False? With many sellers and differentiated products, restaurants and service stations are good examples of monopolistic competition.

Not clear. How many customers actually are basing their consumption decisions on many different restaurants or many different service stations? For most of us it basically comes down to a choice among a few differentiated products with a few sellers. The point here is that concrete distinctions between many forms of markets in economics are difficult to make.

tial variations in quantity sold at any given price. The effect will be to encourage individual sellers to revise their estimates of their demand curves in the light of actual sales experience. Thus a seller will act on the assumption that the maximum price that can be charged for any given level of output is restricted to a range of values in the neighborhood of the prevailing "product group" price level. The seller will revise the estimate of the position of the demand curve with every significant change in sales or in the typical price level. Thus sellers behave as "competing monopolies." Each firm has a less-than-perfectly elastic demand in its own "market," but the demand curve is nearly horizontal and its position shifts significantly as conditions change in other "markets"—that is, as competing firms change price.

By the nature of monopolistic competition, entry into a given industry is unrestricted in the sense that new firms may easily start up production of close substitutes for existing products, though they cannot produce products that appear identical to existing ones in the eyes of prospective purchasers. Because of relatively free entry, excess profits tend to be eliminated in the long run. As we shall see later, this tendency is resisted in a variety of ways. Some firms may earn excess profits even in the long run, and those firms that have earned excess profits may lose them not because prices are forced down but because costs are forced up. (See Box 11-2.)

11.3 MARKET-PERIOD PRICE DETERMINATION

During an interval of time so short that orders to suppliers or other determinants of output cannot be altered, a seller in monopolistic competition has a strong incentive to adjust price to ensure that sales coincide with current rate of output or purchases, particularly to avoid accumulation of inventory. (Because the seller is, by hypothesis, merely one among many, we need not be concerned about possible direct reactions by competitors to a temporary change in the asking price.)

If a change in demand causes sales to lag significantly behind current output, the seller may be expected to reduce price sharply in order to bring about a quick adjustment of sales to output. For while demand may be very elastic in the short run,

---

11-2   If you were opening a new restaurant and wanted to make it different from others, how would you differentiate your product? Can you think of any costs associated with differentiated products?

You could use any of a number of methods to make your restaurant different: location, service, type of menu, quality of food, ambiance, and so on. Note, however, that there are some costs to differentiated products. First, the more differentiated the product the greater the potential monopoly power, and monopolies generally produce a lower output at a higher price than competitive firms. Second, the abundance of variety conflicts with economies of scale. For example, average costs would certainly be lower for one firm producing the same type of automobile than for 100 firms producing 1,000 slightly different models.

additional customers can hardly be found immediately unless the seller makes important price concessions. Accordingly, special sales of goods at attractive discounts from normal prices, combined with advertising that is designed to attract temporary rather than regular customers, is a characteristic feature of monopolistic competition.

If a change in demand causes current sales to exceed current output, rather different considerations apply. The seller will normally distinguish between regular and casual customers and will be reluctant to run the risk of losing a regular customer for the sake of a temporary and probably minor increase in revenue. Thus upward revisions in price in the market period are unlikely to occur. Instead, the seller will adjust sales to output by simply failing to meet demands by casual customers, available output being rationed to regular customers at the prevailing price.

This type of price behavior in the market period could not occur in perfectly competitive markets. Moreover, the phenomenon of frequent temporary reductions in price is unlikely to be found in monopoly or oligopoly. Yet this kind of behavior is so familiar in actual retail markets as to demonstrate the usefulness of the monopolistic competition model for market-period price determination in some types of markets. (See Box 11-3.)

11.4 OUTPUT AND PRICE DETERMINATION IN THE SHORT RUN

Since sellers in conditions of monopolistic competition have some control over setting prices, decisions about short-run levels of output must be made in the light of estimates of the probable prices at which various levels of sales can be obtained in conjunction with estimates of cost. This problem is complicated by the fact that the position of the seller's demand curve will depend on the average level of prices in the industry.

On what basis do the firms estimate what the "industry" price level will be? There are various approaches. One is recent price experience: if other fast food chains are charging $1.50 for hamburgers and $1.00 for milkshakes and have been doing so in recent months, each fast food establishment will assume that other firms will typically continue to charge these figures and will estimate its own potential sales at various price levels on this assumption. Alternatively, a firm may reasonably assume that the

11-3   Imagine you own a clothing shop. Lately demand for your clothing has been tremendous. In the market period, will you increase your price to ration off the available supply of clothing?

Probably not. It is much more likely that if sales exceed output you would give preferential treatment to your steady customers. Therefore, instead of raising price you would probably take care of your preferential customers.

industry price level will be somewhat above average variable cost (AVC), using a markup that has become more or less traditional. It may be assumed that with monopolistic competition, since entry of new firms is relatively easy, variable costs (as, for example, cost of goods sold) constitute the major element of total costs. Each seller knows that these costs must be covered if firms are to stay in business; each seller also knows that certain markups above variable cost are regarded as traditional and will be required to cover fixed costs. Thus, given its estimates of variable costs, the firm can estimate the typical price level that will prevail, and hence its own demand curve.

Given the position of an individual firm's demand curve, we may describe the determination of short-run equilibrium output and price in terms similar to those used in the analysis of monopoly output and price determination. Relevant cost and revenue curves of a typical seller may be represented as in Figure 11-1; the intersection of MR and SRMC indicates that the short-run equilibrium output will be q_0, and the short-run equilibrium price P_0. Because the demand curve is relatively flat, the excess of equilibrium price over marginal cost may be relatively small as compared with the typical monopoly situation. Since different sellers will form different estimates of the level and position of the demand curve, equilibrium prices will typically differ among firms. The differences are unlikely to be extreme, however, because all firms are likely to have rather similar MC curves under the assumed conditions. As in perfect competition, this conclusion is subject to the requirement that price must cover AVC. If, however, failure to cover AVC is regarded as temporary, the firm may continue to operate for a time in order to avoid loss of customers, a consideration not relevant in perfect competition.

FIGURE 11-1

Initial Short-Run Adjustment of Price and Output
In monopolistic competition, the short-run optimum is similar to monopoly except that the AR curve is relatively more elastic. The output level, q_0, is determined where MR = SRMC, and the corresponding price on the demand curve, P_0, is the optimum price. The firm continues to produce as long as AVC is less than or equal to price. This firm earns positive profits as price exceeds SRAC at the current output level.

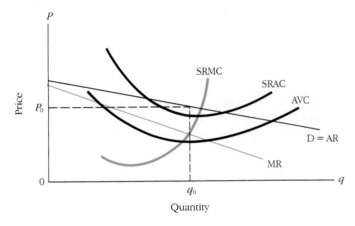

Industry Adjustments

The equilibrium value of output determined by an individual seller on the basis of its current estimate of average revenue prospects may be expected to vary over time in response to changes in the general level of prices in the industry. The mechanism by which such adjustments occur may be illustrated most conveniently by supposing that the actual sales of a typical individual seller at any given price are indicated not by its average revenue curve, AR, as the firm anticipates, but rather by an objective sales curve, represented in Figure 11-2 by the relation DD. The definition of the curve DD poses some logical problems, since it cannot be obtained except by making specific assumptions about the prices charged by all other sellers. For the sake of simplicity— and not too unrealistically—we may suppose that the DD curve shown in Figure 11-2 describes for each level of price what the sales of a typical seller would be if all other firms were charging exactly the same price. That is, the demand curve facing a typical firm—which may be thought of as a "proportional" demand curve—is $1/n$ of the product group overall demand curve, if there are n firms. Our analysis of the probable sequence of adjustments in short-run equilibrium output and price by a typical seller

---

FIGURE 11-2

Final Short-Run Adjustment of Price and Output

At P_0, the firm expects to sell $\bar{q}_0$, but the proportional demand curve, DD, indicates that the firm sells only q_0. Industry demand is less than expected by the firm. The monopolistic competitor adjusts expectations until equilibrium is established at P_2 and q_2, and the anticipated average revenue is equal to actual average revenue on DD when the firm sets MR_2 equal to MC.

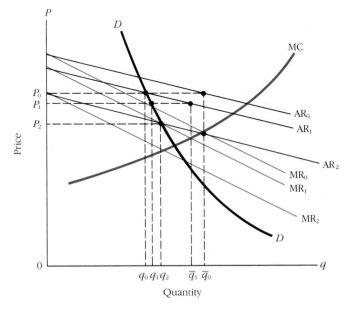

(supposing that other sellers always match the given seller's current price) can then proceed as follows.

Starting with an initial expected average revenue curve AR_0, the seller will choose a value of output $\bar{q}_0$, as indicated by the intersection of the marginal revenue curve MR_0 with the marginal cost curve MC. But if price is thus set at the level P_0, actual sales will be only q_0, or less than $\bar{q}_0$. The seller will therefore revise its estimate of demand. Let us assume that the firm now regards the relevant AR curve to be AR_1 rather than AR_0, defined by the requirement that the curve which is currently relevant must contain the currently "observed" sales-price point (q_0, P_0). Equilibrium output will then be changed from $\bar{q}_0$ to q_1, and the price will be revised downward from P_0 to P_1. Again, however, sales will be less than output $(q_1 < \bar{q}_1)$; so there will be still another expected AR curve. This process will continue until the seller arrives at an estimate of average revenue prospects represented by the curve AR_2 in Figure 11-2. This curve produces an optimum (and equilibrium) value of output: only at price, P_2 and quantity q_2 is what the firm *wishes* it can sell consistent with *actual* sales.

Though this adjustment process is based on very special assumptions, the general character of the process is much the same under less restrictive conditions.[1] Of course, the precise nature of the process depends on the factors assumed to govern each seller's output and price behavior. It cannot be doubted, however, that the simplified analysis presented above contains an important element of truth about the way competing sellers may be expected to adapt to sales experience in almost any imperfectly competitive market. Of particular interest in this connection is the conclusion that the AR curve will shift over time as long as the perceived optimum output at the current price differs from actual sales at the same price. This elementary consistency condition is an essential requirement for any empirically meaningful model of output and price determination. It is therefore interesting to note that the same condition is implicit in the theory of perfectly competitive markets; this is in fact a direct consequence of the proposition that in perfect competition, market equilibrium occurs if and only if price is such as to equate quantity demanded with quantity supplied.[2]

11.5 LONG-RUN PRICE AND OUTPUT ADJUSTMENTS

In monopolistic competition as in monopoly (or perfect competition), existing firms will make adjustments in plant size over a long-run period in an attempt to achieve minimal long-run costs for any given level of output. At any given time, firms seek maximum profits by establishing output at a level such that MR = SRMC with the existing plant. But this level of output will maximize long-run profit only if the existing

---

[1]See R. W. Clower, "Some Theory of an Ignorant Monopolist," *Economic Journal*, Vol. 69 (December 1959), pp. 710–11.

[2]It would be instructive for the reader to derive for perfect competition a figure corresponding to Figure 11-2; the figure would be simpler since MR=P=AR for the perceived demand curve, though actual (proportional) demand would be like that in Figure 11-2.

plant is that which permits production of the optimal output at minimum cost. Plant size will be adjusted over time, therefore, so long as SRMC differs from LRMC. Exactly as with monopoly, attainment of long-run optimization requires that MR = SRMC = LRMC.

While these long-run conditions are necessary, they are not the only conditions that must be met. As individual firms adapt their plant sizes in an attempt to reduce long-run costs, other firms may be considering entry into the industry. Since, as noted earlier, capital requirements are likely to be low and economies of large-scale production rather insignificant in such industries, entry is likely to be fairly free. The main barrier to newcomers is the established reputation of existing firms. The rapid flow of firms into and out of the restaurant field provides a good illustration of this characteristic of monopolistic competition.

To the extent that new firms enter the field, there will be a tendency for any prevailing gap between price and average cost to be closed. Newcomers may find it advantageous to set prices lower than those charged by older firms in order to build up sales volume; and older firms may then find it necessary to reduce prices in order to maintain their sales at a satisfactory level. However, reduction in price brought about in this fashion will not have a significant effect on total sales unless total demand for the product is sufficiently elastic; the existing sales volume may merely be divided among more firms. Whether or not prices fall, the decline in sales that each firm experiences is likely to force operation at a point farther away from the point of lowest cost, and excess profits will therefore be reduced by a rise in average cost.

Tangency in the Long Run

If entry is sufficiently free to lead to complete elimination of excess profits, long-run equilibrium will occur when D is equal to AC for each firm at a level of output at which each firm's D curve is just tangent to its AC curve. For if the revenue curve cuts the cost curve at any point, profits will continue to be earned. The adjustment is illustrated in Figures 11-3 and 11-4. In Figure 11-3, the short-run optimum output is at q_{SR}, and excess profits are being earned. As a consequence, new firms enter, and each firm's demand curve moves to the left until it is tangent to LRAC as indicated in Figure 11-4.[3] The point of tangency is, of necessity, at the same level of output as that at which MC—both short and long run—is equal to MR. The tangency point thus coincides with the point of maximum profit, "competitive" entry or exit ensuring that the maximum equals zero.

Because of the downward slope of the demand curve, the point of tangency will not be at the lowest level of average cost. When long-run adjustments are complete, firms will be operating at levels that do not permit full realization of economies of large-scale production. The existing plant, even though optimal for the chosen volume of

---

[3]The entry of new firms will *rotate* downward the actual (or proportional) demand curve—not shown in Figures 11-3 and 11-4—so that overall market consistency for the product group is obtained, as in the short-run equilibrium of Figure 11-2.

FIGURE 11-3

A Situation of Excess Profits

In the long run, the monopolistic competitor operates the plant that produces the level of output for which MR = LRMC. This firm earns positive economic profits since $P >$ LRAC.

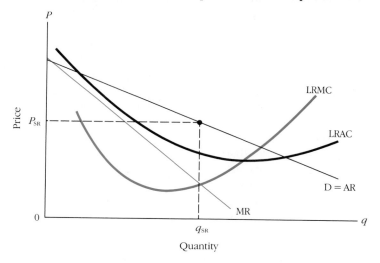

FIGURE 11-4

Tangency in the Long Run

Excess profits attract new firms into the industry. The firm's share of the market declines, and AR shifts down. Profits are eliminated when $P =$ LRAC, that is, when LRAC is tangent to AR.

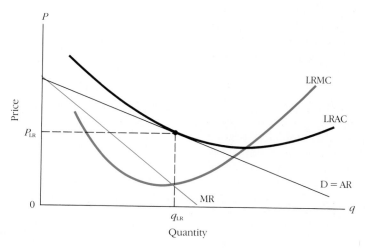

output, will not be used to capacity; that is, excess capacity (downward-sloping SRAC curve) will exist at that level of output. Any attempt to increase output to attain lowest average cost would be unprofitable, since the price reduction necessary to sell the greater output would exceed the cost reduction that it makes possible. In industries of this type, there is a chronic tendency toward too many firms, each producing a volume of output less than that allowing lowest cost. Note that the optimal size plant, while underutilized, is itself smaller (with higher minimum average cost) than would be the case in perfect competition. Thus, there may be too many grocery stores and too many service stations, in the sense that if the total volume of business were concentrated in a smaller number of sellers, average cost and price would be less.

The significance of the difference between the relationship of LRMC to price in monopolistic competition and in perfect competition can easily be exaggerated. So long as preferences for various brands are not extremely strong, the demand schedules for the firms' products will be highly elastic. Accordingly, the points of tangency with the AC curves are not likely to be far above the point of lowest cost, and excess capacity will be minimized. Only if differentiation is very strong will the difference between the long-run price level and that which would prevail under perfectly competitive conditions be significant. (See Box 11-4.)

Excessive Entry of New Firms

In industries in which relatively low capital requirements make entry of new firms comparatively easy, so many firms may enter the industry that few if any sellers can earn even normal profits. The extremely high rate of mortality among firms in some

---

11-4 True or False? The greater the product differentiation, the less elastic the perceived demand curve.

True. Recall the discussion of elastic demand curves in Chapter 3, where it was claimed that an elastic demand curve implied many close substitutes. Greater differentiation means more monopoly power, which in turn means fewer substitutes. Hence the less-elastic demand curve with differentiated products. This also implies that the point of tangency of the demand curve and average cost curve will be further to the left than otherwise at a lower level of output. And this difference between the minimum point of the average cost curve and the tangency point is called **excess capacity**. Moreover, the chosen plant size will be smaller and will have a higher minimum average cost than under perfect competition. Excess capacity is, however, a cost of product differentiation. Have you ever thought about the many restaurants, theaters, and gas stations that have "excess capacity"? Can you imagine a world where all firms were working at full capacity? After all, choice is a good, and most of us value some choice dearly. Thus, excess capacity is the price we pay for differentiated goods, and many of us are willing to pay this price. How do you feel about the choice between low-priced homogeneous goods (say, everyone always wearing drab gray shirts) versus higher-priced but differentiated goods?

lines of retailing, especially in the first two years of operation, suggests a chronic tendency towards excessive entry of newcomers. In part, excessive entry may result when excess profits have been earned temporarily. Because of the time required for operation to get under way, too many firms may start operations, just as farmers may plant too many apple trees when apple prices are high relative to costs. But even when only normal profits are being earned, there may be a tendency for new firms to start, either because newcomers believe they can operate more profitably than existing firms or because they lack adequate knowledge of profit possibilities and are anxious to develop their own businesses. (See Box 11-5.)

Restrictions to Completely Free Entry

Complete adjustment toward equality of price with average cost may be checked by the strength of reputation built up by established firms. Those firms that are particularly successful in their selling efforts may create such strong consumer preferences that newcomers—even though they are able to enter the industry freely and cover their own costs—will not take sufficient business away from the well-established firms to eliminate their excess profits. Thus a restaurant that has been particularly successful in promoting customer goodwill may continue to earn excess profits long after the entry of new firms has brought about equality of price and average cost for the others, or even losses. Adjustments toward a final equilibrium situation involving equality of price and average cost do not proceed with the certainty characterizing perfect competition.

11.6 PRODUCT-GROUP COST CONDITIONS

The cost conditions in which an industry operates have the same general significance for monopolistic competition **product groups** as in perfect competition. A product group is the collection of producers of similar (but differentiated) goods (for example, retail apparel or gasoline) which—were they homogeneous—would be considered

---

11-5   Many restaurants fail every year despite their attempts to equate marginal revenue and marginal costs. Why?

Remember that marginal revenue and marginal costs are based on expectations of the future. And because information is imperfect and costly to obtain, people can and do make mistakes. Nobody opens up a new restaurant *expecting* to go out of business. Thus one must equate expected marginal revenue and expected marginal costs, and those expectations might not be realized.

an industry in perfect competition. In an increasing- or decreasing-cost industry, the height of each firm's cost schedule will be affected by changes in the entire industry's total output. The actual figure of average cost to which price is equal when long-run adjustments have been completed in a situation of free entry will depend upon the volume of output for the industry or product group and thus, in part, upon the total demand for the product. Precise product-group cost curves which would have any significance cannot be drawn, however, both because firms do not operate at levels of lowest average cost and because costs at actual points of operation are not uniform among firms. Likewise, products of different firms are not homogeneous.

11.7 SELLING ACTIVITIES AND MONOPOLISTIC COMPETITION

Differentiation is the key characteristic of monopolistic competition. Thus selling activities play a major role, since consumers must be aware of differentiation for it to matter. Differentiation is created by adjustment of product, including branding and packaging, and reputation is largely created by selling activities. Increased selling activity not only increases demand for the product of the firm but also makes demand less elastic by attaching customers more closely to particular brands. Because of the possibility of taking business away from competing firms, selling activity is likely to be much more significant than it is for a monopolist.

The effect of selling activities upon prices in monopolistic competition is complex, and generalizations are not so obvious as they might appear to be. Expenditures on selling activities constitute costs, which must be covered by revenues if an average rate of profit is to be earned. From the standpoint of business firms, selling costs are not significantly different from production costs. However, selling activities will also alter demand schedules. The combined effect of higher cost and higher demand is almost certain to raise prices. But there are possible exceptions. Sales activities may allow firms to operate nearer the point of minimum cost than they would in monopolistic competition without selling activities. It is possible that the decline in production cost will exceed the sales cost, per unit of output. Unless total demand for the product is affected significantly by advertising, other firms will be forced out of business, and sales will be concentrated in the hands of a smaller number of firms. It should be noted, however, that the new price is lower only by comparison with the price existing with monopolistic competition and no sales activity; the price cannot be lower than would prevail with perfect competition, for in a competitive market there would be no selling costs.

Since firms in monopolistic competition are not likely to experience substantial cost reductions as output increases, lower production cost can hardly be expected to offset selling costs if the latter are at all substantial. The chances of a significant reduction in per unit cost are much greater in oligopoly, as discussed in Chapter 12.

While selling activity may increase demand, it is also likely to make demand less elastic by increasing the degree of preference for particular brands. This effect will tend to bring about higher prices. (See Box 11-6.)

11.8 THE SIGNIFICANCE OF MONOPOLISTIC COMPETITION

The three primary assumptions upon which the analysis of monopolistic competition is based—(1)differentiated products, (2)large numbers of sellers and absence of recognized mutual interdependence, and (3)relatively free entry of firms—are most likely to be approximated in lines of activity where capital equipment is relatively unimportant in production. In these fields, comparatively little money capital is required to commence production and economies of large-scale production are of limited importance, being fully attained at relatively low levels of output. Thus various lines of retailing and small handicraft production and repair would appear to be the types of activity most likely to operate under conditions of monopolistic competition.

However, study of these fields raises some doubt about the applicability of the assumptions. Despite the large numbers of retailers, a particular market area rarely has a substantial number; moreover, feelings of mutual interdependence do not appear to be entirely absent, the firms recognizing that their policies will have some effect upon the policies of their competitors.

The assumption of free entry is regarded by some writers as incompatible with the assumption of product differentiation. It is argued that when consumers have preferences for the products of particular firms, the flow of new firms into a field is inevitably restricted; so the principle that price tends to equal average cost—with the demand curve tangent to the AC curve at a point to the left of lowest average cost—may not be valid. It is also argued that the concept of "an industry" is ambiguous when products are differentiated, and that the empirical implications of an equilibrium analysis of such an industry are correspondingly vague.

Finally, it can be argued that conditions of monopolistic competition can exist only when the initial decline in average cost is of limited magnitude. Thus the principle that firms will not operate at the point of lowest average cost once long-run adjustments have been completed is of little significance, since the difference between price and the point of lowest average cost will be slight. Accordingly, the perfectly competitive analysis is regarded as applicable, even though the firms' demand curves are not perfectly elastic.

11-6   A monopolistic competitor believes advertising is very important. Why is it particularly important to advertise in this type of market structure?

In order for a clothing shop to compete with many similar shops, it must advertise to demonstrate that its clothing or store is somehow different. Remember, monopolistically competitive firms differ from competitive firms because of their ability, to some extent, to set prices and to alter other traits of the product (including color, design, packaging, and service before, during, or after the sale). Thus advertising is important in that it informs consumers of the differences (real or artificial) between one firm's product and those of its rivals.

It may be admitted that these criticisms have some merit. Few markets are completely free of oligopolistic influence, and established reputations undoubtedly are a frequent bar to complete elimination of excess profits. However, monopolistic competition has some interest as a limiting case in which interdependence is relatively weak and entry of new firms is relatively easy. Moreover, the fact that some criticisms of existing monopolistic competition analysis are valid does not mean that we should condemn all conceivable models of this type. Here, as in most other areas of economic analysis, further research is in order.

SUMMARY

1. A monopolistically competitive market is characterized by a large number of independent sellers; barriers to entry are relatively low; and differentiated products (perceived or actual) exist.

2. Product differentiation stems from many different sources including location, physical differences, and differences perceived through advertising and service.

3. Individual sellers in a monopolistically competitive industry view demand for their product as relatively elastic; that is, small price changes will have relatively large effects on quantity.

4. Free entry into the product group has a tendency to eliminate excess profits in the long run.

5. In the market period, a decrease in demand causes sales to lag behind output: prices will fall. If an increase in demand causes sales to exceed output, the seller will most likely ration output to regular customers at the prevailing price.

6. In the short run, the seller's demand curve will depend on the average level of prices in the industry. Estimates of industry price could be derived either from recent price experiences or from some traditional method of markup above average variable costs.

7. In the long run, maximum profits are reached when the level of output is such that MR = SRMC = LRMC. But this is not the only condition that must be met. With the threat of new entrants, established firms may find it necessary to reduce prices in order to maintain a certain level of sales.

8. Because of the downward slope of the demand curve in the monopolistic competitive model, the point of tangency will not be at the lowest level of average costs.

9. Low barriers to entry make it possible for many firms to enter the industry, making it difficult for many firms to earn normal profits.

10. Firms with strong reputations and a customer loyalty may earn excess profits despite the new entrants.

11. Advertising may increase a firm's demand and also make demand more inelastic by creating strong preferences.

WORDS AND CONCEPTS FOR REVIEW

monopolistic competition
product differentiation
tangency in the long run

excess capacity
excessive entry of newcomers
restrictions to free entry

REVIEW QUESTIONS

1. What are the assumptions upon which the model of monopolistic competition is based?

2. In what sense is monopolistic competition a hybrid of monopoly and perfect competition?

3. Suppose that you are considering the purchase of each of the following items, the prices charged by various sellers being the same. What considerations would influence your choice of the particular seller or brand?
a. a new car—make of car;
b. shoes—make of shoe;
c. gasoline in your home area—dealer and brand;
d. gasoline while on a trip—dealer and brand;
e. a motel while on a trip;
f. a restaurant in your home area;
g. an airline for a trip to Europe;
h. a classical record.

4. What is the difference between the demand curve in monopolistic competition and those in monopoly and perfect competition?

5. In a market period in which the seller in monopolistic competition cannot adjust rate of purchases or output, will the firm be more willing to reduce prices if its sales lag behind output or to raise prices if its sales outrun output? Explain.

6. In setting price in a short-run period, on what bases may the firm estimate the "industry" price?

7. Why are fixed costs not likely to be a significant portion of total cost in monopolistic competition?

8. Why does the tangency occur in the long-run in monopolistic competition?

9. Why don't firms in monopolistic competition operate at the point of lowest long-run average cost if all excess profits have been eliminated? Illustrate with a graph.

10. What leads to excessive entry of new firms in some monopolistically competitive markets?

11. Why may some firms in monopolistic competition continue to earn excess profits for long periods even though new firms may easily start up?

12. What is the effect of selling activities upon prices in monopolistic competition?

SUGGESTED READINGS

Chamberlin, Edward. *The Theory of Monopolistic Competition,* 8th ed. Cambridge, MA: Harvard University Press, 1962.

Dewey, Donald. *The Theory of Imperfect Competition.* New York: Columbia, 1969.

Robinson, Joan. *The Economics of Imperfect Competition.* London: Macmillan, 1933.

Scherer, Frederick. *Industrial Market Structure and Economic Performance,* 2nd ed. Chicago: Rand McNally, 1980.

Stigler, George. "Monopolistic Competition in Retrospect." In *Five Lectures on Economic Problems* (New York: Macmillan, 1950).

12

Oligopoly

12.1 INTRODUCTION

Like monopolistic competition, oligopoly lies somewhere between perfect competition and monopoly in its structure. Yet oligopoly is quite different from monopolistic competition. Oligopoly involves a few firms, while monopolistic competition involves many. Whereas product differentiation is critical to monopolistic competition, it may or may not be of importance to oligopolists, some of whom sell standardized products like steel, nylon, or sulfuric acid. Whereas in monopolistic competition the behavior of one individual firm usually has little impact on the behavior of other firms in the industry, in oligopoly each firm's behavior has potential implications for the behavior of other firms. In one vital respect, oligopoly and monopolistic competition are similar: firms in both market structures are price searchers who have some control over product prices.

Oligopoly is also characterized by mutual interdependence among firms. Each seller shapes its policy with an eye to the policies of other firms. Oligopoly is likely to occur whenever the number of firms in an industry is so small that any change in output or price by one firm materially affects the sales of competing firms. In this situation, it is almost inevitable that a firm with rivals who will react directly will take these reactions into consideration when determining policy.

What is responsible for the widespread occurrence of oligopoly? Primarily it is a result of the relationship between technological conditions of production and potential sales volumes. Reasonably low cost of production of many products cannot be obtained unless a firm is producing a large volume of output. Such "internal scale economies" may result in only a few companies being able to supply the entire market demand, as in automobile and steel production.

12.2 CLASSIFICATION OF OLIGOPOLY

Pure versus Differentiated Oligopoly

Situations of oligopoly can be classed into two groups on the basis of the presence or absence of differentiation. If the products of various firms are identical, the term **pure oligopoly** is applied. This model is approximated in some of the capital goods industries such as cement production. Mutual interdependence is greater when products are identical than when they are differentiated, since any price change by one firm is certain to produce substantial effects upon the sales of competitors and will likely cause them to alter their policies in response.

On the other hand, in **differentiated oligopoly**, in which products are not identical to each other, price changes will have less direct effect upon competitors because of the partial isolation of the market for each firm. The stronger the differentiation, the weaker will be the feeling of mutual interdependence. Differentiated oligopoly is characteristic of a very large portion of the total economy, including most manufactured consumer goods and retailing in most areas. Therefore the degree of differentiation and strength of feeling of mutual interdependence vary widely among industries. This makes it very difficult to develop general models for price and output analysis in oligopoly. (See Box 12-1.)

Collusion versus Spontaneous Coordination

Oligopoly situations may also be classified on the basis of whether mutual interdependence reveals itself in outright *collusion* or merely in *spontaneous coordination* of the firms' policies through recognition by each firm of the effects of its actions upon those of its competitors.

Collusion involves *direct* negotiation and agreements among competitors. Such collusion increases the stability of oligopoly. Otherwise, firms may base their actions upon mistaken estimates of their competitors' behavior.

The coverage of agreements made with collusion may vary widely. Agreements may extend to price only, or to both price and output. In other cases, merely the method of

---

12-1 Imagine you have a friend who is a cosmetic surgeon, one of many in the country. She specializes in the tightening of facial skin. Recently, she developed a procedure for her patients that is less painful with less scarring and a faster recovery time. Will price changes by other cosmetic surgeons have much impact on the price your friend charges for facial surgery?

Since the products are not identical there is less likelihood that other cosmetic surgeons will have a *major* effect on the prices your friend charges. If all surgeons were producing identical face-lift operations, then perhaps the rivals' actions would be closely watched.

price determination is agreed upon, such as the rule of following prices set by one firm, which economists call a price leadership model.

Frequently, however, oligopoly involves **spontaneous coordination** rather than outright agreement (particularly since the latter is illegal in the United States and many other countries!) Each firm simply takes into consideration its competitors' *expected* responses to its own actions and determines its policies accordingly. With each firm following similar practices, price and output levels will eventually adjust to figures that are acceptable to all firms. Spontaneous coordination may involve independent adoption by various firms of pricing practices comparable to those agreed upon in situations of collusion, or the acceptance of one firm as a price leader, or adoption of methods of price setting—such as the markup system common in retailing. We will discuss all of these pricing practices in the following paragraphs.

Complete versus Partial Oligopoly

Oligopoly is described as **complete oligopoly** if interdependence among firms is so strong that the profits of the firms as a group are maximized (that is, they succeed in acting like a multiplant monopolist), **partial oligopoly** if this is not obtained. As explained later, complete oligopoly is in all likelihood rarely attained, varying degrees of partial oligopoly being the typical situation. But analysis of the former is important, since it represents the ultimate ideal from the standpoint of oligopolies.

The wide variety of possible situations in oligopoly makes analysis of price and output determination difficult. A broad theory, with assumptions so general as to cover all possible oligopoly situations, offers little specific guidance in analyzing particular situations, while developing separate theories based on all possible assumptions is an impossible task. At present, it is possible only to consider those cases that appear to be of primary importance.

The complexities and diversities of oligopoly make it necessary to divide the analysis of price and output determination in such markets into several sections. As a convenient starting point, we shall deal first with complete oligopoly and then with partial oligopoly.

12.3 COMPLETE OLIGOPOLY

Complete oligopoly exists when relationships among the firms are sufficiently close to permit maximization of the joint profits of the firms, considered as a group. This condition may result from spontaneous coordination of the firms' policies or, more likely, from outright cooperation among officials of the firms. This model does not differ fundamentally from that of monopoly, except that there is more than one firm and that costs are likely to be different.

Maximization of joint profit requires the determination of price on the basis of the total (or market) demand schedule for the product and the horizontal sum of the marginal cost schedules of the various firms, as shown in Figure 12-1. With outright agreements—necessarily secret because of antitrust laws—firms that make up the

FIGURE 12-1

Short-Run Adjustment and Output for Complete Oligopoly
A complete oligopoly maximizes joint profits by equating marginal revenue for the market and the sum of the marginal cost schedules for all firms. The optimum price, P_0, is determined at the profit-maximizing output level, Q_0, along the market demand curve. A complete oligopoly achieves the monopoly price, quantity, and profits.

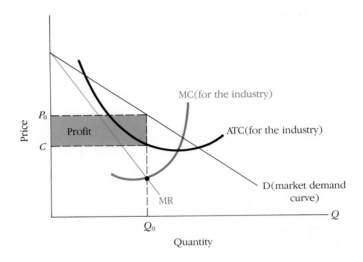

market will attempt to estimate demand and cost schedules, and set optimum price and output levels accordingly. If prices are set by one firm and followed by all others, the price setter will act on the basis of *total schedules* rather than its own situation, and other firms will abide by the decision. When collusive action is absent, maximum joint profits can be obtained only if each firm, acting independently, correctly estimates the price that is optimal from the standpoint of the group.

The manner in which total profits are shared among firms in the industry depends in part upon relative costs and sales of the various firms. Firms with low costs and large sales will obtain the largest profits. Sales, in turn, will depend in large measure upon consumer preferences for various brands if the oligopoly is differentiated. With outright collusion, firms may agree upon market shares and the division of profits. The division of total profits will depend upon the firms' relative bargaining strength, which is influenced by relative financial strength, the ability to inflict damage (through price wars) on other firms if an agreement is not reached, the ability to withstand similar action on the part of other firms, relative costs, consumer preferences, and bargaining skills.

Obstacles to Joint Profit Maximization

There are many obstacles to maximization of joint profit and the attainment of complete oligopoly. The basic difficulty lies in the unwillingness of firms to surrender all freedom of action, combined with the desire of each to increase its own share of total sales and profits.

First, the maximum joint profit price will be optimal (that is, at the best position) for each firm as well as for firms as a group only if marginal cost and demand schedules hence marginal revenue are the same for all the firms. If this is not true (and it is surely unlikely), those firms that will be worse off at the joint-profit maximum must be compensated by other firms or frightened into compliance by threats of punitive action, or they will not accept the optimal solution at P_0 and Q_0 in Figure 12-1. In some instances it would be necessary to close down high-cost firms to attain the highest joint profit, but these firms may resist such a policy. In the absence of adequate compensation, the best that can be obtained is a compromise, a level of profits tolerable to all the firms, but not the joint-profit maximum.

Second, not only is it difficult to determine the exact nature of the demand curve, but different firms will have different opinions about it and compromises will be inevitable.

Third, profit maximization may be checked by strategic moves by one firm designed to force other firms to take certain actions or to discourage them from carrying out policies detrimental to the interests of the given firm. Thus a firm may take action to drive rivals out of business completely or to test their strength and bargaining power.

Fourth, attainment of maximum group profits may be hampered by the firms' inability to agree upon product changes, advertising policies, and new techniques. Typically, it appears that agreements relate only to price. Agreement on nonprice elements is particularly difficult. Each firm may be confident that it will be able to outdo other firms on selling activities and therefore be unwilling to reach an agreement about them. Firms are highly conscious that price changes lead to changes by competitors, so agreements on prices may appear highly desirable. But firms often believe that they will be able to do better than competitors with new methods, products, and advertising procedures. With spontaneous coordination (basing decisions on expected responses of rival firms), firms are likely to be much more conscious of competitors' reactions to price changes than to changes in other variables that affect profits.

A fifth deterrent to the setting of maximum-profit prices is the fear that such prices will stimulate the growth of new firms. Although most oligopolistic industries (like steel, automobiles, and airlines) are characterized by significant barriers to entry by new firms, newcomers may nevertheless seek to enter. High prices and excess profits not only provide great incentive to entry but also make such entry easier. High prices ease the problem of covering heavy initial costs of operations, and good profit prospects facilitate the raising of money capital from investors. As a consequence, existing firms may deliberately hold prices below the short-run maximum profit level, preferring instead a "reasonable" profit that will continue longer because less encouragement will be given to prospective entrants.

Finally, difficulties in coordinating action discourage firms from making frequent price changes in the light of changing conditions. Continuous maximization of joint profits is clearly out of the question, however, if prices are not altered from time to time. (See Box 12-2.)

12-2   Is joint profit maximization more likely in a growing industry or a declining industry?

If firms are close to full capacity (which is more likely in a growing industry than a declining industry)—that is, using their employees and plants sufficiently intensely that average costs are as low as possible—there is less temptation to secretly lower prices or offer special discounts to certain customers. If there is much excess capacity, as is usual with a declining industry, average costs can be lowered by increasing production, hence the temptation to cheat on the agreement.

12.4 PARTIAL OLIGOPOLY

While complete oligopoly may be regarded as the ultimate goal of a group of oligopolists, it is not the typical behavior pattern; partial oligopoly—in which joint profits are not maximized—is the general rule. Spontaneous coordination is probably more common than outright agreement (collusion) in partial oligopoly. Firms set their own prices on the basis of estimates of demand schedules which take into consideration possible reactions on the part of their competitors as well as their own cost schedules. The critical difference between price setting by oligopolists and by other firms is the attention given to possible reactions by competitors. If competitors tend to follow price changes, shifting of customers among firms in response to price changes will be reduced and demand elasticity will be controlled primarily by the elasticity of total demand for the product. As oligopoly develops in an industry, prices may be expected to rise as the demand schedules of firms become less elastic. As in other competitive situations, maximum profit for the firm is determined by the level of operation at which marginal cost is equal to marginal revenue. The problem is that marginal revenue depends on the price reaction of *others* when any one firm changes price.

The mutual interdependence that characterizes oligopoly creates great uncertainty, since a firm can rarely be sure of its competitors' response. Even if a firm suspects that changes in its price will lead to reactions by competitors, it cannot know the extent of these reactions. A small price reduction may cause a large increase in sales if competitors do not reduce their prices, but only a slight increase if competitors meet the cut, or even a reduction in sales if competitors exceed the cut. Under such circumstances, the firm is in a sense confronted not by one demand curve but by an infinity of potential curves, the appropriate one in a particular instance depending upon the exact (but unknown) reactions of competitors. However, the firm must act; it must set some price and must accept one of the potential demand curves. But the uncertainty is itself a major influence upon the firm's policy, encouraging firms to develop techniques of pricing and marketing that minimize the danger of following policies based upon mistaken estimates of competitors' reactions. Uncertainty also encourages firms to minimize the frequency of price changes because of possible dangers (such as price wars) arising out of changes in the status quo.

What means does a firm have to increase knowledge of its relevant demand schedule? One possibility is to study actual sales data over a period during which different prices have been charged. Such a study must be made with great care, since other determinants of sales—consumer incomes and preferences, price of substitutes, weather conditions, and so forth—are constantly changing. Isolation of the effects of price changes from the effects of other changes is very difficult, but careful analysis may yield some useful information. Study of sales volumes of competitors charging different prices (when obtainable) and analysis of the nature of the market in order to estimate elasticity of total demand may also be of assistance. Many large firms devote considerable effort to market research, either by their own personnel or by independent firms specializing in this work. Market research today, however, is devoted primarily to such problems as estimating sales potentials in particular areas, determining new uses and outlets for a product, discovering consumer reaction to quality changes, checking on the effectiveness of advertising and other selling campaigns, and estimating the probable response of a firm's sales to changes in national income. Little attention has been given specifically to price/sales relationships, primarily because of the great difficulties involved. But the information obtained and techniques employed in present market research are valuable in providing further information about price/sales relationships.

Another approach is experimentation with price changes. But firms must use this procedure with great care. Other determinants of sales may change during the period. Far more serious is the danger that if the change proves unprofitable, the firm may be unable to recover its original sales volume if it returns to the old prices. Competitors may meet reductions, or even exceed them, and may not follow the change back to the earlier level. Consumer resistance to returning to the old figure may be encountered; buyers may consider the low price appropriate and may shift to other brands or products should the firm attempt to raise it. Experimental price increases are less dangerous than decreases, since they are less likely to produce defensive reactions on the part of competitors; but they may drive customers permanently into the arms of competing firms. A final difficulty with price experimentation is that the entire effect of the change will not occur instantaneously. Buyers may not shift away immediately when prices are raised, but many may do so over a longer period. Alternatively, reductions may cause temporary sales increases as buyers stock up in anticipation of the return of prices to the original level. Because of these problems, most firms consider experimentation with price changes extremely hazardous. Seldom will they deliberately experiment, but rather will make changes only when they are reasonably certain that the new prices will be more profitable than the old. (See Box 12-3.)

12-3 Imagine you are an executive working for Ford Motor Company. You think it might be appropriate to cut prices on your autos across the board. How do you know whether you should or not?

You don't! What if you cut 5 percent and General Motors reacts by cutting 10 percent?—then you might actually sell less cars at lower prices. Thus, with so much uncertainty about rival behavior, there is a strong incentive to collude.

12.5 THE CASE OF THE KINKED DEMAND CURVE

It has been suggested—more on the basis of commonsense observations than on careful empirical study—that oligopoly demand curves will frequently contain a sharp bend or kink at the level of the existing price. This **kinked demand curve**, illustrated in Figure 12-2, is produced by the greater tendency of competitors to follow price reductions than price increases. A price reduction takes business away from other firms and forces them to cut prices in order to protect their sales, while an increase does not necessitate a readjustment, since other firms gain customers if one increases its price. At the point of the kink the MR curve is discontinuous; thus, in a sense, marginal revenue is not defined. But at higher and lower levels of output the figure is defined, being equal to or greater than r'' for lower output levels and equal to or less than r' at higher levels of output (see Figure 12-2).

The point of maximum profit for the firm is almost of necessity at the output level at which the sharp change in elasticity occurs (q_0 in Figure 12-2). It is likely that marginal cost will not equal marginal revenue at a lower volume of output because the MR curve is so high (and nearly horizontal) in this output range. At output levels to the right of the kink, the MR curve drops—perhaps to a negative figure—and almost certainly will lie below the MC curve. The optimum price (P_0 in Figure 12-2) is indicated by the

FIGURE 12-2

Price and Output Adjustment, Kinked Demand Curve
Assuming rivals do not follow price increases, a firm will lose customers by raising price and the demand curve will be relatively elastic above the prevailing price. If rivals follow price cuts, a firm cannot capture many of its rivals' clients by lowering price and the demand curve tends to be relatively inelastic below the current price. The resulting kink at the prevailing price yields a gap in the marginal revenue curve. Equilibrium price and quantity, P_0 and q_0, correspond to the equality of short-run marginal cost and marginal revenue within the discontinuity of the marginal revenue curve, r'' to r'.

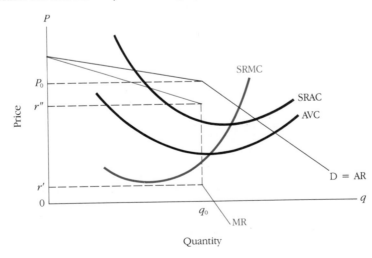

Quantity

point at which the AR curve changes slope. It is obvious to the firm that any other price would be unprofitable given the assumptions about rival behavior, since increases would cause great losses in revenues (as many other firms fail to follow the price increase), while reductions would yield little additional business (since most of the other firms are presumed to follow price cuts). The more standardized the product, the sharper the kink, since customers will shift more readily and thus competitors will react more quickly and precisely.

One important consequence of the kink in the demand curve is that the firm may be slow to adjust price in response to cost changes. Because of the discontinuity in the MR curve, the MC curve can move up or down over a substantial range without affecting the optimum level of output or price.

While the kinked demand curve may be useful for explaining sellers' reactions to various changes, the analysis of the case in itself contributes little to the explanation of existing price and output levels because it doesn't explain why the kink came to be where it is. There appears to be no general principle to explain this level; appeal must be made to historical price trends and to particular techniques used by the firms in setting prices, as noted in subsequent sections.

12.6 COMPLETE OLIGOPOLY REVISITED: COLLUSION

The potential for disastrous pricing decisions is substantial in partial oligopoly since the behavior of rivals may be misjudged. This uncertainty has led some to suspect that oligopolists change their prices less frequently than perfect competitors as implied in the kinked demand curve analysis. It is unclear from examination of the data, however, whether prices are in fact less variable in oligopoly situations.

The temptation is nonetheless great for firms to reduce price uncertainty through collusive activity. Their goal would be to behave as a complete oligopoly, since collusion reduces uncertainty and increases the potential for monopoly profits. However, such **collusive oligopoly** creates a situation (like monopoly) characterized by inefficient allocation of resources (goods having benefits greater than costs are not produced) and inequitable transfers from consumers of the oligopoly good to the (typically) wealthier owners of oligopoly firms.

A complete oligopoly acts as the equivalent of one firm from the standpoint of pricing and output decisions. Hence, the economic effect is exactly the same as a multiplant monopolist's: a single demand curve exists for a group of firms jointly determining the profit-maximizing price and output (the latter allocated in principle according to marginal costs). Disagreements about allocating the output are, however, at the heart of the instability of complete oligopolies.

International complete oligopoly agreements among firms on sale, pricing, and other decisions are usually called **cartels**. We shall illustrate the instability of cartel arrangements with the Organization of Petroleum Exporting Countries (OPEC).

For collusion to work, each firm must agree to some share of the restriction in overall output in order to maintain the profit-maximizing price. However, at the profit-maximizing price there is a great temptation for each of the firms to cheat on the agreement of the complete oligopoly; since collusive agreements are illegal in the United States and in some other countries, the other parties are extremely limited in their ability to punish the offender, though legal considerations do not apply to OPEC.

Organized more than a decade earlier, OPEC began acting as a collusive oligopoly in 1973, in part because of political concern over American support for Israel. For two decades prior to 1973, the price of crude oil had hovered around $2 a barrel in nominal terms, falling substantially in real terms. In 1973, OPEC members agreed to a quadrupling of oil prices in nine months; subsequent price increases pushed the cost of a barrel of oil to over $20. Prices stabilized, actually falling in real terms between 1973 and 1978, as the profit-maximizing price was sought and politics remained relatively calm. But by the early 1980s, prices were approaching $40 per barrel—success from OPEC's perspective but quite difficult for consuming nations, though the wealth of the Western oil companies actually rose since their oil inventories soared in value.

Why were the OPEC nations successful with their pricing policies between 1973 and the early 1980s? First, the worldwide demand for petroleum was highly inelastic with respect to price in the short run for reasons which should be fairly obvious. Second, OPEC's share of total world oil output had steadily increased, from around 20 percent of total world output in the early 1940s to about 70 percent by 1973, when OPEC became an effective cartel. Third, the price elasticity of supply of petroleum from OPEC's competitors was low in the short run; ability to increase production from existing wells is limited and it takes time to drill new ones.

In more recent years, OPEC oil prices have again fluctuated in real terms, due to increases in non-OPEC production and the variable willingness of key suppliers (such as Saudi Arabia) to restrict supply. Moreover at the higher prices of the 1970s, long-run substitution possibilities caused oil consumption to fall almost 5 percent per year, with conservation and alternative energy easing the demands for OPEC oil.

12.7 OTHER APPROACHES TO PRICING: PRICE LEADERSHIP

Firms may lessen the significance of oligopolistic uncertainty by not making any independent price changes, instead adopting and following prices set by other firms. If this policy is so widespread in an industry that all firms follow the prices set by one firm, **price leadership** is said to occur.

Price leadership is most likely to develop when one firm produces a large portion of total output, the remainder being distributed over several relatively small firms. Almost inevitably, the large firm is the one to dominate pricing, the small firms perhaps being in a position to sell as much as they wish at the price set by the "dominant" firm. For maximum profits, the large firm will set its price on the basis of its own cost schedule and the total demand schedule for the product less the expected amounts to be sold by other firms. Price may approach the maximum profit figure, where MR = MC, unless deliberately kept lower to discourage growth of smaller firms.

The easiest way to view this model is shown by the two graphs in Figure 12-3, one

FIGURE 12-3

Price Leadership—Dominant Firm

The dominant firm's demand curve in part (b) is market demand less the expected sales of all other firms in the industry. The corresponding marginal revenue curve intersects the dominant firm's marginal cost curve at the equilibrium level of output for the dominant firm, q_0. The industry price, P_{Df}, is the dominant firm's price at Q_0 on D_{Df}. The followers sell the quantity supplied on S in part (a) at P_{Df}, and the excess demand is supplied by the dominant firm. Note that since the followers are price takers, their supply curve is the horizontal summation of their marginal cost curves.

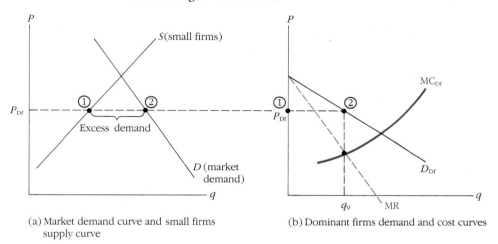

(a) Market demand curve and small firms supply curve

(b) Dominant firms demand and cost curves

for the price leader and the other for the smaller firms. Here we assume that there is only *one* large firm (the dominant firm) and many smaller firms, all selling a homogenous product. The dominant firm is the price leader; it sets the price at P_{DF} and then allows the smaller firms to sell all they want at that price. The dominant firm then sells the residual demand—that is, the excess demand in Figure 12-3(a). Thus it is the excess demand in Figure 12-3(a) that determines the position of the dominant firm's demand curve (the distance between 1 and 2 in both graphs is equal).

In other cases, price leadership might fall into the hands of the lowest-cost firm. One firm in a group of firms of more or less comparable size may come to play the role of price leader, not because of its dominant position in the market but because other firms regard its actions as a suitable barometer of changing market conditions and are willing to follow its policies in order to minimize competitive disturbances.

To visualize most simply price leadership by the low-cost firm, assume there are exactly two firms producing homogeneous products and agreeing to split the market equally (see Figure 12-4). The market demand curve is D and the relevant demand curves once the market is split is each firm's demand curve, d. Firm 1's cost curves are AC_1 and MC_1; Firm 2's cost curves are AC_2 and MC_2.

In Figure 12-4, what would be the maximizing price and output for each firm considered separately? P_1q_1 for Firm 1 and P_2q_2 for Firm 2 would be the respective

FIGURE 12-4

Price Leadership—Lowest-Cost Firm

Assuming a homogeneous product, two firms in the industry, and an agreement to share the market equally between the two firms, the market demand curve, D, is twice as great as the demand curve for either firm, d. The price leader, firm 1, equates its own marginal cost and marginal revenue and sets the price along d accordingly at P_1. To maximize profits independently, firm 2 would have charged P_2. Given that firm 1 sells the same product at a lower price, however, firm 2 would have lost all sales at that price. Firm 2 follows its lower cost rival by charging P_1, and sells the level of output for which P_1 and MC_2 are equal since P_1 is its marginal revenue under these circumstances. Since overall market demand and supply may not be equal at P_1, there may be some "fine tuning" of this price (raising it if $D > q_1 + q_2$, lowering it if $D < q_1 + q_2$).

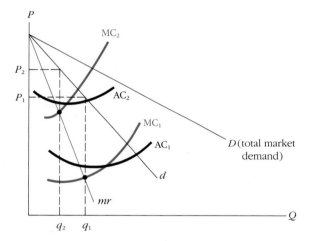

price/quantity combinations. If both are selling homogenous products, then the higher-priced seller, Firm 2, would clearly lose its customers to Firm 1. Therefore, according to this model, Firm 2 must lower its price, accepting the one set by the low-cost firm, P_1. The amount sold by Firm 2 (and whether the overall market will have shortages or surpluses at P_1) depends on where MC_2 intersects P_1.

Of course, Firm 1 could lower its price enough to drive its competitor out of business (any price below AC_2 would cause Firm 2 to shut down in the long run). Why the benevolence, you might ask? One answer might be the fear of being the sole seller in the market—a monopoly is at some risk of being prosecuted under antitrust laws and perhaps even being nationalized in some countries. (See Box 12-4.)

12.8 PRICE FOLLOWING OR IMITATIVE PRICING

In an industry with price leaders, the other firms inevitably are followers. But even in industries without price leaders, there are frequently firms that deliberately adopt no independent pricing policy, merely adapting to the prices of others. Such an **imitative**

12-4   In an industry such as steel where there are dominant firms, is it likely that they will settle on maximizing joint profits?

Joint profit maximization is not as likely when a "dominant" firm is present. The reason is that higher profits can be made if the firm sets its output at the profit-maximizing level, while others with less desirable cost conditions follow the lead of the price setter. Of course, in the presence of substantial international competition one could question the existence of a dominant firm in any one home country.

pricing policy avoids the necessity and cost of calculating prices, avoids any danger of upsetting competitive conditions, and allows the firm to concentrate on nonprice competition.

Price following in some instances involves the selection of a price higher or lower than the typical figure in the industry. Hence a firm stressing high quality and prestige may price at some percentage in excess of the typical industry figure, while cut-rate firms may deliberately set prices below the market.

12.9 AVERAGE COST AND THE COST-PLUS OR MARKUP APPROACH

Empirical studies suggest that the most common approach to pricing is the use of an estimated figure based on average cost. Average cost, in turn, is computed by adding to direct cost a markup that includes the rate of profit regarded as normal or attainable by the firm. This approach is often called the **cost-plus** or target return method.

Calculation of Price

There are several basic steps in the **markup approach** to pricing. First, the firm estimates the direct separable cost per unit of output for which the product is responsible, primarily labor and material costs. These are usually assumed to vary proportionately with output, so that the amount per unit is the same regardless of the volume of output (flat variable cost curves). Second, when (as is typical) the firm is producing more than one product, it must allocate among the various products the *common costs*, costs incurred for the production of more than one product. Indirect labor costs—those of labor not directly engaged in physical production—are often allocated on the basis of hours of direct labor cost per unit of various products. Finally, there is added a markup, usually expressed as a percentage, to cover a return on investment.

The rate of profit included in cost calculations depends upon the attitude of officials of the firm as to the rate which is attainable and appears to them to be the optimum in terms of long-range profit possibilities. A number of firms have set up, on the basis of experience over the years, a *target return* figure which, on the average, they believe they can earn.

Markups in Retail Pricing

Some firms, particularly retailers, use customary markup figures, which are rarely recalculated. Under usual retail pricing techniques, the markup percentage, applied to the purchase price of goods sold, is set sufficiently high to cover all overhead costs in retailing—such as clerk hire, heat, light, rent, and the like—plus expected profit. In some fields of retailing a uniform markup percentage is used on all items, but more typically there are variations. Items requiring refrigeration may be subject to a higher markup to cover additional separable costs for which they are responsible. Prices on other goods are adjusted to bring them to certain price lines at which the goods are traditionally sold; for example, neckties might be carried only at $15, $20, and $25. Other articles, such as electrical appliances and some lines of clothing, are typically priced at figures ending in 95 or 99 cents, in the belief that these have significant psychological advantages. The retailer has no control over prices on some goods, since the manufacturer establishes the resale price. In recent years, however, as a result of the rise of discount houses and the lessened role of state legislation sanctioning maintained prices, substantial shading of manufacturers' suggested prices has become common. Finally, demand considerations may force a retailer to vary a standard markup; some staple goods have come to bear markups typically smaller than the average.

Rigid versus Flexible Markups

In a few industries, firms typically set prices at figures calculated by the average cost plus fixed markup approach. More commonly, though, markups are flexible; that is, average costs serve as a point of departure in price setting but do not determine the actual price. Thus the firm considers demand conditions as well as cost. If the calculated price is higher than prices charged by other firms, the seller must consider whether or not it can charge more than competitors; if not, the seller must adjust the price downward. If, on the other hand, average cost plus customary markup is less than prices other firms are charging, it may be advisable to increase price since rivals may otherwise reduce their figures and all may be worse off. If demand appears to be very inelastic, price increases may be in order. For example, retailers often apply higher-than-usual markups to luxury food items; and automobile manufacturers apparently load expensive cars with a greater share of overhead than cheaper cars, the buyers of which are more price-conscious.

Advantages of the Average-Cost Approach

The widespread use of the average-cost (versus marginal cost) approach to pricing indicates that it must offer significant advantages. One obvious merit is simplicity: when firms have thousands of products, some workable rule-of-thumb pricing technique is imperative. Second, as long as the method is widely employed, it leads to uniformity of pricing and lessens the danger of price wars and breakdown of oligopolistic stability. Especially when markups are customary and uniform among firms—and materials, labor, and other direct costs are comparable—firms will set similar figures.

The average-cost approach to price setting is also furthered by a belief on the part of businesses that this method is "reasonable" and "fair." The notion that all goods should bear their "share" of overhead and that prices should be set at a figure that includes a "fair" profit is widely accepted in the business community, although there are many exceptions.

Average-Cost Pricing and Profit Maximization

The extent to which average-cost pricing consitutes a departure from the assumption of profit maximization has been the subject of much controversy. It is obvious that any method of pricing involving the addition of a fixed percentage to variable costs can hardly maximize short-run profits except by sheer accident. Nevertheless, given the circumstances of oligopoly, the average-cost method, properly employed, may allow firms to come closer to maximum profit than any other pricing system. There are several reasons.

In the first place, as noted earlier, the average-cost technique is an effective means of stabilizing rivalry and lessening the uncertainty characteristic of oligopolistic markets. Second, as long as demand elements are taken into consideration, price may not differ too greatly from the figure that would be selected on the basis of marginal cost considerations. Adjustments made in average-cost estimates in setting actual price bring demand aspects into the picture and thus lead to a price more closely approximating the maximum profit level.

Third, once various firms in an industry have set prices on an average-cost basis, the price so set may actually seem to yield maximum profits—equality between marginal revenue and marginal cost—for any given firm because the kink in each firm's subjective demand curve will be at this level. The price at this level may not yield maximum profit for the firms as a group and may be substantially different from the price firms would set if price determination were initially approached via estimates of marginal revenue and marginal cost. But given prevailing rivalrous relationships and the inability to maximize true joint profits, the price arrived at by average-cost methods may represent a relative if not absolute optimum.

While the use of average-cost pricing may be broadly consistent with profit maximization in oligopolistic industries, total reliance on average cost figures may cause firms to sacrifice profits, particularly if relatively small price reductions would lead to large increases in sales. As indicated above, most business firms consider these factors in setting prices rather than using average-cost techniques alone, but some may overemphasize the significance of average cost.

The Significance of Average-Cost Pricing

From the standpoint of resource allocation and reactions to demand and cost changes, the use of the average-cost pricing techniques has considerable significance:

Effect on prices.   In the first place, the use of this technique results in a different allocation of common cost (or overhead costs, as in the retail example) among various products than would occur with direct use of marginal techniques, and thus in different prices and outputs of particular goods.

Effect on price of an increase in demand.   With the establishment of prices based on estimates of marginal cost and revenue schedules, an increase in demand will usually lead to price increases, as illustrated in Figure 12-5. When the revenue curve shifts from D_0 to D_1, equilibrium price rises from P_0 to P_1. But when the average-cost approach is used, the decline or constancy of average cost consequent on increased sales will lessen the likelihood of price increases and in some cases actually leads to price reductions. Reductions would be more common if average cost were calculated on the basis of estimated sales instead of normal sales. Likewise, when demand falls, strict adherence to average cost price, with actual sales used as a basis for calculating average cost, will tend to bring about price increases.

Reaction of price to an increase in cost.   With marginal-cost pricing, price will not (except under unlikely assumptions) be raised immediately by the full amount of a cost increase. A firm will readjust output until marginal cost and marginal revenue are again equal, thus raising marginal revenue by the amount of the increase in marginal cost. Price will be raised by a smaller amount, as shown in Figure 12-6. Price rises from P_0 to P_1, while the amount of the cost increase is the vertical distance between AC_0 and AC_1. When price is set on the basis of average cost, however, firms are likely to raise

FIGURE 12-5

Short-Run Adjustment to an Increase in Demand
The strategy of pricing according to marginal cost and marginal revenue results in price and quantity increases when demand rises. Average cost pricing, however, may lead to price decreases when demand rises because of economies of scale.

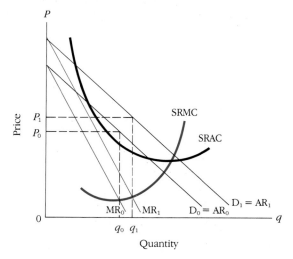

FIGURE 12-6

Short-Run Adjustments to an Increase in Cost—the Marginal Approach
Price rises by the amount of the average cost increase when markup pricing is employed.
Under a marginal cost-marginal revenue pricing policy, however, price will rise (P_0 to P_1)
but by less than the full amount of the cost increase (AC_0 to AC_1).

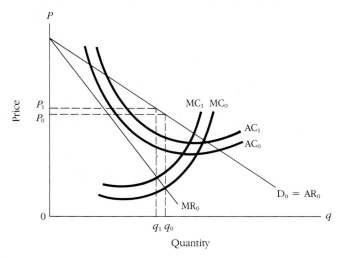

price immediately by the full amount of the cost increase. Suppose, for example, that
wages paid by all firms in an industry increase. Average cost is raised by the amount of
the wage increase per unit of output; accordingly, price is likely to be raised by the
same amount. If all firms follow the same policy, all will be better off (unless they have
already attained maximum joint profits) than they would have been had they raised by
a smaller amount. If the total demand for the product is at all elastic, the firms will not
cover average cost despite the increase (assuming average profit before the wage rise),
but they will more closely approach doing so than if they raised price by a smaller
amount. Some departure of firms from the industry will still be necessary to restore
average profits. It should be noted that such a price increase would have been profitable even in the absence of the wage increase. But, given the competitive situation, no
one firm could raise price because there was no assurance that others would follow.
When a cost increase occurs in all firms, however, each is likely to feel that others will
raise prices if it does, and the increase will take place accordingly. (See Box 12-5.)

12.10 INTRODUCTORY PRICING

For established products, the task of determining prices involves merely the question
of desirable change from existing levels. But with **introductory pricing** of entirely
new products, the problem is more complicated, and the policies followed may vary

12-5   The owners of a regional cement company might merely mark up their prices on cement. How is this firm's behavior in the face of a cost increase likely to differ from a firm employing "marginal-cost pricing"?

If the owners are concerned both about rivals and new entrants in the cement industry, they might be reluctant to pass on additional costs, especially if they were the only ones to incur these higher costs (perhaps having suffered higher costs because of an unexpected equipment breakdown). To raise the price might mean that competitors or new entrants might take away some of their business. However, if there are high barriers to entry, they would be tempted to pass on the cost in the form of higher prices. Remember, the company can't charge as much as it would like because customers can always find substitutes (asphalt, steel, wood etc.) for cement. Thus, instead of equating *expected* marginal revenue and *expected* marginal cost in the short run, the owners may increase price or not change their price, depending on the extent of their competition (from existing competitors as well as potential entrants).

widely. Some firms merely apply their standard pricing techniques. Others set relatively high prices in an effort either to recover very quickly the costs incidental to developing the new product or to take advantage of the temporary lack of competition. Drug manufacturers have, from all indications, tended to price new products relatively high in order to recover heavy research costs in a short period of time, and in so doing have incurred substantial public criticism. Other firms have followed the opposite policy, pricing below average cost (which is typically high until volume becomes substantial) in an effort to stimulate widespread use of new products. The choice of policy no doubt reflects differences in the degree of protection from potential rivals by patent laws, goodwill, and so forth.

12.11   ADJUSTMENT OF PRODUCT TO PRICE

In some lines, there is a definite policy of selecting a price and then adjusting quality and thus cost to allow profitable production at the price selected (provided volume is adequate). The classic example was the ten-cent candy bar, which many firms retained for long periods, despite rising costs, by reducing size. Some firms varied quality from year to year in conformity with varying prices of cocoa and other elements. This phenomenon is encountered in other fields as well. Producers of household electrical appliances and farm implements frequently follow the rule of selecting a price at which they believe a product will sell in profitable amounts, and then adjusting the quality of the product to obtain a cost figure that will allow an adequate profit.

12.12   STRATEGIC MOVES IN OLIGOPOLY

In some respects a situation of partial oligopoly resembles a military campaign or a poker game. Certain actions may be taken not because they are advantageous in themselves, but because they improve the position of the oligopolist relative to its competitors and may ultimately result in an improved financial position. Deliberate price cutting, in itself unprofitable, may be undertaken either to drive competitors out or to scare them sufficiently to discourage them from undertaking actions contrary to the interests of other firms. On the other hand, the desire for security and the ability to hold out against aggressive action on the part of competitors may lead a firm to take action which is itself contrary to profit maximization. Thus a firm may expand in order to increase the absolute size of its financial resources, or to ensure supplies of materials or market outlets during periods of competitive struggle, even though these actions are not in themselves profitable.

Some economists have suggested that the entire approach to oligopoly price and output should be recast in terms of the behavior of participants in a strategic game, replacing the analysis based upon the assumption of attempted profit maximization. This point of view, called **game theory**, stresses the tendency of various parties in such circumstances to minimize damages from opponents. In terms of this approach, there is a set of alternative solutions (with respect to price and output levels, for example), the actual one attained in a particular case depending upon the specific policies followed by each firm. The firm may also seek to ascertain the competitors' most likely countermoves to its own policies and formulate alternative defense measures.

Unfortunately, the chief contributions of this line of thought are merely a novel terminology and a more precise characterization of alternative possible oligopoly situations. It has done little or nothing to improve our ability to predict patterns of behavior in concrete oligopoly situations, largely because it has not led (as originally expected) to an acceptable general solution to the problem of describing "rational behavior" under conditions of limited information. At the present time, there is no reason to suppose that the game theory approach to oligopoly is in very many respects superior to that of traditional economic theory; some specialists would even argue that in most respects it is inferior. (See Box 12-6.)

12-6   Game theory, which looks at decisions in conflict situations, has at least one crucial flaw. What is this flaw?

For the most part, game theory examines firms in conflict, while most of oligopoly analysis stresses the importance of incentives to avoid conflict through cooperation or collusion. Oligopolists cooperate through formal or informal collusion. It might come in the form of a dominant firm that has the greater market share and/or the lowest costs. Or it might come in the form of looking at a published schedule of prices in the industry. The point is that unlike poker (in which wins equal losses), the oligopoly game is not "zero-sum" (or even constant sum); rather, implicit cooperation (never modeled in the simple game theory approach) can make all parties better off.

12.13 OTHER OBJECTIVES OF OLIGOPOLISTS

Some students of oligopoly pricing have argued that profit maximization is not in accord with the objectives of management of large-scale widely owned businesses. William Baumol has stressed the importance of maximizing sales provided that the profit level is regarded as adequate at the maximum sales figure. Thus output is extended until MR is zero, instead of equal to MC, and selling activities are extended to the point at which they will bring no further increase in gross revenue. Thus in Figure 12-7 the point of operation is q_1. Baumol defends this thesis on two basic grounds: management regards total sales and thus its share of the market as the prime measure of success; and salaries of management are more closely related to gross sales than to profits. Adherence to this goal is strengthened by emphasis on "satisfactory" or "fair" profit instead of maximum profit.

Other writers, such as Oliver Williamson, have stressed the personal goals of corporation management. In widely held corporations, management has certain "expense preferences"—types of expenditures that yield benefits to management over and above those yielded to the firms and thus will be carried beyond the profit-maximizing level. Additional expenditures for staff constitute a major example: each subordinate executive seeks to increase the staff working under him, since doing so increases his own salary, prestige, and security. This is a phenomenon frequently attributed to government agencies. It is also argued that management at all levels seeks to increase perquisites—supplements to management salaries that yield direct benefits to the

FIGURE 12-7

Equilibrium Output, Goal of Maximum Sales Revenue
Providing that profits are satisfactory, management may choose to maximize sales revenue. As discussed in prior chapters, total revenue peaks when marginal revenue is zero at q_1. Equilibrium quantity is higher and price is lower when management's goal is sales revenue maximization than when it is profit maximization, since MC is never zero.

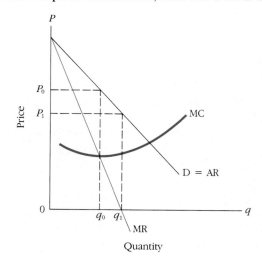

recipients. Management likewise regards the amount of funds available for investment use at their discretion as important. Emphasis on these considerations will lead to price and output policies different from those based on profit-maximization.

The significance of non-profit-maximizing goals is an empirical question, and present knowledge is not adequate for a satisfactory answer. Further studies of decision making, and development of more elaborate models of behavior under diverse and multiple goals, are clearly required.

12.14 PRODUCT VARIATION AND SELLING ACTIVITIES

Oligopoly conditions provide a particularly fertile ground for product variation, advertising, and other forms of selling activities. Price tends to stablize at a certain figure; and though the firm is anxious to increase sales in order to lower average cost, price reductions are not profitable because of the danger that other firms will also reduce prices. Firms turn to various forms of selling activities primarily because competitors' reactions are likely to be less disastrous to the firm than reactions to price reductions. Whereas competitors can meet price cuts almost instantly, they need time to follow selling activities. By the time competitors have discovered the success of nonprice policies and attempted to duplicate them, customers may be so well attached that they do not return to the competing firms. Moreover, there is always a chance that competitors will be unable to devise equally satisfactory selling methods. A price cut is a definite, conspicuous act which competitors can match or exceed if they wish. Sales activities are less obvious in their effects upon competitors. Furthermore, the widespread attitude on the part of businesses that price cutting is unethical encourages the use of selling activities instead of price adjustments. Legislative action, such as sanctioning resale price maintenance or placing restrictions upon selling below "cost," may also direct competition into nonprice lines.

Mutual Interdependence in Selling Activities

While interdependence is less significant with selling activities than with price changes, it is not absent. There is a wide range of possible relationships among oligopolists in the field of product policy and selling activities. At one extreme there may be perfect collusion, the firms agreeing implicitly or explicitly to select those products and selling policies which maximize profits for the group. There is substantial evidence, however, that complete collusion on product and sales activities is rare. From all indications, firms are much less willing to agree on these matters than upon price, partly because each believes that it can carry on these activities more effectively than competitors, partly because the results of failure to agree appear to be less disastrous.

The absence of complete collusion on product and selling activities almost certainly results in a higher level of selling activities than would occur with such collusion. Each firm attempts to increase its share of the market at the expense of other firms. Since competitors follow the same policy, much of the activity will cancel out, and none of the firms will gain anticipated sales volumes. All firms would be better off if all would cut the volume of advertising, yet no one firm can do so independently.

On the other hand, to the extent that firms take into consideration any effects that changes in their own selling activities will have upon the policies of competitors, the level of selling activities will be reduced below that which would otherwise be attained. If a firm believes that initiation of an extensive selling campaign will induce its competitors to follow suit, it will be inhibited from taking any action at all. If competitors follow increases in selling activities but not decreases, retreat from a high level of selling activities will be very difficult.

The Significance of Selling Activities

The success of selling activities among oligopolies has a major influence on the sharing of the total market among the competing firms. The largest shares may go to firms that do the best selling job, rather than to those that attain the lowest cost in manufacturing. The firms that fail may be those which make mistakes in the adjustment of product (such as introducing too-revolutionary changes in style) or fall behind in selling activities. Furthermore, the tendency of firms in oligopoly situations to stress selling activities as a means of increasing sales may lead to a higher level of selling activities than would be carried on in other market structures, making average cost (including selling cost) higher. On the other hand, to the extent that firms take into consideration the effects which their selling activities have upon the sales policies of their competitors, the overall level of selling activities may be less than if the market were one of monopolistic competition. Moreover, successful selling activity may concentrate the total business in the hands of a smaller number of firms and allow operation nearer the point of lowest average cost. Thus the price of the product *could* be lower than it would be if no selling activities were carried on.

12.15   PRICE DISCRIMINATION

Price discrimination is necessary, in all likelihood, for maximum joint profits. However, it is not possible unless the various firms follow uniform pricing policies, because prices in the high-price markets would tend to be pulled down to those in the lower-price markets. Firms must either agree on the prices to be charged in the various markets or spontaneously follow uniform practices. Because of the difficulties of obtaining complete cooperation, effective discrimination is less likely to occur in oligopoly than monopoly.

Some of the most significant instances of price discrimination in the United States have arisen from devices designed to lessen price competition rather than from a pricing policy introduced to adjust prices in terms of demand elasticities in various markets. One of the most important of these devices has been the basing point system, under which the price of the product in each locality was calculated by adding to the price at the basing point the freight from the basing point to the locality, regardless of the actual origin of the goods. For many years, steel prices in all parts of the country were determined by adding to the Pittsburgh price the freight from Pittsburgh, regardless of the actual origin of the steel. A Chicago buyer obtaining steel from a Gary mill would pay the Pittsburgh base price plus freight from Pittsburgh, even though the steel was shipped only a few miles from Gary. In later years, several basing points were used instead of one. The single-point system provided a uniform price in each area for all firms, regardless of the location of the plant, and served as a device to lessen price competition. Ultimately, Supreme Court decisions interpreting the antitrust laws brought an end to most basing point techniques. The use of a uniform price for the entire country, followed frequently in industries in which freight is a relatively unimportant expense, also facilitates the avoidance of price differences and price cutting, yet is seldom interfered with under the antitrust laws.

12.16 LONG-RUN ADJUSTMENTS

In oligopoly, just as in other types of market situations, equilbrium price and output will be different in the long run than at any particular time, partly because of internal adjustments designed to attain the optimum-sized plant and partly because of changes in the number of firms in the industry.

Long-Run Cost Adjustments

Over a long-run period, firms will adjust their plants to the sizes that are most satisfactory in terms of current and expected demand situations. Thus LRMC, including plant and current operating costs, will become a primary determinant of output and price policies. Just as with monopoly, long-run adjustment requires equality of MR with both LRMC and SRMC with the plant that is optimum under the circumstances.

Tendencies toward the Elimination of Excess Profits

The existence of mutual interdependence is no guarantee, in itself, of excess profits. Even if the firms in an industry succeed in maximizing joint profits, the rate of profit might not be greater than average. The extent to which excess profits disappear depends upon the ease with which new firms can enter the industry. When entry is easy, newcomers will be attracted by excess profits. They may break down existing pricing institutions and agreements, as they cut prices in order to establish themselves in the industry. Older firms may reduce prices to avoid excessive losses in sales, and the general level of prices will approach average cost more closely. If the firms' perceived demand curves are kinked, the action of newcomers in setting lower prices will lower the level of the kink for all firms.

On the other hand, new firms may follow the same pricing policies as existing firms, either initially or after a period of price cutting. As a consequence, equality of price and average cost, at least for some firms, will be attained through an increase in average cost rather than a decline in price. The increased number of firms results in a division of total business among a larger number of firms and so in smaller sales volume for each. If loss of sales forces a firm to operate at a higher point on its AC curve, excess profits may be eliminated without a reduction in price.

Figure 12-8(a) illustrates the elimination of excess profits through the entry of new firms: the AR curve moves to the left as new firms enter, until excess profits are eliminated and AR is tangent to LRAC at a price of P_2. Figure 12-8(b) illustrates a completed adjustment with a kinked demand curve. If the curve is kinked, the chances of a price reduction as new firms enter is particularly slight. So long as the new firms follow the prices of the old, none will find a price reduction (or increase) desirable;

FIGURE 12-8

Adjustment of Price toward Average Cost
In the left panel of part (a), an oligopolist earns economic profits because price P_1 exceeds long-run average cost at the equilibrium quantity, q_1. If entry is free, firms will be attracted into the industry and the firm's demand curve will shift to the left. Entry continues until profits are zero and the AR and LRAC curves are tangent. In the kinked demand curve framework shown in part (b), as long as the entrants stand by the pricing policies of established firms, the price will remain the same. The kink will shift to the left, however, as firms lose some of their customers to newcomers. Equilibrium is established when excess profits are eliminated and the LRAC curve is tangent to the AR curve.

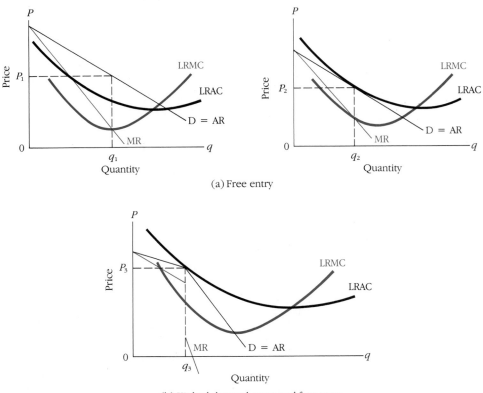

(a) Free entry

(b) Kinked demand curve and free entry

thus the point of the kink will gradually move to the left, but will stay at the same horizontal level, until it is just tangent to LRAC. The use of average-cost pricing techniques also increases the likelihood that excess profits will be eliminated without a price cut. The loss in sales to new firms raises average cost (if it is calculated on the basis of actual sales) and discourages price reductions.

Excess profits may sometimes be avoided deliberately by existing firms, being sacrificed for greater long-run security. If excess profits are earned and new firms enter, there is always a danger that too many will commence operations, with consequent losses (for a period) for many of the firms. To avoid this danger, existing firms may deliberately set prices to yield only a more or less average rate of return, and price may be only slightly above or equal to lowest average cost.

Entry Restriction

To the extent that entry is relatively free, empirical studies of firms' actual levels of operation should indicate that they typically operate on the downward-sloping portions of their LRAC curves, as explained in the previous section. But Joe Bain's study of twenty major, long-established manufacturing industries reveals that, except for a marginal fringe, the firms had reached a scale of plant and firm size great enough to allow lowest cost of operation, and many were well beyond the minimum necessary for low cost. Their positions are shown graphically in Figure 12-9. The maximum-profit price is represented by P_0. Typically, the rate of profit in these industries at actual price was higher than the figure regarded as an average rate of return for the economy as a whole.

FIGURE 12-9

Long-Run Equilibrium, Entry Restriction
With barriers to entry, oligopolists may earn excess profits in the long run. Theoretically, profit maximization occurs at P_0 and q_0. Empirical work, however, suggests that oligopolists actually charge a lower price than the profit-maximizing price (such as P_1). This strategy discourages entry and appears more equitable to consumers.

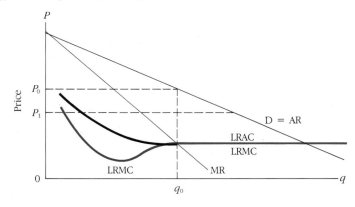

This phenomenon can be explained in two ways. First, firms may deliberately hold prices below the maximum-profit point (illustrated by P_1 being less than P_0 in Figure 12-9) as a means of discouraging newcomers from entering, or because of general acceptance of the idea of a "fair" profit rather than the maximum one. This attitude undoubtedly plays some role. Second, restriction of entry may prevent an increase in the number of firms. The profit rate in these industries suggests that this explanation is the primary one.

In examining entry barriers, the Bain study found three to be of primary importance:

1. Economies of large-scale production, which make operation on a small scale extremely unprofitable during a new firm's early years. A firm cannot build up a large market overnight; in the interim, cost per unit will be so high that losses will be heavy. Recognition of this feature discourages new firms from entering.

2. Product differentiation and established reputations, which make the development of an adequate market by new firms very slow and, particularly when coupled with the first restriction noted, may make entry almost impossible. Bain concludes that, on the whole, differentiation is more significant as a barrier than economies of large-scale production. Among the major features of differentiation noted are durability and complexity of product, which makes consumer appraisal of new brands difficult and leads to reliance on established reputation. A second is dealer relationships: exclusive dealerships and the reluctance of retailers to carry a large number of lines seriously impede the development of a new market. Finally, conspicuous consumption, the desire to be seen using the "popular" make or brand, plays some role.

3. The absolute magnitude of money capital required. The ability to obtain money capital depends primarily upon a satisfactory credit standing. New firms without an established credit position often have great difficulty obtaining necessary capital, even in periods when loan funds are generally plentiful. New businesses must be developed primarily with the capital of the promoters plus reinvested earnings; thus persons lacking adequate resources of their own find the establishment of a business extremely difficult, regardless of profit prospects and their own management abilities. This type of restriction is particularly serious for lines of production which require heavy initial capital investment, such as steel.

In addition, there are certain absolute restrictions to entry, found by Bain to be of little significance in the industries which he studied, but undoubtedly of greater importance in other sectors of the economy. These include:

a. Limited raw material supplies. When necessary specialized resources, such as ores of a certain type, are to be found only in limited areas and existing firms control the entire supply, it is impossible for new firms to commence operation. Entry into nickel production and diamond mining, for example, is severely restricted by this consideration.

b. Legal restrictions. Governmental activity may restrict entry of new firms. Patent rights may interfere with the ability of new firms to develop competing products. Trademarks protect various differentiation devices. Tariffs interfere with the entry of foreign competition into domestic markets. Cities may limit the numbers of certain types of enterprises (taverns, for example) or prevent peddlers from operating. Licensing requirements for various trades are often used to restrict numbers. The most severe legal restrictions are applied to public utilities, where new firms are not permitted to enter without approval of regulatory agencies and sanction is rarely given without substantial proof that existing service is inadequate.

Some of these legal restrictions are established in the interests of general welfare. Control of entry into public utilities might be necessary to prevent excess plant capacity and higher rates, for example. But many of the restrictions, such as most tariffs and many licensing requirements, result from the political activity of interested groups.

Common Costs and the Level of Average Cost

When a firm is producing several products and some of the costs are common, there is no determinate average cost for each product—that is, no average cost figure which price must cover in the long run and to which price will equal if there is completely free entry. The enterprise as a whole must cover common as well as separable costs; and with free entry, total receipts will equal costs for all products, including common costs and a necessary profit. Each particular product must sell for a price which covers its average separable costs (or the firm will cease producing it), but there is no necessary way in which common costs must be shared among the various products. In practice, some articles may carry more than a proportionate share of overhead and others less; yet it is advantageous for the firm to continue to produce items contributing relatively little to common cost, provided they make some contribution. The actual distribution of common costs among the firm's various products will depend primarily upon the techniques employed to allocate common costs, the nature of consumer demands for the various articles, and the extent of competition in various markets.

Elimination of Losses

Mutual interdependence among the various firms in an industry does not ensure that all firms can earn even an average rate of profit, since the number of firms may be so great relative to demand that at each possible output level average cost exceeds the price which can be obtained. There are two possible adjustments when losses are incurred. If price and output are not at the level where joint profits are maximized, increased cooperation may produce a sufficient increase in price to cover average cost. The NRA period of the 1930s was characterized by extensive activity of this sort, when for a short period such cooperation was not illegal. In the absence of greater cooperation, however, restoration of price to the average cost level necessitates the departure of some firms from the field. These are most likely to be the ones that fall behind in the race for customers. They may, however, be firms whose equipment wears out first or whose owners are most pessimistic about the future. As some firms leave the field, the increased sales volumes of remaining firms will allow them to cover cost (assuming that their average cost declines as they increase sales). Prices might not rise at all, as they would under similar circumstances in perfect competition, the losses being eliminated entirely by the decline in average cost of remaining firms.

Nonuniformity of Price

With differentiation, various sellers' prices are not likely to be uniform, even after long-run adjustments. Differentiation often involves deliberate quality differences designed to appeal to different income levels. As a consequence, both cost schedules and the height of demand schedules will differ. Even with outright price agreements, price differentials are almost essential if low-quality-product firms are to remain in business. In other situations, firms without established reputations must maintain lower prices if they are to continue to sell. Most of these sources of difference are not eliminated by the passage of time. Even when all firms in an industry are making a normal rate of profit, prices charged may vary substantially from one firm to another.

12.17 PURE OLIGOPOLY

The analysis in preceding sections rests upon the assumption that products are differentiated. Oligopoly may also be pure, exhibiting standardization of product. This is most closely approximated in markets for capital equipment, building materials, and other factors purchased by expert buyers to meet specific uses in production. Markets for lumber, cement, brick, railroad equipment, industrial machinery, steel, copper, and aluminum provide examples. Rarely, however, is differentiation completely absent, primarily because of differences in service, the personal relations between officials of various companies, and the efforts of sales representatives.

12-7 With all the different models of oligopoly—the joint profit maximization model, the kinked demand curve, the entry limit model, game theory, and so on—it appears that the theory of oligopoly is groping for firmer ground. What makes oligopoly theory so vague?

It is very difficult to predict how firms will react when there is mutual interdependence. No firm knows what its demand curve looks like with any degree of certainty; it thus has no idea about its marginal revenue curve. In order to know anything about the firm's demand curve, you must know how other firms will react to its price. Thus, equating expected MR and expected MC is relegated to guesswork, in the absence of additional assumptions.

With a standardized product, realization of mutual interdependence and tendency toward outright cooperation are greatly strengthened. With no differentiation, prices must be uniform, or the high-price firms will sell nothing. Accordingly, independent price determination on the part of each firm, with no attention paid to competitors' actions, would be suicidal, causing price fluctuations and frequent periods of losses as firms sought to increase sales by price reductions. Hence some type of coordinated action is imperative—much more so than with differentiation, in which each firm has an established clientele and quality differences lessen the severity of price competition. The forms that coordinated action may take are generally the same with standardized products as with differentiation. Price leadership or outright agreements are most likely, since the use of standard pricing techniques may not give the necessary degree of uniformity. Price agreements are of course illegal, but they nevertheless exist, their secret nature preventing effective enforcement of antitrust laws. Occasionally, upon the arrival of a newcomer into an industry or in a period of severe depression, when firms are anxious to increase sales, established pricing institutions break down, and a period of price competition ensues. But such action is not frequent.

The same considerations of price and output determination apply to pure oligopoly as to differentiated oligopoly, except that the greater degree of cooperation in the former may ensure closer attainment of maximum joint profits and temporary excess profits. Lack of differentiation makes the entry of new firms easier, but in many capital equipment industries the heavy capital investment and large volume of output necessary for low-cost operation constitute formidable obstacles to the free flow of firms into the field. (See Box 12-7.)

SUMMARY

1. Oligopoly involves a few firms, each controlling a large segment of the market. Product differentiation may or may not be important; the actions of rival firms are very important.

2. If the products in an oligopolistic industry are identical, this is called pure oligopoly. Price changes are extremely important to rivals in this type of market.

3. If the products are not identical, this is called differentiated oligopoly. In this type of market, prices will have a smaller impact on rival firms.

4. Spontaneous coordination may occur when a firm bases its decision on the expected actions of its competitors.

5. There are many obstacles to maximization of joint profit and attainment of complete oligopoly. Partial oligopoly, where joint profits are not maximized, is the general rule.

6. Most oligopolistic firms consider experimentation with price changes to be dangerous.

7. Oligopoly equilibrium resembles monopolistic competition; in the former, however, the firm is uncertain about the location of its demand and marginal revenue curves, the positions of which depend on pricing decisions of competitors.

8. Collusive oligopolies (cartels) can act much like a monopolist, though such oligopolies often break down when one of the price-fixing members cheats on the agreement in an attempt to enhance profits even further.

9. A most successful collusive oligopoly, the OPEC cartel, benefited from a price-inelastic demand for oil, an inelastic short-run supply of oil on the part of non-OPEC members, and a rising share of the international petroleum market.

10. Price leadership may lessen the uncertainty in oligopolistic industries.

11. The cost-plus, average-cost, or markup approach is computed by adding a markup that includes profits to the firm's direct costs.

12. Important barriers to entry may ensure long-run profits: economies of large-scale production, product differentiation and established reputations, the absolute magnitude of money capital required, limited raw material supplies, and legal restrictions.

WORDS AND CONCEPTS FOR REVIEW

pure oligopoly	collusive oligopoly
differentiated oligopoly	cartels
collusion	price leadership
spontaneous coordination	imitative pricing
complete oligopoly	cost-plus or markup approach
partial oligopoly	introductory pricing
kinked demand curve	game theory

REVIEW QUESTIONS

1. Distinguish between pure and differentiated oligopoly; collusion and spontaneous coordination; complete and partial oligopoly.

2. What are the requirements for establishing price and output at the maximum-joint-profit level?

3. Major obstacles to the attainment of maximum joint profit take what form?

4. What is the kinked demand curve model and why is the optimum price point at the level of the kink?

5. How does the average-cost approach to pricing differ from the MC = MR condition of profit maximization?

6. There is considerable empirical evidence that firms typically increase prices by the amount of an increase in excise or sales tax. Does this reaction suggest the use of an average-cost or an MC-MR approach to pricing? Explain.

7. What is the significance of the goal of maximizing sales revenue for price-output policy?

8. Suppose that entry into a particular oligopoly field is relatively easy. By what process do the excess profits tend to be eliminated?

9. If entry is free, will the oligopoly relationship break down? Discuss.

10. What are the major barriers to free entry?

11. What would appear to be the primary barriers to entry into the following industries in the United States?
(a) farm machinery production
(b) cement production
(c) bus operation

(d) soft drink production

(e) copper mining

(f) beer manufacture

(g) computer manufacture

12. What is the significance of the absence of differentiation for oligopoly behavior?

13. What factors made the OPEC cartel so successful in the past? What would this chapter suggest about the future of this cartel?

SUGGESTED READINGS

Adams, Walter. *The Structure of American Industry,* 7th ed. New York: Macmillan, 1986.

Bain, J. S. *Barriers to New Competition.* Cambridge, MA: Harvard University Press, 1956.

Okun, A. M. "Inflation: Its Mechanics and Welfare Costs." In *Brookings Papers on Economic Activity,* volume 2, 1975. Washington DC: The Brookings Institution, pp. 351–401.

Plott, C. R. "Industrial Organization Theory and Experimental Economics." *Journal of Economic Literature,* December 1982, pp. 1485–1527.

Scherer, F. M. *Industrial Market Structure and Economic Performance,* 2nd ed. Chicago: Rand McNally, 1980.

Stigler, G. J. "The Literature of Economics: The Case of the Kinked Demand Curve." *Economic Inquiry,* April 1978, pp. 185–204.

PART 3

Factor Price Determination

$$13$$

Theory of Factor Pricing

13.1 INTRODUCTION

Much of the analysis of the pricing of consumption goods is also applicable to the pricing of inputs into production called *factors*. However, because factor units are acquired by business firms for use in production rather than by individuals for the satisfaction of personal wants, the determinants of factor demand are different from those of demand for consumption goods. To be sure, the demand for factor inputs is derived indirectly from households' demand for goods. However, the links connecting demand for goods with factor demands are complex, in that a wide variety of different combinations of factor inputs and production technologies may be used. Moreover, the determinants of factor supply are significantly different from those of consumption goods, because factor units (other than capital goods) are supplied by individuals rather than by business firms.

This chapter will analyze the demand for factor inputs and develop some general principles of price determination that are broadly relevant for all kinds of factors. In subsequent chapters, these principles will be applied to particular types of factors: labor, land, capital goods, entrepreneurship, and money capital.

13.2 FACTOR PRICES AND INCOME DISTRIBUTION

In a market economy, the prices paid by producers for factor units constitute the primary source of income available to individuals for purchasing the output of industry. Accordingly, an explanation of factor prices not only completes the analysis of the functioning of the price system and the resource allocation mechanism but also provides an understanding of the forces that underlie the distribution of total income among various groups of factor owners. Wages, for example, are costs from the standpoint of producers but are incomes for the workers; wages give workers the means to buy consumption goods. Wage levels, therefore, not only affect costs, prices, and relative outputs of various goods, but also determine the share of national income received by workers, thereby affecting demand for goods. (See Box 13-1.)

13.3 FACTOR DEMAND

Assuming that the goal of the business firm is to maximize profits, **factor demand** is determined by the firm's desire to produce any given quantity of output at minimum total cost, and to choose that level of output at which total revenue exceeds total cost by the greatest margin. Thus there is a close relation between the theory of demand for individual factor inputs and the theory of production and cost developed in Chapters 7 and 8, and also a close relation between the demand for factors as a whole and the theory of output and price determination developed in Chapters 9–12.

The Basic Rule of Optimum Factor Use

The kernel of the theory of factor demand is contained in the general principle that *a firm will find it profitable to hire any factor unit that "pays for itself."* More precisely, it will be profitable for a firm to hire a factor unit if the addition to total cost resulting from its acquisition will be equaled *either* by an equivalent increase in total revenue *or* by an equivalent decrease in total outlay on other factor inputs. Here the precise meaning of the terms "addition to total cost" and "increase in total revenue" depends on the character of the markets in which factor inputs and the output of goods are traded and on the nature of the firm's production function. In order to develop the implications of the principle stated above, we must therefore first study the nature and significance of these background conditions.

13-1 Does the explanation of factor pricing provide a complete description of the manner in which individuals share in the national income?

Factor pricing tells us little about the manner in which property resources are distributed among individuals and thus about the way in which property incomes are shared by individuals. Likewise, it tells us nothing about nonmarket income transfers. Many persons share in the national income through the receipt of old-age pensions, aid to families with dependent children, federal scholarships, and other transfer payments even though they currently supply no factor units for use in production. Others lose portions of their incomes through tax payments or voluntarily relinquish funds by making gifts to charitable organizations. Description of the forces governing such transfers lies beyond the scope of the present volume, which analyzes factor pricing in order to provide a basic framework for explaining those aspects of income distribution that are market determined.

Average and Marginal Factor Cost

The costs that a firm seeks to minimize in producing a given level of output depend partly on the quantity purchased of each variable factor input and partly on the unit price or **average factor cost** (AFC) that the firm expects to pay for various kinds of factors. If the letters $V_1, \ldots, V_i, \ldots, V_n$ represent quantities of relevant inputs, and $W_1, \ldots, W_i, \ldots, W_n$ represent expected prices of these same inputs, then the total (variable) factor cost (TFC) corresponding to any given set of values of the price and input variables is defined by

$$\text{TFC} = W_1V_1 + W_2V_2 + \ldots + W_iV_i + \ldots + W_nV_n$$

The input quantities in this equation are, of course, decision variables for the firm—ones over which the firm has control—but the values of the average factor cost (price) variables will depend on numerous influences over which the firm has little or no control. In particular, if the input of factor i is purchased in a perfectly competitive market, then W_i will normally be regarded by the firm as fixed—equal to the prevailing market price of the factor. If the factor is purchased in an imperfectly competitive market, however, the value of W_i will depend partly on the quantity of the factor input that is purchased by the firm, as well as on the price at which the factor is currently selling.

In the perfectly competitive case, the addition to total cost or **marginal factor cost** (MFC) associated with a unit increase in purchases of a variable input will be equal to the market price of the factor; that is, marginal factor cost will be equal to average factor cost: MFC = AFC. Thus the "supply curve of the factor as seen by the firm"—the firm's *average factor cost curve*—will be represented by a horizontal line such as AFC ($= \text{MFC} = \underline{W}$) in Figure 13-1; the same line will also represent the firm's *marginal factor cost curve*.

In imperfect competition, MFC on a factor will differ from AFC. For example, if the firm is a *monopsonistic* (that is, exclusive) buyer of the factor (see Chapter 14), AFC will be an increasing function of quantity purchased, as illustrated by the curve AFC_1 in Figure 13-1, and the corresponding MFC curve (MFC_1 in the figure) will lie above AFC_1 at every position level of factor purchases. Alternatively, if the firm receives quantity discounts (calculated, for example, as a fixed percentage of some base price W_2), AFC will be a decreasing function of quantity purchased (AFC_2 in Figure 13-1), and the corresponding MFC curve (MFC_2) will lie below the AFC curve.

As will become clear later, imperfectly competitive conditions in factor markets create serious problems for the definition of factor demand functions. For the sake of simplicity and convenience, therefore, we shall proceed temporarily on the assumption that AFC curves are represented by horizontal lines, with identity of average factor cost and marginal factor cost. However, in order that our statement of general principles may be considered applicable to all cases, competitive or otherwise, we shall use the term "marginal factor cost" rather than "average factor cost" to refer to the expected addition to total cost resulting from the acquisition of one additional unit of a given factor input. Conclusions strictly valid *only* for the case of perfectly competitive factor markets will be so indicated explicitly.

FIGURE 13-1

"Competitive," "Monopsonistic," and "Quantity Discount" Average and Marginal Factor Cost Curve

In competitive input markets, the firm views the input price as given. Average factor cost, marginal factor cost, and factor price are equal, constant, and represented graphically by a horizontal line. In a monopsony, the factor price increases as the firm hires more of the factor. Marginal factor cost rises, average factor cost rises, and marginal factor cost exceeds average factor cost at all input levels. On the other hand, input price declines as factor employment rises when the firm has access to quantity discounts. The marginal factor cost curve lies below the average factor cost curve, and both curves decline throughout.

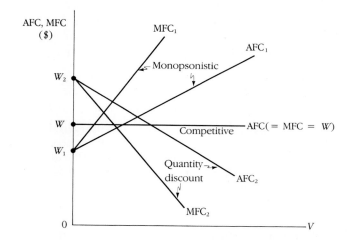

Average and Marginal Revenue Product

As in Chapter 7, we will assume that the firm's output is a given function of the variable factor inputs it uses:

$$q = f(V_1, \ldots, V_i, \ldots, V_n)$$

Hence the total revenue which the firm can expect to realize from using any given set of factor inputs indicated by the total revenue product relation

$$Pq = Pf(V_1, \ldots, V_i, \ldots, V_n)$$

The **average revenue product** (ARP) of any given factor input, say V_i, is then defined by

$$\mathrm{ARP}_i = \frac{Pq}{V_i}$$

—that is, total revenue product divided by the number of units of the factor unit being utilized (such as the dollar value of steel output per person-hour). This relation may be represented graphically (see Figure 13-2). by a curve of the same form as the average (physical) product curve described in Figure 7-1; the vertical coordinates of the ARP curve at any given level of input are those of the AP curve multiplied by the appropriate value of AR (price).

The addition of total revenue that the firm can expect to realize by purchasing and using an additional unit of any particular factor input is simply the marginal physical product (MPP) of the input (as defined by the production function) multiplied by marginal revenue (as defined by the firm's AR curve). In general, of course, AR will vary with the amount of product offered for sale, and so MR will differ from AR. For except in the case of perfect competition, we must distinguish between the price at which a firm expects to sell an additional unit of product and the prevailing price. In every instance, however, the addition to total revenue which concerns the firm when it is considering buying an *additional* unit of any factor input is described by the formula

$$MRP = MPP \cdot MR$$

For convenient reference, we shall call this concept the **marginal revenue product** (MRP) of the factor input. It should be noted that the MRP of one factor need not (and, except in unusual circumstances, will not) be equal to the MRP of another. Where we have to consider more than one MRP in the discussion that follows, we shall therefore

----

FIGURE 13-2

Equilibrium Purchases of a Factor Input Corresponding to Alternative Marginal Factor Cost Curves
A profit-maximizing firm hires units of an input until the marginal factor cost equals the marginal revenue product. The monopsonist employs V_1 amount of the factor, less than the amount hired under perfect competition, V, whereas quantity discounts enable greater employment of the input at V_2.

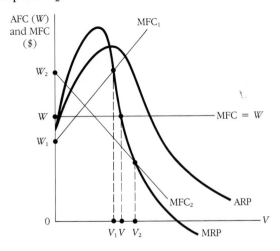

use appropriate subscripts to distinguish among different magnitudes; thus the MRP of factor "1" will be symbolized by MRP_1, the MRP of factor "2" by MRP_2, and so forth.

Cost Minimization and the Demand for Factor Inputs

For a firm to maximize profit, it must produce any given quantity of output with a least-cost combination of factor inputs. The implications of this condition for the theory of factor demand may be indicated most conveniently in terms of the isoquant and isocost diagram in Figure 13-3, which shows the production possibilities and total factor cost alternatives that are open to a firm for a given output (for example, $q = q^*$). As indicated in Chapter 7, the least-cost combination of factor inputs which can be used to produce the given output is defined by the tangency of the isocost curve C^* with the production isoquant q^*.[1] At such a point of tangency, the marginal rate of factor substitution is equal to the (negative) slope of the isocost curve:

---

[1] The isocost curves C_0, C_1, C_2, and so on are necessarily straight lines only if both factor inputs are purchased in competitive markets; that is, if marginal factor cost is identical to average factor cost for both inputs. If one or both markets are not perfectly competitive, the isocost curves will normally be convex or concave to the origin. Quite generally, however, the slope of an isocost curve at any point is measured by the ratio of the MFC of one factor to the MFC of the other at that point.

FIGURE 13-3

Optimal Input Purchase
The least-cost factor combination for output level q^*, V_A and V_S, is determined by the tangency of isoquant q^* and isocost line C^*. The marginal rate of factor substitution equals the slope of the isocost line which is the ratio of marginal factor costs of the two inputs.

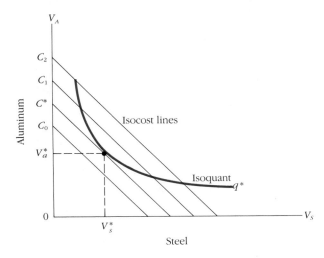

$$\frac{\Delta V_2}{\Delta V_1} = -\frac{MFC_1}{MFC_2}$$

But along the given isoquant, we know that any potential change in output associated with a change in input 2 of ΔV_2 is just offset by a simultaneous variation of ΔV_1 in input 1, so that total output does not in fact alter. The potential changes in output involved are simply the respective MPPs of the two factor inputs. Thus, along the given isoquant, we have

$$\Delta V_2 MPP_2 + \Delta V_1 MPP_1 = 0$$

or, rearranging terms,

$$\frac{\Delta V_2}{\Delta V_1} = -\frac{MPP_1}{MPP_2}$$

or, substituting and again rearranging terms,

$$\frac{MFC_1}{MPP_1} = \frac{MFC_2}{MPP_2} = MC$$

where MC is the common value of the two ratios. Now MC is the marginal factor cost on any factor input divided by the increase in total product associated with the use of the input, and this is the same as what we have earlier called marginal (production) cost. For example, if the cost of hiring one additional worker (MFC) to chop wood is $40 per day, and if his services lead to an increase in output of one-half cord of chopped wood per day (MPP), then the marginal cost of production of one cord of wood is $80. We therefore conclude that *at any least-cost combination of inputs, the firm's marginal factor cost on any factor unit must be equal to the MPP of the input multiplied by the marginal cost*; that is,

$$MFC_i = MC \cdot MPP_i \ (i = 1, \ldots, n)$$

Alternatively, we may say that *total cost will be at a minimum for a given level of output if and only if the marginal productivity of a dollar's worth of any one factor input is the same as the marginal productivity of a dollar's worth of any other factor input;*[2]

$$\frac{MPP_1}{MFC_1} = \frac{MPP_2}{MFC_2} = \frac{MPP_n}{MFC_n} = \frac{1}{MC}$$

---

[2]Note the similarity between this condition and the requirement in the theory of consumer demand (Chapter 5) that the marginal utility of a dollar's worth of one good be equal to the marginal utility of a dollar's worth of any other good.

It is the latter condition which underlies the earlier statement that a firm will find it profitable to hire a factor unit if the additional cost resulting from its acquisition can be offset by a larger or equivalent reduction in total factor cost on other factor inputs. The same condition tells us that it will be profitable to hire (or fire) any factor up to the point where marginal factor cost on the factor is equal to its MPP multiplied by MC. But we know from earlier chapters that *to maximize profit* a business firm must not only combine factor inputs in such a way as to produce any given output at minimum cost, but it must also choose a level of output at which marginal cost is equal to marginal revenue. Thus we arrive finally at the general rule that it will pay a firm to continue hiring any (or all) imputs up to the point where marginal factor cost on the factor is equal to its marginal physical productivity multiplied by marginal revenue; that is,

$$MFC_i = MPP_i \cdot MR \quad \text{where MC} = MR$$

Given the equilibrium condition $MFC_i = MPP_i \cdot MR$, it is a short step to the definition of factor demand functions. For the right-hand term of this condition is the marginal revenue product of a factor (MRP_i) as defined earlier; and the value of the left-hand term corresponding to any particular quantity of an input is given by the MFC curve for the input.[3] So we have only to describe the relation between the quantity of an input purchased and its MRP in order to determine the equilibrium input of the factor corresponding to any given MFC curve.

The Behavior of Marginal Revenue Product in the Short Run

Because plant capacity is given in a short-run period, the MRP of a factor may be expected (based on the theory of production outlined in Chapter 7) to rise initially and then fall. In terms of the assumptions made in the development of that theory, as units

---

[3]The text discussion to this point is simple to characterize formally. Considering that the revenue and cost functions can be written in terms of inputs, labor (L) and capital (K), rather than output, we have that profits (π) can be maximized as:

$$\text{Max}_{L,K} \, \pi = P(Q(L,K)) \cdot Q(L,K) - W(L_,) \cdot L - R(K) \cdot K$$

At a profit maximum, the slope of the "profit hill" with respect to both labor and capital will be zero. Looking only at labor (the condition for capital is exactly analogous) and employing the chain rule (composite function theorem) and the product rule, we have:

$$\left[\frac{dP(Q)}{dQ} \cdot \frac{\partial Q}{\partial L} \right] \cdot Q(L,K) + P(Q(L,K)) \cdot \frac{\partial Q}{\partial L} - \left[\frac{dW(L)}{dL} \cdot L + W(L) \right] = 0$$

Taking the negative term to the other side and rearranging

$$P \cdot \left[\frac{dP(Q)}{dQ} \cdot \frac{Q}{P} + 1 \right] \cdot \frac{\partial Q}{\partial L} = \frac{dW(L)}{dL} \cdot L + W(L)$$

The left side is marginal revenue times marginal product, while the right side is marginal factor cost. Note that with competitive input and output markets this expression simplifies to:

$$P \cdot \frac{\partial Q}{\partial L} = W$$

of a factor are first added, MRP rises because of more efficient utilization of both fixed and variable factor units; thus MRP will rise unless the price reductions necessary to sell the additional output in imperfectly competitive markets outweigh the effect of the rising physical product.

Beyond a certain point, however, and perhaps at a fairly early stage in the adding of units of the factor, MRP will diminish. Several forces are responsible for this behavior, the relative importance of which depends upon the nature of the production process and the type of market in which the firm is selling:

1. If the factor being added is substituted for other variable factors, a decreasing marginal rate of substitution between this factor and others will eventually be encountered; accordingly, beyond this point, the contribution of the additional factor units to net revenue consisting of reductions in costs of other factors will diminish (the marginal product of the factor being added depends on how much of the other factors are present).

2. If the additional factor units are used to increase output, MPP will eventually diminish. Since some factors are fixed in quantity in the short-run period, the addition of further units of other factors will eventually encounter the operation of the Law of Diminishing Returns. A very rapid decline in MPP may occur if the fixed factors are of such a nature that output cannot be increased significantly once all units have been brought into operation.

3. In imperfectly competitive market conditions, the price of the product must be reduced as greater quantities of output are placed on the market; thus, as additional factor units are added, MRP will decline, even if MPP remains constant, since the marginal revenue associated with the larger output is declining. If MPP is declining, MRP will decline at an even faster rate than MPP. The magnitude of the price reduction necessary to sell the increased output depends upon the elasticity of the firm's AR curve.

Long-Run Behavior of Marginal Revenue Product

Over a period of time long enough to allow the firm to adjust the quantities of all factors employed, the MRP of each factor will be substantially different from the period in which some factors are fixed in quantity, primarily because MPP will behave in a different manner. In general, however, in a long-run period as well as in a period in which plant capacity is given, MRP will initially increase and then diminish. The increase results from economies of large-scale production; increasing output initially involves the use of more efficient types of capital equipment and increased special-ization which increases the MPP of the factor. Eventually, however, just as in the short run but at a different level of output, MRP is likely to start falling. In part, the decline is due to the fall in MPP which occurs once decreasing returns to scale (due to problems of large-scale management) are encountered. In addition, just as in the short-run period, the diminishing marginal rate of substitution between this factor and others shifts the MPP down, the tendency of costs of other factors to rise as more units are acquired, and the necessity of reducing the price of the product to sell more units (except in perfectly competitive conditions) all cause MRP to fall.

An Individual Firm's Demand Schedule for a Factor

It is now possible to complete the explanation of the determination of optimum purchases of a factor by an individual firm—that is, to show what quantity of an input will be purchased by a profit-maximizing business firm corresponding to any given (short-run or long-run) MFC curve.

On the basis of the immediately preceding discussion, we may suppose that the relation between the input of a factor and its MRP takes a form such as that illustrated by the curve MRP in Figure 13-4.

Included in the same figure is the corresponding average revenue product curve, ARP (which is AR · AP). For reasons already indicated, these relations are similar in form to the AP and MP curves illustrated in Figure 7-2; the ordinates of each are, in fact, simply the ordinates of the earlier curves multiplied by appropriate value magnitudes (average revenue in the case of the ARP curve, marginal revenue in the case of the MRP curve).

Three alternative MFC functions were shown in Figure 13-2. Applying the rule that units of the factor will be hired up to the point where MFC = MRP, we conclude that V units will be hired (in equilibrium) if the relevant marginal outlay is MFC = W, V_1 units will be hired if the outlay curve is MFC_1, and V_2 units will be hired if the outlay curve is MFC_2.[4]

The effect of large firm size relative to input supply in driving up input prices in the factor market (marginal factor cost curve MFC) is apparently to reduce optimum purchases below the level that would be obtained under conditions of perfect competition. Similarly, the effect of quantity discounts MFC_2 is to increase optimum purchases as compared with the competitive level.

Assuming that equilibrium purchases of a factor corresponding to any given MFC curve are uniquely determined by the MRP curve of the factor, we can derive a demand schedule (or function) for each factor by varying MFC. The demand curve for a factor purchased in a perfectly competitive market, for example, will be identical to the portion of the MRP curve that lies on or below the ARP curve (see Figure 13-4), since in this case the position and form of the MFC curve are determined by a single parameter—namely, the market price of the factor. Only the lower portion of the MRP curve is relevant under competitive conditions, because at factor prices above the highest point on the ARP curve MRP > ARP, and profits are not maximized since the factor amounts involved cost more per unit than their yield in average revenue. This region corresponds to the first stage of production where firms will not wish to operate. At any price above the maximum point on the ARP curve, therefore, equilibrium pur-

---

[4]Technically, this would seem to assume that the marginal physical product of the input under consideration *does not shift* when different relative amounts of *other* inputs are used with various quantities of the input under consideration. That is, if the price of labor falls, one might use less capital if the substitution effect dominates the output and profit-maximizing effect; then with less capital the marginal product of labor might be expected to shift downward. However, these shifts could alternatively be thought of as being built into the MPP curve for the competitive case. This is the view implicitly being taken, for simplicity, in the text. If there is a *single* variable input, the distinction disappears. In footnote 3, this point is reflected in the fact that $\partial Q/\partial L$ is a function generally of the amount of capital present.

FIGURE 13-4

Marginal Revenue Product and the Demand for a Factor
The marginal revenue product curve on or below the average revenue product curve
defines the factor demand curve for a perfectly competitive firm. The equality of factor
price (marginal factor cost) and marginal revenue product ensures profit maximization.
When average revenue product is less than marginal revenue product, the cost of the
factor exceeds the revenues it generates and the firm purchases zero units of the input.

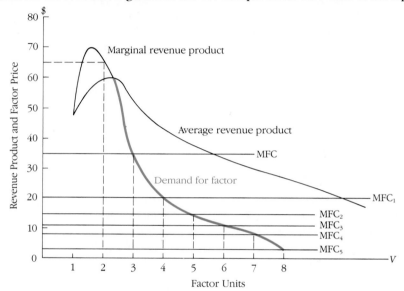

chases of the factor input are zero. (A factor demand schedule corresponding to the
MRP and ARP curves shown in Figure 13-4 is presented in Table 13-1.)

The demand schedule for a factor that is purchased in an imperfectly competitive
market cannot be defined so easily. If quantity discounts were available, we might
regard the base price from which discounts are calculated as a parameter (changes in
the value of which yield different MFC curves) and thus be able to define a corresponding factor demand function.

A firm's demand for any factor input depends then partly on the kind of market in
which the input is purchased (the MFC curve), partly on production possibilities (the
production function), and partly on the kind of market in which the firm's product is
sold (the MR curve). These various influences make it difficult to state any precise
conclusions about the nature of "typical" factor demand curves except that they will
invariably slope downwards from left to right. Some general comments about the
factors that determine the elasticity of a firm's demand for a factor can be made,
however, on the basis of earlier analysis. **Elasticity of factor demand** will be influenced by:

TABLE 13-1

Schedule of Average and Marginal Revenue Product of a Factor and Demand Schedule of the Firm for the Factor

	Revenue Schedule			Factor Demand Schedule	
Units of Factor	Average Revenue Product of Factor	Marginal Revenue Product of Factor		Price of Factor	Quantity of Factor Demanded
1	$47.50	$47.50		>$60.00	0
2	59.50	71.50		> 60.00	0
3	51.33	35.00		35.00	3
4	43.50	20.00		20.00	4
5	37.78	14.90		14.90	5
6	33.27	10.75		10.75	6
7	29.62	7.72		7.72	7
8	26.29	3.00		3.00	8

1. The rate of decline in the marginal rate of substitution between a given factor and all others—that is, the degree of curvature of production isoquants. For example, if steel and aluminum are good substitutes for one another in the production of a certain product, the producer's demand for either metal is likely to be fairly elastic. Any change in relative factor prices will cause substantial substitution of one metal for the other (that is, a significant shift in the point of tangency between the isocost curve and the equilibrium isoquant curve), with a substantial increase in purchases of the metal whose price has fallen.

2. The rate of decline in MPP when additional units of a factor are added to increase output. If the rate of decline is small, and additional factor units add almost as much as previous units to total physical product, small factor price declines will generate substantial increases in the quantity of the factor used (provided that the demand for the product is relatively elastic). If MPP drops sharply, additional factor units will contribute so little that they will not be added unless the factor price falls drastically. As previously indicated, the rate of decline in MPP is less over a longer period, when all factors can be adjusted, than in a shorter interval of time, when some factors are fixed in quantity.

3. The elasticity of the demand schedule for the firm's product. The smaller the reduction in price necessary to sell additional units of output, the greater will be the impact of factor price reductions on sales of the product and thus upon use of the factor. For example, the elasticity of a merchant's demand schedule for merchandise (an input) is controlled almost entirely by the elasticity of the demand schedule for the good. Substitution of this factor for others by the merchant is virtually impossible, and few important economies or diseconomies in the store's operation are likely to result from a change in the volume of one

product handled. Some variations in the rate of purchases compared to the rate of sales may result from the adjustment of inventory in anticipation of price changes, but these are of temporary significance only. (See Box 13-2.)

Changes in Factor Demand

Shifts in the demand schedules of business firms for factors are caused by:

1. *Technological change* that increases the substitutability of the factor with others or increases the MPP of the factor. New types of machinery which increase output per person-hour and per dollar of capital invested may raise the marginal product of both labor and capital goods.
2. *Changes in the prices of other factors.* An increase in the price of one factor will increase the demand for a factor that is easily substituted for it. Where two factors are not readily substitutable, the effect of an increase in the price of the first factor depends upon the relative strength of two opposite reactions. The higher price encourages substitution and an increase in the use of the second factor; the higher cost of the first factor encourages output reduction, which reduces the demand for all factors used by the firm. When factors are complementary, a rise in the price of one will reduce the demand for the other.

13-2   Indicate the effect upon the elasticity of demand for a factor under the following conditions:

a. A rapid decline in marginal physical product beyond a certain point.

b. Reduced elasticity of demand for the product of the firm, due to scarcity of substitutes.

c. Increased scarcity of materials used in conjunction with the particular factor.

a. If MPP of a factor falls rapidly, then the elasticity of demand with respect to the price of that factor will be low; inelastic demand follows from the fact that large price reductions will only result in small proportional increases of optimally-hired inputs, if their MPP falls rapidly with additional hires.

b. Considering the linear case, if the elasticity of demand falls at some initial price/quantity, then marginal revenue falls at a steeper rate over the same ranges of output—hence MRP will fall more rapidly and the elasticity of demand for the factor falls. The demands for inputs, it will be recalled, are *derived* from output demand.

c. As complementary inputs, their higher cost or lower availability will reduce demand for the factor under consideration: the marginal product of the factor will be lower than before the price rise.

Total Demand for a Factor[5]

The **total demand for a factor** can be precisely defined only if the factor is purchased in a perfectly competitive market. If so, the demand might appear to be defined as the sum of the demand schedules of all producers employing the factor. However, at factor prices other than the prevailing level, the total quantity demanded will in fact be different than it would appear to be on the basis of the existing individual schedules. That is, if the factor price changes, the quantity of the factor which each producer finds it profitable to employ at the new price will not be the same as the quantity that would have been employed at the new level had the change affected only the factor prices which one paid and not those that other firms paid. Suppose, for example, that the prevailing wage for a certain type of worker is $40 a day. If it falls to $36 a day for one firm but remains at $40 a day for competitors, the firm may increase its labor force 10 percent, as the lower labor cost allows it to reduce price and increase output. But if the wage rate falls to $36 a day for all firms in the industry, the firm may increase the labor force by only 2 percent; the reason, of course, if all firms expand inputs (hence outputs), price will certainly fall, lowering the MRP curve of each firm as they all expand.

On the whole, the total demand is likely to be much less elastic than it is for the typical individual firm, as shown in figure 13-5. In the first place, when all firms adjust output in response to a factor price change, the demand schedules for their products will be affected. If wages fall, for example, and each firm hires more workers and increases output, the demand schedule for each firm's products will fall because its competitors' prices are lowered. Thus, greater price reductions than those anticipated will be necessary to sell the additional output, schedules of MRP will be lower, and fewer additional workers will be hired. If perfect competition prevails in the market for the output, price will fall as soon as additional production comes on the market.

Second, the adjustment of output and factor purchases by all firms in response to a factor price change will alter the prices and optimal quantities of other factors and thereby modify MRP schedules to a greater extent than would an adjustment by one firm alone. For example, a reduction in the price of raw material A may cause substantial replacement of other materials by A. As a consequence, the prices of the other materials may fall, thereby lessening the substitution and the net increase in the use of factor A.

Third, increased factor employment in one industry due to a decline in factor price may be offset by consequent decreases in the use of the factor in other industries. Reduced wages in the brick industry, for example, might increase employment in that industry. However, the decline in brick prices resulting from the lower wages may increase the use of brick relative to that of lumber and reduce the demand for labor in the lumber industry.

---

[5]Attention is again called to use of the term *factor* in reference to a particular type of homogenous factor unit such as labor of a certain variety, not to broad factor groups such as labor of all types.

FIGURE 13-5

The Industry Demand Curve for Labor
The industry demand curve for labor, D, is less elastic than the sum of the firm labor demand curves, $\Sigma\, d_1$. If the wage falls from W_1 to W_2, each firm anticipates hiring more labor as a result of product price reductions. Total employment along $\Sigma\, d_1$ curve would rise to L_2. However, all firms (in attempting to hire and produce more) would collectively cause price and thus marginal revenue product to decline. The sum of firm labor demand curves shifts to the left to $\Sigma\, d_2$ as wage falls, leading to a smaller actual market factor demand increase, L_3.

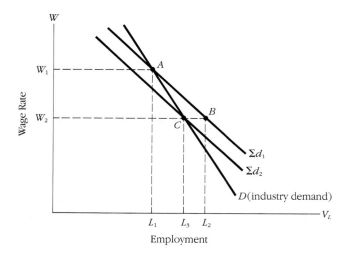

Finally, changes in factor prices may, by altering the pattern of income distribution, affect total spending as well as the composition of spending in the economy. This consideration is an element in macroeconomic theory, and so will not be considered further here. Changes in the composition of spending will themselves, however, affect factor returns.

The Marginal Revenue Product Principle and Business Policy

The principle that business firms adjust the quantity of each factor purchased to the level at which MFC = MRP follows as a matter of logical necessity from the assumption that firms seek to maximize profit. Actually, as previously indicated, this statement is merely a more precise way of expressing the rule that workers will be hired only if they will "pay for themselves." But actual attainment of the principle is obviously not always realized.

In the first place, as noted in earlier chapters, other motives besides profit maximization influence business decisions, and their pursuit may lead to departure from the MFC = MRP rule. If, for example, a firm temporarily determines output and price on the basis of "satisfactory" rather than maximum profits, output may be greater than the level at which MC = MR and the number of factor units acquired will be greater. The desire to avoid taking action which will appear to aggravate a depression may cause a firm to continue to employ more workers than the optimum number, if its finances permit. Or unprofitable expansions, involving the addition of factor units beyond the MFC = MRP figure, may be undertaken in an effort to build a greater business empire.

An analysis of producer demand built upon the assumption of profit maximization, although not entirely adequate because of the exceptions noted, is nevertheless more satisfactory in the present state of knowledge than one built upon any other assumption. (See Box 13-3.)

13.4 FACTOR SUPPLY

For a general theory of factor pricing, generalizations about factor supply must be very broad because of differences in the influences that affect supplies of particular factors.

A sharp distinction must be made between the determinants of the supply of capital goods and other produced inputs, on the one hand, and that of other factor inputs and money capital, on the other. Since capital goods are produced by business firms, the determinants of their output and supply are the same as those of consumption goods, as explained in preceding chapters. Costs of production thus play the dominant role. One difference, however, should be noted: Durable capital goods last over a period of time; once they have been produced, the quantity available is independent of cost of production. But over a period of time, cost is relevant, and plays an important role in the pricing of new capital goods coming on the market.

Other factors are not produced by business firms on a profit-making basis; hence cost of production (at least in the usual sense) has no relevance for supply. The supply depends on the number of units of the particular type of factor in existence at any time and on the willingness of factor owners to allow their factor units to be used in production.

13-3   Actual attainment of the goal of profit maximization in the hiring of inputs is obviously difficult. Why?

The determination of MRP with any degree of accuracy is an extremely difficult task. Often it is not even easy to determine the MPP of an additional factor unit (such as workers not directly involved in physical production). The firm's revenue schedule, knowledge of which is essential for determination of MRP, can at best only be estimated. The various determinants of marginal outlay and marginal revenue product—such as the prices of other factors, techniques of production, and demand schedules—are constantly changing. As a consequence of these difficulties, all a producer can hope to do is to approximate the MFC = MRP rule.

The nature of the supply schedule of the various types of factors will be considered in the next several chapters. One general statement, however, may be useful here. Decisions with regard to the supply of factor units are made by the owners of these units, who may have the option of utilizing the units advantageously to satisfy their own wants. A worker has the option of reserving time for leisure instead of making it available for use in production; an owner of money capital may gain the advantage of liquidity by holding onto the money. Thus there is the possibility of a **"backward-bending" supply curve**; that is, above certain price levels, owners may prefer to hold additional factor units to meet their own personal preferences for them, since those units they do make available will provide income which they regard as adequate. At lower prices for the factor units, owners would supply larger quantities in order to obtain as much money income from the factor units as possible. Thus the supply curve may appear as shown in Figure 13-6.

13.5 FACTOR PRICE DETERMINATION

Given the demand and supply schedules of each type of factor, the price of each factor will adjust to the level at which the quantity of the factor supplied is equal to the quantity demanded, under the assumption of perfect competition in the factor markets. Given the determinants of supply of each factor, at each possible price for the factor there are a certain number of factor units available for use. At each factor price, likewise, there is a certain quantity of the factor demanded—namely, the number which allows equality of MRP and MFC for each firm employing the particular type of factor. The actual price must adjust to the level at which the quantity demanded equals

---

FIGURE 13-6

Backward-Bending Factor Supply Curve
As the price of a factor rises initially, more may be offered for sale. Once the factor price reaches a certain point and factor owners obtain a particular income level, as factor price rises they may begin to offer fewer units for hire. Thus, the factor supply curve may be positively sloped for lower factor prices, becoming negatively sloped at higher prices.

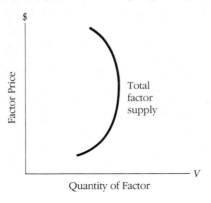

the quantity supplied, since at any higher level more units are available than firms wish to use, while at lower levels the factor price would be less than MRP for some firms, and the firms would seek to add more units. At the equilibrium figure the factor price must equal MRP for each firm, or the firms will seek to obtain either more factor units or less than the number they have, upsetting the equilibrium and causing a change in the factor price.

In other words, equality of MRP and MFC is attained because each firm adjusts the quantity of each factor employed until MRP is equal to the price paid for the factor. Once equality of supply and demand of the factor is attained, as it must be in a perfectly competitive market, the actual price of the factor will equal the MRP of the factor for each firm, with the available number of factor units employed. This explanation of factor price determination is known as the **Marginal Productivity Theory of Distribution** (of income).[6]

In equilibrium, the MRP of each factor will be the same in each use to which the factor is put, apart from the effects of imperfections arising out of difficulties in the calculation of MRP. Likewise, the ratios among the prices of various factors will be equal to marginal rates of substitution among them in all uses, since only this relationship allows the use of optimum factor combinations, and it is attained once each firm adjusts the quantity of each factor to the level at which the MRP = MFC. (See Box 13-4.)

---

[6]It was once argued that income distribution based upon marginal productivity was inherently "just," since each factor was paid according to its contributions to production. It is now recognized that such a conclusion was inappropriate. Justice in income distribution can be evaluated only in terms of a set of value judgments. (See the Chapter 21 on welfare economics.)

13-4 "The marginal revenue product of a factor depends upon the number of factor units used. But in order to know how many factor units to acquire, the firms must know the factor price. Therefore the argument that the factor price depends upon the marginal revenue product involves circular reasoning and explains nothing." Evaluate this argument.

There is no circularity; the confusion stems from *mixing* ideas about market equilibrium with the optimization decision of firms. These are essentially independent in competition. It is true that factor price depends on the interaction of supply and demand in the market for the factor under consideration. But that market demand depends negligibly on the decisions of any one firm—to each firm factor price is given. They then decide how much of the factor to buy given the MRP of the factor. Hence aggregated MRPs (along with factor supply) determine the factor price at which each firm will optimally hire. Everything is determined without circularity. There are, however, some logical traps associated with the simultaneity of the two processes—anything that makes one firm want to hire more of a factor will generally make *all* firms want to hire more. But the collective result will be a higher factor price, partially offsetting their initial desires.

13-5   Why do markets for labor services deviate significantly from conditions of perfect competition?

Before the development of labor unions, wages were sometimes dictated by employers; a very large number of small suppliers (workers) were selling their services to a relatively small number of employers, who exercised monopsonistic domination over wage levels. This situation is still found in some labor markets today. At a later date, the development of labor unions transformed many of the old monopsonistic markets into ones of bilateral oligopoly (oligopoly-oligopsony), in which wages are determined by direct bargaining between unions and employers or employer groups. As a consequence, explanation of wage levels on the basis of any general principles becomes difficult, as is always true with bilateral oligopoly. There is good reason to believe, however, that wage levels in such markets are different than they would be if set by supply and demand forces in a perfectly competitive market. Wages in nonunion industries are patterned to a large extent on union wage levels. An additional problem stems from human diversity and varying skill level. Labor inputs are not homogeneous in the same way that machines are.

Deviations from Perfect Competition

Markets for factors are characterized by substantial deviations from conditions of perfect competition. Probably the least deviation occurs in markets for money capital on a long-term basis, since both the numbers of lenders and the numbers of borrowers are large, the units are standardized, and the market is highly organized. As a consequence, long-term bond interest rates adjust on essentially a perfectly competitive basis. Some rates on short-term money capital, however, are determined in imperfectly competitive markets, with rates dominated by the principal lenders.

The market for land is characterized by a large number of local markets, with a small number of buyers and sellers in each. The average landlord has only one or a few pieces of land to rent and participates in lease transactions only on relatively rare occasions. Direct bargaining is thus significant in land-rent determination; collusive action among buyers or sellers is rare, however, and total supply/demand relationships still play a key role. The total land market is further broken up into small segments because many users prefer to buy land rather than rent it; accordingly, two distinct types of transactions occur. However, as will be explained later, land rents and land sale prices bear a definite relationship to one another. (See Box 13-5.)

SUMMARY

1. The determinants of factor demand are different from those of demand for consumption goods. With the exception of capital and other produced inputs, this is also true for factor supply.

2. In a market economy, prices paid by producers for factors are the primary source of income.

3. Factor price levels affect the costs and relative outputs of various goods; they also determine the share of national income received by persons.

4. Factor pricing does not tell us much about how any particular individual shares in the national income.

5. A firm will find it profitable to hire any factor unit that will "pay for itself."

6. Marginal factor costs will equal average factor costs only in the perfectly competitive case. If a firm is a monopsonistic buyer of the factor, average factor costs will be an increasing function of quantity purchased. If a firm receives quantity discounts, average factor costs will be a decreasing function of quantity purchased.

7. Except for the case of perfect competition, we must distinguish between the price at which a firm expects to sell an additional unit of product and the prevailing price.

8. At any least-cost combination of inputs, the firm's marginal factor costs on any factor unit must be equal to the marginal physical product of the input multiplied by marginal costs.

9. To maximize profits, the firm must combine factor inputs to produce a given output at minimum cost and choose a level of output at which MR = MC. Hence the general rule is that it will pay a firm to continue hiring any (or all) inputs up to the point where $MFC_i = MPP_i \cdot MR$.

10. In general, MPP will rise initially and then fall, both in the short-run period, when plant capacity is given, and in the long run.

11. A firm's demand for any factor input depends on the type of market where the input is purchased, the firm's production function, and the kind of market where the firm's product is sold.

12. The elasticity of the factor demand curve depends on the rate of decline of the marginal rate of substitution between a given factor and all others, the rate of decline in the MPP when additional units of a factor are added to increase output, and the elasticity of the demand schedule for the firm's product.

13. Major causes of shifts in the factor demand schedule include technological change and changes in the prices of other factors.

14. Total demand for a factor is likely to be much less elastic than that for the typical firm.

15. One reason it is difficult for firms to maximize profit is that the marginal revenue product is difficult to determine with any degree of accuracy. The reason is that it is difficult to determine the MPP of an additional factor, and the firm's revenue schedule can be only imprecisely estimated.

16. Factor supply (except in capital markets where cost of production is relevant to supply) depends on the number of units of the particular type of factor in existence and on the willingness of factor owners to allow their factor units to be used in production.

17. It is possible to have a backward-bending supply curve in factor markets. That is, above a certain price level, factor owners may prefer to hold additional factor units to meet their own personal preferences, especially for labor. At lower factor prices, larger quantities would be supplied in order to obtain sufficient factor income.

18. Under the assumptions of perfect competition, given the total supply and demand curve for each factor, the price of each factor will adjust to the level at which the quantity of the factor supplied is equal to the quantity demanded.

19. Markets for factors are characterized by substantial deviations from perfect competition. This is particularly true in the market for labor services.

WORDS AND CONCEPTS FOR REVIEW

factor prices and the
  distribution of income
factor demand
rule of optimal factor use
average factor cost
marginal factor cost
average revenue product
marginal revenue product

elasticity of factor demand
total demand for a factor
factor supply
backward-bending factor supply curve
factor price determination
Marginal Productivity Theory of
  Distribution

REVIEW QUESTIONS

1. Why is it necessary to have a separate analysis of factor pricing, distinct from that of the pricing of consumption goods?

2. Why is the theory of factor pricing often called the theory of income distribution?

3. Under what circumstances does marginal outlay on a factor exceed the price paid for the factor? Under what circumstances is the former less than the latter?

4. What is marginal physical product? Average revenue product? Marginal revenue product?

5. Under what circumstances is:
(a) Marginal revenue product less than average revenue product?
(b) Marginal revenue product zero, yet average revenue product positive?

6. Complete the table.

Units of Factor	Total Output	Marginal Physical Product	Price of Product	Total Revenue	Marginal Revenue Product	Average Revenue Product
1	40	———	$1.40	———	———	———
2	90	———	1.35	———	———	———
3	130	———	1.30	———	———	———
4	150	———	1.25	———	———	———
5	165	———	1.20	———	———	———
6	172	———	1.15	———	———	———
7	175	———	1.10	———	———	———

7. With a given plant, why does MRP decline as units of the factor are added, beyond a certain point? Why will the rate of decline be faster if the industry is one of imperfectly competitive conditions than if it is perfectly competitive (other conditions being the same)?

8. Construct a demand schedule for the factor for which the product data are given in Question 6, above.

9. Plot MRP and ARP data from Question 6, and join the points to represent the firm's demand curve for the factor.

10. Why, if it wishes to maximize profits, will a competitive firm increase the number of units of a factor used up to the point at which the MFC on the factor is equal to the MRP?

11. If marginal factor cost exceeds the factor price, will the firm acquire more or fewer units with a given schedule of productivity than if MFC is flat? Why?

12. What will be the effect upon the demand for a factor of:
(a) Increased substitutability of this factor for others?
(b) A decline in demand for the product of the industry?
(c) Increased prices of other factors?

13. Why is the total demand for a factor likely to be less elastic than the demand for the factor by any one firm?

14. Why, in practice, might firms not always add factor units up to the point at which the marginal revenue product of the factor is equal to marginal factor cost on the factor?

15. What is the difference between the determinants of the supply of capital and other produced inputs and those of other types of factors?

16. How do you determine the price of a certain type of factor, under the assumption of a perfectly competitive market for the factor?

17. Why, under competitive assumptions, must the equilibrium factor price equal the marginal revenue product of the factor?

18. How can the statement that the equilibrium factor price is equal to the marginal revenue product have precise meaning, when the marginal revenue product varies with the number of factor units employed?

SUGGESTED READINGS

Baumol, W. J. *Economic Theory and Operations Analysis*. 4th ed. Englewood Cliffs, N.J.: Prentice-Hall, 1977, Chapter 24.

Bishop, Robert L. "A Firm's Short-Run and Long-Run Demands for a Factor." *Western Economic Journal*, volume 5 (March 1967), pp. 122–40.

Bronfenbrenner, Martin. *Income Distribution Theory*. Chicago: Aldine, 1971.

Kaldor, Nicholas. "Alternative Theories of Distribution." *Review of Economic Studies*, Vol 23, no. 2 (1955–56).

APPENDIX   TWO OVERALL QUESTIONS OF FACTOR PRICING

The Adding-Up Problem: Euler's Theorem

An issue discussed at length in past decades was whether producers' entire revenue from the sale of goods would be paid out to factor suppliers if the price paid for each factor unit were equal to the MRP of the factor, or whether there could be something "left over" as a source of exploitative return for the owners of the business. Or, to consider yet a third possibility, could total revenue from the sale of the product be inadequate to allow all factor suppliers to receive prices equal to MRP? A rule known as Euler's Theorem shows that with a linear and homogeneous production function, total physical product will be exactly equal to the sums of the MPPs of the various factors multiplied by the amounts of each factor used:

$$q = V_1\text{MPP}_1 + V_2\text{MPP}_2 + \ldots + V_n\text{MPP}_n$$

From this identity, it appears that payment of each factor according to the competitive rule MRP = MFC = AFC would imply a set of factor payments that precisely exhausted the total value product. For if we multiply both sides of Euler's identity by the market price of the product P and set P = MR and $\text{MPP}_i \cdot \text{MR} = \text{MRP}_i$, we obtain

$$\text{Total Revenue} = Pq = V_1\text{MRP}_1 + V_2\text{MRP}_2 + \ldots + V_n\text{MRP}_n$$

So if price of each input is equal to its MRP (that is, if each input is hired up to the point where $\text{MFC}_i = W_i = \text{MRP}_i$), we have

$$Pq = W_1V_1 + W_2V_2 + \ldots + W_nV_n$$

and thus the desired "exhaustion of value product" identity.

If factor units were paid less than their MRPs, or if production functions displayed decreasing rather than constant returns to scale, then by similar reasoning it would appear that product would fail to be exhausted; a surplus would be appropriated by entrepreneurs as "rent on institutional advantage" or "gain from monopsonistic exploitation." Alternatively, if production functions displayed increasing returns to scale and factors were paid their MRPs, value product would appear to be more than exhausted; at every positive level of output, average product would be less than marginal product; hence MRP would exceed ARP and no firm could undertake production except at a loss.

Actually, the problems posed by these considerations are of no practical significance. If demand conditions are sufficiently favorable, businesses can earn large profits in a perfectly competitive industry even if MRPs are invariably greater than ARPs, for it is only in a state of competitive equilibrium that questions of revenue and cost can be settled by looking at given ARP and MRP curves. In other than competitive conditions, disequilibrium situations (and so "excess" profits) may easily prevail in practice over indefinitely long intervals of time. It is neither useful nor meaningful, therefore, to attempt to "explain" observed distributive shares by reference to static production possibilities and static revenue and cost relationships. Profits, losses, and distributive shares can be analyzed satisfactorily only in terms of dynamic exit and entry considerations and related market demand and output conditions, following procedures such as those used in our earlier account of short- and long-run adjustments in various kinds of market situations (see Chapters 9–12).

Long-Run Trends in Labor's Share of Output and the Cobb-Douglas Production Function

Time-series data on the distribution of total real income in the United States between "labor" and "capital" indicate that the share of "labor" has been relatively constant over the past 85 years, accounting for some 70–85 percent of total real income (the precise figure depending on what is included in the category of "wage, salary, and other labor income"). Numerous efforts have been made to explain this phenomenon—most of them provocative, but none entirely satisfactory. Perhaps the most notable attempt was that of Paul H. Douglas and C. D. Cobb,[7] who sought an explanation by assuming that the total output of the economy at any given date could

---

[7]See Paul Douglas, *The Theory of Wages* (New York: Macmillan, 1934).

be predicted by inserting appropriate values for labor (L) and capital (K) into an aggregate production function of the form

$$Y = kL^a K^{(1-a)}$$

where Y denotes aggregate real income (product), k and a are given constants, and a is less than unity. It can be shown that this relation, now known as a "Cobb-Douglas production function," implies that the shares of labor and capital will be constant at a and $1 - a$. When Cobb and Douglas first fitted their equation to aggregate time-series data, the points defined by the data clustered closely about the graph of the relation and implied a value for a (labor's share) of about .75 (75 percent).

Like most early empirical studies, that of Cobb and Douglas did not stand up well to later scrutiny. Subsequent attempts to fit a Cobb-Douglas function to more refined time-series data suggested that the constant term should be regarded as an increasing function of historical time, a conclusion that was interpreted to indicate that "technical progress" occurred more or less steadily in the years following 1890. The assumption raised the problem of identifying more precisely the factors responsible for technical progress and clarifying various other ambiguities inherent in the use of aggregate production functions of any variety—for example, how one might arrive at meaningful measures of "capital," "labor," and "aggregate output" in a world where the quantity and quality of all kinds of goods and services are in a constant state of flux. If (as seems inevitable) all aggregate magnitudes must be measured in dollar units, what significance can be attached to a "technological relation" among the various magnitudes such as the Cobb-Douglas production function entails? Results from investigations completed up to now provide little grounds to hope that either of these issues will be well resolved.

14

The Pricing
of Labor Services

14.1 INTRODUCTION

From a formal point of view, markets for labor services are much like markets for personal loans. Workers do not sell themselves; they sell an employment contract that obligates them to deliver a specified period of time in exchange for a series of one or more payments of money wages by the holder of the contract (the employer). An employment contract typically is not negotiable. The buyer (the firm) of such a contract purchases it in the hope that the seller (the worker) will deliver exactly what he or she has promised; but if the seller misbehaves (say by failing to report for work), the contract effectively becomes worthless (unless a court decides otherwise). Unlike consumer goods and capital goods, therefore, markets for labor services are seldom highly organized. Individuals effectively must negotiate the sale of their own "products" (employment contracts), though in many (perhaps most) cases the negotiation process is facilitated by some kind of "broker" such as the firm's personnel department, an employment agency, or a trade union.

14.2 WAGE DETERMINATION UNDER COMPETITIVE CONDITIONS

Let us begin by supposing (contrary to fact) that markets for labor services were perfectly competitive. This procedure allows us to obtain some results that are interesting in their own right but are useful mainly in providing a benchmark against which to compare other conclusions derived from more realistic assumptions.

The Determinants of Aggregate Labor Supply

Labor services differ from other factor services in two primary respects: workers are not produced on a profit-making basis, and the provision of labor services requires the direct participation of human beings. Thus personal preferences between working and leisure as well as personal attitudes towards working conditions significantly influence supply conditions. Accordingly, the determinants of the overall supply of labor available to the economy at any particular time include:

1. The total population capable of working.
2. Institutional factors governing the size of the labor force, such as educational requirements, minimum age and wage legislation, compulsory retirement, and attitudes toward female workers. For example, if two countries of equal population and similar age distribution are compared, one in which women work and the other a Moslem country where wives do not engage in labor outside the home, the market supply of labor will be much greater in the former than in the latter.
3. Preferences for work as compared with leisure. There are only so many hours in a lifetime, and some of these are devoted to sleep and leisure rather than to work. Social customs and physiological requirements limit an individual's freedom of choice among the three alternatives, but much scope remains for individuals to decide for themselves the proportion of total time available for each activity.

Given these considerations, what is the nature of the overall supply function of labor? Wage changes may lure additional supplies into the labor market in one of two ways: (1) by causing existing workers to work more hours per week—by working longer workdays, working on weekends, forgoing vacations, and so on—or (2) by luring into the labor market persons who would otherwise not work. These include persons who are able to subsist on nonlabor income or by dependency upon others—children, retired persons, spouses, and so forth.

If wage changes have some effect on the labor supply, what is the nature of the functional relationship? Will the quantity of labor supplied be greater at high wages than at low (as is true of the supply schedules of goods), or not? (Rules applicable to goods do not necessarily apply to labor, because workers have another use for their time—namely, leisure, an alternative not usually available to suppliers of goods.) The answer is by no means obvious, since there are two conflicting effects:

1. **The substitution effect:** when higher wages are offered, the cost of forgoing labor time to gain greater leisure time becomes greater; thus there will be a tendency to substitute labor for leisure. In other words, higher wages make leisure more expensive—its opportunity cost rises.
2. **The income effect:** at higher wage levels, the income from a given quantity of labor is greater; thus the worker may feel that he or she can afford more leisure; leisure is expected to be a normal good, more being demanded and at a higher income.

Since these forces operate in opposite directions, it is not possible to say what their net effect is, and thus to define the nature of the aggregate supply schedule of labor. This is basically an empirical question that cannot be answered by deductive analysis. On the basis of available evidence, we can make several observations:

1. Most households must obtain wage income in order to maintain desired living standards; therefore at least one family member will ordinarily enter the labor market regardless of the wage rate. This consideration is a force tending to make the schedule relatively inelastic.

2. Because of the requirements of modern production, most persons have relatively little control over hours worked. This is particularly true in manufacturing, where efficient production does not permit individual variance. This "all or nothing" consideration also tends to produce inelasticity in the schedule.

3. Some variations in hours are possible through working overtime, moonlighting, and deferring retirement. Moreover, other members of the household may enter or leave the labor market at various times.

4. The portion of the schedule at relatively low wage rates is likely to be positively inclined, higher wages bringing forth additional labor hours. With wage rates very low, however, workers may not find it worthwhile to work overtime; and other family members may not find it worthwhile to enter the labor market, especially in view of the fact that doing so will often result in additional costs for clothing, transportation, child care, and other expenses.

5. The upper portion of the schedule is more likely to show a negative relationship. As wages reach relatively high levels, people will feel that they can afford additional leisure, since they can do so and yet maintain a relatively high standard of consumption. Thus they will refuse overtime, and will take more time off, and other family members may quit work.

6. The precise nature of the schedule is obviously affected by general cultural patterns and goals. If maximization of income is of paramount importance, higher wages will bring forth additional labor hours. If the primary goal is maintenance of a given standard of living, the reverse will be true: as wages rise, persons will work fewer hours in order to maintain the same living standard.

As a consequence of these considerations, it is generally presumed that the supply curve of labor as a whole is first upward sloping, then backward sloping, as illustrated by the curve *SS* in Figure 14-1. This is merely a presumption, however, for the evidence supporting this conception of the aggregate labor supply function at a point in time is limited and by no means conclusive.

How can we show how much an *individual* will be willing to work at different real wages? To establish an individual's supply curve for labor, we may use indifference curves, placing for example daily income on the vertical axis and hours of leisure per day on the horizontal axis.

Figure 14-2 depicts an individual's preferences between income (assuming for simplicity that all income comes from wages) and leisure.

Higher wages (hence income) can entice someone to give up some leisure for more work, as shown in the movement from L_1 to L_2. This movement is comprised of an income effect and a substitution effect. Recalling consumer theory (Chapter 5), we know that the shape of the indifference curve represents the individual's trade-off between income and leisure.

FIGURE 14-1

Aggregate Labor Supply Curve
The aggregate labor supply curve—the schedule of labor hours supplied from the total populus at different wage rates—bends back if all individual labor supply curves (including those of the nonworking population) turn back at similar wage levels. Generally, the aggregate labor supply curve slopes upward throughout.

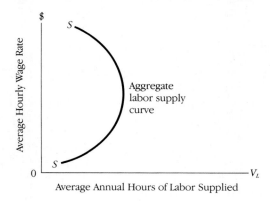

FIGURE 14-2

Preferences between Income and Leisure
The indifference curves chart the combinations of income and leisure that give the individual the same degree of satisfaction. The budget line shows the amounts of leisure and income the consumer can afford, given his or her daily income. The horizontal intercept (the hours of leisure if income is zero) is 24 hours per day; the vertical intercept (income earned with no leisure) is 24 times the hourly wage. The absolute value of the slope of the budget line is the hourly wage. The tangency of the indifference curve and budget line identifies the optimum amount of income y_1, leisure L_1, and work hours ($24 - L_1$). When the wage rises, the budget line becomes steeper and the individual consumes less leisure at L_2 and works more hours.

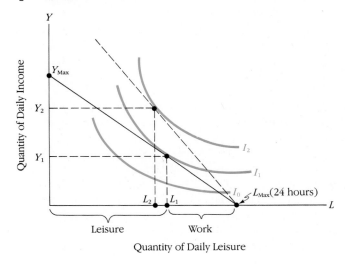

Figure 14-3 shows real wages rising, causing "potential" income (if zero leisure were bought) to rise from y' to y'' and then to y'''.

As real wages (the slope of the budget constraint in Figure 14-3) rise, the individual again trades some leisure ($L_1 - L_2$) for additional income ($y_2 - y_1$); in this case the substitution effect dominates the income effect. However, if real wages were to continue to climb (reflected by ever steeper budget constraints), this individual might cut back on the amount of work per day, presumably because he or she now feels wealthier and is in a position to demand more leisure. In this range the income effect dominates the substitution effect, as shown in Figure 14-3.

Figure 14-4 summarizes these changes in a conventional labor supply curve diagram. This one happens to be backward bending like the aggregate labor supply curve depicted in Figure 14-1. (See Box 14-1.)

Further understanding of the labor supply decision might be provided by historical study of the relationship between changes in wage levels and changes in the average workweek. One such study for the United States showed that as wages rose between 1900 and 1957, the average workweek declined approximately 2.5 percent for each 10 percent increase in wage rates.[1] Similarly, recent years have seen more three-day

---

[1] See A. C. Harberger, "Taxation, Resource Allocation and Welfare," in *The Role of Direct and Indirect Taxes in the Federal Revenue System* (Princeton, NJ: Princeton University Press, 1964), pp. 45–50.

FIGURE 14-3

Preferences between Income and Leisure as Real Wages Rise
The first wage increase rotates the budget line from y' to y''. The worker chooses to reduce leisure hours and increase work effort. Thus, the substitution effect dominates the income effect from a to b. A second pay raise pivots the budget line to y''', raising leisure hours to L_3 and reducing optimum work hours from b to c. In this case, the income effect overwhelms the substitution effect.

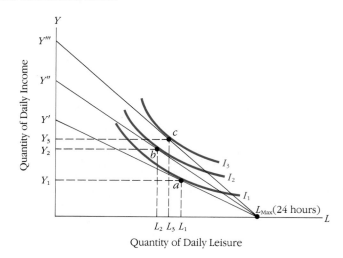

Quantity of Daily Leisure

FIGURE 14-4

Conventional Labor Supply Curve
This individual's labor supply curve is derived from the preference mapping in Figure 14-3. The original wage rate, W_1, is the slope of budget line y'. The person is willing to work $24 - L_1$ hours at that wage rate. When the wage rate rises to W_2, more work hours $(24 - L_2)$ are offered, but an additional pay increase reduces optimal labor hours to $24 - L_3$. Hence, a backward-bending supply curve arises from a dominating substitution effect at low wage levels and a dominating income effect at higher wage levels.

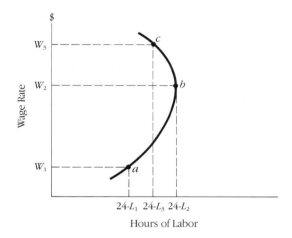

weekends and longer vacations. This might be taken to indicate that labor preferred to take a portion of its gain in greater leisure. Too much weight should not be attached to this conclusion, however, for the period studied was one of great social upheaval; it is entirely possible that average hours worked might have declined even more than they did if wage rates had remained constant! When historical data indicate that variation in two quantities are closely correlated, it is always tempting to argue that variations in one quantity cause variations in the other. Except in cases where environmental and

14-1   If all individuals have backward-bending labor supply curves, does this imply that the labor supply curve to a particular industry or occupation is also backward bending?

No, not at all. While each individual may, above a certain wage (which will depend on the individual), supply *less* labor of a given skill at progressively higher wages, this will be *extremely* unlikely for any particular industry or occupation. As the wage rises within that industry or occupation, labor is attracted to it from other industries and from similar occupations. We may not wish to work *more* at higher wages, but we all want higher wages for the same work! This results in observed labor supply curves of the usual, upward-sloping type.

other background conditions can be shown to be either constant or irrelevant, however, this temptation should be resisted. By and large, it is safe to draw causal conclusions from historical data only when they are supported by other, more compelling evidence.

Supply of Labor of Particular Types

Labor is not homogeneous. The aggregate supply consists of a pattern of supplies of workers of various skills and training. The schedule for any particular type of labor—clerical workers, mechanics, carpenters, and so on—is typically more elastic than the overall supply because of the possibility of workers shifting from one occupation to another. Such transfers depend upon the degree of skill required, the number of persons in other occupations who possess relevant skills, the extent to which seniority and pension rights restrict mobility, and the importance of prestige and other non-monetary considerations in various types of employment.

The supply of any particular type of labor is more elastic over a long period of time than in the short run because, given time, additional persons can gain necessary training and skills. New workers will more readily enter fields in which labor is relatively scarce and wage rates are correspondingly attractive. On the whole, however, regardless of the time period, the possibility of shifting occupations creates a positive relationship between the wage rate and the quantity of labor supplied. Thus if work/leisure considerations for a particular type of labor also produce a positive relationship, the combined effect of the two influences is sure to be positive. Higher wage rates will not only lure workers from other occupations but will also induce additional persons to work or existing workers to work longer hours. If the work/leisure relationship produces a negative effect, however, the net influence will depend on the relative strength of the two conflicting forces. (See Box 14-2.)

Demand Considerations

The **aggregate demand for labor** depends upon the relationship between wage rates and the marginal revenue product (MRP) of labor in the same fashion as the demand for any factor. The aggregate demand consists of a large number of demand

---

14-2   How might the supply of labor facing an individual firm differ from that of the labor force?

While a firm's labor supply curve is quite elastic, the entire labor force supplies labor inelastically, as already indicated. For example, publishing firms might be able to attract additional employees from other industries by offering a slightly higher wage. Other things equal, people will always wish to leave lower-paying jobs for higher-paying jobs even if skill levels are somewhat different. However, this does not affect the labor supply curve for the whole economy. The decision to work or not and how many hours to work will not be as much affected by wages as will the decision of *where* to work which will in some cases involve new skills or training.

schedules for particular types of labor. For each type, an employer will hire workers up to the point at which the MRP of the additional worker is equal to the marginal factor cost on the worker, the latter figure being equal to the wage rate if the market for labor is perfectly competitive.

The elasticity of demand for each type of labor depends upon the rate of decline in MRP of the particular type of labor. The rate of decline is in turn controlled by the nature of the production function, the substitutability of labor for other factors, and the elasticity of demand for the product.

Elasticity will be less to the extent that

1. The nature of production is such that once existing capital equipment is brought into use, additional workers will add little to physical output.
2. Demand for the industry's product is relatively inelastic.
3. Employers cannot easily ascertain MRP of successive workers and thus can only roughly estimate the optimum number. In this case a change in the wage rate may not lead to any change in the quantity of labor services demanded.

On the basis of these considerations, it is commonly argued that the demand for labor is relatively inelastic—that wage reductions will not significantly affect the number of jobs available. This is an empirical generalization, however, for which there is little convincing evidence.

Over a long period of time, the elasticity of demand for labor will obviously be greater, since the quantity of capital and other resources can be altered, as can the quality of capital equipment; thus sharp declines in MRP resulting from the Law of Diminishing Returns can be avoided.

Perfectly Competitive Wage Levels

If labor markets were perfectly competitive, the wages of each type of labor would tend to come to a level at which the demand for and supply of the particular type of labor were equal. Since the demand schedules are dependent upon MRP (each employer hiring workers up to the level at which MRP is equal to the wage rate), the equilibrium wage for each type of labor would be equal to the MRP of that type of labor, with the quantity of the particular type of labor available at this wage rate fully employed. If the wage level were temporarily higher, the number of workers available would exceed the number that employers wished to hire at that wage rate; wages would decline as workers sought the higher-wage jobs and offered to work for somewhat lower wages. If wages were temporarily below the equilibrium figure, employers would seek to hire more workers than were available; they would compete against each other for additional workers and thus bid the wage up toward the equilibrium level.

The equilibrium is illustrated in Figure 14-5. The analysis is based on the following assumptions:

1. Perfect competition in the labor market, and thus the absence of labor unions, on the one hand, and monopsonistic domination of wages by the employer, on the other.

2. Productivity of workers independent of the wage rates paid.
3. Positive-sloping supply curve for labor.
4. Given general price level of goods (thus a change in money wages entails a similar change in real wages).[2]

The assumption of perfect competition is only roughly applicable, of course, in most labor markets. Failure of the second and third assumptions to be realized in particular cases makes possible more than one equilibrium position. If wage increases lead to greater productivity, for example, by allowing workers to maintain a better level of health and efficiency and by raising morale, there may be a range of values of wage rates at which demand equals supply. Within this range, an increase in wages will be accompanied by an increase in MRP, and the new equilibrium wage may be as satisfactory as the old.

Occupational Wage Differentials

As indicated by empirical observations, wages paid for different types of labor vary widely. The differentials at any time will depend on supply and demand conditions for

---

[2]We are implicitly assuming a given total demand for goods, independent of wage rates paid. That is, no macroeconomic aggregate demand problems exist which affect marginal revenue products of particular goods.

FIGURE 14-5
Equilibrium Wage Level for a Particular Occupation,
Perfectly Competitive Labor Market
In perfect competition, the intersection of the aggregate labor demand and supply curves identifies the equilibrium wage rate for a particular type of labor. Wage rates higher than W_0 create unemployment and downward pressure on the wage. If the wage falls short of W_0, there will be a shortage and wages will be bid up by firms. The labor market for each occupation is at full employment in competitive equilibrium.

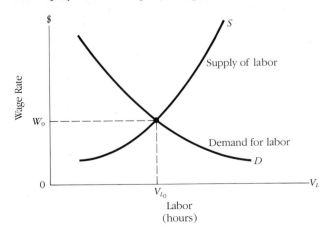

various types of labor (hence on relative MRP figures in different occupations). The strength of the tendency toward a lessening of inequality depends upon the mobility of labor. At any given time, wages will be relatively high in occupations where supply is limited relative to demand and MRP is correspondingly high. The inability of other persons to move into the occupation allows the high wage rate to continue for a period of time. Wages cannot remain relatively high in a field in which immediate entry of large numbers of workers is possible. Entry is, however, often restricted in practice (for example, by formal licensing requirements, by educational qualifications, or by trade union membership rules).

Over a period of time, workers tend to flow toward those occupations offering the greatest advantages relative to the costs of entering them, considering both monetary and nonmonetary factors. Certain occupations require longer periods of training than others, and wage levels must remain sufficiently high in them to induce persons to undertake the added training. Some occupations have greater nonmonetary advantages than others, including prestige, comfort of work, or regularity of employment. At equal wage rates, workers would prefer these to other occupations, and differentials in money wages must remain in order to balance supplies of workers in various occupations with demand for them. Under the assumptions of perfect competition, relative wages will eventually adjust to levels at which wage differentials just compensate for higher costs of training and the monetary values of nonwage differences, so long as entry into occupations is not restricted by lack of sufficient numbers of persons with the appropriate skills to perform the work involved. If there are such restrictions, scarcity of particular types of workers will sustain a higher wage differential than would exist on the basis of different training costs and the like. If the assumptions of perfect knowledge and mobility are dropped, adjustments will occur slowly and may not be complete, but the basic pattern of behavior will be much the same as already suggested. (See Box 14-3.)

Geographical Wage Differences

Distinct from the occupational wage differentials are those among workers in a given occupation in different areas. For almost any type of labor, the labor market is not nationwide but covers a limited region only. At any time the wage level in each market will depend on local supply-demand conditions, with the geographical immobility of labor preventing any immediate regional equalization. Over a period of time, however, labor tends to flow to the high-wage areas, and real wages for a given occupation in various areas tend to be equalized, unless workers find nonmonetary advantages of living in certain areas. Locations having sunny climates, no temperature extremes, and low humidity may, for example, have persistently lower wages for a given skill level since the supply of labor to such areas may outstrip the growth in labor demand. Money wages will not be equalized, moreover, when costs of living differ, as they frequently do, especially between rural and urban areas (or when desirable amenities such as ocean access becomes capitalized in higher rents).

Needless to say, neither labor demanders (firms) nor labor suppliers (households) are completely mobile; hence regional differences in wage rates may continue for long periods. Moving is costly, and many persons are reluctant to leave familiar areas to

14-3   Professional athletes command and receive higher salaries than teachers. Yet teachers, not athletes, are considered essential to economic growth and development. If this is in fact the case, why do athletes receive higher salaries than teachers?

Individuals earn different wages for various reasons, including different skill levels, educational backgrounds, and occupational hazards. Our example of teachers and talented athletes primarily involves skill levels and supply and demand for those skills. For instance, basketball players of professional caliber are in short supply relative to the demand for their services. On the other hand, while the demand for teachers is large, the number of people able and willing to supply teaching services is also relatively abundant. The situation between these two labor markets is depicted in the graphs.

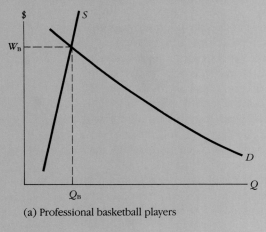

(a) Professional basketball players

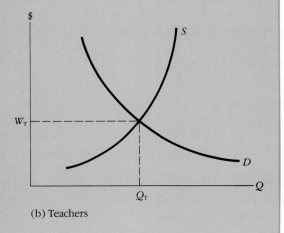

(b) Teachers

look for jobs which might not materialize. Empirical studies show some trend toward equalization, but the process is slow and erratic.

Long-Period Aggregate Supply of Labor

The discussion up to this point has been concerned with the supply of labor over a relatively short period of time, population being given. Over a longer period of time, what is the significance for population and thus labor supply of various levels of real wages? Is there a functional relationship between changes in wages and changes in total population?

Such a functional relationship was developed by T. R. Malthus, whose *Essay on the Principle of Population* (1798) was a major landmark in the development of economics. According to the well-known Malthusian doctrine, any increase in wages above subsistence level will lead to an immediate increase in population, since population is constantly held in check by famine, disease, and war arising out of inadequate food supply. As a consequence, wages are held down to a bare subsistence level—to the "cost of production" of labor.

Malthus wrote nearly 200 years ago, when conditions in many parts of the world gave substantial empirical support to his doctrine. In the 20th century, however, incomes rose and the birth rate fell; higher levels of education and changing standards of social behavior brought substantially smaller families. As persons came to realize the significance of large families for their economic well-being and gained knowledge of birth control methods, they had fewer children. In some areas of the world, however, the population never rose above extreme poverty levels, and the Malthusian rule appeared to apply with some force.

Experience following World War II suggested that once a society had reached a relatively high level of income and education, further increases in wages coupled with easy availability of jobs might lead to higher increase in population growth. However, more recent developments seem to indicate just the contrary conclusion. The declining birth rates in the United States and many other developed and developing countries have made inaccurate even fairly recent predictions of national and global populations. The better part of wisdom in this area, therefore, seems to lie in keeping silent—or at least avoiding strong generalizations.

14.3 MONOPSONY AND OLIGOPSONY

Up to this point in our analysis, the assumption has been made that the number of buyers was large and that sellers had no preference for dealing with certain buyers rather than others. There are, however, situations in which these assumptions are not realized, where individual buyers are able to exert influence on price. Three types of cases fall into this category: monopsony, oligopsony, and monopsonistic competition.

Monopsony with a single buyer, is the counterpart of monopoly. Examples are rare, except for purchases by the government of specialized defense items, or in "company towns" where virtually all labor of a certain skill level is bought by the dominant firm.

Oligopsony is characterized by a sufficiently small number of buyers that each is aware that it can influence price, creating a mutual interdependence among them. For example, an oil refining company may buy so much crude oil in a particular market area that it knows that it can influence market price and that changes in the prices it offers for crude oil will affect prices offered by other firms. Oligopsony may take the form of collusion or spontaneous coordination among buyers.

Monopsonistic competition is characterized by large numbers of buyers, with preferences on the part of the sellers for dealing with particular buyers. This situation does not appear to be empirically significant.

Monopsonistic influences may develop in an industry characterized by homogeneous products and a large number of sellers. Such a market is essentially one of perfect competition from the standpoint of the sellers, since price determination is dominated by buyers and no one seller can influence price. Examples of this situation were once found in the market for crude oil, where a few refineries bought a standardized product from many small producers, and in wholesale markets for tobacco and sugar beets. More commonly, however, oligopsony elements exist in conjunction with differentiation and oligopoly on the sellers' side. Such situations are found in many capital goods markets, where specialized machinery is produced by a few firms and is used by only a few buyers. Labor markets are sometimes influenced on the sellers' side by labor union actions, which coordinate control of supply, and on the buyers' side by a few dominant employers. While oligopsony is not commonly found in final markets for consumption goods, it occasionally exists in wholesale markets for such goods. Three large automobile manufacturers buy approximately half the annual output of tires, which are in turn produced by a small number of firms. Large department stores, mail-order houses, and chain stores frequently dominate wholesale markets for consumption goods.

Monopsony and Large Numbers of Sellers

Suppose that in a certain market there is a single firm buying from a large number of workers or small producers whose products are identical. The buyer has a certain demand for the product, or labor, as indicated by curve DD in Figure 14-6. If this firm acted without regard to the effects of its purchases upon price, it would extend pur-

FIGURE 14-6

Determination by an Employer of the Optimum Number of Workers, Monopsony in the Labor Market

The monopsonist maximizes profits by employing workers until marginal factor cost equals the marginal revenue product at q_1. The labor supply curve shows that these q_1 workers are willing to work for only W_1, the wage rate paid by the firm. If the labor market had been perfectly competitive, the wage and employment levels would be W_0 and q_0, respectively. A monopsonistic competitor determines the employment level in the same manner as the monopsonist.

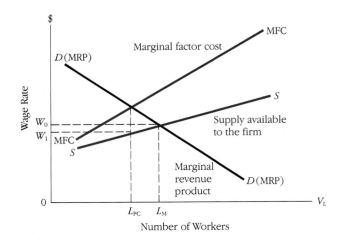

chases to the level at which its demand and the market supply (SS) were equal—q_0 in Figure 14-6. But of course the buyer *will* recognize that the quantity of its purchases affects price. Each additional unit bought will cost not only the price paid but also the additional sum on the units the firm could otherwise have bought more cheaply. Therefore, the *marginal factor cost* of the good—the additional amount it pays as a result of the purchase of another unit—exceeds the price. In Figure 14-6, the marginal factor cost at each possible quantity purchased is represented by the curve MFC. In order to maximize profit, the buyer must extend purchases to the point of equality of marginal factor cost and demand. It will thus buy a smaller quantity (q_1 in Figure 14-6) than it would had it ignored the effect of its purchases upon demand, and the market price of the factor (W_1) will be lower than if the market were perfectly competitive (W_0).

From a long-run standpoint, the effect of monopsony power upon price will depend upon cost conditions of the input being supplied. No amount of monopsony power will allow a buyer to continue to obtain a product for less than average cost, year after year, because production will fall. If an industry is one of increasing cost, price will remain permanently lower than the perfectly competitive figure because of smaller purchases and output. However, if the supplying industry (unlike the case of labor, to which we shall return) is one of constant cost, price will be the same as if the market were perfectly competitive, since average cost, which price must cover, is the same regardless of output. The long-run supply curve is a horizontal line, and thus marginal factor cost and price paid are identical.

Oligopsony with Large Numbers of Sellers

Oligopsony occurs if there is more than one buyer, but so few that each is aware that its buying policies affect those of other firms. Buyers will take the initiative in setting price, provided that there are numerous sellers.

If there is little interdependence, and if the quantities purchased by any one firm have only a slight effect on price, the various firms may bid up price toward the perfectly competitive level. On the other hand, if mutual interdependence is complete, firms may succeed in setting the same purchase price as a monopsonist. If the actual situation lies between these extremes, generalizations about price levels are difficult, just as with oligopoly. The greater the degree of mutual interdependence, the greater the deviation of the supply price of the good from the marginal factor cost of each firm, and thus the closer the price will approach the monopsony figure. In less precise terms, buyers seek to pay the minimum sum for the quantities they desire; but these quantities, in turn, are dependent upon the price that must be paid. If the buyers are business firms, the picture is complicated by the fact that the price the firm must pay for the purchases affects its costs of production and thus the amount of its product that can be sold. Firms seek to determine a purchase price that will allow maximum profit, taking into consideration the supply they can obtain at this price, their costs at this price, and their selling prices and expected sales. The supply of agricultural products depends upon the size of the current crop: if the crop is large, a low price will emerge; if the crop is small, the price will be higher. When the supply is relatively limited, there is a tendency for oligopsony power to disappear as buyers bid against one another to obtain an increased share of the limited quantities available.

Regardless of the power over market prices possessed by oligopsonists, they (like monopsonists) cannot ignore the suppliers' costs of production. In any particular year, very low prices might not affect total supply; but over a period of time, prices must cover the average costs of producers at the equilibrium output level if the supply is to be forthcoming. If the industry producing the product is one of increasing costs, the smaller volume of purchases will hold the price permanently below the perfectly competitive level. If the industry is operating in constant-cost conditions, however, there will be no permanent effect on price, although quantities will be affected.

Bilateral Monopoly and Bilateral Oligopoly

In the two preceding situations, it has been assumed that the number of sellers was large. But monopsony or oligopsony on the buyers' side may be accompanied by monopoly or oligopoly on the sellers' side. Such cases are known as **bilateral monopoly** and **bilateral oligopoly.** If both oligopsony and oligopoly are complete, firms may succeed in setting a price that will maximize the gains of both buyers and sellers and split the gains on the basis of bargaining. But it is perhaps more likely that differences in bargaining strength will result in a figure relatively more advantageous to the stronger party than the maximum-joint-gain figure. No matter how strong buyers are, they cannot keep price below the average cost of the sellers or their supply will disappear. With prices above the maximum, sales of the product produced by buyers will drop sufficiently to cut profits all along the line. Subject to these limits—which may be far apart—the actual price will depend upon bargaining, and no further generalization is possible. The theory of games (discussed in Chapter 12) has been of some use in analysing the strategies that oligopolists and oligopsonists might follow in dealing with each other, but there are few settled questions in this area of economic theory.

14.4 MONOPOLISTIC INFLUENCES IN THE LABOR MARKET

Numerous empirical studies of labor relations, plus everyday observation, suggest the importance of imperfectly competitive forces. In some instances (to a greater degree in the distant past than at present), the employer has a superior bargaining position and takes the initiative in setting wage rates; the worker has the choice of working or not working at the figure set. In the more recent past, unions generally acted as important bargaining agents for many workers. While in a few instances the union may itself dictate the wage, the development of unions ordinarily results in the determination of the wage by bargaining between unions and employers or employer groups. This type of market is essentially one of bilateral oligopoly or, if there is but one union and one group of employers, bilateral monopoly.

Employer Domination

Until unions developed in strength, wages were typically set by the employer, with individual employers exercising substantial influence over the actual level. Employer domination of wages was possible because the number of employers was much smaller than the number of workers. Workers were not highly mobile from one employer to another, and their individual bargaining positions were inherently weaker than that of the employer. In each particular labor market—which, especially in the past, was limited in size—the number of employers was often so small that there was little need for competition among them for workers. In other markets, though the total number of employers was large, a few employers used so much of the total labor force that they were able to dominate the wage level.

Apart from differences in numbers, the tactical position of the employer is superior to that of the individual worker. It is much more important for a worker to obtain and hold a particular job than it is for the employer to hire a particular worker. Failure to obtain a job leaves the worker without income; as a consequence, the worker cannot always wait for a more favorable bargain, as can the employer. The employer will not find his or her own income and living standard greatly impaired by failure to hire any particular person. Moreover, labor service is perishable: the labor service of one day cannot be stored and sold on another day, whereas the property of the employer will not deteriorate in comparable fashion.

The influence an employer can exert on wages depends in part upon the mobility of workers and in part upon the extent of competition for workers by employers. If workers move freely from one firm to another and if firms act independently in determining wage and employment policy, the control over wages by any one employer is small. In practice, however, the mobility of workers is severely limited. Most workers are tied rather closely to a particular firm by various bonds and will not move easily in response to wage differentials. These bonds include privileges (such as pension and continued-employment rights) based upon seniority in the present job, reluctance of workers to leave one job until they find another, preference for living in a particular locality and working with friends, and use by employers of personnel and hiring policies which prevent effective competition between those seeking employment in the firm and those already employed. Most employees are not "job shoppers" as long as they find their present employment reasonably satisfactory.

The control of particular employers over wage rates depends also upon the extent to which employers agree with one another on wage policies or consider the effects of their wage-employment policies on those of other firms. When common action develops, either with or without outright agreement, the situation becomes one of oligopsony. Thus, two cases of employer-dominated wage determination must be distinguished: that in which each employer acts independently but immobility gives them some control over the wage level and that of mutual interdependence. Each case will be considered in turn.

Labor Immobility and Monopsonistic Competition

Workers' lack of mobility among firms reflects their preferences for working for particular firms. If employees act independently, the situation is therefore one of monopsonistic competition. The basic feature is recognition by the employer that the wage that must be paid depends upon the number of workers hired; that is, the supply schedule of labor is not perfectly elastic (as with the upward-sloping input supply of some product, as discussed in connection with Figure 14-6). The less the mobility of workers, the less elastic the schedule will be.

Since additional workers (at least beyond a certain point) can be obtained only by offering a higher wage, the marginal factor cost exceeds the wage paid. In Figure 14-6, the marginal factor cost curve (MFC) is above the supply curve (SS). The employer, in adding workers up to the point at which MFC = MRP, will not reach the point at which the *wage* is equal to MRP. The firm will hire only Oq_1 workers in equilibrium at a wage rate W_1, whereas it would hire Oq_0 workers in equilibrium at the wage rate of W_0 (the rate that would prevail if the market were competitive). Since the same considerations apply to all oligopsonistic employers in the market, the total demand for a particular type of labor at each wage rate will be less than if the labor market were perfectly competitive, and the equilibrium wage will therefore be lower.

It must be emphasized that the supply price—the amount the employer must pay to get a given number of workers—depends primarily upon the exact degree of immobility of labor—in other words, upon the workers' alternative opportunities. Two extreme cases may be noted: If there is but one employer in a certain market (perhaps in an isolated mining town) and workers are immobile, the necessary wage would be an extremely low figure—one just high enough to induce the workers to seek employment instead of starving to death. At the other extreme is the case in which workers are highly (but not perfectly) mobile among employers and regions; the supply schedule will be highly elastic, and competition among employers will bring the wage level close to the perfectly competitive figure, even though the initiative in the setting of wage rates rests with employers. Between these extremes, there is a wide variety of possible cases, differing on the basis of the elasticity of labor supply among firms. (See Box 14-4.)

Oligopsony

The second case of employer wage domination is that in which employers are conscious of wage interdependence: each firm realizes that changes in the wage it pays

14-4 Why does the monopsonist face an upward-sloping supply curve for labor? Is the *marginal* amount the firm must pay for an additional worker greater than the amount it pays all its workers?

Simple mathematics reveals the answer to this one. Say the firm employs 5 workers at $50 each, but the sixth worker will not take the job for less than $51. Now in order to hire the sixth worker, all six laborers must receive $51. Effectively, any already employed worker can quit and become the sixth worker. Thus, the *marginal* factor cost of the sixth worker is

$56 [his or her $51 wage + ($1 × 5 current workers)], while the average factor cost is now $51 per worker. (Marginal factor cost of labor is greater than the average cost when the latter is upward sloping as with all marginal/average relationships.) The supply curve is upward sloping because in order to attract new employees the employers must offer a higher wage.

will result in changes on the part of other firms. Whenever the number of firms in a particular labor market is small, oligopsony attitudes are likely to be common. In this situation, either by outright collusion or merely by independent but coordinated actions, firms will not bid workers away from other firms by wage increases, since they recognize that the increases will be followed and they will gain few additional workers. Under such circumstances, there is no tendency for wages to adjust to equality with MRP, because each firm stops hiring workers short of the point at which this equality is attained. The actual level will be between the competitive and the monopsony outcome, perhaps being a product of historical accident.

If wages are set by outright collusion, the formal principles of setting will be comparable to those of the firm in monopsonistic competition acting independently, as analyzed above; but the MFC curve will be that confronting the firms as a group, which will thus be controlled by the mobility of labor into and out of the particular labor market and will be much less elastic than the curve confronting a particular firm. The degree of elasticity will determine the extent to which the wage level will be less than the purely competitive level.

In practice, however, employers may voluntarily pay considerably higher wages than the minimum figure necessary to obtain the optimum number of employees. In the first place, many employers believe that the quality of the workers they can obtain and the productivity of their labor force will be affected by the wage level. Higher-than-necessary wages will be paid to attract particularly qualified workers, to maintain employee morale and efficiency at high levels, and to minimize costly labor turnover. Secondly, there is the possibility that purely noneconomic considerations, such as ideas about the value of paying "good" wages, may lead an employer to pay more than the minimum. Some employers have been influenced by the principle that a high level of wages increases consumption and the general level of business activity. In depressions, many firms are reluctant to cut wages because of public censure for aggravating the decline in incomes. An even stronger force is the fear that the payment of lower wages will lead to unionization. Thus, wage levels in unionized fields exercise some influence on nonunion wage levels. Finally, for some skill levels, minimum wage laws are relevant rendering firms input price takers.

14.5 LABOR UNIONS AND WAGE DETERMINATION

Typically, wages of union members are set not by the employer but by negotiations between the unions representing the workers and employers or groups of employers. The significance of negotiated wages extends beyond the industries in which such methods are used, since wage rates and employment in nonunion fields are often influenced by union scales.

Employer Policies

Wage determination under conditions of bargaining between union and employer is somewhat uncertain, as it is in most circumstances where outcomes depend both upon bargaining skill and upon countless other psychological and social factors. Nevertheless, we can outline employer and union policies and discuss some of the factors that influence results.

An employer, of course, seeks to pay no more than necessary to obtain the desired number of workers, just as when unions are absent. However, the specific policies adopted are affected by the union's existence, and strategic moves become highly significant. For example, an employer might not grant an otherwise acceptable wage increase simply because the union might then demand still more; on the other hand, an employer may offer more than would be sensible solely in economic terms in order to help keep relatively "friendly" union officials in power. An employer may also offer higher wages in order to persuade a union to drop demands for a union shop, featherbedding, or various fringe benefits. Concessions will likewise be influenced by the employer's estimate of the union's ability to make a strike effective, the probable effect of a strike upon business, the current profit situation, the notion of what is "reasonable," the estimate of the effect of a wage increase upon the ability to raise prices, and prospective sales and profits. (See Box 14-5.)

Union Wage Policies

Analysis of union wage policy is more difficult than the analysis of employer policy, primarily because the union itself is not a seller of labor but essentially a political institution representing the workers and having aims of its own distinct from those of its members. One important union aim is union survival and growth. As a consequence, it is difficult to apply the "maximizing" approach; that is, there is no clearly defined magnitude that unions are seeking to maximize.

The most obvious assumption which may be made about union goals is that of maximization of the total wage bill—that is, the total amount of wages received by all

14-5   Many illegal aliens are motivated to migrate to the United States because of the higher real wages. Do you think labor unions support or object to illegal aliens?

Unions are basically against immigrants because they are a substitute for union workers. Thus immigrants entering into the United States would depress wages. However, on the other side of the coin consumers might benefit from lower prices as a result of falling factor (labor) prices. And if consumers gain more than producers lose, the net economic effect may be positive. Assuming the immigrants are *substitutes* for union labor, the demand for union labor would decline, leading to a lower wage in unionized sectors. The student should, as an exercise, construct an elementary graph of this case. What if unskilled aliens were *complements* with skilled union labor? What have been the historical costs and benefits of the ongoing migration to this country? Would our average incomes be higher or lower with 50 million people than with 250 million? (These are, of course, hard questions—but then the issue of whether aliens are good or bad for the country as a whole is also a very difficult question.)

union members. This is comparable to the profit-maximization assumption applied to business firms and would be clearly acceptable if unions were actually sellers of labor services. But this is not the case. Attainment of the wage-bill maximization goal is likely to cause unemployment of some union members and thus may be regarded as unacceptable, in light of the interests of those losing their jobs. On the other hand, the union may be so dominated by presently employed members that it disregards the interests of unemployed members and seeks a maximum wage bill for those now employed. For example, at a particular level of unemployment, a wage cut might allow reemployment of those out of work and increase total wage payments. But since the incomes of presently employed members would fall, they may through their union refuse to accept the cut.

Pursuit of any of these goals—maximum total wage bill, maximum wage bill for presently employed members, or jobs for all members—requires the union to consider the effects of its wage policies upon the volume of employment available for its members. There is evidence that in some instances unions consider the relationship between the wage and job opportunities, especially when employers are subject to strong competition in the product market and when the industry is not completely organized.[3] However, there is also evidence that unions, especially in periods of full employment, assume that the numbers of employees hired by firms are determined largely by technological requirements and are independent of the wage rate, at least so long as the wage does not force liquidation of the firm—a possibility often regarded as remote. If unions determine their policies under the assumption of a perfectly inelastic demand schedule for labor, the goal of wage-bill maximization is meaningless, since there is no finite value of the wage rate that would satisfy them.

The actual wage demands that unions make depend not only upon their goals but also upon the tactics that union officials believe to be most satisfactory to attain them. These tactics are in turn influenced by union officials' desire to ensure the survival and expansion of the union and the protection of their own positions. (See Box 14-6.)

In determining precise demands, union officials are likely to have in mind two sets of figures—one for which they are actually fighting, another for their initial asking price. The former, which is the really significant figure, is influenced greatly by increases being obtained by other unions. If a $2 hourly increase is being attained by other unions, union officials may feel it necessary to obtain this amount to prevent members from becoming dissatisfied with the existing union, or at least its management. As a consequence, a few wage bargains in major industries—steel and automobile production, for example—are likely to set the pattern for wage increases throughout the economy. Apart from increases obtained currently by other unions, officials will be influenced by their estimate of membership sentiment. The forces molding this sentiment are difficult to analyze. Cost-of-living changes and wage changes of preceding years play a part. Estimates of the employers' willingness to meet demands and their ability to do so—as determined by their present profit position and the possi-

---

[3]See G. P. Shultz and C. A. Myers, "Union Wage Decisions and Employment," *American Economic Review*, Vol. 40 (June 1950), pp. 362–80.

14-6   Is the American Medical Association similar to unions like the Teamsters or Longshoremen? Do you think the wages of American doctors are higher than they would be in the absence of the AMA?

The AMA acts very much like a union with its barriers to entry into the medical profession. The AMA controls the number of entrants into medical schools and other facets of medical education. Thus the restriction of entry into the medical profession leads to higher wages for doctors than would have prevailed in the absence of this "union"—the AMA. The student could profitably graph this case, although as with the case of illegal aliens, the full analysis is more complicated: Does it matter whether supply is restricted according to ability or by random selection? If entry were free would consumers of medical services be better off or worse off? (They would certainly face lower prices, but also more quality variation. But could the latter be *good*? Again, few easy and therefore obvious answers are available to guide social policy.)

bility of raising prices without serious losses in sales—also influence union wage goals. Finally, unions must balance wage goals with other union aims such as dues checkoff, union shop, pension systems, and working rules; smaller wage increases will be accepted in order to obtain concessions on these matters.

A union's initial demands almost inevitably exceed its expected gains; the amount of the difference depends primarily upon the union's bargaining tactics. Most unions prefer to avoid fantastic demands that are obviously far in excess of anything they can obtain. On the other hand, they do usually ask for more than they expect to get. The possibility that a dispute over wages may ultimately be settled by arbitration increases the need for padding original demands, since an arbitrator is likely to produce a compromise award.

There remains the question of the minimum figure a union will accept. There are essentially two minima: the figure below which the union will not go without calling a strike and the figure believed essential for union survival. The minimum without a strike is likely to be the actual demand figure (not the initial inflated demand) if the union feels that it has sufficient strength to carry a strike through effectively. If the union is doubtful about the effectiveness of a strike, it may accept a lower figure than the expected amount. However, it will not go below the amount regarded as essential to the continued maintenance of the union organization. The figure below which union officials will not go without a strike is influenced greatly by the amount which they believe the employer will grant either with or without a strike. If they are certain that the employer will not exceed a certain figure even in the event of a strike, it would be foolish to strike. The absolute minimum the union will accept is essentially the figure below which the union would disintegrate, its members drifting to other employments. If the employer will not accept a wage equal to this amount, then a strike will occur and either the union will break up and the employer will set the wage or else the firm will liquidate and workers will be forced to seek employment elsewhere. But the concept of the absolute minimum is seldom of practical significance.

In summary, union wage demands—both the initial "asking" figure and the far more significant "expected" figure, as well as the minimum figure which the union will accept—must be recognized as the product of a variety of complex factors rather than a figure that will maximize the total wage bill or serve any other simple objective. Frequently, under a widely accepted union assumption that employment is not affected by the wage level, unions seek to drive the money wage figure ever higher, their demands in particular cases being influenced mainly by such considerations as increases being obtained by other unions, estimates of employers' profits and of the figures which employers are willing to pay, the existence of pay differentials regarded as unwarranted, and estimates of union membership sentiment. Wage reductions are often fought to the bitter end, except in rare cases where they are obviously essential to prevent liquidation of the firm. In most situations, wage demands are weighed against the desire for other concessions relating to working rules, maintenance of union membership, and similar considerations. (See Box 14-7.)

The Actual Money Wage Level

Given union and employer wage policies in a particular situation, the actual wage level will be determined by the relative bargaining strength of the two groups and their skill at the bargaining table. If the figure the employer is willing to pay is close to the figure the union is determined to get, an agreement will be reached quickly. If the union is too weak to make a strike effective, the wage is likely not to be far above that initially offered by the employer, regardless of the union's initial demands. If the union's strike minimum is above the maximum figure to which the employer will go in negotiations,

14-7   Is it possible that labor unions might be responsible for prolonged unemployment?

It is often argued that labor unions cause continuing unemployment because they hold wages at artificially high levels and prevent them from falling sufficiently to restore equality of the supply of and demand for labor. This argument appears to have merit; in a sense, unemployment is a surplus of labor supplied over labor demanded, and it would appear that reduction in the wage rate would eliminate this surplus. More careful examination of the argument, however, suggests serious limitations. In the first place, wages fell relatively little in nonunion as compared with unionized industries during the depression of the 1930s; thus it cannot be demonstrated that unions were artificially holding up wage levels. It must

be granted, however, that had there been no unions at all in the economy, the decline in wages might have been greater.

It is no doubt true that in certain instances, groups of workers can preserve their jobs by accepting wage reductions especially when failure to do so may force their employer into bankruptcy. In other cases, marginal types of work, such as various aspects of plant maintenance, may be continued only if wages are sufficiently low. But it cannot be argued that the general level of employment is importantly affected by unions holding up wages in depressions, because of the general tendency in such periods for prices to follow wage changes.

a strike is inevitable. The eventual outcome depends upon the effectiveness of the strike and the employer's ability to withstand it and maintain financial solvency. The union's strength in a strike depends upon the completeness of its membership, the ability to keep nonunion laborers from working and to get other unions to respect its picket lines, the adequacy of reserves to support the members, and the existence of public relief for strikers. (See Box 14-8.)

The Effects of Unions on Money Wage Levels

What is the net effect of labor unions on the structure and level of money wages? This is not an easy question to answer. To the extent that development of labor unions offsets monopsonistic influences of employers over wage levels or gives labor a relative bargaining advantage compared to the perfectly competitive situation, the money wages of the workers affected should be greater than they would otherwise be. If unions alter the flow of labor into various fields in any way, the altered supply/demand conditions may have further effects upon wage levels.

Most empirical studies of unions' effects upon wages have used the technique of comparing wage increases in unionized fields with those in nonunion fields. Such studies have shown that, on the whole, there has been little tendency in recent decades for union wages to rise more rapidly than nonunion wages; some studies have even shown the reverse tendency. There appears to be a greater tendency for unions to affect relative wage levels to the advantage of union members in depressions than in prosperity periods. However, in expansionary periods, some very aggressive unions force increases in excess of those obtained in other fields. Another technique involves comparison of union and nonunion wage rates in the same field. Some studies show a somewhat higher wage level for union than nonunion workers.

The basic limitation of these studies is their inability to take into consideration the effects which wage changes in unionized fields have upon wage levels in nonunion fields. The question of primary interest is: To what extent does union activity cause

---

14-8   Why might unions fight for higher minimum wages even though most of their workers are paid a higher wage rate?

As we have seen earlier, higher minimum wages (above the competitive level) will lead to greater unemployment among low wage earners. If nonunion labor is a substitute for skilled union labor, then an increase in the wage for unskilled labor will increase the demand for skilled union workers. For example, an increase in the minimum wage in the South will help union workers in the North where unions are relatively stronger. The student should again draw a simple diagram depicting this case. Are there parallels between the analysis here and the earlier analysis of illegal (or legal, for that matter) aliens? It turns out (fortunately!) that "the economic way of thinking" renders many different topics of discussion fundamentally similar—one need not "reinvent the wheel" each time.

wage levels to differ from those which would exist if the unions were not present? Studying relative wage trends or levels in union and nonunion labor markets will not provide a satisfactory answer to this question unless the effects of union wage levels upon nonunion levels can be eliminated—and this is impossible. Employers in non-unionized fields are greatly influenced in their wage policies by union wages, not only because of the possible loss of labor supply in periods of labor shortage if they do not meet union levels but also because of the desire to deter unionization of their workers. In periods when demand for labor tends to outrun supply at existing wage rates, the existence of unions may actually slow down wage increases below those which would be attained with perfectly competitive labor markets, and perhaps in some cases even below those which would occur if labor markets were monopsonistic.

It is therefore difficult to generalize about the effect of unions on money wage levels. Theory suggests that unions may raise money wages in those cases where they eliminate monopsonistic wage domination and perhaps may push wages above the competitive figure if they gain sufficient bargaining power, but further empirical work is necessary before any positive conclusions can be reached. (See Box 14-9.)

Labor Unions and Wage Differentials

The development of unions undoubtedly has had some effect upon wage differentials among firms, occupations, and geographical areas.

Interfirm Wage Differences. In the first place, widespread unionization tends to reduce **interfirm wage differentials** in a given region and occupation. These differentials, which would not exist if competition were perfect, are products of employer domination of the labor market, facilitated by the relative immobility of labor. Unions almost always seek to eliminate these differentials which, if continued, would threaten their security. Workers in low-wage plants will insist that the union eliminate the differentials, and high-wage employers may encourage the union to adopt a uniform

---

14-9   The formation of unions may increase wages in union jobs but lower wages in nonunion jobs. Discuss why this is or is not possible.

Suppose you have two labor sectors: the union sector and the nonunion sector. If unions are successful in obtaining higher wages either through collective bargaining or by limiting the number of workers admitted into the union sector (and thus causing wages to be bid up), employment will fall in that sector. With a downward-sloping demand curve for labor, higher wages can only mean less labor is demanded in the union sector. And those unable to find union work will seek nonunion work—increasing supply in that sector and subsequently lowering wages for non-union workers. The student should draw the simple graphs of this case and return to earlier examples to verify that a consistent analytical framework is used to think economically about situations in which your natural sympathies and inclinations differ.

wage policy. If industry-wide bargaining develops, a uniform wage policy is almost inevitable. The elimination of differentials may merely destroy the excess profits of firms that would be able to hold wages to particularly low levels in the absence of unionization. In other cases, however, the low-wage firms are those whose other costs are high, owing to inefficiencies in production or selling activities, poor management, or poor location. If a wage increase stimulates these firms to greater efficiency, workers as well as employers and society gain. If poor management or poor location is responsible, however, high-cost firms may liquidate when forced to pay a uniform wage rate. If workers can shift easily to other plants, there is little loss; the other firms' sales will increase, and society will benefit from the elimination of less-efficient firms. In other instances, however, unions encounter a serious problem: a uniform wage rate may compel liquidation of many firms whose employees cannot easily transfer to other jobs. Should such firms be allowed to continue to operate at lower wage rates? The plants' employees, if they are certain that higher wages will mean liquidation, will almost always favor retention of a differential. National union officials are likely to take the opposite point of view, because pressure for lower wages will develop from other firms. Sometimes one point of view will prevail, sometimes another. In recent years, foreign competition (in, for example, steel and automobiles) has greatly weakened union goals of high uniform wages.

If some firms in an industry become unionized while others do not, the development of unions may actually increase rather than decrease differentials. But this effect is unlikely. Nonunion employers will fear that their plants will be organized if they do not approach union wage levels, while the existence of nonunion firms in the industry will lessen the extent to which the union is able to drive up wages in the unionized plants. There is, however, some evidence that, on the average, nonunion firms pay lower wages than union firms in the same industry. (See Box 14-10.)

Occupational Wage Differentials.   For reasons indicated earlier, the significance of union activity for **occupational wage differentials** is difficult to assess. To the extent that unions are stronger in some occupations than others, it would be expected that differentials otherwise existing would be modified. However, union wage levels affect nonunion levels as well, and the empirical evidence is meager (because other things aren't equal) and somewhat conflicting. It suggests that unions have less significance for wage differentials than might be expected; but it is almost inevitable that particularly strong and aggressive unions may, at least for a time, raise the wages of members relative to those of persons in other occupations.

Likewise, a union may be able to limit the number of workers available for employment in an industry and restrict the competition between employed and unemployed persons. If unions obtain closed shop agreements and limit membership, their control over supply will interfere with the flow of workers into the occupation and thus maintain greater differentials than would otherwise exist. Even if a union accepts all persons wishing to enter, it can ordinarily prevent newcomers from offering to work for lower wages.

Geographical Wage Differences.   The development of widespread unionization tends to lessen geographical wage differences. Wage differentials not offset by other

14-10   Can powerful labor unions be responsible for inflationary pressures?

It has been argued widely since World War II that unions exert a constant upward pressure upon prices and make it impossible to maintain a stable price level with full employment. According to this argument, the unions' continuing insistence on higher money wages leads to increases in production costs and hence in the general price level (providing that the money wage increases are greater than the increases in labor productivity).

This point of view has been seriously questioned by other writers, partly on the basis of evidence that nonunion wages have risen in much the same fashion as union wages in recent years. It is argued, furthermore, that the existence of unions actually retards increases in wages in inflationary periods, primarily because union contracts run for lengthy periods and increases cannot occur during the course of a contract. It is also maintained that employers may be reluctant to give increases they might otherwise offer, in order to be able to concede the increase in subsequent bargaining. Moreover, the most inflationary period in recent history (the 1970s) was a time of *declining* union strength.

Our present state of knowledge does not permit satisfactory conclusions on this issue. From a theoretical standpoint, it is possible for widespread, union-forced money wage increases to cause inflation, *provided* that increases in expenditures or in the nation's money supply take place simultaneously. But whether unions have in the past aggravated inflation or lessened it is an empirical question on which the available evidence is inconclusive. From present knowledge, it does not appear that reasonably full employment, price stability, and labor unions are necessarily incompatible.

differences such as variations in the cost of living create dissatisfaction among union members and injure the competitive position of high-wage firms. Higher wage rates often represent a goal that unions seek to attain in lower wage areas. For example, Canadian unions sometimes refer to higher wage levels in the United States as goals for their own wage negotiations. The tendency toward industry-wide bargaining is also likely to increase the elimination of geographical wage differences. In some instances, unions may obtain uniform money wages despite cost-of-living and amenity differences and may thereby increase real wage utility differences.

When unions are stronger in some areas than in others, the existence of unions may increase wage differentials over what they would otherwise be. Low wage levels in small towns often reflect a difference in the degree of unionization, even allowing for cost-of-living and amenity differences.

14.6 THE REAL INCOME OF LABOR

Recognition of the close relationship between money wages and prices, and particularly of the tendency of prices to change as wages change, brings the discussion back to the original point of departure: What determines the share of labor's real income, given the existing competitive conditions in the labor market? Does union activity, to the extent that it does affect money wage levels, actually alter the level of real wages and the share of labor in total national income?

The level of **real wages**, in total, depends in part on the total level of real income and in part upon the manner in which this total is shared between labor and other factor owners. The level of real national income depends upon the volume and quality of factors available, the techniques of production used, and the extent to which available resources are fully utilized. Increases in national product, in real terms, arise primarily from the development of new methods of production, the introduction of new types of capital equipment, and increases in the skill of workers. Realization of this fact emphasizes the undesirable effects of those union policies designed to restrict output or check the introduction of new methods of production. Such policies may aid a few individual workers, but they obviously injure workers as a group, as well as other members of society, by restricting the growth of national output (which is income). Society cannot become richer by producing less.

Given the level of real national income, the real income of the labor group is determined by the share of the total which labor receives. If all labor markets were perfectly competitive, the real wage of each type of labor would depend upon the MRP of the particular type of labor, and the overall share of labor in national income would depend upon the relationship between the MRP of labor and that of other factors. With monopsony in the labor markets, the real share of labor would be reduced somewhat below this level. The development of unions curtails this monopsonistic "exploitation" of labor and thus tends to restore real wages and the share of labor in national income to the levels which would prevail with perfect competition in the labor market.

Can unions do more than this, so far as wages are concerned, and raise labor's share above the perfectly competitive figure? This can occur, from a long-run standpoint, only if excess profits have been made possible by the restriction of entry of new firms into certain industries. It is also possible for short periods when unions are strong enough to force wages up to the point where all costs are not covered by various business firms. But liquidation of some firms will eventually occur, destroying labor's temporary gains. Beyond these possibilities, the real wage level cannot be forced above the figure determined by the marginal productivity of labor; any increases in money wages beyond this point are accompanied by price changes, with no effect on the real wage level.

SUMMARY

1. Markets for labor services are seldom highly organized because individuals must negotiate their own "product" (though in many cases this negotiation process is handled by a broker).

2. Determinants of the overall supply of labor include the total population capable of working, institutional factors, and work/leisure preferences.

3. Wage changes affect the quantity of labor by causing existing workers to work longer hours and by luring into the labor market persons otherwise not working.

4. There are two conflicting effects between the relationship of wages and an individual's supply of labor: At higher wages the substitution effect results in *more* work, while the income effect leads to *less* work. The shape of the individual's labor supply curve depends on the relative strengths of these two effects.

5. An employer hires workers up to the point where the marginal revenue product of an additional worker is equal to the marginal factor cost on the worker.

6. The elasticity of demand for each type of labor depends upon the rate of decline in marginal revenue product of the particular type of labor, at given initial wage and quantity of labor.

7. If labor markets were perfectly competitive, the wages of each type of labor would tend to come to a level at which the demand for and supply of the particular type of labor were equal.

8. Wages paid for different types of jobs vary widely; these are called occupational wage differentials. There are also geographical wage differentials, which reflect labor's limited mobility as well as regional differences in amenities and living costs.

9. There are three situations in which individual buyers are able to exert influence on price: monopsony, oligopsony, and monopsonistic competition.

10. The influence that an employer can exert on wages depends in part upon the mobility of workers and in part upon the extent of competition for workers by employers.

11. It is difficult to apply the maximizing approach to unions since an important aim is union survival and growth—that is, there is no clearly defined magnitude that unions are seeking to maximize.

12. The total level of *real* income to labor depends in part on the total level of real output and in part upon the manner in which this total is shared between labor and other factor owners.

WORDS AND CONCEPTS FOR REVIEW

determinants of aggregate labor supply
the substitution effect
the income effect
aggregate demand for labor
elasticity of demand for labor
perfectly competitive wage levels
geographical wage differentials
long-period aggregate supply of labor

monopsony
oligopsony
monopsonistic competition
bilateral monopoly
bilateral oligopoly
interfirm wage differentials
occupational wage differentials
real wages

REVIEW QUESTIONS

1. What are the major determinants of the labor supply?

2. Explain the two conflicting considerations which influence the nature of the supply function of labor.

3. What is a backward-bending supply curve? Under what circumstances will the supply curve of labor be of this nature?

4. Why is the supply of labor believed to be relatively inelastic?

5. Empirical evidence shows that as real incomes rose over the years, the typical workweek declined. What significance does this evidence have for the nature of the labor supply?

6. What additional considerations influence the supply of any particular type of labor?

7. What are the major influences upon the elasticity of demand for labor?

8. Explain the level to which wages would come in a perfectly competitive labor market.

9. Indicate the major sources of wage differentials, assuming perfect competition in the labor market.

10. Why is the perfectly competitive model of wage determination of limited significance?

11. What is the nature of the long-run supply schedule of labor, in terms of the Malthusian theory of population?

12. Why did the Malthusian theory prove to be inapplicable to the western world in the twentieth century?

13. Why, in the absence of unions, do labor markets tend to be monopsonistic?

14. What effect does the limited mobility of labor have upon the elasticity of the supply schedule of labor available to a particular firm?

15. Illustrate on a graph the supply curves of labor available to a particular firm (a)when labor is perfectly mobile and (b)when labor is highly immobile.

16. Why, in an employer-dominated labor market, does immobility of labor result in a lower wage level? Illustrate graphically.

17. What effect does the presence of oligopsony in the labor markets have upon wage levels? Explain.

18. Why may employers deliberately pay higher wages than the minimum figures necessary to obtain the optimum number of workers?

19. What factors influence the wage figure the employer is willing to offer, when the workers are unionized? The maximum one is willing to pay?

20. Why are farmers typically much more hostile to the formation of unions among their workers than are manufacturers?

21. Indicate the various alternative assumptions with respect to the wage goals sought by unions.

22. Why cannot the maximization assumption in its usual form be applied to labor unions?

23. What forces influence the minimum figure a union will accept? What forces influence the amount which it initially demands?

24. Under what circumstances can union activity actually improve workers' real standard of living? Even if union activity does not raise the level of real wages, what other advantages may it convey to labor?

25. What are the primary determinants of the level of real wages at any particular time?

SUGGESTED READINGS

Alchian, Armen and Allen, William. *Exchange and Production: Competition, Coordination and Controls,* 3rd ed. Belmont, CA: Wadsworth, 1983, Chapters 14 and 15.

Bellante, Don and Jackson, Mark. *Labor Economics.* New York: McGraw-Hill, 1979.

Ehrenberg, Ronald G. and Smith, Robert S. *Modern Labor Economics: Theory and Public Policy.* Glenview, IL: Scott Foresman and Co., 1982.

Rees, Albert and Schultz, George P. *Workers and Wage in an Urban Labor Market.* Chicago: Chicago University Press, 1970.

Sowell, Thomas. *Markets and Minorities.* New York: Basic Books, 1981.

15

Capital Investment

15.1 INTRODUCTION

Durable capital goods are distinguished from the so-called "basic" production factors, labor and land, in being "produced by people" rather than "supplied by nature."[1] The use of such goods by business firms introduces an important time element into the production process, because the services embodied in them cannot be utilized at the moment the capital good is produced or purchased but must be drawn upon over an (often extended) interval of time. Our discussion will deal only with **fixed capital assets**—relatively long-lived capital goods such as plant, machinery, and buildings. Many other kinds of durable capital goods—previously processed materials, refined fuel, goods in process, stocks of finished goods—are produced and used up in the course of production processes and thus represent a kind of "circulating capital." Such goods are not necessarily short-lived, but in practice they seldom survive more than a few days or weeks. They are excluded from our analysis not because they are unimportant (for they are important), but rather because dealing with them effectively would require us to develop an explicit account of the dynamics of production processing and inventory adjustment—an area of analysis that lies beyond the scope of this book.

The theoretical analysis of the pricing of fixed capital assets involves some complications that do not arise, or arise only to a minor degree, in connection with other kinds of factor inputs. First, fixed capital goods have to be financed prior to the sale of final outputs produced with their services. With labor, the opposite is usually the case,

---

[1] While birth control technology has blurred this distinction a bit for labor, it is still the case that labor (particularly in developed countries) exists for reasons unrelated to current production demands.

payment for services supplied being made after those services have been used in production. Of course, a certain amount of money capital is required to finance purchases of any kind of factor service, since some time typically elapses in any production process between the purchase of factor units and the sale of outputs produced with such units. But financing requirements figure much more prominently in decisions about fixed capital goods than in decisions involving other kinds of factors.

Also, since fixed capital goods are commonly used over a period of several years, there is much greater risk that expected returns will not be attained than in the case of factors which are purchased and used on a more current basis. All production requires prediction, but predictions of sales and prices a week or month in the future obviously have a much greater likelihood of being accurate than predictions about more distant periods.

15.2 SOURCES OF PRODUCTIVITY OF CAPITAL GOODS

Additional capital goods may be desired by a firm for several reasons:

1. *To replace existing capital goods.* A large portion of gross investment each year is designed to replace existing capital goods which have either worn out physically or have become economically obsolete. Calculation of the profitability of replacement investment is essentially the same as that of new investment, with the additional need to consider the relative gain from continued use of old equipment compared with the gain from purchasing new equipment. For example, relative maintenance expenses of new and old equipment must be included in the calculation. (See Box 15-1.)

2. *To permit capital widening.* **Capital widening** refers to an increase in the total stock of capital goods used without a change in capital intensity (as when a transport enterprise that has ten trucks adds another five of the same capacity). Purchases of additional capital goods for widening—that is, to allow the handling of additional output—are dependent primarily upon the *rate of change* of sales. If the capacity of existing equipment has been reached and sales continue to increase, purchase of additional equipment may be advantageous to handle the greater volume.

15-1   True or False?   It is important to note that the original cost of existing equipment is a relevant factor in decisions to retain or replace it.

False. Once money capital has been "sunk" in a particular piece of capital equipment, it can be recovered if at all (over and above the usually nominal salvage value of the equipment) only by using up the equipment in which it is embodied. As with all wise decisions, the decision to retain or replace existing equipment is based on the comparison of expected *marginal* benefits and costs.

3. *To permit capital deepening.* **Capital deepening** involves the introduction of additional capital goods to allow more intensive use of capital relative to labor for a given volume of output. Such a change may become advantageous to a firm when wage costs increase while costs of new capital equipment remain unchanged.

4. *As a vehicle of technological change.* Each type of capital purchase noted thus far may be advantageous even when the state of technology remains unchanged. However, a large proportion of investment in new capital goods is a product of technological change; in modern terminology, the new capital goods *embody* the technological change. Some embodying investments are made for replacement purposes; new techniques may be introduced at the time replacement occurs or may lead to replacement well ahead of the original retirement schedule. Substantial embodying investment is made, however, in order to produce new products, to achieve greater sales through improved quality or lower cost, or because of other dynamic forces. (See Box 15-2.)

15.3 DETERMINANTS OF INVESTMENT

The flow demand for capital goods is directly determined by investment decisions of business firms. The same basic rule applies to capital goods as to other factor units: their purchase will be extended to the point at which the marginal gain (MRP) is just equal to the marginal factor cost. But time and risk considerations create additional complications which call for a variety of decision-making techniques in this realm. Three distinct approaches warrant consideration: direct calculation, discounted present value, and the payback period rule.

Direct Calculation

This technique involves an assessment of the relative return on an additional capital good, compared to the return on earning assets. The result is often called the **internal rate of return**. This may be defined as the rate of return at which the discounted present value of expected net future earnings from a capital good is exactly equal to its initial cost. This rate is defined implicitly by the variable r in the equation

15-2   True or False?   Early replacement of older capital with new capital embodying a technological advance will occur when the revenue added by the new machine exceeds both the cost of the new machine and the revenue which continues to be added by the old machine.

True. As always, the replacement decision depends on expected marginal benefits and costs. Note that the salvage value of the old machine (which the firm gets in either case) does not figure in this decision, apart from minor issues of when it is received.

$$\frac{y_1}{1 + r} + \frac{y_2}{(1 + r)^2} + \dots + \frac{y_T}{(1 + r)^T} - C = 0$$

where T is the life (in years) of the capital good, y_i represents the expected net return during the ith year, (including salvage value in year T), and C represents the initial cost of the capital good. Given the net return figures, $y_1, y_2, \dots, y_T$, and given the cost of the capital good, C, there is normally just one positive (real) value of r that satisfies the equation.[2]

For a simple example, suppose you were thinking about buying a machine that cost $50,000 and is expected to last five years. If in each of the years the MRP is $15,000 (a total undiscounted return of $75,000) then the internal rate of return is slightly more than 15 percent, the figure which when applied to the various MRP's will yield a value of $50,000 when discounted. This figure in effect shows the net gain from the investment, discounting the MRP figure for each of the various years of use back to the present. However, the actual calculation of r can be a very complicated business, particularly if expected earnings figures fluctuate in value from one year to the next or if some values are negative; but the calculation of r is a minor problem by comparison with the task of estimating appropriate values for the y's, because these depend not only on future prices and sales but also on expected future operating costs (which must be subtracted from gross revenues in estimating net returns) and on the expected salvage value of the equipment at the end of its life. Supposing that a firm somehow arrives at an estimate for the internal rate of return on a capital good, however, it is obvious that it will be potentially profitable to purchase the good—assuming the availability of money capital—if it promises to yield an internal rate of return in excess of the rate of interest which must be paid (or forgone) on money capital, since any investment which promises to yield a net return greater than this rate will add more to a firm's revenue than to its cost.

Discounted Present Value

The principal alternative involves calculation of the **discounted present value** of the future returns on the use of the capital equipment (using a given interest rate figure equal to the current rate at which funds can be obtained). Any investment which will yield a discounted present value in excess of the cost of the investment is advantageous. Under usual circumstances, this approach will give the same answer as the internal rate of return method; any investment which will show an internal rate of return in excess of the interest rate will show a discounted present value in excess of original cost (with, of course, the same interest rate figure).

There are at least two situations, however, in which the two methods will not give the same answer. First, projects with highly irregular expected returns may, at certain interest rates, appear profitable with one method and not the other. Second, when the

---

[2]There will be one value for the internal rate of return if costs are paid for the capital good prior to the receipt of returns.

firm cannot obtain all of the money capital required to extend investment to the level at which the internal rate of return is equal to the interest rate, and thus investment must be rationed to a certain dollar figure, the methods may give different answers for the ascertainment of the best projects. If the rationing were necessitated by some other reason than shortage of money capital, clearly the discounted present value method is preferable since it indicates the largest potential gain. But this is not necessarily true if capital shortage is the cause, since the interest rate used in discounting future returns is not the true measure of opportunity cost of money capital to the firm, and some version of the internal rate of return method must be used.

Rule of Thumb—the Payback Period

Uncertainty about expected future yields leads many firms to use a third decision-making technique—the **payback period rule**. The firm calculates the number of years needed to pay for a capital good from its earnings (before subtraction of depreciation). Priority is given to those goods having the shortest payback periods, and projects are not undertaken if the payback period exceeds a specified number of years—five or ten, for example. This method is obviously very crude, for it completely ignores yields from investment in years beyond the payback period, and it also ignores the time distribution of earnings within the payback period. An investment that yields most of its net return in early years is normally preferable (having a higher present value) to one that yields an equivalent return only in later years.

Other firms place primary stress on urgency of needs, on necessity for continued operation of the firm, or on attainment of some other specific goal such as integration of raw material sources of supply. Such criteria are clearly suitable in some instances; if a mile of railroad track is washed out, for example, it must be replaced if the line is to continue in operation. But excessive reliance on such methods can result in piecemeal replacement of extensive capital equipment not warranted by profit considerations. In the long run, this will be disastrous under reasonably competitive conditions and undesirable under other market structures. Careless capital decisions are bad not only for profit-seeking firms but also from the perspective of optimal social use of scarce resources. (See Box 15-3.)

15.4 RISK CONSIDERATIONS

Besides the time dimension, another important and related consideration in investment decisions is the risk dimension. Any investment in capital goods involves risk. Conditions may turn out to be substantially less favorable than anticipated; not only might the expected return not be gained, but the capital sum invested in the equipment may be lost. A new business may find that sales are much less than anticipated, and an existing business may miscalculate the gain from a particular investment. Dynamic forces in the economy are difficult to predict; technological change may render equipment obsolete far ahead of the expected time, or shifts in consumer preferences or development of additional competition may result in lower returns.

15-3 "Capital" is sometimes interpreted more broadly to include *human capital*, the stock of skills and experience embodied in labor. How can we use the preceding analysis in deciding whether or not to pursue a college education?

As in all decisions, the expected marginal benefits must be weighed against the expected marginal costs. On the benefit side is a potentially higher lifetime income: the average college graduate earns over $1,000,000 compared to slightly over $750,000 for the high school graduate. Also on the benefit side is the nonpecuniary aspect of a college education— the social life and the consumption value of education (benefitting from the classics of literature, art history, and so on). On the cost side are the direct costs of education (including tuition, books, and room and board) and especially, forgone employment opportunities. For example, say instead of going on to college you could have driven a truck and made $30,000 a year. Over four years that translates into a $120,000 loss while you were pursuing a college education. Hence one might give up some income now for higher expected income later. But how do we find the value today of an investment that yields returns in the future? In order to look at the benefits over time, we use the rate of return approach. And the present average money rate of return for a college education is estimated to be in the neighborhood of 7.5-10 percent a year. Although the rate of return has fallen in recent years, this is still a good investment, considering that the average rate of return on stocks is between 5 and 7 percent and that education presumably offers greater nonmonetary returns than does stock ownership.

History provides many examples, including a classic case of over $1 billion invested in electric interurban railways which were rendered obsolete by automobiles and buses long before the investment was recovered.

On the other hand, investment may turn out to be much more profitable than anticipated. Sales may be greater, or actual economic life may prove to be longer.[3] It must be recognized, however, that forces of competition tend to set a limit on returns higher than expected, since such returns lead to the entry of new firms.

Though it is obvious that risk is created by capital investment, adjusting for risk in calculations of the profitability of investment is quite another matter. The simplest method is to apply a **risk discount factor** to expected returns, reducing the latter accordingly. The obviously greater risk of later years is taken into consideration by the greater impact of the risk discount for these years. While this discount does approach adjustment for risk considerations, it suffers from a major limitation: there is no basis upon which to select a discount percentage other than sheer intuition. Obviously risk

---

[3]While no one would seriously anticipate the economic life of any transportation equipment at more than 25 years or so, a locomotive built in 1864 and shipped around Cape Horn for use on early California lines continued in regular service until 1950 on the Stockton Terminal and Eastern, a total of 86 years.

considerations differ among various types of industries. Electric power generation, on the one hand, and silver mining and restaurant operation, on the other, are good examples of extremes. Furthermore, investors' attitudes toward risk differ significantly. Sources of funds and the financial situation of an enterprise also affect its risk. As noted below, the risks are greater if the funds are borrowed than if earnings are reinvested; risks are also greater for investments of a given magnitude for a small company with little reserve than for a large enterprise with substantial reserve capital.

Various attempts have been made to simplify or improve risk discounting adjustments. These take several forms:

1. *Use of a cutoff date or finite horizon.* Potential returns beyond a certain date are ignored on the ground that the degree of risk is so high that any prediction would be useless. This technique is quite arbitrary, of course, and could produce very poor results in instances in which it is reasonable to assume that there will be some use beyond the cutoff date.

2. *The Shackle approach*, involving what may be called "potential surprise" instead of a uniform risk discount rate. To take a simple example, suppose that the person believes that there are equal chances of 4, 5, and 6 percent internal returns on a particular investment, and no chance of any other return. If so, there is no risk discount adjustment to be made. Where there is danger of "surprise," an equivalent return figure for the investment which would be riskless may be estimated; the difference between the "risky" and "riskless" rates indicates the appropriate risk discount in the particular case.

3. *Probability adjustments.* A firm faces alternative investment possibilities, with varying degrees of probability of occurence for various returns, the probabilities being projected from previous experience or estimated directly. These alternatives will show different estimated returns. For various alternatives, the most-certain-return projects are those offering lowest potential yield; the least certain are those offering the potential of very high return (as is also true, for example, of certain types of gambling). The situation may be illustrated by considering the indifference curves depicted in Figure 15-1. These are indifference curves between a good and a bad where variance is the bad. Each of these curves indicates various combinations of risk (variance of returns) and earnings (rate of return) between which the firm is indifferent. By hypothesis, the firm prefers higher returns for any given level of risk, lower risk for any given level of returns. Thus all risk-earning combinations that lie on a given iso-return curve are preferred to any combination that lies on a curve to the left of the given curve. The particular investment chosen then depends on the alternative investments available to the firm. If the alternatives are represented by the set of risk-earning points included in the "choice set" shown in Figure 15-1, for example, the investment alternative chosen will be that which is expected to yield an earning rate of $\bar{r}$ at a level of risk $\bar{\sigma}$.

In many instances, of course, risks cannot be projected with any degree of certainty from past experience; intuition and sheer guesswork will determine the relative cer-

FIGURE 15-1

Risk-Earning Alternatives and Preferences

Indifference curves chart the combinations of expected earnings and risk of alternative investments which yield the same level of utility to the owners of the firm. The best investment plans are located in the southeasterly direction of the graph—that is, those with the greatest returns at the lowest risk. The firm will undertake the project associated with the tangency of the choice set (the set of projects available to the firm) and I_3.

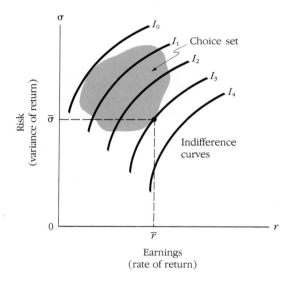

tainty of various returns. Nevertheless, this approach should give more satisfactory results than the risk-discount method, since it entails a more systematic review of investment alternatives.

Estimating the risk of alternative investments may be facilitated by selecting those factors in the situation that appear to be particularly critical and estimating the returns with various figures for these criteria. If the critical factor is the level of raw materials prices, for example, there will be some price level at which the investment would be completely useless and can be eliminated from the choice set because production could not be carried on profitably. Some estimate of the likelihood of such a price level occurring will therefore increase the quality of the predictions.

15.5 THE COST AND AVAILABILITY OF MONEY CAPITAL

As noted above, if profits are to be maximized, the crucial comparison to be made in **capital budgeting** is between the internal rate of return and the cost of money capital. The cost figure— and thus the optimum level of investment for the firm—is influenced somewhat by the source of money capital. There are three possibilities: borrowing money, selling stock, and reinvesting earnings.

1. *Borrowing money, the direct cost being the interest that must be paid on the money.* Borrowing gives rise to an additional risk not incurred with other methods of financing, that of bankruptcy and loss of control of the company should the investment prove so unsuccessful that interest and repayment obligations cannot be met. Thus the owners run the risk of losing their entire investment, not merely the additional investment.

2. *Sale of stock.* No contractual obligations are incurred to pay interest or repay principal, but earnings on the old investment as well as the new are shared with the owners of the new stock. The cost, therefore, may be considered to be the current yield figure on the additional stock issue. If new issues of stock paying $5 annual dividend can be sold at $100, the yield is 5 percent. While no risk of bankruptcy is incurred, there is increased danger of loss of control of the enterprise if too much additional stock is issued.

3. *Reinvestment of earnings, or plowback.* The most important source of investment funds is often money accumulated internally from profits, together with accumulated earned depreciation charges. The cost of such funds is the income forgone by not using the funds for other investments—to buy stocks of other corporations, for example. Since the borrowing rate will exceed the lending rate (because of transactions costs), this "opportunity cost" will be lower than the cost to the firm of acquiring funds from outside sources. In addition, no secondary costs of greater danger of bankruptcy or loss of control are created; the only secondary cost is loss of liquidity, which could endanger the financial stability of the company in the event of losses and which precludes the investment of the funds in more advantageous pursuits that might arise in the future. (See Box 15-4.)

A final but important point relates to the many cases in which firms engage in all or several of the preceding financing possibilities. This point is that *on the margin* the firm must be indifferent between these financing options. Otherwise, the firm would not be observed choosing more than one financing option.

15-4   True or False?   The cost of money capital for additional investment will differ according to the source of the funds and the firm's general credit standing, which affects the rate at which funds may be *obtained from outside*.

True. Actual choice of financing methods will depend upon the relative cost and availability of funds from various sources together with the firm's attitude toward risk and dilution of control. Many firms as a matter of policy will expand only when internal funds are available for the purpose. Others—particularly small enterprises—cannot raise funds by any but internal means, at least beyond a certain point. Thus the availability of various sources of funds will affect the total volume of investment.

15.6 THE FUNCTIONAL RELATIONSHIP BETWEEN THE AMOUNT AND COST OF MONEY CAPITAL

In a perfect market, with no uncertainty, a firm could presumably obtain any desired sum at a given percentage rate. But in practice, market imperfections and uncertainty create a positive functional relationship. Beyond a certain point, as a firm obtains additional funds, it must pay a higher interest rate on borrowed capital or give a higher return to new stockholders; the risks created by additional borrowing of stock financing are increased, as well as liquidity losses from the use of internal capital. Thus the marginal cost of additional investment, which is the relevant cost figure, will rise.

One of the more significant peculiarities of the acquisition of money capital is the prevalence of **capital rationing**; that is, a firm may be unable to raise funds at all beyond a certain point. Every firm has a limited amount of internal funds. Lenders, leery of putting too many eggs in one basket, are frequently unwilling to lend more than a certain amount to a particular firm. Similarly, it may be difficult or impossible to sell stock beyond a certain sum; in fact, some small firms cannot sell stock at all. Many firms will stop short of the absolute maximum they can obtain from the outside; if they follow such a policy, the effect is the same as if they could not raise money at all.

When the quantity of money capital available limits the firm to a volume of investment less than the optimum in terms of the relationship of the rate of return to the cost of money capital, the investment decision becomes a matter of selecting investment projects that offer the greatest potential return. More specifically, the capital available becomes one of the constraints of the problem, and the goal becomes one of maximizing the return from this amount of capital, taking risk into consideration. This problem can be solved rather simply by linear programming, a technique of managerial decision making that has been much in vogue among the business and economics community for a number of decades. Whether the choice proves to be the correct one or not depends upon the accuracy of prediction of returns and upon the appropriateness of the programming model that is used. (See Appendix to Chapter 7—Linear Programming.)

15.7 TOTAL INVESTMENT

The pattern of particular firms' investment decisions determines the total volume of investment in the economy, given the following data:

(a) The prices or supply schedules of capital goods.
(b) The supply schedules of money capital at various interest rates.
(c) The anticipated profitability of various investments.
(d) The anticipated risk of alternative investments.

The information involved in (c) and (d) has been discussed earlier, and the determination of interest rates is discussed later in this chapter. Item (a) warrants further consideration.

15.8 THE PRICE OF CAPITAL GOODS

There is an inverse relationship between the prices of capital goods and the quantity demanded of them, as there is for any type of factor unit. Subject to special qualifications involved in calculations of MRP and to the influence of possible capital rationing, the same considerations apply to the demand for capital goods as to the demand for other factor units. Higher prices of certain types of capital goods, other elements being given, will cause firms to substitute alternative forms of capital equipment and to use more labor-intensive methods; total investment will thus be less. In terms of the economy as a whole, it is difficult for capital goods prices permanently to rise relative to wage rates, since the latter are primary cost elements in the production of capital goods. In the short run, however, capital goods prices (like stock market values) may fluctuate wildly in relation to other prices, because of changing views about the future profitability of such assets.

Since capital goods are produced by business firms on a profitmaking basis, the same considerations apply to output, supply, and pricing policies as are relevant for consumption goods. Many capital equipment industries are characterized by oligopoly, with close implicit or explicit cooperation as a consequence of limited differentiation. But there are no basic differences in pricing policies.

Changes in the Demand for Capital Goods

Several dynamic forces affect the demand for capital goods, and thus the volume of investment. These forces include other factor supplies, the supply of money capital, national income, technology, and expectations about the future.

Changes in Other Factor Supplies. An increase in quantities of other factors available will tend to increase the demand for capital goods. Discovery of new natural resources will lead to purchases of capital goods by firms exploiting the new resources or using products made from them. Population growth makes available an increased supply of labor and requires the use of more capital equipment if least-cost factor combinations are to be maintained, provided the increase in population does not adversely affect the supply of money capital available for investment. This qualification is particularly significant in underdeveloped countries where families use so much of their incomes for consumption purposes that little money capital is available for investment.[4] In highly developed countries, in periods when people tend to seek to save more than the current rate of investment, the effect of population growth in increasing the percentage of income consumed will stimulate investment by increasing sales of consumption goods, apart from the encouragement given to investment by the effect of population growth upon labor supply.

---

[4]If additional money capital is created by bank or governmental action under such circumstances, inflation will result.

Changes in the Supply of Money Capital.   The demand for capital goods and the demand for money capital are complementary to one another, since increased use of capital goods requires additional use of money capital. Accordingly, an increase in the supply of money capital, which tends (temporarily) to lower the interest rate, making money capital more readily available, increases the demand for capital goods.

Increases in National Income Due to Lessened Unemployment of Resources.   As national income rises from recession levels through reemployment of idle factor units, additional investment will be profitable because increasing sales will increase the expected MRP of capital equipment. When recovery first begins, the effect upon investment may be slight, because firms have substantial idle capacity. But once the capacity of existing equipment is approached, sharp increases in investment may be expected.[5]

However, net investment due to a rise in national income will continue only so long as the increase in output (or expectations thereof) continues. As full employment is approached, the rate of increase in national income must slacken; and once full employment is attained, the rate of increase is limited to the rate permitted by increases in factor supplies and technological change. As a consequence, the volume of net investment must fall below the high levels possible during the period in which idle resources were being reemployed. Reinvestment will, of course, remain at higher levels because the total stock of capital goods is greater.

Technological Change.   From a long-range point of view, the most important dynamic force influencing the volume of investment is technological change—the development of *new products* and *new methods of production.* The development of new products will almost always temporarily produce new investment, though over a period of time investment for the production of goods for which the new products are substituted is likely to fall. If the new articles require relatively large amounts of capital goods in their production—as, for example, automobiles—substantial net investment will occur during the period of their development, and annual reinvestment will remain at a permanently higher level. During the past century, the significance for capital investment of a few major new products has been tremendous. The automobile, for example, has led to great investment in factories producing automobiles and their parts and accessories (such as tires), in the oil-refining industry, in service stations, and in highways. The net effect has probably been offset only to a minor extent by consequent reduction in investment in the production of horse-drawn vehicles and in the railroad industry.

Over the last several centuries, most inventions have involved the use of more capital equipment relative to labor and natural resources. In general, inventions have provided means of accomplishing with capital goods tasks formerly performed directly by labor. But there have been exceptions; some technological developments have been capital-saving in that they allow certain tasks to be performed economically with

---

[5]If the various phases of cycles are fully anticipated, these effects will not be observed. Thus, so-called rational expectations will lead to investment based on "typical" growth over time.

less capital investment per unit of output. The replacement of streetcars by buses in local transit service provides an example. But the general pattern of technological change has required the use of progressively more capital goods and thus has made possible continuously positive net investment, except in years of extremely sharp decline in national product.

Not only have new techniques increased investment in industries directly concerned, but by freeing labor and natural resources, they have often made possible increases in output and investment in other industries. Some developments have lessened the cost of producing capital goods and have increased the relative advantages of capital compared to other factors. While the introduction of a series of new techniques will permanently increase the volume of capital goods in use and the annual volume of reinvestment, net investment resulting from technological change will continue only so long as the development of new products and methods continues.

Changes in Expectations. Since capital equipment acquired in one period will be used over succeeding periods of time, changes in expectations about the future will affect estimated MRP and the demand for capital goods. During a depressed period, increased optimism about the future, even if based upon no tangible changes in the current profit situation, can in itself stimulate recovery. Regardless of the initial cause of a recovery movement, once it gets underway the tendency is for expectations to improve and for a general feeling of optimism to develop. This is likely to increase the volume of investment to a much higher level than would be justified on the basis of current sales. That such levels are not sustainable provides a significant cause for the next downturn. Hence capital theory in microeconomics has much to say about the business cycle which, if properly understood, is of concern in macroeconomics. Changes in expectations about future technological change can also alter present estimates of the MRP of additional capital goods.

15.9 PAYMENTS FOR CAPITAL GOODS AND FACTOR INCOMES

The sums paid by business firms for new capital equipment do not in themselves constitute factor income payments; such payments merely serve to cover the costs, explicit and implicit, of equipment-producing firms. The amounts involved are paid out by equipment producers in the form of factor incomes (wages, rent, interest, and profit) to the persons supplying factor units to them, in the same manner as amounts paid for the production of consumption goods.

Capital good purchases by business firms constitute costs from a long-range point of view, since the sums paid out must be covered if operation is to be carried on indefinitely. But the costs of capital equipment acquired in any one year cannot appropriately be regarded as costs for which the year's output is wholly responsible, since the equipment will be used to produce output over a period of years. Accordingly, under usual practice, the purchase price of equipment is depreciated over the period of years of expected life, a formula being used to allocate a share of the total cost to each year. The allocation is inevitably somewhat arbitrary, (especially in light of tax treatments which bear little relation to true depreciation), since there is no way of ascertaining exactly how much the value of the equipment declines in any given year or how long the equipment can actually remain in use. Moreover, these annual depreciation charges are not income; they merely reflect a decline in the value of a firm's capital equipment and thus represent the recovery, in the form of money capital, of earlier investment in equipment. The sums involved are available for the repayment of loans, for replacement of old equipment, for expansion, or for increases in liquid balances or security holdings. Hence the amounts paid for capital equipment do not, in themselves, give rise to a form of income distinct from that which would arise if capital equipment were not used. The distinctive return that arises from the use of capital equipment can be discovered only by considering the money capital that is required to obtain the equipment, for in the final analysis it is the ultimate owner of the capital good (who may be a bondholder or a bank rather than the firm which uses the capital good) to whom the net income yield of the capital good accrues.

SUMMARY

1. Fixed capital assets possess some unique complications as inputs: they must be financed before the outputs produced with their services are sold, and they involve a greater risk in the rate of return, relative to the other factors.

2. Firms desire more capital goods for various reasons: to replace existing capital goods, to permit capital widening or deepening, and to facilitate technological change.

3. Investment decisionmaking under the constraints of uncertainty can be facilitated by the internal rate of return equation, by the discounted present value, or by the payout period rule.

4. To adjust for risk in calculations of profitability of capital goods investment, one can use a risk discounting adjustment. These take several forms: a cutoff date or finite horizon, the Shackle approach, and probability adjustments.

5. The sources of money capital are borrowing money, selling stock, and reinvesting earnings.

6. The marginal costs of additional investments rise; firms may not be able to raise funds at all beyond a certain point.

7. There is an inverse relationship between the prices of capital goods and the demand for them.

8. The demand for capital goods (and thus the volume of investment) is affected by changes in factor supplies, changes in the supply of money capital, increases in national income due to fewer resources unemployed, technological change, and changes in expectations.

WORDS AND CONCEPTS FOR REVIEW

fixed capital assets
capital widening
capital deepening
internal rate of return
discounted present value

payback period rule
risk discount factor
capital budgeting
capital rationing

REVIEW QUESTIONS

1. What major consideration distinguishes capital goods from other factors?

2. What complications are created for the theory of factor pricing by the fact that durable capital goods are used over a period of years?

3. What is the difference between capital widening and capital deepening?

4. What is meant by embodiment of technological change? What role does technological change play in investment decisions?

5. What is the internal rate of return?

6. Why do many firms turn to "rule-of-thumb" methods for investment decisionmaking?

7. What is the payback period rule? What are its limitations?

8. Under what circumstances is use of the "urgency of investment" rule warranted? What danger is involved in its use?

9. Indicate the various approaches to the introduction of risk calculations into investment decision making, along with the limitations of these approaches.

10. Indicate the nature of the cost of money capital under the borrowing, sale of stock, and plowback methods of financing investment.

11. Why are firms more likely to undertake marginal investment projects if they have their own funds for the purpose than if they must borrow the money or sell additional stock?

12. What is capital rationing? Why does it arise? What significance does it have for investment decisionmaking?

13. What are the major determinants of the total demand for capital goods?

14. What is the nature of the functional relationship between the price of capital goods and the quantity demanded? Why?

15. What are the major causes of changes in the demand for capital goods?

16. Why are payments for capital goods not in themselves factor payments? Do earned depreciation charges constitute factor incomes? Explain.

SUGGESTED READINGS

Alchian, Armen and Allen, William. *Exchange and Production: Competition, Coordination, and Controls,* 3rd ed. Belmont, CA: Wadsworth, 1983, Chapter 6.

Baumol, W. J. *Economic Theory and Operations Analysis,* 4th ed. Englewood Cliffs, NJ: Prentice Hall, 1977, Chapters 25–26.

Harcourt, G. C. "Some Cambridge Controversies in the Theory of Capital." *Journal of Economic Literature,* June 1969, pp. 369–405.

Hirshleifer, Jack. *Investment, Interest and Capital.* Englewood Cliffs, NJ: Prentice Hall, 1970.

Jorgenson, D. W. "Econometric Studies of Investment Behavior: A Survey." *Journal of Economic Literature,* December 1971, pp. 1111–47.

Solow, R. M. *Capital Theory and the Rate of Return.* Amsterdam: North Holland, 1964.

16

The Theory of Interest

16.1 INTRODUCTION

Most people think of interest as something that banks pay on savings deposits or that finance companies charge on installment purchases. That is all right; but it is more accurate (and general) to think of interest as the rate of return associated with a loan contract and its sale price. When individuals loan money to banks in the form of savings deposits, the loan contract obligates the seller (a bank) to pay the buyer (depositor) a stated percentage of the amount borrowed at regular intervals of time. In other instances (as with marketable government bonds), the loan contract obligates the seller (the government) to pay stated sums of money at specified dates; the rate of interest that this sum represents then depends on the amount of money (the sale price) that the borrower realizes when the contract is sold. In this chapter, we shall speak (as is customary) as if there existed just one rate of interest—*the* interest rate— at any time, rather than many rates, as is in fact the case. It is easy to see that this makes no substantive difference: the rates will all tend to move together anyway.

16.2 THE NATURE OF INTEREST

In a monetary economy where each individual held and used only assets that were saved and accumulated, interest payments would be nonexistent, for no person would ever be either a lender or a borrower. However, interest payments could (and normally would) arise even in a world without money. In biblical times, for instance, it was common for one person to lend another a stock of seed in return for the borrower's promise to return the wheat, with interest in the form of an additional quantity of wheat, at the end of the harvest season. Accordingly, we may view **interest**, quite

392

generally, as *any payment that is made by a borrower to induce a lender willingly to part with the use of an asset for a specified period of time.*

In modern times, interest seldom takes any form but money because it is normally more convenient to borrow money from one person and buy a physical asset from another than to borrow a physical asset directly from a potential lender. But the ultimate effect is much the same as if the lender of money purchased a physical asset and loaned it, rather than money, to a borrower. In many instances, indeed, the lender of money becomes the legal owner of a physical asset by requiring that it serve as collateral for the loan (a standard procedure in the case of automobile loans).

A person who currently has wealth in liquid form—currency or demand deposits—has three basic alternatives: (1) spend it on consumption; (2) continue to hold it in liquid form; or (3) lend it to another transactor such as a household, business firm, bank, or government. In classical economic doctrine, interest traditionally was regarded as a payment to induce a person to save rather than consume. It is more common today to regard interest as a compensation paid to holders of liquid wealth to induce them to make it available to others rather than hold it idle or use it to purchase resources for their own use. It is sometimes argued that the mere act of saving does not in itself enable a person to obtain interest; and this is true, if by "interest" one means an *explicit* money return. Recognizing opportunity costs, however, a person who decides to hold wealth in money form must obviously receive *implicit* interest in the form of subjective gratification; otherwise he would use the money to purchase consumption goods or to buy an income-earning asset. Thus the "true" nature of interest is best regarded as an issue about which reasonable individuals may agree to disagree. However, as with capital financing, the expected (risk-adjusted) marginal implicit or explicit interest returns of all assets held must be equivalent or some would not be held.

Inflation and Interest Rates

Inflation affects the nominal or money interest rate. The **nominal interest rate** is the one that is often quoted in the media. However, there is another more important interest rate—the **real interest rate**—which is the nominal interest rate minus the rate of change in the price level over the period.

The distinction between nominal and real interest rates is particularly critical during periods of unanticipated inflation. For example, in the late 1970s, when people were clamoring over "excessively high" interest rates of 15 percent, the change in the price level was also close to 15 percent; hence the real interest rate was only slightly positive. In fact, real interest rates were very low from 1960 to 1980 and have only recently risen to the 4 to 7 percent range. Decisions about borrowing and investing are rationally made on the basis of the expected real interest rate, *not* the nominal interest rate. If inflation is always accurately anticipated, the *real* interest rate will not be affected by inflation; the nominal rate will rise and fall with inflation. This chapter deals primarily with real interest rates. The interaction of real and nominal interest rates becomes of importance in the study of macroeconomics. (See Box 16-1.)

16-1   In the first half of the 1980s, the real interest rate has risen sharply. Why?

There is much speculation and debate on this question among economists. The various explanations include: the large budget deficits with the problem of crowding out (public and private sectors competing for loanable funds and driving up the interest rate); long-run prospects of a strong economy inducing investors to borrow even at higher real interest rates, and a high demand for loans because interest was (until recently) tax deductible. However, an important explanation is that high real interest rates will transpire anytime lenders expect higher inflation than actually occurs, because they will only lend money at a nominal rate incorporating their inflationary expectations.

16.3 THE DETERMINANTS OF INTEREST RATES

Putting philosophical issues aside, we can simply define interest as *net sums paid for the use of money capital*. Then the determinants of interest are the demand for and supply of money capital. These in turn will depend on the nature of competition in loan markets. Before entering into detailed discussion of these matters, we shall find it helpful to consider decision making with regard to the allocation of accumulated wealth between money and other assets.

Allocation of Income between Consumption and Saving

A receiver of after-tax income may use it either to purchase consumption goods (consume) or to acquire an asset (save). The allocation of income between consumption and saving will depend directly on an individual's preference for present as compared with future satisfaction—or, as it is usually called, the person's **time preference**. (See Box 16-2.)

16-2   Are time preferences usually regarded as positive or negative?

Positive, because most people will prefer $1000 today to $1000 a year from now, even if they cannot earn explicit interest on any asset; for at worst, they can hold the $1000 until they have a use for it, whereas if they had to wait, they might be deprived of something they would like to buy in the interim (or be killed by a meteor). But few people have an insatiable lust for current consumption; when income rises above a certain level, therefore, almost every individual will put aside some current income for future use: to build a reserve for emergency purposes, to accumulate for old age, to provide for heirs, or for some specific future use such as education of children, purchase of a home, or establishment of a business.

Individuals differ widely in their savings behavior, even at the same level of income and wealth. Some people have a passion for accumulation; they like wealth for its own sake or for the power that it gives them over other people. Other people hate to be hindered by belongings of any kind, particularly earning assets that force them to spend long hours every April preparing tax returns. The great majority of people, however, fall between these extremes. People save a little, or a fair amount, depending on such things as the amount of wealth already accumulated, the number of dependents to support, expectations regarding future income, foresight in planning for the future, availability of desired goods, expectations of future price changes, and the extent of current windfall gains and losses (such as changes in the value of stock-market securities).

The final factor that may influence the choice is the rate of return that can be obtained if the income is saved and loaned. It was once thought that there was a significant positive relationship between the interest rate and the level of saving. Today, however, it is generally believed that the relationship is not strong. That is, of course, an empirical question; but arguments suggest that the interest rate has little significance. It is obvious that most savings are made for reasons largely unrelated to the rate of return. In addition, many families cannot possibly save larger amounts because of pressing "needs" for current consumption. Some savers, seeking a given annual dollar return from their savings, will save more rather than less if the interest rate falls (an income effect). For many families, saving is largely a matter of habit, and the margin is not calculated at all closely.

The actual savings made during a period—that is, the excess of after-tax income over consumption expenditures—may be called *ex post* **(or realized) savings**. This sum may differ from *ex ante* **(or planned) savings**, the amount that persons plan to save at the beginning of a period. The two sums will be identical if all expectations with regard to incomes, prices, and other circumstances are realized, but this is not necessarily the case. For example, suppose that persons on average start to save a higher percentage of their incomes than they did in previous periods. If all incomes remain the same and prices and other determinants are unchanged, people will succeed in saving, *ex post,* the larger sum. But the general increase in saving may reduce production and factor income payments because of the lessened purchase of consumption goods, and so the actual sum of savings during the period may be less than anticipated. The attempt to save more may thus reduce the actual sum saved. While some individuals may succeed in saving larger amounts, this may be more than offset by reduced saving on the part of others—those whose incomes fall because society as a whole spends less on consumption, one component of aggregate demand. (This phenomenon is the "paradox of thrift" referred to in macroeconomics.)

The division of national income between consumption and savings is affected not only by individual decisions in allocating disposable income between consumption and savings but also by decisions of corporate management with regard to retention of profits. These latter decisions are influenced by a number of factors including desires for additional reserves, for expansion, and for stockholder dividends. The influence of the current interest rate on these decisions appears to be slight.

Liquidity Decisions

Savings do not automatically become available for use. Only if individuals and business firms that accumulate liquid wealth are willing to use it in their own enterprises or make it available to others is the supply of money capital actually increased by additional savings. Thus the factors influencing decisions with regard to liquidity are of prime importance for the supply of money capital.

People have a variety of motives for holding portions of their personal wealth in monetary form:

1. **Transactions motive.** Persons must have on hand at any time a certain amount of money for the conduct of day-to-day transactions. Income and outgo of individuals and business firms do not balance exactly in any short period of time. If a worker receives a weekly paycheck and spends the money gradually during the following week, she will have on hand during the week the portion of the money not yet spent. She cannot conveniently lend out half the amount of the check on Saturday and obtain the money back on Tuesday. She will also usually seek to have some margin left over at the end of the week, since it is difficult to calculate exact expenditures in advance. The average amount that she has on hand depends on the size of income, the interval of receipt of the income, and the extent to which she pays in cash. Business firms likewise must keep substantial cash balances to meet current payments. In some enterprises (many types of farming, for example), the entire annual receipts are received over a very short period of time but expenses continue throughout the year. Financial institutions must also keep some portion of their assets in the form of money, since they are under obligation to meet the demands of customers at any time and on short notice.

   The total amount of money required in the economy for transactions purposes is significantly affected by the level of national income. As employment and output or the general price level (or both) rise, the total volume of money desired for transactions will rise (at original interest rates). Individuals will be receiving greater money incomes and therefore holding greater average cash balances; business firms will also desire more money to handle the larger volume of transactions. If the money supply is not increased, these demands will exceed the money supply at the going interest rate, and that rate will therefore rise (or, over a longer period prices will fall).

2. **Precautionary motives.** In addition to amounts needed to meet routine and foreseen expenditures, individuals and business firms typically keep additional sums of money to provide protection in the event of emergency. A firm's expenses may rise sharply, or its revenues may fall; failure to have sufficient money or other highly liquid assets may cause forced liquidation. An individual may suddenly experience loss of income—due to illness, for example—or unexpected expenses; failure to have adequate funds may cause expensive borrowing or loss of personal assets. For either an individual or a firm, one misfortune may lead to another. For example, by reducing income and raising

expenses, illness will necessitate emergency borrowing and thus impair a person's credit standing as well as his ability to meet other emergencies. The holding of money for precautionary purposes is made particularly necessary by the credit-rationing policies of financial institutions. Regardless of credit standing, persons are usually unable to borrow in excess of a certain sum at current interest rates.

3. **Convenience motive.** The making of loans and the reconversion of loans into money are sources of cost and inconvenience. Any type of lending, even making a savings deposit, results in a certain amount of nuisance and loss of time. The purchase of stocks and bonds necessitates the payment of brokers' fees. Persons with relatively small amounts of savings will frequently hold them in monetary form, either indefinitely or until they accumulate sufficiently to warrant purchase of stocks or bonds. Typically, small savers are interested much more in preserving the capital sum of their savings than in return; the easiest and simplest way to keep small amounts is in the form of money.

   The existence of savings accounts—which, in the United States at least, are now usually classified as money (recall the M_1, M_2, definitions of money) since the deposits can now be used directly for making payments—greatly lessens the amounts of cash and demand deposits that individuals hold for both convenience and precautionary motives, since savings accounts offer most of the advantages of currency or demand deposits yet earn interest.

4. **Speculative motive.** Whenever persons expect security prices to fall and thus interest rates to rise, they will prefer to keep their wealth in monetary form at present in order to be able to purchase securities at lower prices in the future. If they lend now, they will be unable to realize the benefits of an increase in interest rates until maturity of the securities purchased; or, if they wish to reconvert their wealth to liquid form prior to maturity, they will suffer a capital loss. When, on the other hand, persons expect security prices to rise, they will wish to lend out larger portions of their wealth at the present time.

The Significance of the Interest Rate for Liquidity Decisions

To what extent is the desire for liquidity influenced by the interest rate? It is generally assumed that the functional relationship between the interest rate and liquidity is much more significant than that between the interest rate and the savings/consumption ratio. Interest is a direct compensation for forgoing liquidity, whereas it is not a compensation for saving, as such. At low rates, the amount received for incurring the inconvenience and danger from loss of liquidity and for taking the risk of decline in the value of securities and of nonrepayment of principal is relatively small. As a consequence, persons tend to keep substantial portions of their wealth in liquid form. At high rates, the sacrifices of income caused by holding wealth in liquid form are great, and persons will be more willing to reduce their cash balances and suffer the consequences of loss of liquidity. If a person can receive only $10 a year from lending out $1,000, she might regard this sum as inadequate compensation for her inconvenience, risk of capital loss, and loss of liquidity. On the other hand, if she can receive $150 a year on the $1,000 loan with the same degree of risk, she is much more likely to consider the return adequate compensation for sacrificing the advantages of liquidity. When interest rates rise, even balances held for transactions purposes will be reduced. (See Box 16-3.)

Finally, when interest rates are low, the current selling prices of securities are relatively high; for example, if the interest rate level drops from 12 percent to 10 percent, bonds issued at 12 percent will sell at higher prices. Thus the total value of a given quantity of securities held will become greater. To the extent that wealth holders seek to maintain a balance between the current value of security holdings and the amount of their liquid balances, a relatively high figure for the former will encourage them to hold relatively larger sums of money than they would at higher interest rates.

Money Creation

Money capital may be forthcoming not only from accumulated liquid wealth but also from money creation—as additional cash issued by the government or as additional demand deposits created via the banking system. If, for example, the central banking system purchases government securities in the open market, commercial bank reserves will rise and the banking system can increase its loans by several times the amount of the increase in reserves (under the fractional reserve system discussed in macroeconomic principles).

The extent to which new money is being created in any period depends upon bank lending policy and upon governmental action in creating new cash. Bank lending policy, in turn, is dependent upon the extent of excess reserves in the banking system, upon the demand for new loans, and upon the reserve ratios that bankers regard as adequate. Bankers' expectations about future business conditions also influence their

---

16-3   True or False?   When interest rates are relatively low, there is greater likelihood that persons will anticipate an increase in rates than they will when rates are already at high levels, and thus greater amounts of money will be held because of speculative motives.

This is generally true. Lenders of money—just like sellers of wheat—become accustomed to certain rates as being "standard"; if the actual rate rises above this figure, expectations that the rate will decline are likely to be stronger than they were when the rate was low. This principle is not necessarily valid in all cases. In some instances a decline in rates may lead investors to believe that further declines are likely. It is widely believed, however, that the principle is a significant determinant of the nature of the bond or money demand schedule. It is commonly argued that the portion of money held for speculative purposes is much more responsive to interest rate changes than that held for other motives.

lending policies. Governmental policy on direct creation of new money is dictated by political considerations that are beyond the scope of the present discussion.

The significance of the interest rate for the rate of expansion of bank deposits depends in large measure upon central-bank policy. If the central banking system were to attempt (over a short period) to hold the interest rate stable at a certain level, it would take measures to increase the supply of money, primarily through open-market operations whenever the rate commenced to rise, and to decrease it whenever the rate started to fall. Over a longer period, banks cannot stabilize interest rates in this way—increasing money supply to lower rates, for example, would cause nominal interest rates to rise as inflation occurred, leaving no change in the real interest rate.

16.4 DETERMINATION OF THE INTEREST RATE

It is now possible to consider the nature of the supply schedule of money capital—the quantities of money capital available for use at various interest rates—and the demand schedule for money capital. Several incidental issues must be noted before the main thread of the argument is developed:

1. *Treatment of money capital from internal sources.* The total amount of money capital held internally by business firms from accumulated undistributed profits, earned depreciation charges, or other sources will be regarded as a part of the total supply of money capital and the firms' use of portions of this sum as a portion of the total demand.
2. *Money capital available through the sale of stock.* This is also regarded as a portion of the total money capital supply.
3. *Amounts borrowed for consumption purposes.* These are regarded as an element in total consumption of the economy, and thus a deduction from savings, rather than as an element in the demand for money capital.
4. *Government borrowing.* This is treated as a form of borrowing for production use, even though a portion is usually obtained for essentially consumption purposes.

The Supply of Money Capital

The supply of money capital may be defined as the schedule of amounts of money available to borrowers (businesses and government) at various interest rate levels in a given period of time. Initially we shall assume a given level of national income; this assumption will be modified subsequently. The supply schedule of money capital, therefore, is dependent upon the following primary determinants:

(a) The propensity to save: the total volume of new savings made during the period, including undistributed profits of corporations, at various interest rate levels. This schedule is assumed to be almost perfectly inelastic.
(b) The liquidity preference schedule: the total amount of money capital offered

at various rate levels. It is assumed, for reasons noted earlier, that a significant positive functional relationship exists.

(c) The schedule of the amounts of new money created by the government and the banking system at various interest rate levels, with a positive functional relationship.

Given these determinants and the assumptions relating to the nature of the schedules, there will be a positive functional relationship between the interest rate and the supply of money capital:

1. Higher interest rates will provide greater inducement to give up liquidity in holdings for transactions, precautionary and, especially, speculative purposes.

2. The higher the interest rate, the more willing banks will be to create additional money and, assuming full employment and the acceptance of the goal of stability by the central banking system, the more money creation that central-bank action will make possible.

In addition, if higher interest rates increase the propensity to save, additional money capital will be available at higher interest rates from this source as well.

The money capital supply schedule is illustrated in Figure 16-1 and is drawn to be upward-sloping as the previous discussion dictates.

FIGURE 16-1

Supply Curve of Money Capital
The funds offered for lending at alternate interest rates in a given time period constitute the money capital supply curve. Determinants of the schedule include the propensity to save, the liquidity preference schedule, and money creation by the government and the banking system. When the interest rate rises, liquidity becomes relatively more expensive, speculative demand for cash balances declines, more money is created, and the propensity to save rises. Thus, the quantity of money capital supplied increases, and the money capital supply curve exhibits a positive slope.

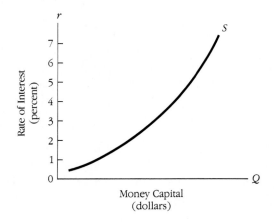

The Demand for Money Capital

The demand for money capital consists of the total amount of money capital which will be invested during the period by business firms (and governmental units) at various interest rate levels. The demand for money for consumption use is excluded from the picture, for purposes of simplicity, and is regarded as a reduction in potential supply. The determinants of demand by business firms have been indicated in Chapter 15. Some money will be desired for additional working capital—for payment of current costs in advance of sales, as total output rises—but most money capital will be desired for investment in capital goods. At each interest rate, the quantity demanded will be the amount which will allow the firm to obtain the optimum level of investment (as defined in Chapter 15). The schedule undoubtedly has some interest elasticity, particularly for longer-range investments, for which time discounting assumes particular significance. Nevertheless, it is widely believed that the interest elasticity is not great; that is, a large portion of investment made in any period is so profitable that it would still be undertaken despite substantial increases in the interest rate, whereas most of the potential *additional* investment is of such low profitability that it would not be undertaken even if the interest rate were substantially lower. The nature of the elasticity of investment is an empirical question, however, and so cannot be answered by deductive analysis.

The Equilibrium Interest Rate

Under the assumption of perfect competition in markets for money capital, the interest rate must come to a level at which the total demand for money capital is equal to the total supply available. Figure 16-2 indicates the determination of the basic equilibrium rate, $\bar{r}$ (5 percent in Figure 16-2). This equilibrium rate of interest will be maintained so long as the determinants (of money capital demand and supply) remain unchanged. If the interest rate went higher than $\bar{r}$, the total supply of money capital would exceed the demand and suppliers would lower the rate; if the actual interest rate were lower than $\bar{r}$, demand would exceed supply and the rate would be bid up by borrowers.

For the equilibrium interest rate thus determined to remain stable through time, two additional requirements must be met. First, changes occurring in the total supply of money (not money capital, but money as such) in the economy must equal the changes in demand for money to hold (not the demand for money capital) for the various liquidity motives; in other words, the total demand for liquid balances must equal the amount of money existing in the economy. Any attempt to hold more than, or less than, exists will cause the interest rate to change.

Second, the level of national income must be consistent with the interest rate. Higher income levels increase the demand for money capital (loanable funds), hence will cause the equilibrium interest rate to rise. Here again, macroeconomics and microeconomics are seen to be inextricably related.

Equilibrium Relationships of the Interest Rate

In equilibrium, the interest rate will equal:

1. The net rate of return on capital goods, since each producer will adjust the volume of investment to the point of equality of these two magnitudes at the margin.
2. The marginal rate of liquidity preference for each individual and business firm; that is, for each, the rate of interest will just balance the gains from keeping the marginal dollar of personal wealth in liquid form.
3. The marginal rate of time preference of those persons, whose allocations of income between consumption and savings are influenced by the interest rate. These persons will adjust their level of savings to the point at which the marginal gain from the use of an additional dollar for present instead of future consumption is just equal to the interest rate obtainable. This adjustment probably has little significance for the adjustment of the overall level of savings, for reasons indicated earlier.

In practice, deviations from competition will interfere somewhat with the attainment of these relationships; these deviations include absence of perfect competition in the money capital or capital goods markets and difficulties of ascertaining MRP. Capital rationing will have the same effect.

Changes in the General Level of Interest Rates

The basic overall interest level will change in response to variations in supply of and demand for money capital. Some of the major causes of shifts in these determinants can be noted briefly.

FIGURE 16-2

The Equilibrium Rate of Interest
In perfect competition, the equality of money capital supplied and demanded determines the equilibrium rate of interest: 5% in this example. Interest rate stability also requires that the total demand for liquid balances equals the existing total money supply and that the interest rate is consistent with the level of national income.

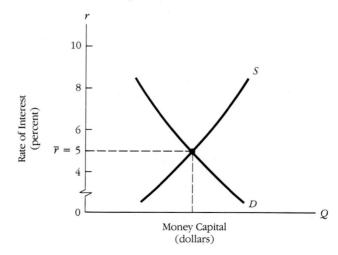

1. *A change in the willingness to part with cash balances.* If persons seek to hold a smaller portion of their wealth in liquid form (but maintain the same consumption/savings ratio), the supply of money capital will increase and the interest rate will tend to fall. This fall will, of course, reduce the willingness to part with liquid balances and restore the equilibrium at a somewhat lower interest level.

2. *A change in the supply of money.* Change in policy relating to creation of new money, either directly by government or central banking action or through expansion of bank loans and deposits, will alter the funds available for loans and affect the interest rate (at least temporarily, until prices rise causing a return to the old *real* money supply). If the central banking system seeks to lower the interest rate, it will purchase securities in the open market, thus raising securities prices and temporarily lowering the interest rate. In addition, such a policy increases the reserves of member banks and places them in a position to make additional loans. If they do so, the supply of money capital is increased and the interest rate temporarily falls still further.

   However, this policy can succeed only if individuals and banks are willing to loan on the basis of the additional money they receive. If all of the additional money is absorbed in cash balances (idle bank reserves), there will be no net increase in money capital and the rate will not fall. There may be certain levels below which the interest rate cannot be driven because of the tendency, at very low rates, for persons or banks to absorb in liquid balances any additional money made available.

3. *Changes in the volume of investment.* A change in MRP of capital will alter the volume of investment and thus the demand for money capital. This increase in demand will in itself tend to raise the rate of interest.

4. *A change in the propensity to save.* An increased desire to save, unaccompanied by an equivalent and simultaneous increase in investment, will tend to reduce the interest rate by depressing the level of national income and lowering the amount of money needed for transactions purposes.[1]

16.5 FUNCTIONS OF THE INTEREST RATE

The major functions that interest performs in the operation of the economy may be summarized briefly. In the first place, and of greatest importance, *the interest rate ensures that the flow of current savings is made available for investment in capital*

---

[1]It might appear that the increased desire to save would have a direct and immediate effect on the interest rate by increasing the supply of money capital relative to the demand for it. But this will not occur: the increase in planned savings will not manifest itself in an increase in the actual supply of money capital unless the volume of national income is maintained. This in turn cannot occur unless investment rises simultaneously with savings—in which event there is no surplus of money capital at the old interest rate level! The only source of the relative increase in the supply of loanable funds is the freeing of money from liquid balances as national income falls.

goods, instead of going into liquid balances. In other words, the interest rate ensures equilibrium of the supply of money capital with the demand for it by inducing persons to make available their liquid wealth for business expansion and other purposes instead of retaining it in liquid form.

Second, *the interest rate rations the total available amount of money capital among various possible uses to those which offer the greatest prospect of return.* This rationing device does not always function perfectly, of course, primarily because some firms undertake expansions with internally acquired capital which might not meet the tests of the market rate (but will tend to—otherwise profit maximizers would loan out internally generated funds).

Third, *the rate establishes equilibrium between the amount of money* (not money capital, but money in existence) *in the economy and the amounts which persons wish to hold in cash balances.*

Fourth, *in full-employment periods, the interest rate is one factor which assists in restricting the total volume of investment to the volume of planned savings and thereby aids in checking excessive aggregate demand.* This function was once regarded as the chief task of the interest rate. But the volume of investment does not appear to be highly responsive to changes in interest rates, especially because of the importance of internal funds for financing of expansion, and because the volume of savings is clearly unresponsive to the interest rate. The rate is still regarded by many economists as a useful tool for dampening inflationary pressures.

In periods of unemployment, the effect of the interest rate in limiting the volume of investment is detrimental to economic recovery. However, this effect is easily exaggerated, since the volume of investment appears to be somewhat unresponsive to interest reductions in such periods.

Finally, interest is one component of income; hence it affects the demand for goods and therefore what is produced in society. Interest is a factor payment for the use of money capital just as a wage is a factor payment for the use of labor.

SUMMARY

1. Interest is the rate of return associated with a loan contract and its sale price. Payment of interest is necessary to induce those persons who have money capital to turn it over to those who wish to use it; hence interest is a factor payment, like wages.

2. The real interest rate is the nominal or money interest rate minus the expected rate of change in the price level.

3. There is a positive functional relationship between the interest rate and the supply of money capital and an inverse functional relationship between the interest rate and the demand for money capital. The equilibrium interest rate equates supply and demand.

4. Decisions affecting interest rates include the allocation of income between consumption and saving, liquidity decisions, the relationship between liquidity and the interest rate, money creation, and firms' attitudes toward the future. Anything affecting either the supply or demand for money capital will affect the interest rate.

5. In equilibrium, the interest rate will equal the net rate of return on capital goods, the marginal rate of liquidity preference for each individual and business firm, and the marginal rate of time preference of those persons whose allocations of income between consumption and savings are influenced by the interest rate.

6. The interest rate ensures that the flow of current saving is made available for investment in capital goods, instead of seeking to go into liquid balances; rations the total available amount of money capital among various possible uses; and establishes equilibrium between the amount of money already in existence and the amounts individuals wish to hold. As income to the recipient, interest rates also affect the demand for goods and services.

WORDS AND CONCEPTS FOR REVIEW

interest
nominal interest rate
real interest rate
time preference
ex post (realized) saving
ex ante (planned) saving

transactions motive
precautionary motive
convenience motive
speculative motive
cash balances

REVIEW QUESTIONS

1. Why is the payment of interest necessary?

2. Why is the payment of interest more satisfactorily regarded as a payment for overcoming liquidity than as a payment for saving?

3. What is meant by liquidity preference? Time preference?

4. What considerations influence individuals' decisions regarding the allocation of income between consumption and saving?

5. Why is it believed today that the rate of interest has little significance for decisions to save or consume?

6. Explain the nature of the transactions motive for maintaining liquid balances. Explain the relationship between changes in national income (in both real and monetary terms) and the amounts of money held to satisfy the transactions motive.

7. Under what circumstances will persons hold wealth in liquid form for speculative reasons?

8. Why will persons tend to hold more money when interest rates are low than when they are high? Answer in terms of the various motives for liquidity.

9. What are some additional sources of money capital in addition to savings?

10. Summarize the primary determinants of the supply of and demand for money capital and the nature of the supply and demand schedules.

11. What will happen if persons seek to hold more money than there is in the economy?

SUGGESTED READINGS

Clower, R. W. "Productivity, Thrift and the Rate of Interest." *Economic Journal*, March 1954.

Fisher, Irving. *The Theory of Interest*. New York: Macmillan, 1930.

Friedman, Milton, *Price Theory*. Chicago: Aldine Publishing Company, 1976, pp. 283–322.

Shackle, G. L. S. "Recent Theories Concerning the Nature and Role of Interest." In *Survey of Economic Theory*. New York: St. Martin's Press, 1967, pp. 48–53.

17

Rents
and Quasi-Rents

17.1 INTRODUCTION

Attainment of the optimum factor combinations requires, in most instances, the use not only of labor and capital inputs but also of natural resources—inputs provided *directly* by nature. Natural resources (or **land**, to use the more common though less descriptive term) differ from capital in that their existence is not dependent on human effort. Accordingly, the supply cannot be increased by deliberate action, although the usefulness of land for production purposes can be increased by various improvements—such as clearing, draining, and irrigating—which require labor and constitute capital goods. Since, however, land available for use is limited relative to demand, a price must be paid for its use, a price which constitutes an income to the owners in a society where natural resources are privately owned. This return, which is not a compensation necessary to overcome any real costs, is known as *land rent*—or, more commonly, **rent**.

17.2 MARGINAL PRODUCTIVITY ANALYSIS APPLIED TO LAND

The basic marginal productivity analysis presented in Chapter 13 can be applied to land as well as to other factors. The demand for land of a particular type is dependent upon the Marginal Revenue Product (MRP) schedule of this type of land to various users of it. As is typical for all factors, land's MRP falls beyond a certain point as additional units are added. For most business firms, the quantity of land in use is not easily adjustable in the short-run period.

The nature of the supply schedule of land is conditioned by the basic characteristics of this factor. Since land is fixed in quantity and cannot be increased by human activity, the potential supply to the economy is perfectly inelastic even over a long-run period.

Relatively high prices paid for the use of the land will of course stimulate the making of improvements to increase the output on given land; but these improvements are capital goods, and the higher output is attributable to them. Of course, these improvements will raise the MRP of land as the land has more of other inputs with which to "work."

Not only is the potential supply of land of various qualities perfectly inelastic, but so will be the actual supply offered to users at positive prices, so long as the market is perfectly competitive. Since the owners of land gain virtually nothing by holding it idle, it is better for them to get the going market return for it, no matter how low this figure is, than to get nothing at all. In contrast, the holders of money capital gain the advantages of liquidity by holding their capital idle, and workers avoid the disutility of labor by not working. But again there is essentially no gain from holding land idle.[1]

Under the assumption of perfectly competitive markets for the use of land, the rent figure for any particular type of land would adjust to the level at which the demand for and the supply of this type of land were equal. At this level, rent would equal the MRP of the land. Because of the perfectly inelastic supply, changes in demand would produce sharp changes in rent; for example, a substantial increase in population (not offset by technological improvements in agricultural production) would result in a significant increase in land rent and thus in the share of national income going to the landowning class. It was this tendency in nineteenth-century England which led to such great interest in the theory of rent, as reflected in the writings of Adam Smith, Ricardo, and Malthus. (See Box 17-1.)

In the absence of imperfections in the land market, the adjustment of rent to equate supply and demand would be rapid. Actually, the land market is somewhat imperfect. A particular market is limited in area, with a relatively small number of tenants and landlords. Knowledge of market conditions may be very limited, and the bargaining position of the various parties may be unequal. The small number of buyers and sellers may well prevent the markets from being perfectly competitive in many cases: monopolistic restriction of supply may sometimes but rarely develop; conversely, monopsonistic influences on price may be present. The rent may be set by direct two-party bargaining, with results difficult to predict by general analysis. If monopoly elements develop, all the available land might not come into use; it may be advantageous for landowners to withhold a portion of land in order to maximize revenue received. The fact that much land may be bought outright by owners, rather than rented, further segments the market, reducing the ease of conversion to its highest valued use and user. When land is owned by users, rent payments cease to be contractual in nature and take an implicit form. (See Box 17-2.)

---

[1]There are rare exceptions, for short periods. Some types of land will increase in productiveness if kept out of use for a few years. Alternatively, if land depreciates with use, at a sufficiently low rent it may be optimal to hold land idle. This may hold for both agricultural and nonagricultural land. For example, development now in a rapidly growing city may preclude later development at a higher, more profitable building density.

17-1   Chart economic rents captured from land in a supply and demand diagram. Would the same quantity of land be available at a low price (rent) as at a high price? And if the supply of land is inelastic, what must determine the amount of economic rent?

Since the supply for land is assumed to be fixed, the supply curve is perfectly inelastic, as seen in the diagram below. Hence even at some minimum positive rent or at any other higher rent, quantity Q_0 of land will be available. The intersection of the vertical supply curve and the demand curve will determine the amount of economic rent. If demand for land is strong, economic rents will be large.

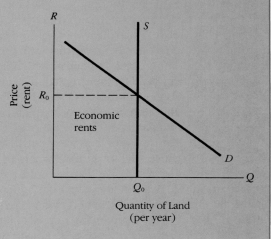

17-2   What, in the long run, is the basic difference between the determination of the cost of land use and the cost of the use of capital?

In the long run, the **cost of land use** depends solely upon the land's potential yield in alternative employments, since no cost of production is involved; whereas the cost of using capital equipment is dependent upon the cost of producing the equipment plus the interest cost element. The supply of land is perfectly inelastic, while that of capital equipment depends upon the relationship between the yield from the equipment and the cost of production of the equipment, and is thus highly elastic over a period of time. The entire sum paid for the use of land constitutes an income to the recipients, while the amounts paid for the use of capital equipment serve, from a long-run standpoint, to cover the costs of the production of the equipment; only the interest constitutes income.

17.3 THE SELLING PRICE OF LAND

Land, like capital equipment, may be purchased outright by the business enterprises using it. The selling price depends on the supply of and demand for the land at a particular time (assuming perfectly competitive conditions in this market). The price the buyer is willing to pay for a particular piece of land and the price at which the present owner is willing to sell are determined by the current and prospective rent (explicit or implicit) that may be gained from the land. Specifically, the selling price will tend to equal the capitalized sum of the expected rental return, the return being capitalized at the interest rate obtainable on other investments of comparable risk.

Suppose, for example, that the current interest rate on such loans is 5 percent. A parcel of land yielding (and expected to yield indefinitely) $600 a year in rent will sell for $12,000 if the market is perfect. If a buyer paid more for the land, she would be getting a return on wealth that was less than she could get from other uses of her wealth. If, for example, she paid $20,000, this would amount to an annual return on the investment of only 3 percent ($600 ÷ $20,000); whereas if she had purchased bonds, interest of 5 percent would have been earned. On the other hand, present owners would not sell for less than $12,000, or they would be getting less return after making the sale than they earn at present.

The markets for the sale of land, like those for its rental, are somewhat imperfect because of the lack of an extensive market organization (comparable to the stock market, for example) and the relatively small numbers of buyers and sellers, each of whom may sell or buy land only at infrequent intervals. Monopoly or monopsony conditions may be rare, but the actual price may be determined in many cases by direct bargaining because the numbers of buyers and sellers are small. Neither party can be certain about the future yield, and estimates of this figure will differ. Furthermore, in some cases, the relative bargaining positions of the buyer and the seller will differ. The seller may be desperately in need of cash and be forced to let the land go for a very low figure. But, except in unusual cases, the buyer would not pay more than the sum representing the capitalization of his estimate of yield; the seller would not part with the land for a figure much less than the capitalized sum of his own estimate of yield. (See Box 17-3.)

The Differential Returns Theory of Land Rent

The supply-demand analysis of land-rent determination, as with the explanation of other factor prices, is not open to question on a logical basis. But for a long time an alternative approach, under which rent was explained in terms of **differential returns** on various grades of land, was regarded as a more satisfactory explanation of

17-3 Why must care be taken when applying the sales price-yield rule to real estate containing both land and buildings?

Because buildings are subject to depreciation. The selling price of existing buildings and other durable capital goods is affected by the yield, but the capitalization must be based upon the limited period of expected remaining useful life, not upon permanent life as in the case of land.

Furthermore, reproduction cost is significant; capital goods cannot sell in the long run for amounts in excess of the cost of building new ones, provided that the construction of new units is possible, even though on a yield basis the value figure might exceed this amount.

rent. This approach arose partly because of the wide variation in quality (and thus productivity) of different types of land and partly from the fixed nature of the supply and the tendency for many producers—particularly farmers—to regard acreage as a permanent fixed factor to which quantities of other factors employed must be adjusted. This is not an unrealistic assumption from the standpoint of the firm in many countries where, for reasons of law or custom, additional land cannot be purchased. Moreover, from the standpoint of an entire economy, the total supply of land is fixed in any country. This **"differential returns" theory of land rent** is often called the Ricardian rent theory after David Ricardo, the early-nineteenth-century economist, who popularized it.[2]

The differential returns approach can be explained most simply by assuming initially that a new area of land, a previously unknown island, is discovered and settled. In this area, all land is equally fertile and equally well located. Further assumptions are made that only one good is produced and is sold in a perfectly competitive market. When the area is first settled and all the land is not yet in use, the price of the product will be equal to the average capital and labor cost, with firms operating at the point of lowest average cost. If the demand for the product increases so that the market price of the product rises temporarily above average cost, additional land will be brought into use as new firms enter production. Since the average cost for the new firms will be the same as that of the old, the supply will continue to increase until the price falls back to the original level. There is no competition among producers for land, since all are making optimum use of labor and capital on their existing land. If some producers were not doing so, they could reach the level of lowest cost by taking up additional land. If a firm increases the amount of land being used beyond the amount which allows lowest average cost, the higher average cost will cause losses. As long as land is not scarce—as long as producers seek no more land than the amount they can obtain by taking up idle land—there can be no rent. Price will equal average and marginal capital and labor costs.

Eventually, however, if population increases sufficiently, the demand for the product will become so great that all land will be brought into use. Beyond this point, further increases in demand for the product will raise the market price, and each firm will increase its output until marginal cost is equal to the new price. So long as the demand is great enough that at the price equaling lowest average cost the quantity demanded exceeds the total amount that can be supplied at that price, the price must remain above this figure (at r in Figure 17-1). Thus a differential arises between price and average capital-and-labor cost (represented by the distance cr in Figure 17-1), which cannot be eliminated by the entry of new firms, since all available land is now in use. This differential between price and average cost arises because of the scarcity of land, once the demand for the product becomes so great that the output cannot be produced on the available supply of land at minimum average cost. In order to meet the high level of demand, output must be produced at a marginal cost ($0C_0$ in Figure 17-1) in excess of average cost. To cover this marginal cost, price must exceed average

[2]See David Ricardo, *Principles of Political Economy* (1817).

FIGURE 17-1

Land Rent Determination, Land of Uniform Quality
When land becomes scarce, its produce becomes more costly. If product demand is greater than the minimum average cost output level, long-run marginal cost will exceed long-run average cost. With a product price of C_0, the firm will produce Q_0 output at a marginal cost of C_0. The differential between price and average cost, cr, is rent per unit of output. The $LRAC^R$ curve incorporates land rent and labor and capital production costs.

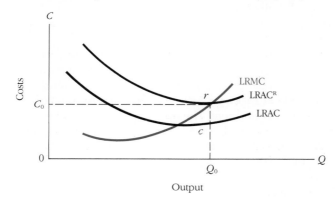

cost (exclusive of rent). The amount of the differential between price (which equals marginal cost) and average cost (exclusive of rent) is the land rent per unit of output. On a given acreage of land, the total land rent will be the amount of rent per unit of output multiplied by the annual yield on the acreage. With rent included in cost, the firm's long-run average cost curve in Figure 17-1 is $LRAC^R$.

Difference in Fertility and Location

The fertility differences of farm land are due largely to variations in the nature of the soil. With a given application of labor and capital, some types of soil will yield more output than others because of physical differences in content. Productivity is influenced also by temperature, rainfall, and other climatic factors as well as by drainage and ease of cultivation. Productivity differences manifest themselves in differences in average cost figures (exclusive of rent) for the firms on various grades of land. On very fertile soil, well drained, with good rainfall and warm climate, the average capital and labor cost per unit of output will be low because of the high yield per dollar spent on these factors. The opposite will be true on poor land.

Though these differences do not modify the theory of rent significantly, they do require some amplification of it. It will be assumed that land falls into certain definite grades, with successively higher cost schedules. In practice, land shades off gradually from the best to the poorest; but classification into grades, with the assumption that producers on all parcels of land in particular grades have identical cost schedules, will simplify the explanation without lessening its significance.

As long as the demand for the product is small, only the very best land—Grade A land—will be used. (The situation will be the same as in the initial stage of the first example above.) If the demand becomes great enough to bring all Grade A land into use, and if the demand still cannot be satisfied at the price equal to lowest average cost on Grade A land, price will remain above the Grade A lowest cost figure. As demand continues to increase, market prices will eventually rise above lowest average cost on Grade B land, and units of this land will come into use. The increased market supply of the product will bring market price to the level of the lowest average cost on Grade B land. Price cannot fall below this figure, with the demand at assumed levels, or all Grade B land would go out of use, and the total supply of the good would be lower than the quantity demanded at the lower price level.

On Grade A land, production will be carried to the point at which price is equal to marginal cost. On Grade A land, price will exceed the old average cost figure (as in Figure 17-1). The differential between price (which equals average cost on Grade B land, the marginal land) and average cost (exclusive of rent) on the Grade A land is, as in the earlier example, the land rent. The firms on Grade A land will be operating at a level of output at which marginal cost is equal to price and thus at a level of output beyond that of the old lowest-cost figure. Note that the rent differential going to owners of Grade A land as demand increases makes these owners wealthier. But the owner-farmers do *not* have a cost advantage over those farmers who rent land from absentee owners! Recall that costs are opportunity costs regardless of whether explicit payments are made or not.

If the demand for the product continues to increase, eventually all Grade B land will come into use; further demand increases will raise the market price until it covers lowest average cost on Grade C land and the latter is brought into use. The price, which must now remain high enough to cover average cost on Grade C land if supply of and demand for the product are to be maintained at equality, will now exceed average cost on Grade B land, and rent will arise on the latter. Grade B land has ceased to be marginal land; Grade C, formerly submarginal, is now the marginal land. The rent on Grade A will be still greater.

Typical cost curves for the firms on each of the three grades of land are illustrated in Figure 17-2. So long as only Grade A land must be used, price will remain at 50 cents. When demand has increased sufficiently to require the use of Grade B land to make supply and demand equal, the price must be 75 cents, or all Grade B land will drop out of use and market demand will exceed market supply. Accordingly, a differential—a rent of approximately 24 cents per unit of output (*nr* in Figure 17-2)—arises on Grade A land.[3] When demand increases still more, so that all B land is used and C land comes into cultivation, the price of the product must be $1.00. There now exists a rent of 24 cents per unit of output (ms) on Grade B land and of 48 cents per unit (*n'r'*) on the Grade A land. The rent per acre would be the rent per unit of output multiplied by the average yield per acre on the particular grade.

In summary, price must equal long-run average cost on the marginal land, the poorest (in the sense of highest cost) land that will be used in production. On better

---

[3]The figure is less than 25 cents because average cost rises slightly as output is pushed beyond the point of lowest cost.

FIGURE 17-2

Land Rent, Land of Varying Quality

Long-run average costs are lowest for Grade A land, are higher for Grade B land, and even higher for Grade C land. If only Grade A land is utilized, product price will be 50 cents in the long run. If product demand is sufficient to allow the use of Grade B land, price will stabilize at 75 cents, and a rent of 24 cents per unit of output accrues for Grade A land. If price is $1.00, Grade C land will be cultivated, per-unit rent on Grade B land will be *ms* in part (b), and per-unit rent on Grade A land will be *n'r'* in part (a).

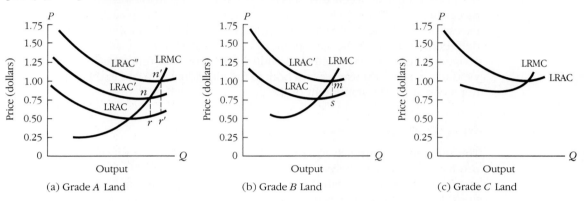

(a) Grade A Land   (b) Grade B Land   (c) Grade C Land

grades of land, the average cost (exclusive of rent) is lower. The difference between this lower average-cost figure and the marginal-land average-cost figure is the amount of land rent on the better land. If land rent were less than this, farmers on poorer land would bid more for the better land.

Once land rent has arisen, it constitutes a cost from the standpoint of the individual producer, regardless (as already emphasized) of whether he owns or rents the land. If he leases the land, he will have to pay rent to his landlord; if he owns the land, his costs include the amount he could have made by leasing the land to someone else, since he must cover this sum (along with his other costs) in order to remain in business. Land rent may be regarded as a differential return from the standpoint of the economy, but it is a cost from the standpoint of the individual producer. (See Box 17-4.)

17-4   Does location affect cost?

Of course. The products of the various parcels of land will be sold in the same market areas; firms using the more remote land and that served by poor and costly transportation facilities will have higher costs of marketing their products than those producing on better located land. Firms in poorer locations cannot sell at prices higher than those obtained by firms located close to market. Hence location advantages, like fertility advantages, will be bid into rents (hence costs) by competitive markets; this fact provides the theoretical foundation of urban economies.

The analysis above, for purposes of simplification, was based upon the assumption that a single product is produced. Actually, a variety of products will be grown in any area; and some land is more suited for one purpose, some for others. For example, wetter parcels might be better suited for rice production, with wheat being produced in drier areas. Each parcel of land will be used for the purpose in which it will yield maximum rent (disregarding the effects of producers' miscalculations); the price of each product will equal average cost on marginal land, and the rent on better land will be a differential between this and the actual cost (exclusive of rent) on the better pieces of land. The rent yielded by the crop actually grown on each parcel of land in excess of the amount of rent which the land would yield in the next-best use is a differential rent from the standpoint of the particular industry as well as that of the economy, but it is a cost to the individual producer. The rent which the land would yield in the next-best use is a cost both to the individual firm and to the industry but is not a cost from the standpoint of the economy as a whole.

Nonagricultural Production

The differential approach to land rent has been explained in terms of agricultural production. A similar analysis can be applied to other types of industries—or, indeed, to existing housing with land rents (and values) being higher at more desirable locations. For manufacturing, rent is typically a minor element in cost. In retailing, however, it is important. The cost differential in such uses arises solely out of considerations of location. Good locations in any city allow lower cost of operation, primarily because the rate of stock turnover is greater than for stores at less-desirable sites. Good locations are limited relative to the demand for them. The faster turnover lowers capital cost, since a given amount of money capital can be invested in a greater total volume of goods during a certain period of time. Faster turnover lessens loss from spoilage and obsolescence. Good locations usually allow better utilization of personnel, greater effectiveness of advertising, and savings in transportation and travel costs. (See Boxes 17-5 and 17-6.)

17-5 True or False? In locations marginal for retailing, no rent will be earned over and above that which the land would yield from nonretailing use.

True. In better locations, the average cost of operations (exclusive of rent) will be less. This differential is the additional rent arising out of the use of the land in retailing. Landowners will be able to extract this amount (plus, of course, the amount of rent that the land would yield in the next-best nonretailing use) from retailers, since the latter can pay this amount and still earn a normal return on their investment.

17-6 **Stores in outlying areas sometimes advertise that they can sell more cheaply because they are outside the high-rent area. Is the lower rent which they pay responsible for the lower prices they charge, or is the rent lower because they must charge lower prices to attract customers?**

The latter answer is correct. The demand for land, like any other input, is derived from the demand for the final product. This example is actually a modern-day version of the famous Corn Law debate in England in the early nineteenth century: Was corn expensive in England because of high corn-land rents, or were corn-land rents high because of the high price of corn? The correct answer, again the latter, had critical bearing on whether a tariff on cheap foreign (French) corn should be maintained. Allowing inexpensive French corn into England would lower the price of corn and hence the size of rental offers for corn land. English farmers on nonmarginal land would not be forced out of business by the high cost of corn land; rather owners would earn less rent and the consumer would benefit.

The Merits of the Two Approaches to Rent Determination

The marginal productivity and differential theories of land rent are merely alternative explanations of the same phenomenon, and they are in no sense contradictory. Actually, the differential theory contributes very little toward a better understanding of the nature of rent; moreover, the use of this explanation for the determination of rent while other factor prices are explained by supply and demand suggests a basic difference between the rent on land and other factor prices which is not realistic. The marginal productivity analysis is adequate; the differential approach was presented in the preceding pages only because of the major role which it once enjoyed in economic theory.

Land Rent as a Distinct Functional Return

Should rent be regarded as a type of return distinct from other income, paid for the provision to business firms of units of natural resources for use in production? This point of view was long accepted in economic theory, but its appropriateness has been questioned in recent decades. The unique characteristic of natural resources is the perfectly inelastic supply, from a long-range standpoint. But from a short-run standpoint, other factor supplies, especially of certain types of capital goods, may also be perfectly inelastic, and the return therefore does not differ significantly from land rent. From the standpoint of the receiver of rent, the income is essentially a return on the money capital value represented by the selling price of the land and does not differ from the usual interest return. Because of these considerations, there has been a tendency in recent years to regard *land rent* as merely one form of return on money capital—that is, as interest in the broad sense of the term. The term *rent* itself was first broadened to include short-period returns from the use of capital equipment—known as **quasi-rents**—and was then extended still further by various writers to apply to all returns that are surpluses over and above the amounts necessary to retain factor units in the industry or available to the economy as a whole. Rent in this broad sense is not regarded as a distinct functional return, but rather as a surplus element in all forms of factor income. (See Box 17-7.)

17.4 QUASI-RENT

Over a long-run period, capital equipment must yield a sufficient amount to cover depreciation—that is, to maintain intact the money capital invested in it—and earn an average interest return (including the appropriate risk premium). If the equipment fails to do so, some units will not be replaced and the return on the remaining equipment will rise. If the return is greater than this, additional equipment will be produced and the return will fall. The depreciation element in the return is not an income, but merely maintains the amount of money capital; the interest element is a return to the suppliers of money capital.

In the short run, however, the actual receipts obtained from use of the equipment may differ substantially from the depreciation-plus-necessary-interest figure, the actual returns to the owners of the equipment being determined solely by conditions of yield

17-7   Some economics professors collect economic rents. That is, they enjoy their work so much that they would work for less than their current salary. Will the supply curve for economists be perfectly inelastic, as it was for land? Draw the hypothetical supply and demand curves for economics professors and indicate which area is economic rent.

The difference between what economics professors would be willing to work for and what they receive is economic rent. However, with an upward-sloping supply curve for economics professors (indicating that more will pursue professing economics at higher wages), part of the payment to the factor is required to keep professors from pursuing other occupations and part is economic rent, as indicated in the diagram.

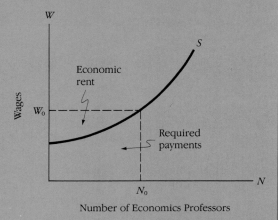

on the equipment. Furthermore, from the short-term point of view, in a sense the cost to the firm arising out of the use of the equipment is not the depreciation-plus-interest-on-investment figure but the amount the equipment could yield in the next-best employment. It is this amount which the firm sacrifices by continuing to use the equipment in the enterprise. If the actual return in the particular firm is greater than the return from the next-best use, the additional amount is a rent, from the standpoint of the firm, attributable to the capital equipment.

From the standpoint of the economy, the entire sum of the return from the use of existing capital equipment is similar to rent, since the equipment is available for use once it has been produced, whether any return is earned or not. If the equipment will yield more in this particular industry than in others, the differential is a rent from the standpoint of both this industry and the economy. Accordingly, the term *quasi-rent* is often applied to the short period return of existing capital equipment. The similarity of land rent is strictly a temporary phenomenon, however, since over a period of time the return must cover the depreciation-plus-interest figure.

In any particular period, the quasi-rent figure may be less or more than the depreciation-plus-interest return on the capital equipment. If, for example, the demand for the product produced with the equipment falls, the return from the use of the equipment will decline below the long-run necessary return figure; the firm now cannot sell the equipment or lease it out except on a reduced basis (due to the lower return) and thus has no better alternative than continued use of the equipment—unless it can be used in another industry more advantageously. On the other hand, if the demand for the product and the return on the equipment rise, the return will exceed the long-run figure in the interval until additional equipment of this type can be produced and placed in operation. (See Box 17-8.)

17.5 THE CONCEPT OF RENT
AS A GENERALIZED SURPLUS RETURN

Many economists expand the concept of rent to include all payments for factor units (and implicit returns attributable to specific factor units owned by the firm) which are not cost elements from the standpoint of the industry or the entire economy, because payments to or earning of them is not necessary to make the factor units available to the industry or the economy. For example, famous athletes and musicians would

---

17-8   Why, in a short-run period, are the determinants of the supply of capital goods similar to those of land?

If the value of the equipment falls, say because of a reduction in the price of the good it produces, it will usually still be supplied to its current use. This is much like the case of land.

The dissimilarity stems from the greater importance of depreciation in use, which renders it more likely that capital will sit idle than is the case with land.

usually continue in their current occupations even if demand for their sport or type of music declined, greatly lowering their earnings. Any return above opportunity cost—perhaps that associated with construction work or musical tutoring of children—would keep them in their current jobs (less than this if construction work or music lessons for children were particularly irritating). In large measure, these elements are costs from the standpoint of the individual firms, since the firms must make the payments to get the factor units away from other firms in the industry, except to the extent that particular factor units offer a greater yield in the one particular firm than in any other. But if the units are available to the industry whether payment is made or not because they have no use in other industries, the payments are rents from the standpoint of the economy. If the units are not available to the industry without payment but are available to the economy as a whole whether payments are made or not, then the payments are costs from the standpoint of the industry but rents from the standpoint of the economy.

Land rent is a rent, in this sense, virtually in its entirety so far as the economy as a whole is concerned; and the excess earned in one industry over the amount the land would yield in the next most advantageous use is a rent from the standpoint of that industry as well. From a short-run standpoint, the returns arising out of the use of capital equipment are rents from the standpoint of the economy; and to the extent that the equipment is usable (or yields a higher return) in one particular industry only, the returns are rents (entirely or in part) from the standpoint of that industry as well. Over a longer period, however, the payments for the use of capital goods are true costs. Wages may consist in part of rents in this sense of the term; if, for example, workers have skills which are of greater value in one industry than another, then the amounts they earn in the industry over and above the amounts they could earn in other lines of work are rents from the standpoint of the industry.

Kenneth Boulding has emphasized that whenever the supply of factor units is not perfectly elastic, a portion of the returns to the factor owners consists of rent because the full amounts are not necessary to make all of the factor units available.[4] If the

---

[4]See K. E. Boulding, "The Concept of Economic Surplus," *American Economic Review,* Vol. 35 (December, 1945), pp. 851–69.

17-9   True or False?   If professors' salaries rise as a result of a temporary increase in college attendance, the salary increases are called economic rents.

True. This occurred in the late sixties, when baby boomers and those attempting to avoid military service contributed to increased college enrollments. As a result of this temporary phenomenon, professors' salaries rose uncharacteristically. Until a larger supply of college professors (new Ph.D's) hit the market, professors enjoyed higher-than-usual salaries because of these short-run rents, called *quasi-rents.*

supply is not perfectly elastic, some factor units will be available at a return lower than the amount their owners actually receive; the differential between the actual return and the one necessary to make them available is a surplus, and thus a rent in this sense. The size of this differential will be different (smaller) if rent is considered from the standpoint of the industry than it would be if viewed from the standpoint of the economy. This is because factor supplies are typically much more elastic to one industry than to the economy as a whole due to the possibility of shifting of factor units among various industries.

17.6 A FINAL NOTE ON RENT

The price paid for the use of land, in the sense of factor units provided directly by nature and therefore nonreproducible, may be regarded as a separate type of return designated as land rent, or it may be regarded simply as an interest return on the money capital equivalent of the land's current sale value. Regardless of the designation, the determination of the sum involved may be explained in terms of the usual marginal productivity approach applied to each type of land or, in traditional terms, as a differential between the average cost (exclusive of rent) on the particular type of land as compared to average cost on marginal land. These approaches are alternative methods of explanation; but there is no particular advantage in applying a method of analysis to land different from that applied to other factors.

The distinguishing feature of land is the fact that, since it is provided by nature and is not producible, the supply is perfectly inelastic. The return is therefore dependent solely upon demand, which depends upon the land's yield. In a short-run period, however, specialized capital equipment is likewise perfectly inelastic in supply, and cost of production is not relevant once it has been produced. Thus, in a short period, the return on capital goods is dependent solely upon the yield of the equipment in production and is similar to land rent; it may be designated as *quasi-rent*. But this is a short-period phenomenon only; since capital goods are produced and wear out, over a long period the return is dependent upon the cost of production of the equipment and must cover this cost plus an interest return on the money capital. If capital goods can be produced at constant costs, the long run is very different indeed from the short run; rather than depending solely on demand, price in the long run depends solely on supply, with demand determining only how much is produced. (See Box 17-9.)

17-10   On which types of land has land rent been increased by the development of the automobile? On which types has it been decreased?

The automobile has raised the demand for land more distant from urban centers. The lower full costs (in money and time) of travel—such as commuting to central work, shopping, and entertainment areas—lowers the value of access to the center. Hence rents have become relatively lower in central urban areas and higher in the suburbs and urban fringe.

In recent years, then, the term *rent* has been extended to cover all returns attributable to specific factors which are surpluses, in the sense that payment of them is not necessary to ensure that the factor units will be available either to an industry or to the economy as a whole. Rent in this sense is not a distinct functional return but an element in all types of factor returns arising whenever factor supplies are not perfectly elastic. (See Box 17-10.)

SUMMARY

1. Rent is a consistent return to a factor of production that is greater than its opportunity costs. That is, rent is the excess of what the factor could earn in the next-best alternative use.

2. In a perfectly competitive model, the supply curve for land is perfectly inelastic; an owner of land gains virtually nothing by holding it idle. Thus it is best to get the market return on land even if that return is very low. This is not true for capital or labor.

3. The position of the demand curve will determine the amount of economic rent when the supply curve is inelastic.

4. The land market is somewhat imperfect. Imperfect information, unequal bargaining powers of buyers and sellers, and small numbers of buyers and sellers may reduce the competitiveness in the land market.

5. The selling price of land will tend to equal the capitalized sum of the expected rental return.

6. Quasi-rents are the returns to factors of production that are greater than opportunity costs in the short run. However, positive quasi-rents disappear in the long run as additional factors are employed because of greater-than-average rates of returns.

WORDS AND CONCEPTS FOR REVIEW

land
rent
marginal productivity theory of land rent
cost of land use
differential returns theory of land rent
location and land rents (costs)

fertility and land rents (costs)
differential approach in nonagricultural
     production
land rent and distinct functional returns
quasi-rents

REVIEW QUESTIONS

1. How does land differ from other types of factors?

2. What is the nature of the supply schedule of land from the standpoint of the economy? From the standpoint of a particular industry?

3. Why is the market for the renting of land imperfect?

4. If a piece of land is yielding $650 a year rent and is expected to continue to do so in the future, what will be the approximate selling price of the land, assuming a real interest rate of 4 percent on investments of comparable risk?

5. Why will the land not sell for more than the figure given in the answer to Question 4? For less?

6. Why will the sale price of a house not equal the capitalized sum of the figure for which it rents?

7. Would rent arise if all land were equally fertile and well located, but limited in amount relative to demand?

8. What is *quasi-rent*?

9. Why is the concept of rent a surplus return attributable to a specific factor?

10. How is it possible for a particular payment for factor units to be a cost from the standpoint of the firm but a rent (in the broad sense of the term) from the standpoint of the economy as a whole?

11. Why is a portion of the returns to a certain group of factor owners rent (in the broad sense of the term) rather than a true cost, unless the factor supply is perfectly elastic?

12. If the supply schedule of a particular factor to a certain industry is perfectly inelastic, what portion of the payment to the owners of the factor unit is rent?

SUGGESTED READINGS

Boulding, K. E. "The Concept of Economic Surplus." *American Economic Review*, Vol. 35 (December 1945), pp. 851–69.

Stigler, George. *The Theory of Price*, 4th ed. New York: Macmillan, 1987, Chapter 16.

Worcester, Dean A. "A Reconsideration of the Theory of Rent." *American Economic Review*, Vol. 36 (June 1946), pp. 258–77.

18

Theory of Profits

18.1 INTRODUCTION

The preceding chapters have analyzed the manner in which contractual payments made to factor owners—in other words, the prices paid by business firms for the services of factor units—are determined. Demand schedules for factor units depend upon marginal revenue products; supply schedules depend upon particular circumstances affecting the availability of factor units and differ widely among various factors. Where markets are perfectly competitive, factor prices depend directly upon demand and supply relationships; where they are not, prices will be affected by the exact nature of competition, by the strength of monopoly and monopsony elements, and, in some instances, by the bargaining policies followed. The same basic analysis applies to all types of factor units and to money capital; differences in the determination of prices of various factors can be traced to differences in supply determinants and competitive conditions. Our final step in analyzing factor pricing and distribution is to explain the determination of residual incomes received by owners of businesses, known as *profit*.

18.2 BUSINESS PROFITS AND OPPORTUNITY COSTS

The term *profit* is used in two distinct senses: (1) in the business or accounting sense, as the excess of receipts over all contractual costs and depreciation; and (2) in the economic sense, as the excess of receipts over all opportunity costs.

As used in accounting practice and in the business community generally, *profit* refers to the sum available to a firm after all payments for factor services acquired on a contractual basis have been made and all other current obligations such as taxes and depreciation charges have been covered. During a given interval of time, a firm obtains a certain sum from the sale of its products. During this period, it also makes various contractual payments for labor services, materials, power, and so forth. It must also meet rent and interest obligations. Since capital declines in value during the period, a portion of the receipts, known as **depreciation charges**, must be regarded as maintenance of capital and must be charged against receipts as a cost. Taxes must be paid. The excess of the total receipts over these various payments and charges is regarded as the profit of the business firm. In a proprietorship, this sum is directly available for the owners' personal use; in a corporation, it may be paid out to the stockholders in the form of dividends or may be retained in the business. Essentially, profits in this business sense comprise the total income that accrues to the business firm as such, and thus to its owners (though in a corporation the owners may not gain access to it).

Examination of business profits reveals that the sum of such profits is made up in large measure of implicit (that is, noncontractual) costs representing the opportunity costs of factor units and money capital provided by the firm's owners. These are true cost elements, in the sense that they must be covered over a long-run period if the firm is to continue in operation. They differ from contractual costs only in that there is no formal, legal obligation for payment of the return. Their cost elements take the form of forgone earnings from other possible uses. Each of the major elements of implicit costs will be reviewed briefly.

Interest Return on the Money Capital of the Owners

In virtually all businesses, a portion of the money capital employed in the enterprise will have been supplied by the owners—directly in a partnership or proprietorship, and indirectly through the purchase of stock or through retention of earnings in a corporation. Since the owners forgo the advantages of liquidity or of a monetary return from placing funds in other investments, a return on the money is an essential cost item from the firm's standpoint. The money would not have been invested in the business initially if a return had not been expected and will not be retained in the business indefinitely if a return is not earned.

This necessary interest return on money capital supplied by the owners may be broken down into two elements. The first is a **pure interest** return equal to the basic rate of interest on the safest investments. The second element is a **risk premium** sufficient to compensate for the greater risk of loss of the capital sum from investing it in the undertaking rather than placing it in high-grade securities. (See Box 18-1.)

Implicit Wages

Especially in smaller firms, a portion of business profits may consist of noncontractual wages for work performed in the enterprise by the owners. The typical farmer or small shopkeeper performs substantial amounts of ordinary labor for which he or she rarely receives a formal wage. A large portion of the sum regarded as business profit is actually an **implicit wage**, equal to the amount which the owner could obtain from selling labor services to another firm.

Closely related are implicit wages of management. In a typical small business, the person or persons controlling the enterprise and making management decisions do

18-1   What is the capital sum upon which the implicit interest rate must be earned?

With unchanged technological conditions and prices, the sum would be the total amount placed in the enterprise by the owners, directly or through retained earnings. But changes in prices and technology alter the amount of money capital required to purchase the equipment to produce a given output. Suppose, for example, that the general price level, including the price of capital equipment, rises. As the present equipment wears out, output can be maintained economically only if additional money capital is invested in the enterprise. Thus the necessary return must be earned on the sum required for *replacement* of the capital equipment, if continued operation is to be maintained, rather than on the sum originally invested. If general price declines or technological developments allow the replacement of the equipment at a lower cost than the original, it is not necessary that the owners earn a return on the larger original sum invested but merely upon the new, lower amount required for replacement. The changes in prices and technology effectively will have destroyed, through nominal (not necessarily real) capital losses, a portion of the money capital originally invested; but operation of the enterprise will continue so long as the going rate of return is earned upon the smaller sum of money capital now invested.

not compensate themselves directly for this activity. A portion of the business profit earned is a compensation for this work, equal to the amount which these persons could earn as hired managers of other firms. Even in larger enterprises, a portion of business profits may represent "wages of management" of officials who are not paid as much as their actual contribution to the business warrants. In this case, however, the sums accrue not to the persons responsible for them but to the owners; therefore, in a sense, they are not necessary cost elements but a form of monopsonistic profits, discussed in the next section. Were markets perfect, these items would become explicit costs; they accrue to owners rather than managers only because of imperfections in market conditions.

Implicit Rents

If rent is regarded as a distinct form of factor return arising from the scarcity of nonreproducible assets, a portion of business profits may fall within the category of **implicit rent**. If a firm owns land or similar nonreproducible assets, a portion of its profits consists of the sum which this land would earn if it were rented out instead of being used in the business. Alternatively, an **implicit interest return** on the current monetary value of the property may be regarded as an implicit cost. The sums involved will be the same regardless of which approach is used.

18.3 THE PORTION OF BUSINESS PROFITS IN EXCESS OF OPPORTUNITY COSTS

Any excess of business profits over and above implicit costs was in the past regarded as a homogeneous return designated as pure or economic profit. More careful analysis of this return, however, has led to increased emphasis on the diversity of the elements that comprise it. Only one segment of the excess may be regarded as a truly distinct return; other segments, particularly those arising from monopoly or monopsony influences, constitute special forms of other types of factor returns and are thus, in a sense, implicit costs. These segments of profit will be considered first, and then we will shift our attention to pure profit—that is, profit that does not become capitalized into the firm's value.

Monopsony Profits

When a particular firm is able to pay factor owners less than their competitive factor incomes, the owners of the firm effectively receive a portion of the factor income attributable to these factor units and thus in a sense "exploit" other factor owners. For example, if one coal mine is able to hire workers more cheaply than other mines, the firm can earn a higher average rate of business profit; the excess consists simply of the wage differential which the owners of the firm have been able to appropriate for their own use because of market imperfections. These **monopsony profits** can be earned only when markets are imperfect—when factor owners lack adequate knowledge of other possibilities or factor units are immobile, or when competition among various firms for factor units is not complete. It should be noted that if all firms in an industry gain similar advantage, such profits will tend to disappear. Only a differential advantage on the part of particular firms enables them to earn profit from this source.

Firms may be particularly likely to obtain monopsony profits from failure to compensate top management personnel for the full contribution they make to the enterprise. The market for such personnel is highly imperfect, and a firm may succeed for a considerable period of time in paying successful managers less than the amounts such persons could obtain from other firms if they sought employment and their abilities were known.

Monopsony profits, though constituting an excess over implicit cost elements as defined in the preceding section, tend to be capitalized in the same manner as monopoly profits, and thus are distinguishable from pure profit. Capitalization will be discussed in the following section.

Monopoly Profits

When a firm is protected from entry of new firms, it will be able to earn profits over and above implicit cost elements, provided average revenue is, in any range of output, above average cost. This higher return protected by entry restriction is known as **monopoly profit**, though the market situation may be variously one of oligopoly, monopolistic competition, or complete monopoly.

Popular thinking attributes a large portion of "excess" profit to monopoly positions, and some economists have regarded monopoly as the primary source of pure profit. However, close examination of monopoly profits suggests that they differ in several respects from pure profits.

Imputation of Monopoly Profits.   In the first place, unlike pure profits, monopoly profits are frequently imputable (that is, attributable) to certain factor units or property rights. Suppose, for example, that entry into a field is restricted because the firm possesses patent rights or established trademarks. Excess profits earned because of the inability of new firms to enter the industry is clearly attributable to the patent right or trademark. The firm could lease these rights to other firms for an equivalent return, and thus the return is in a sense an opportunity cost to the firm as the owner and user of the patent, instead of being a true profit. The amount involved is essentially a rent, in the broad sense of the term, since the asset—the patent right—is not reproducible for the period in which it is valid and other firms cannot find substitutes. The return is not a necessary cost from the standpoint of the industry if the patent has no value outside of the industry, since it would have no rental value if it were freely available to all firms.

Capitalization of Monopoly Profits.   When restriction of entry is due to the large volume of business necessary to produce efficiently, monopoly profits are less clearly attributable to particular factors. However, the firm will tend to capitalize profits if the higher profit rate is expected to continue, the sale value of the enterprise increasing by the capitalized sum of the monopoly return. Thus not only will new purchasers of the firm (or of stock in it) receive only an average rate of earnings on their money capital, but the existing owners, who could dispose of their interest in the firm at the higher price, are in a sense only earning a normal return on the money capital represented by the sale price. The monopoly profit is therefore very similar to rent, in the broad sense of that term, and from the standpoint of the firm itself has some characteristics of a true imputed cost.

An example will serve to illustrate the capitalization of monopoly profits. Suppose that a firm that was established with an investment of $50,000 succeeds in building up a strong reputation that competitors cannot duplicate and earns annual real business profits of $20,000, year after year. If the firm is offered for sale, it may bring as much as $400,000 ($20,000 ÷ .05) if investors regard 5 percent as an appropriate return on investments with the particular degree of risk involved and expect the profits to continue indefinitely. Hence the new purchasers would earn only 5 percent on their money capital, and the monopoly returns would appear to have vanished, having become an implicit cost. Actually, however, the return is greatly in excess of the sum necessary to ensure continued operation of the firm. If entry barriers were broken and profits fell, the enterprise would continue to operate on a permanent basis, so long as the business profits were as much as $2,500—representing a 5-percent return on replacement cost.

Monopoly Profits Distinguished from Other Returns.   As indicated earlier, monopoly profits have certain characteristics of rent and interest returns, since in large measure they are imputable to particular factor units and tend to be capitalized. Thus they resemble implicit costs from the standpoint of individual firms. However, they can be distinguished from true implicit costs in several ways. In the first place, they are not necessary to ration economically scarce resources among competing units; most entry-restricting elements are artificial barriers to the establishment of new firms rather than true scarcity factors. Patent rights could be used by all firms in an industry if the law permitted, and brand names could be shared. Even when limited raw material resources restrict entry of new firms, the restriction is a product of ownership of the available resources by existing firms. Second, the monopoly receipts are not necessary to maintain output of the industry. If the earnings of firms drop to an average-return level through the breaking of barriers to entry, no firm will leave the industry. Finally, the existence of monopoly profits gives rise to constant striving on the part of the other firms to break entry-restricting barriers and enter production in the field. Therefore, while monopoly profits must be distinguished from pure profits, they must also be distinguished from true implicit costs even though they resemble the latter; that is, they must be regarded either as a special form of "return to institutional advantage" or as a major but distinct species of the general category of rents. (See Box 18-2.)

Innovations as a Source of Pure Profits

A third source of an excess of business profits over and above usual implicit costs is the undertaking of **innovations**—deliberate changes in production and demand functions—by business firms. Some economists, of whom the most famous was Joseph Schumpeter, have regarded pure profits as solely the result of innovations.[1] Innovations may be classed into two groups: those affecting production and those affecting marketing. The first group includes all changes that alter techniques of physical production and distribution, and methods of organization and operation. If a firm is successful in introducing cost-reducing techniques, it will earn, at least temporarily, a higher rate of profit. The second type of innovation includes all changes that affect consumer demand for the product, such as the introduction of new products, styles, and advertising techniques. (See Box 18-3.)

Innovational profits, as a form of noncontractual residual income, accrue directly to the firm and ultimately to its owners. In the small firm, therefore, the persons responsible for the innovation usually reap the reward from it; hence it is sometimes argued

---

[1]See J. Schumpeter, *Theory of Economic Development* (Cambridge: Harvard University Press, 1934).

18-2   If you buy the entire stock of a corporation that is earning and expected to earn monopoly profits, will you make a higher-than-average rate of return on the money you place in the enterprise? Explain.

No. Presumably the sellers of the stock that you purchased were aware of the extra-normal profits; they would be foolish if they sold the stock for a price which did not include the capitalized flow of monopoly profit. The former owners may have earned rents from *their* stocks, but you will be earning the going rate of return (assuming the stock was sold under reasonably competitive conditions).

18-3   Can profits due to any one innovation be expected to continue indefinitely? Can they be capitalized?

No. They will continue only until other firms succeed in duplicating the innovations successfully. If an innovation proves difficult to duplicate and other firms are restricted from entering the field, the continuing profits must be regarded as monopoly profits and will be capitalized. Any one firm can continue to make innovational profits, as such, only by continuing to introduce successful innovations.

that innovational profits are essentially a form of managerial wage and not a distinct type of income. However, the complete unpredictability and noncontinuing character of successful innovations suggest that they should be regarded as a distinctive and essentially residual type of income rather than a form of managerial wage. This approach is particularly appropriate for large corporations, in which the persons responsible for innovations typically do not receive direct gains from their success. The argument that their failure to do so constitutes merely a monopsonistic absorption by the owners of gains arising from the actions of the managers obscures the basic difference between innovational gains and other managerial returns.

Uncertainty as a Source of Pure Profits

Pure profits may arise not only from deliberate innovations but also from essentially windfall sources—that is, from unexpected changes in revenues or costs due, for example, to shifts in consumer preferences or declines in raw material prices. If such changes are favorable, they give rise to profits; if they are unfavorable, they give rise to negative profits (that is, losses). If the concept of **uncertainty** is defined broadly, the outcome of innovations may be regarded as one case of uncertainty; thus, uncertainty may be regarded as the major source of pure profits. The tendency in recent years has been to explain profits in this way, following a classic work by Frank Knight.[2] In terms of the uncertainty thesis, pure profits may be defined as the difference between expected net receipts and actual net receipts during a given period—although, as noted below, the term *expected* is subject to more than one interpretation.

Uncertainty arises in two major realms: in circumstances directly affecting the firm's cost and revenue schedules and in changes in the general environment (such as national income or government policies) which indirectly affect cost and revenue schedules. A firm can never be certain about the behavior of sales, prices, and various cost items in the coming period; and pure profits are frequently earned because sales or prices rise, or costs fall, without offsetting unfavorable changes. Even if a firm

---

[2]See F. H. Knight, *Risk, Uncertainty and Profit* (Boston: Houghton Mifflin, 1921).

undertakes a deliberate change—for example, by introducing a new technique or product—it cannot be certain of results. If expectations are exceeded, pure profits will be earned. On the other hand, pure profits may arise as a result of changes extraneous to the firm's immediate circumstances, including changes in anything from the weather to government regulatory or tariff policies. (When the changes are adverse, of course, losses are suffered.)

The Concept of Expected Returns. Clarification of the concept of pure profit requires interpretation of the term **expected returns** in the definition given above. If by this term it is meant the prediction of the firm itself, any foreseen pure profits would not be pure profits at all—since the latter are defined as the difference between expected and realized receipts. If a firm undertakes an innovation in anticipation of a certain profit and actually attains this profit, the sum would not be pure profits, in terms of this interpretation of the term *expected,* but would be an implicit cost. The concept of profits will be more useful, however, if the term *expected returns* is interpreted to mean a forecast accepted with certainty, not only by the firm but by general opinion in the market. Returns expected in this sense will be reflected in factor prices and in the selling or rental price of the firm as a whole, and capitalized in the same manner as monopoly profit, thus they should not be regarded as pure profit. In contrast, those profits that the firm hopes to gain but the market does not accept as certain are not fully capitalized; if realized, these will constitute pure profits, even though the firm may have anticipated them. Hence gains from both innovational and windfall changes that are not market-anticipated constitute pure profits. (See Box 18-4.)

The Absence of Pure Profits and Monopoly Profits in Perfect Competition

For reasons outlined in earlier chapters, neither monopoly/monopsony profits nor pure profits could exist in a static, perfectly competitive market situation. Under such circumstance, business profits would adjust to the level at which necessary implicit wage, interest, and rent costs were covered, the necessary interest return being based

18-4   If profits arising out of uncertainty are foreseen by the market as a whole, are they pure profits, if and when they are earned? Explain. Are they pure profits if they are anticipated only by a particular firm?

If the profits are widely foreseen, this expectation will have caused the value of the firm to be bid up (perhaps resulting in rents being earned on capital in the short run). The profits must in fact occur or losses (below average returns on money capital) will be incurred by those owning the firm. They *are* pure profits if only anticipated within the firm, because they will not be capitalized on the market into a higher firm value.

upon replacement cost of capital equipment and including depreciation. The perfectly competitive nature of such a market would ensure that entry would eliminate any temporary excess returns; if the market were truly perfect, the adjustment would be rapid and there would be temporary pure profits (positive or negative) only in a brief transitional period. If conditions were static (that is, if production and demand functions remained unchanged), there would be no uncertainty and no pure profits. Monopoly profits result from a continued departure of market conditions from perfect competition; pure profits are the result of changes—of the operation of dynamic forces in the economy—which give rise to uncertainty.

18.4 PROFITS AS A FUNCTIONAL RETURN

The question whether pure profits should be regarded as a functional or a residual return has been the subject of much controversy in the field of profit theory. A **functional return** is a compensation for performing a function. A **residual return** is simply a sum which remains to certain factor owners after all costs have been covered, accruing to these persons because of existing institutional relationships rather than as a direct compensation for performing a function. It is obvious that those business profits consisting of implicit wages, interest, and rent are true functional returns, accruing to factor owners for the provisions of factor units made available to the business firm on a noncontractual basis. Monopoly profit, while functional in the narrow sense of the word (because it becomes a type of opportunity cost to the firm upon capitalization), is not functional from the standpoint of the economy, since its receipt is not necessary for continued production of the output of the industry. The controversial issue concerns the functional nature of pure profit.

It was common in the past to regard pure profits, when earned, as a distinct type of functional return received by entrepreneurs as compensation for undertaking innovations and bearing primary risks. As owners of the business, the entrepreneurs also receive implicit cost returns and monopoly profit, if any. But the return distinctive to entrepreneurs was considered to be pure profit, a functional return for innovation and uncertainty bearing.

The usefulness of the functional concept of pure profits can be seriously questioned. In the modern large corporation, separation between ownership and management causes pure profits to accrue largely to persons other than those who perform entrepreneurial functions. In such enterprises, the identity between "entrepreneurs" and profit receivers is lost. Furthermore, pure profits are not *caused* by uncertainty; they arise in conditions of uncertainty when realizations exceed expectations, and they can best be regarded as a residual income. Even in a small enterprise in which the entrepreneur and the profit receiver are identical, pure profits can scarcely be regarded as a reward for bearing uncertainty, since the act of doing so does not in itself ensure pure profits (which arise only if conditions prove to be better than expected). Even when pure profits result from innovations, they can most satisfactorily be regarded as a residual income that accrues to the owners of the enterprise rather than as a functional return for introducing innovations.

The Role of Profits in the Economy

The statement that profits can best be regarded as a residual return rather than a functional return does not imply that pure profits play no role in the functioning of the economy. In the first place, anticipation of pure profits is an important lure that leads firms to undertake innovations of all types and thus to sustain economic progress. While pure profits actually realized cannot be regarded as a functional reward for undertaking change, particularly in the large corporation, the possibility of making such profits is an important source of encouragement to firms. Second, pure profits constitute a signal for the firm to revise its behavior. Failure of expected and realized profits to coincide suggests the need for revision of estimates and policies. Third, the making of pure profits and monopoly profits stimulates other firms to attempt to duplicate successful policies or to develop other policies that will accomplish the same result. In a highly competitive field, firms dare not lag behind or they will soon be suffering losses; the earning of pure profits by some firms constitutes a warning to others to adjust policies in order to avoid future trouble. Likewise, the earning of high profits in a certain field leads additional firms to enter the industry and brings about a reallocation of resources in conformity with changes in consumer demand and other forces.

18.5 NEGATIVE PROFITS

The preceding sections have been largely concerned with positive profits arising when actual results are better than expected. But actual receipts may be less than anticipated, in which case pure profits will be negative. **Negative profits** *occur whenever receipts are less than the sum of contractual obligations, depreciation charges, and implicit interest, wage, and rent costs.* If receipts are so low that contractual obligations plus depreciation are not covered, the situation may be described as one of *business losses,* or losses in the accounting sense. If these items are covered but all implicit costs are not covered, then the firm is earning a business profit but is suffering negative economic profits or an *economic loss.*

Certain types of losses, if expected to continue, will tend to be capitalized, reducing the sale value of the enterprise by the capitalized sum of the loss. It may be argued that the implicit cost element arising out of the investment is the normal return not on the replacement cost of the equipment but on the current sale value. In other words, the quasi-rent on capital goods, not the interest return on their cost, is the appropriate element in cost. From a strictly short-run point of view, this argument has limited merit. But for purposes of analysis, it is preferable to define losses as the excess over receipts of all cost items that must be covered if the firm is to remain in business permanently. It is loss defined in this way that is significant in determining the long-range policies of firms and the flow of resources into and out of various industries.

Types of Losses

It is important to review those loss situations in which firms will cease operations immediately from those in which firms will continue to operate over a short-run period.

1. *Failure to cover explicit (and implicit) variable costs.* If an enterprise is not taking in enough in current receipts to meet variable costs, continued operation is obviously undesirable unless an immediate improvement is expected. Continued operation will be impossible unless the firm or its owners have adequate reserve funds to meet the deficit.

2. *Coverage of variable but not contractual fixed costs.* If receipts cover explicit variable costs but not explicit fixed costs (of which interest is likely to be the most significant), an enterprise will go into bankruptcy unless the firm's reserves are adequate to meet the necessary payments or its owners are able and willing to supply necessary funds. Through reorganization in bankruptcy, creditors will become the new owners of the enterprise and explicit interest costs will be reduced or eliminated; the situation thus becomes one of (3) or (4), below.

3. *Coverage of variable and contractual fixed costs but not depreciation charges.* A firm may, before or after reorganization, be able to meet all contractual obligations involving both fixed and variable costs, but not depreciation. The firm can obviously continue operations as long as existing equipment can be used; but once its equipment wears out, it will lack funds for replacement and will be unable to obtain them unless owners are willing to supply additional money capital. This they obviously will not do unless an improvement in conditions is expected. Prior to the point at which substantial replacement of equipment is necessary, however, liquidation will be advantageous unless improvements are expected. If depreciation charges reflect an actual decline in the current salable value of the capital assets during the period, failure to cover this sum warrants immediate liquidation. If depreciation charges exceed the actual decline in the value of assets, liquidation is desirable if actual earnings toward depreciation charges are less than the sum of the interest return on the salvage value plus the actual decline in the value of the assets.

4. *Coverage of contractual costs and depreciation but failure to earn all implicit costs.* A firm may have adequate receipts to meet all contractual factor payments and depreciation but not enough to cover all implicit costs, the most important of which is likely to be a return on the owners' money capital. Such a firm *can* continue operations indefinitely if the owners wish. But it will not be advantageous for owners to permit continued operations once the point is reached at which cash earnings (receipts in excess of direct operating expenses, taxes, and the decline in salvage value during the period) fall below expected earnings that could be made on the salvage value if the enterprise were liquidated. In other words, the optimum time to liquidate occurs when the ratio of cash earnings to disposable (salvage) value falls below the figure the firm regards as a necessary minimum and there is inadequate expectation of improvement.

Until this point is reached, it is advantageous for the owners to keep the firm in operation, even though they are not making an average return on their capital, since they cannot withdraw their capital from the enterprise. Once money capital has been invested in specialized capital equipment, only a small portion can be withdrawn quickly (the amount equal to the salvage value), and the rental value of the equipment (if rental is possible) will depend upon the earning capacity of the equipment, not its cost. So long as owners make a return in excess of salvage or rental value, there is nothing that they can do to improve their position until the equipment wears out.

In practice, many firms operate far too long from the standpoint of the owners' interests. This is a product of continuing overoptimism about the future and of a reluctance by managers to discontinue an enterprise with which they have long been identified. As a consequence, depreciation funds and such business profits as are made are utilized to maintain or repair equipment, and eventually the stockholders' equity is destroyed.

Causes of Losses

In general, losses may be attributed to uncertainty—to unanticipated events that adversely affect cost or revenue schedules. These events may consist of general changes in the economy, such as a fall in national income or altered governmental policy; or they may be changes in circumstances directly affecting particular firms, such as an adverse shift in consumer preferences or a rise in materials costs. Losses may result from successful introduction of innovations by competitors or from failure of innovations attempted by the firm itself to produce desired results. Or they may result from plain bad management. Where losses are due to obvious managerial errors, it may be argued that the source of the loss from the firm's standpoint is overcompensation of management personnel (the opposite of monopsonistic exploitation). A frequent type of mistake is the establishment of new enterprises under circumstances in which profitable operation is impossible, with promoters being overoptimistic or lacking adequate knowledge of revenue and cost schedules.

Losses lead to readjustments that may serve to eliminate them. Losses constitute a warning to a firm to alter its policies to obtain greater efficiency, to develop innovations, or to make other needed changes. These changes may prove to be successful, and profitable operation may be restored; in other cases, a firm may be unable to escape the losses and thus must eventually liquidate. In large measure, continuing losses may be regarded as a penalty for failure to adapt to changing conditions.

SUMMARY

1. Residual incomes received by owners are called profits. Business or accounting profits are defined as the excess of receipts over all contractual costs and depreciation. Economic profits are the excess of receipts over all opportunity costs.

2. Implicit wages and rents are measures of forgone income from labor and land respectively.

3. Monopsony profits arise when a firm is able to pay factor owners less than their competitive factor incomes. These profits exist as a result of market imperfections.

4. Barriers to entry can lead to monopoly profits if average revenue is greater than average cost in the relevant output range. Often monopoly profits exist because of property rights (such as patents or trademarks) established by the firm. Innovations are a third source of monopoly profits.

5. A functional return is compensation to the factor owner; a residual return is what remains after all costs have been covered.

6. Pure profits are an important incentive to firms, a signal for firm behavior, and an important gauge to potential entrants in the field.

7. Negative profits exist when receipts are less than the sum of contractual obligation, depreciation charges, and implicit costs of interest, wages, and rent.

8. Losses for a firm may result from its failure to cover any of the following: explicit variable costs, contractual fixed costs, depreciation charges, or implicit costs.

WORDS AND CONCEPTS FOR REVIEW

accounting profits
economic profits
depreciation charges
pure interest
risk premium
implicit wages
implicit rent
implicit interest return

monopsony profits
monopoly profits
innovations (and profits)
uncertainty (and profits)
expected returns
functional return
residual return
negative profits

REVIEW QUESTIONS

1. Why does a large portion of business profits consist of elements that are costs from an economic standpoint?

2. Upon what base should the necessary return on the owners' capital be figured?

3. A farmer obtains $17,000 from the sale of his crop; his expenses, including taxes, are $4,000. His farm would sell for $50,000. He could obtain a job in a local feed mill at $10,000 a year, if he wished. Determine his business profits, the implicit cost elements in his business profits, and his pure profit, if any. Use a figure of 4 percent as a real rate of return.

4. What is the source of monopsony profits? Why will they not be attained if monopsony powers extend to all firms in the industry?

5. Define monopoly profit. Why are monopoly profits, in a sense, implicit costs? Why are they not true costs from the standpoint of the economy?

6. Explain the meaning of the term *innovations*, and give examples. How do innovational profits differ from monopoly profits? From windfall profits?

7. Why are innovational profits not regarded as a managerial wage?

8. What is the difference between uncertainty and risk? Give examples of each.

9. What condition is necessary for monopoly profits to continue?

10. Why would there be no monopoly or pure profits in a perfectly competitive market?

11. Why are pure profits not considered to be a functional return?

12. Indicate the major roles that profits play in the economy.

13. Discuss the various meanings of the term *losing money*.

14. Suppose that a particular firm is covering all variable costs and depreciation but not an average return on investment. If the owners are seeking to maximize their gain, at what point will they discontinue operations? Explain.

15. Why do companies sometimes operate far beyond the optimum (from a profit standpoint) time of liquidation?

16. What are the major causes of losses?

17. How would you explain the following:
(a) Losses, despite general business prosperity in the economy, of some textile producers in recent decades?
(b) Frequent failure of small restaurants?
(c) The losses of the New York subway system or the Bay Area Rapid Transit system (BART)?

SUGGESTED READINGS

Friedman, Milton. *Price Theory*. Chicago: Aldine Publishing Company, 1976.

Knight, F. H. *Risk, Uncertainty and Profit*. Boston: Houghton Mifflin, 1921.

Scherer, Frederic M. *Industrial Market Structure and Economic Performance*. 2nd ed. Chicago: Rand McNally, 1980.

PART 4

Efficiency, Exchange, and Intertemporal Issues

19

General Equilibrium

19.1 INTRODUCTION

Preceding chapters analyze the determination of the prices and outputs of *particular* goods and the income and employment of *particular* productive factors. We have, in short, been looking at the "trees" but largely ignoring how they go together to make up the economic "forest." As noted earlier, the "trees" portion of economic analysis is known as **partial equilibrium theory** because it deals with adjustments in isolated sectors of the economy while making only incidental reference to interrelations among different sectors.

Despite its somewhat restrictive assumptions, partial equilibrium analysis is adequate for the study of a surprisingly wide range of practical problems. In the analysis of the effects of a new tobacco excise tax, for example, the assumption that prices are given in all markets other than the market for tobacco is not too unrealistic. Similarly, the effects of a lower price of steel upon the shipbuilding and construction industries can be studied fairly effectively using partial equilibrium methods, even though the total effect on the economy cannot be regarded simply as the sum of the separate effects on individual industries.

To obtain an adequate picture of the functioning of the economic system as a whole, however, and to develop analytical tools suitable for studying problems whose ramifications extend through several sectors of the economy, it is desirable to know something more about interrelationships among the outputs and prices of various goods and the prices and inputs of various factors. The portion of economic theory that deals with these interrelations is known as **general equilibrium theory**.[1] Certain major

---

[1]Although originally developed a century ago in the work of Leon Walras, the impact of the general equilibrium theory on the general body of economic theory was slight until the 1950s. See Walras's *Éléments d'économie politique pure* (Lausanne, 1884), translated into English by William Jaffe and published as *Elements of Pure Economics* (Homewood, IL: Irwin, 1954).

interrelationships in the economy will be noted briefly before the framework of general equilibrium analysis is presented.

19.2 CONSUMER PRICE INTERDEPENDENCIES

The analysis of price and output determination in earlier chapters was based on the assumption that the prices of other goods were given, apart from minor references to the direct effects on the prices or demands of other goods which might result from a change in the price of a particular good. But this type of modification reflects only a small portion of the possible **consumer price interdependencies**. A change in the price of any one consumption good inevitably alters the demand for and possibly the supply of many others. For example, a rise in the price of butter will increase the demand for substitutes such as margarine and lead to increases in the price and output of these goods if markets are perfectly competitive. If they are not, the effect may be solely upon output, with a possible decline in the price of substitutes. The prices of goods complementary to butter, such as bread, may fall because the demand for them will fall if butter becomes more expensive. Changes in the outputs of these other goods will affect factor supplies available for the production of bread, and thus its cost of production and supply, while shifts in the prices of other goods will in turn affect the demand for bread. The changes in prices and outputs of substitute and complementary goods will in turn affect the prices and outputs of other goods.

Thus, complete adjustment in the prices of all goods can occur only when the various prices and outputs attain levels that are mutually consistent with one another. Given the basic determinants of consumption goods prices—namely, consumer incomes, consumer preferences, factor price schedules, production functions, and the nature of competition in various markets—such an equilibrium can be defined. But a shift in some variable affecting any one good may have widespread repercussions on the equilibrium prices and outputs of many other goods, reactions that are largely ignored in partial equilibrium analysis.

The Relationship of the Prices of Consumption Goods and Factors

In the analysis of the pricing of consumption goods, factor price schedules were generally assumed to be given; conversely, consumption goods prices were generally assumed to be given in the discussion of the determination of equilibrium factor prices. Actually, of course, the two sets of equilibrium prices are mutually dependent. For example, a major element in the cost of consumption goods is labor cost, making the wage level a significant influence on the prices of products. But the demand for labor, and thus wage rates, are dependent upon the marginal revenue product of various types of labor, which in turn depends upon consumer goods prices. No circular reasoning is involved in this analysis, as is sometimes claimed. Both wage (and other factor price) levels and commodity price levels must adjust to figures that are mutually consistent, because until such a situation is reached, there will be a tendency for one set of prices or the other to shift.

19.3 THE FRAMEWORK OF GENERAL EQUILIBRIUM THEORY

General equilibrium theory presents an overall framework of the basic price and output interrelationships, including both produced goods and factors, for the economy as a whole. Its purpose is to demonstrate mathematically that, given the basic determinants (factor supply schedules, consumer preferences, production functions, and forms of competition), the prices of all goods and factors and the outputs of various goods *can* adjust to mutually consistent levels; that is to say, there exists in a market economy a consistent pattern of *equilibrium* prices, factor inputs, goods outputs, and consumer purchases.

General equilibrium theory (like conventional discussions of supply and demand) does not deal directly with questions about the process of attaining an equilibrium position. To study problems of this kind, it is necessary to have additional information about the actual *changes over time* in demands and prices under conditions of disequilibrium. This is a problem in economic dynamics rather than economic statics; as such, it lies outside the scope of general equilibrium theory as ordinarily conceived. For most practical purposes, however, it is reasonable to assume that a market economy tends to adjust fairly rapidly to a position of equilibrium. If this assumption is made, it is legitimate to ignore the time required for adjustment. Under these circumstances, we may argue that any given set of basic determinants (factor supply conditions, consumer preferences, and so forth) determines a definite *equilibrium state* for the economy as a whole, and that changes in these determinants will therefore be associated with a widespread pattern of readjustment in the economy until a new equilibrium state is established. Another way of expressing the same idea is to say that any given position of general equilibrium (defined by given determinants) is *stable*. Thus a change in the conditions determining a given equilibrium ultimately will be followed by the reestablishment of a new equilibrium in which prices and outputs throughout the economy are once again mutually consistent.

A simple mathematical explanation of general equilibrium can be based upon the following information and assumptions:

1. An existing pattern of consumer preferences.
2. Factor supplies, independent of factor prices.
3. Techniques of production, with fixed coefficients of production; that is, fixed proportions of various factors are required to produce a unit of output.
4. Perfectly competitive good and factor markets, and thus attainment of equality of price, marginal cost, and average cost for each good; equality of supply and demand for each factor; and equality of supply and demand for each good.

For simplicity, it is further assumed that (1) incomes are derived solely from the provision of factor units, and (2) all income is spent on consumption.[2]

---

[2]These assumptions are not critical, although dynamic adjustments are simplified. The first assumption is quite realistic, upon reflection, while the second could be eliminated by introducing an investment good and savings. However, this would yield *growth* and a moving equilibrium (issues of income elasticities of goods, scale economies relative to the extent of the market, and so on would need to be addressed).

In the mathematical exposition, the following symbols are employed:

$q_1, q_2, \ldots, q_n$ ..... Indicate quantities of various goods, n in number

$P_1, P_2, \ldots, P_n$ ..... Indicate prices of the respective goods

$V_1, V_2, \ldots, V_m$ ..... Indicate the quantities of various factors available, m in number

$W_1, W_2, \ldots, W_m$ ..... Indicate the prices of the respective factors

$\left.\begin{array}{l} a_{11}, a_{21}, \ldots, a_{n1} \\ a_{12}, a_{22}, \ldots, a_{n2} \\ \quad \vdots \quad \vdots \\ a_{1m}, a_{2m}, \ldots, a_{nm} \end{array}\right\}$ ... Indicate the quantities of various factors necessary to produce a unit of each good (in column one, a_{1i} for example, represents the inputs of the m factors needed to produce a unit of the first good).

$MU_1, MU_2, \ldots, MU_n$ ..... Designate the marginal utilities of various goods to a consumer

The Demand Equations

On the demand side of the picture, there are two basic sets of equations:

(1) The budget equation, showing for each person the equality between factor income (that is, the price paid per unit for each factor unit supplied, times the number of such units supplied) and expenditure (which consists of the sum of the quantities of each good one purchases, multiplied by the prices of the goods):

$$V_1W_1 + V_2W_2 + \ldots + V_mW_m = q_1 + q_2P_2 + \ldots + q_nP_n$$

The symbol q_1 refers to the good in terms of which the values of all other goods are expressed; its price, therefore, is unity ($P_1 = 1$). This good is usually referred to as the "numeraire good." Since relative prices are all that matter, the numeraire good could be anything—think of it as a money good, like gold.

(2) The allocation-of-consumption-expenditures equation, showing for each consumer the equality of the ratios of the marginal utilities of all goods to their prices, under the assumption that all persons allocate their incomes among various goods in such a way as to maximize satisfaction:

$$\frac{MU_1}{P_1} = \frac{MU_2}{P_2} = \frac{MU_3}{P_3} \ldots = \frac{MU_n}{P_n}$$

The number of equations of the second type for each consumer is one less than the number of goods ($n - 1$), since the first good (arbitrarily chosen) serves as the unit of measurement of the prices of the others. However, if equation (1), above, is included, the number of equations is equal to the number of unknowns—the amounts of the various goods and the purchases of the various goods by each consumer are in general determinate—given the prices of the goods, the factor prices, and the quantities of the factor units possessed. Since this conclusion is valid for every possible price level for each good, the person's demand schedule for each good is determinate. The demand for each good is thus a function of the price of the good in question, the prices of all other consumption goods (although the influence of many of these is negligible), and the prices of the factors (given the amounts of the factor units supplied). The factor prices and quantities determine the person's income and total expenditures.

The demand functions may be expressed symbolically as follows:

$$q_1 = f_1(P_2, P_3, \ldots, P_n; W_1, W_2, \ldots, W_m)$$
$$q_2 = f_2(P_2, P_3, \ldots, P_n; W_1, W_2, \ldots, W_m)$$
$$\ldots \ldots \ldots \ldots \ldots \ldots \ldots \ldots \ldots \ldots \ldots \ldots \ldots$$
$$\ldots \ldots \ldots \ldots \ldots \ldots \ldots \ldots \ldots \ldots \ldots \ldots \ldots$$
$$q_i = f_i(P_2, P_3, \ldots, P_n; W_1, W_2, \ldots, W_m)$$
$$\ldots \ldots \ldots \ldots \ldots \ldots \ldots \ldots \ldots \ldots \ldots \ldots \ldots$$
$$\ldots \ldots \ldots \ldots \ldots \ldots \ldots \ldots \ldots \ldots \ldots \ldots \ldots$$
$$q_n = f_n(P_2, P_3, \ldots, P_n; W_1, W_2, \ldots, W_m)$$

The equation $q_i = f_i(P_2, P_3, \ldots, P_n; W_1, W_2, \ldots, W_m)$ in this system of equations may be considered to represent the demand for a typical good, q_i. On this understanding, the entire system of equations may be rewritten in a more compact but equivalent form, as follows: $q_i = f_i(P_2, P_3, \ldots, P_n; W_1, W_2, \ldots, W_m)$ $(i = 1, 2, \ldots, n)$. The expression in parentheses following the equation itself indicates the various values of i in successive equations (e.g., $1, 2, \ldots, n$). Thus, if the parenthetical expression were $(i = 1, 2, 3)$, this would indicate that there were three goods to be considered and so a system of equations containing three separate relations. Similarly, if there were five goods in the economy ($n = 5$), the parenthetical expression would be written $(i = 1, 2, \ldots, 5)$, and thus there would be five demand equations in the system as a whole.

As indicated earlier, there is a separate system of demand equations for each consumer, and each system contains as many equations as there are goods in the economy. The entire collection of demand equations, if written out in full (with one equation for each good and for each consumer), would look very complicated and would occupy considerable space. But the basic idea is a simple one—namely, that the quantity of each good demanded by each consumer depends not only upon the price of the good, but also upon the prices of all other goods and upon factor prices, which determine the consumer's income. Given the quantities of the factors owned and the consumer preference schedules, the quantity of each good demanded by each consumer is therefore determinate.

The total demand for each good is the sum of the demands of individual consumers. Since the quantity demanded by each consumer is given by an equation, it is possible to arrive at total quantity demanded by summing the individual demand equations. For each good, the total demand equations can be expressed as follows (capital Q_i and F_i being used to designate total quantities):

$$(1) \quad Q_i = F_i(P_2, P_3, \ldots, P_n, W_1, W_2, \ldots, W_m) \quad (i = 1, 2, \ldots, n)$$

Notice that we are making use of the shorthand expression described above. That is to say, the expression (1) represents a system of n equations rather than a single equation, since the subscript is to be set equal to each of the values $1, 2, \ldots, n$ (as indicated by the expression in parentheses). In other words, Q_i represents the total quantity demanded of a typical good; but the entire set of total demands is represented by the collection of n symbols $Q_1, Q_2, \ldots, Q_i, \ldots, Q_n$, and the numerical value of each of these variables is determined by a separate equation of the general form illustrated by the expression $Q_i = F_i(P_2, P_3, \ldots, P_n, W_1, W_2, \ldots, W_m)$. There is one equation for each good, and thus a total of n such equations in the system of equations would be represented by the expression (1) above.

The Supply Equation

On the supply side of the picture, there are two basic sets of equations. The first relates price to cost of production; under the assumptions of a perfectly competitive market and fixed production coefficients, the price of each good is equal to the sum of the figures obtained by multiplying the price of each factor used to produce the good times the quantity of the factor required to produce a unit of the good:

$$(2)\ P_i = a_{i1}W_1 + a_{i2}W_2 + \ldots + a_{im}W_m \quad (i = 1, 2, \ldots, n)$$

As in the case of the set of equations (1), the present expression describes a system of n equations ($i = 1, 2, \ldots, n$); that is, there is one equation for each good and therefore as many equations as there are goods (n). In the case of good "1," which is the common denominator of value of the others, $P_1 = 1$.

Second, there are equations showing the equality of the total quantities of the factors used to produce the various consumption goods with the total quantities of these factors available, under the assumption of attainment of equality of factor supply and demand. Hence, for each factor, the quantity available must equal the sum of the quantities of the factor used in the production, per unit, of each consumption good, multiplied by the number of units of output of the good:

$$(3)\ V_j = a_{1j}Q_1 + a_{2j}Q_2 + \ldots + a_{nj}Q_n \quad (j = 1, 2, \ldots, m)$$

Here we are using a different symbol, "j," to represent a typical factor input. The expression (3) represents a system of equations ($j = 1, 2, \ldots, m$), for there is one such equation for each factor, and thus m equations in total.

Solution of the Demand and Supply Equations

In total, there are three sets of equations:

n equations (1) relating the quantities of various goods demanded to good prices and factor prices (the latter, in conjunction with given factor quantities, determining incomes) *n* equations (2)   relating the prices of all goods to the costs of producing them (quantities of factor units used multiplied by factor prices)

m equations (3)   relating the supplies of various types of factors available to the total quantities of the factors used in the production of the various commodities

The total number of equations equals twice the number of goods plus the number of factors ($2n + m$). The number of unknowns is equal to the number of goods (n), the number of good prices ($n - 1$, since one good is used as the unit of measurement of the values of the others), plus the number of factors, or $2n + m - 1$. Thus the number of equations appears to be one more than the number of unknowns. But one of the equations in (1) can be eliminated, since, if the prices of all goods are known as well as the quantities demanded of all except one good, the quantity demanded of the remaining good can be deduced by using the budget equations of individual consumers (for these show that the total expenditure on any one good is equal to total income minus total expenditure on all other goods). With this adjustment, the number of independent equations and the number of unknowns are the same: $2n + m - 1$.

From the mathematical point of view, mere equality between the number of equations and unknowns does not guarantee that the equations are solvable for a unique set of equilibrium values of the unknowns. As a general rule, however, this result is attained if the equations are linear in form, as is true of all the equations considered above except the demand equations (1). For a wide range of other actual forms of the equations, moreover, equality between the number of equations and unknowns is both a necessary and a sufficient condition for the existence of a unique equilibrium solution that is meaningful from an economic point of view (that is, a solution in which prices and quantities are all represented by non-negative numbers). Without entering further into questions of this kind, which are mainly of mathematical rather than economic interest, we shall assume that the equations in the general equilibrium system described above are of such a form that the system is determinate. This means that, for given consumer preferences, given supplies of factor units, and given production functions, and under the assumptions noted earlier (with respect to perfect competition and such), the equilibrium prices of all goods and factors (valued in terms of numeraire good "1") are determinate, as are the equilibrium quantities of output of the various goods and the equilibrium allocation of factor units among the production of various goods. If the data on factor supplies, consumer preference schedules, and production coefficients were actually known, all equilibrium prices and outputs could be calculated. As a matter of fact, this information is not obtainable. On our present assumptions, however, there is one and only one set of goods and factor prices and outputs of goods in which the various elements are mutually consistent. Hence a state of general equilibrium may be said to be defined in principle, and the calculation of corresponding equilibrium values of prices and quantities is theoretically possible, were necessary information available.

19.4 A GRAPHICAL REPRESENTATION OF GENERAL EQUILIBRIUM

The preceding discussion may well be unintelligible to many readers. We are sympathetic to this possible confusion: general equilibrium is a complex notion. Figure 19-1, which roughly illustrates this discussion, also appears complicated—but it's not as bad as it looks.

FIGURE 19-1

A Depiction of General Equilibrium with Production and Exchange (dashed lines depict exchange disequilibrium)

The point "General Equilibrium" represents exchange equilibrium (supplies equal demands and $MRS_A = MRS_B$ = price ratios) and production equilibrium (the MRS of each and all individuals in consumption equals MRTS in production). The socially optimal allocation (X_1^*, X_2^*) occurs where the social indifference curve and the production possibilities frontier are tangent and MRS = MRTS. The distribution of output between individuals A and B falls within the box $0_A X_2^* 0_B X_1^*$. The point "General Equilibrium" represents exchange equilibrium (supplies equal demands and $MRS_A = MRS_B$ = price ratios) and production equilibrium (the MRS of each and all individuals in consumption equals MRTS in production). Being *on* the production possibilities frontier means marginal products per dollar factor cost are equated and supplies = demands in input markets. At point M, both individuals can reach a higher level of utility through a redistribution of X_1 and X_2.

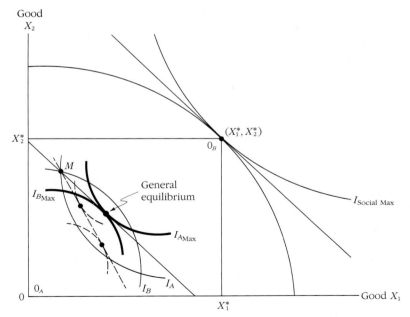

Envision a family of "collective indifference curves" between goods X_1 and X_2 for a society comprised of two individuals, A and B.[3] There will also be a feasible production set showing combinations of goods X_1 and X_2 which can be produced by our two individuals with their resources (labor, capital, and land).

At point (X_1^*, X_2^*) in Figure 19-1 our society is producing the optimal relative quantities of goods X_1 and X_2. We know this since the marginal rate of substitution in consumption (MRS) is exactly equal to the marginal rate of technical substitution in production (MRTS) at this point. Moreover, since we are on, rather than inside, the production possibilities curve, it must be the case that A and B are fully employed and all inputs are optimally allocated between production of X_1 and production of X_2. That is, supply equals demand for each input, and marginal product per dollar spent on each input must be the same considering each good separately.[4]

How about *distribution* of the output of our small economy? The bundle (X_1^*, X_2^*) is produced and *any* point inside the box, $0_A X_2^* \, 0_B X_1^*$, represents a possible allocation.[5] Suppose the marginal products of the resources owned by A and B are such that their earnings (paid in output, although money could be introduced without loss of generality) are represented by point M in Figure 19-1. Individual B has a relatively large amount of good X_1 and only a little X_2 (apparently her resources were better suited, when optimally employed, to X_1 production). Similarly, individual A has relatively more X_2 and less X_1 at M. Clearly, *any* point within the lens-shaped area contained by the indifference curves passing through M will be preferred to M; that is, for any interior point, both A and B can have greater satisfaction. Merely by *reallocating* existing supplies, both A and B are made better off—wealth is created. Where will society end up? If relative prices were as indicated by the dashed line (X_1 relatively expensive, since much X_2 must be given up to get more X_1), then individual A would wish to buy only a small amount of X_1 relative to the amount individual B would wish to sell. The tangencies of the (utility-maximizing) indifference curves of A and B do not occur at the same point. The inconsistency would cause the price of X_1 to fall (there is excess supply at the price indicated by the dashed line). The price will continue to change until the utility-maximizing behavior is consistent—at "General Equilibrium." At the "General Equilibrium" relative price of X_1 the amount individual B wishes to sell of X_1 is exactly equal to the amount A wishes to buy and, indeed, A can pay for the X_1 he purchases with the proceeds from the X_2 he sells.

---

[3] There are severe problems with the idea of a "social welfare function," but don't be unduly concerned at present. The discussion will be seen to have intuitive merit and will clarify what the "invisible hand" is really up to.

[4] An analogous graph with isoquants rather than indifference curves *inside* the box, $0_A X_2^* \, 0_B X_1^*$, could be used to establish these points. The text discussion to follow will clarify how.

[5] Note that one of the difficulties of talking of a "social welfare function" yielding collective indifference curves emerges here: each point of possible allocation represents a particular income distribution. Generally, we will have a different family of I curves for each income distribution—a different (X_1^*, X_2^*) bundle would be optimal. To get around this problem, assume *identical* preferences (indeed, identical cardinal, linear homogeneous utility functions).

Notice that this case is in some respects *more* complicated than the real world. We wrote of prices adjusting as if the economy were competitive, when our example only had two economic transactors, *A* and *B*. If there were in fact only two individuals, the final position would be much harder to determine. Assuming voluntary exchanges (the stronger or meaner of *A* or *B* could just *take* the other's goods—the reason, at heart, for institutions like courts and police), we would know only that the final outcome will be in the lens-shaped area. If *A* were a better bargainer, the final position would be further to the northeast; if *B* were more persuasive, the final position would be further to the southwest.

In the final position—with price-taking, competitive behavior—the prices at which individuals exchange will be equal to the marginal rate of technical substitution in production. Hence the price line passing through "General Equilibrium" must be parallel to that passing through (X_1^*, X_2^*); if exchange were occurring at other relative prices, it would be profitable to alter what is being produced (ending up in a box of different "shape" from that of Figure 19-1).

Just as we have drawn an "exchange box" (called an Edgeworth Box or, sometimes, an Edgeworth/Bowley Box in spite of having been invented by Pareto), we have constructed a "production box" as discussed at the outset. In Figure 19-2, the economy's labor is on one axis and capital on the other. The southwest corner represents zero output of good X_1, while the northeast corner represents zero output of good X_2 (that is, all of the economy's resources being devoted to X_1 production). We reach general equilibrium in production whenever the marginal rate of technical substitution

FIGURE 19-2

General Equilibrium in Production
General equilibrium in production requires the equality of the MRTS for X_1 and the MRTS for X_2, i.e., the tangency of an X_1 isoquant and a X_2 isoquant. The production contract curve maps all of the general equilibrium combinations of labor and capital (*A, B, C,* and *D*).

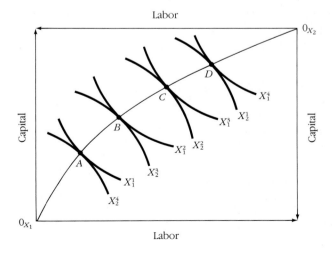

between labor and capital is the same for the production of X_1 and the producton of X_2. This necessitates that the isoquants be tangent to each other in order for efficient production to occur. The curve joining the tangency points is called the **production contract curve**. If not in a tangency position, a higher production of X_1 or X_2 or both can be obtained through reallocation of the inputs. However, once on the production contract curve, no further *net* gains in output can be achieved.

It is easy to derive the **production possibility curve** from the points obtained from the production contract curve. That is, the points on the production contract curve are the boundaries of the production possibilities curve, as seen in Figure 19-3.

The final consideration in general equilibrium (which must occur simultaneously with the considerations of Figures 19-1 and 19-2) would involve the value of marginal product of each input being the same in the production of either good.

Thus we see that the general equilibrium ultimately stems from tastes, technology, and resource endowment. An economy with a great deal of accumulated capital, for example, would (abstracting from international trade and even grander notions of general equilibrium) tend to produce in relatively capital-intensive ways, and the lower relative price of capital intensive goods would favor greater consumption of such goods. If preferences strongly favored good X_2, we would have a very differently shaped box (tall and thin) in Figure 19-1 or 19-3. Even with preferences unchanged, if technology (or resource endowment) was such that the production possibilities curve was "flatter and lower," then relatively more X_1 would be produced and consumed.

The preceding points were, in fact, already well known to you. Recall that even the most elementary discussions of supply and demand indicate that price and quantity are not determined by supply alone (technology, resource endowment) nor by demand alone (preferences) but by their interaction, like scissors.

FIGURE 19-3
Production Possibilities Frontier
The maximum producible quantities of X_1 and X_2, depicted along the production possibilities frontier, can be determined from the isoquants along the production contract curve.

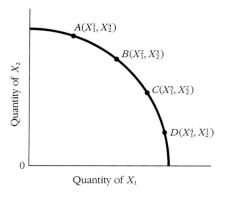

19.5 FURTHER EXTENSIONS

It is a relatively simple matter to extend the preceding analysis to apply to an economic system in which money serves as a medium of exchange, and also to an economy in which individuals hold other kinds of assets (such as bonds, stocks, or capital goods). Moreover, the assumption of perfect competition, which underlies the whole of the preceding argument, can be replaced by the assumption of various forms of competition in all markets, and the analysis can thus be extended to monopolistic and oligopolistic markets. The analysis can also be generalized to consider spatially separated markets in which transportation and location variables are included among the unknowns of the general equilibrium system. Whatever the direction in which the argument is extended, however, the basic conclusions would not be altered. The importance of these extensions—apart from their intrinsic theoretical interest—is that they may reveal interrelationships among economic quantities and so facilitate empirical research by providing a theoretical check on the consistency of observational data.

19.6 THE USEFULNESS OF GENERAL EQUILIBRIUM THEORY

General equilibrium theory is of greatest value in stressing the interdependence of various portions of the economic system, which is easily lost from sight in partial equilibrium analysis. Failure to recognize this interdependence is responsible for many errors in popular reasoning on economic questions. (See Box 19-1.)

General equilibrium theory also provides a useful framework for the organization of empirical research. For effective study of concrete situations, it is essential to approach data with a coherent sense of perspective. Preliminary examination of the data may indicate that only a small portion of one's total stock of theoretical knowledge is relevant for further analysis; but much foolishness and many serious mistakes can be avoided if provisionally relevant theoretical knowledge is retained for use until an explicit reason, based on factual knowledge, can be given for disregarding it. Even though general equilibrium analysis may seldom lead to any directly useful conclu-

19-1 Tariff policy is often considered only in terms of its effect upon output and employment in the particular industry protected (for example, employment in automobile production in Michigan). What else should be taken into consideration in deciding whether to have a tariff?

The effects of the tariff in reducing exports and thus the demand for output and reduced employment in exporting industries should be considered. The analysis calls attention to the fact that changes in one portion of the economy will often have widespread repercussions in other segments, and that commodity and factor prices are mutually interrelated; wage changes, for example, will almost inevitably affect output and prices.

sions, it is an extremely powerful instrument for the orderly arrangement of ideas about the real economic world.

19.7 LIMITATIONS OF GENERAL EQUILIBRIUM THEORY

General equilibrium theory is subject to two major limitations. First, it is essentially static in nature, defining the overall equilibrium in terms of given determinants. While it offers a tool for studying the effect of changes in specific determinants (as illustrated in the following sections), it is of limited value for studying general trends of economic development. In recent years, increased effort has been given to remedying this inadequacy through further analysis of the role of money and other assets, and through work on the dynamics of general equilibrium; but much more work along these lines is required before the analysis can become a truly useful tool for the study of dynamic situations.

The second limitation is a more practical one, relating to the actual body of the theory as it stands—namely, the difficulty of estimating various magnitudes in a general equilibrium system so that the equations may be solved in quantitative terms and so that the theory may be used to predict precise quantitative results of various changes and policies. The tremendous complexity of the actual economic system and the inadequacy of data make this very difficult, though in the last decade various attempts have been made to do so with simplified models.

19.8 CHANGES IN THE DETERMINANTS

Changes in any of the system's basic determinants may have widespread repercussions in the system and will lead to the establishment of a new equilibrium pattern. The effects of several major sources of change will be considered briefly.

Consumer Preferences

Consumer preferences constantly change as styles and tastes and wants vary, partly as a result of deliberate efforts on the part of business firms, partly from endogenous causes (such as consumer income) and exogenous causes (such as technology or governmental action). Increased relative preference for one good (X_1) relative to that for another good (X_2) increases the demand for the former and reduces the demand for the latter. Accordingly, firms will find it advantageous to increase the output of X_1, while the output of X_2 will fall. Thus some resources will be shifted from the production of X_2 to the production of X_1. If all factors involved are equally efficient in the production of either good, factor prices might not change. But this is unlikely; some factors will be more efficient in the production of X_1 and others in the production of X_2. Hence the prices of factors best suited for the production of X_1 will tend to rise, and those best suited for X_2 will fall; as a consequence, the incomes of the owners of the former set of factors will rise, and those of the owners of the latter group will fall. This will, of itself, affect demands for goods and services at this second stage. Over a longer period, factors will shift from one use to another more easily than in a shorter period. Ultimately, the effects will dampen, resulting in new equilibrium—a new pattern of goods production, consumption, and distribution.

Techniques of Production

New inventions produce continuous changes in available techniques of production. These changes alter production functions, the quantities of various factors required to produce a unit of output of particular goods in the optimum fashion, and the prices of finished products. Consequently, the allocation of factors to the production of various goods is affected, as are the prices of goods and factors (and the distribution of income). For example, suppose that a new lower-cost technique used in the production of glass tableware lessens the amount of manpower necessary per unit of output but increases the amounts of certain chemicals required. The reduction in the cost and price of the glassware stimulates increased consumer use, and greater use by the producers of the various ingredients. The quantities of those chemicals and other factors not affected by the technological change will increase; the quantity of labor used will decrease unless increased sales more than offset the substitution of chemicals for manpower. Suppliers of chemicals and other materials will receive increased incomes, at least temporarily, and owners of nonproducible specialized resources used in their production will gain permanently higher incomes. Workers replaced by the new processes will experience declines in wages, unless their skills can be transferred to other industries. The net effects upon factor prices and income distribution will be greatly affected by the ease of transfer of factor units from one line of production to another. (See Box 19-2.)

Technological changes which make new products available likewise produce modifications in the general equilibrium system. Such products alter consumption patterns, the output of substitute and complementary goods, and relative factor prices. The development of the automobile, for example, has had tremendous effects on the economy. The demand for and output of complementary goods (such as highways, gasoline, and tires), have increased greatly, together with facilities to produce them. The demand for and output of substitutes (such as horses and buggies, streetcars, and railway service) have declined. The location patterns of retail stores and dwellings have been greatly altered, as have the nature and location of amusement and recre-

---

19-2 How will the increased use of glassware affect the sales of other products?

Sales of direct substitutes, such as plastic dinnerware, will tend to fall, with consequent repercussions on output and factor prices. If the demand for glassware is relatively inelastic, less money will be spent on the product; and purchases of other unrelated products will rise, with further repercussions on prices, outputs, and factor prices.

ation facilities. Incomes of owners of factors particularly important in the production of automobiles and complementary goods have risen, while those of factor units used primarily to produce the substitutes (and not adaptable to other uses) have fallen. The owners of land containing oil have experienced great increases in their incomes, while owners of land primarily suited to the growing of hay for horses have experienced declines in incomes. The relative incomes of the owners of completely adaptable factors have not been affected by the change.

Factor Supplies

Changes in factor supplies, either in quantity or in quality, have much the same effects as technological developments. An increase in the available quantities of one factor compared to those of others will alter relative factor prices, optimum factor combinations, and prices and outputs of consumption goods. The prices of goods using relatively large amounts of the factor which has increased in supply will fall relative to those of other goods, and consumption and output will increase. The price of the factor which has increased in supply will tend to fall, but the total share of income going to the owners of this factor may rise depending on demand elasticities. A growth in the supply of capital goods relative to the quantities of other factors will increase the prices paid for labor and the incomes of the workers, and increase the relative outputs of goods requiring relatively large amounts of capital goods for efficient production.

Competitive Relationships

Changes in competitive relationships will produce modifications in the equilibrium system. For example, if strong oligopoly replaces perfect competition in the market for a particular good, the relative price of the article will rise, and consumption and output will fall. The demand for all other goods will rise if the demand for this good is elastic and will fall if it is inelastic. The owners of firms producing this good will obtain greater incomes, as long as they are protected from the entry of new firms into the industry. The reduced employment of other factors in the industry will lead to readjustments in factor prices—and in costs, and thus outputs, of other industries. Changes in competitive relations in factor markets will alter relative prices of factors and goods and the relative outputs of various goods.

19.9 THE THEORIES OF CHANGE IN THE DETERMINANTS OF GENERAL EQUILIBRIUM

In the preceding paragraphs, the types of readjustments that occur when the basic determinants of equilibrium change as a result of forces autonomous to the economic system have been indicated in a general way. Relatively little attention has been given to the question of whether or not a theory of change in the determinants, relating this change to certain forces within or outside the economy, can be developed. A few such attempts have been made. T. R. Malthus, for example, developed a long-term relationship between wage levels and population growth, of such a nature that growth in population and thus labor supply were limited to the rate of increase in goods providing a subsistence level of income to the workers.[6] This theory was accepted and developed by various English classical writers after Ricardo. Joseph Schumpeter viewed the rate of change in the introduction of innovations as the primary factor determining the rate of economic development and hence the rate and pattern of change in the determinants of the equilibrium system.[7] One of the most complete theories of economic development was that of Karl Marx. His basic principle of economic change was the thesis that each form of economic system develops within itself internal inconsistencies, which manifest themselves primarily in struggles among various groups in the economy. These ultimately destroy the particular form of economic system, which gives way to a new form, which in turn develops its own internal inconsistencies.

In recent years, renewed attention has been given to the establishment of theories of economic change and development, particularly with respect to the causes and processes of change in the level of employment and the determinants of the rate of long-term economic growth in both underdeveloped and more highly developed countries. For some time to come, however, this subject will probably continue to be one of the weaker areas of economic analysis. The problems involved are so complicated and the stock of established factual knowledge so slight that almost any theory can be considered to have some degree of plausibility. As long as this is the case, substantial progress in understanding concrete problems of economic growth is unlikely.

SUMMARY

1. The study of the interrelationships among the immense number of outputs and prices of various goods and the prices and inputs of various factors is known as general equilibrium analysis.

2. A shift in some variable affecting any one good may have widespread repercussions on the equilibrium prices and outputs of many other goods.

3. Like ordinary supply and demand, general equilibrium theory suggests that there exists in a market economy a consistent pattern of equilibrium prices, factor inputs, outputs, and consumer purchases. However, the theory does not deal directly with the process of attaining an equilibrium position.

4. On the demand side of general equilibrium, there are two basic sets of equations: the budget equation and the allocation-of-consumption-expenditure equation.

5. There are also two basic sets of equations on the supply side. The first relates price to cost of production. The second shows the equality of the total quantities of factors used to produce the

[6]T. R. Malthus, *Essays on Population* (London, 1798).

[7]J. Schumpeter, Theory of Economic Development (Cambridge: Harvard University Press, 1934).

various consumption goods with the total quantities of these factors available (assuming equality of factor supply and demand).

6. We can depict the general equilibrium notion graphically. Exchange equilibrium exists on the consumption contract curve (that is, the indifference curves are tangent) where $MRS_A = MRS_B$ = price ratios. Production equilibrium occurs when the isoquants are tangent along the production contract curve. At this point, $(MRTS_{LK})_{X_1} = (MRTS_{LK})_{X_2}$.

7. General equilibrium in production and exchange in the competitive model requires that the prices which individuals exchange (the slope of the line passing through the point where the indifference curves are tangent) be equal to the slope of the production possibility frontier.

8. General equilibrium theory is subject to two major limitations. First, the theory is static in nature. Second, it is difficult to estimate various magnitudes in a general equilibrium system so the equations may be solved.

9. Several major sources of change—in consumer preferences, techniques of production, factor supplies, or in competitive relationships—may have widespread repercussions in the "system."

WORDS AND CONCEPTS FOR REVIEW

partial equilibrium theory
general equilibrium theory
consumer price interdependencies

production contract curve
production possibility curve

REVIEW QUESTIONS

1. Distinguish between partial and general equilibrium theory.

2. Trace the probable effects of an improved variety of orange, which allows a great increase in yield per acre, upon:
(a) The price of apples (immediate and long run).
(b) The production of apples (immediate and short run).
(c) The income of the owners of land best suited for (1) production of oranges, (2) production of apples.

3. What are some of the probable effects of the development of nylon, dacron, and orlon shirts upon the prices and outputs of other goods, and factor prices?

4. When will a change in consumer preferences *permanently* alter factor prices?

5. Explain the budget equation and the allocation-of-consumer-expenditure equation, and explain how the usual demand function is derived from them.

6. What are the two basic general equilibrium equations, from the supply standpoint?

7. Does equality of equations and unknowns ensure a determinate system? Explain.

8. Is the general equilibrium system regarded as mathematically determinate? On what basis?

9. Note the various assumptions upon which the simplified general equilibrium system is based, and indicate the extent to which these may be modified.

10. What are the advantages and limitations of general equilibrium theory?

11. Trace the effects on the economy of an improved method of producing helicopters, which would allow them to sell for $12,000 and make them as safe as automobiles.

12. Trace through the effect of a shift in demand from oranges to apples.

SUGGESTED READINGS

Baumol, W. *Economic Theory and Operations Analysis,* 4th ed. Englewood Cliffs, NJ: Prentice Hall, 1977, Chapter 21.

Bushaw, D. and Clower, R. *Introduction to Mathematical Economics.* Homewood, IL: Irwin, 1959, Chapter 7.

Kraus, M., and Johnson, H. *General Equilibrium Analysis.* Chicago: Aldine, 1975.

Quirk, J. and Saposnik, R. *Introduction to General Equilibrium Theory and Welfare Economics.* New York: McGraw-Hill, 1968.

APPENDIX   INPUT-OUTPUT ANALYSIS

Introduction

The theoretical framework of input-output analysis is largely the creation of Harvard economist and Nobel Laureate Wassily Leontief. The original purpose of the analysis was to present the essence of general equilibrium theory in a simplified form suitable for empirical study. In terms of techniques, however, input-output analysis is a special type of modern linear programming. In every linear programming problem, two steps can be distinguished. First, a set of feasible plans must be selected, plans which satisfy certain given nutrition, capacity, or other requirements. Second, for the possibly very large set of feasible plans, a particular plan (or at least a more limited set of plans) must be selected which minimizes or maximizes some quantity such as cost or output.

From the standpoint of technique, input-output analysis is the special case of linear programming in which the set of feasible plans, to be determined in the first step of a linear programming problem, *contains only a single plan.* This means that the second step need not be carried out; there is no problem of choosing among alternative feasible plans because there is only one feasible plan. The reasons for this will be explained more fully below. In terms of scope, input-output analysis is concerned with the entire economy, whereas much of linear programming deals with problems of more restricted range.

The following account refers mainly to the foundations of the original version of input-output analysis. Recent developments by Leontief and his co-workers, as well as by other persons, are too varied and complex to be summarized here.[8]

Framework and Assumptions

As indicated above, the first stage in the development of input-output analysis involves little more than a simplification of traditional general equilibrium theory—specifically, the replace-

---

[8]A classic account of some of the developments is presented in R. Dorfman, P. Samuelson, and R. Solow, *Linear Programming and Economic Analysis* (New York: McGraw-Hill, 1958), Chapter IX.

ment of traditionally nonlinear relations by corresponding linear equations. The economy is initially divided into a relatively small number of segments, each including industries producing closely related products (from the standpoint of factor inputs). Equations are then introduced relating the output of each industry to the outputs of industries using the product of this industry and to final, autonomous demand.

In order to make the system manageable, several simplifying assumptions are made:

1. *Given coefficients of production.* That is to say, fixed quantities of various factors are necessary to produce a unit of output of a commodity.
2. *Linear homogenous production functions.* Thus a certain percentage change in the output of one product entails the same percentage change in the inputs of the various factors used to produce it.
3. *Given factor supplies, consumer demands, and prices.* Prices are not variables in the system, which is concerned solely with output adjustments.

Given these assumptions, the output of each sector depends directly upon the outputs of all sectors that utilize its product and upon final consumer and government demands. The assumed linear nature of the equations ensures that, for example, an increase of 10 percent in the output of all industries using steel will result in an increase of 10 percent in steel input, and thus a 10-percent increase in the output of steel (provided, of course, that this increase in steel output is possible with existing capacity). Since there is one equation for each sector relating its output to the outputs of other sectors, there are the same number of equations as there are unknowns (the outputs of each sector), and the system is mathematically solvable under appropriate conditions. If available factor supplies and final consumer demands, as well as the production functions, are known, it is thus possible to determine the equilibrium outputs of all sectors. As a rule, various possible levels of output of the various sectors will be mutually consistent with one another, but only one set of activity levels will be consistent with the actual factor supplies and consumer demands existing at a certain time.

Empirical Content

The second and more difficult step in input-output analysis is to give empirical content to the theoretical framework by determining actual magnitudes in the various equations. A substantial amount of work of this type has been done in recent decades, partly by government agencies or under government auspices and partly by nongovernmental research organizations. Many foreign countries use input-output analysis for central planning or as a guide provided to decentralized firms. The task is a tremendous one, largely because of inadequacy of data, but much progress has been made. As the elements in the equations are given magnitudes, it becomes possible to trace the quantitative effects upon various sectors of changes in determinants such as consumer demand, factor supplies, or governmental purchases. Particular use has been made of the analysis in estimating the reductions in outputs of civilian goods which would be necessary to allow a given output of military equipment in case of war, and the extent of production for military purposes which would be possible with a particular reduction in output of goods for civilian use.

Limitations to the Analysis

Despite its contributions, input-output analysis as it now stands is subject to serious limitations. The basic problem is the development of equations that are simple enough to be manageable yet sufficiently refined to reflect the actual behavior of the economy. The assumption of linear equations, relating outputs of one industry to outputs of others in a unique fashion, is obviously somewhat unrealistic (particularly so for longer-range predictions). Increases in output do not in many cases require proportionate increases in input, mainly because of indivisibilities of various factors. The assumption of fixed production coefficients precludes the possibility of factor substitution. Even in a short-run period, some substitutions may be possible; and over a longer period, the opportunities for substitutions are likely to be relatively great. As a result, it is possible to maintain outputs of some goods at higher levels than would be possible on the basis of given production coefficients when materials currently used in the production of these products are diverted in part to other uses. For example, during World War II, when steel supplies were diverted to war production, it was possible to maintain production of office filing cabinets by making them from wood. Theoretically, of course, the equations could be redesigned to introduce the possibility of factor substitutions, but to do so tremendously complicates the task of establishing the magnitudes in the equations.

The assumption of fixed relationships between outputs of various sectors likewise precludes the possibility of increases or decreases in inventories; as a consequence, changes in inventories which actually occur as production levels change will prevent the attainment of the exact results anticipated in the analysis. The time factor—the lag between inputs and outputs—is also ignored. This is of little consequence in the continuous flow of a static situation but is significant when changes in rates of output occur. The fact that different firms in a sector will employ diverse production techniques is also a complicating factor, since changes in outputs by various firms will have different effects upon the inputs of particular factors. Finally, the treatment of investment demand is troublesome. It would seem clear that inputs of capital goods are not related in a proportionate fashion to changes in outputs of products (particularly in very short-run periods). Some attempts have been made to develop a relationship between investment input and the *rate of change* in the outputs of the products, but this task is by no means simple. More commonly, input-output analysis has been based upon the assumption that investment is an autonomous variable, a procedure which simplifies the system but lessens the significance of its results.

Actual progress in the development of the analysis is of course retarded by lack of adequate knowledge about consumer demand and production technology. Information about both of these is necessary for satisfactory determination of actual magnitudes in the system.

20

Welfare Economics

20.1 INTRODUCTION

Preceding chapters have analyzed the operation of the economic system without attempting to evaluate its performance in terms of given standards of efficiency, justice, or morality. We have considered how the economy works and why it works as it does, but we have not stressed whether particular features of the system are "good" or "bad." We have described how the price system determines output—and thus the composition of national product—without inquiring whether or not realized results meet desired performance goals. We have considered the forces that determine the distribution of income without asking whether the resulting distribution is in any sense optimal. Now, however, it is appropriate to raise some of these questions, to survey briefly that portion of economic analysis—**welfare economics**—which is concerned with evaluation and thus seeks to judge the extent to which the working of the economic system leads to results that are "desirable" by reference to generally accepted social goals.

20.2 SOCIAL GOALS AND THE ECONOMIC SYSTEM

All applications of scientific knowledge give rise to ethical questions of one kind or another. The moral issues raised by the development of nuclear weapons afford some particularly striking examples, but similar instances might be drawn from almost every field of human knowledge. Regardless of the field of study involved, evaluation of either an existing state of affairs or the consequences of a proposed action can be separated into two distinct tasks. First, it is necessary to acquire a fairly comprehensive understanding of the concrete situation to be evaluated. Second, it is necessary to *select* and *apply* standards of evaluation. The first of these tasks, which is concerned with *what is* rather than *what ought to be*, is the main business of science as science. The first step in the second task, the **selection of standards**, is a part of the general field of ethics, since it involves the making of value judgments about the personal and social desirability of alternative actions. The second step, the application of **ethical criteria** to evaluate particular situations, involves a mixture of science and ethics. It is this mixed area of knowledge with which welfare economics deals.

For our present purposes, we shall merely assume certain ethical goals that appear to reflect widely accepted attitudes of contemporary society. The fact that these goals are assumed, not determined by economic analysis, must be stressed, along with the fact that the evaluations which follow are valid only in terms of these goals. If we were to assume other goals, the evaluations would produce different results. It is also worth emphasizing that what is being evaluated are situations described by economic models. The evaluations are relevant so far as the actual economic system is concerned to the extent that these theoretical models provide an adequate description of the real world.

Three primary social goals will be assumed to be desirable:

1. Maximum freedom of choice for individuals, consistent with rights for other individuals.
2. Maximum satisfaction of wants, which requires use and allocation of resources in such a way as to permit the maximum per capita real utility (often proxied by income, for reasons which will become clear).
3. A pattern of distribution of income regarded as most equitable in terms of the standards of contemporary society.

In the remainder of the chapter, these possibly inconsistent goals will be explained more fully, the conditions necessary for their attainment will be indicated, and a brief evaluation will be made of the extent to which the conditions, and thus the goals, appear to be satisfied in the present-day economic system.

20.3 FREEDOM OF CHOICE

Freedom of choice in the sphere of economic activity is the right of individuals to act as they wish in the choice of employment and the purchase and sale of goods and services. Attainment of this goal requires that individuals be free to select the goods they prefer to satisfy their wants. They must be free to make decisions about the use of factor units they own—to make them available to business firms or not, to select the type of work and the place of work they prefer among available opportunities, to divide their time between work and leisure as they please, to establish a business if they wish to do so, and to make decisions of their own choice in the operation of the business. Contemporary western society regards freedom of action to be desirable in itself, apart from the role it may play in facilitating attainment of optimum standards of living.

It must be recognized, however, that freedom of choice is a relative matter, since absolute freedom would result in serious injury to others. Freedom of choice must be exercised within a framework established to protect the interests of society as a group, and sometimes individuals by themselves. If all persons were free to hunt deer without restriction, there would soon be no deer to hunt, and the right to hunt would become worthless. The greatest overall freedom is obtained through the establishment of certain restrictions in the interests of the group. Over the years, there has been a tendency to increase the number of restrictions of this type. Yet, in the market form of economic system (as found in the United States, Canada, much of the western Europe, and elsewhere), a substantial degree of personal freedom of choice remains. In general, people are free to buy anything they please except for a few goods, such as certain drugs, which could bring injury to the consumer and/or others. Legally, they may work or not as they wish, obtain jobs anywhere they can find them, and move from one area to another. People are free to start any type of business (with a few exceptions) and to select products, prices, and methods of production as they desire.

20.4 MAXIMUM SATISFACTION OF WANTS

The second goal is the maximization of the **satisfaction of wants**—in other words, the attainment of the highest possible level of economic well-being for society as a whole through the use and allocation of resources that allow the highest per capita real income with given resources, technology, and preference schedules of factor owners regarding the use of their factor units. We assume that maximization of economic well-being requires maximum per capita real utility; it must be recognized that this in itself is a value judgment—one which would not be acceptable to some social groups such as the Amish communities. If income becomes higher (in a noncoercive society that doesn't make factor suppliers supply more than they wish), then utility will become higher because more goods and services are consumed at higher incomes. There are analytical problems here relating to the measurement of increases in per capita real income, particularly as the relative output of various goods changes, and there are significant questions relating to the manner in which the increase is distributed among various individuals. But for the moment we shall disregard the question of the distribution of real income, discussing resource use and allocation in terms of the prevailing pattern of distribution. The question of the optimum pattern of distribution will be raised later in the chapter.

Given the pattern of income distribution, the requirements for optimum use and allocation of resources are often called the "marginal conditions." These are noted in the following paragraphs.

Optimum Efficiency in the Use of Resources

In the first place, optimum want satisfaction requires that resources be efficiently utilized in production. This, in turn, requires:

1. Use of the most efficient production techniques and the most satisfactory available methods of administrative organization and physical distribution.
2. Attainment of least-cost factor combinations in short-run production, and thus the adjustment of factor combinations until the marginal rate of technical substitution between any two factors is equal to the ratio of their prices.
3. Operation of firms at the point of lowest long-run average cost; they must not only expand plant to the size allowing lowest cost, but must also operate at the optimum capacity (lowest-cost point) of this plant.

Only if these requirements are met can maximum output be obtained from given resources. If obsolete methods are used, least-cost combinations are not attained, plants are too small, or firms are not operating at lowest average cost, then the total output obtained from given resources will be less than the potential. (See Box 20-1.)

Theoretically, when markets are perfectly competitive, firms will operate at the point of lowest LRAC (see Chapter 9). But imperfections, especially lack of knowledge, undoubtedly interfere with the attainment of lowest average cost. In imperfectly competitive markets with free entry of new firms, operation at the point of lowest LRAC is impossible since the downward-sloping demand curves for the products of the firms cannot be tangent to the ∪−shaped average cost curves at their lowest points. Hence there are too many firms in terms of the market (but too few to permit the markets to be perfectly competitive); resources are poorly utilized, and costs could be lower if the market were divided among a smaller number of firms. The waste, however, may be less than is sometimes argued. In these industries, the demand curves of the firms are likely to be highly elastic, and thus the departure from perfectly competitive conditions may not be very substantial. Furthermore, the product diversity of monopolistic competition may itself be valuable, hence worth some departure from least-cost production of a homogenous good.

In imperfectly competitive markets in which entry is not entirely free, firms may of course operate at the point of lowest cost (although price does not equal average cost); but there is no necessity for this to be so (indeed, it would be a fluke if MR = MC at this point). If an industry is dominated by a few large firms, they may easily expand to the point of lowest LRAC or even beyond. If the typical LRAC curve contains an extensive

---

20-1   To what extent is the optimum organization of production attained in a market economy?

This is not an easy question to answer. The profit motive provides a continuous incentive to reduce costs—one which is, of course, strongest when competition is effective, but which is present even with complete monopoly. Yet the exact least-cost combination of factors, in all aspects, is rarely attained. It is an extremely difficult task for a firm to accomplish, especially with complex industrial processes.

horizontal segment, as is now believed to be common, the likelihood that many firms may be operating at or near the lowest average cost figure in imperfectly competitive conditions is increased.

Whenever product is differentiated, a new element in cost is introduced—that of advertising and other selling activities. Though these activities inevitably raise cost schedules above perfectly competitive levels, they do convey certain benefits to consumers. Evaluation of the relative advantages of the higher costs and benefits is very difficult. In some instances in which markets would not be perfectly competitive even without selling activities, the development of these activities may allow the firms to operate nearer the point of lowest average cost by increasing their sales volumes.

Optimum Adjustment of Production in Terms of Consumer Preferences

The second requirement is the attainment of a pattern of relative outputs of various goods that conforms to consumer preferences. That is, the composition of total output—and thus the allocation of resources—must be such as to best satisfy consumer preferences. For example, if consumers desire some shoes and some luggage, all of the available leather should not be used for luggage production while people go barefooted or wear wooden shoes. The leather supply must be allocated in such a manner that consumer preferences for the two products are satisfied as completely as possible given constraints. If consumers desire both cake and bread, all flour should not be used to produce bread; some should be utilized in cake production as well.

Optimum adjustment of production can be obtained only if, for each consumer, the *marginal rate of substitution* between each two goods purchased is equal to the **marginal rate of transformation** between the two goods in production—that is, to the number of units of one good that must be sacrificed if an additional unit of the other good is to be produced. If this relationship is not attained, consumer preferences will be more fully realized by shifting some resources from the production of goods with output excessive relative to consumer preferences to the production of goods with inadequate output. For example, the relative output of bread and cake must be such that consumers are indifferent between bread made with the marginal units of wheat going into bread production and cake made with the marginal units of wheat going into cake production. If the preference for bread is greater at the margin, more wheat must be used for bread production and less for cake production.

This relationship at the margin between rates of substitution and rates of transformation will be attained only if several requirements are met:

1. Consumers must allocate their incomes in such a manner that marginal rates of substitution among all goods they buy are equal to the ratios of the prices of the goods; in other words, the marginal utilities of all goods purchased are proportional to their prices. Consumers who fail to accomplish this adjustment will not have reached the highest indifference curve possible subject to their income and thus will not be maximizing satisfaction.

2. Relative prices of various goods must reflect marginal rates of transformation among them, so that if consumers allocate incomes in such a manner that marginal rates of substitution are equal to price ratios, marginal rates of substitution will also equal marginal rates of transformation.

   Relative prices will reflect marginal rates of transformation only if:

   (a) Factor prices equate the supply of and demand for the factors, and are uniform to all producers. If factor prices exceed the levels at which supply and demand are equal, for example, they will not reflect the real costs involved in the production of an additional unit of a good in terms of the sacrifice of other goods necessary to obtain another factor unit for the production of the particular good. The same is true if factor prices are not uniform to all users.

   (b) Marginal costs to firms for the production of a given product must reflect all costs to the economy arising out of its production; in other words, there must be no external diseconomies. If certain costs to society do not enter into the firms' marginal production costs, the price of the good will be too low and an excessive amount of the good will be produced. The traditional example is the damage from factory smoke, which does not become a cost to the business firm operating the factory but is a cost to society as a whole. As patrons pour out of a football stadium parking lot at the end of the game, they congest traffic on the highway, cause accidents, and delay motorists and truckers. These are real costs for which the football game is responsible, but they are not borne by those operating it and are not reflected in the prices charged the patrons. Air pollution by motor vehicles is another example.

3. All benefits from the use of goods must accrue to the person acquiring them; that is, there must be no external economies of consumption. If some indirect benefits are gained by other persons, too little of the good will be purchased and thus produced, since the indirect benefits do not influence the actions of persons purchasing the units. For example, if a person kills dandelions in his lawn, his neighbors will benefit as well. But the person is not likely to consider the latter (except in the interests of neighborhood goodwill) when he makes the decision whether or not to buy the weedkiller. More significant examples of indirect benefits include social or community goods such as national defense, which convey their benefits to the community as a whole rather than to individuals separately.

Realization of These Requirements. Complete attainment of these requirements would ensure an optimum allocation of resources, an optimum "product mix" given the pattern of income distribution. In a perfectly competitive economy, with perfect knowledge on the part of consumers and business firms and with no external economies or diseconomies, these conditions would be attained. Each consumer would allocate income according to the MRS-price ratio rule. Factor prices would equate factor supply and demand; prices of all goods would be equal to their marginal factor costs (which, in the absence of external diseconomies, would include all real costs); marginal rates of substitution would therefore equal marginal rates of transformation. This conclusion is essentially a statement of the "invisible hand" doctrine: the economy, left to its own devices, will, under the assumed conditions, best serve the interests of society as a whole. It must be stressed, however, that *the conclusions are valid only in terms of a static context and in terms of the assumption of a given pattern of income distribution.*

However, the actual economy is far removed from one of universal perfect competition and absence of external economies and diseconomies. Some of the major deviations and their significance for economic welfare are noted below:

1. *Consumer allocation of incomes.* Even though consumers may seek to maximize satisfaction gained from their incomes, there are many obstacles to succeeding at this goal. Inadequate information about the ability of particular goods to meet various desires prevents attainment of maximum satisfaction. In part, this is inevitable by the very nature of consumer wants: a person cannot tell if she likes guava pie until she tastes it; and if she doesn't like it, she will have not maximized satisfaction. But the economic system does not do as effective a job of informing the consumer as it might. Advertising accomplishes this in part, but it is by no means adequate and may be misleading. Some rules for the labeling and description of contents have been imposed by governments, although there are counterarguments to the merits of such rules.[1]

2. **(a)** *Factor prices do not always equate supply and demand.* The most extreme deviation is that of mass unemployment: the real social cost of additional units of output may be almost nil when unemployed workers and resources can be used to produce them; but the marginal private costs, reflecting existing factor prices, will be very much higher. Such situations may be explained partly by imperfectly competitive elements in factor markets but primarily by the inability of factor owners to adjust their real factor prices. If workers agree to work for lower wages, the competitive forces may cause prices of products to fall; thus real wages may change slowly, if at all.

    Similarly, factor prices are not always uniform to all users. Wages for a given type of labor may be higher in one area than in another, perhaps because of the varying strength of local unions, and thus uneconomic location of industry will result. Price discrimination practiced by monopolist or oligopolist producers or materials may also cause failure to attain this requirement, as may monopsony influences exercised by buyers over price.

    (b) *Marginal costs do not always reflect all costs for which production of additional units is responsible.* Examples were given above in the discussion of this requirement; many others could be supplied. The social

---

[1]For example, if labeling requirements have benefits to the consumer *greater than costs,* why would firms be required to label—it would be in their own interests to do so.

costs of alcoholism do not become factor costs to liquor producers, for example. If a factory is built in a residential area, the decline in the value of residential property is not borne by the business firm.

Governments have sought to meet this problem in several ways with varying degrees of success. They have prohibited the production of certain goods, such as narcotics, which have heavy social costs not borne by the producers. They have placed taxes on the sale of other products, such as liquor, to shift some of the additional social costs to the users and thus reduce consumption. City zoning ordinances are primarily designed to prevent losses in property values through indiscriminate location of particular types of activities without reference to other property uses. The danger, of course, is "overcorrection" or correcting in inappropriate ways (ways having costs greater than benefits).

(c) *Equality of marginal costs and prices is attained only if firms are selling in perfectly competitive markets.* The greatest advantage of perfectly competitive market conditions, from the standpoint of economic welfare, is the attainment of equality of price and marginal cost.

In imperfectly competitive conditions, price will exceed marginal cost. Under such conditions, characterized by downward-sloping demand curves for the products of the individual firms, at the output level at which MR = MC, price will be in excess of marginal costs, as illustrated in Figure 20-1. Therefore the prices of goods exceed the figures which reflect the real factor costs, in the sense of the sacrifice of output of other goods, and outputs of goods are held to uneconomically low levels. This result is encountered whether excess profits are earned or not; the source of the difficulty is the downward-sloping demand curve, which causes marginal revenue to be less than price at the point of most profitable operation.

In other cases, artificial deviations between marginal factor cost and price are caused by the levying of excise taxes on the sale of particular goods. These taxes result in prices for the goods in excess of their factor costs—and hence in uneconomic reductions in output (if the other requirements for optimum economic welfare are attained)—unless, of course, the excises reflect costs to society that are not borne by the producers. Liquor taxes may perhaps be justified on this basis. (See Box 20-2.)

3. *There are many types of goods which yield important benefits to persons other than those who acquire them, or yield all or most of their benefits to the community as a whole, rather than separately to individuals.* National defense is the traditional example. By its nature, it cannot be broken up into small pieces and sold to individuals. Education directly benefits the recipients but also yields important community benefits such as greater social and political stability, more rapid economic development, and cures for disease and other inventions having benefits not captured fully by those responsible.[2]

---

[2]An additional benefit is that people become more interesting to talk to as they increase their education. This "cocktail party" externality is not trivial.

FIGURE 20-1

Relationship of Price and Marginal Cost, Imperfectly Competitive Conditions
In imperfect competition, firms face downward-sloping demand curves. Consequently, price exceeds marginal cost and too little output is produced.

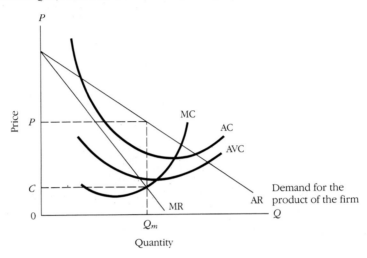

Because of the importance of indirect benefits from many types of activities, governments (representing the community as a whole) have found it desirable to provide such services to the community and to cover the costs of producing them from compulsory levies in the form of taxes. Private enterprise cannot produce many of these services at all, because they cannot be sold to individuals. Others, such as education, are publicly and privately produced, but the total output would be uneconomically small if production were left in private

20-2   Are there cases where price is equal to marginal cost but average cost is not covered, and thus all costs of production cannot be recovered?

Yes. An obvious example is a public utility enterprise which, although possessing a monopoly in a particular geographical area, does not have a sufficient market to allow it to reach the point of lowest cost. As explained in earlier chapters, in ranges of output less than that of lowest average cost, marginal cost is less than average cost. An extreme example is provided by a toll bridge not used to capacity. Marginal cost of use of the bridge by another car may be almost zero, yet the average cost may be substantial. If prices are set at a level equal to marginal cost, the deficit must be made up by a subsidy financed by taxation or by a fixed charge for the ability to use the bridge. Since virtually all taxes presumably have some adverse effects upon the economy, the decision about pricing must be made by weighing the disadvantages of taxes against those of departure from marginal-cost pricing.

hands—if there were *no subsidies*—because the indirect benefits would not influence purchases. However, subsidies such as "education vouchers" could make the output optimal and open up the education industry to greater private competition.[3]

Optimum Degree of Factor Utilization

The third general condition necessary for the attainment of optimum satisfaction of wants, given the pattern of income distribution, is an optimum degree of utilization of factors such as labor, capital, and natural resources. Several aspects of this condition are discussed below.

Avoidance of Cyclical Unemployment. Optimum use of factor units requires that all factor units whose owners wish to have them employed at the equilibrium factor prices should find employment (perhaps after some optimal search process, in the case of frictional unemployment). Unemployment of factors obviously reduces overall output and real income per capita below the optimum level. This affects savings levels, hence growth. Furthermore, unemployment causes severe distress for the individuals concerned, since their source of income vanishes.

Optimum Division of Time between Work and Leisure. Optimum economic welfare does not require the absolute maximum possible output, but rather a level consistent with the generally preferred allocation of time between work and leisure. Thus, as real income rises as a result of increased productivity, optimum economic welfare does not require that the entire gain be taken in the form of greater output, if individuals prefer to take a part or all of the benefits of greater productivity in the form of increased leisure. The argument against shorter hours—that output will be reduced—is not a convincing one. If society prefers more leisure and less output, it cannot be argued that such a choice is undesirable in terms of the assumed goals.

In practice, the requirements of efficient production make it impossible for each individual to decide the number of hours he or she will work. In general, individuals must accept the working period that is standard in their particular line of employment, or else work elsewhere. Trends before and during the 1980s, however, are to greater flexibility as the economy becomes increasingly less reliant on large-scale, mass-production industrial processes. In many occupations, it is not unusual for individuals to work some days at home, perhaps communicating via computer modem to other centralized resources.

On the other hand, it may be argued that the growth in the importance of certain taxes has interfered with the attainment of an optimum division of time between work and leisure. Income taxes apply to gains from work but not to those from leisure, and sales and excise taxes apply to gains from work to the extent that income is spent on taxable goods. Thus the relative gains from work and leisure are altered somewhat;

---

[3]This is not necessarily "good," although it might be a great improvement on our present educational system.

some persons may seek to work more because of taxes (to maintain a standard of living), while others will seek to work less (substituting toward leisure). It may be argued that the consequent distortion interferes with the attainment of optimum economic welfare. Tax reforms occurring in the mid-1980s, along with earlier reductions in maximum marginal tax rates, may well reduce these distortions in the future.

Optimum Rate of Capital Formation.   The optimum rate of capital formation is particularly difficult to define. It may be argued that economic welfare requires the division of total income between consumption and savings in a manner which conforms to the relative preferences for present and future consumption on the part of individuals. However, this requirement is subject to two important modifications.

First, an increased rate of capital formation allows a more rapid increase in output of consumption goods in the future. Particularly in countries with very low per capita incomes, relatively small increases in savings now may lead to very sharp rises in consumption in the future—rises that are not foreseen by the people of those societies. It may be argued, in such cases, that a higher rate of capital formation than would occur on the basis of the preferred division of income between consumption and savings would greatly increase economic welfare, at least for future generations.[4]

Second, the preferred allocation of income between consumption and savings may prevent the maintenance of full employment and stable economic growth. If persons seek to save greater sums at high income levels than can be rapidly absorbed in investment, unemployment will develop, and optimum economic welfare will not be attained. Under such circumstances, a compromise is necessary between the requirement of allocating income on the basis of individual choice and the desire for maintaining full employment.

Optimum Rate of Utilization of Scarce Natural Resources.   Economic welfare requires an optimum rate of utilization of scarce resources such as petroleum and iron ore. But this optimum rate is very difficult to define because of the conflicting interests of present and future generations. An extremely rapid rate of exploitation would exhaust supplies otherwise available for the future, while an excessively slow rate involves heavy sacrifice of present welfare for future welfare, one which may prove to have been unnecessary as new resources or alternative methods of production are developed in the future.

It is sometimes argued that the perfectly competitive outcome of the free market is short-sighted regarding the utilization of scarce natural resources. In their single-minded pursuit of short-run profits, greedy profit maximizers purportedly do not care about future generations. Is this likely to be a correct view? It is not: The market efficiently allocates resources intertemporally in much the same way that it allocates resources efficiently at any one time. Indeed, it is "greed" (the attempt to maximize profit) that generates this desirable result. Let's see how.

---

[4]Issues of intergenerational equity are very complex and, of course, normative. Are large gains in consumption to future people sufficient justification for even small reductions in consumption on the part of those living now? What if those in the future will be richer anyway, while present populations are desperately poor?

Suppose you owned an oil well. If you believed that we were using our scarce resources too fast, what would you expect to happen to future prices of oil? Clearly, you would expect those prices to be very high as the larger future demand (from greater numbers of higher-income households) confronted the smaller supply. Similarly, if we were using scarce resources too fast, present prices would be relatively low. Would it not, then, be stupid for you to sell your oil *now*, when merely by holding it in the ground you could be much better off in the future? Presumably, you could borrow to finance "high living" today on the collateral of your oil wealth.

But, of course, every other oil well owner would be just like you. They (and you) would in fact end up keeping oil off the market (holding this asset) in an amount necessary to guarantee that the oil "asset" earned the going risk-adjusted rate of return. How can oil earn *any* return? (It certainly has no coupon yield, like a bond.) The answer is that the price of oil and other scarce natural resources must rise at the rate of interest.[5] If some resource-owners *were* to use them up too fast, prices would be depressed today and would be expected to be larger in the future; the greed of other resource-owners would cause them, then, to hold their resources off the market to gain the extranormal rate of return. It is profit-maximizing that guarantees that resources *are* used efficiently over time. The value of scarce natural resources to future generations is indeed considered by present owners, *so long as* they care about maximizing the present value of their wealth (the latter occurring if they make the most discounted profits from future periods).

The preceding should cause worry to those suspecting that government intervention will improve the temporal pattern of resource usage. This is true even if government were not short-sighted. Yet evidence suggests that our elected representatives have very short time horizons (even Senators face reelection every six years, others more frequently). Political pressures to keep prices low *now* are more likely to cause intertemporal resource misallocation, undesirably harming future generations, than would be the case if society relied on market forces.

Attainment of an Optimum Rate of Economic Growth

Traditionally, the theory of economic welfare has been established in terms of static conditions, merely seeking to define the requirements for optimum welfare in terms of given determinants of equilibrium positions. In recent years, however, increased attention has been given to the significance of dynamic considerations for economic welfare. This attention has centered primarily on two elements: stable growth and increasing real national income.

Maintenance of an Equilibrium, Full-Employment Rate of Growth.   Generally speaking, an economy can continue to expand at a stable rate, without continuing or frequently recurring unemployment, only if balance is maintained among various determinants of the rate of development. In particular, aggregate demand for

---

[5]This is a bit of a simplification, ignoring marginal storage costs and so on. But the basic point is unaffected by various sophisticated "add-on" notions.

output must keep pace with growth in aggregate capacity to produce. The theory of economic development has not reached a sufficient stage of advancement to prescribe more fully the specific requirements for stability in growth.

Attainment of an Optimum Rate of Increase in the Real Level of National Income. The economic system must provide optimum incentive for the discovery and introduction of new techniques, new methods of organization and operation, and new products, which increase the real level of national income and aid in maintaining the volume of investment at sufficiently high levels to permit full employment.

One of the greatest advantages of the private enterprise market economy relates to innovation. A major means by which firms can gain a higher-than-average rate of profit is to introduce innovations that will yield excess profits until competitors are able to duplicate the change. If competitors are unable to duplicate the change, this may give rise to continuing monopoly profit. The pressures of competition likewise force other firms to meet innovations in order to escape losses.

Imperfectly competitive conditions may be somewhat more advantageous for economic growth than perfectly competitive ones, so long as some elements of competition remain. The typical firm selling in perfectly competitive markets may be too small to undertake the research and experimentation necessary for innovations. Largely for this reason, most agricultural research in the United States has been undertaken by the federal government. It is the larger firm, in situations of oligopoly and related cases, that may best be able to develop and introduce improvements which allow real increases in national income.

However, pressures toward improvement and efficiency will slacken if the entry of new firms into various industries is limited and if existing firms gain monopoly or semimonopoly positions. Many innovations are made by newcomers. If these cannot start, and if existing firms are already making a high rate of profit, development may be checked. Restrictions on entry of new firms may be more detrimental, from the standpoint of overall economic welfare, than are mere differentiation of product and the presence of relatively few firms in an industry. Likewise detrimental to economic progress are outright agreements among firms on prices, methods of production, shares of output, and so on, as permitted in the cartel systems of some countries.

20.5 INTERPERSONAL COMPARISONS AND WELFARE CRITERIA

The analysis thus far has abstracted from the problem of the relative economic positions of various individuals; we have in effect assumed that all individuals have the same capacity for satisfaction—in other words, the same utility functions relating to money income. We have also assumed a given income distribution. The second assumption will be considered later in this chapter. The first assumption, if considered carefully, is seen to be essentially meaningless. It is now universally recognized that with the present state of knowledge, there is no possibility of making **interpersonal utility comparisons**,—that is, of comparing relative satisfactions received by different persons. There is, for example, no way to compare the relative satisfactions gained by two persons drinking cups of coffee.

Once it is recognized that interpersonal utility comparisons are impossible, it becomes evident that the rules advanced above are inadequate to allow us to state with certainty that various changes in the economy would of necessity increase economic welfare, even many changes which are universally regarded as doing so. Almost any type of change will benefit some persons and injure others—even, for example, readjustment of factor combinations to bring them to the optimum as defined above, or elimination of monopoly. Since the relative gains and losses of satisfaction by various individuals cannot be compared, we cannot say that the changes *necessarily* increase economic welfare, even though they bring the economy more closely in conformity with the rules of optimum efficiency and resource allocation. (See Box 20-3.)

Thus if welfare economics is to be at all meaningful as a basis for evaluation of the economy and determination of economic policy, it is necessary to establish a suitable welfare criterion to meet this interpersonal comparison problem. There have been several approaches, including the Pareto optimum, the compensation principle, and the social welfare function.

The Pareto Optimum

The **Pareto optimum** has played a major role in the development of general equilibrium theory and welfare economics. According to this criterion, a change may be regarded as necessarily desirable in terms of economic welfare only if the change benefits someone without injuring anyone else. This is, of course, a highly restrictive

---

20-3   Suppose that the building of a new highway will bring benefits to thousands of motorists in the form of saved time, fewer accidents, and more pleasant driving. But the building of this highway will necessitate moving the home of one family from a site for which it has strong preference and does not wish to leave, regardless of the compensation offered. Is there a way to relate the satisfaction received by the family and the motorists?

There is no scientific basis for stating that the total satisfaction gained by the thousands of motorists exceeds the dissatisfaction suffered by the one family. An additional criterion is necessary for determining on welfare grounds appropriate policy for building the highway. A common approach, benefit/cost analysis, does compare the dollar willingness-to-pay of those affected. If, in the example, the aggregate willingness-to-pay of the motorists were $30 million and the cost of the road were $20 million, *most* people would suspect that the net benefits of $10 million are greater than the loss in satisfaction the family would experience by having to move. There is no way to prove this definitively, however, apart from bribery (and this would presume that the family would not lie!).

assumption; even elimination of monopoly, for example, while benefiting many persons, will injure the owners of monopoly enterprises. Changes covered by the criterion might be restricted to such instances as the lessening of unemployment (if this could be done without costs to others), or alteration of factor inputs in such a way to increase output with a given quantity of factor inputs, there being no change in factor prices (and incomes) as a consequence. Thus, as a basis for judging efficiency or recommending policy, welfare economics is of very little assistance if we hold rigidly to the definition of Pareto optimum.

The Compensation Principle

In the years immediately after World War II, British economists Kaldor and Hicks and others developed the so-called **compensation principle** in an effort to broaden the applicability of welfare economics. This involved adding to the Pareto optimum case those situations in which the persons benefiting from the change would be willing to compensate those losing to a sufficient extent that the latter would no longer oppose the change. Thus, for example, owners of business firms and consumers benefiting from the introduction of improved technology might be willing to pay enough to induce those workers displaced by the technological change or forced to take jobs at lower pay to end their resistance to the change. It is *willingness* to pay that is significant, not actual payment. If the latter occurs, the Pareto rule applies.

Various criticisms have been advanced against this rule. One is a technical question, as noted by Scitovsky: In some instances, once the change had been made, it would be advantageous for those who had been willing to allow the change to compensate the other group to return to the original situation. Scitovsky argued that the rule was valid only if after the first change it would not be advantageous to change the situation back to the original.

More fundamentally, the compensation principle is based upon the implicit assumption that a given number of dollars represents equal utility to all persons; otherwise the fact that those benefiting are willing to pay an amount in excess of the figure which the injured would regard as adequate compensation for their injury does not demonstrate that there is a net gain in economic welfare. In effect, interpersonal utility comparisons have entered in. Furthermore the rule cannot be implemented: there is no easy way in which the compensation that persons would be willing to offer and to accept could be ascertained (though much recent work has made progress in revealing demands in such situations).

Social Welfare Function

Today, the most widely accepted welfare criterion is the **social welfare function**, as developed by Bergson, Samuelson, Arrow, and others. Such a function would express the optimum pattern of distribution of benefits among individuals as viewed by the consensus of thought in contemporary society.[6] The welfare function would thus

---

[6]The function could, of course, be based upon the opinion of a dictator or some other source.

establish the basis for weighing benefits and injuries of various persons—perhaps in terms of the relative numbers of persons benefiting or losing, for example, or in terms of the nature of the gain or loss (such as cheaper products in preference to monopoly income). The task of ascertaining an overall social welfare function embracing all aspects of the economy is obviously an impossible one, given the present (or likely future) state of knowledge. But it is not impossible to develop major segments of such a function; this is constantly being done as persons make judgments about the desirability or undesirability of certain policies.

Thus, we typically conclude that the benefits from the elimination of monopoly power, with a consequent improvement of resource allocation, exceed the injury to those losing their monopoly profits. Restricting the rights of smelters, refineries, or chemical manufacturers to pour out noxious fumes is accepted because the social welfare function dictates that benefits to those living in the surrounding area outweigh the injury to the owners of the smelter and their customers, who must pay higher prices as a result of the costs of pollution-control devices.

The principle of the social welfare function criterion has great merit in making explicit the fact that virtually any change does benefit some persons at the expense of others and that society must weigh these benefits and injuries, not in terms of any scientific principle but upon a social welfare function based on value judgments. Unfortunately there are many difficulties involved in ascertaining consensus of thought, and the rule could lead to what an outsider might regard as flagrant violation of the rights of a minority segment of the population. But given the present state of knowledge there is no suitable alternative, and it is preferable to recognize that there is no scientific basis for the judgments than to make implicit assumptions which result in attaching scientific support to purely value judgments.

20.6 THE OPTIMUM PATTERN OF INCOME DISTRIBUTION

The definition of optimum efficiency in the use and allocation of resources given in the preceeding sections is based upon the assumption of a given distribution of income; this is true even with the Pareto optimum and compensation welfare criteria. If conformity with the efficiency and allocation rules has been attained, the economy may be said to have attained optimum economic welfare in terms of the pattern of income distribution which prevails after all adjustments have been made—but only in terms of this pattern. Moving beyond this given, what can be said about the **optimum pattern of income distribution**?

Aggregate Total Satisfaction?

Were utility measurable, and interpersonal utility comparisons warranted, it would be meaningful to say, in conformity with the accepted goals, that the optimum pattern of income distribution would be that which would maximize aggregate satisfaction. But satisfactions are not measurable and are not comparable among individuals, and thus such a statement is meaningless. As a matter of practice, rough comparisons are frequently made; most persons would accept the argument, for example, that the transfer of one dollar from a millionaire to a starving family would increase the satisfaction of the latter more than it would decrease the satisfaction of the former. But this is strictly a value judgment—perhaps the reason the millionaire became one was because of his intense love for dollars or the things they can buy! Similarly, at least some of the poor could make themselves better off if they valued goods more intensely; being poor is not in all cases involuntary.

The Lerner Argument

Abba Lerner has argued that, in the absence of knowledge of the actual pattern of distribution which will maximize satisfaction, the most satisfactory assumption we can make is that an equal distribution would be the one more likely to maximize satisfaction from a given level of national income. Lerner's argument is based upon the principle that capacities for satisfaction are distributed normally around the mode of a frequency distribution and that an equal distribution would involve only random error, whereas any other would involve a definite bias. But this assumption likewise has no scientific foundation. Satisfaction may depend to a large extent upon the ability to be able to outdo other persons in consumption, or to keep up with them, in a society in which such "keeping-up" is not ensured by equality of distribution. Furthermore, an equal distribution is obviously not consistent with the maintenance of a high level of national income (because of effects upon incentives[7]) nor with prevailing attitudes in contemporary Western societies.

The Attitudes of Society—the Social Welfare Function

The only feasible approach to the problem is the principle that the optimum pattern is that which is regarded as the most equitable by the consensus of opinion in the particular society—which is, in other words, embraced in the social welfare function. This is a value judgment that cannot be derived from economic analysis, but it appears to reflect most satisfactorily contemporary thinking on the question. This criterion cannot be defined; it is simply one which accords with the concept of equity accepted in the particular society.

How can the consensus of thought on this question be determined? No precise method is possible; evaluation of legislation, as reflecting (perhaps rather imperfectly) the will of society, represents the only tangible approach. On this basis, certain general statements about the current consensus of opinion are possible:

1. *Excessive inequality of income is regarded as undesirable.* This point of view is reflected in (among other legislation) progressive taxation; the provision of

---

[7]Indeed, if guaranteed $1/n$ of GNP (where n is the number of people) regardless of work effort, the realization that GNP won't be significantly affected by individual work/leisure decisions implies that GNP—hence income—would go to zero!

old-age pensions, relief, and aid to housing; antipoverty programs; and in the sentiment behind (if not the actual outcome of) minimum wage legislation. Opinions differ on the question of what constitutes excessive inequality, but the general principle is widely accepted that the extent of inequality which develops in the absence of governmental interference is excessive.

2. *The attainment of large incomes from monopolistic "exploitation" of the public is regarded as particularly objectionable.* An attempt is made to check this by antitrust legislation, public utility regulation, and other legislation. From the standpoint of resource utilization, the basic objection to monopoly is its restriction of output below the level at which price is equal to marginal cost. But legislation on the question has been greatly influenced by the desire to eliminate monopoly profits.

3. *Complete equality of income is regarded as undesirable from the standpoint of its effects on production, and as inequitable because it denies the more efficient, hard-working persons the attainment of a higher reward for their skill and effort.*

The lack of a more precise definition of the optimum pattern of income distribution reduces the significance of contemporary welfare theory, the precision and strength of its conclusions, and the force of policy recommendations based upon them. For example, on the basis of welfare principles relating to optimum use of resources, it can be argued that subway fares should be higher in rush hours than in off hours because marginal cost is higher in the former (when extra cars and trains must be added to carry more passengers) than it is in the latter (when trains are half empty). But the distribution of passengers by income group is different in the two periods, with a heavy concentration of workers in the rush hours. Therefore, opponents of such a fare system condemn it on the grounds of its effects on distribution of the costs of providing subway service by income group. Welfare theory can offer no conclusive answer to this argument.

20.7 CONCLUDING OBSERVATIONS

Welfare economics is admittedly one of the least satisfactory portions of the overall subject of economics. The rules for attainment of optimum efficiency in the use and allocation of resources—given the pattern of income distribution—are clearly definable and generally acceptable; but their significance is dependent upon the nature of the social welfare function relating to gains and losses of particular individuals and groups and the optimum distribution of real income. The concept of a social welfare function is clear enough; but the determination of its empirical content—which must rest upon consensus of thought in the particular society—encounters serious theoretical and practical difficulties. Thus decisions as to the desirability or undesirability of certain policies or features of the economy rest in part upon individual interpretations about the nature of the social welfare function. Here differences of opinion are inevitable. Judgments will be made and policies adopted; welfare economics can make significant contributions to these actions, even if it cannot provide answers based entirely on scientific analysis. It is of utmost importance, however, that the value judgments involved in these evaluations and recommendations be made explicit, and that they not be given a scientific validity they do not possess.

SUMMARY

1. Welfare economics is the portion of economic analysis that evaluates the working of the economic system by reference to generally accepted social goals.

2. Evaluation can be separated into two distinct tasks: first, acquiring a fairly comprehensive understanding of the situation; second, selecting and applying standards of evaluation.

3. Three social goals are assumed to be desirable: freedom of choice, maximum satisfaction of wants, and an optimum pattern of income distribution.

4. Freedom of choice is the right of individuals to act as they wish in the choice of employment and the purchase and sale of goods and services.

5. Another social goal is the attainment of the highest possible level of economic well-being for society as a whole through the use and allocation of resources that allows the highest per capita real income given the resources, technology, and preference schedules of factor owners regarding the use of their factor units.

6. Optimum want satisfaction requires that resources be efficiently utilized in production.

7. Composition of total output must be such as to best satisfy consumer preferences.

8. Optimum adjustment of production can be obtained only if, for each consumer, the MRS between each two goods purchased is equal to the MRT between the two goods in production.

9. It may be difficult to attain optimum product mix because of imperfect information in consumer and factor markets and external economies or diseconomies.

10. An optimum degree of utilization of factors would include the avoidance of cyclical unemployment, an optimum division of time between work and leisure, an optimum rate of capital formation, and an optimum rate of utilization of scarce natural resources.

11. There is no possibility of making interpersonal utility comparisons (comparing relative satisfactions received by different individuals).

12. The Pareto optimum is desirable in terms of economic welfare only if the change benefits someone without injuring anyone else.

13. The social welfare function expresses the optimum pattern of distribution of benefits among individuals as viewed by the consensus of thought in contemporary society.

WORDS AND CONCEPTS FOR REVIEW

welfare economics
selection of standards
ethical criteria
freedom of choice
satisfaction of wants

consumer allocation of incomes
optimum degree of factor utilization
optimum rate of economic growth
interpersonal utility comparisons
Pareto optimum

optimum efficiency in the use of resources
optimum adjustment of production
marginal rate of transformation

the compensation principle
social welfare function
optimum pattern of income distribution

REVIEW QUESTIONS

1. What is the nature of welfare economics?

2. How are the goals selected for evaluation of welfare?

3. What are the major goals which are generally employed as a basis for welfare economics?

4. Why can freedom of choice never be absolute?

5. What does the term "maximum satisfaction of wants" mean?

6. What are the requirements for optimum efficiency in the use of resources?

7. Why is the operation of firms at the point of lowest LRAC essential for optimum efficiency in the use of resources?

8. Why, in perfectly competitive markets, will firms operate, over a long-run period, at the point of lowest LRAC? Will they necessarily do so in imperfectly competitive markets? Explain.

9. Why does optimum adjustment of production require equality of the marginal rate of substitution and the marginal rate of transformation? What requirements must be fulfilled for this equality to be attained?

10. Indicate some examples, other than those given in the chapter, of divergence between costs to the economy and costs to the individual producer.

11. Give examples of external economies of consumption.

12. What is the significance for economic welfare of the failure of price to equal marginal cost in imperfectly competitive conditions?

13. How would you justify, in terms of welfare economics, the following government policies?
(a) high excise taxes on liquor
(b) municipal zoning ordinances
(c) financing subway construction by taxes on motor vehicle use
(d) prevention of price discrimination
(e) restriction of entry of competing firms into the public utilities field
(f) provision of funds for agricultural research
(g) legislation prohibiting "featherbedding"

14. In what respects is perfect competition superior to imperfect competition from the standpoint of welfare economics? In what respects is it inferior?

15. Why is it difficult to state categorically that any particular change increases economic welfare of society? What type of change is regarded as desirable in terms of Pareto optimum? Why is this a very restrictive rule?

16. What is the compensation principle? What are the limitations of the rule?

17. What is meant by a "social welfare function"?

18. Explain the various approaches to the definition of the optimum pattern of income distribution.

SUGGESTED READINGS

Bator, Francis. "The Simple Analytics of Welfare Maximization" *American Economic Review* (March 1957) pp 22–59.

Baumol, W. J. *Economic Theory and Operations Analysis*, 4th ed. Englewood Cliffs, NJ: Prentice-Hall 1977, Chapter 21.

Bergson, A. *Essays in Normative Economics*. Cambridge: Harvard University Press, 1965.

Graff, J. de V. *Theoretical Welfare Economics*. Cambridge: Cambridge University Press, 1957.

Little, I. M. D. *A Critique of Welfare Economics*, 2nd ed. Oxford: Oxford University Press, 1957.

Scitovsky, T. *Welfare and Competition*, Homewood, IL: Irwin, 1957.

21

Asset Management and Intertemporal Choice*

21.1 INTRODUCTION

Until recently, the theory of consumer demand constituted not just one branch but virtually the sum and substance of the theory of household behavior. During the past few decades, however, economists have recognized that the allocation of given sums of expenditure among alternative purchases—the main concern of demand analysis—is only one part of the household story. By almost any practical reckoning, household problems of asset management and **intertemporal choice** (borrowing or saving to change consumption patterns) appear to be at least as important. Unfortunately, these problems do not lend themselves to precise analysis except at a high level of abstraction. In the discussion that follows, therefore, we shall be concerned more with clarifying particular kinds of asset- and income-management decisions than with elaborating a unified theory of household behavior.

21.2 INTERTEMPORAL CHOICE: BASIC IDEAS

At any given time, a typical household possesses a certain amount (possibly zero) of previously accumulated wealth in the form of money and other assets. Some part of this wealth (for example, stocks and bonds) will be held mainly for the sake of expected future income, which may consist partly of dividend and interest payments, partly of gains in capital value. Another part (including houses, cars, furniture, and appliances)

---

*The material in this chapter is a bit more difficult than are those chapters leading up to it: the applications are to intertemporal choice and human capital, one or both of which may be omitted without loss of continuity.

will be held for the sake of current and prospective yields of consumption services. Yet another portion (specifically, money and inventories of consumer goods) will be held not for the sake of direct income or service yields but to avoid costs that would otherwise be incurred in synchronizing receipts and expenditures.

In addition to marketable physical and financial assets, the typical household possesses a certain amount of **nonmarketable human wealth**—personal services that members of the household can dispose of in exchange for payments of money income. Considered in the abstract, **human capital** is analogous to a plot of land that cannot be sold outright (for legal or other reasons) but can be used to produce food for a household or be leased out to other individuals in exchange for rent payments. Like such a plot of land, human capital can be improved in various ways (through education, for example) to enhance the market value of its services; it can also be allowed to deteriorate (through laziness or lack of care). It differs from most forms of nonhuman capital in that its "capital value" can only be realized over an extended period of time and its "quantity" cannot quickly be altered.

Every asset (human or nonhuman) held by a household constitutes a potential source of immediate purchasing power. In effect, therefore, a household that holds wealth of any kind incurs a certain cost in the form of forgone consumption. This is obvious in the case of currency, which yields no objective income but which might be used to purchase interest-bearing bonds, the income from which could be used to finance a permanent flow of consumption expenditure. The proposition is no less true of interest-bearing bonds: these could be sold for money that could, in turn, be used to finance an immediate increase in consumption. One can even raise a certain amount of cash from human capital by borrowing against expected future earnings (as with student loans). (See Box 21-1.)

Our immediate task is to translate the general rules found in Box 21-1 into principles that are applicable to particular cases.

21-1   Other things being equal, how would a rational household maximize its satisfaction from consumption over the course of its lifetime?

This can be accomplished only if the household manages its asset holdings in such a way as to maximize the present expected value (as calculated by the household) of their (implicit and explicit) income yield. This requires that the anticipated marginal net income yield from any given asset be at least as great as that from any alternative asset of equal market value and risk (otherwise it would be sensible to exchange the asset with the lower yield for the asset with the higher yield). It also requires that the marginal yield (explicit or imputed) of any asset held by the household be sufficiently high to offset the explicit and implicit costs associated with holding it. The first of these rules provides a basis for analyzing the factors that govern holdings of particular assets in relation to holdings of other assets; the second provides a basis for analyzing total holdings of particular types of assets in relation to consumption expenditure.

21.3 THE CHOICE BETWEEN CONSUMPTION AND INCOME-EARNING ASSETS

It is convenient to begin by considering a simple model involving just one kind of consumption good and one kind of marketable asset—interest-bearing bonds that pay a coupon of $1 per period (such as month or year) in perpetuity. (Bonds of this type, called "Consols," are actually issued by the British government.) We shall assume that the current dollar income of the household consists partly of interest earnings from accumulated holdings of bonds and partly of wage income derived from sales of labor services.

If the wage income of the household is constant from one period to another, total dollar income in any given period will depend on holdings of bonds at the beginning of the period, as indicated by the **income locus** Y shown in Figure 21-1.[1] Starting with a given number of bonds, say B^0, at the outset of some initial period $t = 0$, the household has to decide how to allocate its total income $(m + B^0)$ between current consumption and bond purchases (we abstract here from cases in which the household uses current income to add to its holdings of money balances). If the dollar price of bonds is fixed at P_B and the price of a unit of consumption goods is fixed at $1, the choice alternatives confronting the household in the initial period are represented by the budget line L^0 in Figure 21-1, the slope of which is equal to $-P_B$.[2] But a bond that pays $1 per period in perpetuity may be said to yield a current rate of interest, r, equal to the reciprocal of its current market price; if $P_B = 100$, for example, then $r = \$1/\$100 = 1$ percent; if $P_B = \$25$, then $r = \$1/\$25 = 4$ percent. In the present model, therefore, the slope of the line L^0 varies inversely with the current bond rate of interest, being relatively steep at low rates and relatively flat at high rates.

Which choice alternative the household selects depends (we shall assume) on its preferences between **present and future consumption**. On our assumption, future consumption (viewed as a quantity per period in perpetuity, starting at the beginning of the next period) is represented by distances along the bond axis, because each bond pays $1 per period in perpetuity and this will buy one unit of consumption goods per period in perpetuity. If its preferences are defined by the indifference curves in Figure 21-1, therefore, the household will plan to purchase a quantity C^0 of consumption goods and a quantity $(B^1 - B^0)$ of bonds in the initial period.

21.4 TIME PREFERENCE

At the utility-maximizing level of consumption and bond purchases, the subjective rate of substitution between present and future consumption (as measured by the slope of

---

[1] The equation of the income locus is $Y^i = m + B^t$, where m denotes the real number of dollars M/P received as wage income at the beginning of each period and B^t denotes the quantity of bonds (each paying $1 per period) that the household has carried over from the preceding period.

[2] The equation of the budget line is $C^t = -P_B(B^{t+1} - B^t) + m + B^t$.

FIGURE 21-1

Short-Run Allocation of Income Between Consumption and Saving
The budget line L^0 shows the maximum affordable allocations of current consumption and future consumption (bond purchases). When the price of a unit of consumption goods equals $1, the slope of the budget line equals minus the bond price which varies inversely with the rate of interest. The indifference curves characterize a household's preferences between current and future consumption. The household maximizes utility at point A, consuming C^0 and purchasing B^1 less B^0 amount of bonds. The indifference curve and budget line are tangent, and the marginal rate of time preference equals the current rate of interest (assuming a bond yield of $1 per period).

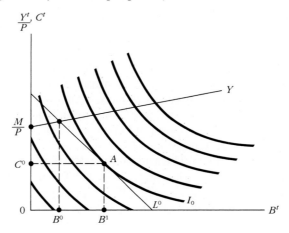

the indifference curve I_0 at the point A) is equal to the interest rate (as measured by the slope of the budget line). This indicates that the household's (marginal) **rate of time preference**—that is, the ratio between the marginal utility of a flow of consumption in perpetuity to the marginal utility of current consumption—is equal to the current rate of interest. This conclusion accords with the second of the rules set out earlier, to the effect that a household will hold an asset only if its marginal income yield is sufficient to offset its cost in terms of forgone consumption. At any point on the budget line to the left of the tangency point, the household's rate of time preference would be less than the rate of interest; at any point to the right of the tangency point, the household's rate of time preference would be greater than the rate of interest. The future consumption yield of bond holdings is just sufficient at the margin to offset the implicit cost of forgone consumption only at the point of tangency between the budget line L_0 and the indifference curve I_0.

21.5 THE SAVING PROCESS

The allocation of income between current consumption and bond purchases depends, of course, upon the household's initial wealth as well as its wage income and the prices of bonds and consumption goods. If the household purchases additional bonds in period $t = 0$ and carries them over to the beginning of the next period, its income will be larger in period $t = 1$ than in period $t = 0$, so its allocation of income in period $t = 1$ will differ from its allocation in period $t = 0$. This result is illustrated in Figure 21-2, where L^0 represents the budget line of the household in period $t = 0$, L^1 represents its budget line in period $t = 1$, L^2 its budget line in period $t = 2$, and so on. In this example, the household will increase its holdings of bonds in each period until (in the limit as time tends to infinity) it attains a position of stationary equilibrium at the point B^*, after which further increases in future consumption are considered undesirable. Having reached such a position, the household will consume in each period the whole of its income from sales of factor services and interest payments on its holdings of bonds.

The adjustment process illustrated in Figure 21-2 merits close examination. The process would work in the reverse direction if the household were endowed initially with a stock of bonds that exceeded the stationary equilibrium level; that is, the household would gradually dissave (sell bonds to finance consumption in excess of current

FIGURE 21-2

Asset Accumulation Process Leading to Stationary Level of Wealth and Consumption

The income locus, Y, shows all stationary combinations of consumption goods and bond holdings. Along Y the household spends all wage and interest income, neither saving nor dissaving. Below Y, the household is saving and will increase current consumption until the budget line and indifference curve are tangent on Y. Dissaving occurs above Y. In this case, the household will decrease consumption in the long run.

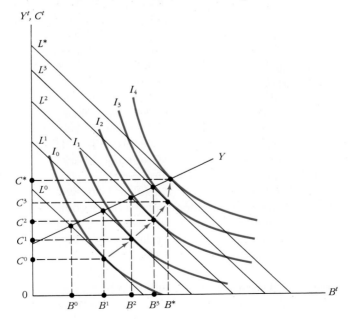

income) until its final holdings provided a permanent income just sufficient to offset its rate of time preference. In effect, the household has a choice *in the long run* between all wealth/income combinations that lie on the income locus. Any combination that does not lie on the income locus cannot represent a stationary point because it will entail either current saving or dissaving. The household cannot immediately adjust its bond holdings to achieve a stationary position, because in general the choices available to the household in the short run (defined by the current budget line) will not include a stationary combination. Given sufficient time, however, the household will arrive at a final situation in which its total income from bonds and factor services is in keeping with its long-run preferences between current and future consumption—that is, a situation in which it sees no advantage at the margin in sacrificing even a single unit of current consumption in order to increase future consumption by r per annum.

21.6 REALISM AND RELEVANCE

The extent to which this simple model faithfully portrays salient aspects of reality is open to question. Merely as an illustrative example, however, its implications are interesting. Among other things, the model suggests that household accumulations of wealth are not entirely a matter of historical accident. No doubt it helps to inherit cash and earning ability from one's parents; but if our model makes sense, a person who inherits wealth will quickly become a candidate for welfare assistance if his rate of time preference is sufficiently high (he has only to eat up his capital in riotous living and then refuse to work for wages!). Similarly, even someone who inherits nothing can, if she so desires, steadily increase her income and wealth and perhaps even become rich if she is sufficiently greedy or lucky and lives long enough.

The model also indicates relevant factors affecting the allocation of income between current consumption and current additions to assets. Evidently, this choice will depend in the short run on current income (from all sources), on the current rate of interest, on the price level of consumption goods, and on current holdings of wealth. It seems clear that if consumption and wealth are both normal goods, an increase in income or initial wealth or a reduction in the current interest rate or price of consumption goods will *tend* to increase current consumption. However, since any of these changes may set in motion a process of asset adjustment (by shifting either the income locus or the current budget line), no firm conclusion can be reached about the *actual* consequences of changes in data other than bond and consumption goods prices, and only then in relation to positions of stationary equilibrium. In our model (and surely too in the real world), income and wealth are *not* given data in the long run; on the contrary, they are chosen by the individual household in accordance with prevailing prices and in conformity with its own preferences between present and future consumption.

The only implication of our model that seems obviously contrary to experience and common sense is the conclusion that the household will, in the long run, attain a stationary state in which consumption is equal to income. It is a familiar fact that most households save at least part of their income some of the time and that American households historically have saved substantial, though declining percentages of, aggregate income in every decade since 1900. This apparent inconsistency between theory and fact disappears, however, once we introduce into the model steady changes in real wages associated with technological progress. Such changes imply a continual upward shift in the income locus—at a rate of about 2 percent per annum, if we go by the historical experience of the United States. The effect of these shifts is to produce a continual process of asset accumulation among households at a rate that is a multiple of the rate at which real wage income grows. The outwardly contrary result implied by our model is valid only in a world that does not experience technological progress. There may be an important moral in this for students of underdeveloped economies: perhaps the solution to the problems of backward nations lies not in providing them with resources (which they may simply consume) but rather in assisting them to change social attitudes that currently inhibit rapid assimilation of new techniques of production.

21.7 DURABLE CONSUMER GOODS

The preceding analysis is applicable in detail only to assets that yield an explicit money income, but its conclusions should also be broadly applicable to highly **durable assets** that yield an implicit income in the form of services. In dealing with assets of this kind, such as paintings or jewelry, we might assume that future service flows are approximately proportional to quantities held, so that such assets are effectively analogous to perpetual bonds except that the "coupon" accrues in the form of services rather than money. Since the yield of such assets is implicit (rather than an upward-sloping line, as in Figure 21-1 for bond income), the household cannot vary its explicit income by varying its holdings of such assets. The analysis of the preceding section then applies: In the short run, purchases of additional durable goods (saving) will occur so long as the household's rate of time preference is less than the implicit income yield provided by holdings of the durable good at the beginning of each period. In the long run, the household will gravitate towards a stationary situation in which the implicit income yield from holdings of any durable good is such that the household sees no advantage in reducing current consumption in order to increase its future flow of services.

The analysis can also be extended to include semidurable consumer goods that are costly to store or maintain. In this case, the income locus becomes a downward-sloping line (or possibly a downward-sloping curve), for we can treat costs of maintenance and storage as deductions from money income available for expenditure on current consumption. This change in our diagrammatic apparatus has potentially amusing implications. For example, if the consumption good is "bread" and the durable good is "housing," the stationary equilibrium position of the household might be at a point where the household is "house poor"—where it spends so much on home maintenance that it purchases no bread! Short-run and long-run adjustment processes operate in qualitatively the same fashion, however, regardless of the form of the income locus.[3]

21.8 HUMAN CAPITAL

In principle, a household could survive without earning any income from personal services, provided that it could somehow manage to acquire an initial endowment of income-earning nonhuman wealth. In practice, however, most households derive the bulk of their current income from personal services, for these derive from the one kind of wealth with which every household is endowed at its inception.

If human wealth were simply a matter of historical accident—that is, if the quality and quantity of services associated with human wealth could not be altered by individual action—then describing the factors governing household management of this portion of its asset portfolio would be a simple matter. The only choice confronting the household would be to decide what quantity of services to offer in exchange for money income in each period. The household's current choice alternatives might be represented by a line such as $m(w)/p$ in Figure 21-3, which indicates for each possible level of work (represented by the variable L) the amount of real income (money income, m, divided by the price level of consumption goods, p) that the household could expect to earn if the money wage rate were fixed at level w. If expected earnings were associated with positive utility while expected work was associated with negative utility (disutility), the household's preferences between current work and current real income would be represented by upward-sloping indifference curves ($I_0, I_1, \ldots, I_9$ in Figure 21-3). Household satisfaction would be maximized by choosing a point on the income line $m(w)/p$ at which the marginal rate of substitution between work and real income was just equal to the real wage rate (point A in Figure 21-3).

In general, the nature of the preference map would depend upon current holdings of wealth. A household with substantial wealth in the form of income-earning stocks or bonds, for example, would be unlikely to value an increment of current wage income as highly as a household that had no other means of financing future consumption. Note that nonwage income shifts upward the $m(w)/p$ curve in Figure 21-3: there is more income at any level of labor supply than in the absence of nonwage income. It is conceivable, however, that work of some sort might be largely a matter of personal habit and social conditioning for most households, in which case the household's

---

[3]Readers may find it instructive to work out for themselves the effects of an increase in maintenance costs upon long-run holdings of durable goods. Intuitively, one would expect stationary holdings to be smaller, but situations can occur in which an increase in maintenance costs leads to increased holdings.

FIGURE 21-3

The Work-Leisure Decision
In this example, households have no control over the quantity or quality of their human capital. Real income *(m/p)* directly relates to the employment services supplied by the household. With income considered a "good" and labor a "bad," indifference curves slope upward. The household maximizes utility at the tangency of the budget line and indifference curve, point *A*, providing N^* labor services and earning $(m/p)^*$ income.

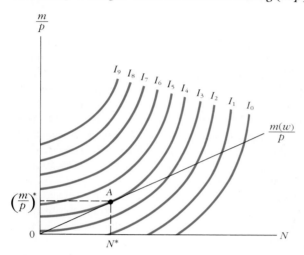

preferences might be such that its desired sales of labor services were virtually independent of both current wealth and the real wage rate.[4]

We have little definite knowledge about matters of this kind or about related issues such as the effect of income taxes on work incentives. Generally speaking, people seem to be relatively insensitive in the short run to changes in wealth or real wage rates; habit and social circumstances tend to dominate work/leisure decisions over relatively short time periods (say, less than five years). The crucial question is whether economic factors significantly affect work/leisure decisions in the long run. If real wage rates are high and rising decade after decade, for example, will this encourage people to work more in order to consume more, or will it encourage people to work less in order to enjoy more fully the pleasures of high-level consumption? If income tax rates are maintained for a generation at very high levels on incomes above a certain magnitude, will this tend ultimately to discourage highly skilled people from working

---

[4]The sale of labor services may be very inelastic *to the economy,* but certainly not to any one *industry* or *firm*. Small wage increases by any one firm will lead to a large increase in labor supplied to it. One's decision to work 35 or 40 hours a week may not be much affected by wage, but *where* one does that work will be!

long hours or will it encourage them to work even harder? Theory provides no clear answers to questions of this kind since theory allows for both income and substitution effects, which work in opposite directions in this case. Empirical research is almost equally uninformative as of the present time.

As a rule, human capital is not a fixed quantity; individuals, particularly during earlier years, can to some extent alter the future sale value of their services by investing resources currently in education and training. The factors governing choices at this level are extremely complex, and much work remains to be done before we understand even partially the technology and economics of such decisions. At a descriptive level, however, the problem is relatively easy to characterize.

At any given time, an individual has a choice between current work and activities that increase future earning power. The more currently available time that is devoted to work, the larger will be the current real income, but the smaller will be the difference between expected earnings in future years and the income currently received. If a person accepts a reduction in current income, devoting some portion of current effort to education and training, that person can expect to realize a certain return on the investment, for in later years a somewhat higher wage rate will be earned (the amount of the increase depending on the nature of the education and training as well as the individual's natural ability).

If one could forecast exactly the consequences of alternative programs of investment in human capital, it would be a relatively straightforward matter to compare expected returns with expected costs and decide whether the investment promised to be economically worthwhile. If the yield of an investment of $30,000 in a college education were equivalent to, say, $6,000 per annum (20 percent) for a period of 45 working years, a person obviously would be foolish to forgo the investment if she could obtain the necessary funds at something less than 20 percent (say, 15 percent per annum). By the same token, she would be acting unwisely (in a purely economic sense) to invest in a college education if the expected yield from it were less than the prevailing rate of interest on secure loans. (See Box 21-2.)

21-2   True or False? Education and training activities are always undertaken purely with a view to economic consideration.

False. A person might well invest in a college education even if it yielded a negative return in money income, provided that it gave him or her personal satisfaction (an implicit income that might offset a very substantial loss of money income). It may also be argued that even where an individual does not benefit financially from increased education, society may benefit in cultural and other respects (such as lower crime rates or more informed voters) from having its members highly educated. Even if investment in human capital could be shown to be privately unprofitable, therefore, such investment might still be considered profitable from a social point of view. This explains the prevalence of subsidized education in the United States and elsewhere.

The main difficulty in all discussions of investment in human capital is that both costs and returns are highly unpredictable. The problem is not simply that explicit costs and returns cannot be estimated; even if this complication were not present, there would remain the far more serious problem of evaluating implicit (subjective and social) costs and benefits. As matters stand, empirical studies stimulated by economic theory have contributed few answers to the many questions that might be posed. Proper strategy would seem to require that research be directed first towards ascertaining explicit costs and returns, which involves (among other things) research into the technology of education and training. Judging from work already done in this direction, such a strategy would yield much useful information about present patterns of private behavior in relation to investment in human capital and could also provide worthwhile guidance to social planners. It is of some interest, after all, to be able to say more or less definitely whether a particular kind of educational program (such as free high school education for all children) seems worthwhile in terms of strictly economic considerations. If it is, that should settle the issue (unless it were thought that educated people are undesirable, per se!). In the contrary case, policy decisions would have to be based in part on noneconomic considerations.

21.9 MONEY AND CONSUMER GOOD INVENTORIES

A typical household in the real world maintains sizable average inventories of canned goods, milk, soap, vegetables, bread, coffee, gasoline, shirts, dresses, typing paper, towels, and other nondurable consumer goods; indeed, the aggregate money value of such inventories may be anything from 2 to 20 times the value of the household's average money balances. Such inventories are costly to hold, partly because of explicit expenses of storage and deterioration, partly because of implicit costs in terms of forgone interest income. To rationalize what at first sight might be regarded as uneconomic behavior, we have only to observe that if a household did not hold inventories of most of the goods that it regularly consumes, someone in the household would have to spend a great deal of time and effort making frequent trips to market. Rational behavior on the part of the household requires that its average holdings of nondurable consumption good inventories be maintained at a level such that the value to the household of marginal units of released energy and other resources that would otherwise be devoted to trading activity is just equal to the marginal storage and interest costs associated with such holdings.

In a money economy, it is possible to trade goods in organized markets only by paying or receiving money in every exchange. A household's recurrent shopping activities thus involve certain indirect as well as direct inventory costs; for in addition to holding inventories of physical goods, the household must maintain an inventory of cash as a passport for entry into organized markets. In general, a household will avoid holding large cash balances for much the same reasons that it avoids holding excessive inventories of goods. Very rarely, however, will a household attempt virtually to do without cash by shopping and paying bills only on days when it receives cash income, for such a procedure would force the household to carry huge inventories of consumer goods, and the costs of such holdings would outweigh any real or monetary savings associated with lower cash balances and fewer trips to market. What the typical household does (though certainly not consciously) is to choose the frequency and timing of its shopping trips in the light of both direct costs of holding inventories of goods and related indirect costs of holding money balances.

This verbal description of factors governing average holdings of goods and money inventories may be clarified by a diagram. Let the dashed horizontal line $L(q)$ in Figure 21-4 represent the dollar value of the household's rate of consumption of a particular good (assumed constant in each period); and let the vertical distance between the line $L(q)$ and the curve $R(q)$ represent the implicit dollar cost (per unit of time) of leisure and energy devoted to trade, corresponding to alternative possible dollar values of average holdings of inventories of the same good. The curve $R(q)$—henceforth called the **trading returns curve**—may be considered to represent the *net* money value of the consumption flow q, after deducting relevant trading costs. Trading returns are positive only after average inventory holdings reach a certain finite level (q_0 in Figure 21-4); this reflects the assumption (and fact) that low levels of average inventories imply frequent trips to market—so frequent in the limiting case that trading costs exceed the value of goods acquired.

If trading costs depended simply on the frequency of shopping trips per unit of time, the trading returns curve would approach the line $L(q)$ asymptotically as average

---

FIGURE 21-4

Optimal Inventory Holdings
The trading returns curve, $R(q)$, depicts the value of the consumption flow q (shown by $L(q)$) less trading costs. Total waiting costs, W, consist of direct waiting costs, W_q, plus indirect waiting costs, W_m. The optimum stock of inventories, q^*, maximizes the difference between trading returns and total waiting costs. At q^* marginal trading returns, the slope of $R(q)$, equals marginal waiting costs, the slope of W.

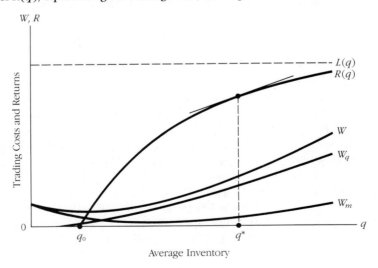

Average Inventory

inventories increased, for by purchasing in sufficiently large lots at sufficiently infrequent intervals, the cost of each shopping trip could be spread over so many time periods as to become insignificant. In practice, however, trading costs will depend in part upon the quantity of goods purchased per shopping trip, and this quantity will be directly related to average inventory holdings. For example, if no reserve inventories are held, the quantity purchased at any one time will be just twice the average inventory; thus, if one smokes a carton (ten packs) of cigarettes every week and purchases a new carton every Saturday, one's average inventory of cigarettes will be five packs. Although the trading returns curve therefore rises steadily at relatively low levels of average inventory holdings, beyond a certain point the costs of purchasing in large quantities may offset returns associated with less-frequent purchases, in which case the curve $R(q)$ will somewhere attain a maximum and thereafter turn down.

Direct waiting costs (storage and deterioration charges plus forgone interest income) associated with alternative holdings of inventories of goods are represented in Figure 21-4 by the curve W_q, while **indirect waiting costs** (forgone interest income on money balances that are held to facilitate commodity purchases) are represented by the curve W_m. Direct waiting costs are a strictly increasing function of the dollar value of average inventory holdings. Indirect waiting costs depend, however, upon the timing and frequency of purchases in relation to the timing and frequency of income receipts. In general, these costs will decline up to a point as purchases and income receipts become more closely synchronized, but they will thereafter rise indefinitely. Except in special cases, indirect waiting costs will be small compared with direct waiting costs, partly because the money value of commodity inventories will be large compared with money inventories, partly because money balances cost little or nothing to store whereas deterioration and storage costs of commodity inventories may be substantial. Therefore, when we add direct and indirect waiting costs to obtain the *total waiting cost curve*, W, the result is a relation that differs only moderately from the direct waiting cost curve, W_q.

The choice of an optimal stock of commodity inventories (equivalently, the choice of an optimal transaction period) requires that the household maximize the difference between total trading returns as defined by the curve $R(q)$ and total waiting costs as defined by the curve W. For the relations illustrated in Figure 21-4, the optimal stock of inventories is q^*. At this value of Q, the rate of increase of trading returns (the slope of $R(q)$) is just equal to the rate of increase of total waiting costs (the slope of the curve W); in technical parlance, *marginal* trading returns are just equal to *marginal* waiting costs, a condition that will be familiar to students who recall standard conditions for profit maximization. In effect, the household's choice of commodity inventories is a technical production problem, the solution to which naturally is analogous to the solution of similar problems in the theory of business behavior.

Our diagrammatic and verbal analyses grossly oversimplify the problem of inventory choice as it occurs in actual experience. What we have described as a decision process involving just one good appears in practice as a large collection of interrelated decision processes, one for each good purchased or sold. Average holdings of inventories of all goods and of money are determined jointly in accordance with the general principles set above, but the formal details of the solution differ significantly (particularly in complexity) from the simple picture presented here. We shall not attempt to elaborate a more general model, for such a procedure would not produce any essentially new insights. We have gone far enough already to assert what is important for our purposes—namely, that equilibrium holdings of money balances are inextricably linked with equilibrium holdings of commodity inventories, and vice versa. This means, among other things, that we cannot establish any definite conclusions about the probable effect of changes in interest rates or prices upon holdings of inventories of money or individual goods. A rise in interest rates, however, should induce a household to diminish *aggregate* holdings of money and goods.

21.10 PLANS AND REALIZATIONS

The whole of our discussion of household problems of income allocation and asset management is concerned with states of equilibrium or (in the few instances where we have dealt with adjustment processes) with situations in which we take it for granted that the household's plans can be executed as scheduled. In a sense, therefore, we have been concerned with "virtual" rather than with "real" decision processes; for in any realistic account of household behavior, provision obviously should be made for the possibility that plans cannot be realized—that quantities of consumption goods or assets demanded for purchase might exceed or fall short of quantities offered for sale. To be sure, if the economic system always adjusted smoothly and quickly to remove prevailing inconsistencies in trading plans, it would hardly be purposeful to analyze transition states of disequilibrium, for such states would be too short-lived to merit serious consideration. However, one does not have to be a professional economist to have serious doubts about the validity of this conception of economic adjustment processes. The daily newspapers would not be full of worried editorials about unemployment, inflation, and high interest rates if the economic system worked as well in fact as it is customarily conceived to work in theory.

21.11 UNSETTLED ISSUES

The deeper one goes into the fine details of household behavior, the more complicated the entire subject appears to become. We are reminded of the problems physicists have encountered in trying to explain the nature of the atom. Around the turn of the present century, it seemed that the atom was like a miniature solar system, consisting of a hard central nucleus around which various electrons circled in regular orbits. Thirty years later, the nucleus no longer seemed hard, appearing rather to consist of a large number of more basic particles—neutrons, protons, mesons, and other strange objects. The electron no longer seemed to have any particular orbit, and it was associated with numerous other particles whose behavior could be characterized but not really explained. Physicists have not given up the search for some kind of order in the chaos that now confronts them, but many of them have given up the idea that the search will yield practical fruit and have turned their thoughts to alternative ways of describing microphysical phenomena. Broadly speaking, they seek for regularities in the average or statistical behavior of atomic processes and no longer attempt to describe the behavior of individual atomic particles in a literal fashion. Economists have not yet reached the stage at which they are willing to confess their inability to characterize accurately the details of human decision processes, but present indications are that such a stage will be reached in the not-too-distant future. Modern work in this area tends more and more to be focused on mathematically complicated descriptions of empirically trivial problems, such as the consumption and saving behavior of an individual with given and unchanging tastes who has certain knowledge of all future income and prices. Such problems pose countless logical puzzles, but they do little to advance economics as an empirical science except to the extent that they help convince economists of the practical futility of most such exercises.

These observations should not be interpreted as an attack on rigorous analysis of precisely defined models of human behavior. Even when such analysis has no direct payoff, it can produce useful negative results—as the example of physics illustrates. Our suggestion is not that economics can do without rigorous analysis, but rather that economics cannot do without models that are designed to describe ongoing economic processes and are correspondingly endowed with empirical content. The existing body of theory dealing with household behavior is all very well as a description of an imaginary situation, and it has much value in indicating where we are likely to run into problems in attempts to describe less-fanciful cases. It does not carry us very far, however, towards an understanding of actual household behavior; and it becomes seriously impaired when it is elaborated in finer and finer detail without reference to any kind of empirical data.

SUMMARY

1. Accumulated wealth is held in the form of money and other assets. Some of these assets are held for the sake of expected future income, or to provide a stream of consumption services (like cars) or inventories of goods or money to ward off problems of uncertainty.

2. In addition to the marketable physical and financial assets, households possess a certain amount of nonsellable (but rentable!) human wealth, called human capital.

3. Human capital differs from nonhuman capital because its "capital value" can only be realized over an extended period of time and because its "quantity" cannot quickly be altered.

4. Households will hold an asset only if its expected marginal income yield is sufficient to offset its costs in terms of forgone consumption.

5. In order to maximize utility between consumption and bond purchases, the subjective rate of substitution between present and future consumption must be equal to the interest rate.

6. The marginal rate of time preference is the ratio between the marginal utility of a flow of consumption in perpetuity and the marginal utility of current consumption.

7. Households' marginal rate of time preference is equated to the current rate of interest.

8. The allocation of income between current consumption and bond purchases depends on the household's initial wealth level as well as its wage income and the prices of bonds and consumption goods.

9. In the long run, households have a choice between all wealth/income combinations that lie on the income locus. Any combination off the locus is a position of either saving or dissaving.

10. The introduction of changes in real wages in our model will shift the income locus upward at a rate of about 2 percent per year. This will produce a continual process of asset accumulation at a rate that is a multiple of the rate at which real income grows.

11. In dealing with durable assets like jewelry, we might assume that future service flows are approximately proportionate to quantities held.

12. At any given time, individuals have a choice between current work and investment in human capital. However, because of future uncertainties, it is difficult to compare expected returns with expected costs of a particular investment in human capital.

WORDS AND CONCEPTS FOR REVIEW

intertemporal choice
nonmarketable human wealth
human capital
income locus
present and future consumption

rate of time preference
durable assets
trading returns curve
direct waiting costs
indirect waiting costs

REVIEW QUESTIONS

1. How much do you think you could borrow from a bank on your present stock of human capital? From your parents? From a finance company?

2. Suppose that someone owns outright a house whose current market value is $100,000. If this person told you that he lived "rent free," what might you tell him to correct his delusion?

3. What is meant by the term "rate of time preference"?

4. Would the rate of interest on saving deposits be an appropriate measure of the rate of time preference to a person who is currently paying an interest rate of 18 percent per annum on an automobile loan? Explain your answer.

5. Each of us knows people who spend everything they earn as fast as they get it and also borrow as much as their friends will lend out. Does this tell you anything about the probable magnitude of these persons' rate of time preference? Explain carefully and illustrate your answer with a diagram.

6. Some people save a positive percentage of their income throughout most of their lives. Draw a diagram to illustrate the preferences of such people as between present and future consumption. (*Hint:* The locus of points representing short-run consumption/saving decisions should not intersect the income locus, however wealthy such people might become.)

7. Discuss the mechanics of asset accumulation for a person who is an avid collector of old coins (treat coins as goods that cost something to maintain).

8. During much of human history, some people have been "human capital" in a literal sense—that is, marketable as slaves. What factors would enter into calculations of the market value of such capital goods? Would any of these factors be irrelevant in the case of nonhuman capital goods? Discuss.

9. Why are you going to college? Is it costing you anything but time (and forgone income)? What does it cost your parents? What does it cost your school? Will the value of your services be increased sufficiently as a result of your education to offset its cost to you and others?

SUGGESTED READINGS

Becker, G. *Human Capital.* New York: Columbia University Press, 1975.

Friedman, M. *A Theory of the Consumption Function.* Princeton, NJ: Princeton University Press, 1957, Chapter 2.

Johnson, M. *Household Behavior: Income, Wealth, and Consumption.* London: Penguin, 1971.

Schultz, T. "Investments in Human Capital." The *American Economic Review,* March 1961, pp 1–17.

22

Market Failures: Public Goods and Externalities

22.1 INTRODUCTION

Supply and demand, in concert, perform an extremely complicated and valuable function. These forces coordinate the optimizing activities of a large, diverse set of economic agents and provide answers to the basic economic questions of WHAT? HOW? and FOR WHOM? The answers are, moreover, often socially optimal (given an appropriate income distribution, as discussed in Chapter 21), in the sense that a larger output level has marginal costs greater than marginal benefits, whereas a smaller output level would leave unproduced goods having benefits greater than costs.

22.2 SUPPLY AND DEMAND REVISITED

Let us now examine more carefully the efficiency aspects of the supply and demand outcome under idealized conditions. Suppose that demand or willingness to pay accurately represents marginal social values of additional output. Similarly, suppose that supply or the marginal willingness to produce represents the marginal social cost of output. As seen in Figure 22-1, the intersection of these two curves indicates that quantity (Q^*) at which the marginal social value of the last unit produced is equal to the marginal social cost of that last unit produced. As seen in Figure 22-1, output levels higher than Q^*, say Q_{High}, represent output levels having costs greater than benefits (inefficiency). On the other hand, at output levels below Q^*, say Q_{Low}, output having benefits greater than cost goes unproduced (inefficiency).

When would the desirability of the Q^* outcome in Figure 22-1 be called into question? The answer must clearly be that Q^* will be wrong if the supply and/or demand curves do not measure what they are presumed to measure in the usual analysis. The demand curve purportedly depicts the **social marginal value** of various quantities of

FIGURE 22-1

The Desirable Efficiency Features of the Supply and Demand Equilibrium, When Demand Represents *True* Marginal Social Values and Supply Represents *True* Marginal Social (Opportunity) Costs

Equilibrium price and quantity (P^*, Q^*) are socially efficient when demand reflects marginal social benefits and supply reflects marginal social costs. If output exceeds Q^*, marginal social costs exceed marginal social benefits, and efficiency requires a reduction in quantity. Conversely at output rates less than Q^*, marginal social benefits exceed costs and society would gain from additional output.

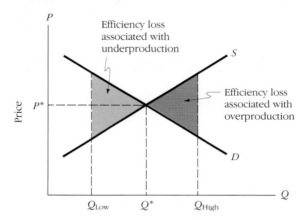

the good in question, while the supply curve is intended to reflect the **social marginal cost** (forgone opportunities) of alternative quantities of the good. Unfortunately, these curves do not always measure what is intended.

There are three important reasons why the invisible hand might "mess up," one of which will be considered in detail in this chapter. But first a brief review of the other two sources of resource misallocation is in order.

Suppose you believe that the current income distribution is "wrong." You may feel that income is distributed either too equally or too unequally, or merely that the wrong individuals have particular incomes (say, your own is too low). What difficulties does this cause to the optimal provision of goods through market forces? Suppose that you think that the income distribution is too unequal and that this is unfair. To clarify how this matters, further suppose that the good under consideration is yachts. Since this good is quite superior over the relevant (high) income range, redistributing income (as you deem appropriate) would result in a leftward shift in the demand curve: with fewer millionaires, the number of yachts demanded would also be smaller. Hence, after your desired income redistribution, the optimal quantity of yachts would fall, and you could infer that the pre-distribution quantity was not optimal.

Economists, in their role as economists, find little wrong with the preceding argument; in a sense, efficiency becomes a meaningless concept. But more can be said.

First, with a representative form of government, the existing income distribution may fairly closely parallel what most people think appropriate. If income were very unfairly distributed (either too equal or too unequal), politicians advocating various tax (and other) reforms would get elected. Such an evolutionary (or even revolutionary) outcome would push the system closer to the collective ideal.

Second, the income elasticity of demand for many goods is unity or close to unity. For such goods, redistributing income among people with similar preferences will lead to reductions in the demands of those losing income that are completely offset by increases in demands from those gaining income. The market outcome is, for such goods, optimal regardless of the income distribution. Note that since all income is spent (counting savings as a good), the collective income elasticity is 1, and this is your best guess for any single good (lacking other information, as for example the intuitive knowledge we have about yacht-buyers). So, not knowing whose ethical judgment about the appropriate income distribution is correct, economists tend to treat the existing distribution as satisfactory, particularly since optimal overall quantities will often be unaffected in any event.

Another source of misallocation stems from noncompetitiveness on either the supply or demand side of the market. Since monopolists must lower their prices to sell additional output, their marginal revenue is below their average revenue curve. In the competitive case, demand or average revenue (the marginal value of additional output to society) gets set equal to marginal cost, since average revenue equals marginal revenue to each firm. For the monopolist, however, setting marginal revenue equal to marginal cost fails to produce output having value (average revenue) greater than the marginal cost of production. Hence we get too little of those goods produced under monopolistic (or oligopolistic) conditions.

But our focus here is on a third circumstance under which the unconstrained workings of the market will lead to inappropriate quantities of goods produced. Even if the economy is competitive and the income distribution is correct, it is still possible for the market supply and demand curves to wrongly characterize the marginal social benefits and costs of production. How might this happen?

22.3 EXTERNALITIES

Consider first the market supply curve. As you will recall, this curve is the (horizontal) sum of the marginal cost curves (above the minimum of the average variable cost curve in the short run) of each firm in the industry.[1] But the marginal costs being summed are marginal *private* costs—firms' payments (explicit or implicit) to acquire the factors to produce various quantities of the good. These payments will, indeed, represent the opportunity costs of forgone other goods—as they are supposed to *if* the

---

[1]This abstracts from the possibility that industry expansion will drive up certain input prices that would be unaffected by an individual firm's expansion. This refinement does not materially affect the text discussion.

firm must pay for all of its inputs. But sometimes, unlike with labor and other inputs, the firm uses some input which is socially valuable (has an opportunity cost) yet costs the firm nothing. The classic example is air used by an air-polluting factory. The firm uses clean air in production and returns dirty air to the atmosphere. The loss of air quality is felt by members of society as worsened health, material damage, and aesthetically unappealing views. Such damages are real costs associated with the firm's use of the air, yet since nobody owns the air (unlike other inputs) there is no charge placed on its use. As a consequence, too much of it is used in producing too much of the polluting good. This leads to a definition.

Externalities: An *externality* is said to occur whenever a physical impact on third parties to a transaction takes place without compensation. This definition may be abbreviated to "uncompensated spillovers."

The presence of externalities, and their implications for actual versus optimal resource use, may be seen in Figure 22-2.

In Figure 22-2, $S_{Private}$ represents the private costs of the polluting good, say steel.[2] Hence the actual competitive outcome, Q_A, would occur with steel selling for P_A. Notice that the last unit of steel produced had a true social cost of P_S, greatly in excess of its price. The full efficiency loss is seen as the shaded region in Figure 22-2. This area shows the sum of the amounts by which full social cost exceeds private benefits for the (excess) output from Q^* to Q_A. If the firm were to produce Q^*, marginal social cost would equal marginal social benefit; this ton of steel (and all inframarginal tons) would have social value equal to (or greater than) social cost.

The output level Q_0 represents the output level at which emissions from the smokestack first result in nonnegligible damages to people and things downwind. Of note is the fact that it is socially desirable to produce the steel between Q_0 and Q^* even though that production results in environmental damages. Hence the paradoxical result that there is an "optimal level of pollution" which is not generally zero! This result is rather disgusting to environmentalists (though they may themselves use a great deal of products which directly or indirectly pollute), but it is logically unassailable.[3] It is easy to see the efficiency loss to society of requiring steel producers to produce at Q_0; indeed a zero-pollution outcome would generally be much *less* desirable than would be the uncontrolled outcome (compare the appropriate efficiency loss triangles).

While there are many similar examples of **negative externalities** in production, there can also be **positive externalities** on the supply side and especially on the demand side. For many goods, the individual consumer does not receive *all* of the benefits of their having been purchased. This is not the case for, say, a hamburger; if

---

[2]While we suspect that the steel industry is competitive due to foreign competition, the skeptic may think of, for example, dry cleaners which emit carcinogenic benzene compounds, or even "miles of travel" with private automobiles (it is not just firms which pollute). See Mills and Graves (1986), especially Chapters 2–4, for a more in-depth treatment of environmental economics.

[3]Note that we are assuming that the social cost of production in Figure 22-2 includes all damages which are not compensated under the private supply curve.

■■■■■■
FIGURE 22-2

Negative Externalities and Resource Misallocation
The social supply curve includes the marginal costs of production, reflected by the private supply curve, plus the external costs (such as pollution). Market production is greater and market price is lower than is socially desirable. The shaded area designates the efficiency loss due to overproduction.

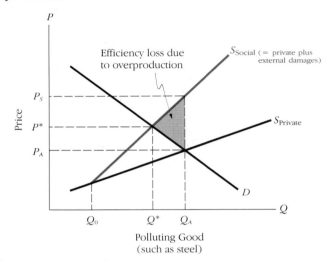

you buy it, you get all of the benefits associated with it. But consider education, well-kept home exteriors, beautiful art, or even the purchase of praying mantises and ladybugs as an alternative to pesticides. Certainly when you "buy" an education you receive many of its benefits, which may take the form of greater future income, more choice of future occupations, and the consumption value of knowing more about life as a result of classroom (and extracurricular) learning. But these benefits, great as they may be, are not all of the benefits associated with your education. You may end up curing cancer or solving some other social problem of importance, or you may just be more interesting to everyone who talks to you for the rest of your life. These nontrivial benefits may be thought of as the *positive* external consumption benefits of education (see Figure 22-3).

In the case of positive externalities, the private market will supply *too little* of the good in question (such as education). With negative externalities, *too much* is produced. In either case, the result stems from the fact that economic agents are receiving the wrong signals: the apparent benefits or costs of some action differ from the true social benefits or costs. The economic agents—producers and consumers—are *not* doing what they do because they are evil; rather, well-intentioned people or ill-intentioned people will behave according to the incentives they face.

Why, then, does the free market work fine in providing most goods but do quite

FIGURE 22-3

Positive Externalities and Resource Misallocation
The private demand curve plus external benefits constitute the social demand curve. The market price falls short of the socially optimal price, and the market underproduces the commodity. The shaded area indicates the associated efficiency loss.

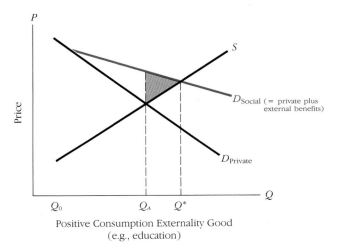

Positive Consumption Externality Good
(e.g., education)

badly (without regulations, taxes, and subsidies) in providing others? The problem, at heart, lies with a concept closely related to the concept of externalities.

22.4 PUBLIC GOODS, THE FREE RIDER, AND PROPERTY RIGHTS

As used by economists, the term *"public goods"* refers not to how particular goods are purchased—whether by some government agency or by some private economic agent—but to the properties which characterize them. A private good, say a hamburger, has two critical properties in the present context. First, if you buy it, it's yours—nobody else can have it (unless you let them, in which case you no longer have it). This property is referred to as **excludability**, meaning that your use of the good excludes others use of the same good. Second, and closely related, is the fact that the user of a private good receives *all* the benefits of its consumption—consumption of a private good is therefore **rivalrous**

Many goods are not like this, having quite different properties. Such so-called "public goods" are defined by two characteristics.

Public Goods: A good is said to be a *public good* whenever its consumption is (1) nonexcludable and (2) nonrivalrous.

Two classic examples of public goods are national defense and lighthouses. Whatever the level of national defense, we all get it (consumption is nonrivalrous) and we can't be prevented from receiving it (consumption is nonexcludable).[4] The light emanating from the lighthouses exists for all boat owners: it is technologically impossible to keep certain boat owners from looking at it while letting others see it (nonexcludable). Similarly, one boat-owner's decision to use the light as a guide does not diminish the ability of the light to guide other boat owners (nonrivalrous).

Public goods are closely related to externalities and to something called the **"free rider"** problem. Suppose the quality of the air where you live is undesirable to you. Since air quality (unlike land quality) is largely a public good, you know that if you clean up the air (say, reducing your own pollution by substituting a cleaner wood-burning stove for a highly polluting one, or even by placing a huge filtering apparatus upwind of your home), others will benefit. It might well be advantageous from society's perspective for the air to be cleaned up in this way, but what incentive do your neighbors have to pay for the benefits they will receive?

The answer, of course, is very little. They know that if you choose to clean up the air, they cannot be prevented from receiving the benefits which accrue to them. They also know, individually, that no one of them would honestly be willing to pay enough to affect your decision. They may attempt to become what are known as "free riders." Since you do not receive compensation for the benefits accruing to them, you will pollute more than otherwise, giving rise to externalities.

Now suppose a "Save the Whales" group came around your neighborhood collecting funds with which to lobby for protection of the blue whales (whose existence is a public good—recall the definition). You may have a genuine interest in the whale's continued existence, but what incentives do you face? Suppose the whale's survival is actually worth $100 to you. If the 100 million households in the United States each made a similar contribution, this would add up to about $10 billion. But will you write a check for $100? Or will you reason as follows: "If I give $100, there is no guarantee that the whale gets saved, because my contribution is negligible relative to the amount required to convene conferences, pass legislation, buy up existing boats, and so on. Furthermore, if I *don't* give $100, the whale may get saved anyhow and I'll continue to receive the benefits of its existence plus the benefits of the $100." Taking the latter course represents a rational attempt to become a free rider. The rub is that if everyone attempts to take a free ride, the ride won't exist.

How do property rights figure into this discussion? This is easy to see by pursuing the previous examples. If air quality were like land quality, where rights of ownership and use were easy to prescribe and enforce, each "owner of air" would have an incentive to protect the value of his or her asset just as people paint their homes, rotate their crops, and so on to maintain and enhance the value of other assets. The technological nature of air, however, precludes this. (See Box 22-1.)

---

[4]Actually, there are few "pure" public goods. National defense really is not identical everywhere, and at some very high cost it may be possible to exclude individual households from consuming defense. Indeed, many goods are mixed public/private goods—congestion at a national park or on the Santa Monica Freeway, for example, means that your consumption is rivalrous with others. Similarly, an endangered species may have a value both as a private good (for furs) and as a public good (for ecological stability or scientific research).

22-1 Why are blue whales, condors, and bighorn sheep endangered when cows, chickens and ordinary sheep are not?

The property rights associated with cows give their owners the incentive to care for these animals. Nobody owns whales (or acts as if they did), hence whale users are not charged a price to reflect the scarcity of whales unlike the case with cows. An ironic conclusion emerges: It is often believed that the price system of capitalist economies is responsible for our environmental woes, when in fact the opposite is the case. The problem is a *lack* of prices (charging a zero price for the use of socially scarce air or wildlife); where prices work properly, we do not have environmental problems.

There is a caveat to this assertion that there would be no environmental problems if the price system worked properly. The assertion takes, as seems appropriate to us, negative externalities to be synonymous with environmental problems. This means that it is human values that matter and that some environmental degradation may be optimal: when the benefits of producing a polluting good are greater than the full social costs, there are no "environmental problems" in the sense that efforts to improve the environment further make us worse off.

How do we arrive at proper levels of public goods? It is clear, on both the supply and the demand side, that we will get too little of the public good without some intervention. On the supply side, nonexcludability precludes charging consumers for benefits received, hence producers will not be able to cover their costs of producing public goods from revenues. On the demand side, individual consumers have an incentive to be free riders, further reducing the likelihood that goods having benefits greater than costs will be produced.

22.5 EFFICIENT PROVISION OF PUBLIC GOODS

The marginal social value of a pure public good is readily seen to be the vertical summation of individual demand curves. Thus it differs from a private good, for which the appropriate question is: "How much will be demanded at various prices in the market (**horizontal summation**)?" The corresponding question for the public good, due to its nonrivalrous nature, is: "How much will be offered in aggregate for various quantities (**vertical summation**)?" The first lighthouse should be built if the present value of the benefits (say $500,000) exceed the present value of the costs (say $200,000); and similarly for the second, third, and fourth lighthouse until the benefits no longer exceed the costs. But from the previous discussion it is clear that the proper number of lighthouses is not likely to be forthcoming in a voluntary exchange economy because of the peculiar nature of public goods.

We can show this graphically. Imagine a small coastal community of 10,000 people that is considering investing in the services of a lighthouse. For simplicity let us assume that there are three income groups (the poor, the middle class, and the rich) in the community, having demand curves for the lighthouse represented by d_H (high income), d_M (middle income) and d_L (low income) in Figure 22-4. The low-income group, containing 1,000 individuals, are infrequent seafarers, but would enjoy the aesthetics of a lighthouse on the point and are willing to pay 50 cents per person or a total of $500 for the first lighthouse. The second group, which is the largest, is the middle-income class. Some members of the middle class are fishermen; others enjoy boating. They are willing to pay $3 each; with 8,000 members, the middle class as a whole is willing to pay $24,000 for the first lighthouse (this is the reason d_M is the d curve furthest to the right). The last group are the rich, who primarily use the services of a lighthouse while yachting. The group members, 1,000 individuals, are willing to pay $20,000, or $20 per person. In sum, the three groups are willing to pay $44,500 for a lighthouse. The social value (D_{Social}) is derived by summing vertically (at one lighthouse) each group's marginal benefit or demand curve.

With the construction of the social demand curve D_{Social}, we can determine the efficient output of lighthouses. To the left of the intersection of the MC (drawn horizontally for convenience) and the D_{Social} curve, the community is willing to pay more for a lighthouse than the marginal costs required to produce it; hence the lighthouse should be built. This will continue to be the case until marginal social benefits fall to marginal social costs, at two lighthouses in Figure 22-4.

Note that two practical policy difficulties emerging from an example such as the preceding are present in many similar cases. First, it will be difficult to get people to

---

FIGURE 22-4

The Efficient Output of a Public Good
The social demand curve for a public good is the vertical sum of individual demand curves. The social optimum occurs when marginal social costs equal marginal social benefits, i.e., 2 lighthouses at $30,000 each. In practice, consumers understate their willingness to pay and public goods are often underproduced.

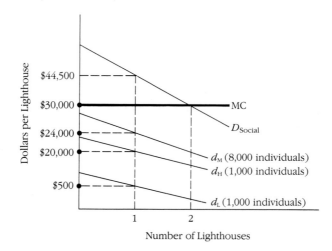

honestly reveal their preferences for the public good: they will attempt to be "free riders," trying to get the good for nothing (their individual valuations will have a negligible impact on the overall decision on the number of lighthouses). As a result, the right number of lighthouses won't get built. Second, the average cost per resident of the lighthouse is $3. Since the poor value the first lighthouse at $.50, they will be harmed by the decision to build one, unless equity is considered in the financing mechanism chosen (say, through fees based on assessed value of boat, rather than financing the lighthouse with general tax revenues).

Many public goods like national defense are provided directly by governments. In other cases, some combinations of taxes, subsidies, and direct regulations have been employed to move toward the socially optimal quantity of various goods.

Consider, by way of another illustration, the case of air pollution control. Airborne emissions come from many sources including the transportation sector, industrial stationary source emitters, and power plants. Because the uncontrolled emissions tend to lead to externalities,[5] the output of the polluting sources is too large and the public good "air quality" is underproduced. How might one increase the level of air quality in ways that would be socially desirable? Some methods may have costs greater than benefits. The classic solution of Pigou, dating back to the early 1900s, is to tax the polluter per ton of emissions an amount equalling the external damages associated with a marginal ton of emissions. This would effectively internalize the externality, sending the appropriate signal to the producer that using air in such a way as to dirty it has an opportunity cost. The social supply curve (S_{Social} in Figure 22-2) would then become the private supply curve, and the market failure would be corrected in a way that largely maintains the desirable features of market exchange.

For other public goods, such as education, subsidies might be a desirable approach. Return to Figure 22-3 and note that by subsidizing the cost of education to certain individuals, the supply curve which represents the private marginal cost *to the education buyer* could be shifted down enough to encourage the purchase of the socially desirable quantity of education, Q^*. Alternatively, the private demand could be subsidized (through education coupons called "vouchers"). Such an approach would effectively lower the price to the education buyer enough so that he or she would desire the socially optimal quantity of education, Q^*.

In some cases, technological difficulties or cost considerations suggest that other approaches be taken. It was historically difficult or very costly to monitor actual emissions into the atmosphere or water bodies. As a result, when environmental legislation was being introduced in the 1960s, the approach of requiring certain pollution control devices to be in place was adopted. Hence automobiles are required to have exhaust gas recirculation systems, catalytic converters, and so on, while certain industries must

---

[5]They will not always lead to externalities. The emissions may be so small relative to the large absorptive capacity of the environment (for example, squirrel droppings) that there is a negligible impact on environmental quality, hence on people. Also, as discussed in the text, the emissions which remain after optimal control policies are in effect will not represent externalities if the controls involve full compensation for those experiencing the emissions. Recall that externalities are "uncompensated spillovers."

install wet limestone scrubbers, electrostatic precipitators, or baghouses on their smokestacks.

Such direct-control-device approaches suffer from certain drawbacks that the economic incentives approaches of taxing or subsidizing do not possess. First, there is no incentive for the user to be sure, even if possible at low cost, that the device is working properly.[6] The law requires only that it be present. This means that whatever environmental gains occur are more expensive than they should be. Second, there is no incentive for polluters to do *more* than required, even if some could do so at very low cost. There are many other problems with the direct-control-device approach that are more administrative in nature.[7]

One approach sometimes advocated is of almost no help at all. "Moral suasion" (for example, in the form of television or newspaper ads exhorting people to not drive, to recycle, or to use less water) is hardly ever effective. There are two situations when this approach is useful: in short-run emergency situations and when no other policy has benefits greater than costs. An example of the first type would be during unusual air pollution inversion conditions, when people would be asked not to drive and firms asked not to operate for a brief time. An example of the second situation would be policies dealing with litter in wilderness areas—not only would they not be "wilderness areas" if antilitter signs and policemen were present, but the cost would be prohibitive over the vast areas involved.

As is no doubt apparent by now, dealing with market failures to provide public goods is a complex issue. The "free rider" problem makes it difficult to determine values for public goods; lack of ownership, hence lack of prices on scarce goods, means that people do not face the proper incentive to economize on them; and policies commonly used to improve the situation sometimes make it worse! Are there any circumstances in which one can be more optimistic about market performance?

22.6 THE COASE THEOREM AND THE IMPORTANCE OF TRANSACTION COSTS

Fortunately, environmental problems (and other public good problems) are more scarce than one would initially suspect from the preceding discussion. Ronald Coase, in a classic paper, observed that if there are benefits greater than costs for some course of action (say, environmental cleanup), there must be potential transactions that can make some people better off without making anyone worse off.[8] To appreciate this important insight, consider the following problem.

---

[6]Indeed, there is sometimes an incentive to ensure that control devices do *not* work. For example, unleaded gasoline is more expensive than leaded, hence a significant fraction (perhaps 10 percent) of drivers put leaded gas in "unleaded only" cars. Two tankfuls ruin the catalytic converter, rendering the car about 100 times dirtier than if unleaded were used.

[7]See Mills and Graves, Chapters 8–10, for more detail on United States environmental policy, criticisms of it, and alternative approaches.

[8]This is the Pareto efficiency criterion. Note also that if an action exists which can make some people better off without making anyone worse off, it must also be possible to make *all* people better off by redistributing the benefits.

A cattle rancher lives downstream from a paper mill. The paper mill dumps sulfurous compounds into the stream which damage the rancher's cattle. The rancher is not compensated; hence an externality exists. The question is: Why does the externality persist? Suppose the courts have established (perhaps because the paper mill was there first) that the property rights to the use (abuse) of the stream reside with the mill. If there are benefits greater than costs of cleanup, the rancher should be willing to pay the mill owner to stop polluting. The benefits of cleanup (say $10,000) being greater than the costs (say $5,000) means that there is *some* offer (say $7,500) which will make *both* the rancher and the mill owner better off than with continued pollution.[9] If, on the other hand, the property rights to the use of the stream resided with the rancher, the mill owner would have an incentive to pay the rancher for the right to pollute, up to the point where the marginal benefits to the mill owner of polluting equaled the marginal damages to the rancher from pollution. Apart from the wealth effect associated with who owns the right to use the stream (which would usually be fairly small), the outcome would be the same either way! Hence, apart from property rights issues (about which there is much legal controversy), the socially desirable stream quality should be forthcoming.

The example hinges critically on low **transaction costs** of negotiation between mill owner and rancher. Transaction costs are the costs of negotiating and executing an exchange, excluding the cost of the good or service bought. For example, when buying a car, a great deal of time is usually spent finding the car to be bought and negotiating a mutually agreeable price.

Suppose that instead of one rancher there are a thousand, and instead of one mill owner there are ten—but with the *same* total benefits and costs of cleanup. The desirable outcome that the workings of voluntary exchange will eliminate the externality—equivalently that optimal emissions will be present—disappears. Not only are there complicated issues of how to assign observed damages to specific mill owners, but each individual rancher may try to become a free rider. The $10,000 of benefits are now only $10 per rancher, and the transactions costs of successfully dealing with the several polluters (either to bribe them or bring suit, depending on property rights assignment) will be far higher than that. Now imagine the complexities inherent in more realistic cases: There are, for example, 12 million people within 60 miles of downtown Los Angeles. Each of them is damaged a little by each of a very large number of firms and other consumers (for example, automobile drivers).

So it becomes apparent why the inefficiencies resulting from pollution control are not solved by private negotiations. First, there is ambiguity regarding property rights in air, water and other environmental media—firms with historical ability to pollute resent controls, giving up their rights to pollute only if bribed—yet consumers feel they have the right to breathe clean air and use pristine water bodies. These conflicting positions must be resolved in court, with the winner being, of course, wealthier. Second, transaction costs increase greatly with the number of transactors; this, as indicated by our example, is most critical. Finally, the properties of air or water quality

---

[9]In the terminology of the Edgeworth Box diagram, which is used to demonstrate the benefits of voluntary exchange, the initial position represents a position off the contract curve.

(and similar public goods) are such that additional people can enjoy the benefits at no additional cost and cannot be excluded from doing so. Hence, in practice, private agreements are unlikely to solve many problems of market failure.

It is, however, an easy jump to the conclusion that governments should solve any problems not properly solved by private actions. It may be that no solution is possible, or that all solutions involve costs that exceed benefits. In any event, the concepts developed in this chapter should enable those who wish to think carefully about such problems to formulate better policies than would otherwise be the case.

SUMMARY

1. Sometimes the unconstrained workings of the market will result in the "wrong" levels of output for particular goods. While monopoly, monopsony, income distributional problems and tax distortions may also be of importance, this chapter focuses on public goods and externalities as causes of resource misallocation.

2. Externalities are "uncompensated spillovers" which cause the private benefits or costs of an action to differ from the social benefits or costs. As a consequence, too little or too much is produced, from society's perspective.

3. Since the use of a public good is nonexcludable, no private supplier receives sufficient incentive to produce it; producers would be unable to cover costs with revenues because of the "free rider" problem.

4. Externalities and public goods are closely related: a firm producing a good involving negative externalities (such as pollution emissions) tends to cause the level of some public good (air or water quality) to be nonoptimally low.

5. The efficient provision of a public good may be accomplished either by direct government production or by some method of making the private benefits and costs correspond to the true social benefits and costs (with subsidies or taxes, for example).

6. *If* property rights are well defined and transaction costs are small, externalities will tend to become internalized by either legal action (if rights to use the air or water reside with households) or "bribes" (if rights to use the environmental media reside with owners of firms). However, the large number of those emitting pollutants and, especially, of those being damaged greatly reduces the practical significance of this observation.

WORDS AND CONCEPTS FOR REVIEW

social marginal value
social marginal cost
externalities
negative externalities
positive externalities
public goods

excludability
rivalrous
free rider
horizontal summation
vertical summation
transaction costs

REVIEW QUESTIONS

1. Why is the outcome of voluntary exchange in the market *usually* considered to be socially optimal? When would this outcome *not* be appropriate?

2. What properties characterize a public good? If such properties hold for a good, what is the socially optimal price to charge for this good? What problem results from actually charging the socially optimal price?

3. Why doesn't recognition of the "free rider" problem in providing public goods cause people to contribute, on the grounds that they know they won't get the good at all without doing so? Since they all know this, they might contribute enough to get the good. Would the likelihood of this happening be greater or less if there were a small number of people affected?

4. How might one design a social policy relating to loud fraternity parties? Suppose the fraternity were taxed an amount, per party, that would just compensate those damaged (leaving them on the same indifference curve with the party and compensation, or without the party and compensation). Suppose further that the fraternities traditionally had two types of parties— either loud rock music/beer bash dancing parties (now subject to tax) or quiet classical background music/wine and cheese conversational parties (not subject to tax). What impact would you expect the tax to have on (a)the overall number of parties and (b)the ratio of beer bashes to wine-and-cheese parties? (*Hint:* Employ indifference curve analysis.)

5. Would the results in Question 4 depend on whether the revenues from the loud party tax were *actually* redistributed to the neighbors? Or is that a value judgment about which people could have different opinions? (*Hint:* This is a complicated question. For simplicity, assume the tax revenue collected would be sufficiently small per neighbor as to negligibly affect any neighbor's income, hence demands for quiet.)

6. Can you think of any *positive* externalities from a firm's production?

7. Suppose there is substantial *variation* in air quality within an urban area. If people are aware of both the nature of pollution damages and the air quality at each location, will the resource misallocation be less severe or more severe than if the same average air quality were distributed uniformly everywhere? (*Hint:* If people are affected differently, with some greatly damaged and some harmed very little, will the bidding in land markets reduce external damages by, in effect, partly converting a public good to a private good?)

SUGGESTED READINGS

Coase, Ronald. "The Problem of Social Cost." *Journal of Law and Economics,* October 1960, pp. 1–45.

———. "The Lighthouse in Economics." *Journal of Law and Economics,* October 1974, pp. 357–376.

Mills, Edwin S. and Graves, Philip E. *The Economics of Environmental Quality,* 2nd ed. New York: Norton, 1986.

Ruff, Larry E. "The Economic Common Sense of Pollution." *The Public Interest,* Spring 1970, pp. 69–85.

Schorerer, F. M. *Industrial Market Structure and Economic Performance,* 2nd ed. Chicago: Rand McNally, 1980.

Index

Italicized page numbers indicate reference to a figure caption or a table.
Bold-faced page numbers indicate reference to an application box.